D1096299

POLITICAL ATTITUDES & PUBLIC OPINION

edited by

DAN D. NIMMO
University of Tennessee, *Knoxville*

CHARLES M. BONJEAN
University of Texas, *Austin*

DAVID McKAY COMPANY, INC.
NEW YORK

Unless otherwise noted, selections are reprinted from the *Social Science Quarterly*, 51 (December, 1970). "Perceptions of Ghetto Riots" by Harlan Hahn and Joe R. Feagin is reprinted from *Social Science Quarterly*, 51 (September, 1970). "The Use of Magnitude Estimation in Attitude Scaling: Constructing a Measure of Political Dissatisfaction" by Robert E. Welch, Jr., and "The Vietnam War and Student Militancy" by Robert B. Smith are reprinted from *Social Science Quarterly*, 52 (June, 1971).

Library of Congress Catalog Card Number: 72-75643
Manufactured in the United States of America

Preface

Despite a growing number of multi-disciplinary projects in recent decades bringing together social scientists with mutual research interests, many college courses in the social sciences remain "departmentalized"; that is, each discipline through its specialized course offerings presents its unique perspectives, theories, and findings as though no cross-disciplinary concerns exist. All too often the advanced undergraduate student finds that if he is interested in, for instance, public opinion, the price he must pay for an introduction to all dimensions of the subject is to enroll in separate political science, sociology, psychology, social psychology, journalism, and other courses. Finding the price too high, he usually despairs and accepts a narrower outlook.

One way of exposing students to the varieties of cross-disciplinary research bearing upon selected aspects of human behavior is, of course, to provide a collection of materials prepared by specialists representing several disciplines. The contributions in this volume have been chosen with such a view in mind—to bring together articles reflecting the concerns, research, and findings of various behavioral scientists working in the areas of political attitudes, opinions, and behavior. As the volume's co-editors one of us is a political scientist and the other a sociologist. We hope that our joint efforts avoid the conventional images of man as but a "social" or "political" animal by viewing him as both; moreover, although this compilation of articles is intended to assist primarily our colleagues and students in political science and sociology, by including contributions reflecting other perspectives, we believe the volume conveys the multi-disciplinary character of current research in political attitudes.

Most of the contributions contained herein were selected by the co-editors and others from among more than 150 articles submitted by social scientists in 1969–1970 for possible inclusion in a special, topical issue of the *Social Science Quarterly.* In the preparation of that special issue of *SSQ*, we noted that certain trends and themes typified the manuscripts reporting *contemporary* research in political attitudes and behavior regardless of the scholarly discipline of the researchers. It was particularly noteworthy, for example, that many articles dealt with controversial matters outside the conventional problem area of political attitude research, voting behavior. Hence, this volume contains studies of several matters of current (and we think lasting) interest as exemplified by selections dealing with the politically relevant attitudes of blacks, the poor, the unskilled, and students; attitudes toward the Vietnam war, student demonstrations, and local issues; or the attitudinal bases of movements among black militants or supporters of George Wallace. Thus, our perspective is not only interdisciplinary, but our focus is on events of *contemporary* significance.

In selecting the articles for this volume we tried not only to supply a sampling of cross-disciplinary and topical research into political attitudes; we also endeavored to provide students with selections introducing critical conceptual and methodological problems in attitude research. These include such matters as the conceptual and operational distinctions between attitudes, opinions, beliefs, and behavior; relationships of attitude-learning and change to status consistency and cognitive balance; principles and techniques of attitude measurement; and the sources of data available for the study of political attitudes. This necessitated the inclusion of contributions in addition to those from the December, 1970, issue of the *Social Science Quarterly*. We have included 13 selections previously published elsewhere because they focus on important matters not dealt with in *SSQ* articles or provide useful supplements to those originally selected. Final gaps were filled by three articles written especially for this volume.

To be sure, the articles in this volume fall far short of exhausting the number of available pieces of reported research deserving of either original or republication. We feel, however, that they communicate the richness of inquiries currently being conducted into political attitudes by behavioral scientists with common concerns transcending differing backgrounds, training, skills, and disciplines.

In addition to the authors and the publishers who graciously consented to the republication of their works, we are indebted to many. Contributions by Thomas J. Cook, Frank P. Scioli, and Norval D. Glenn appear for the first time in this volume. We are especially appreciative of their efforts to fill what would otherwise have been several important gaps in this collection. Helpful in undertaking many of the administrative chores associated with a volume such as this one was Paula Jean Miller, who also contributed valuable editorial suggestions. We are also highly indebted to the office and editorial staffs of the *Social Science Quarterly*, without whose efforts this volume would have been impossible. Among these individuals, special gratitude is due Harry Holloway, Robert L. Lineberry, Harold Osborne, Norval D. Glenn, Cynthia Gardner, and Jan Hullum.

Any errors or shortcomings are exclusively our own.

Dan D. Nimmo
Knoxville, Tennessee

Charles M. Bonjean
Austin, Texas

January, 1972

Contents

IV. The Distribution of Attitudes and Opinions   379

Introduction

V. Attitudes and Opinions as Independent   489   Variables: Social and Behavioral   Consequences

Introduction

PART I

Basic Concepts and Methods

INTRODUCTION

Only a decade ago, the late V. O. Key asserted, "Without doubt the conditions affecting the relations between government and public opinion have been radically altered during the past half century."[1] Noting that governmental decision-making had become more centralized, more classified, and more concerned with foreign policy matters, he suggested that while mass views still had some place in the shaping of policy, the average person had become more bewildered, repelled, and ignorant of public policy.

While some of the contributors to this volume offer views not inconsistent with Key's (e.g., Hennessy), events of the last decade suggest that the relationships between government and public opinion—if not the nature of public opinion itself and its modes of expression—may have been altered as much since 1961 as they were in the preceding half century. The traditional linkages between government and public opinion—elections, pressure groups, press conferences, letters, "trial balloons," etc.—were supplemented in the 1960s by such non-institutionalized "innovations" as sit-ins, marches, and even collective civil violence. Public opinion was perhaps more intense and divided than in any decade since the Civil War. Blacks and liberal whites squared off against segregationists and conservatives (and occasionally against each other) on race-related issues which, although secondary in the 1964 election,[2] erupted into black-initiated violence and a white backlash sufficiently intense to be associated with the appearance of a third party later in the decade. Vietnam further divided the nation and demonstrations which had earlier focused on civil rights became peace marches and confrontations between "hawks" and "doves." Violence in the ghetto was replaced by violence on the campus. Traditional distinctions between liberals and conservatives and Democrats and Republicans remained important, but radicals and reactionaries came to occupy more central positions in the political arena. The 1960s offered new challenges for the American political system as well as for those social scientists who during the previous three decades had assembled an impressive battery of concepts, theories, techniques, and data on public opinion and political attitudes.

The number of selections in the current volume dealing with the unique political events of the last decade—ghetto violence, Vietnam, Kent State, student dissent, and the Wallace phenomenon—attest to the flexibility and durability of the concepts and techniques developed earlier to deal with more regular and recurrent phenomena—local and national elections, attitudes toward foreign policy, party identification, product choice, and similar phenomena. To be sure, there have been modifications and innovations in both conceptualization and methods of investigation. Many of these will be explicit in the selections which follow, as will the points of disagreement among scholars, but perhaps more obvious will be the considerable amount of *continuity* in the study of political attitudes and public opinion.

[1] V. O. Key, Jr., *Public Opinion and American Democracy* (New York: Alfred A. Knopf, 1961), p. 6.
[2] See Samuel A. Kirkpatrick, "Issue Orientation and Voter Choice in 1964," *Social Science Quarterly*, 49 (June, 1968), pp. 87–102.

The purpose of Part I of this anthology is to offer an overview of basic concepts and to provide a description of some of the methods widely used by social scientists in the study of political attitudes and public opinion. The reader will again encounter the concepts and methods in substantive contexts in the remaining sections of the book.

In most areas of social scientific endeavor, precise agreement in regard to the meaning of terms and concepts is absent. Indeed a perusal of the relevant literature suggests that in the late 1920s there was some disagreement in regard to whether the concept "attitude" should refer to mental phenomena such as feelings[3] or to overt behavior.[4] Later efforts often combined aspects of both of these definitions and it has been suggested[5] that the following definition offered by Allport in 1935 is the point of departure for most current orientations: "A mental and neural state of readiness organized through experience, exerting a directive or dynamic influence upon the individual's response to all objects and situations with which it is related."[6] Thus, used in its most general sense, an attitude is a constellation of perceptions, beliefs, and sentiments making for a relatively stable predisposition to respond to a set of related objects. Such a definition includes several components (not all of which are used by different investigators).[7] First, there is a *cognitive* component—what a person perceives and believes to be true. A seismologist and a medicine man, for example, would neither perceive an earthquake in the same manner nor would they share the same beliefs about that phenomenon. Certainly related to cognitive elements—but frequently conceptualized and studied independently—are *affective* components. There is probably more agreement among social scientists that attitudes involve a judgment along the lines of good-bad, fair-unfair, attractive-unattractive, etc. than there is in regard to whether or not the concept should also incorporate cognitive and *conative* (action tendency) elements. Even though the concept attitude has been equated with the probability of recurrence of behavior of a given type or direction, research attempting to link attitudes to different types of behavior has not always supported the linkages expected and recently there has been considerable critical discussion concerning this component of the concept. For example, it has been suggested that "... there is no reason to expect consistency of response

[3] L. L. Thurstone, "Attitudes Can Be Measured," *American Journal of Sociology*, 33 (Jan. 1928), p. 531.

[4] Read Bain, "An Attitude on Attitude Research," *American Journal of Sociology*, 33 (May, 1928), p. 950.

[5] See, for example, William J. McGuire, "The Nature of Attitudes and Attitude Change," in Gardner Lindzey and Elliot Aronson, eds., *Handbook of Social Psychology* (Reading, Mass.: Addison-Wesley, 1968), p. 142.

[6] Gordon W. Allport, "Attitudes," in C. Murchison, ed., *A Handbook of Social Psychology* (Worcester: Clark University Press 1935), p. 798.

[7] The following discussion is based on Daniel Katz and Ezra Stotland, "A Preliminary Statement to a Theory of Attitude Structure and Change," in Sigmund Koch, ed., *Psychology: A Study of a Science*, Vol. 3 (New York: McGraw-Hill, 1959), and M. Brewster Smith, "The Personal Setting of Public Opinion," *Public Opinion Quarterly*, 11 (1947), pp. 507–523.

where there is no consistency of stimuli" and thus while paper-and-pencil attitude tests do offer relatively consistent stimuli, actual behavioral situations are far more variable.[8] Still, a number of the selections in Part V of this anthology do show a relationship between attitudes and behavior and it is there that the reader will find the conative component of attitudes stressed. While it may be useful, for analytical purposes, to differentiate between the cognitive, affective, and conative characteristics of attitudes, their inter-relatedness should be kept in mind. That is how a person perceives an object and what he believes to be true about it will influence his feelings toward it and how he is likely to react to it.

Standard discussions of attitudes—and especially of their affective or evaluative components—suggest the further complexity of the concept by indicating they have at least four dimensions:[9]

Direction simply emphasizes the evaluative component of attitudes suggesting that they may be positive (favorable), negative (unfavorable), neutral, or ambivalent.

Degree reminds us that individuals may be *more or less* favorable or unfavorable toward objects, events, persons, or ideas. Thus, while the statement on the part of one person that "Once you learn how the American political system actually works, it's a hell of a disappointment" and another on the part of a second person that "At present the American political system is making a mockery of the ideals upon which it was supposedly founded" both represent negative attitudes, the latter indicates a greater degree of negativism than the former.[10]

Intensity refers to how strongly an individual holds an attitude. Intensity is low if he is able to modify it in different social contexts and it is high if it motivates him to immediate action or if he refuses to change it even when offered considerable rewards to do so. Thus, if the person suggesting that our political system makes a mockery of the ideals upon which it was founded finds it convenient to take this stance when with his peers but experiences no discomfort in adopting a more positive stance when with his parents, we would consider his attitude intensity low even though the degree of his negativism may be considerable. Although degree and intensity refer to quite separate phenomena, they have been found to be related. Ordinarily, those with the most extreme attitudes hold them most intensely.

Salience refers to the centrality of an attitude within the individual's constellation of attitudes. At any given time, individuals hold many attitudes and not all are equally important to him. Often, individuals find themselves in situations where different attitudes that they hold prescribe (perhaps contradictory) modes of behavior. In such situations, the most salient attitudes will become manifest. In other situations, attitudes may be so peripheral

[8] Donald E. Tarter, "Attitude: The Mental Myth," *The American Sociologist*, 5 (Aug. 1970), p. 276.

[9] The following discussion is based on E. L. Hartley and Ruth E. Hartley, *Fundamentals of Social Psychology* (New York: Alfred A. Knopf, 1952), pp. 665–674.

[10] See Robert E. Welch, "The Use of Magnitude Estimation in Attitude Scaling: Constructing a Measure of Political Dissatisfaction," Selection 7 in this volume.

that they will remain at a subconscious level until stimulated by a direct probe.

Several distinctions have been made between the concepts attitude and opinion. Some investigators see attitudes as more general and enduring states than opinions, which are defined as positive, negative, neutral, or ambivalent reactions to specific issues, individuals, events or other phenomena at one point in time.[11] Frequently, the definition of opinion is further specified as a verbal expression of an attitude, a point originally made by Thurstone in an early discussion of attitude measurement.[12] That attitudes and opinions are thought to be related should be obvious—the latter are often viewed as specific indicators of the former. Because the latter are more accessible to measurement and interpretation, studies of collectivities—as opposed to individuals—almost invariably deal with public *opinion* rather than public, group, or societal *attitudes*. Katz, for example, in the first essay differentiates between attitudes and public opinion in this manner, indicating that the former is defined at the individual level and the latter refers to a description at the collective level.

"Attitude Formation and Public Opinion" summarizes trends in attitude research from the 1930s to the early 1960s and introduces the reader to several theoretical perspectives currently used by social scientists to guide, describe, and explain their observations. The alert reader will recognize variations on these perspectives in many later selections in this volume. Thus, there are some parallels between Katz's description of the "suggestion and stereotype" models and the approach used by Hamilton in his study of open housing and Orum's discussion of the relationship between religion and Wallace support in 1968. That which Katz terms the consistency models are explored in detail by the selections comprising Part III of this anthology. Wilker and Milbrath criticize the consistency model and then elaborate on still another orientation discussed by Katz—field theory. Katz himself attempts to bring together the several perspectives by incorporating them in a scheme based on the functions that attitudes fulfill for individuals.

A more skeptical introduction to the study of political attitudes is offered by Bernard Hennessy in "A Headnote on the Existence and Study of Political Attitudes." After offering some preliminary definitions of key concepts and a description of the three most common methods for the study of attitudes (survey research, deductive speculation from psychological theory, and experimentation), Hennessy summarizes the findings from a number of key studies. From this evidence, he suggests that most individuals are able to respond to specific stimuli with *ad hoc*, unintegrated, temporary opinions, but they do not hold the more consistent, more enduring and more general orientation labeled attitudes. Finally, he suggests that not more than 10 to 30 per cent of the voting adults in the United States have political *belief systems* (coherent patterns of attitudes). Hennessy uses these assumptions

[11]Bernard Berelson and Gary A. Steiner, *Human Behavior: An Inventory of Scientific Findings* (New York: Harcourt, Brace and World, 1964), p. 558.
[12]Thurstone, "Attitudes Can Be Measured."

as the basis for a critique of much contemporary and recent research and as a springboard for suggesting the types of research that should be undertaken.

Wilker and Milbrath also explicitly differentiate between beliefs and attitudes in "Political Belief Systems and Political Behavior." They reserve the former term for feelings of credulity or incredulity and the latter for feelings characterized by valence (direction). Using the attitudinal dimensions discussed above, Wilker and Milbrath would suggest that attitudes are characterized by direction and degree, while the central component of beliefs is intensity. They note, as has been suggested above, that most research has been on attitudes and that it is time to re-orient priorities since seldom have attitudes been placed within the larger belief context from which they derive. Unlike Hennessy, they believe that most ordinary citizens *have* belief systems and they argue that the existence of stable loyalties and stable political behavior support this assumption. They further suggest that previous theoretical orientations—especially consistency models—are not sufficiently inclusive to be able to identify all types of belief systems. They call for the use of a different theoretical orientation—field theory—and an attempt to understand the purposes pursued by political activity—especially symbolic ends—to lead to an understanding of the belief structure underlying this activity.

"Politics, Ideology, and Belief Systems" by Giovanni Sartori parallels the first three selections in that it is basically a conceptual-theoretical analysis, yet in other ways it departs from them. Unlike Wilker and Milbrath, Sartori uses the concept "belief systems" to include what the former authors would also term attitudes. Specifically, he differentiates between two types of belief elements—cognitive and emotive (other investigators would, of course, term the latter "attitudes"). He then notes that the cognitive elements may be organized in such a manner that individual cognition will be open or closed—that is, the individual may or may not be receptive to empirical proof or the demonstration of logical relationships that are not already a part of his belief system. Similarly, the emotive or affective aspect of an individual's belief system may also vary—from strong to weak. The two dichotomies, then, suggest four types of belief systems: adamant (strong beliefs, closed mind), firm (strong beliefs, open mind), resilient (weak beliefs, closed mind) and flexible (weak beliefs, open mind). Only the first type of system represents an *ideological* orientation which Sartori then contrasts with the fourth type—*pragmatism*. Both types of belief systems are said to be better developed among political elites than mass publics and, in fact, it is suggested that the nature of belief systems among the latter will be determined by the nature of their exposure to the former. The utility of the conceptualization is further demonstrated by a discussion of the "end of ideology" argument, political conflict, and mass manipulation.

The first four selections collectively represent some of the theoretical-conceptual issues in the study of attitudes and public opinion. These selections and others suggest that there is basic agreement in defining the concept "opinion" and that the vast majority of individuals are able to express them. There is somewhat less agreement in regard to the concept attitude. The most general definitions give the concept cognitive, affective, and conative elements, while the most restrictive orientations focus only on the second dimension, or at least give it primacy. Obviously, the generalizations an investigator makes about political attitudes will be, at least in part, a function of the manner in which he has defined them. The greatest amount of disagreement among students of political attitudes and public opinion is, then, as one would expect, at the most abstract and general level—in the realm of belief systems and ideologies. That part of the problem may be associated with conceptualization is suggested by a comparison of the Hennessy, Wilker and Milbrath, and Sartori contributions. That comparison will also indicate that each of these selections is characterized by a different theoretical orientation. As the reader continues his way through the selections in this anthology, he will find that these perspectives may not only be more or less valid, but that they sensitize the investigator to look for and emphasize *different* parts of the empirical world.

How social scientists investigate political attitudes and public opinion is the basic thrust of the last five articles in Part I. There are basically three research designs (and variations on each) used by social scientists in their attempts to describe and explain individual, group, or societal phenomena. The most primitive is the case study—the systematic and intense observation of a single individual or social unit. This strategy of investigation is ordinarily used when the investigator knows very little about what he is seeking to describe or explain. Thus, the emphasis is upon gathering a large amount of information on one or a few individuals or groups by using a variety of data gathering techniques including existing records, interviews, direct observation, and sometimes, participant observation. The very full body of data resulting from such inquiry is then analyzed primarily to provide a rich *description* of that about which little was previously known and to suggest relationships between variables which can be tested by more rigorous research designs. Anthropologists' accounts of primitive tribes, sociologists' early descriptions of small groups, and some of the political scientists' and sociologists' initial descriptions of community power structures offer good examples of this approach. As Hennessy suggests in his essay and as a perusal of this volume indicates, the case study approach is not used extensively in the study of political attitudes and public opinion. The major shortcoming of the case study is especially critical given the aims and orientations of most opinion studies—there is no basis for generalizing beyond the case studied. This volume includes no "pure" case studies, although several of the studies presented may be regarded as a blend of this orientation and that design most frequently used by opinion researchers, the sample survey.

Viewed in terms of logical rigor and function, the controlled experiment stands in sharp contrast to the case study. If an investigator is to use this research design, he must know a great deal about the probable relationships among the variables he plans to study. The definitive characteristics of experimentation—the manipulation of one variable and the use of a control group to precisely assess the effect of the manipulated variable (the independent variable) on one or more consequent variables (dependent variables)—requires information about the temporal sequence of events, indications that concomitant variation does exist, and data suggesting which control variables (other factors that may influence the value of dependent variables if they are not held constant) demand special attention. In opinion research, all of these factors are problematic. In spite of the inherent logical rigor of this research design, its greatest drawback for attitude and opinion research is that both manipulation and control frequently require a laboratory situation which, while excellent for the study of the inter-relationships among a few selected variables, takes both the variables and the subjects out of their usually more complex social context. Thus, the results from many laboratory experiments may be laboratory specific. Recent criticisms of the conative component of the concept attitude (discussed above) are also applicable to the laboratory experiment—laboratory stimuli are characterized by a degree of consistency and intensity not found outside the laboratory. Occasionally, it is possible to adapt the experimental design for use in behavioral settings outside of the laboratory, in which case the design is termed a "field experiment." Such a design is used in several of the selections in this anthology. Kolson and Green, for example, were able to manipulate several independent variables in a classroom situation to assess response-set bias in political socialization research. Their findings are used as the basis for a criticism of some aspects of that type of research which is almost synonymous with the study of attitudes and opinions—survey research.

As Hennessy notes, the survey research approach to the study of attitudes and opinions is "charmingly direct." The purpose of selections 5–9, all dealing with specific aspects of or variations on survey research, is to introduce the student to some of the complexities of this research design so that he will not assume the methodology exemplified by the vast majority of the selections in this anthology is also "charmingly simple." Indeed, the essence of the survey approach simply involves asking a respondent what he thinks about political objects; but how the respondents are selected, what they are asked and in what manner, and how the responses are analyzed have produced a body of literature on survey research technology much too detailed and varied to be summarized adequately in the space offered here. Thus, our approach will be to identify two general problems basic to any study employing the survey design, look in more detail at aspects of each, and indicate where, in the later substantive parts of this anthology, the student will be re-acquainted with these problems and introduced to others. The two basic problems inherent in any survey are sampling—deciding who the respondents will be, and scale construction—determining what they will be asked and in what manner.

In Parts II–V of this anthology, research findings will be presented describing aggregates as diverse as black veterans, voting-age citizens living in private households within the 48 contiguous states, Atlanta metropolitan area voters, Detroit ghetto residents, and students at the Santa Barbara campus of the University of California. Obviously, the nature of a research problem dictates the *universe* to be studied. If one were concerned with attitudes toward a community-specific referendum, gathering data from all voting-age adults in the United States would be just as inappropriate as studying college students if one were concerned with the general public's feelings about campus disorders. Unless the universe is relatively small and geographically compact (e.g., community leaders), practical limitations prevent the investigator from gathering information from all elements making up the universe he has defined. When this is the case—and in most instances of survey research it is—a limited number of respondents are selected from the universe and the data gathered from them are generalized to the universe. The selection process is, of course, termed "sampling" and it may assume one or a combination of several different forms. "The Variety and Characteristics of Sampling Procedures" are described by Stephan and McCarthy. Their discussion provides the reader with sufficient information to be able to understand the discussions of sampling techniques offered later in the volume as well as with some clues for the assessment of the adequacy of these techniques.

Sampling is only one of several steps in the survey research process where an investigator is likely to encounter pitfalls which may render his findings suspect. No less than 11 problems associated with the construction of instruments designed to measure attitudes are discussed by John P. Robinson, Jerrold P. Rusk, and Kendra B. Head in their paper, "Criteria for the Construction and Evaluation of Attitude Scales." As can be inferred from our conceptual discussion above and as several of the earlier selections make explicit, belief systems, attitudes, and even opinions are not directly observable. Rather they are inferred from respondents' behavior, usually responses to a question or set of questions comprising an index or a scale. The degree to which it is likely that the question or set of items actually measure what the investigator purports to measure is that instrument's *validity.* Related to validity is *reliability,* the stability of responses to an item or scale or the degree to which it gives the same results consistently. The problems and criteria discussed in this essay all relate to these two key characteristics of attitude and opinion measurement and they are organized around three basic steps associated with this process: (1) writing or finding items to include in attitude scales; (2) constructing the scales in such a manner so that a "response set" will be avoided; and (3) the statistical techniques involved in scale construction processes. All three of these steps—and many of the more specific problems discussed by Robinson, Rusk, and Head—are illustrated by Robert Welch in "The Use of Magnitude Estimation in Attitude Scaling: Constructing a Measure of Political Dissatisfaction." He illustrates in detail how subjects themselves may offer the most valid and useful items to be incorporated in a scale and he further describes one statistical technique for selecting items and assigning them scale values. The reader will note in subsequent selections that not all investigators are as careful as Welch nor do they consider all of the criteria discussed by Robinson, Rusk, and Head in constructing their interview schedules or questionnaires. To the degree that some previous research may have incorporated invalid or unreliable scales, the current criticism of the attitude-action orientation relationship (discussed above) may be, in part, an artifact of poor methodology and especially the measurement techniques employed.[13]

Juxtaposing some of the ideas central in sampling with problems in attitude measurement, Steven R. Brown and Thomas D. Ungs note that while the idea of representativeness has been central in the selection of respondents, it has been overlooked in the selection of those stimuli presented to respondents. "Representativeness and the Study of Political Behavior: An Application of Q Technique to Reactions to the Kent State Incident" criticizes previous research from this standpoint and offer examples of the kinds of results that can be obtained when the criterion of representativeness is extended to areas beyond sampling.

It should be emphasized that both the problems discussed and the techniques suggested for meeting them in selections 5–8 are neither inclusive nor exhaustive. Still, the nature of the problems and the solutions discussed there are indicative of the types of problems one may encounter during other stages of the survey research process. Once a sample has been selected and measurement techniques have been constructed, the process of interviewing or mailing questionnaires must be undertaken with the same care as that required by earlier steps. Some problems likely to be encountered are interviewer cheating (selection of readily available individuals rathers than those designated by the sampling procedure or possibly the interviewer filling out the schedule himself), interviewer bias (a conscious or subconscious misinterpretation of responses), or respondent bias (cues the respondent may pick up that yield reactions to questions that more closely reflect what the respondent believes is expected of him than his actual feelings). Much of the time, if interviewer bias or respondent bias is present, it is unintended. A black respondent, for example, may respond differently to black and white interviewers asking the same questions even though both interviewers adhere to the same professional standards in their work. Finally, interviewers themselves may vary in the skill with which they can establish rapport with respondents, maintain their interest, avoid an aborted interview, ask questions without giving cues, etc. In many cases, these skills are developed by interviewer training sessions conducted immediately before the field research is undertaken. If a questionnaire, rather than an interview, is used to obtain attitude or opinion data, the major problem is the response rate, which if low is usually associated with bias and thus makes it difficult for the investigator to generalize to the universe originally selected for study.

The data analysis step of survey research is so varied that it defies description in a limited amount of space. Fortunately, the articles in Parts II–V of this anthology expose the student to a wide variety of strategies and

[13]Charles R. Tittle and Richard J. Hill, "Attitude Measurement and Prediction of Behavior: An Evaluation of Conditions and Measurement Techniques," *Sociometry*, 30 (June, 1967), pp. 199–213.

techniques. Some, for example Smith's discussion of current knowledge about Asian affairs, are simple and straightforward because they are primarily descriptive. Total sample responses are compared with the responses of sub-groups classified by sex, age, education, and similar variables and percentage comparisons convey all the information necessary to accomplish the author's purpose. On the other hand, those selections concerned with explanation as well as, or instead of, description involve much more complex analyses including the use of tests as diverse as chi-square and factor analysis to determine how two or more variables are related to one another, the introduction of statistical controls for still other variables, and frequently even a comparison of results based upon different types of statistical manipulation. The various statistical tests and the manner in which data are arranged in tables represent the survey researcher's attempt to approximate the model of the laboratory experiment by seeing how different levels of an independent variable relate to one or more dependent variables while the influences of still other variables are *statistically* controlled. At this point, the reader need not worry about the mechanics involved in computing the various statistics associated with data analysis. *Why* they have been used and what they enable the investigator to conclude is made explicit in most of the articles selected for inclusion in later sections.

Not all investigators design and execute their own surveys because of the time and expense involved, especially if the concern is with a national or international universe. In recent years, there has been an increasing tendency to rely upon and re-analyze a growing body of existing data readily available from several major data archives. Several of the selections in this volume (including half of those in Part III) attest to the success of this strategy. The major data sources, the kinds of data available from them, and how more detailed information about them may be obtained are described in "Archival Data on Political Attitudes: Opportunities and Pitfalls," by Norval D. Glenn. As his title indicates, not only are the research opportunities provided stressed but so are some of the cautions that should be observed in the secondary analysis of these data. The discussion may stimulate the reader to do his own secondary research or, at least, will alert him to the problems associated with those secondary analyses included in this volume.

Part I of this anthology does not purport to expose the reader to all of the theoretical and methodological problems inherent in the study of attitudes and opinions. As an introduction to this topic, it should serve as a sensitizer for the remainder of the book which, in addition to substantive concerns, will illustrate the material covered here as well as introduce other aspects of conceptualization and methodology.

ATTITUDE FORMATION AND PUBLIC OPINION*

DANIEL KATZ
The University of Michigan

THE CONCEPTS OF "ATTITUDE" AND "PUBLIC OPINION" ARE RELATED BUT not identical. Attitude is defined at the individual level, namely, the specific organization of feelings and beliefs according to which a given person evaluates an object or symbol positively or negatively. Public opinion, or more appropriately the public-opinion process, is a description at the collective level and refers to the mobilization and channeling of individual responses to affect group or national decision-making.[1]

There are four stages in the process of public-opinion formation: (1) the salience of some problem for a number of people, even a small minority; (2) the discussion of the problem resulting in increased salience; (3) the formulation of alternative solutions and the narrowing of alternatives; and (4) the final mobilization of opinion to affect the collective decision either through a majority vote, as in an election or referendum, or through the assessment by leaders of the strength of mobilized opinion in coming to a decision. The census-taking of poll-takers in ascertaining the opinions of a representative sample of the public may or may not be a measure of the public-opinion process as defined. It depends upon whether there is a common salient problem about which discussion has taken place and alternative courses of action have been formulated.[2] (Thus, if polled during a period of freedom from international tension, the overwhelming majority of people may express strongly their wishes to remain out of war. Once there is common awareness of some threat to the nation, discussion in the mass media, and a proposed solution of a warlike character by leaders, the picture may change markedly.)

Attitude formation is relevant in the public-opinion process, however, both for the background attitudes which limit the alternatives formulated and for understanding how these attitudes are aligned to give support or rejection to the alternatives for action. A knowledge of existing attitudinal structure of the public can indicate the general directions in which peo-

---

*Reprinted by permission of the author and publisher, from Daniel Katz, "Attitude Formation and Public Opinion," *Annals*, 367 (Sept., 1966), pp. 150–162.

[1] Floyd H. Allport, "Toward a Science of Public Opinion," *Public Opinion Quarterly*, 1 (1937), pp. 7–23.

[2] In the political sector the public-opinion process is institutionalized with respect to electoral behavior. Thus, we do not enter the later stages of the public-opinion process in a presidential year until the conventions have been held, the candidates nominated, and the campaigns joined. Hence, polling the public about candidates before the convention furnishes background data which in themselves are an inadequate basis for the prediction of the outcome. Polling when the public-opinion process is well launched, that is, after the convention, does afford an excellent basis for prediction.

ple can move. The right wing of the Republican Party in 1964 incorrectly
assessed the basic values and attitudes of the American public in assuming
that a strong, clear enunciation of conservative doctrines would win supporters to their candidate and secure an unrivaled turn-out of millions of
previously apathetic conservatives. And even where the crystallized public
opinion of the group is at variance with the aggregate of individual opinions at an earlier stage of the process, the discrepancy can still be accounted for by the general principles governing individual attitudinal
change. For example, people may favor public health measures, but in the
course of a campaign to fluoridate the water supply in their community
the arguments about introducing foreign substances into the water may
engage the defensiveness of anomic individuals who feel victimized and
manipulated and who hence reject the poison symbolism of fluoridation.[3]

TRENDS IN ATTITUDE RESEARCH

A brief review of significant theoretical and research trends in the study
of attitudes may suggest the problems as well as the progress in an understanding of the mechanisms of attitude change.

Suggestion and Stereotypes. The early research on attitude formation in the 1920s and 1930s came at a period during which ideological
models of man were being rejected. Man was viewed as a creature whose
cerebral cortex was the servant of emotional forces rather than their master. The prestige of authority, of numbers, and of social status were the
key concepts in understanding man's suggestibility and irrationality. The
Freudian movement gave depth and substance to this approach, in which
the logic of the unconscious replaced the logic of the conscious and
rationalization received more attention than rationality. There were those,
however, who still clung to a more rational utilitarian model, save that
rationality was still the means for achieving need satisfaction rather than
an ideological force in its own right. In recent years, however, the pen-
dulum has swung in the other direction. Present-day research is heavily
occupied with cognitive processes, and the most popular models are those
of cognitive consistency. Some documentation of these trends will contribute to an understanding of the complexities of the factors in attitude
formation and will suggest the need for a broader framework for predicting attitude change.

Research on attitudes in the 1930s piled up evidence to demonstrate
that the ideational content of communications was less significant than
their association with prestigeful sources. For example, literary passages
would be judged less on their merit than on their alleged authorship.[4] The
same selection attributed to Robert Browning in one group and Edgar

[3]In fact, Gamson found that the opponents of a fluoridation campaign were
much more suspicious and helpless than the proponents. Willam A. Gamson, "The
Fluoridation Dialogue," *Public Opinion Quarterly*, 25 (1961), pp. 526–537.
[4]Muzafer Sherif, "An Experimental Study of Stereotypes," *Journal of Abnormal
and Social Psychology*, 29 (1935), pp. 371–375.

Guest in another received radically different evaluations. Moreover, this prestige effect was found not only among undergraduates in science courses but also among English majors. Similar experiments concerned with communications about political, economic, and social beliefs yielded the same type of outcome.[5] When a statement appeared over the name of John Adams, its true author, it received a much more favorable evaluation than when it appeared over the name of Karl Marx.

The experiments just cited dealt with the prestige of the source in affecting the evaluation of messages. Even earlier experiments had shown that attitudes could be changed by the prestige of numbers, that is, that people would modify their beliefs and attitudes to accord with majority opinion—the so-called band-wagon effect. The study of compliance and conformity thus has a long history. During the 1930s, moreover, research demonstrated that Lippmann's doctrine of stereotypes[6] could be substantiated even among sophisticated audiences. The ready-made stereotypes of the culture or of the subculture did, in fact, furnish coding categories for people, so that they responded to new information not by assimilating it in terms of its meaningful content but by distorting it to fit their stereotyped codes.

The Authoritarian Personality. The doctrines of suggestion and stereotypes had pretty well run their course when a new input into the emotional concept of man came from researchers following a neo-Freudian point of view. In the 1940s and 1950s, the work of the California investigators on the authoritarian personality explored the motivational sources of attitude formation at a depth level.[7] The major assumptions in these studies were that attitudes reflected the basic value patterns of the individual and that these value patterns were the product of his unconscious conflicts and his defensive mechanisms for handling such conflicts. Thus, prejudices toward out-groups reflect suppressed hostility deriving from childhood experiences in the socialization process. When the child is punished for aggression, thwarted by parents but still dependent upon them for affection and security, he learns to repress his aggressive tendencies. He may, however, become a hostile person and as an adult express his hostility toward socially approved scapegoats. The authoritarian personality, lacking insight into the conflict between his aggressive and social needs, and not aware of the source of his insecurity, develops a rigidity of cognitive structure and an intolerance of ambiguity. He tends, moreover, to fall back upon conventional stereotypes, dichotomous thinking, and power-oriented identification. He is both more submissive to those above him in the pecking order and more exploitive toward those below him. His attitudes thus are determined at two levels: emotionally, his

[5] Irving Lorge, "Prestige, Suggestion and Attitudes," *Journal of Social Psychology*, 7 (1936), pp. 386–402.

[6] Walter Lippmann, *Public Opinion* (New York: Macmillan, 1922).

[7] T. W. Adorno, Else Frenkel-Brunswik, Daniel J. Levinson, R. Nevitt Sanford, *The Authoritarian Personality* (New York: Harper & Brothers, 1950).

substantive values are congruent with acts of hostility toward less-favored groups and, cognitively, his mode of thinking is simplified, restricted, and accepting of in-group–out-group distinctions.

Research support for this general hypothesis is highly suggestive though not conclusive. In general, significant correlations have been found between social prejudice and the F-scale—the measure designed as a test of authoritarianism. This positive relationship is not as clear a confirmation as might be desired, in that the F-scale is not a pure measure of personality disposition. It also taps a conservative ideology, so that the correlations found may be more a demonstration of the consistency of ideological patterns than a relationship between personality mechanisms and prejudice.[8] Nonetheless, the consistencies predicted by the proponents of this view are many and striking. It has been demonstrated, for example, that attitudes toward international affairs are also significantly correlated with the F-scale, with the more internationally minded people scoring lower on authoritarianism.[9] In addition some laboratory studies have confirmed the rigid character of thinking of the high F-scorers. People low on this measure are better able to handle problem-solving in dilemma-type situations than people high on the measure.[10] Finally, attempts to arouse and to change emotionally held attitudes based upon a recognition of their ego-defensive basis, as postulated in this approach of Adorno and his colleagues, have been successful. Thus, high-F subjects have been found to respond more to authoritarian appeals from people in positions of authority than people who score lower on the scale.[11] And subjects who are given some understanding of the psychodynamics underlying prejudice maintain a significant change in attitude over time, whereas those who are presented the usual information materials show a great deal of backsliding in the same time period.[12]

[8] Herbert H. Hyman and Paul B. Sheatsley, " 'The Authoritarian Personality': A Methodological Critique," in Richard Christie and Marie Jahoda, eds., *Studies in the Scope and Method of "The Authritarian Personality"* (New York: Free Press, 1954), pp. 50–122.

[9] Daniel J. Levinson, "The Authoritarian Personality and Foreign Policy," *Journal of Conflict Resolution*, 1 (1957), pp. 37–47.

[10] Milton Rokeach found that subjects high in authoritarianism were more rigid in solving a problem in which the effects of mental set have to be counteracted than were those low in authoritarianism, Milton Rokeach, "Generalized Mental Rigidity as a Factor in Ethnocentrism," *Journal of Abnormal and Social Psychology*, 43 (1948), pp. 259–278. R. Brown corroborated this finding, but only when subjects worked under conditions of stress, Roger Brown, "A Determinant of the Relationship Between Rigidity and Authoritarianism," *Journal of Abnormal and Social Psychology*, 48 (1953), pp. 469–476. Other investigators have not been able to replicate the Rokeach resesults.

[11] Morton Wagman, "Attitude Change and the Authoritarian Personality," *Journal of Psychology*, 40 (1953), pp. 3–24.

[12] Daniel Katz, Irving Sarnoff, and Charles McClintock, "Ego Defense and Attitude Change," *Human Relations*, 9 (1956), pp. 27–46. Also Katz, Sarnoff, and McClintock, "The Measurement of Ego Defense as Related to Attitude Change," *Journal of Personality*, 25 (1957), pp. 465–474.

Instrumental Character of Attitudes.   Another trend in attitude research has studied the instrumental character of attitudes for need satisfaction of a more obvious kind, as in the utilitarian model of Jeremy Bentham. For example, people are said "to vote their pocketbooks," that is, to support the political candidates and parties representative of their economic interests. More broadly, attitudes are the means for reaching any recognized goal. Thus, people will change their attitudes to insure acceptance in a group and to rise to positions of leadership. Soldiers in combat in World War II gladly accepted Negroes as replacements in their platoons; some American leaders have changed their attitudes about racial segregation because of the needs of a different image of the United States in the non-white world.

With the rise of field theory in psychology the utilitarian model more explicitly became a model of subjective or psychological perceptions and probabilities. Field theory maintained that objective realities become important only as they are perceived and cognized by the individual and that the field of forces responsible for behavior consist of the individual's own interpretation of his experiences and external influences. Hence, one could no longer assume that people would adopt attitudes to advance their own self-interest as objectively defined. Rather, their own conceptions of desirable goals would have to be ascertained as well as the perceived instrumentality of attitudes for achieving these goals.[13]

Consistency Models.   Field theory thus directed attention to perception and cognition. Since people seem to organize their perceptions and beliefs in meaningful and sensible patterns, one outcome has been the development of models of cognitive consistency. These models postulate that inconsistent beliefs create imbalance and that there is a push toward balance or symmetry. In other words, the assumption is that man has a strong need for consistency and that he changes his attitudes to eliminate some incompatibility in his cognitions. The incompatibility may result from discrepancies between belief and behavior or from contradictory attitudes, as long as the behavior and attitudes have cognitive representation.[14]

Consistency models stem from the work of Heider, who dealt with the ways in which people view their relations with other people and with their environment.[15] He distinguished between relations of liking and disliking and unit-forming relations such as similarity, proximity, causality, and ownership. A positive unit relationship calls for a positive sentiment relationship. Things perceived as similar should be similarly evaluated. Moreover, if a given person P likes another person O, and P likes some object X, then a

---

[13]Cf. Dorwin Cartwright, "Some Principles of Mass Persuasion," *Human Relations*, 2 (1949), pp. 253–267.

[14]For a cogent presentation and discussion of models of cognitive consistency, see Robert B. Zajonc, "The Concepts of Balance, Congruity and Dissonance," *Public Opinion Quarterly*, 24 (1960), pp. 280–296; also Roger Brown, *Social Psychology* (New York: Free Press, 1965), pp. 549–609.

[15]Fritz Heider, "Attitudes and Cognitive Organization," *Journal of Psychology*, 21 (1946), pp. 107–112; Fritz Heider, *The Psychology of Interpersonal Relations* (New York: John Wiley and Sons, 1954).

balanced state exists if O also likes X. Other balanced conditions would be that P likes O and dislikes X, and O dislikes X; or that P dislikes O and likes X and O dislikes X. Unbalanced conditions are unstable and generate forces for change to achieve balance. Jordan's research reports that balanced relations are evaluated as more pleasant than unbalanced states.[16] De Soto found that subjects learned sets of hypothetical relationships among individuals with respect to mutual attraction more readily when the structures were symmetric than when asymmetric.[17] In a follow-up study Zajonc and Burnstein reported two findings: (a) that an unbalanced structure was more difficult to learn than a balanced one, but only when the issue was an important one, and (b) negative relationships were more difficult to learn than positive ones.[18]

Newcomb has adapted the Heider model to his study of changes in attitudes and mutual attraction among students living together in a university house. They were complete strangers to one another before their recruitment for Project House, and their attitudes on a number of issues as well as their perceptions of one another were measured over a semester. These students did change in the direction predicted by balance theory in the four-month period, in that they did move toward favorable evaluation of those whose attitudes accorded with their own. There was no significant change in attitudes, however. Balance was achieved for most subjects by changing their preferences for their colleagues, though in a few cases students maintained their preferences and their attitudes, but distorted their perceptions of the orientations of others.[19]

The most interesting applications of the consistency principle, however, come from the work of Festinger and his students in testing predictions based upon their theory of cognitive dissonance.[20] This theory asserts that dissonance is produced by any logical inconsistency in cognitions. The strength of the dissonance is a function of the importance to the individual of the cognitive elements in conflict, the proportion of relevant elements that are dissonant with the one in question, and the degree to which the consonant and dissonant elements weighted by their importance are equal in magnitude. The greater the dissonance, the greater will be the resulting change in attitudes, beliefs, or behavior.

One example of the type of non-obvious prediction generated by dissonance theory is the experiment of A. R. Cohen, who recruited students at Yale University to write essays against their attitudes toward the New Haven

[16] Nehemiah Jordan, "Behavioral Forces That Are a Function of Attitudes and Cognitive Organization," *Human Relations*, 6 (1953), pp. 273–287.

[17] Clinton B. DeSoto, "Learning a Social Structure," *Journal of Abnormal and Social Psychology*, 60 (1960), pp. 417–421.

[18] Robert B. Zajonc and Eugene Burnstein, "The Learning of Balanced and Unbalanced Social Structures," *Journal of Personality*, 33 (1965), pp. 153–163.

[19] Theodore M. Newcomb, *The Acquaintance Process* (New York: Holt, Rinehart and Winston, 1961).

[20] Jack W. Brehm and Arthur R. Cohen, *Explorations in Cognitive Dissonance* (New York: John Wiley and Sons, 1962).

police.[21] Following a student riot at New Haven, there had been accusations of police brutality, and student opinion ran high against the actions of the police force. Cohen asked students to furnish arguments on the police side of the issue, since he already had full information on the other side, and offered different groups of students rewards ranging from fifty cents to ten dollars for writing the essays. A control group received no reward. Then students were asked to fill out attitude scales concerning the justification for the police actions in the riot. On the basis of reward theory, one would expect the most favorable shift away from the baseline of the control group for the highest reward condition. Dissonance theory, however, would predict that there would be greater dissonance created by writing an essay against one's beliefs under conditions of low reward and hence that there would be greater attitude change in the groups receiving fifty cents and a dollar than in the groups receiving five dollars and ten dollars. This, in fact, was the case, with the ordering of groups on attitude change in inverse proportion to the amount of reward.

Similar experiments have confirmed the basic finding that participating in a task for little external incentive creates more change than for high incentive. This could also be explained by the greater arousal of internal or self-motivation where people carry out the assignment for minimal external rewards. But the Festinger school would argue that the more precise, parsimonious explanation is one of dissonance reduction. Moreover, other experiments have demonstrated that individuals who voluntarily perform disagreeable tasks tend to assess these tasks favorably.

Dissonance theory, thus, is not concerned with the factors often studied in attitude change, such as situational determinants of a rewarding or a punishing kind or personality predispositions in and of themselves. It is concerned with the internal stress produced by cognitive inconsistencies. By focusing upon this area of tension it calls attention to sources of attitude change which have been ignored or which contradict the usual assumptions about the conditions under which beliefs and attitudes can be modified. Two instances of such novel predictions can be cited. In the first place, it is assumed, not without evidence, that a communicator highly acceptable to an audience and representing some of their values will be more influential than a communicator who has more social distance from the group. According to dissonance theory, however, the communicator closer to his audience will produce less change than the distant speaker if one condition can be met, namely, that the audience can somehow be committed to really listen and consider the arguments of the speaker. If they do listen, greater dissonance will be created by the speaker less acceptable to the audience than by the one more acceptable.

In the second instance a very similar prediction is made, namely, the more strongly an attitude is held, or the more extreme the individual's position, the greater the change will be. Again, however, the necessary condition is sufficient commitment on the individual's part to receive new inputs or en-

21 *Ibid.*, pp. 74–78.

gage in some form of activity inconsistent with his attitude. Most theories of attitude hold to the opposite view, namely, that the more extreme an attitude position or the more firmly it is held, the more difficult it is to change the individual. The critical condition, then, is one in which the person experiences some incongruity between his original position and new inputs because he has had some choice in taking action which brings him into conflict. Personality conversion, though its incidence is not great, has been a problem for attitude theorists. Dissonance theory may fill this gap.

In general, dissonance theory would maintain that any factor contributing to the strength of an individual's cognitive discomfort would lead to change either of behavior or belief. The limiting condition for producing dissonance is choice or commitment, that is, the individual himself agrees to engage in some activity which makes salient the contradiction in cognitions. Without such commitment, the individual will merely ignore the more hostile communicator, avoid the punishing or effortful task, and persist in his own convictions.

The qualification of choice and commitment does limit the general usefulness of the dissonance notion. The major battle is often one of securing commitment or consent to a course of action in the first place. On the other hand, such engagement does not necessarily mean a profound decision on the part of the individual. All it implies is a willingness to enter a situation, assume a role, or take some action. So long as he perceives that he has acted voluntarily, the requirement is met. Advertisers have long employed techniques to elicit such behavior by securing some response through return mail or by getting people to try their product. Moreover, the commitment does not always have to be obtained in full by the communication itself. The message may capitalize upon some partial previous commitment. Though national political campaigns give some attention to converting the opposition, a great deal of political work concentrates upon maximizing support from those already partially and even marginally committed to the party.

In general, then, dissonance theory would argue for shifting from heavy external pressures to smaller inducements but with more perception of choice by the individual and more effort on his part.

RESOLUTION OF DIFFERING THEORETICAL CONCEPTIONS: THE
FUNCTIONAL APPROACH

Though we have witnessed a variety of models for dealing with attitude formation and change, they have not been dramatically opposed to one another in many of their major aspects. Hence, with some modification, they can be brought together within a more comprehensive framework which recognizes different types of motivational needs and their interaction with cognitive processes. A move toward a more complete model is the Kelman theory of social influence. He postulates three different processes in acceptance of social influence: *compliance*, in which the influencing agent has control of rewards and punishment; *identification*, in which the person is attracted to the influencing agent; and *internalization*, in which the ideas of the communicator are accepted as congruent with the values of the recipient. Moreover, to use Kelman's own words:

> When an individual adopts an induced response through compliance, he tends to perform it only under conditions of surveillance by the influencing agent. When an individual adopts an induced response through identification, he tends to perform it only under conditions of salience of his relationship to the agent. When an individual adopts an induced response through internalization, he tends to perform it under conditions of relevance of the issue, regardless of surveillance or salience (p. 54).[22]

A more ambitious attempt to handle the complexities of the factors affecting human behavior is the functional approach, which has been espoused, in somewhat different formulations, by Smith, Bruner, and White[23] and by Sarnoff and Katz.[24] Both formulations center about the functions which attitudes serve for the individual and deal more specifically with the motivational bases of belief systems. Smith, Bruner, and White have postulated three basic types of roles which attitudes play: social adjustment, externalization, and object appriasal. An example of the first process would be the taking over of the norms of the individual's reference group to insure acceptance by other group members or a sharing in group rewards. The second process of externalization refers to the role of unresolved internal problems in attitude formation. Externalization deals, for example, with the depth basis of prejudice in repression and projection as described by the psychoanalytic approach to authoritarianism. The third process of object appraisal is more cognitively oriented and shows how attitudes serve the individual's need for understanding the realities of his social world. Social adjustment and externalization thus distinguish between the adjustment to environmental pressures and the ego-defensive needs of the individual.

Sarnoff and Katz have independently made similar distinctions among the adjustment, defensive, and knowledge functions. In addition, they have included the function of value expression (which is very much like Kelman's internalization). This framework thus differentiates between the more negative ego motivation built around defense mechanisms where the individual is driven by anxiety and the more positive ego motivation of value expression where the individual embraces and develops new ideas to accord with his basic values and self-concept.[25] The latter need is akin to the motivation emphasized in the self-actualization and self-realization doctrines of Rogers[26] and Maslow.[27] Attitudes in the service of value

---

[22] Herbert C. Kelman, "Compliance, Identification and Internalization: Three Processes of Attitude Change," *Journal of Conflict Resolution*, 2 (1958), pp. 51–60.

[23] M. Brewster Smith, Jerome Bruner, and Ralph W. White, *Opinions and Personality* (New York: John Wiley and Sons, 1956).

[24] Irving Sarnoff and Daniel Katz, "The Motivational Basis of Attitude Change," *Journal of Abnormal and Social Psychology*, 49 (1954), pp. 115–124.

[25] Daniel Katz, "The Functional Approach to the Study of Attitudes," *Public Opinion Quarterly*, 24 (1960), pp. 163–204.

[26] Carl R. Rogers, "Toward a Modern Approach to Values," *Journal of Abnormal and Social Psychology*, 68 (1964), pp. 160–167.

[27] Abraham H. Maslow, *Motivation and Personality* (New York: Harper, 1954).

expression are not so much instrumental as they are intrinsic to this function. Their substantive content has meaning for the individual in itself, whereas an attitude serving a utilitarian need is only a means to an end. This fourfold approach to attitude dynamics further specifies the conditions for arousal and change as is indicated in Table 1 below.

TABLE 1

Determinants of Attitude Formation, Arousal, and Change in
Relation to Type of Function[a]

Function	Origin and Dynamics	Arousal Conditions	Change Conditions
Adjustment	Utility of attitudinal object in need satisfaction. Maximizing external rewards and minimizing punishments	1. Activation of needs 2. Salience of cues associated with need satisfaction	1. Need deprivation 2. Creation of new needs and new levels of aspiration 3. Shifting rewards and punishments 4. Emphasis on new and better paths for need satisfaction
Ego defense	Protecting against internal conflicts and external dangers	1. Posing of threats 2. Appeals to hatred and repressed impulses 3. Rise in frustrations 4. Use of authoritarian suggestion	1. Removal of threats 2. Catharsis 3. Development of self-insight
Value expression	Maintaining self-identity; enhancing favorable self-image; self-expression and self-determination	1. Salience of cues associated with values 2. Appeals to individual to reassert self-image 3. Ambiguities which threaten self-concept	1. Some degree of dissatisfaction with self 2. Greater appropriateness of new attitude for the self 3. Control of all environmental supports to undermine old values
Knowledge	Need for understanding, for meaningful cognitive organization for consistency and clarity	1. Reinstatement of cues associated with old problem or of old problem itself	1. Ambiguity created by new information or change in environment 2. More meaningful information about problems

[a]From "The Functional Approach to the Study of Attitudes" by Daniel Katz, *Public Opinion Quarterly*, 24 (Summer, 1960), p. 192.

The functional approach has many advantages in furnishing a more comprehensive framework for taking into account the complexities of attitude formation and opinion change. By definition, it does not throw out personality predispositions and motivational factors, and permits dealing indirectly with these determinants. In the cognitive-consistency models, motivational conflict is handled tangentially, if at all. The need for consistency is not ignored in the functional approach, in that knowledge and utilitarian needs are included. It is thus better able to account for conditions under which inconsistent as well as consistent behavior occurs. And it also makes possible a consideration of the interacton between cognitive and motivational factors. More specifically, in at least four ways, the functional model can help to synthesize theorizing and research in social psychology.

1. If we examine the functional basis of attitudes we are better able to answer the question of the nature of cognitive consistency: consistency for what? In the various models of cognitive consistency it is assumed that elements which are logically incompatible exert a pressure toward change. If I love my dog, I want my friends who like me to love my dog. But there are very restrictive limits to this type of consistency. An academic intellectual may heartily dislike his colleagues in a political party, but may accept them because he and they are both working for a common objective. Here the logical inconsistency of smaller matters is tolerated because of the logic of the larger purpose. If we take into account the basic utilitarian and value commitments of the individual we have a better criterion for dealing with problems of consonance and dissonance.[28] Take the example of Senator Fulbright, whose conservative views and behavior on civil rights have been incongruent with his liberal and humanitarian values on international relations. Once it is realized that the Senator is from Arkansas and must be elected by the people of that state the problem of inconsistency is easily understood. In accounting for the behavior of people outside of the constraints of a laboratory situation we need a theoretical framework which can handle some of the major sources of variance.

A more general type of example of the importance of moving toward a broader model can be seen in the old distinction between public and private attitudes. To maximize the utilitarian or adjustment function, people may display attitudes in public settings which are inconsistent with their personal beliefs which serve their own value systems. They readily compartmentalize these areas of cognition if the situational factors permit. They realize that they are living in a complex world which makes conflicting demands upon them.

2. Rational models of man give greater weight to his consistent seeking to maximize gains and minimize losses than a fuller understanding of motivation and cognition justifies. The facts are that men do not seek for optimal solutions but are content for given periods with satisfactory solutions, as March and Simon have so ably pointed out in their concept of *satisficing*.[29]

[28] William A. Scott makes a similar point in showing that inconsistencies in beliefs about international affairs which are remote from the person may not be inconsistent with his major personality system, "Rationality and Non-Rationality of International Attitudes," *Journal of Conflict Resolution*, 2 (1958), pp. 9–16.

[29] James G. March and Herbert A. Simon, *Organizations* (New York: John Wiley and Sons, 1958).

This is due, in part, to the many needs which people have, so that they do not pursue economic goals or other single-type objectives exclusively, It is also due to the limitations of the cognitive process, which is essentially near-sighted. Immediate and obvious factors are over-weighted compared to more temporally and spatially remote factors.

3. Older research findings on the compelling force of majority opinion and of the prestige of status and authority can be assimilated within a functional framework by considering the types of motivation and cognition involved. It is not sheer numbers that produce an impression of majority opinion to which people conform but the character of the majority in relation to the individual's psychological group membership. If the majority lie outside the individual's own group the effect upon him will be much less than if it is a majority of his own group. The concept "reference group," introduced by H. Hyman, specifically deals with this phenomenon.[30] The reference group is not necessarily the group in which the individual has formal membership. It is the group with which he identifies, the norms of which furnish the frame of reference for evaluating ideas and making decisions. Motivationally, it furnishes social support for the person and cognitively it meets his needs for object apprisal and mental structure.

H. Cantril and R. Centers, in studying the role of social classes on attitude formation, utilized this concept.[31] Instead of placing individuals in social classes according to objective measures of income and occupation, people themselves were asked about their subjective class identification. In his famous Bennington study, T. Newcomb also demonstrated that the girls who made the Bennington group their frame of reference took on the norms of that subculture more readily than those who did not accept this frame.[32] Stouffer and his associates employed the concept of reference group in developing their notion of relative deprivation of men in the armed forces during World War II.[33] Satisfaction and discontent were not as strongly related to favorable or unfavorable conditions as they were to the relative expectations of men determined by their group frames of reference. Though better-educated soldiers had a higher promotion rate than the less-well-educated group, the former were more dissatisfied about their chances of promotion than the latter.

The prestige of authority when considered in relation to a functional approach also becomes a more complex phenomenon. People will conform to pronouncements of authority, but not necessarily in a blind irrational fashion. The demands made upon them must fit their cognitive structures, which help them understand and operate in the real social world. They are much

[30] Herbert H. Hyman, "The Psychology of Status," *Archives of Psychology*, No. 269 (1952).

[31] Richard Centers, *The Psychology of Social Classes* (Princeton: Princeton University Press, 1949).

[32] Theodore M. Newcomb, *Personality and Social Change* (New York: Dryden Press, 1943).

[33] Samuel A. Stouffer, *et al.*, *The American Soldier, Combat, and Its Aftermath*, Vol. 2 (Princeton: Princeton University Press, 1949).

more likely to accept authoritative requests which are in accord with their notions of legitimacy and relevance. Thus, the union leader's stand on issues related to labor-management negotiations will be more readily folowed by union members than his stand on political issues. Similarly, the American people will obey laws which affect behavior in the public domain more readily than laws about private and personal matters. This was the problem at issue in enforcing the old Volstead Act. Civil rights legislation is easier to pass and enforce when it is directed against discrimination in the public domain than when it is aimed at private behavior.

4. Finally, the psychoanalytic model can be contained within a functional approach as one set of basic determinants of emotionally held attitudes. It would be an error, however, to equate all discriminatory behavior against races and minority groups with prejudice of an ego-defensive character. Discriminatory practices can bring material and psychological rewards to the dominant group of a more obvious type than the expression of repressed hostility. What has made ethnic and national prejudice such a powerful force is the combination of motives it can service for so many people, thus producing an over-determination of social behavior. Moreover, the emotional determinants of racial prejudice receive rich cognitive support in a culture in which prejudice has had a long history. Since aggression is repressed by social stimuli, that is, the significant others in the child's socialization, its release against minority groups is facilitated by social support for discrimination in one's own group and subculture. This is reflected in the cognitive pattern accompanying prejudice, namely, that the minority group is seen as a threat to law and order, to property values, to jobs, to health, and the like. Recent studies have yielded evidence supposedly supportive of a belief-congruence theory of prejudice.[34] Experimental subjects are asked to evaluate people varying from themselves in different dimensions such as race, social class, religion, and characteristic beliefs. In general, subjects are less affected by the race of the target person than by his belief system. If he is a Negro but of their social class and of their own persuasion in his beliefs, he is more acceptable than a member of their own race but of different social class and different belief patterns.

The results of these studies have been interpreted as showing that prejudice is not a negative evaluation of race membership as such, but a rejection of people of different beliefs and characteristics from the person making the judgment. This an over-generalization of the findings, for they are also consistent with the theory that racial prejudice is supported by belief systems congruent with the prejudice. It is easier to show discrimination against people who are perceived as inferior, threatening, and characterized by beliefs of an undesirable type than against people who are like oneself save in racial identification.

[34]Milton Rokeach, ed., *The Open and Closed Mind* (New York: Basic Books, 1960), pp. 132–168; David D. Stein, Jane A. Hardyck, and M. Brewster Smith, "Race and Belief: An Open and Shut Case," *Journal of Personality and Social Psychology*, 1 (1965), pp. 281–289.

The implications of the functional model for attitude change are clear. In the first place, the methods and types of influence which will affect existing attitudes must be differentially geared to their motivational basis (see Table 1, p. 22). Emotionally held beliefs in the service of ego defense will be the most difficult to change. Change here requires some acquisition of insight into one's own internal conflict. Attitudes linked to basic value systems can be modified through an approach which first seeks understanding of the nature of the value systems of the person and the linkage of attitudes to these values. In the second place, the nature of attitudinal change varies for the functions already described. It is easier to substitute one attitude for another when the attitude is a means to an end than when it provides consummatory satisfaction in itself. Instrumental attitudes for helping the individual to meet utilitarian needs are easier to replace with other attitudes than are the beliefs central to the individual's value system. In the third place, more enduring change will result when ego defenses have been breached or value systems restructured than when situational forces require instrumental conformity. Finally, an understanding of the attitudes of people and prediction about their modification must begin with a much more thorough assessment of the functions they serve. Campaigns to influence the public resort to attempts to saturate the market with information, or to a variety of devices in the hope that some one of them will be effective, or that they will somehow have an additive effect. Little is done before such campaigns to assess the motivational basis of existing attitudinal structures.

A HEADNOTE ON THE EXISTENCE AND STUDY OF POLITICAL ATTITUDES

BERNARD HENNESSY

California State University, Hayward

THIS IS MEANT TO BE A QUESTION-RAISING PAPER. IT IS NOT A REVIEW OF the literature, nor is it a systematic attempt to explore any piece of that vast area of speculation-research-inference that we call "political attitudes."

Instead, I ask some simple questions: what are political attitudes? who has political attitudes? how do we know about them? what do we know about them? and what more do we want to know about them?

I advance the proposition that political attitudes are an elite phenomenon. Most people do not have political attitudes. Even in modern high-energy societies most people do not have political attitudes. When we accept that fact, and accept the epistemological and research implications that flow from it, we will be able to make more sense of attitude formation and change, of leader-follower relationships, and of the public policy-making processes.

ATTITUDES AND POLITICAL ATTITUDES

Attitudes are relatively enduring orientations toward objects (including, of course, ideas, other people, etc.) that provide individuals with mental frameworks for making economical sense of the world.[1]

Attitudes may be distinguished as being less intense and less central-to-the-personality than beliefs, as being less specific in their referents than opinions, and as being conceptually useful only at the individual level of analysis—although they may be, and of course are, aggregated for de-scriptive-statistical purposes.[2]

Political attitudes, then, are relatively enduring orientations toward *political* objects. I define political as phenomena having to do with the authoritative allocation of values for the community as a whole.

The perceptive reader of article introductions will note that I have opted for a narrower definition ("the *authoritative* allocation of values") rather than the wider definition ("the exercise of power") in defining the domain of politics. It is part of the hard line I take in this article—partly as provocation—that "political attitudes" have come to mean everything

---

[1] I think the attitude experts would generally agree to this summary definition; for more thorough considerations see the classic discussion by Gordon W. Allport, "Attitudes," in C. Murchison, ed., *Handbook of Social Psychology* (Worcester, Mass.: Clark University Press, 1935), pp. 798–884; and William J. McGuire, "The Nature of Attitudes and Attitude Change," in G. Lindzey and E. Aronson, eds., *Handbook of Social Psychology* (Reading, Mass.: Addison-Wesley Publishing Co., 1969), 3, pp. 136–314, esp. pp. 141–149.

[2] My interpretation of attitudes and opinions is essentially that of Leonard Doob, *Public Opinion and Propaganda* (New York: Holt, Rinehart and Winston, 1948).

from penis envy to existentialism, and that, smart as we political analysts
are, we probably shouldn't undertake to study everything that everybody
thinks about. The article is, among other things, a request that we keep
our eyes on what most people regard as politics, namely, the structures,
roles, processes, and policies of governance. I regard political attitudes to
be relatively enduring orientations toward the structures, roles, processes,
and policies of governance.

When political attitudes cohere in larger patterns exemplifying beliefs,
then ideology may be present. Ideology becomes, then, the most inclusive
concept of those we deal with here. Still limiting the discussion to the individual level—the only level at which psychological concepts can be
actually investigated[3]—we can think of an order of concepts that consists of: (1) opinions, as immediate orientations toward contemporary
controversial political objects; (2) attitudes, as more diffused and more
enduring orientations toward political objects not necessarily controversial at the moment; and (3) ideologies, as networks of related attitudes and
opinions that exemplify basic beliefs with regard to political objects.

HOW DO WE KNOW ABOUT POLITICAL ATTITUDES?

The short answer to the subhead is: we know about political attitudes
only inferentially. That is, attitudes are inferred from behavior. Attitudes
are not apparent. Attitudes don't happen. Attitudes are not real.

Yet we all know that attitudes—or something identical in function, whatever its name might be—have to be called into existence if we are to make
sense of human behavior. However skeptical the social scientist might be
about the reality of attitudes he is in the position of the faith healer in the
celebrated English limerick:

> There was a faith healer from Deal
> Who said, "Although pain isn't real,
> When I sit on a pin
> And it punctures my skin
> I dislike what I fancy I feel."

There are three methods for the study of attitudes. They are (1) survey
research, (2) deductive speculation from psychological theory (often
supplemented by clinical observations), and (3) experimentation. Each
will be briefly commented on.

Survey Research. Of the three methods survey research is by far the most
important for political attitudes—most important, that is, in bulk of work
and in acceptance (or at any rate, diffusion) of findings among social scientists. One measure of the wide use of survey research on political attitudes is the compendium of over 100 scales published by the Survey Re-

---

[3] Which is another comment on the level-of-analysis dilemma: psychological variables can be investigated only at the individual level, because that's where they really
happen; but findings at the individual level can be aggregated in such a way that we
can make social-level statements about them.

search Center in 1968.[4] The editors point out that, when political attitude scales alone number over 100, the mere listing of single-item attitude questions would be a "gigantic and perhaps hopeless task."

The typical survey research approach to political attitudes is charmingly direct: the respondent is asked what he thinks about a political object. Thus attitudes about Communists, for example, are elicited by questions like: "Do you think we can trust the leaders of Communist countries to keep their word?" And if *respondent Americanus* says "no," as most do, then we infer an attitude called "mistrust of Communists."

Often, and increasingly by more sophisticated researchers, a number of questions are asked about a political object; these presumably all tap an orientation that we call an attitude, and if there is some logical coherence in the answers (that is, if the respondent's answers fit together in the same way as did the scaling-sample by which the questions were "standardized") then we infer an attitude. And we quite rightly have more confidence in our inference if we have used a scale (that is, a number of questions that cohere logically, and if pretested, empirically) than if we have used only a single question.

It might appear that, in being so simpleminded and didactic, I am making fun of survey research on political attitudes. Not at all. As a believer and a user it's far from my intention to ridicule our best efforts. For I do think that survey research on political attitudes is more fruitful for our objectives—which I take to be understanding of man and his social works —than either of the other two methods.

But I seek simplicity in the service of humility. The study of political attitudes by survey research falls lamentably short of the criteria of empiricism. It is a tissue of assumptions and inferences.

The remarkable fact is that the assumptions and inferences work. They do help us understand many (but not all) individuals, and help us make sense of much (but not all) political behavior.

Deductive Speculation From Psychological Theory. The oldest method for attitude study, and the one still favored by those with therapeutic or learning orientations, is that of deductive speculation from psychological theory.

The origin of the word "attitude" may be instructive in thinking about its meaning. Through the first three quarters of the nineteenth century "attitude" meant, essentially, body posture. Lewis Carroll employed the word in this older sense in *Through The Looking Glass* when he describes Haigha, the Anglo-Saxon messenger, as going into "curious attitudes . . . skipping up and down, and wriggling like an eel."

Attitude as a body posing (or, even better, as a body *poising*) became

---

[4] John P. Robinson, Jerrold G. Rusk, and Kendra B. Head, *Measures of Political Attitudes* (Ann Arbor: University of Michigan Institute for Social Research, 1968). A familiarity with this book, and especially with the introductory chapter by the editors, would be of much use to the person wanting an efficient overview of the scope and the dangers, as well as the challenges, of political attitude study by survey research.

by a simple transfer a mental poising—a psychological orientation, or readiness to act. The early behaviorists needed a bridging inference between perception of stimulus and response. That is, organisms needed to have some stored propensities to respond in certain ways to stimuli, once the stimuli were perceived as having meaning. The alternative to the notion of stored propensities was the postulation that every perception was reasoned about *de novo*—and of course such a suggestion was on its face absurd and behaviorally most improbable. Thus the need for an economy concept—the attitude—to sort out stimuli perceptions according to ready-made categories.

In this way S-R theorists bootlegged attitudes into their theories. And then, having got one (of several) concepts *induced* into their "black box," the organism, they began to *deduce* theoretical expectations, that is, hypotheses about attitudes. Attitudes to the more orthodox S-R theorists are clustered conditioned traces (electrochemical or molecularly-patterned in their biological base), products of earlier experience, that predispose the organism toward responses. Therefore if one knows enough about earlier experience one can, theoretically, predict attitudes.[5]

The story of psychoanalytic concern with attitudes is also, to oversimplify considerably, the story of bootlegging the concept into the original theory. Freud's concept of drive, an hydraulic analogy, was his functional substitute for attitude—a drive was a patterned tendency to act. The drive concept, however, as everyone now knows, was incapable of handling culturally-induced behavior, and the later Freud, as well as all the latter-day Freudians, found it *necessary* to accept a broader concept of "tendency to act," and found it *convenient* by the middle thirties to accept the common term "attitudes." As would be expected, attitudes were incorporated into the psychoanalytic framework as adjuncts to the ego, the regnant and organizing element of the individual. Attitudes served as cognitive and affective "defenses" for the individual. Daniel Katz's and Irving Sarnoff's recent statements may be taken as illustrative of the theoretical place that attitudes have in the neo-psychoanalytic frame. Attitudes, they say, serve a number of personality needs: the first two being *instrumental* (getting along in everyday life), and *knowledge* (organizing the environmental data), both of which are straightforwardly cognitive in nature, and of relatively little interest to psychotherapy. The third and fourth are more heavily affective: the *value expressive* needs served by attitudes are those that project the individual's self image; and the *ego-defensive* needs that attitudes may serve are those that preserve the individual's basic sense of selfdom.[6]

---

[5] Although the hard-line S-R theorist might say there's no point in predicting an intervening variable like attitude because if one knew *that* much about earlier experience one could predict behavior (response) directly. Which is why hard-line S-R theorists never spent much time on attitudes, but left it to personality psychologists and social psychologists (especially personality-in-culture theorists) to develop attitudes as patterned links between individual-level and social-level phenomena.

[6] Daniel Katz, "The Functional Approach to the Study of Attitudes," *Public Opinion*

Political attitude study in Freudian theory has been principally of derivative concern in considerations of "the political personality." The main lines of those investigations have been extrapolations of basic Freudian personality types to political activists. Freudian insights, especially those related to resolutions of infancy and childhood conflicts over sexuality, parents, and general authority relationships, are applied to real or ideal-type political activists. Earlier social science speculators on psychoanalytic political personality include Lasswell[7] and Almond.[8] The *genre* has received sporadic attention since the middle 1920s, with the most concentrated work being by Adorno and disciples on the authoritarian personality[9] and by Erikson and his followers in their two-pronged attack on political leadership—one historical, exploratory of political greats such as Luther[10] and Wilson,[11] and those who might be charitably described as near greats such as Chicago Mayor Anton Cermak[12]; the other cultural, developmental, and aggregative, exemplified by Pye on the Burmese[13] and the Chinese,[14] and McClelland on the entrepreneurial personality in general.[15]

Experimentation. There have been very few direct *experiments* on political attitudes. Gosnell's early study of controlled campaigning is almost alone in the literature, and even that did not focus on attitudes primarily.[16] Of course, political objects, especially those presumed to be ideology-related, have served along with non-political objects in a number of laboratory efforts at attitude change. Thus Hovland and his collaborators used attitudes toward German and Japanese political activity, toward civilian production effort, toward social responsibility of the steel in-

---

Quarterly, 24 (Spring, 1960), pp. 163–204, and Irving Sarnoff, "Psychoanalytic Theory and Social Attitudes," *Ibid.*, pp. 251–279. See also M. Brewster Smith, Jerome S. Bruner and Robert W. White, *Opinions and Personality* (New York: John Wiley & Sons, 1956).

[7] Harold L. Lasswell, *Psychopathology and Politics* (Chicago: University of Chicago Press, 1930).

[8] Gabriel A. Almond, "The Political Attitudes of Wealth," *Journal of Politics*, 7 (Aug., 1945), pp. 213–225.

[9] T. W. Adorno, *et al.*, *The Authoritarian Personality* (New York: Harper and Row, Inc., 1950).

[10] Erik H. Erikson, *Young Man Luther* (New York: W. W. Norton & Co., Inc., 1958).

[11] Alexander L. George and Juliette L. George, *Woodrow Wilson and Colonel House* (New York: John Day Co., Inc., 1956).

[12] Alex Gottfried, *Boss Cermak of Chicago* (Seattle: University of Washington Press, 1962).

[13] Lucien W. Pye, *Politics, Personality and Nation Building: Burma's Search for Identity* (New Haven: Yale University Press, 1962).

[14] Lucian W. Pye, *The Spirit of Chinese Politics: A Psychocultural Study of The Authority Crisis in Political Development* (Cambridge, Mass.: M.I.T. Press, 1968).

[15] David C. McClelland, *The Achieving Society* (Princeton, N.J.: Van Nostrand, 1961); and David C. McClelland and David G. Winter, *Motivating Economic Achievement* (New York: The Free Press, 1969).

[16] Harold F. Gosnell, *Getting Out the Vote: An Experiment in the Stimulation of Voting* (Chicago: University of Chicago Press, 1927).

dustry, and toward draft policy in their studies on communication and persuasion, 1944–1952.[17] Their conceptual efforts and research designs simply teem with suggestions for experimentation on political attitudes— especially with hints to quasi-experimental field designs.[18] Similarly, Lasswell's discussion of "Experimentation, Prototyping, Intervention"[19] links some scattered experimental and field studies on, for example, executive decision-making and political self-perception; more importantly, he suggests the increased use of "prototyping" ("an innovation, typically small-scale, made in political practice primarily for scientific purposes") as a policy-science device somewhere between laboratory experimentation and public reform program. So far social science seems unwilling and/or unable to employ prototyping to that level where its potential uses and its limits could be provisionally evaluated.

In the absence of greater experimental or field-experimental research there remain many questions about the diverse and often conflicting findings of experimentalists and survey researchers. Those who wish to reflect on these questions should see Hovland's article, "Reconciling Conflicting Results Derived from Experimental and Survey Studies of Attitude Change," for observations on communications research, but also for possible extrapolations to more *general political* attitudes.[20]

WHAT DO WE KNOW ABOUT POLITICAL ATTITUDES?

Political attitudes, we agree, are orientations toward political objects. They are related, in logic clearly—and in practice, too, but less clearly— to antecedents and to consequences. That is to say, political attitudes come from somewhere; from the biological facts and the life experiences of the individual.[21] And political attitudes go somewhere; to expression in language and in behavior like voting, or maybe even to repression and psychopathology. This section is a commentary on some problems in the linking of political attitudes with antecedents and consequences.

[17] See Carl I. Hovland and Irving L. Janis, eds., *Personality and Persuasibility* (New Haven: Yale University Press, 1959); Carl I. Hovland, Irving L. Janis, and Herbert H. Kelley, *Communication and Persuasion* (New Haven: Yale University Press, 1953); and Carl I. Hovland, Arthur A. Lumsdaine, and Fred D. Sheffield, *Experiments on Mass Communication* (Princeton: Pirnceton University Press, 1949).

[18] Thus the chapter "Group Membership and Resistance to Influence," in *Communication and Persuasion* (pp. 134–165) contains dozens of researchable propositions about political leadership and followership.

[19] Harold Lasswell, "Experimentation, Prototyping, Intervention," in his *The Future of Political Science* (New York: Atherton Press, 1963), pp. 95–122.

[20] Carl Hovland, "Reconciling Conflicting Results from Experimental and Survey Studies of Attitude Change," *The American Psychologist*, 14 (Jan., 1959), pp. 8–17. See also Philip E. Converse, "Attitudes and Non-Attitudes: Continuation of a Dialogue," Paper read at the Seventeenth International Congress of Pyschology, Washington, D.C., August, 1963.

[21] Of course, in this brief essay, I must avoid the nature-nurture argument. The expression "biological facts and life experiences" is the phrase-blanket that covers all: from double-Y chromosomes, aggressivity, male-bonding and all such possible physiological roots of political attitudes, to the most delicate, even subliminal, stimulus of the environment.

Not Everyone Has Political Attitudes. But first, before linkages, a direct query about the reality of political attitudes. Some of the more perceptive literature in the last decade has suggested that there may be many people who do not have political attitudes. However, the proposition has not been made directly and explicitly that political attitudes are found only among minorities characterized by certain cognitive and integrative capacities. I think that proposition could be made—and by so making it social science might achieve some conceptual clarification, as well as considerable understanding of research findings that are now confusing and contradictory.

Converse first put the pieces together in his perceptive and much-quoted article "The Nature of Belief Systems in Mass Publics."[22] He says that mass publics don't have belief systems. A belief system he defines as "a configuration of ideas and attitudes in which the elements are bound together by some form of constraint or functional interdependence." He points out that many historical and social science observations presume that the "constraint among idea-elements visible at an elite level is mirrored by the same lines of constraint in the belief systems of their less visible 'supporters.' *It is our argument that this assumption not only can be, but is very likely to be, fallacious"* (emphasis added).

There were some earlier hints from survey research that average Americans didn't put political things together in any interdependent whole. McClosky *et al.* reported that "followers of each [major American] party, often ignorant of the issues and their consequences, find it difficult to distinguish their beliefs from those of the opposition and have little reason to be concerned with the consistency of their attitudes. . . . In short, if we mean by ideology a coherent body of informed social doctrine, it is possessed mainly by the articulate leadership, rarely by the masses."[23] And Prothro and Grigg found that there was very little consistency between responses to general statements about democracy and responses to specific applications of those statements. Although voters in Ann Arbor, Michigan, and Tallahassee, Florida, agreed almost to a person on democratic principles, on applications of those principles they "were closer to complete discord than to complete consensus."[24] Converse's explanation for the Prothro-Grigg findings is simply that "the individual lacks the contextual grasp to understand that the specific case and the general principle belong in the same belief system: in the absence of such understanding, he maintains psychologically independent beliefs about both."

Compare Converse's explanation for the Prothro-Grigg finding with the

[22] Philip Converse, "The Nature of Belief Systems in Mass Publics," in David Apter, ed., *Ideology and Discontent* (New York: The Free Press of Glencoe, 1964), pp. 206–261, esp. p. 210.

[23] Herbert McClosky, Paul J. Hoffman, and Rosemary O'Hara ,"Issue Conflict and Consensus Among Party Leaders and Followers," *American Political Science Review,* 54 (June, 1960), pp. 420–421.

[24] James W. Prothro and Charles M. Grigg, "Fundamental Principles of Democracy: Bases of Agreement and Disagreement," *Journal of Politics,* 22 (May, 1960), p. 291.

explanation by McPhee *et al.* for their similar finding from 1954 congressional election data:

> [An apolitical] person has an observable opinion only when he is prompted
> to react, for example, by a dinner party, interview, or whatever. Thereafter,
> "out of sight, out of mind," that is, he soon forgets these casual responses. . . .
> [W]hen some months later he is again prompted to respond on this topic,
> it is a *new* response independent of the first. . . . If another opinion on a
> related topic was also elicited at the first time, it is not only independent
> of the first opinion . . . but independent "of itself" when a new version of
> it is given at some second time a month or two later.[25]

McPhee *et al.* argue, consistently with Converse's view, that two or more
expressed opinions, given casually and in an offhand manner by a person
who has little interest in the subject, may be logically inconsistent. They
are not part of any definable belief system.

Converse effectively refutes every interpretation that could save the
notion that political belief systems exist through all educational and SES
strata of American society. It might be thought that the proportion of
Americans who have no political belief system is tiny and insignificant,
but the data show that not more than 12 per cent have logically (or culturally) interrelated idea-patterns about politics, and not more than perhaps 40 per cent more have group-related patterning of political opinions
(what Converse calls "ideology by proxy"). Thus the paucity of political
belief systems is "not a pathology limited to a thin and disoriented bottom
layer of the *lumpenproletariat*, [but] immediately relevant in understanding the bulk of mass political behavior."[26]

He shows that even ideology by proxy—that is, the relating of attitudes
and preferences to group memberships—is not demonstrable in 30 to 50
per cent of the American public. On pro- or anti-Negro questions a full 30
per cent of Americans have insufficient contextual information to pattern
their responses[27] and on political party questions not more than 50 per cent
of the public can put together the liberal or conservative label, and their
meanings, with the appropriate major party.

Converse finds that tau-gamma coefficients of responses from SRC surveys reveal no correlations that could reasonably be elements of belief systems among the population at large.[28]

[25] William N. McPhee, Bo Anderson, and Harry Milholland, "Attitude Consistency,"
in William N. McPhee and William A. Glaser, eds., *Public Opinions and Congressional
Elections* (New York: The Free Press, 1962), p. 91.

[26] Converse, "Nature of Belief Systems," p. 213.

[27] *Ibid.*, pp. 236–237.

[28] With a smaller and a different kind of sample Luttbeg argued that factor analysis
does distinguish ideological clusterings in mass publics, and suggests that Converse
should have subjected his data to factor analysis. Luttbeg's study of attitudes and
beliefs of citizens on local questions in Eugene and Springfield, Oregon, alerts us to the
need for more intensive, controlled research on opinion-attitude-belief integrations (or
lack thereof) in differing publics, milieus, and issue-areas. Norman R. Luttbeg, "The
Structure of Beliefs Among Leaders and the Public," *Public Opinion Quarterly*, 32
(Fall, 1968), pp. 398–409.

It might be argued, also, that individuals in the mass public do have political belief systems, but they are idiosyncratic—that they interrelate internally to the individual's own psychological scheme of things, but since they are different individual by individual they cannot be aggregated, and therefore aggregate measures would not find them. To test that argument, implausible and logic-chopping as it is, Converse looked at survey responses by the same people to the same questions at two different periods of time. And over time there was no important consistency such as there would have to be if the members of mass publics had genuine, although idiosyncratic belief systems.[29]

Where does that leave us? I submit it leaves us with the high probability that (1) not more than 10 to 30 per cent of the voting adults in America have even a rudimentary sense of how political things should go together;[30] that many people do not have political attitudes, for we have said that attitudes are tendencies—tendencies that rest upon some sense of *categorization and appropriateness* that necessitates a minimum of integration of things political; and therefore (3) that political opinions may, and for some significant number of average people, do, exist as more or less *ad hoc* and unintegrated responses to stimuli of the moment.

It is thus necessary to distinguish opinions from attitudes, and both from belief systems, in the psychological analysis of political phenomena. The distinctions have been around for several years, of course, but the reasons for making them have been heretofore regarded as definitional (semantic), aesthetic, or one of emphasis-giving.

But belief systems, I am arguing, require some yet-to-be-specified but clearly essential level of knowledge, capacity for concept integration, and interest-arousal; all three probably, and not merely one alone or two in combination. Further, I am arguing that attitudes, like belief systems, require both integration of similar-dissimilar stimuli and a background of biocultural readiness-to-respond. *Therefore, in most, even the most advanced, political communities a significant fraction of the citizens are unlikely to possess political attitudes, just as they are innocent of political belief systems.* For them political opinions may or may not be held, and may or may not be expressed (though they probably will be expressed only upon direct provocation),[31] but most of those opinions will be psychological epiphenomena.[32]

[29] Converse, "Nature of Belief Systems," p. 239.

[30] By "should go together" I mean should go together in *any* sense, logically, culturally (as patterns of received ideas and behaviors), or idiosyncratically.

[31] Converse also suggests that a majority of American survey respondents will "fabricate" an attitude, even when they are asked not to or when screening questions are used. "Attitudes and Non-Attitudes," p. 15.

[32] If I read Milton Rokeach right he would agree that many adults do not have political belief systems (or ideologies), and that many do not have political attitudes. Moreover, his definition of "opinion" seems to indicate that many adults can not have political opinions either—because opinions, to him, are "verbal expression(s) of some belief, attitude, or value." See Milton Rokeach, *Beliefs, Attitudes and Values: A Theory of Organization and Change* (San Francisco: Jossey-Bass, Inc., 1968), *passim,*

What does this mean for the study of political opinions, attitudes, and belief systems? I submit it means we are naive and inconsequential if we waste time with mass belief systems and mass attitudes. Beyond the concern for some outer cultural limits to what elites may do, we should not try to investigate that which isn't. We should, instead, research attitudes and belief-systems in three contexts: (1) descriptive, mapping their existence among elites; (2) dynamic, which means (2a) individual elite change processes and (2b) aggregate attitude change among elites and the creation of political attitudes and belief-systems among those not formerly possessing them (that is, political socialization and political education investigations, broadly); and (3) policy-relatedness, by which I mean research on how attitudes descriptive and dynamic relate to governmental outputs under various environmental and input conditions.

Political Attitudes and Political Parties. Political attitudes strongly reflect the influence of group identifications. The orientations individuals have toward political objects tend to be consistent with (and mutually to reinforce) the individuals' perceptions of group positions toward those same political objects. The dynamics appear to be something like this: (1) political object becomes salient for the individual; (2) he looks for clues with which to make cognitive and/or affective evaluations of the political object; (3) among the important clues—probably the *most* important source of clues—is the individual's assessment of how the political object is regarded by groups he identifies with; (4) his perception of the way such groups regard the political object is made consistent with his own orientation toward the object.

All the research on American political attitudes finds that the party is the dominant group clue-giver. More than any other groups, party identification "explains" political attitudes—which is a loose way of saying that many otherwise independently held stimuli seem to be given meaning in political party terms. If the income tax is being promoted by the Democratic Party that knowledge alone may be enough for the Democrat to firm up his attitude toward income taxes. For the loyal Republican it may be enough that his party's spokesman, President Nixon, says Vietnamization is desirable to make Vietnamization in fact desirable. As a lodestar for fixing political attitudes the party seems to be paramount wherever it has gained the status of an enduring political institution; it is an attitude-organizing group of great importance.

It's not surprising that the political party is the main group referent for political attitudes. It is the relevant organizing agent for clue giving on political attitudes. And that is, of course, one of its manifest and explicit goals. All successful party leaders see the party as a giver of meaning to the masses, as a simplifying device for the economy of thought among vast

---

and for definitions, pp. 123–126, and 132. What I am saying is that in research on political psychology we often get responses that appear to be opinions but that are in no way expressions of, or linked to, beliefs, attitudes, or values, but rather are psychologically meaningless.

numbers of people whose limited thinking-resources will be largely devoted to nonpolitical objects. It seems clear whenever large numbers of people participate in political decision-making that some economical ordering-group like the political party is indispensable. If parties didn't exist they would have to be invented.

Thus it seems to me that the recent predictions of the disappearance of political parties are not very likely to be borne out. It seems certain that the relative importance and differential attitudinal meanings individuals attach to parties, and to other political or potentially-political groups, are changing and will continue to change. If it turns out to be the case that, because of vast socioeconomic (especially educational) changes, a larger proportion of the world's adults acquire political attitudes, then it may be that more and more groups will be wholly or in part politicized in the sense that they become clue-givers. Conceivably all adults could achieve political attitudes, even—why not?—a full set of opinions-attitudes-beliefs-values on things political. If that were to happen many political attitudes would no doubt be related to a vastly-proliferated set of non-party groups; but at some point economy would reassert itself, and the need would be recognized for some overarching group to coordinate/integrate things political. *Voilà*, the political party! The political party as attitudinal anchor is as durable, it seems to me, as is the political party as interest aggregator; and both are inevitable in any society that offers freedom for the play of conflicting demands.

Attitudes Change, But We Know Very Little About When and How. Common sense and everyday observation confirm that people sometimes change their attitudes. If, as I argue above, many adults do not have *political* attitudes, then the investigation of political attitude change must exclude such adults. That seems like a most obvious and useless statement. But is it? Individuals who do not have political attitudes must be eliminated from the objects for which attitude change phenomena are relevant. On the other hand, persons who do not have political attitudes may gain them, and are of great interest for the study of the creation of attitudes even though they are irrelevant to a study of attitude change.

I have earlier drawn attention to the importance of distinguishing attitude creation from attitude change.[33] It may be that the differences between creation and change are insufficiently recognized in part because of the differences in the traditions and perspectives between attitude-creation researchers and attitude-change researchers. The development of *new* attitudes is a central concern of developmental psychologists, learning theorists, and socialization social-psychologists; their research emphasizes stimulus-response measurements, effects of differential conditioning, imitative behavior, and the habit principle. Attitude *change*, however, seems to have become the province of the social and experimental psychologists who

---

[33] Bernard Hennessy, "Public Opinion and Opinion Change," in James A. Robinson, ed., *Political Science Annual I* (Indianapolis: Bobbs-Merrill Co., 1966), pp. 268–269.

emphasize equilibrium or Freudian models, perception-cognition activities, problem-solving, along with rationality and/or psychotherapy.

Leaving political socialization (that is, attitude creation) aside, for the moment, I can only say here that, in my view, attitude change is best explained by a combination of functional and balance theory in which change-promoting stimuli are seen as inducing sufficient cognitive and emotional imbalance (discomfort) that adjustment becomes necessary for maintaining the minimal functions that the attitudes are designed to perform.[34] But suggesting a possible general framework for thinking about attitude change is a very far thing from understanding it. I can only suggest that those who wish further enlightenment on the attitude-change literature should see McGuire's recent exhaustive essay on the subject. I agree with his gloomy conclusion about all the contemporary theories of attitude change: "Each has an appreciable *a priori* plausibility; each has given rise to intriguing predictions; each has provoked admirable research. In short, each deserves to be true. Unfortunately, none seems to have any great deal of empirical validity."[35]

WHAT MORE DO WE WANT TO KNOW ABOUT POLITICAL ATTITUDES?

We want to know a great deal more about distributions of political attitudes. As I argue above, this is partly a question of finding out who has political attitudes. Much more attention should be given to the development of survey devices and experimental techniques that screen out respondents who fabricate opinions and attitudes. Once we disenthrall ourselves of the notion that every adult has manifest (or at least latent) political attitudes, then we can develop adequately sensitive indicators.

At the same time it is of interest to note what is characteristic of those who have no political attitudes, because comparative descriptions of those who have with those who haven't will tell us much about how political attitudes may be generated. I have suggested on the basis of the existing literature that minimal cognitive activity, integrative capacity, and motivational arousal—all three—are necessary for the generation of *any* attitudes. Political attitudes come into being when all three prerequisites are focused on political objects.

The mapping of distributions, and the construction of adequate measuring devices, should be followed (or accompanied) by attention to the creation and to the change of political attitudes. Much work has been done on the creation of political attitudes in the school-age child in America. Almost all of it, as its devotees admit, is limited and uncritical in its methodology (interview-provoked responses that are likely to be fabricated) and in its objects (white public school children of average means and conformist orientations).[36] Merelman's recent article breaks new

[34] See Bernard Hennessy, *Public Opinion* (Belmont, Calif.: Wadsworth Publishing Co., 2nd Edition, 1970), pp. 361–379.

[35] McGuire, "The Nature of Attitudes and Attitude Change," p. 271.

[36] The Greenberg and the Kolson-Green articles in this issue are exceptions. See

ground in its integration of a Piagetian developmental model with a number of findings from experimental psychology on self-identification and child rearing; much fruitful research could be undertaken in the directions he suggests.[37]

We need more rigorous and more critical explorations of the relations between political attitudes and political behavior. When, among political elites, will attitudes determine behavior? There is evidence that political elites, especially those in representative roles, base their behavior on their assessments of the attitudes of "significant others" such as powerful constituents.[38] I suggest that political leaders generally follow a "law of anticipated reaction" which often leads to behavior that is inconsistent with their own attitudes. Bargaining, logrolling, and the capacity to delay gratification are especially likely to result in inconsistencies between simple attitudes (such as those that might be measured by single items or Guttman scales) and behavior. The point is that the attitudes of political activists are likely to be more complex, interrelated in strategic/tactical ways as well as in logical/substantive ways, and therefore understanding the links between attitudes and behavior may require much more situational and idiosyncratic information than survey research is able to make available.[39] We should perhaps increase our use of participant observation and other techniques of more complete researcher involvement.[40]

Finally, among this small list of large questions about political attitudes, we would like to know more about leader-follower relations. A usually unspoken but root premise of the pluralist democrats, as distinguished from the populist democrats, is that leaders have considerable free choice and wide discretion in the policy outputs they can generate. That premise, hinted at by pluralists (often apologetically) and regretted by populists,

---

Jack Dennis, "Major Problems of Political Socialization Research," *Midwest Journal of Political Science*, 12 (Feb., 1968), pp. 85–115.

[37] Richard M. Merelman, "The Development of Political Ideology: A Framework For The Analysis of Political Socialization," *American Political Science Review*, 63 (Sept., 1969), pp. 750–767. Merelman seems ready to accept the view that many (most?) adults do not have political attitudes:

We should not ignore the effects of our making attitudinal inconsistency and slippage a primary assumption in the study of politics. Accepting such a premise makes our tasks doubly difficult. Many of our most cherished findings, not only from the "behavioral" sides of political science—such as public opinion and electoral behavior —but also from the more institutional areas of the discipline, become problematic.

[38] See, for example, Charles F. Cnudde and Donald J. McCrone, "Constituency Attitudes and Congressional Voting: A Causal Model," *American Political Science Review*, 60 (March, 1966), pp. 66–72; and G. R. Boynton, Samuel C. Patterson, and Ronald D. Hedlund, "The Missing Links in Legislative Politics: Attentive Constituents," *Journal of Politics*, 31 (Aug., 1969), pp. 700–721.

[39] Samuel A. Kirkpatrick, "Political Attitudes and Behavior: Some Consequences of Attitudinal Ordering," *Midwest Journal of Political Science*, 14 (Feb., 1970), pp. 1–24, esp. pp. 13, 15, and 22.

[40] See James A. Robinson, "Participant Observation, Political Internships, and Research," in James A. Robinson, ed., *Political Science Annual II* (Indianapolis: Bobbs-Merrill Co., 1969), pp. 71–110.

makes a good deal more sense if we accept the notion that the masses typically do not have political attitudes or belief systems. Policy-making becomes something like the thieves' midnight distribution of booty while the victims remain asleep; as long as those with interest, attitudes, and shared power bargain successfully among themselves the deed is done without any wide social or cultural constraints being invoked. That image (elite minorities with political attitudes and mass majorities without them) goes far to explain most of the recent findings about voting behavior in local referenda.[41] It also complements nicely Schattschneider's insightful observations about when and why the scope of political conflict ebbs and flows from restrictive to widely participative.[42] Further, it helps to clarify the use of political public relations, and underscores again the importance of massive media campaigns for the selective manipulation of communications that *look like* mass attitudes but are in fact aggregated Pavlovian responses, psychologically epiphenomena even when they are tactically powerful and/or successful.

All of which leads me, in concluding this too-short and oversimplified "headnote," to return to my opening *caveat* against an over-psychologizing approach to the study of political attitudes. We—at least we political scientists—have probably followed our curiosity too far down the garden path, away from the realities of political life, into that corner where Bentley feared there was mere "soul stuff . . . which starts with a rough, untested guess, and comes out in a rough, untested guess, with nothing but metaphysics in between."[43]

[41] See, among others, Robert L. Crain, Elihu Katz, and Donald B. Rosenthal, *The Politics of Community Conflict* (Indianapolis: Bobbs-Merrill Co., 1969).

[42] E. E. Schattschneider, *The Semi-Sovereign People: A Realist's View of Democracy in America* (New York: Holt, Rinehart and Winston, 1960).

[43] Arthur F. Bentley, *The Process of Government* (Bloomington, Ill.: Principia Press, Inc., 1949, Reprint of 1908 Edition), p. 30.

POLITICAL BELIEF SYSTEMS AND POLITICAL BEHAVIOR

HARRY R. WILKER
State University of New York at Buffalo

LESTER W. MILBRATH
State University of New York at Buffalo

T HIS PAPER IS ADDRESSED TO SEVERAL CONCEPTUAL INADEQUACIES IN THE way that social scientists have looked at political attitudes, political beliefs, political behavior, and the way that the interrelationships between these concepts have been viewed. One set of these difficulties derives from our confusion of civic myth and empirical reality. Present in contemporary American society is the myth of the "informed citizen." The "informed citizen" takes an interest in political matters, thinks about and discusses politics with his neighbors, weighs all sides of all issues, and takes appropriate political action in pursuit of his rational self-interest. Research into the substance of this myth shows slight empirical foundation upon which a conception of the "informed citizen" might rest. Some scholars have reacted to such findings by suggesting that since this assumption of democratic theory is incorrect the theory is in need of revision.[1] Other scholars have responded by asserting that we must find ways to make this myth a reality.[2]

In later studies the problem has been recast in terms of the development of political belief structures in ordinary citizens. Such studies have focused on the ability of citizens to recognize and be informed about public policy questions; and on their ability to see some relationship between a political action that they take (for example, voting) and the political outcome that they wish to achieve. Large numbers of people show by questions on policy issues that they cannot link the policy outcome that they desire with the stands of the public officials that they support. Philip Converse has shown, in a very extensive and competent discussion, that the great mass of people cannot recognize many policy issues, do not have a clear position of their own, cannot link a stand on one policy with stands on other policies, and cannot link their policy stands to appropriate political actions that will help to realize them.[3] He finds by a very broad defini-

---

[1] See Bernard Berelson, et al., Voting (Chicago: University of Chicago Press, 1954); Robert Dahl, Who Governs? (New Haven: Yale University Press, 1961); V. O. Key, Public Opinion and American Democracy (New York: Knopf, 1965); Gabriel Almond and Sidney Verba, The Civic Culture, (Princeton: Princeton University Press, 1963); and Walter Lippman, Public Opinion (New York: The Free Press, 1922).

[2] See Peter Bachrach, The Theory of Democratic Elitism (Boston: Little, Brown, 1967); Graeme Duncan and Steven Lukes, "The New Democracy," Political Studies, 11 (June, 1963), pp. 156–177; and Robert J. Pranger, The Eclipse of Citizenship (New York: Holt, Rinehart and Winston, 1968).

[3] Philip Converse, "The Nature of Belief Systems in Mass Publics," in David Apter, ed., Ideology and Discontent (New York: The Free Press, 1964).

tion of ideology that only about 10 to 15 per cent of American adults could be considered to have a political ideology.

While we do not dispute these findings, we do challenge a conclusion that might be derived from them: that most citizens do not have political belief systems. We shall suggest later, and support our contention, that such a conclusion is inaccurate. If one were to conclude that most people do not have political belief systems he would have to devise an explanation for behavior which is largely unguided by beliefs. We contend that an explanation which discards a linkage between beliefs and behavior is theoretically untenable.

THE NATURE OF BELIEFS AND ATTITUDES

If any theoretical progress is to be made we must begin with the relationship between beliefs and attitudes. Beliefs and attitudes generally relate to an object or to a linkage between objects. For both attitudes and beliefs an individual must cognize an object or group of objects. Given the cognition, however, two kinds of feelings may attach to the object. If the feeling is like or dislike (for example, a valence) we may say that that feeling of a valence is an expression of an attitude. If the feeling is credulity or incredulity, however, we may say that a person has a feeling of believableness about the object.[4] It is important to note that it is the feeling about the cognition which makes it believable or not; credulity does not inhere in the cognition itself. Belief and attitude, then, are distinctive kinds of feelings toward an object that an individual cognizes. Belief may also apply to cognitions about the relationships between objects (for example, if I hit the ball over the fence I'll be able to make a home run).

Our purpose in making the distinction between beliefs and attitudes is to try to reorient our research priorities. It seems to us that we have been getting the cart before the horse. We have been studying attitudes without placing them within the larger belief context from which they derive. In our perspective, belief systems are broader and more inclusive than are attitudes; they are the context from which attitudes derive and in which they must be understood. (This point will become clearer as we develop our perspective on belief systems in the succeeding pages).

Fishbein and Raven have empirically demonstrated the separate domains of attitudes and beliefs.[5] Subjects were asked to rate three concepts using the semantic differential. Ten adjective pairs were used for each concept. Five pairs represented the evaluative dimension, which we may view as an operational definition of valence or attitude. The other five adjective pairs, representing the belief or credibility dimension, were

[4] Lester W. Milbrath, "Beliefs: A Neglected Unit of Analysis in Comparative Poltics," in Edward Pinney, ed., *Comparative Politics and Political Theory* (Chapel Hill: University of North Carolina Press, 1966); Lester W. Milbrath, "The Nature of Political Beliefs and the Relationship of the Individual to the Government," *American Behavioral Scientist*, 12 (Nov.–Dec., 1968), pp. 28–36.

[5] Martin Fishbein and Bertram Raven, "The AB Scales: An Operational Definition of Belief and Attitude," *Human Relations*, 15 (1962), pp. 35–44.

called the B (Belief) scale. The B scale is comprised of the following five adjective pairs: impossible-possible, false-true, existent-nonexistent, probable-improbable, unlikely-likely. The B scale was shown to be independent of the attitude dimension when, over the set of three concepts, the two scales correlated −.168, −.069, and +.120.

Fishbein and Raven describe their B scale as measuring "belief in" an object; it is the subjective probability that the object exists. They point out that there are a great many concepts over which existence is not really at issue. Thus it is a waste of time to ask subjects to rate the credibility of "The U.S.A." on the B scale. The B scale has greater potential value when it refers to a "belief in the existence of a relationship between that object and some other object or some quality."[6] Belief in the existence of the United States may not be an important question but belief in a positive relationship between the United States and world peace is certainly an important question. The B scale, in a semantic differential, can measure the degree to which an individual believes such a relationship to exist by placing the assertion "the U.S. fosters world peace" as the semantic object to which the respondent reacts.

BELIEF SYSTEMS

When we speak of belief systems we are speaking of something more than a collection of beliefs which occur in the same individual at the same point in time. Rokeach defines belief systems as "the beliefs, sets, expectancies, or hypotheses, conscious and unconscious, that a person at a given time accepts as true of the world he lives in."[7] This definition seems to us to be too broad and unspecific to be maximally useful for theoretical purposes. Converse more explicitly adds the notion of systematic constraint. Constraint refers to ". . . a configuration of ideas and attitudes in which the elements are bound together by some form of constraint or functional interdependence."[8] When we refer to a belief system we imply that it has structural properties which hold it together.

Having defined a belief system as having interrelated parts we must now confront the evidence presented by Converse and others that large portions of the mass public can scarcely be said to have any belief system so defined. Ordinary people respond to attitude items in what resembles a random fashion. Careful observation rules out the possibility that most people organize their beliefs around a liberal-conservative continuum since items intercorrelate poorly. One must entertain the possibility that a variety of organizing principles are used for personal belief systems, but even this hypothesis seems dubious in that the over-time test-retest correlations are very low.[9] If belief systems were idiosyncratic but stable

---

[6] *Ibid.*

[7] Milton Rokeach, *The Open and Closed Mind* (New York: Basic Books, 1960).

[8] Converse, "Nature of Belief Systems in Mass Publics," p. 207.

[9] Steven Brown has recently presented some evidence which he claims contradicts these findings about over time stability in his article "Consistency and the Persistence

these correlations would be high. (This point assumes good measurement of attitudes; an assumption which may not be true in all cases but which surely should be true in some of the cases).

One might be tempted to conclude from the findings just presented that for most people their political belief systems are so poorly structured that they have no relevance for explaining their political behavior. We find this conclusion theoretically untenable. The research team of which Converse is a part, as well as many other research projects, have demonstrated that there is considerable stability in several kinds of mass political beliefs and behaviors. Most notably, people have stable reactions to and identifications with such political elements as parties and groups. In contrast to attitudes about policies, their attitudes toward parties and groups have considerable stability. It is interesting that loyalties to parties and groups are not transferred very readily into the area of policy, but this should not obscure the significance of the stability of these loyalties.

There are two reasons why it is important that we find considerable stability in the political universe of ordinary citizens. First, stable loyalties are associated with relatively stable political behavior patterns; the very strong relationship between party identification and voting direction is a case in point. More importantly, it is difficult to conceive of stable behavior occurring without some kind of stable belief structure lying behind that behavior. The skeptic might respond, "couldn't their stable response patterns be simply a function of habit?" Our answer would be that habits must be seen as functioning elements of a stable belief system. A "habit" to vote Democratic in all elections must rest on a set of beliefs about the Democratic party which is supportive of that habit.

Perhaps we have failed to find the political belief structures of ordinary citizens because we have looked for them in the wrong way. Converse focused primarily upon attitudes toward policy questions and sought to find a structure resembling a political ideology as envisioned by academics and political elites as they introspect about their own belief structures. Converse found a high frequency of such belief structures only among the college educated.[10] The fact that ideological belief systems are rarely

---

of Ideology: Some Experimental Results," *Public Opinion Quarterly,* (Spring, 1970), pp. 60–68. However, two points should be made. First, Brown's major evidence lies in showing that the relationship between an individual's response pattern at time 1 is correlated with his response pattern at time 2 to a statistically significant degree. This tells us only that such responses are not *statistically* random. Such evidence does not deal with the real question of the strength of the relationship between over time responses. That they could not have occurred by chance does not demonstrate that Converse is wrong and that people are truly capable of organized thinking as demonstrated by over time stability. Second, and more importantly, Brown deals not with the stability of items dealing with public policy issues, as does Converse, but rather with matters relating to equality, efficacy and the power of various groups (judging from the items presented). As we shall hopefully demonstrate later it is entirely reasonable for masses to have stable beliefs in these areas while they conform quite well to the chaotic patterns of response to issues of policy that Converse has described.

[10] Converse, "Nature of Belief Systems in Mass Publics," p. 225.

found in the mass public does not lead to the conclusion that ordinary people do not have belief systems that are relevant for understanding their political behavior. We believe that a different and somewhat broader conception of belief system can be delineated which will sharpen our inquiry into the ways these systems are organized and may help to explain elite-mass differences in belief structures and behaviors. To do this we will look briefly at a conception of a belief system which is implied by Converse's work. The inadequacies of this theory lead us to an alternative which we hope will elucidate some of the difficult theoretical issues that we now face.

BELIEF SYSTEMS AS BALANCE STRUCTURES

Converse's analysis leads him to conceptualize belief systems in terms analogous to balance theory. In balance theory, beliefs exist within a framework of relationships which may be in varying degrees of balance or imbalance. In a balanced structure there are no inconsistent relationships. If the belief elements "go together" the system is said to be in balance; inconsistent belief elements throw the system out of balance.

Different balance theorists conceive of balance in slightly differing ways. Festinger defines two elements to be in a dissonant relationship, not in balance) "... if, considering these two alone, the obverse of one element would follow from the other."[11] Cartwright and Harary take a more structural approach.[12] In their perspective at least three elements are examined to see whether they go together by looking at the signs connecting the objects.

Figure 1 shows two balanced and one unbalanced structure portraying the attitudes of three different individuals toward U.S. policy in Vietnam and their attitudes toward President Nixon. The person depicted in Figure 1-A has a favorable attitude toward Nixon, a favorable attitude toward U.S. policy in Vietnam, and perceives Nixon to favor the U.S. policy in Vietnam. The individual in Figure 1-B has an unfavorable attitude toward Nixon, an unfavorable attitude toward U.S. policy, and perceives Nixon to favor U.S. policy. Both these structures are balanced in that we can conceive of people comfortably holding either set of views. Cartwright and Harary formally define balance by showing that if, in a connected belief structure, all possible circular paths yield positive signs when subjected to consecutive multiplication, then the structure is balanced. If all such paths are not positive (if at least one is negative) then the structure is unbalanced. In structures of only three elements there is only one circular path and we can obtain the sign of that path by multiplying the sign of each connecting link together. Thus, the three links of Figure 1-A yield a positive path; Figure 1-B contains two negatives and one positive which also yields a positive path. Both systems may be considered to be in balance. Figure

[11] Leon Festinger, *A Theory of Cognitive Dissonance* (Stanford: Stanford University Press, 1957).

[12] Dorwin Cartwright and Frank Harary, "Structural Balance: A Generalization of Heider's Theory," *Psychological Review*, 63, (1956), pp. 277–293.

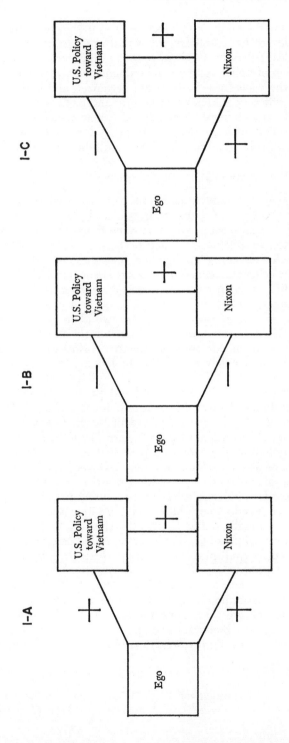

FIGURE 1
Models of Three Belief Structures From Cartwright and
Harary's Balance Theory

1-C has two positives and one negative which yields a negative value in successive multiplications. The structure is unbalanced in that the individual favors Nixon, is against U.S. policy in Vietnam, and perceives Nixon as favoring U.S. policy.

A more sophisticated conception for mapping belief structures as balanced structures, is provided by Rosenberg and Abelson's "psycho-logic."[13] Their approach can deal with a broader range of phenomena than could Cartwright and Harary's approach. Furthermore, the latter's approach could only express Ego's attitude toward Nixon via a plus or minus sign and could not represent the larger context of beliefs which undergirded that simple attitude. Rosenberg and Abelson enrich our understanding by showing us how we may represent attitudes as summations of beliefs about objects and values connected with those beliefs. This is illustrated in Figure 2, where the belief structures of three people are represented. In Figure 2-A, the individual holds the following sets of beliefs: (1) the U.S. policy in Vietnam fosters inflation, (2) the U.S. policy hurts American prestige, (3) the U.S. policy hurts international stability, and (4) the U.S. policy fosters domestic unrest. The verbs used are somewhat arbitrary; others such as increase, decrease, hinder, help, could be substituted. The power of this mode of representation is that it enables us to deduce an individual's *attitude* toward a focal object (U.S. policy in Vietnam) from a larger context of *beliefs* about that object.

The reader can see in Figure 2 that the linkages as well as the objects have signs indicating affect. If the sign of the linkage is multiplied by the sign of the object we can compute the direction of the impact of a given belief upon the individual's general attitude toward U.S. policy. A negative result for a given belief implies that the focal object hinders the attainment of a positively valued object (in Figure 2-A, U.S. policy hinders attainment of international stability), or it implies that the focal object fosters the attainment of a negatively valued object (in Figure 2-A, U.S. policy leads to inflation). A positive computational result indicates that the focal object hinders the attainment of the negatively valued object (in Figure 2-B, U.S. policy hinders Communist aggression), or it implies that the focal object fosters the attainment of a positively valued object (in Figure 2-B, U.S. policy fosters American prestige). If we compute these signs for all three individuals portrayed in Figure 2, we can see that in Figure 2-A, the belief structure shows a consistently negative attitude toward the war; Figure 2-B shows a consistently positive attitude toward the war; Figure 2-C portrays a belief system with conflicting elements.

The relationship among belief elements that Converse discusses is constraint. The notion of constraint can be seen to be essentially the same as the notion of balance. He states ". . . 'constraint' may be taken to mean the success we would have in predicting, given initial knowledge that an individual holds a specified attitude, that he holds certain further ideas and

[13] Robert Abelson and Milton Rosenberg, "Symbolic Psycho-Logic: A Model of Attitudinal Cognition," *Behavioral Science*, 3 (1958), p. 1–13.

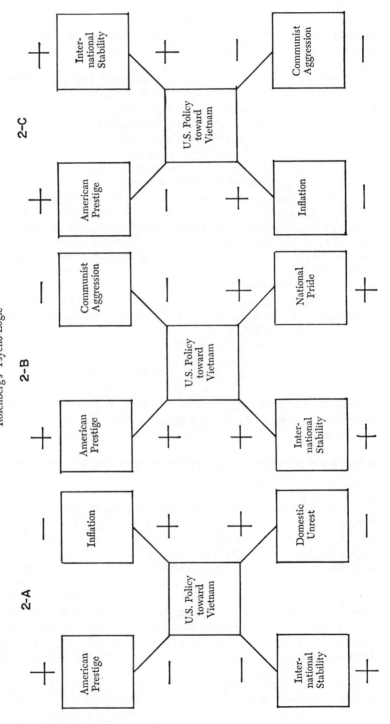

FIGURE 2

Models of Three Belief Structures From Abelson and
Rosenberg's "Psycho-Logic"

attitudes."[14] As a corollary he suggests that we can operationalize constraint in terms of correlation and measures of goodness of fit to a cumulative scale; but he cautions that these criteria apply only in a static world. "In the dynamic case 'constraint' or 'interdependence' refers to the probability that a change in the perceived status (truth, desirability and so forth) of one idea-element would *psychologically* require, from the point of view of the actor, some compensating change(s) in the status of idea-elements elsewhere in the configuration.["]

This definition of constraint implies that some kind of "psycho-logic" holds between belief elements. While Converse is quick to point out that logical constraint is but one kind of constraint, the context of his work makes it clear that beliefs in constraint are in some kind of quasi-logical, psychologically rational relationship with one another. Elements are related through a quasi-logic of cogent argument. He points out that the key factor in psychological constraint ". . . is that the elites familiar with the total shapes of these belief systems have *experienced them as logically constrained clusters of ideas* within which one part necessarily follows from another."[16]

There are several reasons to be dissatisfied with a framework that restricts the analysis of belief systems to balance structures. Balance theory has little power when the belief structure is poorly developed; indeed, it is difficult to think of it as a system at all. We have already indicated that this forces us to speak of political action as if it did not have a belief system underlying it, a posture which we find unsatisfactory. But there are other reasons as well for seeking an alternative formulation. It was apparent in the preceeding discussion that there was a nagging ambiguity when dealing with elements as "related" or "going together." Balance theory seems to posit very formal relationships and requires the researcher who would use the theory to deal with many empirical ambiguities. In certain contexts this aspiration may be burdensome and unproductive. A half-truthful query, reportedly attributable to Festinger, asks whether he ought to like chicken feed since he likes chickens and chickens like chicken feed. Such inferences seem intuitively unreasonable and yet, the model does not indicate how the researcher chooses between reasonable and unreasonable conclusions.

Balance models are well suited for dealing with quasi-logical relationships, but this is also their limitation. Ideas may be related in many other ways than that implied by balance theory. Elements may be related because of their relationship to a common desired outcome. For example, the adjustment function of attitudes as postulated by Smith, Bruner and White implies that a person may hold two contradictory beliefs because he hopes to be liked by two different groups who happen to hold contradictory positions.[17] Ideas may also be related through the need of the individual to

[14] Converse, "Nature of Belief Systems in Mass Publics," p. 207.
[15] *Ibid.*, p. 208.
[16] *Ibid.*, p. 211.
[17] M. Brewster Smith, Jerome Bruner, and Robert White, *Opinions and Personality* (New York: John Wiley, 1956).

express complementary emotions. For example, in order to hold one belief successfully, one often holds another; for example, we believe that the president is good if we believe the country is good. Logically contradictory beliefs can even be related by a need to express ambivalence toward an object. For a system to have inter-related parts it is not necessary that the interrelationships be of a quasi-logical nature. If we can find a framework for dealing with belief systems which allows us to use a broader conception of relationship, we can deal more effectively with mass belief systems and the impact of belief systems upon behavior.

FIELD THEORY

Such an alternative view of belief systems can be extrapolated from Kurt Lewin's field theory which views behavior as a function of the structural characteristics of the field at the time of the behavior one is studying.[18] In its Lewinian psychological sense field theory reduces to the statement that ". . . any behavior or any change in a psychological field depends only upon the psychological field at that time."[19] Thus behavior cannot be caused *directly* by objects which are not part of the field. This does not mean that past experiences aren't important, but only that they become important because of the effect they have on the structure of the field. "The effect of the past on behavior can only be an indirect one: the past psychological field is one of the 'origins' of the present field and this in turn affects behavior."[20]

Field theory views a field as a perceptual space. Objects themselves are not part of the field, only the perceptions of them may be accorded status as part of the field. Happening to walk into a wall does not make that wall part of the field if the individual is not aware that he is about to do so. The wall's existence will not influence the behavior of an individual unless its existence is perceived by that individual as a barrier. Colliding with the wall, in all likelihood, establishes the perception of the presence of a barrier, and the field will be structured accordingly.

From the perspective of field theory all behavior is motivated by the field underlying it. Objects in that field are interrelated by their existence in that field as the individual sees them. Objects might be interrelated through a common purpose, because they fulfill a common need, because they are in close proximity or at a distance, indeed they may be related by being perceived as in balance. The point is that objects may be related in the field in a much broader theoretical context than in balance theory. The field has a boundary and the elements are related because they lie within these boundaries.

When looking at an individual political act we can speak of the field surrounding that action as the political region of an individual's field. Such a

[18] Kurt Lewin, *Field Theory in Social Science* (New York: Harper Torchbooks, 1951).
[19] *Ibid.*, p. 45.
[20] *Ibid.*, p. 64.

field will include the purposes and behavioral intentions of the actor, beliefs about the nature of authority, government, etc., beliefs about the intentions of others, beliefs about the effectiveness of different kinds of behavior, as well as many other elements. We might refer to this political field as the individual's belief system. Belief systems conceived in this way make it possible for us to conceive of political behavior as flowing from the political beliefs held by that individual. It also enables us to look directly to differences in the structural characteristics of belief systems to account for differences in behavior.

STRUCTURING BELIEF FIELDS

Understanding the structure of a given field is essential to understanding the reasons underlying an action taken by an individual. If we wish to understand why a particular field developed in that way we would have to trace the developmental pattern of causative factors back in time. Personality factors may be important for determining the shape of a field. Taste, for example, may explain why one person has a well-developed field for understanding football while another has a well-developed field for understanding modern music. No doubt intelligence and education also play a role in that they facilitate the structuring of any given field.

These personal factors are likely to have small impact compared to what we may term situational factors. These refer to goals, purposes, and needs of the actor in his specific environment. Field theoreticians contend that a field can only be described by referring to the goals, purposes, and needs that are involved. These purposive factors are the prime motivating forces and provide the impetus for structuring the field. If we wish to understand why political elites have well-developed fields in terms of issue orientation, while the masses have poorly developed fields, we may find the answer by looking to the differences in the purpose of political activity for the two groups.

Successful navigation in an environment requires a well-structured and differentiated field. If a field is poorly structured, it ". . . means that that region is not differentiated into clearly distinguishable parts. It is not clear therefore where a certain action will lead and in what direction one has to move to approach a certain goal. . . . [T]he lack of a cognitively clear structure is likely to make every action a conflicting one. The individual, not knowing whether the action will lead him closer or farther away from his goal is necessarily uncertain as to whether or not he should carry it out."[21] Lewin uses the example of a newcomer to a city. In the first few days the newcomer's field, representing the physical layout of the city, may consist of nothing more than the train station, his rooming house, and the bus line that leads from one to the other. If he intends to settle down in the city, we may assume a need to be able to move around the city with ease. This need will motivate him to fill in the details of his cognitive map.

[21] *Ibid.*, pp. 137–138.

What is true of navigation in a largely physical environment is no less true of navigation in a purely social environment. An inadequately structured political region of a field would spell disaster for a lobbyist, political candidate, political columnist or public official. These kinds of persons have goals which can only be achieved if their political field is adequately structured. It is little wonder that investigations of their attitudes toward political issues disclose a well-developed political belief system.

But what do the political regions of the field of the mass man look like? Converse has shown, as have many others, that the ordinary citizen does not have a well-structured political field in the same sense as persons who are highly involved in politics. The contextual grasp of issues is poor; political information is very low; predictability from one attitude to another or over time is poor. This characterization of mass belief systems is incompatible with the fact that the political actions of most people are relatively stable. It is unlikely that consistent patterns of action will emanate from a poorly structured field.

EXPRESSIVE ACTIVITY IN POLITICS

If fields can best be understood by reference to the goals that an individual hopes to realize, it follows that we may be able to make better headway toward understanding mass political behavior by looking at the goals that ordinary people pursue. The myth of the "informed citizen" in democratic theory suggests that every member of the polity wishes to pursue policy goals as he engages in political activity. He has a field which is highly structured and in which policy plays a strong role. A few persons corresponding to that myth do exist in our society (most typically people who occupy political roles); but, we must entertain the possibility that many people are seeking different goals as they engage in political activity. If that is the case we may be looking for structure in the wrong place. In short, if political action may serve goals other than the achievement of policy, the political region of their fields will be structured by those other goals. The field arising from these needs may provide the necessary stability for consistent action, and we have missed it to this point only because we have been looking for structure in the wrong place.

Much of the political activity of ordinary citizens involves the pursuit of expressive goals[22] in contrast to other persons who may pursue instrumental goals through their political activity. Political role occupants pursue such tangible things as obtaining passage of a bill, seeking a tax break, obtaining a favorable ruling from an administrative agency, or winning public office. These tangible goals are the hard "stuff" of politics, goods which are distributed via political means, which various authors have identified as the essence of politics.[23] It should be clear that in order to compete in this

[22] Ulf Himmelstrand, *Social Pressures, Attitudes, and Democratic Processes* (Stockholm: Almquist and Wiksell, 1960).
[23] See Harold Lasswell, *Politics: Who Gets What, When, How* (Cleveland: World Publishing Co., 1958).

realm of contention over public policy, a well-defined cognitive map is necessary so that the actor knows who is likely to want what, what goes with what, and what route through the barriers in the field is likely to bring him to his goal.

But if the goals of political action are expressive in nature, then we may expect a different kind of structure. Edelman has suggested a variety of ways in which symbolic goals may be pursued by political action.[24] As a rather complex being, man has a variety of needs to be satisfied, at least some of which are likely to be psychic or symbolic. An obvious need is engendered by living in a complex hostile world with which one has to cope. Faced with that challenge, most people develop a necessity for believing that they understand their world and that their life has meaning within that world. Edelman calls our attention to the role of ritual and myth in satisfying such needs. Speaking of ritual in primitive society he states: "In rain dances and victory dances men achieve symbolically something they collectively need or want by reaffirming their common interest, denying their doubts, and acting out the result they seek. The motor activity, performed together with others, reassures everyone that there are no dissenters and brings pride and satisfaction in a collective enterprise. A simplified model or semblance of reality is created, and facts that do not fit are screened out of it."[25]

Edelman argues that political activity of ordinary citizens in modern society plays an analogous role to the dances of primitive culture in that it is mainly ritualistic. "They (election campaigns) give people a chance to express discontents and enthusiasms, to enjoy a sense of involvement. This is participation in a ritual act, however; only in a minor degree is it participation in policy formation. Like all ritual, whether in primitive or modern societies, elections draw attention to common social ties and to the importance and apparent reasonableness of accepting the public policies that are adopted."[26] Participation in political ritual serves to demonstrate that the order is a rational one, that we all control our destiny, and that the world is indeed a friendly place.

In contemporary democratic cultures these myths are embodied largely in what we have been calling the myth of the "informed citizen." They embody "the rational character of the voting act, the reality of the controls elections exert over governmental policy directions, the rational and even mechanical character of judicial and administrative enforcement of the laws."[27] Myths in all cultures serve to make the world safe, fair and intelligible. By voting an individual "proves" the veracity of the civic myths that give him a sense of well-being.

The point that voting is a symbolic act for most citizens finds empirical

[24] Murray Edelman, *The Symbolic Uses of Politics* (Urbana: University of Illinois Press, 1964).
[25] *Ibid.*, p. 17.
[26] *Ibid.*, p. 3.
[27] *Ibid.*, p. 18.

confirmation in a recent study of political behavior in Buffalo, N. Y.[28] In this study respondents were interviewed about a variety of instrumental and expressive inputs individuals can make to a political system. It is theoretically significant that in a factor analysis of these inputs, voting in elections loaded heavily on a "patriotism and love of country" factor which included such other items as "love my country," "show my patriotism by flying the flag, attending parades or some other way," "respect the police," "support my country in wars that I don't agree with." Voting did not load very heavily on a more instrumentally oriented "party and campaign activity" factor which included such items as "take an active part in a political campaign," "give money to help a party or candidate," "work to get people registered to vote," "join and support a political party," "be a candidate for public office." The latter, more instrumental activities, are engaged in by a relatively small proportion of the population (about 10 to 15 per cent) whereas the more expressive activities (voting, love of country, keeping informed) are pursued by nearly all citizens and are considered to be very important by them. One can imagine a very different psychological field for the person who believes he fulfills his civic duty by voting, keeping informed, and being patriotic; in contrast to the psychological field of a person with instrumental goals in politics which require him to become active in groups, parties, and campaigns.

Many ordinary citizens also have a need to use the outside world to express feelings that cannot, for one reason or another, be expressed directly. This process of displacement is at the heart of Freudian theory; symbols serve to allow the release of feelings that cannot be directed toward the original object. The resolution of the Oedipal complex involves displacement (this kind of process). The young male child learns that he cannot express openly either his love of his mother or his hatred of his father. Similarly, many kinds of feelings may be repressed and may be forced to gain expression through other objects.

The process of displacement through symbolization is the mechanism through which these other objects come to stand for the original. The specifics mechanisms (projection, sublimation, etc.) all act through their ability to make symbols of other objects, and political objects are not immune from being used for these purposes. Indeed, Edelman argues they are eminently suited for this purpose in that political objects are remote, the feedback necessary to modify impressions is lacking, and they are heavily laden with affect. "The parade of 'news' about political acts reported to us by the mass media and drunk up by the public as drama is the raw material of such symbolization. It has everything: remoteness, the omnipresent state, crises and detentes. More than that, it has the blurring or absence of any realistic detail that might question or weaken the symbolic meanings we read into it."[29] The key word here is drama. Political events are seen as

---

[28] Lester W. Milbrath, "Individuals and Government" in Herbert Jacob and Kenneth Vines, eds., *Politics in the American States*, rev. ed., (Boston: Little Brown, 1971).

[29] Edelman, *The Symbolic Uses of Politics*, p. 8.

remote acts in a powerful dramatic battle. Edelman points out that the objects in this symbolic drama are seen as either threatening or reassuring; threatening symbols may be hated and feared, while reassuring symbols may be loved and trusted.

EMPIRICAL BASIS FOR THIS PERSPECTIVE

If we can accept these expressive purposes as important to the political action of many ordinary citizens, it follows that the belief systems underlying this activity will be very different from the issue orientation common to elite political actors. The configuration of expressive orientations, and some notion as to their frequency in the population, needs thorough investigation. The designers of many previous studies have not expected such orientations and, not surprisingly, they have not found them. It is possible, however, to reanalyze some familiar data from the perspective of field theory and thereby find that the field theory notion is at least tenable.

Chapter V of *The American Voter*[30] deals with several factors affecting turnout: intensity of preference, interest in the campaign, perceived closeness of the election, degree of concern over election outcome, sense of political efficacy, and sense of citizen duty. The data show that the percentage of people voting is high when: the intensity of preference is great, the election is perceived as close, the degree of interest in the campaign is high, the degree of concern over outcome is high, sense of efficacy is high, and sense of citizen duty is strong. These psychological characteristics are treated as motivational factors which explain why some people vote while others do not. People vote *because* their involvement is great, *because* their sense of efficacy is high, and so forth.

But, to repeat an oft-used caveat, causation cannot be shown by correlation. It is just as plausible to assume that causation runs in the opposite direction. Perhaps it is the decision to vote that leads people to be highly involved and to feel highly efficacious. There is also a third possibility, that citizens make a basic decision that they wish to try to be a good American. Strongly identifying with what it means to be a good American, they turn out to vote, they develop an interest in the election, they get informed about politics, all with the purpose of making themselves feel good about fulfilling their role as American citizens. Viewed in these alternative ways, the data from *The American Voter* fit very well into the field theoretic framework proposed by this paper.[31]

Having hypothesized that beliefs are structured by purposes and that the purposes of many political actions are symbolic and ritualistic, we can go further and hypothesize that the more firm the behavioral intention the better structured the field will be in terms of that intention. The intention to vote, or more likely the intention to be a good citizen,, mobilizes the body

---

[30] Angus Campbell, *et al.*, *The American Voter* (New York: John Wiley, 1960).

[31] The authors of this work also see their theoretical perspective deriving from field theory. Their interpretation, however, is strongly influenced by their perspective that voting is a dependent behavior.

of myth that lies behind the society's definition of what it means to be a good citizen. Familiar political scales such as "efficacy" and "citizen duty," embody in their rhetoric much of the myth of being a good citizen. Hoping to fulfill that role well, the individual believes that he should be efficacious, believes that he should fulfill his citizen duty by voting, believes that he should stay informed, believes that he should patriotically support government officials as they try to carry out their assigned duties. This commitment to the role of good citizen also affects the way an individual may structure his phychological field of politics. Believing that his vote is important he tends to perceive the election as close and therefore that his vote counts; he believes that the system is responsive to his wishes (at least the wishes of the majority of the people); he believes that elections will be conducted according to prescribed procedures and that his vote is counted along with everyone else's. The point is that ordinary citizens choose their role and structure their field of politics so that their fit into the field "makes sense"; their purposes and roles as structured in the field are attainable and are designed to reassure them and make them pleased with themselves as they go about their daily business.

The Buffalo Study, alluded to above, shows relatively high correlations between what a person believes he ought to do in politics and what he claims he does.[32] In other words, it would be very difficult psychologically for a person to believe it was important to do something and then fail to do it.

The data that can be supplied at this point are not adequate to confirm our perspectives. Data may be compatible with several perspectives and it often requires a special research design to choose finally between perspectives. We do feel that the data brought to bear on our perspective are supportive enough to warrant a study which would test these theoretical notions directly. Most specifically, we are arguing for a theoretical perspective which views attitudes as part of a larger belief structure. We feel that such an approach, if it is to be successful, must not impose upon respondents the researcher's own conception of what a belief system should look like. To restrict one's notion of belief systems to issue-oriented systems is simply not fruitful. It leads us to miss much of the meaning of mass political behavior.

Attitude research has a well-developed tradition and methodology; but what kinds of methods can one use to empirically investigate political belief systems? Our discussion so far has indicated that we do not think it wise for academic investigators to impose their own structure on the beliefs of ordinary citizens. Our own predisposition would be to approach this topic in a very open-ended fashion and interview respondents in a relatively free wheeling and unstructured way so that they could tell us about their purposes and how they cognitively structure their political world. In the early stages we would urge respondents to self-define their attitudes and beliefs. Once these self-definitions had been obtained from a wide variety of per-

---

[32] Milbrath, "The Nature of Political Beliefs."

sons, the researcher might attempt to construct some items which could be used to measure attitudes and beliefs across individuals. We would be careful not to freeze the structure of the research instrument too soon and we would be cautious to open the inquiry frequently so as to catch changes in structure as time goes by.

To put the problem another way we believe that the first scholarly task is to declare our theoretical need. Once that need is recognized and agreed to, we can obtain the resources necessary so that we can be inventive about new techniques. If it makes sense to think about political belief systems as fields, we can probably find the methods required for discovering, measuring, and comparing these fields. Typically, scholars move from conceptualization to operationalization and back to conceptualization. This back and forth process is mutually reinforcing and leads to sharpened inquiry. We hope that our thoughts may stimulate others to join us in the next stages of this search.

POLITICS, IDEOLOGY, AND BELIEF SYSTEMS[*]

GIOVANNI SARTORI
University of Florence

T HE WORD "IDEOLOGY" POINTS TO A BLACK BOX. AS A PHILOSOPHER PUTS IT, ideology "signifies at the same time truth and error, universality and particularity, wisdom and ignorance."[1] Likewise, for the political scientist the term ideology points to a cluster concept, i.e., belongs to the concepts that bracket a variety of complex phenomena about which one tries to generalize; and the growing popularity of the term has been matched, if anything, by its growing obscurity.[2] All in all, one is entitled to wonder whether there is any point in using "ideology" for scholarly purposes.[3] And my specific question will be whether there is a technical meaning, or meanings, of "ideology" which constitute a necessary tool of enquiry for a science of politics.

Discussions about ideology generally fall into two broad domains, namely, *ideology in knowledge* and/or *ideology in politics*. With respect to the first area of inquiry the question is whether, and to what extent, man's knowledge is ideologically conditioned or distorted.[4] With respect to the second area of inquiry the question is whether ideology is an essential feature

[*]Reprinted by permission of the author and publisher, from Giovanni Sartori, "Politics, Ideology, and Belief Systems," *American Political Science Review*, 63 (June, 1969), pp. 398–411. This is an abridged draft of a paper prepared for the meeting on "Ideology and Politics" of the *Institut International de Philosophie Politique*, Chatillon, June, 1967.

[1] Remo Cantoni, *Illusione e Pregiudizio* (Milano: Mondadori, 1967), p. 103.

[2] Concerning the popularity it is symptomatic that while the 1930–1935 *Encyclopedia of the Social Sciences* did not include the item "ideology," its successor, the 1968 *International Encyclopedia of the Social Sciences*, contains two articles on ideology. For the bibliography see Norman Birnbaum, "The Sociological Study of Ideology 1940–1960: A Trend Report and Bibliography," *Current Sociology* (Oxford: Blackwell, 1962); and Kurt Link, "Bibliographische Einfürung," in *Ideologie, Ideologiekritik und Wissensoziologie* (Neuwied: Luchterhand, 1961).

[3] See the conjecture of Arne Naess that "the movement of the term 'ideology' into social science, social psychology and political science will, within a generation, be followed by a movement in the other direction. It will continue to be used in headlines, in summaries and popularizations, but scarcely in statements intended to express . . . theories, hypotheses or classifications of observations." *Democracy, Ideology and Objectivity—Studies in the Semantics and Cognitive Analysis of Ideological Controversy* (Oslo: Oslo University Press; and Oxford: Blackwell, 1956), p. 171. The book also reviews many current definitions of ideology, esp. pp. 141–198.

[4] Marx and Mannheim are the obvious references, and the literature is extensive. See esp. I. L. Horowitz, *Philosophy, Science and the Sociology of Knowledge* (Springfield: Charles C. Thomas, 1961); and Jacques J. Maquet, *Sociologie de la Connaissance—Etude Critique des Systèmes de K.* Mannheim *et de P. A. Sorokin* (Louvain: Nauwelaerts, 1949). A particularly brilliant criticism is Robert K. Merton, *Social Theory and Social Structure* (Glencoe: Free Press, rev. ed., 1957) Chaps. 12 and 13. See also Raymond Aron, *La Sociologie Allemande Contemporaine* (Paris: P.U.F., 2nd ed., 1950) pp. 74–94. My own position (*Democratic Theory*, New

of politics and, if so, what does it explain. In the first case "ideology" is contrasted with "truth," science and valid knowledge in general[5]; whereas in the second case we are not concerned with the truth-value but with the functional value, so to speak, of ideology. In the first sense by saying ideology we actually mean *ideological doctrine* (and equivalents), whereas in the second sense we ultimately point to an *ideological mentality* (also called, hereinafter, "ideologism").

The distinction between ideology in knowledge and ideology in politics is not necessarily neat, for a number of issues draw from both domains. For instance, if one asks whether the various "isms" of politics—e.g., liberalism, socialism, nationalism, etc.—are *only* ideologies (there is no quarrel that in some sense of the word they also are ideologies), it can be readily conceded that our treatment of the "isms" of politics will be more perceptive if it presupposes a stand vis-à-vis the sociology of knowledge. But the distinction is neat when one is exclusively concerned with the question: what does ideology explain about the nature of politics?

For the sake of brevity a number of preliminary points will have to be laid down axiomatically.

First, there is no object in adopting new terms unless they are employed to cover new phenomena or new sets of observations. I take it, therefore, that the word ideology has been increasingly adopted in response to, and as a pointer of, the development of politics—if not the development of an unprecedented aspect of politics. To be sure, one may choose to apply "ideology" to any time and place; but not without loss of conceptual substance.

Second, either we dispose of a notion of ideology that lends itself to falsification, or we do not dispose of an empirically usable term. We are logically required, then, to declare what ideology is not, i.e., to qualify the notion *a contrario*. In other terms, we are required to conceive ideology as a dimension or an aspect of politics which may, or may not, be found to apply to the real world. For this purpose "ideological politics" will be opposed here to "pragmatic politics," i.e., pragmatism will be used as a designation for non-ideology. To be sure, I am not saying that we *must* oppose ideological to non-ideological politics. My argument is, rather, that if no such opposition is justified, then the notion of ideology loses much of its interest and has little explanatory value.

Third, I take the methodological view that *awaiting contrary proof* (subsequently called the a.c.p. clause) no concept should be used as a synonym

York: Frederick A. Praeger, 1965, pp. 455–460) is that the Mannheim type of sociology of knowledge attacks the consumer's end of the problem, thereby explaining the success, the spread of mental products. How mental products are produced is, however, an entirely different matter.

[5] This is actually the major and more persistent controversy. The theme has been especially pursued by analytical philosophy. See Theodore Geiger, *Ideologie und Warheit: Eine Soziologische Kritik des Denkens* (Stuttgart: Humboldt Verlag, 1953); Gustav Bergmann, "Ideology," now in *The Metaphysics of Logical Positivism* (New York: Longmans Green, 1954); E. Topitsch, "Begriff und Funktion der Ideologie," in *Sozialphilosophie zwischen Ideologie und Wissenschaft* (Neuwied: *Luchterhand*, 1961).

for any other concept. Ideology is generally qualified by how it relates to idea, belief, opinion, creed, myth, utopia, ethos, and similar or derivative concepts. However, I shall not be content with implying that the aforementioned concepts are largely interchangeable and tend to overlap. This way of handling conceptual problems I call "superfluous coextensiveness," and represents an intolerable waste for the economy of language and clarity of thought. The more a set of concepts is closely interlinked, the more their meanings need to be specified and distinguished. And the point is that under the a.c.p. clause, it is the equivalence between two concepts, not their difference, that requires demonstration. Therefore, unless it can be demonstrated that "ideology is nothing other than X,"[6] I shall aim at using ideology to signify something that no other neighboring concept signifies.

Fourth, the relation between ideology and "idea" (i.e., conceptual thinking) bears on the genesis of ideological doctrines, on how they originate and are born, and is eventually conducive to an epistemological discussion. It will suffice to note here that ideologies are no longer ideas, in the sense that ideological doctrines no longer fall under the jurisdiction of logic and verification. When we pass on to consider ideologies we are confronted with "the conversion of ideas into social levers,"[7] i.e., with a *persuasive treatment* (not a logical treatment) of ideas leading to action-oriented ideals.[8] However, for the present inquiry ideological doctrines are givens—they exist in their distinctiveness, whatever their *genesis* in relation to "idea." I propose, therefore, to investigate a different relationship, namely, the relation of ideology to "belief" and belief systems, under the assumption that this is the pertinent focus for discussing the *structure* and *function* of ideologism. By saying structure I refer to *how* one believes; and by speaking of function I shall be concerned with the *efficacy*, or effectiveness, of belief systems.

A final clarification is in order. Given the fact that we are confronted with a black box, it will be necessary to begin with a pure and simple *semantic explanation*.[9] My first assignment is, then, to clarify the various meanings of the term ideology as they stand in actual usage.

A term may have a "notational use," i.e., it may be a useful shorthand, an economizing device, and yet explain nothing.[10] This is notably the case

[6]This is called by Abraham Kaplan the "pattern model of explanation," as against the "deductive model of explanation." *The Conduct of Inquiry* (San Francisco: Chandler, 1964), esp. pp. 332–341. The pattern model of explanation does not necessarily coincide with Hempel's "reduction to the familiar." *Aspects of Scientific Explanation* (New York: Free Press, 1965), pp. 430–433.

[7]Daniel Bell, *The End of Ideology* (New York: Collier Books, 2nd rev. ed., 1962), p. 400.

[8]See C. J. Friedrich: "It is confusing . . . to call any system of ideas an ideology. . . . Ideologies are action-related systems of ideas. . . ."*Man and His Government* (New York: McGraw-Hill, 1963), p. 89. In a similar vein Z. B. Brzezinski qualifies ideology as "essentially an action-program suitable for mass consumption." *Ideology and Power in Soviet Politics* (New York: Frederick A. Praeger, 1962), pp. 5–6.

[9]Kaplan, *The Conduct of Inquiry*, p. 327.

[10]Kaplan contrasts *notational* and *substantive* terms as follows: "Substantive terms cannot be eliminated without loss of conceptual content, but notational terms are fundamentally abbreviations, and could be replaced." *Ibid.*, p. 49.

with the authors that are satisfied with saying that ideology amounts to the views of any and all social groups, or that everybody has political beliefs which amount to everyman's ideology. To abridge "social views" or "political beliefs" into "ideology" is perhaps convenient, but we are simply left to describe what people believe or have to say in political matters. If the term ideology were not employed, no loss of conceptual content would follow. Moreover, the foregoing definitions are not falsifiable: they simply lead to the conclusion that everything (or, conversely, nothing) is ideology.

This is not to say that the notational use of the term ideology is necessarily trivial. Not only do we need notations, but we equally need "explanation stoppers," i.e., terms defined in such a way as to avoid endless regression of inquiry. Ideology is, however, an ambitious term; it does belong to the concepts that are supposed to have broad and farreaching causative significance. Hence, if the eminence attributed to the notion of ideology is justified, it must be justified, because the term *explains*, not merely because it abridges and/or provides a regression stopper. Therefore, as the discussion proceeds the focus will be progressively shifted to the *explanatory value* of the various meanings of ideology, for my ultimate purpose is to probe and single out the conceptualizations that are cognitive instruments, that do have explanatory-causative potency.[11]

I. THE IDEOLOGICAL MENTALITY

If ideology is linked to "belief," it is readily apparent that the general class is "belief systems" and that ideology is the narrower conceptualization. Properly speaking, "a person's belief-disbelief system is really a political-religious-philosophic-scientific-etcetera system,"[12] i.e., a total and diffuse framework; whereas ideology indicates only the political *part* of a belief system. Whatever the psychological functions of a belief system, for the present discussion it can be simply defined as the system of symbolic orientations to be found in each individual. Correlatively, a *political* belief system consists of the set of beliefs according to which individuals navigate and orient themselves in the sea of politics.

It is not sufficient to say, however, that ideology is the political slice, or part, of a belief system. Under the a.c.p. (awaiting contrary proof) clause, I assume that ideology indicates a particular state, or structure, of political belief systems. By definition, then, not all political belief systems are ideological.

Two corollaries follow. First, pragmatism is also a state of belief systems.

---

[11] I purposely avoid saying "explication" on account of the technical meaning attributed to the term by Carnap followed by Carl K. Hempel, *Fundamentals of Concept Formation in Empirical Science* (Chicago: The University of Chicago Press, 1952), pp. 11–12. For the sake of simplicity I equally neglect the more sophisticated test suggested by K. R. Popper with regard to the "informative content" of scientific statements. *The Logic of Scientific Discovery* (London: Hutchinson, 1959), pp. 119–121. For an introductory overview see Ernest Nagel, *The Structure of Science* (New York: Harcourt, Brace and World, 1961), Chap. 2: "Patterns of Scientific Explanation."

[12] Milton Rokeach, *The Open and Closed Mind* (New York: Basic Books, 1960), p. 35.

Indeed to contrast ideologism and pragmatism as representing, repectively, a belief versus a belief-less orientation toward politics is to preempt the issue from the outset. The first corollary is, therefore, that *both* ideologism and pragmatism are possible states of belief. Second, and conversely, the presence of beliefs does not suffice to qualify, *per se*, the ideological nature of such beliefs: the pragmatic actor also is belief-oriented. The second corollary is, then, that beliefs are, as such, a *common*, not a discriminating element. While not every polity need contain ideological publics, no polity can exist without publics that have beliefs.

A number of authors seemingly agree to the effect that not all political belief systems are ideological, but they founder on the reefs of definition by failing to provide a discriminating element. According to Talcott Parsons, for instance, ideology is "a system of beliefs, held in common by the members of a collectivity . . . which is oriented to the *evaluation integration* of the collectivity (emphasis added)."[13] But the discriminating power of the notion of evaluative integration, and, in general, of having recourse to the value dimensions, is almost nil.[14] Beliefs are inextricably value-laden—they precede the analytical distinction between value and fact—and any belief system serves the purpose of integrating (axiologically or otherwise) the belief-collectivity.[15] It is not without reason, therefore, that I propose to search for structural elements of differentiation bearing on *how* one believes.

Speaking of belief systems, both the notions of "belief" and "system" must be taken seriously. Under the a.c.p. clause a *belief* is neither an opinion nor an idea. Opinions include and characterize the more ephemeral and superficial level of discourse, and can be safely set aside, therefore, with reference to belief systems. On the other hand, in the strict sense ideas are *thought of*, they typically belong to the more self-conscious dimension of discourse, to reasoning and theorizing. If the sentence is understood *cum grano salis*, beliefs can be defined as "ideas that are no longer thought,"[16] to signify that beliefs are idea-clusters that routinize the cost of decisions precisely because they are taken for granted. Beliefs are *believed*—not explored, tested, and held under the searchlight of consciousness.[17]

[13] *The Social System* (New York: Free Press, 1964 ed.), p. 349.

[14] This applies also to the attempt, notably pursued by Bergmann and Geiger, to qualify ideology (vis-à-vis scientific truth) as any value judgement mistaken for, or disguised as, statement of fact. This view makes ideology far too broad.

[15] Let alone the fact that the "integration" of a belief group may well be a "disintegration" vis-à-vis other groups. We are forcefully reminded of this other side of the coin by Ben Halpern: "The function of ideologies [is] to segregate and consolidate competing groups around rival ideas." "Myth and Ideology in Modern Usage," *History and Theory*, 1 (1967), p. 136.

[16] I paraphrase from Wladimir Weidle, "Sur le Concept d'Ideologie," *Le Contrat Social* (March, 1959), p. 77. The author speaks of ideology, but the sentence applies more directly to beliefs.

[17] *Contra*, among others, Clyde Kluckhohn, "Values and Value-Orientations in the Theory of Action," in T. Parsons and E. Shils, eds., *Toward a General Theory of Action* (Cambridge, Mass.: Harvard University Press, 1951), p. 432: "*Belief* refers primarily to the categories, 'true' and 'false,' 'correct' and 'incorrect.'" This intellectualistic conceptualization overlooks the difference between idea and belief.

As for the notion of *system*, a first obvious caution is that the system may have properties which are not exhibited by its parts. But it is more important to underline that a "belief system" points to a state of *boundedness*, to the fact that beliefs hang together. This belief-linkage is presumably what a number of authors have in mind when they define ideology as a more or less coherent set of ideas. Now, logical (or rational) attributes such as "coherence," "consistency," and the like, are hardly applicable to a belief-linkage. Indeed the single belief-elements can be logically contradictory. But there is no question that beliefs are "bound together by some form of constraint or functional interdependence."[18] Beliefs, then, cluster in *systems*, though not in rationally congruent and organized systems.

Having issued the *caveat* that the system should be taken seriously, no harm follows if one decomposes belief systems in a number of ways. Following Rokeach, one may distinguish between (1) primitive beliefs, (2) intermediate, and (3) peripheral regions of belief.[19] I propose to dwell briefly on the intermediate region, and then to decompose the more peripheral regions of belief into single belief-elements.

The first problem is to pinpoint the discriminating element, the mentality (*forma mentis*) that qualifies an ideological structure of belief in its difference from a pragmatic structure of belief. Following Rokeach again, it appears that the crucial single factor resides in so-called authority beliefs, and more precisely in the beliefs concerning cognitive authority: the beliefs that tip us off to what is true or false about the world and its events.[20] More concretely one may say that the crucial factor is "the authorities," those on whom we rely for information.

Since nobody can avoid reliance on cognitive authorities, the difference must reside in how authorities are chosen and how the instructions emanating from these authorities are assessed. It is on this basis, in effect, that Rokeach draws the distinction between the *closed* and *open* mind. His initial basic definition is as follows: "A person's [belief] system is open or closed . . . [to] the extent to which the person can receive, evaluate and act on relevant information . . . on its own intrinsic merits."[21] The closed mind is defined, accordingly, as a cognitive state in which a person does not discriminate substantive information from information about the source. Hence the more closed one's belief system, the more he is unable to evaluate relevant information on its own intrinsic merits. In substance, the closed mind relies on, indeed yields to, absolue authority, and is hardly in a position to select and to check its authorities.

Doubtless the association of the ideological mentality with the closed mind can be accused of representing an anti-ideological bias. However, ideological closedness is bad and pragmatic openness is good only according to an intellectual yardstick—and one could well say an intellectualistic

[18] Philip E. Converse, "The Nature of Belief Systems in Mass Publics," in D. Apter, ed., *Ideology and Discontent* (New York: Free Press of Glencoe, 1964), p. 207.
[19] *The Open and Closed Mind*, pp. 39–51.
[20] *Ibid.*, esp. p. 44.
[21] *Ibid.*, p. 57, and *passim*, pp. 54–67.

prejudice. If we are reminded that the pertinent yardstick is "efficacy" the evaluation could be reversed, for reliance on absolute authorities does obtain the kind of efficacy praised by the man of action and is surely in keeping with the purpose served by ideologies. In short, the ideologist cannot have it both ways, he cannot claim at the same time an intellectual and a practical primacy.

The foregoing underpins nicely the common opinion according to which the ideological mentality represents a typically *dogmatic*, i.e., rigid and impermeable, approach to politics. On the other hand, it should be noted that a cognitive closed structure fails to justify the other characteristic generally imputed to the ideological mentality, namely, its typically *doctrinaire* bent. Should this characterization be dropped? Or does it draw from another source? I shall abide by the latter suggestion, thereby shifting the focus to the notion of *ideological culture*.

When we speak of ideology as a "culture"—or a cultural pattern—we are more or less implicitly referred to the anthropological notion of culture. Perhaps we may say that we are referred once again to the intermediate regions of belief, though no longer to the "authority-beliefs" but to the "processing-coding-beliefs." The simplest and closest analogy appears to be, however, the *Gestalt* analogy: a cultural pattern is characterized by the forms, or the matrixes, with and within which our mind stores and orders whatever it apprehends. For our purposes these processing-coding *Gestalten* will be labeled "rationalism" and "empiricism," and the assumption will be that these cultural matrixes help explain why only certain polities characteristically display, over time, an ideological patterning.

What strikes me in this connection is the extent to which the typically ideological *isms* of politics—Marxism being the outstanding current example—were born and have developed (before being exported) in the cultural area qualified by the notion of *rationalism*, hardly in other cultural contexts, and surely not in the cultural area of *empiricism*.[22] I find it equally striking that only the "rational ideologies"—I mean, the ideologies drawn from rationalistic philosophies and nurtured in a rationalistic soil—travel easily throughout the world.[23] Hence my hypothesis is that ideology and pragmatism *qua* "political cultures" are related, respectively, to the "cultural matrixes" rationalism and empiricism.

Rationalism and empiricism are generally associated, respectively, with a "coherence" theory of truth as against a "correspondence" theory of truth.

---

[22] If "liberalism" is conceived as an ideology, I suggest that it represents the ideological apex attained by the empirical mind; and surely liberalism has been a poor competitor, ideologically speaking, of socialism, communism, equalitarianism, and the like.

[23] In this connection it should be noted that the ideologies of the developing nations and, in general, of the third world have been hardly nurtured and taught in London and Oxford, and even less in the United States. A perusal of Paul E. Sigmund, ed., *The Ideologies of the Developing Nations* (New York: Frederick A. Praeger, 1963), suffices to confirm, in spite of nebulous and bizarre melanges, their unmistakably rationalistic Western source.

Oakeshott equally makes a good point when he writes that "Rationalism is the assertion that . . . practical knowledge is not knowledge at all."[24] But, however sweepingly, let us attempt to qualify rationalism and empiricism in more detail, with the understanding that the following characterizations represent a syndrome, so that the full enumeration is required to appreciate the meaning of the separate assertions.

The *rationalistic* processing-coding tends to approach problems as follows: (i) deductive argumentation prevails over evidence and testing; (ii) doctrine prevails over practice; (iii) principle prevails over precedent; (iv) ends prevail over means; and (v) perceptions tend to be "covered up," doctrine-loaded, typically indirect. Hegel's famous sentence, "The rational is real," goes to the very heart of the rationalistic mind,[25] for the rationalistic attitude is to argue that if the practice goes astray, there must be something wrong with the practice, not with the theory.

Conversely, and symmetrically, the *empirical* processing-coding can be described as follows: (i) evidence and testing prevail over deductive argumentation; (ii) practice prevails over doctrine; (iii) precedent prevails over principle; (iv) means prevail over ends; and, therefore; (v) its perceptions tend to be more "direct." Consequently the empirical attitude is to argue that if the practice goes astray, something is likely to be wrong with the theory, not with the practice.

The *ad hoc* implications for our subject are that the rationalistic *Gestalt* is characterized (relatively speaking, of course) by openness to deductive axiomatization and deafness to empirical evidence, by low *practical* problem-solving flexibility and by high *theoretical* problem-solving ability. Also, and consequently, the rationalistic mind soars at a higher level of explicitness and especially of abstraction than the empirical mind. This implies, in turn, that rationalism is able to embrace and to cover in terms of *Weltanschauung* a comparatively broader "space," either with long deductive chains or with acrobatic leaps—a quality that I shall call "comprehensiveness."

The foregoing can be easily translated into a "cultural" characterization of the ideological mentality. If we assume ideologism to result from a rationalistic cultural matrix, it follows that to the extent that the ideological mentality is "open," it is open to rational, deductive argument, hardly to evidence: the sentence "experience proves" proves nothing to an ideologically minded actor. An ulterior implication is that the ideological mentality identifies *par excellence* with highly "abstract" and "comprehensive" be-

---

[24] *Rationalism in Politics* (New York: Basic Books, 1962), p. 11. I cannot follow Oakeshott, however, in his positive identification of rationalism with technical knowledge. ("The sovereignty of 'reason,' for the rationalist, means the sovereignty of technique." *Ibid.*) It seems to me, rather, that technical knowledge represents the point at which rationalism and empiricism converge. On its own premises, rationalism looks down at technical knowledge as an inferior knowledge.

[25] To be sure, Hegel's sentence had a dialectical circular formulation. But "the rational" is the subject: it is rationality that qualifies reality, not the reverse. Hegel's philosophy was a realistic *rationalism*, hardly a rationalistic *realism*.

lief systems. In particular an important feature of the ideological mentality that neatly flows from its rationalistic matrix is that the central elements of an ideological belief system are necessarily "ends," not "means."

I shall revert to these characteristics later. For the moment let us simply retain that to the extent that the ideological mentality is characterized by the rationalistic cultural matrix, to the same extent it can be legitimately qualified as a typically principled and doctrinaire way of perceiving political problems and of constructing their solution.[26] It should be clear that I am *not* saying: given a rationalistic cultural matrix, the ideological mentality necessarily follows. I am simply saying that a rationalistic culture is particularly vulnerable on this score. It should be equally clear that a number of individuals react to the culture to which they belong. Therefore, an ideological culture will contain non-ideological minority groups, just as an empirical culture will breed ideological minorites.

Bringing our two threads together, the ideological mentality now results in both a *personality trait* and a *cultural trait*, and the following conclusion appears reasonably warranted: ideologism can be legitimately understood to mean not only a rigid and dogmatic approach to politics, but also a principled and doctrinaire perception of politics. Needless to say, the two characterizations reinforce one another but can exist disjointly. However, for the simplicity of the argument in the following section, the ideological mentality will be reduced to a "closed" cognitive structure, and cognitive closedness will be defined as a state of dogmatic impermeability both to evidence and to argument. Conversely, the pragmatic mentality will be simplistically identified with an "open" cognitive structure, and cognitive openness will be defined a state of mental permeability.

II. A FRAMEWORK FOR ANALYSIS

Thus far the analysis has been confined to a single dimension—cognition. But beliefs and belief systems vary not only along a cognitive but also along an emotive dimension. Along the former a belief system can be, as we know, closed or open. Along the emotive dimension beliefs can be intense or feeble, passionately or weakly felt. Possibly, in each individual cognition and affect are tightly interlinked, but with reference to mass phenomena—e.g., abrupt transitions from "hot politics" to "cool politics," and vice versa—cognition and affect seem to vary independently. Assuming cognition to be constant, we can still have formidable oscillations of emotional intensity.

The difference between cognitive structure and emotive status underpins two different conceptions of ideology: *ideologism*, i.e., the mentality on the one hand, and *ideological passion* on the other hand. *Per se* the ideological mentality is not necessarily conducive to an active involvement and thereby to "ideological activism." Thus, whenever we find a mobilized polity

---

[26]The rationalist matrix also explains the "logicality of ideological thinking" forcefully highlighted—perhaps in an overly speculative vein—by Hannah Arendt, "Ideology and Terror: A Novel Form of Government," in *The Review of Politics* (July, 1953), pp. 303–327.

displaying a high degree of political activism, reference should be made to the emotional component, and thereby to the notion of ideological affect, or passion. This is also to say that the effectiveness of ideology, its capacity of activation, of arousing and unleashing energies, does not reside in the ideological mentality as such but requires, in addition, "ideological heating." Likewise, whenever politics is depicted as a matter of faith, as a religion or even as a mystique, reference is made more often than not to a particular itensity of feeling, of emotional involvement, and we should speak, therefore, of ideological passion.

The overall scheme of analysis is thus the one recapitulated in Figure 1.[27]

FIGURE 1

Scheme of Analysis

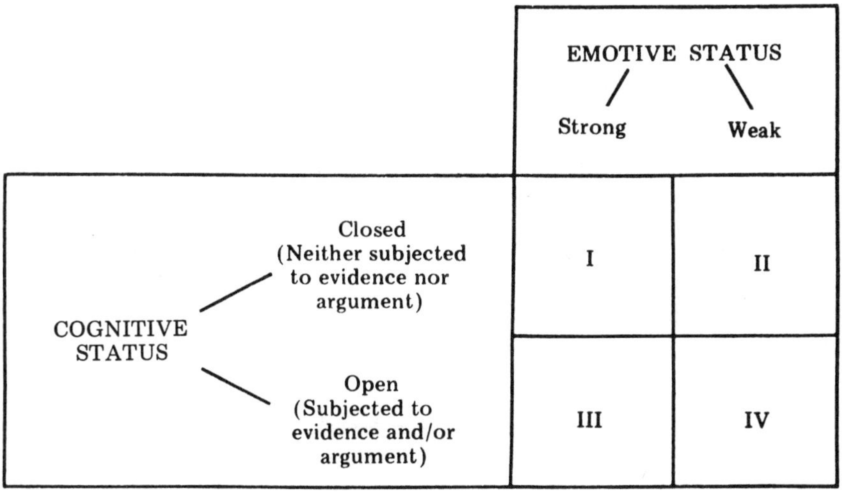

| | | EMOTIVE STATUS / \ | |
		Strong	Weak
COGNITIVE STATUS	Closed (Neither subjected to evidence nor argument)	I	II
	Open (Subjected to evidence and/or argument)	III	IV

Let us now enter the peripheral regions of belief and decompose belief systems into distinguishable belief-elements which are generally expressed in a slogan form. As Dahl introduces the argument, "it is convenient to think of the content of a belief system as made up of identifiable elements or components" (e.g., beliefs expressed by propositions like "Democracy is the best form of government," "Bourgeois democracy must be replaced by a dictatorship of the proletariat," "A capitalist economy is more efficient than a socialist economy.")[28] With reference to the four combinations afforded

[27] The scheme is largely inspired by Robert E. Dahl, *Ideology, Conflict and Consensus: Notes for a Theory* (mimeographed), a paper prepared for the panel on "Consensus and Dissent," VII IPSA World Congress, Bruxelles, September 18–23, 1967, p. 2. This essay is particularly indebted to Dahl's intellectual stimulation.

[28] *Ibid.*

by the scheme of Figure 1, the belief-elements can be broken down, follow-
ing the roman numerals of the previous table, as follows.
   (I) Closed and strongly felt. These elements will be called *fixed.*
   (II) Closed but weakly held. These elements may be called *inelastic.*
   (III) Open but strongly felt. These elements will be called *firm.*
   (IV) Open and wealkly felt. These elements will be called *flexible.*
   The scheme of Figure 1 can thus be filled with the typology of belief-ele-
ments represented in Figure 2.

FIGURE 2

Typology of Belief-Elements[a]

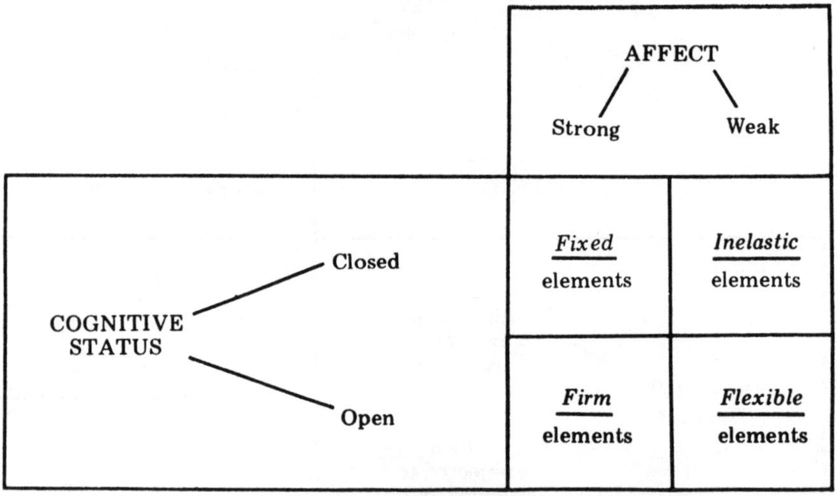

[a]This table repeats, in substance, Dahl's scheme on page 3, *Ideology, Conflict
and Consensus.*

   Some additional but in no way exhaustive qualifications are as follows. (I)
The *fixed* elements are rigid, dogmatic, impermeable to argument and evidence. One may also call them "adamant" elements. As such, they are subject only to traumatic change under conditions of great stress. Given the
fact that they are emotively participated in, the dynamic, activistic potential of the adamant elements is high. (II) The *inelastic* elements are still impermeable to argument and to evidence, but display a low dynamic potential, for they are not passionately felt. Furthermore, even though they tend
to be persistent over time, they can fade away, or be dismissed, without
traumatic consequences. (III) The *firm* elements are firmly held, but are
open to evidence and/or to argument. Even though they tend to be persistent, they are not impermeable and are, therefore, changeable, at least in
principle. On the other hand, firm elements have a stronger dynamic potential than the inelastic elements. (IV) The *flexible* elements are feebly held,

open to argument and/or to evidence and, furthermore, to convenience. They are changeable by definition. On the other hand, their dynamic potential is very low.

It can be easily seen that the foregoing typology of belief-*elements* can be turned into a typology of belief-*systems* tentatively labeled as in Figure 3.

FIGURE 3

Patterns of Belief Systems

I *Adamant* "fixed-strong" elements prevail	II *Resilient* "fixed-feeble" elements prevail
III *Firm* "flexible-strong" elements prevail	IV *Flexible* "flexible-feeble" elements prevail

Conceivably, the simplest way of establishing the nature of a pattern is provided by the following criterion: which type of element prevails in terms of intensity. However, we are also reminded by Converse that "the idea-elements within a belief system vary in a property we shall call centrality."[29] Whenever possible, therefore, one should use centrality as a criterion.

The individuals imbued with an *adamant* belief system are impenetrable vis-à-vis external influence and are strongly motivated toward outward expansion, either in the form of proselytism or of overt aggression. The individuals imbued with a *resilient* belief system resist change and support the internal *status quo*, but lack dynamism and outward orientation. The individuals sharing a *firm* belief system are both open to change and motivated toward outward expansion. Finally, the individuals sharing a *flexible* belief system easily accept changes but lack outward dynamism.

Be that as it may, we are now in a position to perceive clearly the *placement* of the ideological and pragmatic varieties of belief systems, and to *define* them accordingly (regardless of *what* one believes).

Having reference to our initial scheme (Figure 1), *qua* ideal types or, better, *qua* polar opposites, a "perfectly ideological" belief system falls in quadrant I, whereas a "perfectly pragmatic" belief systems falls in quadrant IV—as shown in Figure 4.

Definition: Whenever ideology and pragmatism are confronted dichot-

[29]"The Nature of Belief Systems," p. 208.

FIGURE 4

Ideology and Pragmatism as Polar Opposites

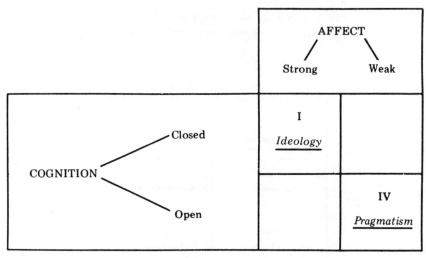

omously, and thereby conceptualized as polar types, *ideology* is a belief system based on (i) fixed elements, characterized by (ii) strong affect and (iii) closed cognitive structure. *Pragmatism* is, conversely, a belief system based on (ii) weak affect and (iii) open cognitive structure.

Granted that pure types seldom, if ever, are approximated in the real world, this means only that we are also required to define ideology and pragmatism as "concrete" systems. It does not follow that it is logically erroneous, and even less that it is logically superfluous, to define concepts *ex adverso*. I would argue, on the contrary, that the logical error is to hold that if ideology and pragmatism are conceived as blends of a same continuum, they should not be defined as opposites. A continuum of what? Unless the ends of a continuum are defined, the continuum itself remains undefined. Hence, even if one abides by the "continuum language," polar definitions remain the *sine qua non* condition for having a continuum at all.

The usefulness of these mappings, and the extent to which crucial distinctions are often by-passed, can be illustrated with reference to the decline or end of ideology debate.[30] If the question is, what do we mean by *decline of ideology*, Figure 5 shows that we are liable to confuse, in this connection, two very different processes.

A shift from box I to box II merely reflects a decline of emotive intensity and amounts to a relatively easy and easily predictable transformation. On the other hand, this shift does not necessarily indicate a point of no return.

[30]Jean Meynaud's book on the *Destin des Ideologies* is actually a review and a discussion of the decline of ideology literature. See it, transl., *Destino delle Ideologie*, (Cappelli ed., 1964), esp. pp. 37–112. Raymond Aron, Daniel Bell and S. M. Lipset are the standard references on the subject.

FIGURE 5

Decline of Ideology Hypothesis

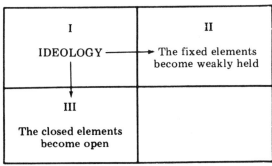

At least in short run terms (from one to two generations), returns from box II to box I, i.e., from cooler to warmer politics, are only to be expected and not difficult to obtain. Moreover, in this respect the argument largely hinges on the point in time chosen as parameter. E.g., with respect to the base 1918–20 the thirties represented a decline of ideology, but the 1946–50 period represented an increase of ideology with respect to a pre-war base; and it seems to me that the late sixties reveal no decline, but resurgence, with respect to the late fifties. A real decline of ideology is safely indicated, then, by the passage from box I to box III. However, a transformation of fixed into firm belief-elements is not an easy transformation, for it involves a radical change in the mental posture, a shift from closedness to openness.[31]

The expression "end of ideology" pushes the matter further, at least in forecasting terms. If "end" is meant seriously, it calls for an overall transformation of an ideological belief system into a pragmatic belief system. If so, Figure 6 underpins how many conditions need to be satisfied and, by implication, the hazardous nature of the prediction.

Let us now turn to the problem of defining ideology and pragmatism as *concrete* belief systems. In the real world, an ideological pattern can be identified as such when the overall distribution of the belief-elements gravitates—with reference to the scheme utilized so far—around quadrants I and II. Conversely, when the overall distribution of the elements gravitates around quadrants IV and III, the polity can be identified as being pragmatic.

---

[31] Another possibility is that the decline of ideology amounts—all other conditions remaining equal—to a convergence among different ideologies, either in the sense that the opposed "disbelievers" come to share a greater number of beliefs in common, or in the sense that the distinctive elements which oppose the various belief systems become feebly or more feebly held. This is the suggestion perceptively set forth by Dahl ("Ideology, Conflict and Consensus," pp. 5–8). However, in this case the "decline" would be an optical illusion, for the process described is, in reality, a mere process of growing "affinity" or of diminishing distance between two or more ideologies.

FIGURE 6

End of Ideology Hypothesis

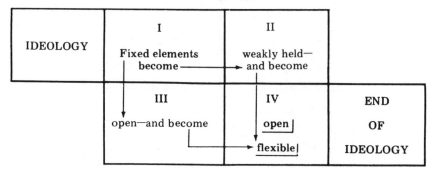

This is not to deny the possibility of spill-overs in other boxes as well. Varieties and variations within each concrete belief system can be very great, as suggested by the following rule of thumb: an ideological polity will be *less ideological* the lesser the elements contained in quadrant I; conversely, a pragmatic polity will be *less pragmatic*, the lesser the elements contained in quadrant IV. The two patterns fall wide apart with reference to their respective centers of gravity; but the feebler the gravitational attraction of each *noyeau*, the greater the diffusion, and therefore the overlaps. This is, admittedly, very vague. But one can hardly be more specific until an additional set of distinctions is brought to bear on the discussion.

If belief systems are broken down into elements, they can be classified with respect to the following properties: (a) their relative articulation, or richness; (b) their correlative constraining power; (c) their divisibility in belief strata corresponding to belief publics.

(a) With reference to the first property, a belief system can be *rich* (articulate) or *poor* (inarticulate).[32] A rich belief system is necessarily explicit and contains a relatively large number of elements. Conversely, a poor belief system has a low degree of explicitness and consists of relatively few elements. (b) With regard to the second property, a belief system may be *strongly constraining* or *feebly constraining*: in the former the elements are tightly related in a "quasi-logical" fashion, while in the latter the elements are loosely connected and follow, at best, an "idiosyncratic" syntax.[33] (c) As for the *stratification* aspect, the various "belief strata" can be identified by the amount of political information received and absorbed by each belief-public.

These properties, or aspects, appear highly correlated. The correspondence between the richness of a belief system and various levels of belief publics is hypothesized by Dahl as follows: "In every country the number of identifiable elements ('richness') in the political belief system of different

---

[32] *Ibid.*, p. 3.

[33] As Converse puts it, "The Nature of Belief Systems," esp. pp. 210–211 and 241.

individuals is most highly related to (1) the amount of political activity an individual engates in; (2) the level or extent of his political interest, and (3) the amount of formal education he has had."[34] The hypothesis is highly plausible on the ground of its sheer logical force, and is supported on empirical grounds by the factual evidence reviewed by Converse. Furthermore, if the argument of Dahl is combined with the "constraint argument" of Converse, two conclusions appear reasonably warranted:

(a) A rich, articulate, quasi-logical—and therefore constraining—belief system corresponds to an elite belief system.[35]

(b) In comparison, mass publics are likely to display, in whatever country, a poorly explicated, inarticulate, disconnected—and therefore relatively unconstraining—belief system.

If the foregoing is correct, a number of consequences follow. First, investigations are rewarding only if the public under investigation is clearly identified, if we deal with one belief public at a time, and only if each stratum is measured in accord with its standards. Second, the order of investigation suggests that precedence should be given to the rich elite belief systems. Third, mass belief publics appear to be dependent variables of elite belief publics.

The last suggestion is not only crucial, but also appears, at first, hazardous. Yet the thesis is largely implied in the basic finding of Converse that at the lower levels individuals "lack the contextual grasp of the [belief] system to recognize how they should respond to it without being told by elites who hold their confidence."[36]

On the one hand, belief systems are "diffused in 'packages' which consumers come to see as 'natural' wholes"; i.e., they are constraining in that they are presented in such terms: "If you believe this, then you will also believe that, for it follows in such-and-such ways."[37] On the other hand, however, what "follows in such-and-such ways" is not easy to follow—I mean, the argumentative chain is grasped only by the attentive, articulate citizen. The inarticulate public not only lacks, without guidance, the grasp of *what goes with what* in the deductive chain of a highflown, abstract argument; it equally and especially lacks the information and the inductive capability of deciding on his own how a *specific* event relates to a general principle, and specifically to *which* principle.

The thesis is, then, that a poorly articulated belief system becomes constraining if and when subjected to "linkage-guidance." This means that elite rich belief systems tend to be *self-constraining*, whereas poor and poorly articulated belief systems are basically *hetero-constraining*. The first provide a self-steering, inner-directed system of orientation; the latter re-

---

[34] Dahl, "Ideology, Conflict and Consensus," p. 4.

[35] See Converse, "The Nature of Belief Systems," p. 248: "Ideological constraints in belief systems decline with decreasing political information, which is to say that they are present among elites at the 'top' of political systems . . . and disappear rather rapidly as one moves 'downward' into their mass clienteles."

[36] *Ibid.*, p. 216.

[37] *Ibid.*, p. 212.

quire, *at least for dynamic purposes*, other-direction. The implication is
that elite publics are largely in a position to manipulate mass publics. It
should be clear, in this latter connection, that "elites" also include so-
called counter-elites; the term applies to whichever authorities happen to
be recognized by a distinct belief-group.

The argument can be recapitulated as in Figure 7.

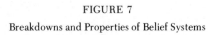

FIGURE 7

Breakdowns and Properties of Belief Systems

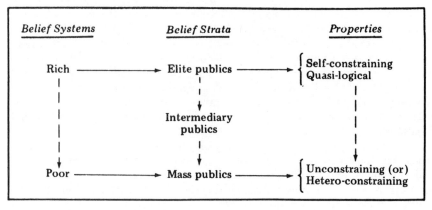

I propose to elaborate on the relevance of these points in the final section.
Meanwhile, I only wish to make the point that unless one distinguishes
among the various belief strata he is hardly in a position to discuss ideology
and pragmatism *qua* concrete belief systems. Indeed I would go as far as to
say that this discussion edges on meaninglessness unless the distinction is
sought at the elite belief level.

My conjecture is, in fact, that under unexposed "rest conditions" any
mass public would display at best a latent political belief system. If so, and
always assuming a hypothetical "non-exposure," mass belief systems are
likely to be largely undifferentiated, largely amorphous with respect to the
ideology-pragmatism distinction. This is to suggest, then, that the ideologic
or pragmatic qualification of mass publics—of the *latent* beliefs—is largely
decided by the *forensic* beliefs, by the elite belief systems to which mass
publics are exposed.[38]

The argument should be placed, however, in perspective, in the sense that
the ideology-pragmatism bifurcation should be traced back to the original
impetus with which a belief system was launched by the founding fathers.
Assuming that the take-off point of an ideological elite is likely to be situ-

[38] The distinction between "latent" and "forensic" is borrowed from Robert E.
Lase, *Political Ideology* (New York: Free Press, 1962), p. 16. In line with my pre-
occupations, I would say that Lane's "latent ideology" can either become, at
the forensic level, an ideological or a pragmatic type of political belief system.

ated in quadrant I, whereas the take-off point of a pragmatic elite is likely to be in quadrant III, *over time* an ideological elite public is likely to vary across a mix of "closed" strong-weak elements (boxes I and II); whereas a pragmatic elite public is likely to vary across a mix of "open" strong-weak elements (boxes III and IV). Therefore, to the extent that each elite remains as it is—either ideological or pragmatic—the respective areas of variation can be represented as in Figure 8.

FIGURE 8

Mixes and Variations of Elite Belief Publics

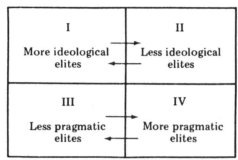

By contrast, the *independent* area of variation of mass belief publics is more likely to be the one suggested in Figure 9. According to the hypothesis, at the lower belief stratum there is no reason to assume that in response to a situation of stress shifts from quadrants II to I necessarily represent, in themselves, an increase of ideologism: they are more likely to signify a sheer growth of intolerance. Likewise, shifts from quadrants II to III do not necessarily indicate, in themselves, the acquisition of a pragmatic mentality: they may simply mean a loss of beliefs and thus increased apathy and indifference. As for the blank of quadrant III, the suggestion implicitly conveyed by the table is that an "open-firm" political belief system typically represents an elite achievement. For a latent state of belief left to itself, this appears to be a very unlikely pattern.

FIGURE 9

Mixes and Variations of Mass Publics

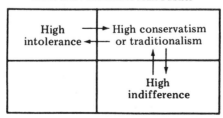

III. IDEOLOGY AND CONFLICT

It should be acknowledged that so far we have been explaining "ideology" more than using "ideology" to explain. Hopefully we have thrown light in a compartment of our black box. Yet the question remains: having explained the term, what does the term explain? I suggest that the question can be squarely met at least in two respects. First, I shall argue that ideology is an important variable in explaining conflict, consensus and cohesion. Second, I shall argue that ideology is the decisive variable in explaining mass mobilization and manipulation.

With regard to the problem of conflict and consensus the question is: how do two or more belief systems relate to one another? If belief systems are compared among themselves, some belief-elements may be shared, and they are the *common elements*; whereas the elements that differentiate one belief system from another are the *distinctive elements*.[39] It is also convenient to assume that the belief-elements that really matter are the "central" ones. On these premises our earlier distinctions between fixed, firm and flexible belief-elements[40] immediately outline three typical patterns of interrelation between different belief-systems and belief groups.

(i) If the distinctive elements are *fixed* (i.e., closed and strongly held) two belief systems are *incompatible* or mutually exclusive, and the relations between the corresponding belief groups will definitely be *conflictual*: conciliation is impossible. However, the intensity and scope of conflict may vary greatly, for the more numerous the (central) distinctive elements, the greater the hostility; the less numerous, the lesser the occasions of conflict.

(ii) If the distinctive elements are *flexible* (i.e., open and weakly held) two belief systems are *coalescent* or fusible, and the relations between the corresponding belief groups will be *consensual*: cooperation is likely. Of course, the fewer the distinctive elements, the greater the amalgamation and the convergence.

(iii) If the distinctive elements are *firm* (i.e., open but strongly held) two belief systems are *compatible*, that is, capable of peaceful coexistence, and the relations between the corresponding belief groups will be of the *bargaining* type: mutual adjustment is possible. Of course, the fewer the (central) distinctive elements, the easier the coexistence.

In essence, then, political conflict (in its autonomy vis-à-vis economic conflict, or conflicts of interest) largely depends on *which* distinctive elements are distributed *how* within a national community or across nations. With regard to the pure and simple distribution—i.e., disregarding for the moment the nature of the elements—political conflict reflects the rise of a controversy which taps the distinctive elements of two (or more) belief systems. Conversely, the sharing of common belief-elements indicates the area in which we obtain political consensus. This preliminary argument can be reformulated also along the lines suggested in Figure 10.

[39] Dahl, "Ideology, Conflict and Consensus," p. 2.
[40] *Supra*, Figure 2: "Typology of Belief-Elements." For the present discussion the "inelastic elements" will be neglected.

FIGURE 10

Conflictual Versus Consensual Politics

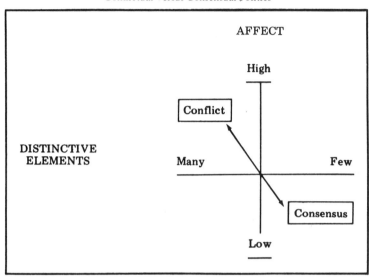

However, Figure 10 accounts for two variables—the numerical magnitude and the emotional intensity of the elements—but fails to account for
a third, crucial variable: the nature of the distinctive elements. We are thus
referred to the question: which is the distribution of *which* elements? If the
central distinctive elements are "closed," the controversy will be ideological; if they are "open" it will be pragmatic. In either case controversy is
inevitable, but the chances and the ways of conflict resolution are conspicuously different.

At one end, if the distinctive elements are not only closed but also passionately held we shall have "ideological warfare," the relation is incompatibility and conflict is unmanageable. At the other end, the more the
distinctive elements are open and feebly felt, the more we shall obtain
"pragmatic transactions" and relations of mutual adjustment.

The same applies to the shared elements. At one end, a belief group
whose common elements are closed and strongly held will display "ideological cohesion," that is, strong and lasting solidarity ties, discipline and
active dedication to the whole. At the other end, a belief group whose
common elements are open and feebly held will display "pragmatic consensus," which means low cohesion, ephemeral and feeble solidarity ties,
and a tendency to dissolve into multiple loyalties.

Thus far we have hypothesized relations among homogeneous belief sy-
tems, i.e., between two belief systems which are both ideological or both
pragmatic. We can also obtain, however, heterogeneous interrelations between pragmatic and ideological belief groups. In this case the additional
complication is a serious communication lag. The two mentalities simply do

not fit: their very logic, their *Gestalten,* are different. On the other hand, each belief group is inevitably prompted to project its own *forma mentis* on the opposing group. A blind game results in which misinterpretation, misperception, frustration and a spiral of distrust play the major roles.

For instance, the pragmatic actor tends to assume that interests and conflicts of interests—along a continuum ranging from total coincidence of interest to zero-sum conflict—suffice to explain and to predict political behavior.[41] But in the ideological actor the "logic of interest" combines with a "logic of principles." In fact, ideological politics represents a situation in which the utility scale of each actor is altered by an ideological scale. Hence, and much to the bewilderment of the pragmatist, in this case the logic of interest no longer suffices to explain, and even less to predict, political behavior.

In conclusion, unless we are sensitized to the existence of distinctly ideological publics and belief systems we are likely to miss the very nature of "big conflict." For instance, we are easily misled into believing that ideological conflicts can be reduced to underlying economic conflicts which can be cured with economic medicines. Likewise, we are likely to miss the fact that the dialogue of politics may well be a dialogue among deaf men. On the other hand, the foregoing equally alerts us to the fact that ideological censensus is not the same as pragmatic consensus, and that the in-group cohesion of an ideological community is a far cry from the in-group solidarity of a pragmatic community.

IV. IDEOLOGY AND MASS MANIPULATION

Before turning to the explanatory value of "ideology" vis-à-vis the unprecedented scale of contemporary mass manipulation—which is also my major and most comprehensive point—it will be necessary to recapitulate, however sweepingly, the route traveled thus far.

Having reference to the more basic features, belief systems vary, as we know, along the following dimensions: (i) closed and open cognition, (ii) emotive intensity, (iii) rich-poor articulation, and (iv) constraining power.

With respect to their cultural matrixes belief systems vary, in addition, with respect to the following characteristics: (i) accessibility either to argumentative demonstration or to factual evidence; (ii) centrality of the belief-elements; (iii) level of abstraction; and (iv) comprehensiveness.

It is unnecessary to elaborate further on the first set of basic characteristics. As for the additional underpinnings, attention should be called to the following hypotheses.

With regard to *accessibility,* the hypothesis is that to the extent that the ideological mentality receives external communications, it is receptive to rational demonstration, hardly to empirical proofs. Conversely, the pragmatic mentality is open to evidence far more than to the "reasons of reason."

[41] Interest is understood here as the utility scale of each individual, as perceived by the interested party according to the culturally accepted standards of economic rationality.

With regard to the *centrality* of the belief-elements, the hypothesis is that in ideological belief systems the "ends" constitute the central elements; whereas in pragmatic belief systems the "means" tend to be more central.

With regard to the *abstraction* ladder, ideological belief systems soar on a far more remote, abstruse and high-flown level of discourse than the pragmatic belief systems.

Correlatively, and finally, with regard to *comprehensiveness*, the coverage, or the space for expansion, of ideological belief systems is far more universal and "totalistic" than the coverage of the pragmatic belief systems.

The import of these qualifications is readily apparent in the light of the most crucial aspect of belief systems, namely, their *constraining power*. It was suggested earlier that mass publics are, in general, easily hetero-constrained, in the sense that poorly articulated believers need guidance not only for the horizontal inter-belief linkage, but also for the vertical event-principle linkage.[42] But now the argument can be pinned down, according to the following three points.

First: The greater the centrality of the belief elements designating *ends*, the more a belief system will elicit normative, goal-oriented, if not futuristic or even chiliastic responses and behavior.

Second: The more *abstract* a belief system, the more "what follows from what" (inter-belief linkage), and "which event goes with which principle" (event-principle linkage) escape the grasp of mass publics and require elite guidance. Hence, the more abstract a belief system, the more it allows for elite manipulation and maneuvering.

Third and correlatively: The more a belief system transcends common-sense spatial and temporal boundaries, that is, the more it obtains a totalistic *comprehensiveness*, the more it calls for elite interpretation and facilitates elite control.

The foregoing forcibly suggests, then, that the hetero-constraining potentiality of belief systems increases the more the system is ideological, and diminishes the more the system is pragmatic. In short, ideologies are the *hetero-constraining* belief systems par excellence. And this is the same as saying that ideologies are the crucial lever at the disposal of elites for obtaining political mobilization and for maximizing the possibilities of mass manipulation. This is, it seems to me, the single major reason that ideology is so important to us. We are concerned about ideologies because we are concerned, in the final analysis, with the power of man over man, with how populations and nations can be mobilized and manipulated all along the way that leads to political messianism and fanaticism.

The focus on ideology as a lever of political mobilization, as an instrument of mass manipulation, satisfies the requirement of causal explanation. At this stage we are not merely saying, "this is *what* the term indicates";

[42]The need, if not the inevitability of guidance is also the conclusion implicitly conveyed by the literature on the closed and open mind. In particular Rokeach brings out neatly the extent to which cognitive closedness is exposed to manipulation from the authorities.

we are also saying "this is *why* we have ideological politics." Yet the reader may feel that this is a too narrow conclusion, and surely a conclusion that requires some justification.

At the outset of this exploration I had two queries in mind. One was: what should we seek to explain? The other one was: what is it that remains unexplained? Clearly these are the two sides of a same question. But the first query is virtually limitless, whereas the second narrows the problem, thereby providing the guideline that I have resolved to follow. By now we know a great deal about why individuals act and react in politics the way they do. Nevertheless we are still at a loss when we come to macro-phenomena and try to understand why the distribution of the "open" and "closed" minds, of high or low affect, does not follow any statistical logic and varies as it does. If so, the concept of ideology still has an important explanatory role to play—under the condition, however, that we sharpen it for the purpose of explaining what other convergent conceptualizations and disciplines leave unexplained. My view is, then, that ideology is crucial to an empirical theory of politics because, and to the extent that, it is conducive to the understanding of *variations* and *varieties*.

Politics is not a monotonic phenomenon. At times it is a mystique, a matter of faith, a secular religion; at other times the logic of politics is no less practical, no less "matter of fact," than the logic of economics. Some political systems display a high extractive capability and succeed in eliciting enthusiastic, passionate and trustful allegiance; other political systems display a low mobilizational and extractive capability. In certain instances we are confronted with monolithic political units characterized by extraordinary cohesiveness; but in other instances we find equivalent political units characterized by a hopeless lack of solidarity ties. Finally, the dialogue of politics is confronted with very different types of "deafness."

Does political science need the variable ideology to explain, at least in part, these varieties and variations? My reply has been in the affirmative, provided we do not overload the concept in pursuing ambitious attempts to explain (worse) that which other disciplines or conceptualizations explain better; and provided, therefore, that the use of "ideology" is restricted to the meanings that appear to have a *unique* explanatory value.

THE VARIETY AND CHARACTERISTICS
OF SAMPLING PROCEDURES*

FREDERICK F. STEPHAN
Princeton University

PHILIP J. McCARTHY
Cornell University

O UR PRIMARY CONCERN ... IS THE USE OF SAMPLING TO OBTAIN INFORMATION relating to the distribution of various measures of attitudes, opinions, consumer wants, and related variables among the members of a specified human population. Many different procedures have been suggested and used for choosing samples of persons from such populations. Some of them are widely known and well understood. Many of them can only be described in vague and superficial terms. Some require a rather technical description to make clear the manner in which they operate to produce samples and their relative strengths and weaknesses for this purpose. This chapter will describe some of the types of sampling that are frequently reported and discuss certain of their characteristics. It will also outline a broad classification scheme and then indicate the general features that appear to be common to all sampling operations.

Sampling methods have frequently been labeled in papers and reports with very general titles such as "representative," "random," "quota control," "purposive," "judgment," "stratified," "area," "precision," "unbiased," "probability," and the like. Actually, such general labels have little meaning, either because there is no commonly accepted and precise definition of the term applied or because there exist many variations of the general method, both in concept and application. For these reasons it is important that survey operators provide adequate descriptions of the procedures they use. Moreover, each description should include an account of the way the sampling was actually done and how it differed from the way it was planned. Even here, however, we must acknowledge that there is an arbitrary element in stating what constitutes an adequate description, since it is never possible to set forth every relevant detail of a sample survey.

REPRESENTATIVE SAMPLES

The first aim of most sampling procedures is to obtain a sample of people that will *represent* the population from which it is selected. In other words, it is expected that results obtained from the sample will agree "closely" with the results that would have been obtained had the entire population been subjected to study. This same idea has frequently been stated by saying that a sample should be a miniature population or universe.

*Reprinted with permission of Philip J. McCarthy, from Frederick F. Stephan and Philip J. McCarthy, "The Variety and Characteristics of Sampling Procedures," in *Sampling Opinions* (New York: John Wiley and Sons, 1958), pp. 30–52.

Many different procedures, arising from intuition or common sense, have been suggested and used for obtaining representative samples. Thus it seems fairly obvious that the sample should be scattered evenly throughout the population being sampled. A simple illustration of such scattering is the sampling of cars which cross a bridge during a fixed interval of time, every tenth car being drawn into the sample. Bowley obtained such a scattering of his sample in 1912 when he selected every twentieth household in Reading by counting down the street lists in the directory. Another intuitively appealing method of obtaining representative samples is to select the sample in such a manner that it *must* agree with the population in certain respects. Illustrations of specific applications of this type will be given later in this chapter.

The foregoing remarks have been phrased as though the quality of representativeness were absolute, that is, as though any given sample of people could be classified as either entirely representative or entirely non-representative of the population from which it is drawn. Actually, this is not the case. In the first place, a sample may represent the population with respect to one characteristic or variable and may not represent the population with respect to other variables. For example, suppose that in selecting a sample of pupils from a school, only those pupils in the first grade were taken. Such a sample would certainly be very far from representing the school population with respect to age. However, the fraction of pupils in the first grade having blue eyes might be very close to the corresponding fraction in the entire school. Consequently we see that representativeness must be specified not only with respect to a population but also with respect to one or more variables. In the second place, it is clear that representativeness is also a matter of degree. A sample selected from the children in each of the first three grades would be more representative of the school with respect to age than a sample selected only from the first grade, though neither sample would be as representative as the sample made up of all the blue-eyed boys in all the grades in the school.

The problem of the relative nature of representativeness is particularly marked when human populations are being sampled for the measurement of opinions, attitudes, and consumer wants. The difficulties arise because in practice we must first obtain a sample of individuals in order to obtain a sample from the population of all opinions or attitudes on a specified topic, even though it is only the population of opinions in which we are interested. This means that a sample of persons may be quite representative according to some individual traits but still not yield a very representative sample of opinions when the measurements have been made. Moreover, it is a rare survey in which only one variable is studied. Consequently, it is necessary to balance the requirements for representativeness, one variable against another.

In view of these considerations, it is quite clear that the term "representative sample," by itself, can never be given a precise meaning. Accordingly, we offer the following definition:

A *representative sample* is a sample which, for a specified set of variables, resembles the population from which it is drawn to the extent that certain specified analyses that are to be carried out on the sample (computation of means, standard deviations, etc., for particular variables) will yield results which will fall within acceptable limits set about the corresponding population values, except that in a small proportion of such analyses of samples (as specified in the procedure used to obtain this one) the results will fall outside the limits.

Any individual or agency is, of course, free to adopt its own standards of representativeness, and these may well vary from investigation to investigation. However, it is only when these standards are set forth in detail, together with the reasons for assuming that the sample conforms to them, that the term takes on a precise meaning. Thus the mere statement or claim that a sample is representative of a population tells us nothing. This is not necessarily a condemnation of the sample itself but only of the incompleteness of the description of the sample.

SAMPLING FROM LISTS OR OTHER NATURAL
ORDERINGS OF POPULATION ELEMENTS

A sample can be drawn from a list by taking items from the list at regular intervals—say, every fifth or every twenty-third or in general every kth, where k is some integer that will yield a sample of the right size. When every kth element is taken from a list or from some other form of natural ordering, we say that a *systematic sampling procedure* is being used. Systematic sampling has a strong intuitive appeal, for it spreads the sample elements uniformly over the population. This appeal is particularly strong when the ordering is a geographic one, but it also exists in many other cases. Thus the salesgirl who hands out a questionnaire to every tenth person making a purchase spreads her sample out evenly over all her customers with respect to the order in which they appear at her counter.

Even with a simple procedure such as systematic sampling, intuition is not always an adequate guide to the degree of representativeness that may be achieved by a given sample. For example, there may be a relationship between the order of occurrence and an element's characteristics that will produce unexpected or "queer" results. As a simple example, consider the following. During World War II, there was a research agency connected with the Army which was engaged in finding out how the soldiers felt on particular subjects. When a member of this organization went into a camp, he obtained a list of the soldiers in the camp from which to draw a sample. An obviously convenient procedure was to draw a systematic sample from this list. In one particular instance in which such a sample was being drawn, some of the characteristics of those men drawn into the sample were examined. It was found that much too great a proportion of master sergeants was selected for the sample. Upon learning this, the surveyor had no trouble in finding the reason. The men in the camp were listed barracks by barracks. Within each barracks the men were listed in order of their military rank. Also there were the same number of men in each barracks. Unfortunately, the chosen sampling interval was such that it stepped off the same line numbers on list after list, and in this way it happened to fall again and again on lines that usually contained the names of master sergeants.

In addition to problems such as the above, many practical difficulties may arise in applying systematic sampling. For example, in sampling from lists or schedules, some of the records may be out of the file, in use, or waiting to be refiled and consequently may be overlooked entirely. Further accounts of such difficulties will be found in a paper by Stephan.[1] Moreover, in any large-scale undertaking, problems of time and cost are of the greatest importance.

If the data are to be obtained not only from the list but from further inquiry about each case in the sample, new problems arise. It is one thing to select a systematic sample of 1,000 names from a list, and it is quite another thing to obtain a sample of data by personal interviews with each of these persons when they are located in 700 or 800 towns scattered across the United States. These practical problems of time and cost require modifications in the selection procedure for their solution, and these modifications are usually designed to obtain some geographic clustering of the sample elements. In other words, one interviewer can obtain six or seven interviews in one town much more quickly than he can obtain the same number of interviews if they are scattered over two or three counties.

A relatively simple example of this type of sample design was used to select a sample of names from the list of subscribers to the magazine *Country Gentlemen*, each selected subscriber to be visited for personal interview. Stripped of details, the procedure was as follows. First a systematic sample of names was selected from the list. Since the names were arranged in a geographic fashion, this imposed a geographic spread on the sample. The size of this sample was determined by the number of *different geographic areas in which it was feasible to conduct interviews*. After these names had been selected, an automatic procedure was devised to associate with each of them an additional group of names such that (*a*) the total sample was of the required size and (*b*) the additional names were "geographically close" to those originally chosen. Most samples used in personal interview surveys are necessarily subject to similar considerations, except when the population is confined to a very compact geographic area. The use of mail questionnaires avoids this problem of "scattering," but as is well known, mail questionnaires present other problems.

RANDOM SELECTION

Some of the difficulties that may arise in the use of systematic selection can be traced directly to the fact that the inclusion or exclusion of any given element may not be independent of certain characteristics of the element which are associated with its position or order in the list. The same statement can of course be made even more strongly in instances where *self-selection* is operative (e.g., where an individual decides whether or not he

[1] Frederick F. Stephan, "Practical Problems of Sampling Procedure," *American Sociological Review*, 1 (1936), pp. 569–580.

will respond to a mail questionnaire), where *convenience selection* is used (e.g., where those elements are taken which are conveniently located with respect to the sampler), or where *judgment selection* is used (e.g., where the sampler decides whether or not an element will be included in the sample).

It is therefore natural that we should look for a method of selection which bears no relation to the properties or characteristics of individual elements, and in which no subjective influence is allowed to affect the determination of what elements will make up the sample. Such procedures can be obtained by considering the operation of games of chance, lotteries, and other related activities. A simple procedure for performing this type of selection comes to mind immediately. Suppose we assign a number to each population element and write the numbers on identical cards. Having done this, we shuffle the cards thoroughly and draw "blindly" a number of cards equal to the required sample size. The population elements with the corresponding numbers will then complete the sample. It is quite clear that this process removes all subjective influences from the selection procedure, and also that the characteristics of individual elements have no bearing on whether or not they are included or excluded from the sample.

When such a selection procedure as this is used, we say that every element in the population has an equal chance of being drawn into the sample and, furthermore, that each of the possible sets of elements of the required size has the same chance of being selected. We call it *random selection.*

Even when systematic selection may be assumed to give a representative sample, it is sometimes preferable to use random selection. For example, suppose a garage wished to survey customers' attitudes toward repair work done in the shop. This could be done by questioning every fifth customer. However, this might allow shop employees to figure out in advance which jobs would be followed up, and consequently to give these jobs special attention. The use of random selection would remove this difficulty.

Random selection is one example of a method which conforms to theoretical principles from which deductions can be made about the performance of the method. In this instance, the principles assume that there is assigned to each population element, in advance of the draw, the same probability of being included in the sample. Provided that a mechanical procedure can be devised for selecting elements in accordance with this principle, probability theory can then be helpful in predicting how the method will work in practice and thus assessing the representativeness of the chosen sample.

If random samples are drawn repeatedly from the population, estimates made from the samples will vary from time to time around an average value. Probability theory permits us to deduce how closely these estimates will agree with the results that would have been obtained if the entire population were subjected to the same measurement and estimation procedures. A similar approach can be made to systematic sampling, but the methods are necessarily more complex.[2]

[2]Lillian H. Madow, "Systematic Sampling and Its Relation to Other Sampling Designs," *Journal of the American Statistical Association*, 41 (1946), pp. 204–217.

WHY COMPLEX SAMPLING PROCEDURES MAY BE REQUIRED

The simple procedures of random and systematic selection described in preceding sections can frequently be applied if lists of population elements exist. Even when such lists are not available, there may still be a possibility of using these procedures, provided the population is of relatively small size and is confined to a relatively compact geographic area. For example, we might walk along every street in the area that contains the population and draw every *k*th dwelling unit into the sample. However, even here we must proceed with care in the application of the scheme. Some of the dwelling units may be missed because they are located in alleys, in the rear of stores, and so on. Moreover, it is necessary to specify exactly what population is being sampled. If we are interested in dwelling units, then information can be obtained from any responsible person in each of the selected units. On the other hand, if we are interested in the population of individuals living in the dwelling units, there is the further problem of obtaining respondents from among the people living in the selected dwelling units. If we always take the person who comes to the door, the sample will contain too many housewives and other persons who are usually at home. In this instance it is possible to use random selection to obtain one person from each dwelling unit, or we may wish to interview every person in the selected units. Probability theory and experience must serve as the guides in deciding what is to be done.

In the event that the population is large and scattered over a wide geographic area, it is frequently too costly in terms of time, money, and personnel to carry out a procedure such as that outlined above. Consequently, some other form of sampling must be devised. The general outlines of the procedures that are currently being used under such circumstances are relatively easy to describe and understand. We shall now consider a number of illustrative examples. For the sake of simplicity, we shall confine our attention to city sample designs. The procedures that will be described can be carried over, with little change, to the sampling of populations which are located in rural areas or in areas of both urban and rural population.

QUOTA SAMPLING

For a long time the dominant form of sample design in opinion surveys has been "quota sampling." This procedure was developed by Cherington, Roper, Gallup, and Crossley, whose sample surveys of opinion became widely known after the presidential election of 1936, and by other market research and opinion survey organizations whose studies received less publicity. Its basic features have been widely adopted, partly in imitation of the more widely known surveys and partly because of their attractiveness with respect to costs and convenience. In recent years it has been superseded in many surveys by various forms of "probability sampling."

As with many other sample designs, a quota sampling procedure starts with the premise that a sample should be scattered over the population and should contain the same fraction of individuals having certain characteristics as does the population. Census data and other information are used to divide the total population into a number of mutually exclusive and exhaustive sub-populations or *strata* and to determine or estimate (depending on the adequancy of these external data) the fraction of the population in each of these strata. The total sample is then allocated among these strata—geographic regions, age and sex groups, racial groups, and the like—in proportion of their real or estimated size.

The imposition of controls on the sample, which are external to the survey, is carried out through stratification in many other types of sample designs. Therefore, the mere statement that a quota sample is a "stratified" sample is not sufficient to distinguish it from other sampling procedures. Many other considerations have to be raised. What strata were used? How were the strata defined? How was the sample allocated among them? How was sampling carried out *within the strata?*

The final step in quota sampling is to apportion the sample among the interviewers and tell each the number of persons he is to obtain in each one of the strata. Thus he is told to obtain so many men and so many women, so many persons of high income, and so many of low income, and similarly for the other characteristics used to control selection. Interviewers are free to choose the particular respondents they will interview, subject only to the restriction that the quota requirements be fulfilled.

If it were true that the interviewers selected their respondents in a purely random fashion within each stratum or "quota control" group, then quota sampling could be labeled as stratified random sampling. Actually, it is extremely difficult to see how we can regard interviewers as completely random selecting devices. There are many ways in which the conscious or unconscious likes, dislikes, and habits of the interviewers may influence their selection of respondents. For example, an interviewer may be attracted or repelled by the appearance of a house; he may concentrate his work in certain sections of a city and miss others; and he may fail to reach certain kinds of people because he selects those who are most convenient to interview.

This lack of full control has long been recognized as a fundamental weakness of quota sampling by both proponents and opponents of the method. It has led to various modifications in the method intended to make the interviewer operate like a mechanical selecting device. This may be done by specifying more definitely the procedures he is to follow in selecting people to interview, or by narrowing the group from which he makes his selection to such an extent that the subjective element can have little effect. The instructions issued to interviewers caution them against neglecting the lower education and income groups, request them to make their interviews in the home or on the farm, stress the necessity for making evening calls, and so on. Many of these points are covered in the manual prepared by the National Opinion Research Center[3] and in similar manuals used by other

[3]National Opinion Research Center, *Interviewing for NORC* (Denver: University of Denver, 1945).

survey organizations. The group from which the interviewer selects his respondents is usually narrowed by telling him to obtain interviews only on specified blocks, in specified sections of a city, etc.

There are many different ways in which the foregoing considerations, and others that have not been mentioned, may be translated into a definite quota sampling procedure. Therefore it is not sufficient simply to state that quota sampling was used in a survey and expect anyone to have more than a very general idea of how the sample was drawn. A substantial portion of the design must be described before we can even state that two such procedures are roughly similar. . . .

PURPOSIVE SELECTION OF AREAS

There are many situations in which it may be necessary to conduct interviews in a relatively small number of compact groups or areas. That is, it may be impossible to identify individual population elements, whereas groups of elements can be specified (workers in a plant, members of social or professional organizations, people living in defined geographic areas, and the like); also, the geographic "clustering" of sample elements will tend to reduce the amount of time and the number of personnel required for obtaining a given number of interviews. Under these circumstances, we may wish to conduct the sampling in two stages. A sample of groups or areas is chosen first, and then a sample of elements is taken from each of the selected groups.

There are many ways in which this sampling of areas, or groups, can be accomplished; at this point we shall present a brief description of one approach which is closely related to the fundamental premise of quota sampling, namely, that forced agreement between sample and population on a number of characteristics or *controls* is desirable. The particular example to be considered ultimately ends with the assignment of quotas to interviewers. However, prior to the determination of these quotas, a sampling of areas was carried out by what we may call *purposive selection*.

In making predictions for the 1948 presidential elections, the *Philadlephia Evening Bulletin* used the following sample design.[4] Philadelphia has a total of 52 election wards, each of which is divided into a number of voting divisions. After each election the Registration Commission publishes detailed reports on voting and registration by wards and divisions. The *Bulletin* selected 25 wards from the city which, when combined, voted in the same proportions as did the city as a whole, over the three election years 1942, 1944, and 1946. From each of the selected wards, two divisions were chosen which, when combined, voted over the three election years in exactly the same pattern as the ward itself. The total number of interviews to be obtained was then allocated among the divisions in proportion to the total voting population. The interviewers were given maps showing the

[4] Frederick Mosteller, Herbert Hyman, Philip J. McCarthy, Eli S. Marks, and David B. Truman, *The Pre-election Polls of 1948*, Bulletin 60, Social Science Research Council, New York, 1949.

boundaries and the number of interviews to be obtained from each division, and the sampling proceeded from this point in a fairly typical quota fashion. The interviewers were not given specific addresses within the divisions but were instructed to scatter the calls, one or two to each block. White-Negro quotas were assigned to each division and checks were maintained on the sex and economic composition of the sample.

A procedure very similar to this (at least as far as the selection of areas is concerned) was used by the American Institute of Public Opinion (AIPO) to design state samples in connection with the 1944 and 1948 presidential elections. It has been described by Benson, Young, and Syze[5] who refer to it as a "pinpoint" sample. The current method of "precinct" sampling that is used in Gallup election polls appears to be a development of "pinpoint" sampling.

It is quite clear that many variations of this fundamental approach are possible—depending on how the areas are defined, how the *control* variables are chosen, and how the sample of individuals or households is taken from each of the selected areas. Therefore it is not sufficient merely to state that a purposive sample of areas has been taken. The details must be specified so that others will know what was done.

SELECTION OF AREAS IN ACCORDANCE WITH A PROBABILITY MODEL

When a list of the population elements is available, the methods of random and systematic selection may be used, and they may be made to conform to theoretical models from which deductions can be made about the long-run performance of the method. We may well ask whether such models exist in the more complex situation where population lists are not available. As has been shown by the work of the Indian Statistical Institute, the Bureau of the Census, the Bureau of Agricultural Economics, and Iowa State College, and many other agencies too numerous to mention, the answer must be in the affirmative. In the material which follows, we shall speak of a sampling method as conforming to a probability model if it is possible, in advance of the actual selection of the sample, to assign to each possible set of population elements a known probability. These probabilities give the fraction of times that each possible set would be drawn if the sampling procedure were repeated an indefinitely large number of times.

These concepts can be illustrated by considering a probability model design which might be used in a city. We could first obtain maps and divide the city into a large number of smaller areas, or *primary sampling units*, as they are usually called. These primary sampling units might be blocks, portions of blocks, or any other areas which seemed desirable. The areas must be mutually exclusive, must be easily identifiable, and must include between them all the population. From the totality of these units a sample of units is selected. In the event this is done by simple random selection, the probability that any given unit will be in the sample is simply n/N, where

[5] Edward Benson, Cyrus Young, and Clyde Syze, "Polling Lessons from the 1944 Election," *Public Opinion Quarterly*, 9 (1945), pp. 467–484.

N is the number of units in the city and n is the number of units to be drawn into the sample.

Once the primary sampling units have been chosen for the sample, field workers are sent out to prepare a list of every dwelling unit located within their boundaries. Then a random sample of dwelling units is selected from this list. If, for example, a 10 per cent sample of dwelling units is to be selected from within each primary unit, then the probability that any given dwelling unit is included in this sample is equal to $(n/N) \times (1/10)$—i.e., the product of the area selection probability multiplied by the dwelling unit selection probability. If all the eligible persons within each chosen dwelling unit are to be included in the sample, this probability is also the probability that a specified individual will be chosen; but if further sampling is performed within the dwelling unit, the number obtained must be multiplied by still another factor to determine the probability for an individual. A step-by-step account of such a procedure as this for obtaining a city sample has been provided by Kish[6]

As far as practical application is concerned, this procedure accomplishes the following things: (a) it makes it possible to state in advance the probability that any given individual will be included in the sample and the relation of this probability to the probabilities for other individuals, without requiring preparation of a complete list of all population elements, thus conforming to our concept of a probability model sample; and (b) it clusters the selected respondents from a geographic point of view and thus effects economies in the amount of travel required to contact the selected respondents.

Once a probability model of this kind is set up, a mechanical procedure is devised to select elements from the population in accordance with the model. This is frequently done by means of random-number tables.[7] It designates the elements that are to be included in the sample. As the final step, interviewers are sent to obtain information from the predesignated respondents.

Sample designs of this general type have frequently been referred to as "area samples" because we first select a sample of geographic areas. However, the term is not particularly apt because it is possible to make use of areas without having a probability model sample. An example of such a sample design was given in the preceding section. Also, we can apply similar techniques to groups of population elements which are not defined on an area basis. Thus a sample of workers in a particular occupation could be obtained by first selecting a sample of firms that employ such workers and then choosing a sample of workers from within each firm.

MULTI-STAGE SAMPLING PROCEDURES CANNOT BE CLASSIFIED SIMPLY

As illustrated in the preceding sections, many sampling operations are carried out in successive stages, a member of the defined population being

---

[6]Leslie Kish, "A Two-Stage Sample of a City," *American Sociological Review*, 17 (1952), pp. 761–769.

[7]The RAND Corporation, *A Million Random Digits* (Glencoe: Free Press, 1955).

TABLE 1

Possible Combinations of Sampling Procedures in a Three-Stage
Sampling Operation

Sampling Stage	Unit of Sampling	Procedures That Might Be Used in Selection
1	Blocks	*a.* Random
		b. Systematic
		c. Purposive
2	Dwelling units within blocks	*a.* Random
		b. Systematic
		c. Selection left up to interviewer
3	Adults from within dwelling units	*a.* All adults interviewed
		b. Random selection of a single adult
		c. Selection left up to interviewer (subject to quota restrictions)

obtained only at the final stage. This means, among other things, that an extremely large number of sampling procedures are possible in even a simple situation. For example, Table 1 shows what might have to be considered in drawing a sample of adults from a city.

Any of the procedures given for one of the three stages may be used in combination with any of the procedures given for another stage, and thus it is possible to conceive of 27 different sampling methods in this situation. Moreover, some of the procedures that we might wish to consider have not been included in this table. Further variations could be obtained by imposing external controls on the sample. Thus we might wish to stratify blocks with respect to geographic location, or with respect to average rental, or with respect to estimated size.

This example emphasizes the point made in the opening portions of this chapter, namely, that general titles can tell us little concerning the actual procedures used in selecting a sample. It is essential that the producers of survey information provide a complete description of sample design, and that the consumers of such information expect this description as a matter of course. Otherwise there is no basis on which to evaluate the accuracy and reliability of the data.

THE ACTUAL APPLICATION OF THE PROCEDURE

We have already noted that a sample of individuals is important only insofar as it leads to a sample of data. Two surveys may use the same type of sampling procedure but apply it in different ways and so get markedly different samples of data. They may use identical sampling procedures to select persons, and yet the ultimate results may not be comparable for a variety of reasons. There may be essential differences in the methods that are used to obtain information from the sample elements such as mail questionnaires, personal interviews, group interviewing (where sample elements are called into a central location and fill in their own questionnaires), or telephone interviews. There may be important differences in the extent to which information is actually obtained from the intended sample. Thus some of the individuals may refuse to be interviewed; it may be impossible to contact others without a prohibitive expenditure of time and money; or persons sent a mail questionnaire may not respond. These latter eventualities often mean that we do not obtain information from an important fraction of the people in the sample originally selected. Consequently our advance predictions about the behavior of the sampling procedure may no longer be correct. All these points must be included in the evaluation and comparison of sample survey results. . . .

A BROAD CLASSIFICATION OF SAMPLING OPERATIONS

The kinds of sampling that have been described in this chapter are those that have been distinguished and discussed most frequently. A review of the reports of sampling surveys and studies of attitudes, opinions, and wants reveals many instances in which the processes by which the data were obtained do not seem to correspond to any of these methods. It would be fruitless to set up a large number of specific classifications to include the many varieties of sampling, but several broad classifications are useful. They will be illustrated by a discussion of three examples: (A) classification by the method of selection, (B) classification by the type of contact or connection between sampler and sample, and (C) basis for cooperation or compliance of persons in the sample.

A. *The Method of Selection*

The methods of selecting samples of people and of data may be grouped into four broad classes:

1. Taking what is readily available.
2. Expedient choice.
3. Selection constrained by group quotas, matching, and other purposive controls.
4. Probabilized selection.

1. Taking What Is Readily Available.   In this class the sample is scarcely selected at all. It is merely discovered or picked out of the immediate environment. Although this may seem a careless or slipshod method, it is not necessarily so. Its application often consists of a prolonged and careful search for available cases. This is essentially the method used in a study of letters received by members of Congress.[8] It is the method by which Thomas and Znaniecki obtained a large collection of letters written by and to Polish immigrants in America to form a principal part of their pioneering study of attitudes at the time of the First World War.[9] Another similar

[8] Hilda Hertzog and Rowena Wyant, "Voting via the Senate Mailbag," *Public Opinion Quarterly*, 5 (1941), pp. 359–382 and 590–624.
[9] W. I. Thomas and Florian Znaniecki, *The Polish Peasant in Europe and America*, 2 vols. (New York: Alfred A. Knopf, 1927).

application occurs in the interrogation of prisoners of war and refugees,[10] in analyses of captured correspondence,[11] and in studies of excommunists such as Gabriel A. Almond's study, *The Appeals of Communism.*[12] It is also the method that must be used in the studies of the reactions of civilian populations to major disasters. Thus the sampler may have no other choice than to take the sample that is offered to him ready-made by the force of circumstances.

In other instances, however, the sample seems not so much a rare opportunity or scarce set of data as it does a windfall or a convenient by-product that frees the user from more costly or arduous methods of obtaining his sample. Thus the selection of readily available cases is the method used by innumerable psychologists and sociologists who have made studies of attitudes by giving questionnaires to the students in their classes or members of other readily available groups.[13] It is the method used in some of the voluntary panels of consumers, correspondents, and crop reporters, in which people are accepted who have been recommended, are willing to cooperate, and are qualified according to some general criteria.

2. Expedient Choice. In this category would be placed methods which recognize that the elements of a sample should be "chosen" from among all elements in a defined population but which permit this choice to be made in the most expedient manner. This may not be very different from taking readily available persons, but it does include active steps to make more members of the population available or it rejects some that are readily available. For example, a questionnaire may be published in a newspaper with a request that everyone cut it out, answer the questions, and then mail it to a central office. A card may be attached to a product so that the users of the product can report their reactions to it.

People have been approached for their opinions when they are assembled at meetings, county fairs, conventions, women's club meetings, bus stations, hospital clinics, and other places. There are two selective processes that are usually involved: first, the sampler's selection of the place and the occasion, and second, the processes of attraction that bring people to it. These processes introduce obvious possibilities of bias and distortion that may make it impossible to obtain a fair sample. On the other hand, certain types of places and occasions will produce mixtures of persons who are widely dispersed with respect to place of residence and ordinary daily activities. Dr. Kinsey's sampling methods appear to have been of this kind.

---

[10]Alexander H. Leighton, *Human Relations in a Changing World* (New York: Dutton, 1949); Margaret Mead, *Soviet Attitudes Toward Authority* (New York: McGraw-Hill, 1951).

[11]The United States Strategic Bombing Survey, *The Effects of Strategic Bombing on German Morale*, Vol. 2 (Washington, D.C.: U.S. Government Printing Office, 1947).

[12]Gabriel A. Almond, *The Appeals of Communism* (Princeton: Princeton University Press, 1954).

[13]Quinn McNemar, "Opinion-Attitude Methodology," *Psychological Bulletin*, 43 (1946), pp. 289–374.

He traveled about seeking all who would agree to be interviewed; he attempted to interview all the members of various groups; he even interviewed many hitchhikers. The results of his sampling procedure may be fairly representative of the population he was interested in studying in some characteristics but quite different in some others.[14] How good they were is still debatable.

An element of expediency appears even in some of the more rigorous methods of sampling. For example, some surveys exclude people who live in institutions, are migrating, or are homeless. The selection is thus confined for the most part to private households when it is believed that the results are substantially the same as would be obtained by more refined and difficult methods attempting to cover the whole population. Relative to the other problems involved in the survey, the distorting influence of such exclusions is regarded as negligible. This assumption may be unwarranted. Some test of it is always needed.

3. *Selection Constrained by Group Quotas, Matching, and Other "Purposive" Controls.* There are methods of selection in which the taking of readily available individuals or the active search for individuals is regulated by definite instructions that aim to make the whole sample similar in a number of ways to the population that it is to represent. The instructions may be negative so as to avoid certain kinds of unrepresentative persons; or they may be positive and seek to provide specified numbers of persons of particular kinds. They may specify that no children are to be included and that specified numbers of men and of women are to be obtained. They may warn interviewers against taking people who are too readily available, such as their friends, members of their own households, or persons who all live in the same district of a city. The instructions may be given in such general terms as "Interview people who are regarded in their communities as typical citizens" and "Try to pick a representative sample with the right proportion of rich and poor, old and young, well educated and poorly educated, and members of the important religious and social organizations."

The indefiniteness of these general instructions, plus the latitude that is left by even the more specific instructions of a positive kind, leads many statisticians to call these methods "judgment sampling." Judgment is used in many phases of sampling operations, but here it is used rather freely in the actual determination of the individuals to be included in the sample. Sometimes the element of judgment is subordinated in some degree to definite rules. For example, a set of cities or counties or other areas may be selected provisionally and then tested by comparing its average values on each of several population characteristics with the averages for the whole population. Next some of the areas are removed and others added until the set of areas compares quite closely with the whole population in these characteristics. Some judgment is involved in the choice of areas to be removed

[14]William G. Cochran, Frederick Mosteller, and John W. Tukey, *Statistical Problems of the Kinsey Report on Sexual Behavior in the Human Male* (Washington, D.C.: American Statistical Association, 1954).

and added but the entire procedure could be reduced to a set of formal rules that involve no judgment in their application. Several decades ago this method was tried under the name of "purposive sampling" with somewhat disappointing results.

Some more recent developments have shown the usefulness of exercising judgment in the stages of sampling prior to the final choice of the sample rather than in the actual choice itself.[15] The selection by a group of judges or experts of "typical" cities, or regions, or districts within a city, or individuals is still and will continue to be a common form of sample selection. It aims to use what is known by the best-qualified persons in putting together a better sample than could be obtained without that knowledge. Undoubtedly there are many instances in which the neglect of expert knowledge, or indeed of any pertinent information, will seriously weaken the sampling operation. Expert judgment has limitations in the selection of samples, however, and even some biasing tendencies and defects. Therefore this class of methods is often based on a somewhat optimistic appraisal of the effectiveness of the expert. It may also over-estimate the effectiveness of the control variables on which the sample is matched to the population.

4. Probabilized Selection. In methods of this type chance is deliberately given a principal role in the determination of the individuals who are to go into the sample. Since, in the simpler varieties of this method, every individual in the population has the same chance of getting into the sample, this may seem to involve no selection at all. In fact it almost seems like an instance of the class discussed first, in which the sample is not chosen by the sampler but just happens. With these methods, however, the sampler does actually accomplish certain definite purposes by delegating the selection to a definite system of chance. Under some specific conditions, his action could be fully justified by the recently developed theory of games and statistical decision theory. It is "blind selection" only in a restricted sense, for ordinarily the sampler knows quite a bit about what he is doing. By utilizing known facts and principles, he can *channel* the operation of chance and gain the advantages it offers while avoiding the losses and disruption that it might otherwise introduce. Probabilized selection is favored by people who are relatively pessimistic about the effectiveness of choice by experts and relatively optimistic about rigorous methods. It opens up, as none of the other methods does, the possibility of analyzing the operation of the sampling procedure in terms of probability theory and of applying the theory of mathematical statistics to the design, operation, and analysis of the results of a specific sampling procedure.

When we attempt to classify a particular selection procedure, the line of division between these categories will be found to be blurred. Many surveys use a mixture of two or more types. The classification scheme should be useful, however, to bring some order into the variety of methods that are used.

[15] Roe Goodman and Leslie Kish, "Controlled Selection—A Technique in Probability Sampling," *Journal of the American Statistical Association*, 45 (1950), pp. 350–372.

B. *Type of Contact or Connection*

The two other examples of principles for classifying various sampling operations stem from and qualify the foregoing system for categorizing selection methods. The first of these concerns the nature of the contact or connection between the sampler and the individuals in the sample. This contact is the means by which the final sample of data is extracted from the sample of persons. We might make a distinction between obtaining the data: (a) through other persons, (b) through communication in writing, (c) through direct contact by talking, and (d) through observation of behavior. This classification would not be wholly satisfactory, however, and hence a somewhat more extended one will be outlined. It follows a scale of increasing involvement of the sample of persons in the process of obtaining information about them. We distinguish the following classes of contacts:

1. Indirect connection.
2. Semi-direct contact.
3. Direct impersonal contact.
4. Direct personal contact.
5. Participating contacts.

This classification is based on the relation between the sampler and the sample of persons. It generalizes the answers to the question, "How did the sampler get the data from the persons in the sample?"

1. Indirect Connection. Ordinarily this type of contact occurs without the knowledge of the persons who are in the sample. It taps their attitudes and wants through knowledge and information which already exist in the minds of people who know them, or which exist in records in the possession of other persons. For this reason this type of contact usually does not offer any opportunity to improve the records and knowledge, or to discover and correct misunderstandings. In some recent studies, for example, the people in the sample were asked how their friends and relatives voted in an election. They had no opportunity to ask their friends and relatives but could only reply out of knowledge they had gained previously in conversation.

The use of letters and documents is also an example of indirect connection. Sometimes, of course, it is believed that such records provide more accurate and franker replies than could be obtained by direct questioning. However, the record may be one that tends to conceal the "true" intentions and attitudes of the people who contributed to it. For example, the record is not assumed to be a frank one in "content analysis" when we attempt to see behind the mask of propaganda. In this type of contact the possibility of using standard questions and measuring devices is severely limited.

2. Semi-direct Contact. In this second type of contact, there is some degree of "individualizing" of the contact. The most meager step in this direction may be a request to each individual for his permission to use existing records or to furnish records in his possession pertaining to his own opinions, experiences, and actions. Records requested might be correspondence, diaries, professional and institutional records, recordings of interviews and private meetings, etc. The essential point is that the individual usually has some control over the material and may refuse to assent to its inclusion in the sample. Of course his control may not be fully effective. The material may be used in an anonymous manner or in such summary form that the objections are overcome. There are important questions of legal and moral rights in such instances that may be more prominent in the future than they have been in the past.

A second feature of semi-direct contact is the opportunity afforded for supplementing the recorded material with explanations, descriptions of changes that took place after the time covered by the record, and personal interpretations of a stated position. The individual concerned may also provide clues to the location of other material related to the original records. Such opportunities for further communication will often lead to more direct contacts, though they may remain on a relatively impersonal and indirect basis. Even though such subsequent contacts are developed, the contact can be regarded as being primarily semi-direct so long as the principal data are those that were recorded in some form for another purpose. If they are shaped to the purposes or circumstances of the current inquiry, then the type of contact changes.

3. Direct Impersonal Contact. The third type of contact involves a request to specific individuals, or to all members of some population collectively, to furnish information about their own individual attitudes or wants. Ordinarily the individual or organization making the request is known to, or is at least identifiable by, the members of the population.

The responses are influenced by the respondents' attitudes toward the source of the request as well as the indicated use to be made of the results. The request may be ignored or it may be definitely refused. Questionnaire surveys that are broadcast to widely dispersed groups may find the percentage of refusals and other failures to reply going well above 75 per cent. This is very likely to produce a strong biasing of the selection process so that the sample of replies is quite different from the replies that would have come if all the questionnaires had been returned. Thus, even though the sample of persons selected to receive the requests may have been closely representative of the population in the characteristics to which the questionnaire applies, the actual sample of replies is not representative of the characteristics or of the desired reponses concerning them. It might be observed that a low rate of response is not inevitable. Many questionnaire surveys are made in which 90 per cent or more of the sample of persons is covered successfully.

4. Direct Personal Contact. The fourth type of contact is one of person-to-person communication. Ordinarily it is an interview, but it could be conversation and correspondence, or a combination of the two, over a period of time. An example of this combination is the contact of a biographer with a person whose biography he is writing. The biographer has an opportunity to go beyond the examination of records, letters, and writings, and beyond collateral interviewing of persons who have known or been associated with the biographee. He can arrange for a period of personal contact for the mutually recognized purpose of improving the biography. An interesting example in early studies of attitudes is the analysis of an immigrant autobi-ography by W. I. Thomas and F. Znaniecki.[16] There are many studies of a similar nature.

Interviewing takes many forms. It may be done by telephone, by visit to the home of the interviewee, by appointment at the office of the interviewer, or casually in some public place. It provides a full opportunity for supple-menting each major question with further questions designed to clear up ambiguities, fill gaps, explore the background of important material, check interpretations, and otherwise enrich the data by using the responses to develop further questioning. If carried far enough, the respondent may even be able to contribute to the determination of the questions that should be asked in order to develop the essential information. This of course requires that the interviewer give the interviewee a reasonably complete account of the purposes and problems of the survey.

It should be noted that direct and personal contacts are not necessarily "face-to-face." Moreover, not all face-to-face contacts are direct and per-sonal. The mere fact that a person hands a questionnaire to the people in the sample and receives it when it is filled out is not sufficient. Even though something is said about the purpose of the study and the method of com-pleting the questionnaire, this kind of contact has only a remote and modest relation to the answering of the questions. It is not essentially different from direct impersonal contact, even though the spoken words may be im-portant as a means of increasing cooperation.

5. *Participating Contacts.* In some studies the persons in the sample take an active part in the prosecution of the study. The method of partici-pant observation is a well-known example. In contacts of this type the par-ticipant may only be a passive subject during part of the data-collecting process. However, his connection with it is such that his performance as a subject is influenced substantially by his participation in the planning of the study, in contacts with other subjects, or in similar phases of the work.

The manner in which information is obtained about his attitudes, wants, and reactions is usually altered considerably by this connection. He is not merely better informed about the purposes and methods of the study, but his responses are likely to be formalized to some extent by his knowledge of the theoretical implications of the study and of the analytical scheme according to which it will be carried from data to conclusions. Some of the recent studies of community life in new housing developments and of pre-ferences with respect to various features of residential construction are examples of this kind of contact. So too are some recent studies of rumor and organization.

C. Basis for Cooperation or Compliance

The preceding principle of classification of sampling operations is largely concerned with the degree of personal involvement of the subjects in the production of the final sample of data. It measures the opportunity they

---

[16] *The Polish Peasant in Europe and America.*

have to determine what data are to be obtained, to formulate it for the record, and to participate actively in the research undertaking. It necessarily involves the particular means of communication and measurement, and it goes beyond these means to the character and limitations of the communication involved in eliciting responses on the one side and responding on the other. Communication, when fully developed, requires quite as much initiative on one side as the other. Some cooperation is usually necessary, even when the process involves little or no relation beyond the implicit linkage established by a researcher in discovering and gaining access to records from parties other than the persons to whom they refer. We may find it useful to include a third principle to classify sampling operations by the influences that enable the sampler to obtain from other people the sample of data, including his ability to motivate individuals to provide information about themselves or about other persons in the sample. This somewhat elusive facet of sampling is essential to the operation of obtaining a sample of data.

The influence may be simply that of calling on the good nature of people to help a stranger, or it may be strong pressures that compel replies. It may be exerted directly through the contact or indirectly by calling on the prestige and authority of some generally influential agency. Some of the interviewing of civilians in occupied countries by survey organizations that work for the occupying forces are examples of the latter type of influence.

The nature of the pressure, and the personal reactions of individuals to various kinds of pressure, not only affects the degree to which the sample of persons is covered but determines the kind and amount of distortion of the data that will result from this aspect of the sampling. If strong influence is brought to bear on the entire sample of persons solely to induce a small number of reluctant respondents, the biases produced in willing respondents may prove a heavy price to pay for the cooperation of the unwilling. Even a very friendly approach or the awarding of money and prizes may sometimes have undesirable effects on the accuracy and completeness of the data obtained.

The sample of data will also be affected by the motivations of the people in the sample, whatever the kinds of influence used to obtain the data. Thus in indirect contacts the motivations that lead the originating persons to write the letters they wrote, to keep a diary and write in it what they did, to submit for recording the statements and other information they gave all have an effect on the subsequent processes of sampling and measuring attitudes, opinions, wants, and related variables.

D. Other Principles of Classification

There are other principles of classification that are useful in grouping together the many varieties of sampling operations that have been employed in the study of human populations. For example, the sampling may be done at one time, at successive times, or continually. It may also be classified according to the technical means used to record the responses of persons in the sample, such as by standard questionnaires, speech-recording devices, interviewers' notes, and self-written replies. It may be done publicly or with various degrees of privacy and anonymity. All such means are part of the production of data and have a characteristic effect on it. Selection of what to put into the record, losses from faulty memory, misunderstandings, self-consciousness about the contact, outright deception, and many other processes are involved in the recording of data.

No attempt will be made to develop the classification scheme to include these other phases, but their effects and the problems of controlling them deserve attention in a thorough study of the operations of sampling and in valid assessment of the reliability of the results they produce. . . .

CRITERIA FOR THE CONSTRUCTION AND EVALUATION OF ATTITUDE SCALES[*]

JOHN P. ROBINSON
The University of Michigan

JERROLD G. RUSK
The University of Michigan

KENDRA B. HEAD
The University of Michigan

T HE EVALUATIVE CRITERIA WE HAVE CHOSEN ARE LISTED IN THE ORDER THAT may represent the ideal, but not absolute, chronological sequence in which attitude instruments should be constructed.

The first step for the scale-builder, and the first criterion on which his work can be evaluated, is writing or finding items to include in the scale. It is usually assumed that the scale-builder knows enough about the field to construct an instrument that will cover an important theoretical construct well enough to be useful to other researchers in the field. If it covers a construct for which instruments are already available, the author should demonstrate sound improvements over previous measures. There are three further preliminary considerations which represent the minimum that an adequately constructed scale ought to possess. These are:

Proper Sampling of Content. Proper sampling is not easy to achieve, nor can exact rules be specified for insuring that it is done properly (as critics of Guttman's phrase "Universe of content" have been quick to point out). Nevertheless, there is little doubt of the critical nature of the sampling procedure in scale construction. Future research may better reveal the population of behaviors, objects, and feelings which ought to be covered in any attitude area, but some examples may suggest ways in which the interested researcher can provide better coverage in designing scales. Investigators of the "authoritarian personality" lifted key sentiments expressed in small-group conversations, personal interviews, and written remarks and transformed them into scale items; some of these items in fact consisted of direct verbatim quotations from such materials. In the job satisfaction area, we gave detailed consideration to the analysis from representative samples of responses to open-ended questions which ask the respondent, "What things do you like best (or don't you like) about your job?" We feel that these responses offer invaluable guidelines to the researcher both as to the universe of factors he should be covering and the probable weight that should be given to each factor. Other instruments in the job-satisfaction area were built either on the basis of previous factor analytic work, or on responses to

[*]Reprinted by permission of the authors and publisher, from John P. Robinson, Jerrold G. Rusk, and Kendra B. Head, *Measures of Political Attitudes* (Ann Arbor: Institute for Social Research, 1968), pp. 9–21.

questions about critically satisfying or dissatisfying situations at work, or on both of these.

Difficult decisions remain to be made about the number of questions needed to cover each factor (probably a minimum of two in any lengthy instrument) but the important first step is to make sure that the waterfront has been covered.

Simplicity of Item Wording. One of the great advantages of securing verbatim comments from group discussions or open-ended questions (as people in advertising have apparently discovered) is that such attitudes are couched in language easily comprehended and recognized by respondents. One of the most obvious advantages of more recently constructed scales is that item wording has become far less stuffy, lofty, or idealistic. Even today, however, survey researchers still must adapt items developed from college samples for use on heterogeneous populations.[1]

There are other item-wording practices that are, thankfully, going out of style as well: double-barreled items which contain so many attitudes that it is hard to tell why the person agrees or disagrees with it (e.g., "The government should provide low-cost medical care because too many people are in poor health and doctors charge so much money"); items that are so vague they mean all things to all people ("Everybody should receive adequate medical care"); or items that depend on knowledge of little-known facts ("The government should provide for no more medical care than that implied in the Constitution"). Other considerations about writing items, such as negative vs. positive wording, will be covered under our discussion of response set.

Item Analysis. While item wording is something the investigator can manipulate to insure coverage of attitudinal areas, there is no guarantee that respondents will reply to the items in the manner intended by the investigator. Item analysis is one of the most efficient methods whereby the investigator can check whether people are responding to the items in the manner intended. We have encountered too many instances in the literature where authors inadvertently assume that their *a priori* division of scale items corresponds to the way their respondents perceive these items.

There have been many methods of item analysis proposed, and, in fact, complex multi-dimensional analyses (described below under homogeneity, in our detailing of statistical procedures) can be seen as the ultimate item analytic procedure. The researcher need not go so far as factor analyzing his data to select items to be included or discarded, but an item inter-correlation matrix (on perhaps a small subsample or pretest sample) is certainly the most convenient basis of doing item analysis. If it is hypothesized that five items in a large battery of items (say those numbered 1, 2, 6, 12, and 17) comprise a scale of authoritarianism, then the majority of the ten inter-item correlations between these five items should be substantial. At the minimum they should be significant at the .05 level. While this mini-

---

[1]The process is often referred to as "farmerization," i.e., making items intelligible to the less sophisticated.

mum may seem liberal, it is in keeping with the degree to which items in the most reputable scales inter-correlate for heterogeneous populations. If items 1, 2, 12, and 17 inter-correlate substantially with each other but 6 does not correlate well with any of them, then item 6 should be discarded or rewritten.

Measuring the degree to which each of the five items correlates with some external criterion is a further valuable device for the selection of items. This is usually referred to as the "item-validity method."

We learned one valuable lesson about writing items from a certain item analysis we performed. A previous study had uncovered four dimensions of value—authoritarianism, expression, individualism, and equalitarianism— and we wished to incorporate measures of these factors into a study of political attitudes. One individualism item, "It is the man who starts off bravely on his own who excites our admiration," seemed in particular need of farmerization. Accordingly, the item was reworded, "We should all admire a man who starts out bravely on his own." Item analysis revealed this revised statement to be more closely associated with *authoritarian* items than with the other individualism items. It became clear that a seemingly logical wording change can unexpectedly alter the entire implication of an item.

Often a researcher does not have the benefit of pre-test groups in order to eliminate or revise unsatisfactory items. In such a case, the item-analysis phase of scale construction should be incorporated into the determination of the dimensionality, scalability, or homogeneity of the test items. This will insure that there is empirical as well as theoretical rationale for combining the information contained in various items.

The second large area of evaluation is the concern that the scale-builder has given to the avoidance of "response set" in the items. Response set refers to a tendency on the part of individuals to respond to attitude statements for reasons other than the content of the statements. Thus, a person who might want to appear agreeable and thus fail to disagree with any attitude statement is said to show an "agreement response set." Only through experience and by constant revision can the researcher insulate his scale from this potentially dangerous side effect. As a basic guard against response set, the researcher should try to make the scale as interesting and pleasant for the respondent as possible. If the respondent finds the instrument to be dull or unpleasant, there is a greater chance that he will try to speed through it as quickly as possible. It is in such a setting that the scale is most liable to response set contamination, such as indiscriminate agreement or checking off in a certain column.

There are two main sources of response set that are most difficult to control:

Acquiescence. Most of us have seen (or perhaps been) people whose attitudes change in accord with the situation. Such people are said to "acquiesce" in the presence of opposition from others. In the same way, some people are "yea-sayers," willing to go along with anything that sounds good, while others (perhaps optimists) are unwilling to look at the bad side of anything. These dispositions are thus reflected in people's responses to attitude questions. How then is it possible to separate their "real" attitudes from their personality dispositions?[2]

There are various levels of attack, all of which involve forsaking simple affirmative item format. The first involves at least an occasional switching of response alternatives between positive and negative. For simple "yes-no" alternatives, a few "no-yes" options should be inserted. Similarly, for the "strongly agree-agree-uncertain-disagree-strongly disagree" or Likert format, the five alternatives occasionally should be listed in the opposite order. This practice will offer some possibility of locating people who choose alternatives on the sole basis of the order in which they appear. It may also alert an overly casual respondent to think more about his answers.

It is more difficult to vary the item wording from positive to negative, as those who have tried to reverse authoritarianism items have found. A logician can argue that the obverse of "Obedience is an important thing for children to learn" is not "Disobedience is an important thing for children to learn," and the investigator is on shaky ground in assuming that a respondent who agrees with both the first statement and the second is completely confused. Along the same line, the practice of inserting a single word in order to reverse an item can produce some pretty silly-sounding items, while changing one word in an unusual context has produced items in which the ordinary respondent will not notice a change. In sum, writing item reversals requires sensitivity. The interested researcher would be well advised to check previous competent work on the subject[3] before undertaking such a task. However, the literature is still ambiguous as to the real value of item reversals.[4]

A third and more difficult, yet probably more effective approach concerns the construction of "forced-choice" items. Here two (or more) replies to a question are listed and the respondent is told to choose only one: "The most important thing for children to learn is (obedience) (independence)." Equating the popularity or "social desirability" of each alternative requires even more intensive effort for both the scale constructor and the respondent. Since the factor of social desirability is an important response set variable in its own right, we give it individual attention next.

Social Desirability. In contrast to the theory that the acquiescent person reveals a certain desire for subservience in his willingness to go along with anything, Edwards has proposed more positively that these people are just trying to make a good impression.[5] As yet research has been unable to determine clearly whether the overly high incidence of positive correlation

---

[2] L. Rorer, "The Great Response Style Myth," *Psychological Bulletin*, 63 (1965), pp. 129–156, points out many relevant objections to attempting separation of the acquiescent response set from item content.

[3] R. Christie *et al.*, "Is the F Scale Irreversible?" *Journal of Abnormal and Social Psychology*, 56 (1956), pp. 143–159.

[4] L. Wrightsman, *Characteristics of Positively-Scored and Negatively-Scored Items from Attitude Scales* (Nashville: Peabody Teachers College), 1966.

[5] A. Edwards, *The Social Desirability Variable in Personality Assessment and Research* (New York: Dryden Press, 1957).

among questionnaire items is ultimately due more to bias from acquiescence or to social desirability.[6] The methods of lessening social desirability bias, in any event, usually involve the use of forced-choice items in which the alternatives have been equated on the basis of social desirability ratings. In more refined instruments, the items are pretested on social desirability, and alternative-pairings (or item-pairings) which do not prove to be equated are dropped or revised.

One further method consists of using the respondent's score on the Crowne-Marlowe social desirability scale as a correction factor. Smith gives an explicit example of the mechanics of this approach.[7]

We have mentioned the major sources of response-set contamination but there are others of which the investigator should remain aware. One of the more prevalent sources of contamination is the faking of responses according to some preconceived image that the respondent wants to convey. On a job-satisfaction scale, for example, the respondent may try to avoid saying anything that might put his supervisor in a bad light or might involve a change in work procedures. College students may be aware of a professor's hypothesized relationship between two variables and try to answer so as to make this prediction work out or fail. Other undesirable variations of spurious response patterns that the investigator might want to minimize can result from the respondent's wanting (a) to appear too consistent, (b) to use few or many categories in his replies, or (c) to choose extreme alternatives.

The third and final area of evaluation for each instrument is the various statistical and psychometric procedures incorporated into its construction. While each of these statistical considerations—sampling, norms, reliability, homogeneity, and validation—is important, an inadequate performance on any one of them does not render the scale worthless. Nevertheless, inadequate concern with most of them certainly does indicate that the scale should be used with reservation. Fortunately, scale-constructors in the past few years appear to have paid more heed to these considerations than did the vast majority of their predecessors. Still, even today few scales rate optimally on all these factors. It is very seldom indeed that one runs across scales that overcome (or even attempt to overcome) the distortion due to restricted samples or incomplete validation procedures.

We have chosen seven statistical standards which we hope cover the basic requirements involved in the construction of competent scaling instruments. These are:

Representative Sample. In this day and age, it is hoped, researchers are aware of the fallacy of generalizing results from samples of college students[8] onto an older and much less well-educated general population.

---

[6]R. Christie and F. Lindauer, "Personality Structure," *Annual Review of Psychology*, 14 (1963), pp. 201–230.

[7]D. Smith, "Correcting for Social Desirability Response Sets in Opinion-Attitude Survey Research," *Public Opinion Quarterly*, 31 (1967), pp. 87–94.

[8]Some statisticians contend that a sample of a single class should be treated as having a sample size of one, not the number of students in the class.

Significant differences are even likely to be found between freshmen and seniors, engineering and psychology students, and college A and college B, so that one must be careful in expecting results from one class to hold for all college students. In the political attitude area, we shall see that there are great dangers in expecting findings from political elites to hold for typical citizens (or even in using scales developed on elites with such typical samples).

This is not meant to discourage researchers from improving the representativeness of whatever populations they do have available for study, but rather to caution them against implying that their findings hold for people not represented by their samples. Nor is it meant to imply that samples of college students are a useless basis on which to construct scales. In some areas (attitudes toward foreign affairs, for example), one might well argue that college exposure is probably the best single criterion of whether a person can truly appreciate the intricacies of the issues involved.

But an instrument constructed from replies of a random cross-section of all students in a university has much more to offer than the same instrument developed on students in a single class in psychology (even if there are many more students in the class than in the university sample). The prime consideration is the applicability of the scale and scale norms to respondents who are likely to use them in the future.

Normative Information. The adequacy of norms (e.g., mean scale scores, percent agreements, etc.) is obviously dependent on the adequacy of the sample. The absolute minimum of normative information, which should be available for the researcher to be aware of any differences between his sample and the sample on which the scale was developed, is the mean scale score and standard deviation for the sample on which the scale was constructed. There are further pieces of statistical data that are extremely useful: item means (or percent agreements) and standard deviations, median scores (if the scale scores are skewed), or more obscure statistics like the inter-quartile range.

Most helpful are means and standard deviations for certain well-defined groups (men or women, Catholics or Baptists) who have high or low scale scores. When such differences have been predicted, the results bear on the *validity* of the scale, which is discussed below. Validity, reliability, and homogeneity also constitute needed normative information, of course, and they are covered below in the detail required by their complexity.

Reliability (Test-Retest). Unfortunately, one of the most ambiguous terms in psychometrics is "reliability." There are at least three major entities to which the term can refer: (1) the correlation between the same person's score on the same items at two separate points in time; (2) the correlation between two different sets of items at the same time (called "parallel-forms" if the items are presented in separate format, and "split-half" if the items are all presented together); and (3) the correlation between the scale items for all people who answer the items. The latter two indices refer to the internal structure or homogeneity of the scale items (the next criterion), while the former indicates stability of a person's item responses over time. It is unfortunate that test-retest measures, which require more effort and sophistication on the part of the scale developer and show lower reliability figures for his efforts, are available for so few instruments in the literature. While the test-retest reliability level may be approximately estimated from indices of homogeneity, there is no substitute for the actual test-retest data.

Homogeneity. In addition to split-half, parallel forms, and inter-item indices of the internal homogeneity of the test items, there exist other measures of this desirable property. Some of these item-test and internal consistency measures, as Scott has shown,[9] bear known statistical relationships with one another. Included in this collection are certain indices of scalability for Guttman items, although not the most often used Coefficient of Reproducibility. Even between such "radically" different procedures as the traditional psychometric and Guttman cumulative, however, there likely exist reasonably stable relationships between indices based on inter-item, item-test, and total test characteristics; as yet, however, these have not been charted. For now, the major difference between the indices seems to lie in the researcher's preference for large or small numbers. Inter-item correlations and homogeneity indices based on Loevinger's concepts seldom exceed .40; if one prefers larger numbers, a Reproducibility Coefficient or split-half reliability coefficient computed on the same data could easily exceed .90. Thus, since it seems at present to be the only way of relating the various indices, one is apparently forced to rely on the imperfect criterion of statistical significance in order to evaluate instruments for which different indices have been employed. To make the job even more difficult, statistical distributions of these various indices are not always available so that significance can be ascertained.

Of all the indices that have been proposed, however, probably none combines simplicity with amount of information contained as well as the inter-item correlation matrix. Computing Pearson r correlation coefficients for more than five items is certainly a time-consuming operation on a hand calculator. However, for the researcher who does not have access to a computer that prints out such a matrix, there are some simple rank-order correlation formulas that can be calculated by hand in a few minutes, so that even a ten-item scale inter-item correlation matrix can be put together in a few hours. The job is too lengthy if there are too many alternatives or over 100 subjects, but in the case of dichotomous items, the coefficients Y or γ (defined in a statistical appendix to this chapter) can be easily calculated to determine inter-item significance. These, however, constitute only rule-of-thumb procedures for deciding whether a group of items deserves to be added together to form a scale or index. Similarly, the criterion of significance level is proposed only because it is a standard that remains fairly constant across the myriad of measures that are now, or have been, in vogue. Probably it is only the minimum to be expected before one can talk about a

[9]W. Scott, "Measures of Test Homogeneity," *Educational and Psychological Measurement*, 20 (1960), pp. 751–757.

scale which can be reasonably called "homogeneous." Hopefully, more satisfactory norms may be proposed in the future.

When the number of items goes beyond ten, however, the inter-item matrix is indeed quite cumbersome to compute by hand calculator for any coefficient, and the researcher is well advised to look for a computer specialist and a correlation matrix program. Computers have the ability to generate 50- to 100-item inter-correlations in less than ten minutes, given a reasonably sized sample. This does not work out to burdensome cost if the researcher has put much effort into his data collection. At this level of analysis (i.e., more than ten items), the researcher might as well proceed to invest in a factor analysis or cluster analysis of his data. This type of analysis will help him locate the groups of items that go together much faster than could be done by inspecting the correlation matrix.[10] There are many kinds of factor analysis programs and options; under most circumstances, however, the differences between them usually do not result in radical changes in the structure which is uncovered.

To say that factor analytic programs do not usually vary greatly in their output is not to imply that structures uncovered by factor analysis may not lead to serious ambiguities in the interpretation of data. There is one common type of attitudinal data arrangement in particular for which the factor structure seems indeterminant. This is the case where almost all the items are correlated from say .15 to .45. Sometimes only a single factor will emerge from such a matrix and sometimes a solution will be generated which more clearly reflects item differentiation on a series of factors. We have encountered one instance where an instrument—supposedly constructed carefully to reflect a single dimension of inner- vs. other-directedness, according to a forced-choice response format—was found when analyzed in Likert format to contain eight factors. Thus, one can offer no guarantee that inter-item significance will always yield unidimensional scales. Nor does it seem possible to offer any better advice or to recommend any competent practical literature on the inconsistencies into which factor analysis can lead one. On balance, however, one is further ahead performing such analyses than not doing so.

The length of this discussion clearly shows that we feel the determination of homogeneity to be a crucial step in scale construction. Only by these procedures can the analyst properly separate the apples, oranges, and coconuts from the salad of items he has put together.

One final word of caution is in order: it is possible to devise a scale with very high internal consistency merely by writing the same item in a number of different ways. Sampling of item content then can be a crucial component in internal consistency.

Discrimination of Known Groups.   This is where the value of a scale is truly tested—the aspect of validity. Nevertheless, group discrimination is

---

[10] However, the researcher should not be deceived by what appear to be high factor loadings. Items having factor loadings which reach levels of .50 or .70 are equivalent to correlation coefficients of .25 and .49.

not necessarily the most challenging hurdle to demonstrate validity. It is pretty hard to construct a liberalism-conservatism scale that will *not* show significant differences between John Birchers and Students for Democratic Society, or a religious attitude scale that will not separate Mormons from Jews or ministerial students from engineers. The more demanding hurdle is the ability of the scale scores to reliably single out those liberals or conservatives, agnostics or believers, in heterogeneous groups—or to predict which of them will demonstrate behavior congruent with their hypothesized attitudinal state. A still more definitive test is cross-validation, a test to which very few attitudes scales have been subjected.

Cross-Validation. A test of cross-validation requires two different samples and measures of some criterion variable on each sample. The question to be answered by the test is whether the combination of items for sample A that best correlates with the criterion variable in sample A will also work for sample B's criterion, and whether the best set of sample B items works on the sample A criterion. Note that the crux of the procedure involves picking (and, if necessary, weighting) the *items* from the sample A experience which work best on sample B.

An even more refined method, and probably the ultimate standard now available, is the multi-trait multi-method matrix as proposed by Campbell and Fiske.[11] The method requires more than one index of each of the several constructs (say, x, y, and z) we want to measure by our instrument. It is best to include as many measures or indices of each construct as possible, as well as to measure for control purposes such variables as intelligence or agreement response set which could be at the root of any apparent relationship. In the resulting correlation matrix, the various indices of the single construct (say, x) should correlate higher among themselves than any index of x correlates with any indices of y, z, or the control variables.

Needless to say, this comprises a gross over-simplification of the Campbell-Fiske method. The reader should peruse the authors' article thoroughly before attempting comparable analyses. It is worth noting that the authors find only a couple of personality scales that meet their conditions. To our knowledge, no attitude scales have as yet advanced the claim.

Other Procedures. Since there are many methods used in constructing scales beyond our recommended procedures, we should also note alternative methods that may be employed. Such alternatives may include special precautions taken to ensure better items, better testing conditions, or adequate validation—although at times the precautions have had the opposite effect from that intended.

One interesting procedure to which researchers have become increasingly attracted involves the use of positive and negative items. Sometimes, as we have noted, items intended as negative are responded to as negative correlates of positive items; in other instances, this does not work. A procedure which may provide valuable insights into the response patterns of the

---

[11] D. Campbell and D. Fiske, "Convergent and Discriminate Validation by the Multi-trait Multi-method Matrix," *Psychological Bulletin*, 56 (1959), pp. 81–105.

sample is the separation of the high and low scores on both the positive and negative scales. There are four groups to be examined: *yea-sayers* (who score high on both the negative and positive items), *nay-sayers* (who score low on both), *assenters* who score high on the positive items and low on the negatives, and the *dissenters*, who follow the opposite pattern. This division can be seen more clearly in the following diagram:

		Positive Items	
		Low	High
Negative Items	Low	Nay-sayers	Assenters
	High	Dissenters	Yea-sayers

A parallel analysis for Likert scales (or procedures which demand more than a simple dichotomous item response) is the separation of the group at the mean into those who are ambivalent (combining extreme positive responses with extreme negative responses) from those who fall in the middle by taking an extreme position on very few items. . . .

It is very important that the reader realize that even this extensive list of proposed criteria is not exhaustive. The actual choice of an instrument, where possible, should be dictated by decision-theoretic considerations. Thus, the increasing of homogeneity by adding questionnaire items needs to be balanced against corresponding increases in administrative analysis and cost (and against respondent fatigue and non-cooperation) before reaching a decision about how many attitude items to use. For assessing general levels of some attitude state (e.g., merely to separate believers from atheists), well-worded single items may do the job just as well as longer scales no matter how competently the scales are devised. For an excellent theoretical exposition of the decision-theoretic approach for psychometric problems Cronbach and Gleser is recommended.[12] In this extended version of their earlier volume, the authors provide a number of relevant examples.

STATISTICAL APPENDIX: COMPUTATION OF Y TO DETERMINE INTER-ITEM CORRELATION

Item 1

$$Y = \frac{\sqrt{ad} - \sqrt{bc}}{\sqrt{ad} + \sqrt{bc}}$$

and

Item 2

	Yes	No	
Yes	a	b	$a + b$
No	c	d	$c + d$
	$a + c$	$b + d$	N

[12] L. Cronbach and Goldine Gleser, *Psychological Tests and Personnel Decisions* (Urbana: University of Illinois Press, 2nd ed., 1965).

The significance of Y can be computed by calculating its standard error for the case where Y is hypothesized to be 0. Thus when Y exceeds

$$Y = \left(\frac{N \sqrt{N}}{4}\right) \left(\frac{1}{(a + b)(b + d)(a + b)(c + d)}\right)^{1/2}$$

by a factor of 2, the items are significantly related at the .05 level, and when it exceeds Y itself by a factor of 2.5 the items are related at the .01 level (assuming the number of respondents is greater than 30).

Goodman and Kruskal's gamma, γ, is a measure that can be called into use when the number of item alternatives is greater than 2.[13] Approximate sampling distributions for this statistic have recently become available.[14] The reader may be interested to know that for the dichotomous case, gamma reduces to the formula for Y with the square root signs removed; hence, gamma tends to take on larger values than Y for the same data.

[13] Leo A. Goodman and William H. Kruskal, "Measures of Association for Cross Classification," *Journal of the American Statistical Association*, 49 (December, 1954), pp. 732–764.

[14] Irene Rosenthal, "Distribution of the Sample Version of the Measure of Association, Gamma," *Journal of the American Statistical Association* (1966), pp. 440–453.

THE USE OF MAGNITUDE ESTIMATION IN ATTITUDE SCALING: CONSTRUCTING A MEASURE OF POLITICAL DISSATISFACTION

ROBERT E. WELCH, JR.[1]

The University of Texas at Austin

THE IMPORTANCE OF ACCURATE MEASUREMENT FOR THE SUCCESSFUL study of attitudes is widely recognized. In this article we will first describe a powerful yet relatively unknown procedure—magnitude estimation—which can be productively employed in the scaling of attitudes. Then, primarily for purposes of illustration, this technique will be utilized in the construction of a measure of dissatisfaction with the American political system; and the resulting index will in turn be used to examine the relationship between such dissatisfaction and the intensity of an individual's political activity.

AN OVERVIEW OF MAGNITUDE ESTIMATION

Magnitude estimation is simply a method of measuring the subjective, or perceived, magnitudes of "real" variables.[2] The general technique originated in the 1930s with the experimental efforts of psychophysicists to scale human perceptions of sensory stimuli such as loudness of sound, heaviness of weight, and lightness of color—all of which were already measurable in terms of some accepted physical unit such as decibels or grams.[3] In these experiments small groups of subjects were presented with a number of different stimuli (various shades of a color, for example), one of which was assigned an arbitrary magnitude and designated as the standard. The subjects were asked to estimate the relative magnitude of the remaining stimuli by comparing each to the standard. These judgments were then averaged across subjects, and the means obtained were plotted against the corresponding physical magnitudes. This process almost always resulted in a smooth curve of the form

$$R = kS^n,$$

where R is the subjective, or response, magnitude in arbitrary units; S is the stimulus magnitude in physical units; n is an empirical but nonarbitrary exponent; and k is an empirical constant dependent on the value assigned to the standard.[4]

[1] I am grateful to Judy Hanson, Warren Bradley Moody, and Anne Welch for their help in assembling much of the data on which this study is based; and to Allen M. Shinn, Jr., for his critical but cheerful comments on numerous occasions.

[2] This basic approach has several minor variants, among which are magnitude production, ratio estimation, and ratio production; see S. S. Stevens, "On the Psychophysical Law," *Psychological Review*, 64 (May, 1957), pp. 162–165.

[3] It had long been known that subjective and physical magnitudes were not, as most of us would probably suppose, linearly related.

[4] The notation used here and elsewhere in this paper closely follows Allen M. Shinn,

The above equation, of course, describes a simple power function. As investigations involving magnitude estimation have continued, this same general relation has been found to hold for more than three dozen sensory continua. These findings have led Stevens to propose the "psychophysical law," which states that equal stimulus ratios produce equal perceptual ratios (a necessary consequence of the power-function relations observed). In fact Stevens has recently argued that this psychophysical or power law has now achieved the status of a natural law, ". . . so that henceforth it becomes the exception to the power law that calls for solid demonstration."[5]

The relevance of all this for the measurement of attitudes is simply this: Subjective magnitude has been found to be a power function of stimulus magnitude not only for sensory stimuli but for several *social-psychological* continua as well.[6] This suggests that the latter sort of responses, insofar as they are non-voluntary, also conform to the stimulus-response power law. Given a related body of evidence which indicates that this law is equally applicable to continua not associated with physical metrics, there appears to be a strong theoretical case for using magnitude estimation procedures to scale such social variables as norms, attitudes, and opinions.[7]

A number of other factors recommend magnitude estimation. The first of these is the technique's overall simplicity. Not only does it require relatively little of the scale builder, but subjects seem to grasp the logic of the method more clearly than is sometimes the case with other measurement models.[8] A second advantage is the exceptional discriminatory capacity of magnitude estimation, especially in comparison with that of simple category scales such as the widely used semantic differential and Thurstonian equal-appearing intervals methods.[9] Finally, magnitude estimation procedures seemingly produce genuine ratio-level data.[10]

Despite its advantages the method of magnitude estimation has almost completely escaped the notice of those concerned with the measuring of

---

Jr., *The Application of Psychophysical Scaling Techniques to Measurement of Political Variables*, Working Papers in Methodology, No. 3 (Chapel Hill: University of North Carolina, Institute for Research in Social Science, 1969).

[5] S. S. Stevens, "Neural Events and the Psychophysical Law," *Science*, 170 (Dec. 4, 1970), p. 1050.

[6] See Robert L. Hamblin *et al.*, "The Interference-Aggression Law?" *Sociometry*, 26 (June, 1963), pp. 190–216; Thorsten Sellin and Marvin E. Wolfgang, *The Measurement of Delinquency* (New York: John Wiley and Sons, Inc., 1964); Robert L. Hamblin, "Ratio Measurement and Sociological Theory: A Critical Analysis" (St. Louis: Washington University, Department of Sociology, n.d., Mimeographed); Allen M. Shinn, Jr., "An Application of Psychophysical Scaling Techniques to the Measurement of National Power," *Journal of Politics*, 31 (Nov., 1969), pp. 932–951; and Shinn, *Measurement of Political Variables*.

[7] S. S. Stevens, "A Metric for the Social Consensus," *Science*, 151 (Feb. 4, 1966), pp. 530–541.

[8] Shinn, *Measurement of Political Variables*, pp. 123 and 131–132.

[9] *Ibid.*, pp. 110–111.

[10] While some social scientists question the value of ratio measurement, others consider it a requisite for successful theory building; see Hamblin, "Ratio Measurement," pp. 1–16.

attitudes.[11] We will now demonstrate the relevance of the approach by using it to construct a measure of dissatisfaction with the American political system.

AN APPLICATION: MEASURING POLITICAL DISSATISFACTION

In recent years social scientists have devoted considerable energy to the task of identifying the determinants of mass political activity. As this research has progressed, a variety of psychological variables have been put forth as influential; and it is one of these, an attitude which might be labeled "political dissatisfaction," that is of interest to us here.[12] While most students of participation seem to feel that political dissatisfaction and political activity are causally related, there appears to be considerable confusion as to the nature of this relationship. Some, including Campbell and Dahl, see the connection as a direct one, with greater dissatisfaction producing increased participation.[13] Others like Lane think just the opposite—that dissatisfaction results in reduced political activity.[14] Curiously, in light of the importance of the matter for democratic thought, very little empirical effort has been expended in trying to ascertain which of these viewpoints is correct.[15]

Hypotheses, of course, cannot be tested until variables can be measured; and, whereas indices of political involvement abound, direct measures of political dissatisfaction have not heretofore been available. Accordingly, before we could examine the relationship between dissatisfaction and participation, it was necessary to construct a measure of the intensity of an individual's dissatisfaction with the political system. In doing so our first

[11] Some exceptions are Gösta Ekman and Teodor Kuennapas, "Scales of Conservatism," *Perceptual and Motor Skills,* 16 (April, 1963), pp. 329–334; Teodor Kuennapas and Monica Sillén, "Measurement of 'Political' Preferences: A Further Study of Direct and Indirect Scaling Methods," *Scandinavian Journal of Psychology,* 6 (1965), pp. 162–172; and Shinn, *Measurement of Political Variables,* pp. 112–138.

[12] Many scholars prefer to call this variable "political *satisfaction.*" In our opinion, however, *dissatisfaction* is the more appropriate term since it is this attribute which actually varies. For example, a given individual may be described as slightly, moderately, or even totally dissatisfied; but it makes little sense to speak of these same gradations with respect to satisfaction. One simply is either satisfied or not satisfied, and a person who is less than satisfied is clearly to some degree dissatisfied. In short, satisfaction is merely the zero point on the continuum "dissatisfaction."

[13] Angus Campbell, "The Passive Citizen," *Acta Sociologica,* 6 (1962), pp. 15–16; and Robert A. Dahl, *Modern Political Analysis* (2nd ed.; Englewood Cliffs, N. J.: Prentice-Hall, Inc., 1970), p. 83.

[14] Robert E. Lane, *Political Life* (Glencoe, Ill.: The Free Press, 1959), pp. 156–157. Lane also sees two more general types of dissatisfaction—life and community dissatisfaction—as inversely related to political activity.

[15] Only a few studies have even touched upon this question; see Gordon M. Connelly and Harry H. Field, "The Non-Voter: Who He Is, What He Thinks," *Public Opinion Quarterly,* 8 (Summer, 1944), pp. 181–182; Morris Rosenberg, "Some Determinants of Political Apathy," *Public Opinion Quarterly,* 18 (Winter, 1954–55), p. 366; and William Buchanan, "An Inquiry into Purposive Voting," *Journal of Politics,* 18 (May, 1956), pp. 281–296.

task was to collect a large number of candidate scale items. This we did by assembling what might be called a "subject-generated item pool" (that is, a set of potential scale items gathered from a sample of those persons whose attitudes a scale is being designed to measure).[16] Specifically, since in this instance we intended to administer the finished instrument to assorted groups of University of Texas students, we asked over 500 undergraduates the following question: "In one or two sentences, what is your opinion of the American political system?"[17] Each subject was also asked to indicate his attitude toward the system by checking the appropriate point on a nine-interval self-rating scale which ranged from "satisfied" to "totally dissatisfied." The responses obtained were then sorted into nine categories according to the self-ratings of the respondents. Finally the statements were edited and pared to five per category,[18] the 45 survivors constituting our item pool (see Table 1, Column 2).

Next we turned to the problem of selecting and weighting the final scale items. Combining the method of magnitude estimation with the item selection criteria originally proposed by Thurstone in connection with his equal-appearing intervals model,[19] we proceeded as follows: First, the statements comprising the item pool were presented to a panel of 81 student "judges," along with these directions:

> Recently a large number of your fellow students were asked their opinions of the American political system. A sample of their responses accompanies these instructions. What we would like you to do is to estimate the

[16] Item pools generated in this manner tend to be more meaningful and more interesting than statement sets authored by but one or two individuals. Moreover, they are usually more *inclusive*; that is, they encompass a wider range of opinion. This matter is more important than is generally realized. If one's item pool is not inclusive—say, for instance, that it wholly eschews extreme statements in favor of those of a more moderate variety—then, no matter how sophisticated one's subsequent manipulations, only a truncated scale can be constructed. Truncation clearly decreases the *sensitivity* (that is, the discriminating power) and thus the precision of a measuring instrument. One questions the worth of a scale which rates both Democrats and Weathermen as "very liberal" and both Republicans and Minutemen as "very conservative." For a discussion of these issues with reference to the measurement of political attitudes, see John P. Robinson, Jerrold G. Rusk, and Kendra B. Head, *Measures of Political Attitudes* (Ann Arbor: University of Michigan, Institute for Social Research, 1968), pp. 9–12.

[17] Only students enrolled in "required" courses were questioned. Such classes, though populated largely by underclassmen, tend to be as politically diverse as any sample one might draw.

[18] In editing the statements we followed many of the helpful guidelines suggested in Allen L. Edwards, *Techniques of Attitude Scale Construction* (New York: Appleton-Century-Crofts, Inc., 1957), pp. 13–14; A. N. Oppenheim, *Questionnaire Design and Attitude Measurement* (New York: Basic Books, Inc., 1966), pp. 113–117; and L. L. Thurstone and E. J. Chave, *The Measurement of Attitude* (Chicago: University of Chicago Press, 1929), pp. 22–23. Our purpose in choosing five statements from each self-rating category was, of course, to ensure the inclusiveness of the item pool.

[19] For a discussion of these criteria, see L. L. Thurstone, "Attitudes Can Be Measured," *American Journal of Sociology*, 33 (Jan., 1928), pp. 529–554; and Thurstone and Chave, *Measurement of Attitude*.

degree of *dissatisfaction* expressed by each response. You can easily do this by following a simple two-step procedure. First, assume that one of the responses, which we shall call the "Base Statement," has a value of *100 units of dissatisfaction.*

Base Statement: "The American political system is far from perfect, but it is also far ahead of whatever system is in second place."

Second, rate all of the other responses in terms of this one statement. Thus, if in your judgement a given response expresses five times as much dissatisfaction with the American political system as does the "Base Statement," assign it a value of 500 units. Similarly, if a response indicates only one third as much dissatisfaction as the "Base Statement," give it a value of 33 1/3 or 33.3. You may use whole numbers, fractions, decimals, or whatever you need to be accurate. If a response expresses no dissatisfaction at all (i.e., perfect satisfaction), give it a value of zero. . . .[20]

After each of the judges had rated all 45 statements,[21] their estimates were collected and examined for obvious signs of carelessness or non-cooperation. On the basis of this screening, the judgments of four students were rejected as defective. We then averaged the remaining 77 sets of ratings (item by item, across subjects) in order to determine the scale values of the statements.[22] As is customary when dealing with data produced by magnitude estimation, geometric means were computed (see Table 1, Column 3) because the geometric mean, which here is simply the nth root of the product of the judges' ratings for a given item, is an unbiased estimate of the central tendency of pooled ratio information. The arithmetic mean, on the other hand, consistently overestimates this value.[23]

In addition to the geometric mean, a "corrected" standard deviation was computed for every statement in the item pool (see Table 1, Column 4). This measure, which is obtained by multiplying the familiar standard deviation about the arithmetic mean by the ratio of the geometric to the arithmetic mean, is more easily calculated than the standard deviation about the geometric mean (for which it is thus a convenient substitute) yet better suited for use with geometric means than the conventional arithmetic standard deviation.[24]

[20] With subjects who do not thoroughly grasp the notion of proportionality (which is central to magnitude estimation), the researcher should follow these instructions with a practice exercise in estimating the lengths of lines or the distances between points; see Stevens, "Metric for the Social Consensus," p. 531; and Hamblin, "Ratio Measurement," pp. 72–73.

[21] In order to minimize possible sources of systematic bias, the statements were presented in a different order to each judge.

[22] The assumption here is that one is averaging out random error so as to obtain the "'true" scale values.

[23] For a more extensive discussion of this point, see Shinn, *Measurement of Political Variables*, pp. 37–40. Note that geometric means cannot be computed for data sets which contain the value zero. Thus, following Shinn, we arbitrarily increased all zero ratings to the lowest non-zero response otherwise obtained (in this case .001).

[24] The use of "corrected" standard deviations was originally suggested by Teodor Kuennapas and Inger Wikstroem in their article "Measurement of Occupational Prefer-

From this point on, constructing the final index of dissatisfaction was simply a matter of applying Thurstone's three well-known criteria to our data. First, in order to satisfy the requirement that the items comprising the completed scale be evenly spaced across the full range of the continuum being measured, we ranked all 45 statements according to their scale values (geometric means) and then grouped them into 20 contiguous clusters—the finished instrument to consist of one item from each cluster.[25] Then, in keeping with but modifying Thurstone's "criterion of ambiguity," we compared each statement's corrected standard deviation to its geometric mean and deleted as ambiguous those items having standard deviations larger than their means.[26] Finally the remaining items were presented to a politically diverse panel of 90 students who were asked to mark those statements with which they personally agreed. On the basis of these responses, coincidental acceptance distributions were plotted for each item paired with every other item; and those statements evidencing random or non-unimodal scatter patterns (see Table 1, Column 5) were excluded as "irrelevant" in the Thurstonian sense.[27]

Fortunately at least one statement within each of our twenty clusters survived this double-barreled elimination process. Where *only* one survived, of course, that item automatically became part of the final index of political dissatisfaction. In cases where there were two or more survivors, the item having the lowest standard deviation relative to its mean was selected for inclusion (see Table 1, Column 6).

THE RELATIONSHIP BETWEEN POLITICAL DISSATISFACTION AND POLITICAL ACTIVITY

Having thus developed an index of political dissatisfaction, we were able to investigate the relationship between this attitude and political activity. First, in connection with an extensive study of political activists, we administered the dissatisfaction scale described above to more than 150 students attending regularly scheduled meetings of five campus political organizations: Young Republicans, Young Democrats, New Party, Ameri-

---

ences: A Comparison of Scaling Methods," *Perceptual and Motor Skills*, 17 (Oct., 1963), pp. 611–524. See also Shinn, *Measurement of Political Variables*, p. 100.

[25] The 20 clusters, which were delimited arbitrarily, are identified in Column 1 of Table 1.

[26] In practice this amounted to eliminating those statements with coefficients of variation greater than one. (However, Statements A and B in Cluster 1 were excepted from this general rule because their means were so extraordinarily low.) Such a procedure, as opposed to one which would exclude items having standard deviations greater than a certain fixed value, is recommended inasmuch as the variability of magnitude estimations increases with the magnitude of the stimulus.

[27] For a full explanation of the "criterion of irrelevance," see Thurstone and Chave, *Measurement of Attitude*, pp. 45–56. In recent applications of the final scale, statement 15-B has displayed a more or less random response characteristic; hence now it should probably be excluded as irrelevant too.

TABLE 1

An Index of Political Dissatisfaction

1 Cluster No.	2 Statements	3[a] Geo Means	4[b] SD-C	5[c] Plots	6[d] Final Scale
1	A. Let's give credit where credit is due: the American political system is the best in the world. I support it 100 per cent!	0.02	0.02	+	✻
	B. The American political system is a perfect model for the rest of the world to imitate.	0.16	0.28	+	
	C. The American political system does a good job of meeting popular demands for change.	3.76	5.86		
	D. I cannot think of a single major change that would improve the American political system.	4.35	14.59		
2	A. The only thing wrong with the American political system is that too many people are criticizing it.	6.05	7.40		
	B. I certainly would not want to live in any other political system	13.6	11.1	+	✻
3	A. Well, we hear a lot of complaints about our political system these days, but I challenge anyone to find a better system elsewhere.	28.6	17.2	+	✻
	B. The American political system is as democratic as one could reasonably expect.	33.6	19.6	−	
4	A. I don't think the American political system is as bad as various groups and individuals try to make us believe.	49.1	30.7	−	
	B. Sometimes I get a little upset with the American political system; but then I look at other systems and I can hardly believe how lucky I am to be here.	56.5	25.4	+	✻
	C. The American political system is certainly not a utopia, but then what system is?	59.5	29.0	+	
5	A. Considering its great size and diversity, I think the American political system works fairly well.	69.4	43.7	+	✻
6	A. The American political system is the best in existence, but I still feel it could be improved upon.	81.4	30.4	+	✻
	B. While the American political system has numerous defects, it is probably the best that human nature and 20th century conditions will permit.	83.9	51.1	+	

7 A. The American political system has
      problems, but I still feel that it is well
      worth the effort necessary to correct
      these problems.   108   71.4   +   *
   B. To paraphrase Winston Churchill, the
      American political system is the worst
      such system ever devised by man,
      except for every other political
      system devised by man.   129   322.9

8 A. The American political system is not
      any paradise, but since I'm here I
      guess it will do.   165   83.7   +   *
   B. Somehow the American political system
      manages to muddle through.   178   494.6
   C. I wish the American political system
      was like it used to be.   190   130.0   —

9 A. I'm not wild about the American
      political system; however, it has
      possibilities.   206   109.0   +   *
   B. Our political system is becoming increas-
      ingly involved in matters which do
      not concern it.   228   169.8   —
   C. For the most part the American political
      system disgusts me, but I'm learning
      to live with it.   293   721.3

10 A. The American political system does not
      meet the needs of those who are
      most in need.   358   184.0   +   *
   B. Man, I love the American political system.
      There's so much freedom here—as
      long as you aren't "different."   386   376.0   —

11 A. The American political system is the
      genuine, original "Excedrin headache."   430   791.3
   B. I never see it but I feel it lurking, and
      I am always wondering when it
      will pounce.   432   716.0
   C. Once you learn how the American
      political system actually works, it's
      a hell of a disappointment.   459   230.2   +   *

12 A. Some political systems need tune-ups;
      ours needs a massive overhaul.   533   433.2   +   *
   B. If the sound of two hands is applause,
      what is the sound of one hand?   566   560.9   —
   C. Because it tries to make everyone equal,
      the American political system is a
      dehumanizing monstrosity.   577   702.9

13 A. If political systems go to heaven or hell,
      ours had better start changing its ways.   613   588.3   —

TABLE 1—Continued

1 Cluster No.	2 Statements	3[a] Geo Means	4[b] SD-C	5[c] Plots	6[d] Final Scale
	B. If I had the power to completely change the American political system, I would do so in a moment.	688	670.0	+	*
14	A. If I were grading the American political system, I would give it about a D+.	746	619.2	+	*
	B. The American political system reminds me of Limburger cheese—it reeks.	783	782.1	−	
15	A. I no longer even care about having an opinion of the American political system.	896	709.9	−	
	B. At present the American political system is making a mockery of the ideals upon which it was supposedly founded.	899	395.6	+	*
16	A. The American political system is devoid of morality; it ought to be renamed "Corruption Unlimited."	958	866.3	−	
	B. I suppose the American political system is a great place—if you're big on concentration camps.	993	850.5	+	*
17	A. The American political system is a hollow hypocrisy dedicated only to the perpetuation of itself.	1150	1045.7	+	*
	B. I salute the American political system—with the clenched fist of REVOLUTION!	1161	1128.9	−	
18	A. The American political system is an obsolete oligarchy run by senile bastards.	1351	1189.1	−	
	B. The American political system scares the shit out of me; we need to start over.	1375	1215.4	+	*
	C. The American political system is merely the greatest tragedy in the history of the world.	1398	1399.4		
19	A. The American political system sucks!	1737	1673.3	+	*
20	A. If there was ever a political system that deserved to be wiped off the face of the earth, the American political system is it.	2151	2143.3	+	*

[a] These geometric means are the scale values of the statements.

[b] These "corrected" standard deviations were obtained by multiplying the standard deviation about the arithmetic mean by the ratio of the geometric to the arithmetic mean.

[c] A plus in this column signifies that a statement is "revelant" in the Thurstonian sense; a minus indicates that it is not. (A blank indicates that a statement was so clearly ambiguous that it was not even tested for relevance.)

[d] The twenty items which comprise the final index of dissatisfaction are designated by an asterisk.

TABLE 2

Political Dissatisfaction by Activity Levels

Activity Level	N	Average Mean Score	Average Median Score
Activist	156	497.1	422.2
Transitional	97	427.1	365.7
Spectator	100	318.0	253.8
Apolitical	30	164.9	127.4

can Independent Party, SDS.[28] The same measure was also administered to a much less politicized segment of the general student population (viz., some 200-plus students enrolled in an assortment of required courses). In both cases the subjects were asked to indicate those statements with which they agreed.[29] These data were then used in calculating two dissatisfaction scores—the mean and median values of the items checked—for each respondent.

In addition every subject was asked a series of questions concerning the extent of his political activities and, on the basis of the answers given, was assigned to one of four activity levels: apolitical, spectator, transitional, or activist.[30] The average dissatisfaction scores for each of these strata (computed for both mean and median individual scores) are presented in Table 2. By themselves, the figures would seem to indicate that political dissatisfaction and political activity are *directly* related, for dissatisfaction clearly increases as we move up the hierarchy of involvement. However, if we divide the activist level into its component political groups and compute new average dissatisfaction scores for each, this relationship immediately breaks down (see Table 3). Instead we find that Young Democrats are generally less dissatisfied than transitional students; that Young Republicans are less dissatisfied than both transitionals and spectators; and that student supporters of the American Independent Party are less dissatisfied than transitionals, spectators, and even those classed as apolitical. Only New Party and SDS members fit the positive pattern exhibited in Table 2.

[28] We also attempted to survey the membership of Young Americans for Freedom but were thwarted by their leader.

[29] Alternately, the subject may be instructed to mark the *one* statement which he agrees with most or to indicate how strongly he agrees or disagrees with *each* statement. A number of scoring options are available in conjunction with the latter procedure; see Rensis Likert, Sydney Roslow, and Gardner Murphy, "A Simple and Reliable Method of Scoring Thurstone Attitude Scales," *Journal of Social Psychology*, 5 (1934), pp. 228–238.

[30] These categories and their defining characteristics were adapted from Lester W. Milbrath, *Political Participation* (Chicago: Rand McNally and Company, 1965), pp. 16–22. Our classification differs from Milbrath's primarily in that *activists* were specifically defined as students who on the average devoted at least one hour a week to some sort of organized political activity; and in that participation in marches and demonstration was classed as a type of transitional activity.

TABLE 3

Political Dissatisfaction among "Activist" Groups

Activist Group	N	Average Mean Score	Average Median Score
Young Republicans	35	207.2	143.0
Young Democrats	41	322.9	259.9
New Party	15	459.8	378.5
American Independent Party	12	87.8	64.1
SDS	53	926.5	825.5

Given these findings, one might conclude that political dissatisfaction and political activity are simply not related, either directly or inversely. Another possibility, however, is that political dissatisfaction is a multi-dimensional attitude, one or more facets of which are not tapped by our index. Research in process, in fact, suggests that this is the case. Evidently the scale developed in this paper measures a sort of symbolic, regime-level dissatisfaction which is apparently unrelated to political activity. On the other hand, we have found that measures of a more concrete, policy-directed dissatisfaction correlate highly and *positively* with political activity.

CONCLUSION

In this paper we have sought to demonstrate the value and the relevance of magnitude estimation for the measurement of attitudes. While we are convinced of the usefulness of this procedure, we also realize that it has its limitations. For example, the method can only be used to scale continua which can be readily conceptualized by those asked to "judge" the statements comprising the item pool. Also, it can be used only with difficulty by subjects who have had little experience in manipulating ratios.

Likewise the index of dissatisfaction which we have constructed is certainly not universally applicable. Indeed it may well be that the scale as a whole is ill-suited for use beyond the borders of the campus community.[31] However, we do not view this limited applicability as a consequence of the methods by which the measure was constructed; rather we see it as occasioned by the more fundamental fact that styles of expression and ranges of opinion vary from population to population and even from sub-popula-

---

[31] Aside from the fact that some of the scale items would probably provoke considerable hostility in certain quarters, a more serious problem is that many of the statements just do not have the same meaning for different groups of people. In fact, recent research suggests that the index is not even suited for use on non-white college campuses.

tion to sub-population.[32] That this is so constitutes a formidable obstacle for those who would seek to overcome the existing state of discontinuity in the measurement of social perceptions.[33]

[32] See Herbert Jacob, "Problems of Scale Equivalency in Measuring Attitudes in American Subcultures," *Social Science Quarterly*, 52 (June, 1971), pp. 61–75.

[33] On the pervasive lack of continuity in the measurement of social variables in general (including attitudes), see Charles M. Bonjean, Richard J. Hill, and S. Dale Mc-Lemore, *Sociological Measurement* (San Francisco: Chandler Publishing Company, 1967), pp. 2–9.

REPRESENTATIVENESS AND THE STUDY OF POLITICAL BEHAVIOR: AN APPLICATION OF Q TECHNIQUE TO REACTIONS TO THE KENT STATE INCIDENT

STEVEN R. BROWN
Kent State University

THOMAS D. UNGS
Kent State University

THE REPRESENTATIVE SAMPLE HAS BECOME THE METHODOLOGICAL BACK-bone of empirical political research, for as every political behavioral-ist knows, if one wishes empirical results to have generality, the sam-ple of respondents must be representative of the population to which the results are to apply. Despite this recognition, however, the point we wish to make is that representativeness has not been extended far enough into political research.

The concept of representativeness has been employed primarily for the useful, but limited, purpose of selecting respondents. In the opinion-attitude domain, for example, a recent Survey Research Center publication states that a representative sample of respondents is one of the five basic requirements in scale construction.[1] However, in our view the concept has broader applicability. Might it not be, for example, that representativeness could apply equally well to the stimulus side of the stimulus-response situation—to the items as well as to the respondents? If representativeness is required in order to ensure responder generality, then perhaps the same kind of representativeness is required to ensure stimulus generality. If so, then previous applications of sampling theory to respondents only may have produced results of unknown generality and, perhaps, of questionable replicability; indeed, perhaps it has led to erroneous conclusions and con-ceptualizations regarding the functioning of human beings in a political context.

What follows is a discussion of the extension of the concept of repre-sentativeness and examples of what we regard as substantive-theoretical errors which have resulted from inadequate representativeness in research design. Empirical illustrations are also presented to illustrate the kinds of results which can be obtained when representativeness is extended to other areas outside respondent sampling. The examples concern a Q-technique approach to attitudes toward the shootings of four students at Kent State University in May 1970 but the principles apply to virtually all domains of empirical political inquiry. Since representativeness as applied to the

---

[1] J. P. Robinson, J. G. Rusk, and K. B. Head, *Measures of Political Attitudes* (Ann Arbor: Survey Research Center, Institute for Social Research, 1968), pp. 14–20.

sample of respondents is already an accepted principle, the examples will emphasize the application of representativeness to other domains.

BRUNSWIK'S CONCEPT OF REPRESENTATIVE DESIGN

More than 20 years ago, Egon Brunswik pointed to an apparent double standard employed in psychological research insofar as the sampling of subjects and the sampling of objects were concerned. Noting that psychologists were accustomed to dealing with responder (subject) samples of sufficiently large ns, he pointed to a failure to extend sampling theory to the object side of the stimulus-response situation: Experiments with large ns as far as respondents were concerned were inadequate insofar as the ecological (stimulus, situational) Ns were concerned[2]—that is, the number of responders was adequate, but the number of objects to which the responders were reacting was inadequate.

The relationships of person-sample to object-sample (of n to N) may become clearer in reference to Figure 1. In the stimulus-response situation of the typical social science experiment or study, at least two questions are pertinent, although usually only one of them is asked. The first question is whether or not the sample of persons performing the behavioral tasks is adequate and fairly drawn in such a way as to ensure generalizability to the parent population of persons. The second question concerns the sample of objects-of-perception and their adequacy to a population of such objects. A third question may also be pertinent, depending on the nature of the study, and concerns the sample of situations in which the sample of responders perceive the sample of objects.

Brunswik asks: If it is necessary, according to sampling theory, to have a random sample of respondents in order to ensure generality of results on the responder side of the study, is it not also necessary, by the same logic, to have a random sample of stimuli (scale items, questionnaire questions, and so forth) and/or situations in order to provide generality on the stimulus side of the study as well? How do we know, for example, that a single stimulus object presented to a suitably large respondent sample is truly representative, in a sampling sense, of the stimulus domain?

To provide an illustration: Inkeles reports a cross-national study concerning participant citizenship which involves an assessment of such things as allegiance, interest in politics, and political information. Large respondent ns were taken from each of six developing countries—for example, $n = 1300$ from India. Brunswik, however, would have raised questions about the $N = 3$ allegiance questions, the answers to which Inkeles used

---

[2] Following Brunswik, n will be used to designate the responder sample, N to designate the object, or ecological, sample. Brunswik's major work, "Systematic and Representative Design of Psychological Experiments," is in E. Brunswik, *Perception and the Representative Design of Psychological Experiments* (Berkeley and Los Angeles: University of California Press, 1956). See also, K. R. Hammond, ed., *The Psychology of Egon Brunswik* (New York: Holt, Rinehart and Winston, 1966), and "Symposium on the Probability Approach in Psychology," *Psychological Review*, 62 (May, 1955), pp. 193–242.

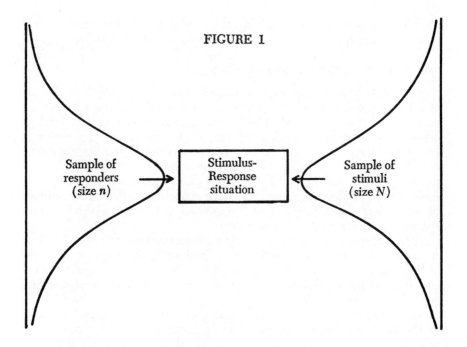

FIGURE 1

to determine whether the respondents' identities were primal or political. Brunswik, if we understand him, would suggest that identity involves a wide distribution of behaviors of more or less "primalness-politicalness" and would wonder whether the $N = 3$ items were representative of this behavioral domain, in the same sense that the $n = 1300$ respondents were representative of the human domain of India.[3]

A good deal of contemporary social research is single-variable in orientation; the investigator looks at one variable at a time (Inkeles' aforementioned "primalness-politicalness" for example) while holding all else constant. For example, considerable effort goes into attitude scale construction to ensure that only one attitude, or trait, is being measured. Modern experimentalists, however, have noted that factors are rarely independent and that they frequently vary depending on the context of other variables. Fisher's introduction of multivariate factorial design sought to cope with

[3] A. Inkeles, "Participant Citizenship in Six Developing Countries," *American Political Science Review*, 63 (Dec., 1969), pp. 1120–1141. In a similar way, Sigel asked $n = 1349$ children for their reactions to the death of President Kennedy, using their responses to this N of 1 as an indication of their orientations to the *political world*, a universe with an N of thousands and of which Kennedy could hardly be said to be representative in any methodological sense. See R. S. Sigel, "Image of a President: Some Insights Into the Political Views of School Children," *American Political Science Review*, 62 (March, 1968), p. 216.

diverse possibilities and to overcome restrictions in the single-variable approach. Independent variables were therefore cross-classified with one another, allowing for an analysis of both simple effects as well as more complex interactions.[4] Fisher's experimental innovation was radical in many respects and of great importance—political science has not yet begun to look at his work, first published in 1935—but Brunswik's approach was even more radical, for it was his feeling that Fisher's design did not go far enough, at least in the realm of the human sciences. For Brunswik, the narrow range of environmental boundaries which might be structured factorially according to Fisherian schema was too formalistic and "systematic" to bring out the essentials of behavioral functioning. What was necessary was to observe the human organism under a wide range of situations, that is, under conditions more life-like and natural in character. As Brunswik summed up this position:

> The call for unrestricted vicarious functioning in studying gross behavioral adjustment . . . injects a new element into the discussion of these issues. It is the requirement of normalcy, naturalness, "closeness to life," or, with a more methodological slant, that of "situational representativeness." According to the much-stressed requirement of "representative sampling" in differential psychology, individuals must be randomly drawn from a well-defined population; in the same manner, the study of functional organism-environment relationships would seem to require that not only mediation but especially also focal events and other situational circumstances should be made to represent, by sampling or related devices, the general or specific conditions under which the organism studied has to function. This leads to what the writer has suggested to call the "representative design of experiments."[5]

Some examples from contemporary research may help clarify Brunswik's position and point to its relevance for future research in political science.

REPRESENTATIVENESS AND POLITICAL ATTITUDES

In most political attitude studies, a representative sample of respondents is asked to respond to a number of items which are defined as measures of this or that attitude or trait. Respondents are sometimes asked to give their intensity of feeling about items (agree strongly, agree, etc.), and each person's scale score is obtained for the particular attitude. Analysis typically proceeds in terms of comparisons of means between categorical groups (males-females, Republicans-Democrats). The attitude itself is never seen, but left to inference.

The difficulty with some attitude measures is that certain statements can frequently mean different things to different people. Stephenson, for example, observes:

---

[4] See R. A. Fisher, *The Design of Experiments* (7th ed.; New York: Hafner, 1960).
[5] E. Brunswik, *The Conceptual Framework of Psychology*, International Encyclopedia of Unified Science, Vol. 1, No. 10 (Chicago: University of Chicago Press, 1952), pp. 29–30.

The sentence "I hate men" covers very different attitudes with different emphases. "*I* hate men" indicates *hauteur;* "I *hate* men," irritation; "I hate *men,*" deep anger; "I hate men," flat despondency; "*I hate men,*" desperation; "*I* hate *men,*" theatricalness—and so on.[6]

However, most people will agree that an irritated woman is quite different from a desperate one—that is, they behave differently, and a more extensive sampling of their respective behaviors will enable the observer to distinguish the one from the other. In addition to saying "I *hate* men," for example, the irritated woman is apt to remark what a bother men are, how they always go to needless ends to impress, and what undependable little boys they really are. The desperate woman, on the other hand, may say how men persecute her, how they gain her trust through false promises only to deceive her, and so forth. The irritation and desperation, therefore, need not be inferred from test scores, but can be demonstrated directly as two separate kinds of overt (and, in this case, verbal) behaviors.

Rather than asking the respondent for information from which to make inferences, therefore, what is necessary is to induce him to display his attitude directly. Stephenson's view is that the respondent, with a little assistance from the investigator, is quite capable of expressing his attitude overtly. This is accomplished through the use of Q technique whereby a respondent is presented with a sample of statements which he is instructed to rank from, say, those he agrees with down to those with which he disagrees. Through this ranking of the statements, the respondent provides a replica or model of his attitude. As Stephenson says, "I do not make attitude scales, therefore, but get each person to operate with the opinions he holds and to produce for himself a replica or model of his overall attitude about a matter."[7] In terms of our present concern, care must be exercised to assure the sample of statements is representative of the topic under consideration.

After each respondent has provided his own ranking of the statements, the various ranks are correlated, and the correlation matrix is factor analyzed. A factor in this case represents a group of persons who have ranked the statements in essentially the same order—persons who have displayed

[6] W. Stephenson, "Definition of Opinion, Attitude and Belief," *Psychological Record,* 15 (April, 1965), p. 281. Response equivalence has also been questioned by T. R. Williams, "A Critique of Some Assumptions of Social Survey Research," *Public Opinion Quarterly,* 23 (Spring, 1959), pp. 55–62.

[7] W. Stephenson, "The Contribution of Q to Attitude Research," in L. Adler and I. Crespi, eds., *Attitude Research on the Rocks* (Chicago: American Marketing Association, 1968), p. 160. The most complete statement on Q technique is in W. Stephenson, *The Study of Behavior* (Chicago: University of Chicago Press, 1953). A good introduction is in F. N. Kerlinger, *Foundations of Behavioral Research* (New York: Holt, Rinehart and Winston, 1964), pp. 581–599. Applications of Q to political research are discussed in R. C. North, O. R. Holsti, M. G. Zaninovich, and D. A. Zinnes, *Content Analysis* (Evanston, Ill.: Northwestern University Press, 1963), pp. 55–77, and a recent (and interesting) attempt to apply Q-technique-type procedures to survey work is in E. F. Cataldo, R. M. Johnson, L. A. Kellstedt, and L. W. Milbrath, "Card Sorting as a Technique for Survey Interviewing," *Public Opinion Quarterly,* 34 (Summer, 1970), pp. 202–215.

a common attitude. Thus, the statements to be ranked have the status of discrete *opinions* about a topic; they are the opinions which are selected, as Brunswik says, by sampling or related devices. The factors represent *attitudes* which exist with respect to the issue under consideration. The factors which result from a Q study, therefore, in a very real sense are results of behavior—that is, they exist as the consequence of a group of respondents having responded in the same fashion. An attitude for Stephenson is not a hypothetical construct, but an operant in the Skinnerian tradition: Factors in Q technique studies arise from the actual concrete operations of persons as they model their attitudes; a factor is the result of behavior. The factor-categories are genuine, as opposed to *ad hoc* categorical, and reflect true attitudinal segmentation. They are more genuinely "operational definitions" of this-or-that attitude, since whatever it is they are definitions of—for example, a pro-labor attitude—has been made manifest by virtue of behavioral operations expressed through the medium of Q technique.

Of importance in Stephenson's Q technique procedure is the employment of a representative sample of statements and the use to which they are put. The more statements with which a person has to operate, the more often will he be able to demonstrate his attitude. A respondent may be asked for his pro or con response to $N = 10$ items regarding labor unions. If these 10 items are sprinkled throughout the questionnaire, then the responses may be regarded as 10 discrete bits of information relative to the respondent's attitude about labor unions. If, on the other hand, he is asked to rank those same 10 statements from agree to disagree, he will (however implicitly) have to make $\frac{1}{2}N(N-1) = 45$ judgments which represent a far richer sampling of his behavior.[8] (Most Q studies employ at least 40 statements.) When ranked, the items are no longer discrete bits of information independent of one another since in the ranking process they interact with one another, each item influencing the placement of all others as it finds its place in the overall context. The resulting correlations and factors may indicate the pro and con dichotomy to be too simple, that is three factors may result, two of which may be attitudinally positive.

The principles involved and the kind of results which might be expected from this approach can be illustrated by a study, to be reported in more detail subsequently, concerning the public's reaction to the May, 1970,

---

[8] This coincides with Glaser and Strauss' concept of the *depth* of sampling from each respondent. See B. G. Glaser and A. L. Strauss, *The Discovery of Grounded Theory* (Chicago: Aldine, 1967), particularly their chapter 3 on "Theoretical Sampling," pp. 45–77. A fundamental distinction between the typical attitude-scale approach and the *Q-method* approach concerns the source of the unit of measurement: In responding to an attitude scale, the respondent *receives* a score (which is passive), whereas in Q the respondent *assigns* scores to items. The difference is that in the attitude-scale approach, what a response is to mean is defined prior to its utterance, whereas a Q factor is inductive and evaluated as to its meaning after its occurrence. This is one of the fundamental distinctions between the methods of expression and impression as discussed by J. G. Beebe-Center, *The Psychology of Pleasantness and Unpleasantness* (New York: Russell and Russell, 1965), pp. 9–57.

shooting of four students by the Ohio National Guard on the campus of Kent State University. The event generated a good deal of controversy and provided the occasion for persons to express their attitudes on a concrete issue. Although thousands of statements were undoubtedly made, our population of statements consisted of about 600 taken primarily from 70 depth interviews and from newspaper accounts and comments. From these 600 statements was taken a sample of $N = 75$, drawn according to a Fisherian design in such a way as to represent, so far as possible, the major aspects of the situation: to provide for Brunswik's situational representativeness.[9] There were statements supportive of the National Guard ("As far as the National Guard is concerned, right or wrong I back them 100 per cent") as well as statements antagonistic to the Guard ("The Kent shootings were cold-blooded murder; the Guard should never have been allowed on the campus"). Likewise, there were statements pro and con the students, pro and con the university's administration, and so forth.

The 75 statements were each printed on small cards and placed in a Q sort for administration. To help the respondent model his viewpoint vis-a-vis the Kent State situation, he was provided with an opinion continuum ranging from +6 (most agree) to —6 (most disagree), with 0 in the middle, along which he was to distribute the statements according to their degree of characteristicness for his viewpoint. As is customary, respondents were requested to adhere to a forced, quasi-normal distribution with, for example, 3 items being scored +6, 4 being scored +5, 9 being scored 0, and on down to 3 being scored —6.

Under Q-factor-analytic conditions there is generally little reason to employ large numbers of respondents—40 to 50 are typically quite sufficient—since the major relationships tend to stabilize with just a few cases and are little changed with additional observations. The law of diminishing returns tends to assert itself rather quickly in correlational and related work. *Representativeness* is still a criterion, however, for in an inventory of the public's attitudes on an issue of controversy one must make certain that all parties are *represented*. If students have a point of view specific to their group, for example, their noninclusion will mean that their point of view will not exist in the factor matrix; however, 10 students may be sufficient in providing a stable student factor, and the addition of another 100 students will only serve to fill up the factor space without having any effect on the factor itself.

Rather than randomly, therefore, sampling is accomplished on a theo-

9 See Brunswik's quote referred to in footnote 5. By "related devices," Brunswik provided room for selection on other than a random basis and, indeed, specifically made room in his scheme for Q methodology. See Brunswik, *Perception and the Representative Design of Psychological Experiments*, pp. 30, 36, and S. R. Brown, "On the Use of Variance Designs in Q Methodology," *Psychological Record*, 20 (Spring 1970), pp. 179–189. As Herbert McClosky, a leader in survey research, also observes, samples need not always be representative of a general population, but may be purposefully restricted. See H. McClosky, "Survey Research in Political Science," in L. D. Hayes and R. D. Hedlund, eds., *The Conduct of Political Inquiry* (Englewood Cliffs, N.J.: Prentice-Hall, 1970), pp. 120–127.

retical basis by judiciously selecting various individuals for purposes of assuring a hearing to certain viewpoints. Selection of individuals for this controversy was accomplished within the theoretical structure of the public as presented in one of Lasswell's[10] earliest papers. Prior to the shooting, the *public*, particularly the *participative public*, by and large was limited to persons on the campus, with various *attention groups*, especially townspeople, looking on with interest. The participative public contained many special *interests*: students, faculty, administration, and the National Guard. More than 80 respondents from the major interests took the KSU *Q* sort. (Only three Guardsmen participated since they had been placed under orders to remain silent.)

The *Q* sorts were correlated and factored, producing two factors which accounted for all respondents—that is, all respondents had significant loadings (p < .01) on one or the other or both of the factors. The first factor represented primarily the radicalized student point of view; only students were purely defined on this factor (had significant loadings on this factor and insignificant loadings on the other factor). The second factor primarily represented a more moderate, restrained, and system-oriented point of view held disproportionately by members of the university administration; only two students were purely defined on this factor, one of them being a Marine officer sent back to school by the military. Faculty members tended to have significant loadings on both factors, or to have pure loadings on the second (nonstudent) factor. An indication of the stances taken by these two factors can be obtained through examination of the statements attaining the highest (+6) and lowest (−6) factor scores. The factor scores for each statement in factors A and B, respectively, are shown in parenthesis:

Factor A (students)

6. The Kent shootings were cold-blooded murder. The Guardsmen were not trapped, not shot at, not threatened. They should never have been allowed on the campus. (+6, −4)
10. If the Guard had not been on campus, none of the shooting would have occurred. (+6, +2)
58. Anyone who claims it is justifiable and exemplary to kill innocent citizens just to protect law and order is ideal bait for a fascist regime, and this, more than riots, terrifies me. (+6, −1)
26. This is all very tragic; yet, if this is what it takes to teach law and order to students, then this is the high price that must be paid to keep our country free. Freedom ends when laws are broken and authority threatened. (−6, 0)
27. As far as the National Guard is concerned—right or wrong, I stand behind them 100 per cent. (−6, −2)

[10] H. D. Lasswell, "The Measurement of Public Opinion," *American Political Science Review*, 25 (May, 1931), pp. 311–326. The specific application of *Q* technique along these lines is in W. Stephenson, "Application of *Q*-Method to the Measurement of Public Opinion," *Psychological Record*, 14 (July, 1964), pp. 265–273.

33. The only way to stop those degenerates is for those who believe in the flag to band together and kick the hell out of some people. Brute force is the only answer. $(-6, -6)$

Factor B (administrators)

3. What I mourn, more than the needless death of four young people, is the slow death of reason, understanding, compassion, and respect in relations between people. $(+4, +6)$
11. The working together of faculty, administrators, and students within the established framework would help prevent recurrences of these kinds of things. $(0, +6)$
44. Reform and change should move forward cautiously and should take place in the form of education, not revolution. $(-1, +6)$
18. I have become radically shifted. I don't like violence, but right now I can't see any other way. They didn't give peace a chance. $(+2, -6)$
33. Same as in Factor A above.
67. They should shoot those who perpetrate violence and destroy property. The radical core can't be changed—they have to be shot to be stopped. $(-5, -6)$

These two factors may be regarded as the two major attitudes which existed on the Kent State campus. As might be expected, many of those who were in the group fired upon gave the factor-A viewpoint which expresses more anxiety and concern than does more restrained factor B. Given these two unrelated (orthogonal) points of view, despite the fact statement 33 obtained the same—6 score in both factors, different meanings must be attributed—just as different meanings attend the phrase "I hate men." In this case, we suspect that factor-A students responded to 33 with a −6 because of the expectation that they would be the recipients of the brute force; this flows from the sense of being threatened which permeates the entire factor array. Factor B, however, does not feel personally threatened—administrators are only subject to verbal potshots—and so one suspects the strongly negative −6 flows from a different emotion, namely, a feeling that use of brute force would be improper—the kind of expression consistent with a restrained attitude. This is mentioned to draw attention to the distinction to be made vis-à-vis attitude-scale items whose status is logico-definitional; the Q items are interpreted *a posteriori* and are defined contextually.

The Kent State incident enlarged the attention group and created *sentiment groups*, composed of persons who emotionally identified with certain of the interests, and the *crowd*, which Lasswell defined as those who became actively intolerant of dissent. An additional $n = 132$ respondents geographically removed from the Kent State campus were sampled. Most respondents were obtained by Kent State students who were sent home immediately following the incident. Respondents in the second phase were as close as the Kent, Ohio, community, and as distant as California, New York, Florida, Missouri and elsewhere. Q sorts from these respondents were then compared to the factor structure obtained on the Kent State campus.

Again, two factors accounted for almost everyone: 126 of the 132 respondents were significantly loaded ($p < .01$) on one or the other or both of the two factors. This would indicate sentiment groups in the public at large which were commensurate with the two factor groups on the Kent State campus. The factor-A response emerged as strongly as in the first study, and again was dominated largely by students—from Ohio, New York, California, Virginia, and Pennsylvania, illustrating indentification across geographical distances—who tended to express an attitude virtually identical to the one expressed by students who were fired upon. Likewise, factor B re-emerged in the general public and was again dominated by the "grown-ups"; only two students were loaded purely on the factor.

A grouping which emerged in this second study and which was not visible on the Kent State campus itself was the *crowd*, that group which was triggered into active intolerance by the shooting incident and which, apparently coast to coast, took an attitudinal position bipolar to the student factor A. The factor-analytic relationships among the three groups are shown in Figure 2. Group C represents another point of view, but not a new factor since it is merely the reverse of factor A which had already been obtained. Factors A and B were described previously; the following statements (with scores obtained in groups A, B, and C, respectively, in parentheses) give an indication of the viewpoint held by group C:

2. Although I wouldn't want to hurt anyone myself, nevertheless when those New York construction workers plowed through those students like a Sherman tank . . . well, I must admit, I found it a bit refreshing.   ($-4, -2, +5$)

47. The students at Kent had a choice where they wanted to be; the members of the Guard did not. Therefore, it's the weirdos who are to blame, and as far as I'm concerned they got what they deserved.   ($-5, -2, +5$)

50. Kent State was a clear-cut and classic instance of outsiders planning and manipulating a series of events: outsiders dedicated to only an out-and-out revolutionary purpose used President Nixon's decision to invade Cambodia as a trigger for violence.   ($-3, 0, +6$)

1. As much as I disagree with them, I still don't think radical groups like SDS should be banned; that just causes them to go underground. As long as this is a free country, they should be allowed to try to get support for their ideas, just like everybody else.   ($+1, +1, -5$)

43. The ROTC building was proof of the University's bias and lies about academic neutrality. Maybe burning it was the wrong answer, but I wouldn't have put the fire out.   ($+4, -5, -6$)

68. Agnew is an ignorant slob, a rhetoritician for Nixon's insipid policies. His invective after the Kent murders served more to fan the flames of indignation than to appeal to reason.   ($+5, -3, -5$)

The results are of some interest for both theoretical and methodological reasons. Theoretically, many observers regarded the Kent State situation as an indicator of the depth of the generation gap, with the anti-establish-

FIGURE 2

Factor Structure and the Location of Some Factor Representatives

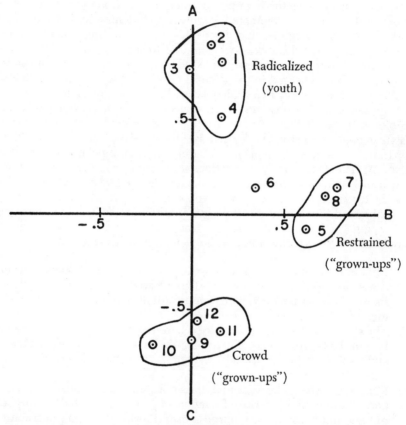

ment youth pitted against the "older folks," and our findings support this to some degree: The average age in groups B and C is much older than that in group A, and so far as A and C are concerned there is a polarization evident. What has been overlooked is the schism in the adult culture, between groups B and C. The reason may lie in the fact that group B has no opposite point of view—similar to the relationship between A and C— to help throw its position into sharper relief. When the students (group A) and construction workers (group C) clashed on nationwide television, the polarity was obvious, but college administrators (group B) have no group with which to fight on network TV. (However, as a theoretical matter, we could reverse the signs associated with the statements in group B and see what a group opposite to B would have to look like if it existed.[11]

[11] Of some additional theoretical interest: in a Q technique study of another student disruption on the Kent State campus a year earlier (spring, 1969), the same factor

Methodologically, attitudes regarded as Q factors allow the investigator to determine true audience segmentation. Since it is frequently the case that Q factors cut right across traditional sociological categories—social class, party preference, sex—it is wise to know what genuine groupings exist before a survey is initiated so that one knows what is worth counting and what is not. For example, an attitude study on the Kent State situation which compares average responses of persons under 30 with those over 30 will yield statistically significant results but will miss the distinctions between groups B and C. In addition, if we were interested in a deeper interrogation of the factors in this study, statistical criteria exist which would enable us to select respondents to interview further. In terms of Figure 2, for example, respondents 2 or 3 would be more valuable than 4 in providing additional data relevant to the factor-A point of view since 2 and 3 are better approximations to the factor. In Glaser and Strauss' terminology, respondents 2 and 3 are more *theoretically saturated* than 4.[12]

CONCLUDING REMARKS

An investigator doing social research these days with a large number of subjects (n) but a small number of objects (N) is a bit like a one-armed man trying to lead applause: The proper spirit is being entered into, but there seems to be something lacking which will make people take notice. The preoccupation with the application of random procedures to the responder side of research has been to the detriment of the application of these principles to the object side, and so, as Hammond has noted, while the conditions under which our results are *obtained* are well defined, we are unable to define the frame of reference to which our results *apply*.[13]

---

structure was generated as was found in the 1970 study: one bipolar factor involving the major antagonistic groups, and an orthogonal and non-bipolar factor. (See Brown, "On the Use of Variance Designs.") Therefore, despite the fact that issues may vary from conflict to conflict, the possibility exists that the *structure* of conflict may be relatively invariant, and it may also be that a representative sampling of the elements of conflict must be assured before such structural similarities emerge.

[12] Glaser and Strauss, *Discovery of Grounded Theory*. Likewise, respondent #6 is significant on factor B (Figure 2), but #7 and #8 are more highly saturated and could therefore better represent the factor B point of view since they are more similar to it in a descriptive sense. On descriptive representation, see A. P. Griffiths and R. Wollheim, "Symposium: How Can One Person Represent Another?" *The Aristotelian Society*, Suppl. Vol. 34 (London: Harrison and Sons, Ltd., 1960), pp. 187–224. In survey work, respondents are of very little theoretical interest since all were included accidentally and since comparisons are usually in terms of group averages on a scale. No one is really interested in respondent #472's viewpoint. Where whole person-responses are correlated and factored, however, as in Q technique, a single respondent may be very important since his view may be closest to a modal view to which all others in the study are lesser approximations.

[13] K. R. Hammond, "Relatively and Representativeness," *Philosophy of Science*, 18 (July, 1951), pp. 208–211. See also E. Brunswik, "Note on Hammond's Analogy Between 'Relativity and Representativeness'," *ibid.*, pp. 212–217. These concepts are applied to political science in S. R. Brown and R. W. Taylor, "Objectivity and Subjectivity in Concept Formation: Problems of Perspective, Partition, and Frames of Reference,"

If the stimulus-response situation depends for its overall generalizability both on the representativeness of the respondent sample and the representativeness of the object sample, he who foregoes representativeness in either, foregoes generalization.

This is particularly apt to be the case when situations are more numerous and variable than persons, which Brunswik suspected was typically the case. In Figure 2, above, after one has sampled four or five highly saturated representatives from each of the three groups, the amount of additional information gained with subsequent sampling is greatly reduced. It is possible that for any given issue the audience segmentation is very limited and that persons are more alike than different; if so, then it may be that the concerns of random sampling have been devoted to the wrong side of the stimulus-response situation.

The effect of the environment within which behavior occurs cannot be assumed to be neutral, such that it can be ignored, but must be experimented with. Brunswik's conceptualizations provide a framework for dealing with what before was a problematical aspect of social research, and the procedures associated with Q methodology, as illustrated above, indicate how these matters can be dealt with instrumentally. Given the complex dimensions of the study of political attitudes in particular, and of behavior more generally, no single approach or instrument can claim a monopoly on conceptualization or measurement. The need to develop more systematic, comprehensive, and varied ways of examining political behavior is still manifest. Political attitudes are one dimension in the study of political behavior, and Q methodology appears to provide a way to model the subjective aspects of attitudes that does not appear to be available through survey research. Q technique is not a tool for the manufacture of attitude scales—although it may be used for that purpose—but is best regarded as a set of procedures and instructions by way of which individuals can produce for themselves a replica of their own attitudes toward particular matters. In its emphasis on subjective reflections as opposed to the researcher's reflections, Q technique opens new paths not only for examining the product of survey research in political attitudes, but also for the development of broader conceptualizations of the role of attitudes in the political process.

---

a paper presented at the American Political Science Association meetings, Los Angeles, September, 1970.

ARCHIVAL DATA ON POLITICAL ATTITUDES: OPPORTUNITIES AND PITFALLS*

NORVAL D. GLENN

The University of Texas at Austin

IDEALLY, EACH RESEARCHER INTERESTED IN POLITICAL ATTITUDES WOULD SEND interviewers into the field to gather precisely the data he needed from a sample of respondents of adequate size, representativeness, and willingness to cooperate. In fact, however, he often does not have the funds to do that, and even if he does, the margin of superiority of new data often would not justify the time and money required to gather it. Furthermore, if one is concerned with political attitudes at some earlier point in time, he must rely upon evidence already in existence, although not necessarily in the form of data gathered for social scientific purposes.

Fortunately, vast quantities of data on political attitudes are available, and the researcher familiar with the major sources can usually obtain the data most useful for his purposes quickly and without excessive cost. Recent years have seen a proliferation of social scientific data archives, both in the United States and in other countries. There are three major sources of data on political attitudes in the United States, and one of these has political data from hundreds of studies conducted in other countries. This paper describes briefly these major data sources, to inform the reader, in general terms, of the kinds of data available from them, and how more detailed information about them may be obtained. Also discussed are some of the research opportunities provided by the archival data and some of the cautions that should be observed in the secondary analysis of these data.

THE DATA ARCHIVES

The three data archives with which any good researcher on political attitudes should be familiar are the Inter-University Consortium for Political Research at the University of Michigan, the Roper Public Opinion Research Center at Williams College, and the Louis Harris Political Data Center at the University of North Carolina at Chapel Hill. Although I choose to concentrate on these three major sources, I do not mean to imply that they are the only important sources of data on political attitudes. At least half a dozen other archives have considerable bodies of political data, including, for instance, the International Data Library and Reference Service at the University of California at Berkeley, which specializes in data on Asia and Latin America.[1]

The Inter-University Consortium for Political Research (ICPR) is the data source with which political scientists and political sociologists are likely

---

*Written for this volume.

[1] For a listing of several other data archives in the United States that have some data on political attitudes, see David Nasatir, "Social Science Data Libraries," *American Sociologist*, 2 (Nov., 1967), pp. 207–212.

to be most familiar. Unlike most data archives, it is associated directly with a data-gathering and analyzing organization, the University of Michigan Survey Research Center. A large proportion of the survey data available through ICPR were gathered by the Survey Research Center and are from U.S. national sample surveys. For instance, data from the well-known University of Michigan election studies, which have been conducted periodically for more than 20 years, are available through ICPR. These surveys exemplify the highest-quality academic research. Questions are carefully worded, interviewers are well trained, and the samples are about as representative as current sampling techniques will allow. In most of the election studies, each of the 1,200 or so respondents was asked a wide variety of questions in addition to those dealing with voting, political attitudes, and political party identification, so the political variables can be related to many other variables. For instance, some of the studies have asked for each respondent's father's occupation, thereby relating political attitudes to intergenerational occupational mobility. Data on such variables as occupation, education, age, and religious preference were gathered in all the studies.

In addition to the University of Michigan election studies, ICPR has data gathered by survey organizations other than the Michigan Survey Research Center and data on countries other than the United States. For instance, it has data on political attitudes in Italy, the United Kingdom, Germany, and Mexico, and data gathered by the National Opinion Research Center at the University of Chicago. It also has data from several local studies within the United States.

Although the ICPR data archive is at the University of Michigan, most major universities in the United States are members of ICPR, and information about ICPR data are usually available from the department of political science or government of a member institution. Persons not affiliated with a member university may write for information directly to Richard Hofferbert, Director, Inter-University Consortium for Political Research, University of Michigan, P. O. Box 1248, Ann Arbor, Michigan 48106.

The Roper Public Opinion Research Center has a much greater quantity of data on political attitudes than ICPR, although the quality is more uneven. The Roper Center has the greatest collection of survey data in the world, and a large proportion of these data are on political attitudes and other political variables. As of this writing, the Center has more than 8,000 survey data sets contributed by 110 survey research organizations in 66 countries, and the collection is growing by about 400 data sets per year. The U.S. data alone include the coded responses to about 55,000 questions. Unfortunately, the name of the Roper Center has led some people to believe that it contains only the opinion data gathered by The Roper Organization, Inc. (the Roper poll). Although the Center started in 1946 with 177 Roper studies, the "Roper poll" data are now a minor portion of its U.S. holdings. For instance, it has almost 800 studies conducted by the American Institute of Public Opinion (the Gallup poll), 20 studies conducted by the Bureau for Applied Social Research at Columbia University, and around

600 studies conducted by state-wide polling organizations in California, Texas, and Minnesota.

Researchers interested in nationwide political data in the United States will find the Gallup polls especially valuable, in spite of their several limitations.[2] There has been an average of almost two Gallup polls per month since 1936, and the sample size for each survey has ranged from about 1,500 to more than 3,000. Most of these have gathered information on party identification, voting in the previous presidential election, and preferences among major candidates or probable candidates for the following presidential election. If one is interested in the first two of these variables,[3] he can combine data from several polls conducted within a short period of time to form a huge N that will largely overcome the problems of sampling variability and insufficient N for needed controls. For instance, one can easily amass an N of around 30,000 (in contrast to the 1,200 or so respondents to the University of Michigan election studies), so that age, religious preference, occupation, and so forth can be simultaneously controlled.

Data from the 25 Gallup affiliates in other countries are valuable for cross-national political studies, since each one regularly gathers data on party identification and voting. Occasionally, several of the organizations simultaneously ask the same or similar questions,[4] and a few of these are on political or politically relevent topics.

The International Survey Library Association (ISLA) is an organization of colleges and universities formed to provide access to the Roper Center data and to information about those data. Membership entitles faculty and students to request data decks, data tabulations, and searches for specific kinds of data. These services, up to a certain level, are paid for by the membership fee, and there is usually no charge to the individual. Several of the member institutions maintain a topical index of the U.S. data. The unit for indexing is the individual question rather than the study, and each index card gives the exact wording of the question, the survey organization, and the number and date of the study. Items in each category are arranged chronologically, so it is easy to detect questions repeated at intervals of weeks, months, or years by the same survey organization.

Many of the major categories used in the index are of interest to students of political attitudes. A few relevant categories and the number of items

[2] The limitations of commercial opinion poll data are well known, so I need not discuss them in detail here. The researcher who uses these data must usually resign himself to one-item indicators of beliefs and attitudes, and the two or three response alternatives to most of the questions do not distinguish between perfunctory, routinized responses and responses based on deeply felt convictions and beliefs. Deficiencies in the earlier poll samples are discussed in some detail below.

[3] Data from different polls concerning preferences among candidates should not be combined, because these preferences may shift appreciably even in a two- or three-week period.

[4] The Gallup affiliates that most often ask the same questions are in the United States, Greece, Canada, France, Uruguay, Finland, Switzerland, Austria, Norway, Great Britain, the Netherlands, and Sweden.

indexed under each (as of 1969) are as follows:

Communism, 834

Congress, 611

Government, state and local, 640

Government, U.S., 2,319

International relations, 2,453

Military affairs, 1,249

Politics, general, 629

Politics, practical, 9,963

Taxation, 903

United Nations, 770

Information about ISLA can usually be obtained from the departments of sociology and political science of member institutions. The U.S. index is usually maintained by the library or by the local data archive, if there is one.

Although ISLA facilitates access to the Roper Center data, access is not limited to faculty and students at ISLA institutions, nor is it limited to academicians. Anyone interested in the Roper Center data may get more information by contacting Philip Hastings, Director, The Roper Public Opinion Research Center, Williams College, P.O. Box 624, Williamstown, Massachusetts 01267.

The third major source of data on political attitudes, the Louis Harris Political Data Center, needs only brief mention. Its importance lies in the fact that political data gathered by the Harris poll, which along with the Gallup poll is now one of the two major nationwide commercial polling organizations in the United States, is ordinarily available to academic researchers only through the Harris Center. The Center's specialty is data on individual states, and most of the data were gathered within the past decade. Information may be obtained by writing the Center in care of the Department of Political Science, University of North Carolina, Caldwell Hall, Chapel Hill, North Carolina 27514.

SOME CAUTIONS

For the inexperienced researcher, there are a number of pitfalls in the secondary analysis of existing data on political attitudes. For instance, he may apply statistical tests that are not appropriate to the sample design, fail to take into account the considerable systematic bias in the earlier poll data, or use national survey data for inappropriate purposes.

A common error is to apply textbook formulae for tests of significance and confidence intervals, which assume a simple random sample, to national survey data. In fact, it is virtually impossible to draw a simple random sample from a nationwide or a state-wide population, and many local surveys do not utilize a simple random sample. Most national and state-wide surveys employ quota-control sampling, area-probability sampling, or some combination of those two.[5] Quota-control sampling was used by all

---

[5] For a detailed but understandable treatment of the various survey sampling techniques, see Frederick F. Stephan and Philip J. McCarthy, *Sampling Opinions* (New York: John Wiley and Sons, 1958).

of the major commercial polling organizations and by most academic survey organizations through the early 1950s, and it is still used occasionally. There are several kinds of quota-control samples, but all use quotas to assure that the percentage of respondents having certain characteristics is the same or about the same as the estimated percentage in the total population. For instance, quotas may be set for sex, region, race, and age. Usually, each interviewer is assigned quotas of respondents having certain characteristics, and within the limits imposed by the quotas, he uses his discretion in selecting the respondents. The sampling variability of quota-control samples varies according to the specific techniques employed, but usually it is around 1.5 or 1.6 times the variability with simple random samples. Therefore, in computing the significance of a difference between two proportions, a difference at least 1.5 times the difference needed for simple random samples should be required for significance at a given level.

The greater sampling variability of the quota-control samples poses no major problem, provided the researcher is aware of it and takes it into account in computing tests of significance and confidence limits, since the pollsters typically used large samples that kept variability at an acceptable level. For instance, the Gallup quota samples usually contained at least 3,000 respondents. A more serious problem is that most of the quota samples used by the pollsters systematically under-represented people in the lower income, educational, and occupational strata.[6] Therefore, kinds of opinions, attitudes, and behavior more characteristic of the lower strata were rather consistently under-estimated by the early opinion polls. Obviously, it is important that the researcher who conducts secondary analysis with these data be aware of this systematic error.

An area-probability sample is drawn by dividing the nation (or other geographic unit to be sampled) into a number of geographic areas with similar numbers of people and drawing a random sample of these areas. Each of these areas, in turn, is divided into smaller areas, which are again sampled randomly. This "multiple-stage" process is continued through two or three stages until there is a sample of "sampling points," which are usually city blocks and portions of townships in the open countryside. Within the sampling points, respondents may be selected by the quota method, or some random or systematic process may be used to select households and respondents within households·. Gallup, for instance, uses a modified-quota method, which differs from the older quota techniques in that the interviewer selects respondents through a systematic process and has no discretion in the choice of respondents.

Area-probability samples are superior to quota-control samples in that they lead to little systematic error and are subject to less sampling variability. However, sampling variability is usually 1.3 to 1.4 times the vari-

[6] Ibid., Chaps. 7 and 8; and Norval D. Glenn, "Problems of Comparability in Trend Studies with Opinion Poll Data," Public Opinion Quarterly, 34 (Spring, 1970), pp. 82–91. Obviously, use of the right kind of quotas for income, education, and occupation could largely overcome this deficiency in the quota control samples.

ability with simple random samples. Furthermore, it is important to keep in mind that many survey organizations sample households rather than individuals, and therefore the kinds of people who are likely to live in households with more than two adult members may be slightly under-represented.[7] Furthermore, the institutionalized population—people in prisons, mental hospitals, and the like—are usually not represented at all. Nevertheless, comparisons of recent samples drawn by the Gallup organization, the National Opinion Research Center, the Michigan Survey Research Center, and other major survey organizations usually show very close correspondence with census data in terms of age, sex, education, race, region, and other demographic variables.[8]

Most of the data available through ICPR are from area-probability samples, and ICPR will furnish users with complete information about sampling techniques. In contrast, the code sheets obtained from the Roper Center may contain little or no information about sample design, and the Center may be able to supply no additional information. Therefore, it is advisable to write directly to the organization that conducted the study for information about the sample.

Most of the decks for U.S. Gallup studies conducted since 1960, and some of the other decks from the Roper Center, contain weighting cards, so the number of cards is more than twice the number of respondents. This weighting procedure is used as a substitute for calling back at dwelling units where no one is found at home.[9] Of the people who are found and interviewed, the responses of those who say they often are not at home during the hours when the Gallup interviewers call are weighted more heavily than others, that is, two or more cards on these respondents are included in the deck. This procedure should make the percentages derived from the weighted deck more representative of the population than those from the unweighted deck. However, the weighting cards, which are identified as such in one column, should not be counted in arriving at the N for tests of significance and confidence intervals.

Since the earlier poll data are very valuable for trend and cohort studies, the fact that they contain systematic error should not discourage their use. In fact, most kinds of political attitudes differ so little by social level that the systematic error resulting from the under-representation of the lower social levels will not be more than one or two percentage points, which is of little or no importance for most purposes. However, if it seems likely that there is

[7] So far, this has been of negligible importance, but when and if an appreciable percentage of the population participates in communal living arrangements, the sampling of households will no longer be adequate, and indeed the traditional concept of the household will have to be modified. By "communal" living arrangements, I mean not only hippie communes but such arrangements as four single working girls or college students sharing the same apartment.

[8] Of course, it is now well known that the census data contain some errors, the most notable of which is an under-enumeration of young low-status males.

[9] The Gallup organization has also added weighting cards to some of its decks to compensate for an under-representation of low-education persons in the unweighted samples.

appreciable systematic error, percentages can be adjusted to correct for it.[10] For instance, if one is using data for 1950, he can obtain a correct, or approximately correct, educational distribution from the 1950 census reports and standardize the responses from the study to the census educational distribution. If the date of the study is not a census year, he can arrive at an approximately correct educational distribution by interpolation from decennial census data or from data from the Current Population Survey, which provides annual estimates of population characteristics in the United States.[11]

The U.S. Gallup data provide excellent opportunities for cohort analysis, that is, for tracing characteristics of a birth cohort as it grows older. This procedure is valuable not only for studying the aging process but also for assessing the relative importance of different components of social and cultural change. Therefore, it is an especially valuable tool for political analysis. For instance, Ted Hefner and I recently did a cohort study of political party identification using data gathered at four-year intervals from 1945 through 1969.[12] Cohorts that aged from young adulthood to middle age and from middle age to old age during this period exhibited virtual stability in party identification, although in the total population the percentage of Republicans declined and the percentage of independents increased. Except for a shift to independence between 1965 and 1969, which to some extent involved people at almost all ages, the changes in party identification in the total adult population were largely a function of mortality, that is, of the dying off of the older, more Republican cohorts.

In a study of this kind, it is especially important to take into account changes in sampling techniques from the earlier to the later studies. In the study on party identification, for instance, the unadjusted data showed a small but steady increase in Democratic identification within the aging cohorts. This apparent change was not real but rather was strictly a function of the more adequate representation of lower-stratum people, who as a whole are more Democratic, in the later samples. Adjustment for systematic sampling bias is easy in a cohort study, since the estimate of the correct educational distribution is the same for a cohort at all dates and may be derived from the later and presumably more representative samples.[13] For instance, in the study referred to above, we standardized the responses for all

[10]Detailed instructions for this adjustment are given in Glenn, "Problems of Comparability."

[11]These estimates are published periodically in U.S. Bureau of the Census, *Current Population Reports* (Washington, D.C., Government Printing Office, annually).

[12]The results of this study are reported in "Further Evidence on Aging and Party Identification," *Public Opinion Quarterly*, 36 (Spring, 1972). Earlier cohort analyses of party identification are reported in John Crittenden, "Aging and Party Affiliation," *Public Opinion Quarterly*, 26 (Winter, 1962), pp. 648–657; and Neal E. Cutler, "Generation, Maturation, and Party Affiliation: A Cohort Analysis," *Public Opinion Quarterly*, 33 (Winter, 1969–1970), pp. 583–588.

[13]Of course, the educational attainments of a cohort increase somewhat as it grows older, but the change is so small after about age 25 that it may be ignored. For detailed instructions on adjusting the cohort percentages to correct for

of the dates to the educational distribution shown for each cohort by the 1965 data.

Probably the greatest danger in the ready availability of vast bodies of survey data is that they are likely to be used for purposes for which they are not appropriate. A few scholars have taken the extreme position that survey data are of practically no value for any purpose, and although their arguments are not convincing to most social scientists, the more sophisticated survey researchers readily admit some serious limitations of survey data and concede that the most valuable use of survey techniques is in conjunction with other methods of inquiry, such as depth interviewing.

Unfortunately, past practice is not an adequate guide to the appropriateness of survey data for specific research purposes. In recent years, for example, one of the most common applications of secondary analysis of survey data has been in research on the consequences of status inconsistency. I do not claim that survey data are of no utility for this purpose, but analysis of the usual kinds of survey data—the kinds available for secondary analysis—will never produce convincing evidence on the effects of status inconsistency. A major breakthrough in status-inconsistency research awaits the development of techniques and data especially for that kind of research.

A person is status inconsistent when he ranks differently on the different dimensions of stratification, such as income, occupational prestige, education, and racial or ethnic prestige. Since one can "rank" only in relation to others, status inconsistency is not an inherent characteristic of the individual that he possesses independently of other individuals. He is status inconsistent only in relation to others. Everyone is status inconsistent in relation to certain others, that is, everyone can find some others who rank higher than he on some dimensions of stratification but lower than he on other dimensions. However, the person who is labeled "status inconsistent" in social scientific research is judged to be inconsistent to an important degree in relation to a large proportion of the others in the population under consideration.[14]

According to most authors who write about status inconsistency, its alleged consequences result from interaction between individuals who are inconsistent in relation to one another. According to this hypothesis, each of the individuals expects the other to react to his higher ranks, whereas in fact the other tends to treat him in terms of his lower ranks. In other words, each person, seeking his own self-interest, expects to be superordinate in the relationship and to receive deference from the other. The incongruities between expectations and actions lead to strain in the relationship, and if a person has a large number of such relationships the strain will pro-

---

changes in sampling techniques, see Norval D. Glenn and Richard E. Zody, "Cohort Analysis with National Survey Data," *Gerontologist*, 10 (Autumn, 1970), pp. 233–240.

[14]Obviously, whether or not a certain individual is labeled status inconsistent or status consistent may depend upon what population is under consideration. For instance, a person may be inconsistent with reference to the national population but consistent in his home community.

duce an important degree of psychological stress. According to the various versions of the hypothesis, the psychological stress will lead, in turn, to such consequences as political liberalism, political extremism, social isolation, and psychosomatic illness.

It should be obvious that an adequate test of the various versions of this hypothesis would have to utilize information on interaction patterns, which the usual kinds of survey data do not provide. A respondent who is status inconsistent in relation to most other respondents in a survey sample may not be status inconsistent in relation to most people with whom he interacts, and vice versa. Two respondents to a national survey who are inconsistent in relation to one another have usually never interacted, and, what is more important, they often represent categories of people who rarely interact with one another. For example, the differing relationship between formal education and income in small towns in the Deep South and in large cities in the Northeast makes most people in the former communities status inconsistent in relation to most people in the latter communities. However, these two categories of people rarely interact with one another, so it makes no sense to expect a great deal of social strain and consequent psychological stress to result from this kind of status inconsistency that will show up in national survey data.

This difficulty can be partially overcome by restricting status-inconsistency studies to local samples or by controlling for region and community size in studies with national samples. These procedures can at least reduce the probability that respondents who are status inconsistent in relation to one another will represent categories of people who do not interact because of lack of spatial proximity. However, lack of spatial proximity is not the only barrier to interaction, and the Ns of national samples are rarely sufficient for all of the needed controls.

The problem of inadequate N for controls is exacerbated by the fact that controls for such variables as age and religious preference are also usually needed. In fact, age should almost always be controlled, since status inconsistency means something very different in young adulthood than in middle age or advanced maturity. Among young adults, a higher rank in formal education than in income is normal, and young adults probably typically compare themselves with other young adults rather than with older people. Controls for age also are important because the consistents and the inconsistents may differ in average age, and this difference may lead to differences in such dependent variables as political orientation.

An example of status-inconsistency research in which controls for age were needed but not used is Gerhard Lenski's study of status inconsistency and voting in four nations.[15] His two "status" variables were religious preference (Catholic or Protestant) and occupation, the assumption being that Catholics received less prestige than Protestants in all of the nations.[16] He

[15] "Status Inconsistency and the Vote: A Four-Nations Test," *American Sociological Review*, 32 (April, 1967), pp. 288–301.
[16] This assumption is questionable, but its validity or invalidity is not relevant to the point I am making.

used an occupational dichotomy, so that "working-class" Catholics and "middle-class" Protestants were considered status consistent and "middle-class" Catholics and "working-class" Protestants were considered status inconsistent. He then summed the percentages of "liberal" voters in the two consistent categories and did the same for the two inconsistent categories. If the sum was greater for the inconsistent categories (as it usually was), Lenski considered this to be evidence that status inconsistency leads to liberalism.

One of the nations included in the study was the United States, and in the case of the U.S. data, it can be shown that lack of controls for age and use of the crude occupational dichotomy would have produced a greater sum of Democratic voters for the two inconsistent categories in the absence of any inconsistency effect whatsoever.[17] People in each inconsistent category were younger on the average than people in each consistent category, and of course youth is associated with voting Democratic. Furthermore, "working-class" Catholics were more highly concentrated in the higher-prestige manual occupations than "working-class" Protestants, and "middle-class" Protestants were more highly concentrated in the higher-prestige non-manual occupations than "middle-class" Catholics. When one remembers that Democratic voting is inversely related to occupational prestige, a moment of reflection will reveal that both of these Catholic-Protestant occupational differences tended to produce greater Democratic voting in Lenski's status inconsistent categories than in his consistent categories.

Many other examples could be given, but the lesson from status-inconsistency research is clear: there are research problems for which the usual kinds of survey data may appear to be appropriate but are not—at least not without elaborate controls which the sample size often will not allow. It should also be clear that the abundance of readily available survey data is not an unmitigated blessing to social science. Researchers who gather their own data not only have more control over the characteristics of their data; they also have greater familiarity with them, through long and intimate experience, and it is likely that they are typically more aware of the limitations of their data than researchers who receive data decks through the mail and plunge immediately into the analysis. The data archives have opened up tremendous opportunities for important research at moderate cost, but they may also lead to a considerable increase in carelessly conducted and mediocre studies.

[17]The statements in this paragraph are based upon analysis of Gallup poll data from the early 1960s, which are similar to the U.S. data used by Lenski. One of the major advantages of research with archival data is that other researchers can easily replicate and refine the studies by using the same or similar data.

PART II

*Attitude Formation
and Development:
Political Socialization
and Political Knowledge*

INTRODUCTION

If the description and measurement of political attitudes and public opinion is the first concern of social scientists interested in these phenomena, then explanation is certainly their second. How and why individuals develop certain ideologies, attitudes, or opinions has long been of concern to social psychologists and is treated more than incidentally in the first four selections of Part I. Further, in a general sense, it is the basic question asked by most of the contributions in Parts II–IV of this anthology. This section explores two aspects of the attitude-formation process that are treated only incidentally in other sections of this volume: political socialization and political knowledge.

Socialization can be viewed from two perspectives: as the way culture is transmitted from one generation to the next, or as the process by which the individual learns his social roles and acquires a personality. Only in the past dozen years, however, has the process by which individuals learn *political* values, attitudes, beliefs, and behaviors received much attention from social scientists.[1] The major contributions during this period are organized and summarized by Thomas J. Cook and Frank P. Scioli, Jr., in "Political Socialization Research in the United States: A Review." The double-edged significance of the socialization process is reflected by the dominant methodological approaches used to study it—a micro approach (called "methodological individualism" by Cook and Scioli), where the focus is on how individuals learn political phenomena and the effects of this learning on their political behavior, and a macro approach (called the "political-system orientation"), concerned primarily with how this same process maintains or transforms society. The complementarity of the two perspectives should be obvious. If one generation socializes the next so that there is little or no change in political values or behavior, the probability that the society will be characterized by change from within will be low. Where there is a "transmission failure" and thus a "generation gap," there is likely to be some advocacy of radical change. Cook and Scioli present the major research questions that both the macro and micro perspectives have generated and they summarize the general tenor of the answers found thus far. Much of their discussion is organized around the *agents* of political socialization—those groups and institutions centrally engaged in instilling political beliefs and behavioral responses. The family, school, peer groups, secondary groups, and the mass media have all been the foci of different investigators and the roles thought to be played by each are succinctly summarized.

Of the various socialization agents, the family is generally considered the most important. Studies indicate, for example, that as many as 70 to 80 per cent of those voters who know their father's party identification report the same identifications for themselves.[2] Other studies have shown consider-

---

[1] Often cited as the pioneering work in this area is Herbert H. Hyman, *Political Socialization* (New York: Free Press, 1959).
[2] See the sources cited in note 11 of Goldberg's article.

able agreement among parents and their children concerning attitudes toward governmental policies, toward communism, and toward other political phenomena. The importance of the family is stressed by Richard M. Merelman in "The Development of Political Ideology: A Framework for the Analysis of Political Socialization." Merelman proposes a developmental theory which suggests that few individuals in American society experience the prerequisites necessary for the attainment of political ideology. After offering a more complex definition of ideology than that set forth by Sartori in Part I of this anthology, Merelman notes that *cognitive skills* allowing an individual to see linkages between ideas and events and a *developed morality* allowing him to evaluate consistently the ethical meanings of political events are both prerequisites to becoming an ideologue. It is then argued that these processes are so complex that they are not fully experienced by most individuals. In addition, it is noted that child-rearing practices may retard cognitive and moral development and, in some cases, may even cause behavior to regress. Specifically, parental warmth, the early delegation of responsibility and disciplinary practices which make some sort of appeal to the child's inner needs, may foster moral development. The frequent use of physical punishment is cited as a major factor probably inhibiting the development of cognitive skills. Merelman demonstrates the utility of his scheme by showing how it explains previous research findings and by suggesting some of the research questions it raises. The reader can test parts of the scheme himself by applying it to several of the selections that follow.

The low level of cognitive development of concern to Merelman is also stressed by Kenneth L. Kolson and Justin J. Green in "Response Set Bias and Political Socialization Research." Their data from 289 elementary school children suggest that a low level of cognitive development creates a high probability of response sets. This finding, in turn, leads the authors to criticize that mode of investigation which has been the foundation of the study of attitudes and opinions—survey research. They are especially skeptical of the type of questions most frequently used by researchers (Likert-type scales) and thus they question the validity of many of the generalizations concerning political socialization set forth to date. A balanced presentation of many research *issues* may be obtained by comparing this selection with the related topics discussed by Robinson, Rusk, and Head.

Harrell R. Rodgers, Jr., and George Taylor are primarily concerned with moral development. "Pre-Adult Attitudes Toward Legal Compliance: Notes Toward a Theory" analyzes survey data to assess the sophistication and antecedents of students' attitudes toward compliance with laws. Several aspects of their findings support the orientation suggested by Merelman. A comparison of high school with elementary school students suggests that attitudes toward law and compliance become more subjective and less idealistic over the school years (offering evidence supporting the developmental aspect of Merelman's scheme). But in spite of indications of development, Rodgers and Taylor also note that a large number of high school students have not internalized any values by which they can *evaluate* decisions concerning compliance, an observation supporting Merelman's attempt to relate the difficulty of moral development to the relative absence of ideologues. Rodgers and Taylor are also concerned with some of the attitudinal antecedents to compliance and the difference between white and black children. Again their findings support the Merelman perspective. Among the strongest correlates of non-compliance are above-average cognitive skills suggesting, according to the authors, that the more developed such skills are, the more inclined the student is to develop personal standards by which he will judge both his and the system's behavior.

Whether new cognitive skills are likely to lead to an increased level of political participation consistent with the Western liberal democratic model or to a negative evaluation of the system and thus the possibility of revolutionary activity is the major concern of "Political Response to New Skills: The Conforming and the Deviant." To provide a preliminary answer to this question, Dean Jaros studied 513 students at two eastern Kentucky vocational schools. Jaros notes that although the purpose of these schools is not overtly political, they are designed to counter the withdrawal of a disadvantaged people and the skills taught there are likely to be translated into political resources. New admissions were thus compared with students having one and two years of training. Among those students who were identified as conformists, additional training led to feelings of greater political efficacy and a higher level of participation in conventional activities (registering and voting). On the other hand, among students who had rejected legitimate means for the attainment of social goals, the effects of new cognitive skills were quite different. Not only was there a slight negative relationship between training and conventional political activity, but the data indicate that new skills among such persons may be translated into political deviancy.

The effect of cognitive skills in changing political orientations is also the concern of Arthur S. Goldberg in "Social Determinism and Rationality as Bases of Party Identification." Goldberg accepts the research evidence suggesting that most individuals develop the same party identifications as their parents early in their childhood but he moves on to attempt to explain why there is *some* defection. Both the effectiveness of parental political socialization and the conditions under which children will change their party identification can be explained, according to Goldberg, by examining the concept of rationality and its relationship to education (perhaps the most widely used indicators of cognitive development). Rationality is first applied to the political preference of parents. That is, most parents identify with that party assumed to be oriented toward the goals of the groups to which they belong (e.g., one would expect Catholics, blacks, those identifying with the working class, and Southerners to be more likely to express a Democratic than Republican preference) but some do not. The former are described as typical and rational, while the latter are classified as "sociologically deviant." Whether or not parental (especially paternal) deviance will contribute to party defection on the part of offspring is, in turn, suggested to be related to the cognitive development of the offspring. Specifically, the well-educated should perceive more accurately the expected utility associated with the paternal party identification. Thus, according to Goldberg, one would expect defection rates in the following order, from highest to lowest: (1) paternal party identification deviant and respondent well educated, (2) paternal party identification deviant and respondent poorly educated, (3) paternal party identification normal and respondent poorly educated, and (4) paternal party identification normal and respondent well educated. This prediction is confirmed by data and several other tests of propositions derived from the "rationality model" also provide support for it.

Goldberg's contribution reminds us that socialization (political as well as other types) is a process continuing beyond childhood. Attitudes may be modified or changed completely during adulthood by significant experiences requiring adjustments to new situations. Marriage, parenthood, becoming a home owner, moving to a new region or a different type of community, and perhaps simply the process of aging itself contribute to the development and modification of political attitudes. As Goldberg suggests, the extreme views in regard to attitude development are a social-determinism perspective stressing the affective nature of attitude acquisition and the rational-political-man perspective suggesting an instrumental goal-attainment orientation on the part of the actor. Attributing rationality to a political actor implies an ability on his part to select from among alternative goals, those which will be of the greatest utility to him. It implies also the ability to select the most efficient means for the attainment of those goals. Thus, one important prerequisite to rational political decisions is a relatively high level of knowledge about political issues, the political system designed to cope with them, and the key officials in the system. Several of the preceding selections dealing with political socialization suggest that low levels of cognitive development may not yield sufficient knowledge for rational political behavior; and a similar observation was made by Hennessy in Selection 2 of this anthology. The final selections of Part II deal explicitly with political knowledge. Both raise questions regarding the extent to which the typical American adult is capable of engaging in rational political behavior. While cognitive development may be sufficient for him to identify with a party as a rational cost-reducing mechanism, his knowledge of events and persons may be at a sufficiently low level to raise questions about the basis for his orientation toward specific issues.

" 'Dark Areas of Ignorance' Revisited: Current Knowledge about Asian Affairs" brings together findings from many national surveys to assess the American public's level of knowledge about several significant political events taking place during the 1960s. American adults were found to have incorrect perceptions concerning the number of American troops in Vietnam, the number of American casualties there, and the positions on the war taken by various national figures. Misperceptions were also widespread in regard to events in Communist China (in fact, as late as 1964, 28 per cent of the American people were still unaware that mainland China *had* a Communist government). Comparing his findings with those set forth a generation earlier, Don D. Smith concludes that adults are as poorly informed on foreign affairs today as they were in the 1940s. Public ignorance in regard to other topics is documented by Norval D. Glenn in "The Distribution of Political Knowledge in the United States." After suggesting that a large proportion of the American public cannot participate intelligently in the democratic process, Glenn compares the knowledgeability of different population sectors. As one would expect, education and political knowledge are closely related, but some rather surprising conclusions are also presented. When education is controlled, young adults are found to have less knowledge of political events and personalities than middle-aged and older persons. Individuals living in middle-size communities are more knowledgeable than those living in large cities or small towns. Both of these findings are explained by the "distraction" hypothesis—that younger persons and persons in large cities experience a great number of stimuli, many of which impinge more directly on the individual than political stimuli.

The two basic themes exemplified by the articles in this section—the social determinism-political socialization and rationality-political knowledge perspectives—may also be identified in the contributions in Part III and, especially, Part IV.

THOMAS J. COOK
Pennsylvania State University

FRANK P. SCIOLI, JR.
University of Illinois–Chicago Circle

LTHOUGH THE PHRASE "POLITICAL SOCIALIZATION" DESIGNATES A RELATIVELY
new approach to the systematic analysis of political behavior, an emphasis on citizen training for civic participation is not new to the literature of classical political theory. In Plato's *Republic*, we find considerable discussion of early childhood training in civic affairs as a necessary prerequisite to the continued maintenance of the well-ordered state. Aristotle
stressed the necessity of considering the characteristics of the citizenry in
the selection of a constitutional framework. Bodin's assertion that "Children
who stand in little awe of their parents, and have even less fear of the wrath
of God, readily set at defiance the authority of the magistrates" presages
the current discussion of the so-called generation gap between parents and
their children.[1] Later writers have reiterated in various ways a similar concern for the process whereby the political culture is transmitted from
one generation to the next. The principle departure from the scholarly concern for civic training sketched above has been the more recent emphasis
upon the construction of systematic theory based on empirically verifiable
assertions.

The first attempt to review and integrate research findings and discuss
the significance of political socialization for the explanation of political behavior is found in Herbert Hyman's *Political Socialization*.[2] At that time,
Hyman wrote that "One seeks far and wide for any extended treatment of
political behavior as learned behavior, despite the fact that this is patently
the case."[3] Hyman's pioneering work signaled a twofold advance in the
study of political socialization. First, he relied almost exclusively on empirical data to substantiate his theoretical assertions.[4] Second, he called for
an inter-disciplinary approach to the study of political socialization. This is
apparent from his emphasis upon *political learning* as the central component of the political socialization process. Several other concepts endemic
to the field of psychology were incorporated into Hyman's discussion: mo-

---

*Written for this volume.
[1] Fred I. Greenstein, "Political Socialization," *International Encyclopedia of the
Social Sciences* (New York: Crowell-Collier, 1965), p. 552.
[2] Herbert Hyman, *Political Socialization* (Glencoe: Free Press, 1959).
[3] *Ibid.*, p. 17.
[4] The primary data sources were a vast accumulation of research reports (mainly
surveys) from both political scientists and social psychologists, (e.g., pp. 70–71). The
book serves as a valuable reference of pertinent literature on the topic up to that
time.

tivation, emotion, perception and cognition.[5] Subsequent to Hyman, numerous political scientists have similarly relied upon existing psychological and social-psychological concepts in their discussions of the subject.[6] This is particularly evident relative to the concept of political learning. Research has progressed under the general conceptualization of political socialization as the process whereby the individual learns his political values, attitudes, beliefs, and behaviors.

PROMINENT RESEARCH ORIENTATIONS

In general terms, political socialization theory has progressed under two general research orientations. The first general direction may be described as a "people-oriented" approach to the study of political events. According to Dawson and Prewitt:

> Political socialization is a concept directing attention towards the knowledge, values and beliefs of the average citizen. What is it that the citizen wants of his government? Is he willing to support the political rules and rulers? Under what conditions? . . . These questions share a basic assumption. A nation's political life is linked closely to the moods, manners and values of its people. What citizens feel about politics both reflects and shapes the politics of their period.[7]

This approach may be characterized as that of "methodological individualism." The focus is on the behaviors of *individuals* and the attempt is to specify the conditions under which individual behavioral acts will occur. George Homans has discussed the concept of methodological individualism in terms of explanation:

> Explanation is the process of showing how empirical findings . . . can be deduced from general propositions under particular given conditions. The general propositions of all the social sciences are psychological propositions about the behavior of men rather than about societies or other social groups as such.[8]

Under this approach, the "political system" concept is a referent for the collection of individuals within the political boundaries of the system. An

[5] Hyman, *Political Socialization*, pp. 18–19.
[6] For excellent inventories and critiques of the research on political socialization see the following: Richard E. Dawson, "Political Socialization," in James A. Robinson, ed., *Political Science Annual: An International Review*, Vol. I (New York: Bobbs-Merrill, 1966), pp. 1–84; Richard E. Dawson and Kenneth Prewitt, *Political Socialization* (Boston: Little, Brown, 1969); Jack Dennis, *Recent Research on Political Socialization: A Bibliography of Published, Forthcoming, and Unpublished Works, Theses, Dissertations, and a Survey of Projects in Preparation* (Medford: Lincoln Filine Center for Citizenship and Public Affairs, 1967); Jack Dennis, "Major Research Problems of Political Socialization Research," *Midwest Journal of Political Science*, 12 (Feb., 1968), pp. 85–114; Roberta S. Sigel, "Political Socialization: Some Reflections on Current Approaches and Conceptualizations," a paper presented at the annual meeting of the American Political Science Association, New York, Sept. 6–10, 1966; Greenstein, "Political Socialization," pp. 552–557; Kenneth P. Langton, *Political Socialization* (New York: Oxford University Press, 1969).
[7] Dawson and Prewitt, *Political Socialization*, pp. 4–5.
[8] George C. Homans, *The Nature of Social Science* (New York: Harcourt, Brace and World, 1967), p. 79.

explanation of the behavior of the political system (as a single unit) necessitates research which leads to an understanding of the political behavior of the individual's interacting within the political system. These individuals are the primary units of analysis, and it is their behaviors that constitute the collective behavior of the political system. To a very large extent, therefore, the political socialization process refers to the training of individuals for political participation through the inculcation of politically relevant attitudes, values, beliefs, and behaviors. Students of political socialization are interested in, among other things, the effect of the individual's political training experience upon his relationship with his government.[9]

The second general direction of political socialization research has defined the *political system* as the primary unit of analysis. Writers emphasizing this aspect of political socialization theory have focused their attention on the concepts of system stability and system maintenance. How important are the political attitudes, values, beliefs, and behaviors of the citizens of a country to the continued functioning of the political system? In much of the political socialization literature, the answer to this question is centered around concepts extracted from the sociological writings of Robert Merton and Talcott Parsons.[10] Merton and Parsons concentrated much of their attention on the formulation of theoretical propositions about the necessary requisites to system maintenance and societal perpetuation. The influence of these writers on political socialization theory is reflected in current conceptualizations which stress the system maintenance function.

Gabriel Almond, for example, writes that the end-product of political socialization, which he defines as "induction into the political culture," is "a set of attitudes, cognitions, and value standards—toward the political system."[11] Almond's "induction process" serves the purpose of perpetuating the cultural and structural elements of the political system. Thus, the political system is maintained by the stable transmission of the political culture from one generation to the next. Does this mean that the political system cannot be maintained without some form of induction process to train the citizenry for civic participation? David Easton and Robert Hess answer that ". . . no system is able to function, much less maintain itself for any length of time, without educating its young po-

[9]The work of David Easton and others exemplifies this type of concern. See, for example, David Easton and Jack Dennis, "The Child's Acquisition of Regime Norms: Political Efficacy," *American Political Science Review*, 16 (March, 1967), pp. 25–38; David Easton and Robert D. Hess, "The Child's Political World," *Midwest Journal of Political Science*, 16 (Aug., 1962), pp. 229–246; David Easton and Jack Dennis, "The Child's Image of Government," *The Annals of the American Academy of Political and Social Sciences*, 361 (Sept., 1965), pp. 40–57.

[10]Talcott Parsons, *The Social System* (New York: Free Press, 1951); *Toward a General Theory of Action* (Cambridge, Mass.: Harvard University Press, 1951); Robert Merton, *Social Theory and Social Structure* (New York: Free Press, 1949).

[11]Gabriel Almond, "A Functional Approach to Comparative Politics," in Gabriel Almond and James S. Coleman, eds, *The Politics of the Developing Areas* (Princeton: Princeton University Press. 1960), pp. 27–28.

litically . . . it must undertake to transmit some of its political heritage. . . ."[12] For example, the individual's acquisition of a supportive attitude toward formal positions of authority (e.g., the President of the United States) may be related to the presence or absence of constraints on public decision-making. The importance of the support-acquisition function is underscored in the statement by Easton and Dennis that ". . . if a political system is to exist, one of its major tasks is to provide for the input of at least a minimal level of support for a regime of some kind. . . ."[13] Current discussion of the so-called generation gap between the political values of parents and their children may benefit from an analysis of the support-acquisition function in political socialization terms.

We may consider the generation gap as a "transmission failure" in the socialization process. The key to an understanding of the transmission failure lies in an analysis of the complex interactions of the various agencies (e.g., family, peer groups, school, mass media, etc.) involved in the political learning process. What are the conditions associated with the advocacy of radical political change? What are the conditions associated with the expression of unqualified system support? According to Kenneth Langton, the political socialization process may serve as the vehicle for *both* system maintenance and system change:

> This [political socialization] process may serve to preserve traditional norms and institutions; on the other hand, when secondary socialization agencies inculcate political values different from those of the past, or when children are raised with political and social expectations different from those of their forebearers, the socialization process can be a vehicle of political and social change.[14]

Langton's statement indicates that an understanding of the generation gap requires an explication of the conditions associated with the expression of system support or the advocacy of radical political change. As we shall see in later discussion, the concept of political socialization, whether the focus is on the individual or the political system, affords a research approach which is highly appropriate to the type of questions raised above.

It should be stressed that the two general research orientations outlined above—the individual and the political system—do not represent mutually exclusive (or antithetical) approaches to the study of political socialization. They more accurately reflect the preference of scholars for the analysis of political learning at different levels of theory construction. The distinction between micro- and macro-levels of analysis in economics is appropriate here.[15] At the micro-level, the individual constitutes the primary unit of analysis and research is directed toward the explanation of the individual's acquisition of politically relevant behavior. The macro-level

[12]Easton and Hess, "A Child's Political World," pp. 231–232.
[13]Easton and Dennis, "The Child's Acquisition of Regime Norms," p. 25.
[14]Langton, *Political Socialization*, p. 4.
[15]Paul A. Samuelson, *Economics: An Introductory Analysis.* (New York: McGraw-Hill, 6th ed., 1964), pp. 371–372.

approach identifies the political system as the primary unit of analysis and the attempt is to identify the correlates of system maintenance. As was pointed out above, the maintenance of a stable political system is largely dependent upon the ability of the political system to transmit its political culture from one generation to the next.

The authors are cognizant of the present debate over which of the two approaches to the explanation of social events is the more theoretically sound.[16] Rather than engage in the debate, we perceive the two approaches as complementary aspects of the same general phenomenon. We are in agreement with Dawson and Prewitt that research should proceed at both levels of analysis, each type of approach drawing upon the findings of the other.[17] For if one wishes to explain the behavior of the political system as a whole, it is necessary to conduct research that leads to an understanding of the behavior of the individuals within the political system. By the same token, individual political learning is relevant to political science as the vehicle for the transmission of political values, beliefs, attitudes and behaviors from one generation to the next. The importance of the transmission process lies in the consequences of individual political learning for the continued functioning of the political system.

POLITICAL SOCIALIZATION AS A CONTINUOUS PROCESS

In their attempts at theory-building, political scientists have become involved in both national and cross-national investigations of political socialization.[18] This research has largely focused on the relationship of attitudes and values to various types of political activity such as voting, decision-making, political participation, and feelings toward the political system. An examination of the literature reveals a significant point regarding the nature of the political socialization process: political socialization is a continuous process operative at all stages of the individual's life cycle.[19]

This perspective allows us to consider a phenomena such as political attitudes within a developmental framework. Given this view of political

---

[16] For a discussion of the issue see Ernest Nagel, *The Structure of Science* (New York: Harcourt, Brace and World, 1961), Chap. 14; Heinz Eulau, *Micro- Macro Political Analysis: Accents of Inquiry* (Chicago: Aldine, 1969); and Robert L. Lineberry, "Approaches to the study of Community Politics,"in Charles M. Bonjean, Terry N. Clark, and Robert L. Lineberry, eds.; *Community Politics: A Behavioral Approach* (New York: Free Press, 1971), pp. 16–25.

[17] Dawson and Prewitt, *Political Socializations*, p. 13.

[18] For studies investigating political socialization cross-nationally, see Gabriel A. Almond and Sidney Verba, *The Civic Culture* (Boston: Little, Brown, 1965); Lucian Pye, ed., *Communications and Political Development* (Princeton: Princeton University Press, 1963); Langton, *Political Socialization;* Stein Rokkan, "Cross-National Studies in Political Participation," *International Social Science Journal*, 12 (1960), pp. 7-14; Robert D. Hess, "The Socialization of Attitudes Toward Political Authority," *International Social Science Quarterly*, 15 (1963), pp. 542–559.

[19] Greenstein, "Political Socialization," p. 1.

socialization as a continuous process, we are then able to investigate attitudinal development and change, as well as attitude acquisition.[20]

If we recognize that the individual may receive specific information at one point in his socialization experience and then be exposed to additional, but perhaps contrary, information at a later point, we can determine whether the individual accepts or rejects the new information. A change in the individual's behavior pattern suggests acceptance of the contrary information and prompts the inference that attitude change has occurred. The amount of attitude change observed may be a function of several diverse factors such as the amount of discrepancy between the different bits of information, the characteristics of the communicator, or the conditions of information transmission.[21] Given the emphasis on attitude development and change, it is not surprising that the political socialization is of interest not only to political scientists but to psychologists, social-psychologists, and sociologists as well.[22]

The conclusion that political learning is a continuous, or developmental, process should not mask the significant differences in interpretation that exists in the literature relative to other aspects of the general concept. As Greenstein points out, scholars have not yet agreed on a model that provides a firm conceptual basis for the organization of research.[23] Thus, there has not yet emerged a single agreed-upon theory of political socialization which either delineates the important components of the concept or specifies the effect of each component on the socialization process.[24] Instead, we find that there are numerous competing "theories" of political

[20] Implicit in this view is an understanding of the issues involved in the study of attitudes and attitude change. Recent attempts at incorporating social-psychological principles in the study of political attitudes and behavior include: Michael J. Shapiro, "Rational Political Man: A Synthesis of Economic and Social Psychological Perspectives," *American Political Science Review*, 63 (Dec., 1969), pp. 1106–1119; Samuel A. Kirkpatrick, "Political Attitudes and Behavior: Some Consequences of Attitudinal Ordering," *Midwest Journal of Political Science*, 14 (Feb., 1970), pp. 1–24; James W. Dyson and Frank P. Scioli, Jr., "Linkage of Alternative Attitude Theories: An Experimental Test of a Model Interrelating Consistency Theory and Behavior Theory," a paper presented at Southern Political Science Association Convention, Atlanta, Ga., Nov., 1970; Giuseppe DiPalma and Herbert McClosky, "Personality and Conformity: The Learning of Political Attitudes," *American Political Science Review*, 64 (Dec., 1970), pp. 1054–1073.

[21] See Arthur R. Cohen, *Attitude Change and Social Influence* (New York: Basic Books, 1964).

[22] For an example of this inter-disciplinary concern, see Dennis, *Recent Research on Political Socialization*. The interested reader should consult, in particular: Jean Piaget, *The Moral Judgment of the Child* (New York: Free Press, 1966); Barbel Inhelder and Jean Piaget, *The Growth of Logical Thinking* (New York: Basic Books, 1958); Jean Piaget, *The Language and Thought of the Child* (New York: Meridian Books, 1955); and Albert Bandura and Richard H. Walters, *Social Learning and Personality Development* (New York: Holt, Rinehart and Winston, 1963).

[23] Greenstein, "Political Socialization," p. 552.

[24] For an attempt at providing a general framework in which data on political socialization can be integrated, see Selection 11 in this collection: Richard Merelman, "The Development of Political Ideology: A Framework for the Analysis of Political Socialization."

socialization, each of which ascribes differing importance to each of the agents of political socialization.

PROMINENT AREAS OF RESEARCH

A significant proportion of the research on political socialization has been concerned with answering the following questions: (1) when does the political socialization process begin? and (2) what, if any, is the most important stage in the political socialization process?

As was pointed out in the previous section, political scientists have attempted to answer these questions by treating political socialization as a developmental process. These research efforts have mainly centered on: (1) ascertaining at what age the individual first begins to learn political attitudes, values, beliefs, and behaviors; (2) how these political orientations develop; and (3) whether this learning process occurs mainly within specific age boundaries.

A review of the political socialization literature reveals little agreement as to the exact age at which the political socialization process begins. On the following three points, however, most of the political socialization researchers agree: (1) political socialization occurs before adulthood; (2) the political socialization that occurs in childhood has important implications for later political behavior; and (3) the political socialization process is a continuous process beginning with abstract notions about politics in childhood and developing into more concrete attitudes, values, and beliefs.

In regard to the early learning of political attitudes and behaviors, Hyman writes that: "It is clear that in all [these] areas of inquiry political participation, political orientation, and authoritarian versus democratic tendencies, differences among adults have their origins in earlier stages of development."[25] Hyman's assertion has received subsequent empirical support in a number of research efforts. Fred Greenstein came to a similar conclusion based on a study of elementary school children in New Haven, Connecticut. Greenstein states that ". . . the importance of political roles is learned early; just how early cannot be determined by this sample."[26] He found that differences between male and female adults (relative to issue positions, candidate familiarity, and levels of participation) can be traced to similar differences observed in children in the fourth through the eighth grades.[27] His research further revealed that by the fourth grade children were able to express a discernible political party preference.[28] The finding on the early learning of party identification was supported in a study reported by Easton and Hess on children in the second

---

[25] Hyman, *Political Socialization*, pp. 45–46.

[26] Fred I. Greenstein, "The Benevolent Leader: Children's Image of Political Authority," *American Political Science Review* (1960), p. 936.

[27] Fred I. Greenstein, "Sex-Related Differences in Childhood," *Journal of Politics* (May, 1961), pp. 353–371.

[28] Fred I. Greenstein, *Children and Politics* (New Haven: Yale University Press, 1965), p. 21.

through the eighth grades. The latter authors found that children in as early as the second grade could express a political party identification.[29]

As the above studies suggest, a general conclusion found in the literature is that the political socialization process begins at an early point in the lifetime of the individual. Moreover, this early political learning has profound consequences for later adult political development. Easton and Dennis underscore the importance of the early learning experience in their statement that "What is learned early in the life cycle is more difficult to displace than what is learned later."[30] Dawson and Prewitt identify the early political socialization experience as the crucial factor in determining the adult's political orientation. They contend that ". . . adult political behavior is the logical extension of values, knowledge, and identifications formed during childhood and youth."[31] Easton and Hess have narrowed the crucial time period down to the years between the ages of three and thirteen.

> It appears that by the time a child enters high school at the age of 14 his basic political orientations to regime and community have become quite firmly entrenched . . . the truly formative years of the maturing member of a political system would seem to be the years between the ages of three and thirteen.[32]

A similar conclusion was reached by Hess and Torney in their study of 17,000 children in grades two through eight. They found a strong positive attachment to the country develops quite early and shows almost no change through the elementary years.[33]

The evidence that early political training is related to later political behavior is to be expected from the general theory of socialization. Political socialization is, after all, a subset of the general phenomenon of socialization and operates in much the same way. Dean Jaros points this out in his statement that "Childhood experiences are known to be determinants of many kinds of adult behavior; it is unlikely that political behavior enjoys independence of such influence."[34]

While there is general agreement that the political socialization process begins quite early and is important for later political behavior, there is some doubt as to the number and quality of these early political orientations. Lewis Froman contends that children's values and beliefs about politics and political figures are relatively few in number and that their political attitudes are not very resistant to change. He attributes this to the early stage in their learning and the lack of sufficient reinforcement for

[29] Easton and Hess, "The Child's Political World," pp. 229–246.
[30] Easton and Dennis, "The Child's Acquisition of Regime Norms," p. 238.
[31] Dawson and Prewitt, *Political Socialization*, p. 205.
[32] Easton and Hess, "The Child's Political World," p. 246.
[33] Robert Hess and Judith Torney, *The Development of Political Attitudes in Children* (Chicago: Aldine, 1967).
[34] Dean Jaros, "Children's Orientations Toward the President: Some Additional Theoretical Considerations and Data," *Journal of Politics* (May, 1967), p. 369.

these values, beliefs, and attitudes.[35] Greenstein argues in a similar vein that children tend to learn political roles (such as the President) quite early yet they have very little specific knowledge about political figures or political events. He states that "Evaluations and affective knowledge about political leaders precede the factual information on which one might assume they would be based."[36] Research by Easton and Hess indicates that the attachments to country which the child learns quite early are essentially emotional, affective ties:

> As we find in most other aspects of the child's political world, and as we would expect, the responses are highly colored with emotion and occur long before rational understanding or even the capacity to rationalize political orientations are evident.[37]

Thus, the available research suggests that the political socialization process begins early in childhood where vague, affective notions about politics and political figures are acquired.

The fact that political orientations have their origins in childhood does not mean that the individual is then impervious to later change in his political behavior. The individual's political socialization experience does not end when he reaches his fifteenth birthday. According to Hyman, "He may show further changes with cumulative experiences in the large society or in a particular segment of the society."[38] The study by Prewitt, Eulau, and Zisk points out that adult political socialization may be quite influential in the decision, for example, to choose a political career. Their study of state legislators revealed that interest in a political career developed in adulthood for a large number of the legislators interviewed. They account for their findings by stating that adult political behavior is a function of *both* childhood socialization and adult political experience. In fact, they suggest that much of adult behavior may be independent of childhood socialization. They state that "Intervening between initial political socialization and incumbent behavior are political experiences that condition subsequent behavior irrespective of initial socialization."[39]

The five-nation study by Almond and Verba provides a further example of the need to consider political socialization within a developmental framework. In their conclusions, the authors were careful to stress the importance of the adult's socializing experiences (e.g., job satisfaction) as a potential contributor to adult political behavior. In each of the five nations (United States, Great Britain, Germany, Mexico, and Italy), the authors found that a sense of political competence in adulthood was more closely related to a feeling of job competence than to a feeling of competence, as

---

[35] Lewis Froman, "Learning Political Attitudes," *Western Political Quarterly*, 15 (1962), p. 309.

[36] Greenstein, *Children and Politics*, p. 235.

[37] Easton and Hess, "The Child's Political World," p. 236.

[38] Hyman, *Political Socialization*, p. 151.

[39] Kenneth Prewitt, Heinz Eulau, and Betty Zisk, "Political Socialization and Political Roles," *Public Opinion Quarterly*, 30 (1966–1967), p. 582.

the individual could recall it, in childhood or school.[40] We have support, therefore, for the conclusion that the political socialization process continues into adulthood, with the possibility that many important dimensions are learned in adulthood.[41]

In summary, the research to date indicates that the political socialization process begins in childhood, prior to the start of formal education, and prior to the time when the child has developed the ability to understand and cognitively order abstract political symbols and relationships. The child's early political orientations are in the form of vague emotional attachments and identifications which are not highly resistant to change. As the child grows older, however, his attitudes toward law and compliance become less and less idealistic.[42] It seems that the early orientations function as a screen through which later political information and experience is filtered. The psychological concept of "selective perception" is appropriately applied to this filtering process. The individual's perception of political events is a function of his previous political learning experience. He perceives, in effect, what he has learned to perceive.[43] It is this early learning experience which has the greatest consequences for the transmission of the political culture and maintenance of the political system. The fact that, for a large segment of the population these early political orientations are favorable toward the established institutions of political authority is highly significant relative to the previously discussed concept of support acquisition. One need only look at the rise in public support for presidential action during "crisis" periods to gain an appreciation of this point.[44]

AGENTS OF SOCIALIZATION

A consideration of the temporal aspects of the political socialization process leads to the question of *how* the individual acquires his political values, beliefs, and attitudes. This necessarily involves a discussion of two interrelated facets of the political learning experience: (1) the conveyers of the socialization experience; and (2) the psychological mechanism incorporated within the political learning process. The first involves a de-

[40]Almond and Verba, *The Civic Culture*, pp. 370-373.

[41]For a general treatment of adult socialization, see Orville G. Brim, Jr., and Stanton Wheeler, *Socialization after Childhood: Two Essays* (New York: John Wiley and Sons, 1966); Orville G. Brim, Jr., "Adult Socialization," *International Encyclopedia of the Social Sciences* (New York: Crowell-Collier, 1965), pp. 555–561.

[42]For research supporting this proposition with elementary school children, see Hess and Torney, *The Development of Political Attitudes in Children*, pp. 50–59; and for research supporting this proposition with high school children, see Harrell R. Rogers, Jr., and George Taylor, "Pre-Adult Attitudes Toward Legal Compliance: Notes Toward a Theory," Selection 13 in this volume.

[43]For a discussion of this point, see Bernard Berelson and Gary A. Steiner, *Human Behavior: An Inventory of Scientific Findings* (New York: Harcourt, Brace and World, 1964), pp. 100–101.

[44]Nelson Polsby, *Congress and the Presidency* (Englewood Cliffs: Prentice-Hall, 1964), pp. 25–26.

termination of the factors within the environment of the individual which are related to his acquisition of politically relevant behavior. These factors are generally discussed in terms of the "social agents" responsible for politically socializing the individual. The second aspect involves an explication of the psychological mechansims subsumed by the "learning" concept in socialization theory. In other words, what do we mean when we say that political behavior is "learned" behavior? What is the nature of the empirical phenomena referred to by the use of the term, learning? In this section, we will briefly discuss the agents that have been identified as prominent contributors to the political learning experience. Albeit there are disagreements as to which of the socializing agents is most important, the research literature generally notes the following components as significant agents of political socialization: family, school, peer groups, secondary groups (e.g., occupational organizations, political parties, religious groups, etc.), and mass media.

Family.   As with the rest of his initial learning experiences, it is in the family that the individual experiences his initial political training. The family is the first social group to which the individual belongs and, thus, the first potential socializing influence that he experiences. It is the family, Hyman states, that transmits the generalized political orientations to the child.[45] V. O. Key emphasized the child's early family experiences as having important consequences for his adult political behavior.[46] Relative to a particular type of political act, party loyalty, McClosky and Dahlgren conclude from their research that ". . . the family is a key reference group which transmits, indoctrinates, and sustains the political loyalties of its members."[47]

Some authors have gone so far as to cite the family as the primary agent of political socialization. Greenstein, for example, contends that the family is the most important source of political attitudes. He writes that: "Political learning progresses during the adolescent years. . . . This learning has many sources. The most important of them—at least as a determinant of attitudes—undoubtedly is the family.[48] While not all students of political socialization share Greenstein's point of view, the general thrust of the research to date is supportive of the family as a key agent in the transmission of political values and beliefs.[49] Richard Dawson has succinctly summarized the family's role as a socializing agent in the following three propositions:

[45] Hyman, *Political Socialization*, p. 95.

[46] V. O. Key, Jr., *Public Opinion and American Democracy* (New York: Alfred A. Knopf, 1961), p. 294.

[47] Herbert McClosky and Harold E. Dahlgren, "Primary Group Influence on Party Loyalty," *American Political Science Review* (Sept., 1966), p. 775.

[48] Greenstein, "Political Socialization," p. 940.

[49] For a review of the pertinent literature on this topic, see Steven L. Wasby, "The Impact of the Family on Politics: An Essay and Review of the Literature," *The Family Life Coordinator*, 15 (1966), pp. 3–24; James C. Davies, "The Family's Role in Political Socialization," *The Annals*, 361 (Sept., 1965), pp. 10–19.

1. In American society there is a high degree of congruence between parent and offspring political orientations.

2. Whenever clues concerning parental party identification are not present in the home, the individual is less likely to form an identification with a political party himself, than when partisan ones are present.

3. The closer the relationship within the family and the more uniform the orientations among other members of the family, the more political influence the family is likely to have on a given individual family member.[50]

While a considerable body of research supports these propositions and the assertions of the authors cited, we must caution against an overemphasis of the family as a socializing influence. The family is but one of a number of socializing agents within the environment of the individual. Recently, scholars have begun to question the extent of the family's socializing influence. Hess and Torney contend that ". . . the effectiveness of the family as an agent of political socialization has been over-estimated in previous research."[51] They limit the direct influence of the family to political party identification. Beyond party identification, the family's role is that of support for other institutions in teaching political information and orientations. Strong support for this limiting interpretation of the family's socializing influence is found in the study by Jennings and Niemi. In a survey of 1,669 high school seniors, randomly selected from 97 secondary schools (public and private), the authors found parental influence on children's political values limited almost solely to party identification. They state that:

> . . . any model of socialization which rests on assumptions of persuasive current of parent-to-child value transmissions of the types examined here is in serious need of modification. Attitude objects of the concrete, salient, reinforced terrain of party identification lend support to the model. But this is a prime exception. The data suggest that with respect to a range of other attitude objects the correspondences vary from at most, moderate support to virtually no support.[52]

The over-emphasis of the family's socializing influence is a function of two main factors: (1) the type of political behavior studied (e.g., party identification); and (2) the model of parent-child interaction prominent in the political socialization literature. As the Jennings and Niemi article indicates, we need to consider parental influence across a wider range of political behaviors (attitudes on a number of different issue areas) rather than just party identification. Second, the unidirectional model of parent-child interaction implicit in political socialization research (which portrays the child as a passive receptacle for parental influence) is unrealistic.[53]

[50]Richard E. Dawson, "Political Socialization," p. 29.
[51]Hess and Torney, *The Development of Political Attitudes in Children*, p. 217.
[52]M. Kent Jennings and Richard Niemi, "Transmission of Political Values from Parent to Child," *American Political Science Review* (March, 1968), p. 182.
[53]Richard Q. Bell, "A Reinterpretation of the Direction of Effects in the Study of Socialization," *Psychological Review*, 75 (March, 1968), pp. 81–95.

The School.   The educational system in our society also plays a significant role in the process of political socialization, for it is through the educational system that the society attempts formally to instruct the young. This
formalized instruction is transmitted to the young through specifically
designated institutions created for the purpose of teaching the skills that
the child needs in order to function in the adult world. Moreover, the educational system may be a vehicle for the shaping of political attitudes and
political orientations.

As an agent of political socialization, the school provides content, information, and concepts that expand the early learning experiences of the
family. In a family environment the individual may be exposed to both
positive and negative comments about the political system and its leaders.
Conversely, the politically relevant content of the grammar or high school
curriculum generally stresses the benevolent character of governmental
institutions and leaders. Greenstein contends, for example, that the grammar school training of children in the United States tends to promote the
notion that government and governmental officials are to be trusted.[54]
Thus, in a very basic sense, the grammar school training of children reinforces the child's basic trust in government. The primary emphasis is on
the development of citizen support for established authority.

Recent research findings suggest that the school experience is particularly important for children from lower- and working-class familes.[55]
In their study of the high school civics curriculum in the United States,
Langton and Jennings concluded that civics courses are limited in their
effect mainly to children from culturally deprived families. The authors
hypothesize that these children are more susceptible to influence because
of the relatively low level of political interest, knowledge, or involvement
in their family environment. Langton and Jennings report, however, that
"For the great majority of high school students, our findings certainly do
not support the thinking of those who look to the civics curriculum in
American high schools as even a minor source of political socialization."[56]

While these scholars argue that the effect of specific course instruction
does not play an important role in political socialization process, others
assert that the general values of the school, as represented in the instruc-
tional material, constitute a major factor in the political socialization process. Hess and Torney, using data collected on children in grades two
through eight, cite the school as the primary agent of political socialization. They state that:

> It is our conclusion from these data that the school stands out as the central
> salient and dominant force in the political socialization of the young child . . .

[54] Greenstein, "The Benevolent Leader," pp. 934–945.
[55] Kenneth P. Langton and M. Kent Jennings, "Political Socialization in the High
School Civics Curriculum in the United States," *American Political Science Review* (Sept., 1968), pp. 852–867.
[56] *Ibid.*, p. 965.

[this] suggests a need for greater attention and more systematic evaluation of the methods, curriculum, and timing of political socialization.[57]

A resolution of this apparent conflict in interpreting the influence of the school curriculum awaits further research. Hopefully, this research will be based on comparative research designs and similar population groups. The contradiction cited above, for example, may be a function of the simple fact that results from grammar school children were compared with data obtained from high school students. It is quite possible that the findings are not contradictory, but rather, reflect the fact that the effect of the formal school curriculum is limited to the grammar school population. Thus, by the time the child enters high school he is only marginally susceptible to influence by the formal curriculum, and other kinds of agents (e.g., peer groups) have become more important as sources of political socialization. This type of possibility suggests the need for both longitudinal designs (where the same population is studied over time) and comparative analysis where similar groups (i.e., same grade level) are studied under a wide variety of conditions (e.g., region, socioeconomic status, type of curriculum, etc.).

Greater agreement exists in the research which has focused on effect of educational attainment on the individual's political involvement and information. V. O. Key reports, for example, that "Persons with college education show themselves to be markedly more active in politics than are persons whose education has been restricted to grade school."[58] The authors of The American Voter note that "The educated person is distinct from the less educated, not only in the number of facts about politics at his command, but also in sophistication of the concepts he employs to maintain a sense of order and meaning amid the flow of information."[59]

The available cross-national data investigating the effect of education on political involvement and attitude suggests similar conclusions. Almond and Verba summarize these findings from their five-nation study in the following points:[60]

> 1. The more educated person is more aware of the impact of government on the individual than is the person of less education;
> 2. The more educated individual is more likely to report that he follows politics and pays attention to election campaigns than is the individual of less education;

[57] Hess and Torney, The Development of Political Attitudes in Children, pp. 219–220.

[58] Key, Public Opinion and American Democracy, p. 329. See also Selection 15 in this collection: Arthur S. Goldberg, "Social Determinism and Rationality as Bases of Party Identification," in which the author notes that he is able to predict party identification, on the basis of sociological characteristics, with greater accuracy for the better-educated than for the less-well-educated.

[59] Angus Campbell, et al., The American Voter (New York: John Wiley and Sons, 1960), p. 251.

[60] Almond and Verba, The Civic Culture, pp. 380–381.

3. The more educated individual has more political information;

4. The more educated individual has opinions on a wider range of political subjects; the focus of his attention to politics is wider;

5. The more educated individual is more likely to engage in political discussion;

6. The more educated individual feels free to discuss politics with a wider range of people. Those with less education are more likely to report that there are many people with whom they avoid such discussions;

7. The more educated individual is more likely to consider himself capable of influencing the government; this is reflected both in responses to questions on what one could do about an unjust law and in respondent's scores on the subjective competence scale;

8. The more educated individual is more likely to be a member—and an active member—of some organization; and

9. The more educated individual is more likely to express confidence in his social environment; to believe that other people are trustworthy and helpful.

It appears, therefore, that the formal educational experience must be considered as an agent of political socialization, even if recent research questions the formal curriculum as a major source of political socialization.[61] While the evidence concerning the effect of the high school and civics curriculum on political attitudes, beliefs, values, and behaviors is mixed, the research literature does reveal a clear difference, in terms of political involvement and information, between those individuals who have had only a primary school education and those who have gone to high school and college.

Peer Groups.   Several scholars maintain that it may be the presence of peer groups (and the general social climate) that accounts for the importance of the school as an agent of political socialization. The function of the peer group is essentially to expand the experiential background of the individual beyond that of his family circle. According to Roberta Sigel, ". . . it offers youth the first opportunity to look to a non-familial reference group that can teach him how to play his role and to socialize him into new ways of thinking, feeling, and behaving."[62] Thus, the peer group may or may not act to reinforce the behavior learned in the familial environment. The extent of non-congruence between the family and peer-group values and norms is an indicator of the potential attitudinal change that the individual may evidence as a result of his exposure to peer group influence and his identification with peer-group values.

One of the most prominent research investigations in the area of peer-group influence was the four-year study at Bennington College conducted

[61] An interesting study reporting the use of anomie theory to explain various kinds and levels of political behavior that accompany education and vocational training is reported by Dean Jaros, "Political Response to New Skills: the Conforming and the Deviant," Selection 14 in this collection.

[62] Roberta Sigel, *Learning About Politics* (New York: Random House, 1970), p. 413.

by Theodore Newcomb.[63] Newcomb interviewed students (all women) at various periods in their four-year college program and discovered a marked difference in the attitude distributions of students over the four-year period. He explained his findings in terms of peer-group identification. According to Newcomb, those individuals who had evidenced the greatest amount of attitudinal change had formed new reference groups while at the college. These individuals came, in time, to accept the norms and values projected by the new reference groups. Conversely, those individuals who did not indicate this kind of reference-group identification did not evidence a significant attitude change at the completion of their four-year college program. Moreover, in a follow-up study 20 years after the initial interviews, Newcomb located 130 of the original 141 girls interviewed, reinterviewed them, and found that the attitudinal differences observed during the first interview period had remained stable over the intervening time period. He concluded that:

> In terms of party or candidate preference in 1960, the degree of individual stability is startling . . . these data provide no support for a prediction of general regression (to the attitude held at the beginning of their college career).[64]

Thus, according to Newcomb, peer-group identification resulted in a significant attitude change for the particular population studied and this attitude change persisted after a period of 20 years.

Newcomb discussed peer-group identification as the vehicle for changing the individual's political orientation or attitudes from those acquired within the family experience. In this regard, attitude change refers to the individual's deviation from the modal norms and values represented within his immediate family environment. As Langton has pointed out, a primary function of the peer group is to expose the individual to a wider set of norms and values than those represented in his immediate family. Thus, according to Langton, ". . . the peer group may provide a social system in which the individual learns new attitudes and behavior."[65]

The peer group may also serve to promote or reinforce those basic orientations learned within the immediate family environment. The peer group may, in effect, function as an extension of the individual's family in the type of orientation and attitudes it reinforces. For example, the child who grows up in a poverty-stricken family environment will most likely interact with children experiencing a similar-type condition. The effects of such interaction may result in the acquisition of attitudes and values

[63]Theodore M. Newcomb, "Attitude Development as a Function of Reference Group: The Bennington Study," in E. E. Maccoby, Theodore M. Newcomb, and E. L. Hartley, eds., *Reading in Social Psychology*. (New York: Holt, Rinehart, and Winston, 3rd ed., 1962), pp. 265–275.
[64]Theodore M. Newcomb, "The Persistence and Regression of Changed Attitudes: Long-Range Study," *Journal of Social Issues*, 19 (1963), p. 7.
[65]Kenneth Langton, "Peer Group and Schools in a Political Socialization Process," *American Political Science Review* (Sept., 1967), pp. 751–758.

quite different from those evidenced by children raised under more ad-
vantageous circumstances (i.e., more economically secure). Recent studies
indicate that this is, in fact, what occurs. Studies of ghetto children and
children raised in the impoverished region of Appalachia suggest that their
perceptions of political institutions and political figures are significantly
less favorable (or trusting) than those of children raised in middle-class or
upper-middle-class family environments.[66] Edward S. Greenberg points
out, for example, that there is a small but significant difference between
white and black children's support for the political system with black
children becoming less supportive as they grow older.[67]

Kenneth Clark contends that the effect of the ghetto socialization
experience is the child's acquisition of negative attitudes not only toward
political institutions, but more importantly, toward his own worth as an
individual. The potential reinforcing effect of peer-group interaction on the
perpetuation of these attitudes is suggested in the following statement by
Clark:

> Human beings who are forced to live under ghetto conditions and whose daily
> experience tells them that almost nowhere in society are they respected and
> granted the ordinary dignity and courtesy accorded to others will, as a matter
> of course, begin to doubt their own worth. Since every human being depends
> upon his cumulative experiences with others for clues as to how he should
> view and value himself, children who are consistently rejected understand-
> ably begin to question and doubt whether they, their family, and their group
> really deserve no more respect from the larger society than they receive.[68]

Clark's statement underscores the need to take into account the peer-
group influence not only within the school setting but also within the
individual's total environment. The peer-group structure is an important
component of the individual's political socialization experience. Moreover, the peer-group characteristics vis-à-vis the individual's family environment generally determine the importance of the peer group as an
agent of political socialization.[69]

[66] For an example of this research, see Schley R. Lyons, "The Political Socialization of Ghetto Children: Efficacy and Cynicism," *Journal of Politics* (May, 1970),
pp. 288–304; Dean Jaros, *et al.*, "The Malevolent Leader: Political Socialization in
American Sub-Culture," *American Political Science Review* (June, 1968), pp.
564-575; Edward S. Greenberg, "Children and Government: A Comparison Across
Racial Lines," *Midwest Journal of Political Science* (May, 1970), pp. 249–275.

[67] Edward S. Greenberg, "Black Children and the Political System," *Public Opinion Quarterly* 34 (Fall, 1970), pp. 333–345. See also his article, "The Orientations
of Black and White Children to Political Authority Figures," *Social Science Quarterly*, 51 (Dec., 1970), pp. 561 to 571.

[68] Kenneth B. Clark, *Dark Ghetto* (New York: Harper & Row, 1965), pp. 63–64.

[69] By importance of the peer group as an agent of political socialization, we mean
the potential socializing influence of the peer group away from the modal
tendency of values represented within the family environment. The greater the
discrepancy between peer group and family values, the greater the potential change
in the individual as a result of peer-group identification.

Secondary Groups and Mass Media. While researchers generally cite the family, school, and peer groups as the most important agents of political socialization, other factors have also received prominent mention as being important to the political learning process. In particular, secondary groups and the mass media play an important role in the development of politically relevant behavior.

Secondary groups such as political parties, religious groups, labor organizations, and professional associations affect the political socialization process by both direct and indirect means. For example, it is not uncommon for a secondary group such as the American Bar Association to devote direct energy toward advancing a political cause that will benefit the Association (the recent statements made by the ABA on President Nixon's replacement for Justice Abe Fortas is a case in point). Likewise, in an indirect way labor unions have inculcated a dedication to the Democratic Party among their members. As a result, it would generally be uncommon to find a worker, at his job, overtly promoting a Republican candidate.[70]

These secondary groups promote a conformity to the norms of the group and individuals are generally reluctant to deviate from these norms due to the fear of social ostracism. If an individual belongs to more than one secondary group (for example, a physician belonging to the AMA, a church group, and a country club) it is entirely possible that the various groups to which the individual belongs will each espouse different political views. If this should be the case then the individual is indeed in a conflict situation. Robert Lane comments on such a situation by stating:

> It is usual for a person to identify with a number of groups. . . . These reference groups usually exert pressure in predominantly the same political direction . . . . But where this is not true, where the system of group identification involves conflicting pressures (liberal vs. conservative, Democratic vs. Republican, isolationist vs. internationalist) a problem of choice arises for the individual. Such choices involve not only the solution of a political problem, but also the accompanying loss of solidarity within a given group.[71]

The large body of research on voting behavior generated over the last 25 years has paid considerable attention to the concept of "cross-pressures." Lane, in his review of these findings, concluded that cross-pressures affect the political behavior of the cross-pressured individual in various

[70]William H. Flanagan, *Political Behavior of the American Electorate* (Boston: Allyn and Bacon, 1968), pp. 55–57; Fred I. Greenstein, *The American Party System and the American People* (Englewood Cliffs: Prentice-Hall, 1963), p. 25; Robert E. Lane and David O. Sears, *Public Opinion* (Englewood Cliffs: Prentice-Hall, 1964), pp. 33–42; Sidney Verba, *Small Groups and Political Behavior* (Princeton: Princeton University Press, 1961), pp. 22–23.

[71]Robert E. Lane, *Political Life: Why People Get Involved in Politics* (New York: Free Press, 1959), pp. 197–198.

distinct ways.[72] According to Lane, withdrawal from the conflict situation is only one of several possible reactions:

> Withdrawal from a decision involving conflicting reference groups is only one of several means of solving the conflict problem; others included (a) identification with one of the conflicting reference groups (sometimes because of frustration in the other), (b) moderation in viewpoint, a moderation which may be either confused and eclectic or synthesized, (c) minimization of the issue, (d) failure to "see" the conflict, (e) generalized apathy (when the conflicting groups embrace many aspects of life).[73]

Subsequent research on voting behavior has also revealed that, as in the case of peer-group influence, the impact of the individual's secondary-group associations on his political orientation is mainly a function of the extent to which the individual identifies with the group values or objectives. A second important factor is the scope of promotional activity that the group undertakes in attempting to influence its membership.[74]

We find, also, that the various communications media (television, radio, newspapers, magazines, etc.) may have an affect on shaping the individual's political attitudes, values, beliefs, and behaviors.[75] A vast body of research on the influence of the mass media on political behavior has followed upon the research conducted by Elihu Katz and Paul Lazarsfeld.[76] Katz and Lazarsfeld found that while the mass communications media have an effect, the media generally transmit their messages to the mass public through "opinion leaders." These "opinion leaders" (community activists, ministers, schoolteachers, etc.) are particularly attentive to the mass media and transmit information they receive from the media to those individuals in the community whom they know and can influence.

Thus, we have a "two-step flow" of communication where the flow of information from the media source to the mass audience is filtered through

---

[72]The reader should note that the findings on the effects of cross-pressures on voting behavior largely parallel the theories of balance and cognitive dissonance originating in the field of social psychology. See, for example, Fritz Heider, "Attitudes and Cognitive Organizations," *Journal of Psychology*, 21 (1946), pp. 107–112; Leon A. Festinger, *A Theory of Cognitive Dissonance* (Stanford: Stanford University Press, 1960), pp. 112–163.

[73]Lane, *Political Life*, p. 203.

[74]Campbell, *et al.*, *The American Voter*, Chap. 12; An excellent discussion of this general point may be found in Cohen, *Attitude Change and Social Influence*, pp. 81–99.

[75]Richard R. Fagen, *Politics and Communication* (Boston: Little, Brown, 1966); see also Walter Weiss, "Effects of the Mass Media of Communication," in Gardner Lindzey and Elliot Aronson, eds., *The Handbook of Social Psychology*, Vol. 5 (Reading, Mass.: Addison-Wesley, 2nd ed., 1969), pp. 77–195, esp. pp. 155–177 on "Mass Media and Voting Behavior."

[76]Elihu Katz and Paul Lazarsfeld, *Personal Influence* (New York: Free Press, 1965).

the group opinion leaders.[77] Moreover, recent studies suggest that the result of this phenomena may be the perpetuation of a "knowledge gap" between the opinion leaders and the mass audience. Based on a review of the literature on the topic and field experiment, Tichenor, Donohue, and Olien suggest the following hypothesis:

> As the infusion of mass media information into a social system increases, segments of the population with higher socioeconomic status tend to acquire this information at a faster rate than the lower status segments, so that the gap in knowledge between these segments tends to increase rather than decrease.[78]

A second major finding is that the mass media do not generally change already existing political attitudes, values, and beliefs. Rather the mass media serve to reinforce the individual's political orientations.[79] The explanation for this phenomenon lies, to a large extent, in cognitive dissonance theory which states that individuals tend to pay more attention to the mass-media messages with which they agree than those with which they disagree. Research by V. O. Key and others tend to substantiate the reinforcing, rather than changing, function of the mass media. Key states that "without the benefit of the findings of any large-scale analysis of the content of the media, it is safe to conclude that the major influence of the media upon political attitudes is by and large reinforcement of the status quo."[80]

Finally, any attempt to assess the influence of the mass media must recognize the fact that groups vary both in their exposure to different types of mass media (i.e., radio, television, newspapers, etc.) and their attitudes toward different media as sources of information. Greenberg and Dervin, for example, found that a "culture of poverty" existed relative to mass-media usage.[81] Low-income whites and blacks evidenced significantly different media-usage behavior from that of the general population. These findings point out the need to analyze the mass media as a multidimensional concept and consider the differential effects of various media sources on different population groups.

CONCLUSION

It is our hope that the foregoing discussion has provided the reader with some understanding of the development of the socialization concept in

[77] Elihu Katz, "The Two-Step Flow of Communication: An Up-to-Date Report on a Hypotheses," *Public Opinion Quarterly*, 21 (1957), pp. 61–78.

[78] T. J. Tichenor, G. A. Donohue, C. N. Olien, "Mass Media Flow and Differential Growth in Knowledge," *Public Opinion Quarterly* (Summer, 1970), pp. 159–160.

[79] David O. Sears, "Political Behavior" in Lindzey and Aronson, *The Handbook of Social Psychology*, pp. 315–458.

[80] Key, *Public Opinion and American Democracy*, p. 396.

[81] Bradley Greenberg and Brenda Dervin, "Mass Communication and the Urban Poor," *Public Opinion Quarterly* (Summer, 1970), pp. 225–235.

political science research in the United States. We have attempted to introduce the reader to the types of research questions that have been posed, and the general tenor of the answers found thus far in investigations of the political learning process.[82] Political socialization research is currently a vital part of the political science research that is being conducted in the United States. The need for more cross-national comparisons and investigations of political socialization looms as an important factor aiding in the further development and refinement of the concept.

[82] This review has primarily focused on the non-methodological aspects of political socialization research; we feel that the reader should be constrained against the interpretation that the research to date has been free of methodological criticism. The interested reader may consult the following sources for further discussion: Thomas J. Cook, "The Application of Operant Learning Theory Principles to the Study of Political Socialization," Ph.D. dissertation, Florida State University, 1969; Frank P. Scioli, Jr., "Political Attitude, Verbal Behavior, and Candidate Selection in Experimental Small Groups," Ph.D. dissertation, Florida State University, 1970; Kenneth L. Kolson and Justin J. Green, "Response Set Bias and Political Socialization Research," Selection 12 in this volume.

THE DEVELOPMENT OF POLITICAL IDEOLOGY: A FRAMEWORK FOR THE ANALYSIS OF POLITICAL SOCIALIZATION[*]

RICHARD M. MERELMAN[**]
University of Wisconsin

"MYSELF, I GET CONFUSED. THE PRESIDENT TELLS YA THAT HE DON'T WANT no war, it's peace. You pick up a paper, they're bombing children. And television, the guys being interviewed, talking about peace, and the picture shows where the women and children are being bombed and slaughtered and murdered. How long if I think that way and I have had a bad feeling, how long will other people that their mentality's not strong enough, to separate the cause of it? Fear. What's gonna happen to our kids, our grandchildren?

"Lotta them are afraid of their jobs, losing their jobs. Because the government's maybe got some contract with some company. For example, we got one fellow here works with the government, with this here carbonic gas or whatever it is. If he opens his mouth up too much, he can lose his job. And the senators or congressmen, they personally don't take interest in their own country, right here, what's going on.

"The colored. We had a tavern on Sixty-first and State, three and a half years, Negro neighborhood. I tell you I never was insulted no place by not a Negro person over there. They respected me highly. It took a white fella to come in and insult me because I wouldn't serve him beer, he was too drunk. And if it wasn't for these poor Negro fellas, I'd a probably killed this man. [Laughs.] Because he called me a dirty name."

Eva Barnes, 56, citizen of Chicago.[1]

I. FOUR THEORIES ABOUT THE SOURCES OF IDEOLOGY

Mrs. Barnes is trying to understand the political world, but she suffers from a common problem. She has no intellectual handle on it. She blames the government for acting inconsistently, but she herself is inconsistent. She deplores war and its slaughter; yet she can imagine herself killing a man who has merely called her "a dirty name." She rambles from war to governmental control of employment to the problem of race. There are no explicit intellectual links in this chain. Rather, her choice of topics seems almost randomly martialed. For example, "them" in the first sentence of

[*]Reprinted with permission of the author and publisher, from Richard M. Merelman, "The Development of Political Ideology: A Framework for the Analysis of Political Socialization," *American Political Science Review*, 63 (Sept., 1969), pp. 750–767.

[**]I wish to thank Fred Greenstein for his comments on an earlier version of this piece. He is absolved of any responsibility for what follows.

[1]Studs Terkel, *Division Street: America* (New York: Pantheon Books, 1967), p. 65.

the second paragraph has no clear referent; therefore, we have no way of knowing the logic that led her from war to the involvement of government in employment. And, of course, she speaks primarily from and about personal experiences, which she uses to illustrate her generalizations. There is the "fellow . . . [who] works with the government," and the incident in the barroom. Each single case must support by itself the general principle. Finally, her remarks include no familiar political concepts by which we can connect one observation to the next. We can understand why Mrs. Barnes yearns for "the cause of it."

Is Mrs. Barnes atypical? Yes, but in an unexpected way. She has been a political activist. She helped unionize the Chicago stockyards under conditions which might well have made her reflective about her political world.[2] The vast majority of her fellow citizens have never done anything as political as union organizing. Consequently, their conversations about politics might be even more fragmented than hers.

Although Mrs. Barnes' discussion of politics evidences a desire to understand, it is uninformed by any basic ideational framework which would permit comprehension. This framework may be called "ideology." It is by now a commonplace that the mass of Americans do not have a sophisticated conceptual organization by which politics may be understood. Perhaps the aptest description of this situation is contained in Philip E. Converse's "The Nature of Belief Systems in Mass Publics."[3] Converse defines political ideologies as belief systems characterized by high constraint, great range, and a centrality of political items.[4] These belief systems provide conceptual and terminological canals into which the flood of political events which overwhelms Mrs. Barnes can be diverted and managed.

Political scientists have emphasized different components of ideology. The concept of constraint is vital to Converse's analysis. Constraint "may be taken to mean the success we would have in predicting, given initial knowledge that an individual holds a specified attitude, that he holds certain further ideas and attitudes."[5] But ideologies also provide standards by which political events may be evaluated, allowing a person to approve some and deplore others. While Converse's discussion of ideology stresses cognition, Lane's definition of ideology emphasizes evaluation. To Lane, ideologies "are normative, ethical, moral in tone and content."[6]

My understanding of ideology encompasses both panels of this picture. Let us think of ideology as involving: (1) a considerable number of con-

---

[2] *Ibid.*, pp. 61–62.

[3] In David E. Apter, ed., *Ideology and Discontent* (New York: Free Press of Glencoe, 1964). pp. 206–262. For an interesting attempt to rebut Converse, see Norman R. Luttberg, "The Structure of Beliefs Among Leaders and the Public," *Public Opinion Quarterly*, 32 (Fall, 1968), pp. 398–410.

[4] In Apter, ed., *Ideology and Discontent*, pp. 207–213.

[5] *Ibid.*, p. 207

[6] Robert E. Lane, *Political Ideology* (New York: Free Press of Glencoe, 1962), p. 15. The uses of the term "ideology" are legion. Therefore, we have defined the term in our own way. For further elucidation, see *Ibid.*, pp. 13–17.

strained political ideas. By "constraint" let us mean, with Converse, that if one idea changes, those others related to it in the ideology will change as well. (2) An evaluational and prescriptive system. The ideology sets forth a statement of political preferences. (3) Persistence. An ideology must have some arbitrary, but considerable, duration in order for us to distinguish its components from passing whims. (4) Global standards. The judgments applied to any sub-category of political events within the ideology are exhaustive and consistent. (5) Boundaries. Political events which fall into different sub-categories within the ideology are sharply distinguished from each other and are, therefore, judged differently by and within the ideology. (6) Deductive consistency. Given inherently non-logical premises, deductions must occur in accordance with the rules of logic. For example, if a person, because of some views of individual morality, favors a balanced budget, he cannot, at the same time, believe in extra-budgetary social welfare payments to his own group. In short, ideological prescriptions must not produce logical absurdities. (7) Activist directives. Political ideologies do not produce apathy.

According to Converse, no more than 2.5 per cent of Americans meet our qualifications as ideologues.[7] There is no clear understanding among political scientists as to why so few Americans think ideologically. After all, our society is characterized by the largest percentages of college students and graduates in the world, great affluence, and instant contact with political events through the mass media. Shouldn't these things help to produce more ideologues? Four attempted explanations of this paradox exist, but, as we shall see, none is successful.

A favorite hypothesis notes a relationship between political activity and the development of political ideologies. More generally, the argument may be formulated as follows: the greater his proximity to politics at any time, the greater is the likelihood that a person will become an ideologue. Few people participate; therefore, few are ideologues.[8] According to this hypothesis, the more active a person is in politics, the more familiar with political life he becomes. His familiarity leads him to forge the informational links between political events which encourage and sustain the growth of a political ideology. Furthermore, the more active he becomes, the more he associates with others who speak in terms of and group themselves around political ideologies, such as liberalism or conservatism. These are only a sample of the supporting arguments for the hypothesis, but they suffice for our purposes.

No one doubts the high correlation between sustained political activity and the existence of political ideologies.[9] But even if all the ideologues so defined by Converse were political "gladiators,"[10] many other political

---

[7] "The Nature of Belief Systems," p. 218.
[8] For a thoroughly tangled statement of the interrelationships of participation and cognition, see Lester W. Milbrath, *Political Participation* (Chicago: Rand-McNally, 1965), pp. 62–66 ff.
[9] *Ibid.*
[10] *Ibid.*, p. 21.

participants would not be included. Nor in reality should we expect that all ideologues engage in sustained political activity. In short, many political gladiators are no doubt able to function without the benefit of tightly knit political ideologies; and some ideologues do not become regular political participants.

The hypothesis may also be attacked even when we take the case most favorable to it. We would certainly expect, under the terms of the argument, that the sons and daughters of the politically active would be themselves especially likely to become both politically active and ideological. Politics becomes proximate to them at particularly early ages, and they, surrounded as they are by political influences and having a set of ready-made contacts, should naturally fall into a political life. However, the process is neither so simple nor so encompassing as it seems, for we can observe many sons and daughters of politicians who resist the political siren. No compelling political ideology pushes them into politics. On the other hand, there are many people from backgrounds of political apathy who, moved by motives divorced from the proximity of political decisions, enter into political careers. Indeed, it is often those from the most unpromising backgrounds who become the most ideologically deviant and politically militant in their society. For all these reasons, it would appear that the proximal politics hypothesis is insufficient. It cannot tell us why the proximity of politics is not sufficient for ideological development among all the politically active. It cannot tell us why some children of politicians become active themselves and others do not. It cannot tell us why some people from backgrounds in which politics is only dimly perceived become political ideologues. Nor can it tell us why some ideologues do not engage in sustained political activity.

A second, weaker hypothesis concentrates on sociological factors. This argument asserts that the development of political ideologies is associated with particular positions in the social structure. For example, as Converse and others stress, ideology is closely related to educational level.[11] It also appears that extremist ideologies often originate in social positions which are exposed to sociological discontinuities, such as, for example, status inconsistency.[12] People experiencing status inconsistency are accepted by society in some respects and rejected in others. A case in point, in terms of European society, involves the early marginal status of the Nazi ideologues, numbers of whom felt themselves worthy of respect as ex-soldiers and German patriots, but could find no place in the Weimar Republic. In addition, many of the early Nazi leaders came from geographically marginal areas of

---

[11] Converse, "The Nature of Belief Systems," p. 213. See also Angus Campbell, *et. al., The American Voter* (New York: John Wiley, and Sons, 1960), p. 476.

[12] See, for example, the pieces by Seymour Lipset and Richard Hofstader in Daniel Bell, ed., *The Radical Right* (Garden City: Doubleday Anchor Books, 1964); and Joseph R. Gusfield, *Symbolic Crusade* (Urbana: University of Illinois Press, 1963). For an early statement of the theory underlying these formulations, see Gerhard Lenski, "Status Crystallization: A Non-Vertical Dimension of Social Status," *American Sociological Review*, 19 (Aug., 1954), pp. 405–413.

the Reich.[13] Another European case involves the many middle-class Jewish ideologues, such as Karl Marx, whose financial standing was more than respectable, but whose religion set them apart.

Unfortunately, these sociological hypotheses suffer from the same difficulties encountered in our earlier discussion of the proximal politics argument. For example, there are many more people in positions of status inconsistency, particularly in an upwardly mobile, highly fluid society such as ours, than there are ideologues. Furthermore, a respectable body of sociological theory suggests that the modal response to status inconsistency and cross-pressures is withdrawal rather than activism.[14] There are, of course, many more educated men than there are political ideologues. We are forced to conclude that while this theory may provide clues to help us discover those positions in society where ideologues are most likely to cluster, it can do little more. It does not explain the existence of ideology any more than the arrival of clouds explains the consequent rain.

A third suggested explanation is also heavily sociological, though it is not so well defined as the previous two arguments examined. It may, therefore, be dealt with more rapidly. Some observers feel that while ideology in the United States and Western Europe once flourished, fed by the class antagonisms of stratified industrial societies, the age of ideology has come to a close.[15] The social basis of ideological thought has simply disintegrated under the impact of widespread affluence and the lowering of class barriers. This position may be faulted on two counts. It assumes that ideological thought was more characteristic of nineteenth-century than twentieth-century America, an assumption for which it is impossible to gain reliable evidence. But, in addition, it implies that contemporary American politics is not marked by ideological divisions. Yet we are living in a comparatively rich time for the generation of ideology. Black Power, Student Power, New Left Radicalism, and their conservative counterparts fill the news and shape the nation's politics. Furthermore, the segment of our population most indulged by our affluence—college students—has been disproportionately responsible for the development of these new ideologies. For these reasons, the end of ideology hypothesis is unpersuasive.

Finally, we may take brief note of an hypothesis which attributes the absence of large numbers of American ideologues to the American "national character."[16] Americans are alleged to be "pragmatic" people whose

[13] Daniel Lerner, *The Nazi Elite* (Stanford: Stanford University Press, 1951), p. 85.

[14] For a review and empirical test of the two theories, see Richard M. Merelman, "Intimate Environments and Political Behavior," *Midwest Journal of Political Science*, 12 (Aug., 1968), pp. 382–400. A case study of the same phenomenon is E. Franklin Frazier, *Black Bourgeoisie* (New York: Collier Books, 1962).

[15] The fullest statement of this position may be found in Daniel Bell, *The End of Ideology* (New York: Collier Books, 1961), pp. 393–407.

[16] For one of the best national character treatments of Americans, see Max Lerner, *America as a Civilization* (New York: Simon and Schuster, 1957).

instincts do not lead them into the airy realms of ideology. We can see immediately that this position is no explanation; it is, rather, another way of saying the same thing. Even if true, it does not tell us *why* Americans are the way they are. Therefore, the national character hypothesis is of no use for our discussion.

If none of these attempted explanations is sufficient, where can we turn? The answer is simple. The four arguments fail primarily because they are unable to account for the development of an ideology in some people and not in others. The key word, in this formulation, is *development*. A person must be psychologically capable of ideological thought. We must uncover and describe both those developmental patterns which produce ideologues and those which hinder the growth of ideology. Our definition of ideology tells us where to begin the search for these patterns. To become an ideologue, a person must: (1) have cognitive skills which allow him to see linkages between ideas and events. Such linkages determine the amount of constraint in his belief system. (2) Have a developed morality which allows him to evaluate consistently the ethical meanings of political events. In order, therefore, to explain the development of political ideologies, we must explore the course of cognitive and moral development. So far, this developmental process and the literature which studies it is largely uncodified and unintegrated into the study of both political science as a whole and of political socialization in particular. This omission is particularly important for the latter area, because political socialization is the branch of our discipline most concerned with human development. Indeed, as we shall see, knowledge about the development of moral and cognitive skills not only enlightens us about the question of ideology but also has broader import for the entire study of political socialization. Therefore, let us see if we can understand and describe the growth of those cognitive and moral skills which are prerequisites for ideological thought.

II. A MODEL OF IDEOLOGY FORMATION

We will begin by sketching an ideal-typical psychological development culminating in the ability to think ideologically. The pattern is characterized by a passage through a series of psychological stages. It is true that psychological theories relying upon developmental stages are subject to Bandura and Walter's criticism that "Stage theories have at best specified only vaguely the conditions that lead to changes in behavior from one level to another."[17] However deficient such theories are, their division of a complex process of growth into distinct phases does provide an unusually clear model against which real-world development may be compared.

Let us first turn to the cognitive side of ideological development. As Adelson and O'Neil put it, ". . . the growth of cognitive capacity allows *the birth of ideology* [emphasis in original]. . . . What passes for ideology in . . . younger-respondents is a raggle-taggle array of sentiments. . . . When

[17] Albert Bandura and Richard H. Walters, *Social Learning and Personality Development* (New York: Holt, Rinehart and Winston, 1963), p. 25.

younger subjects are cross-questioned, however gently, they are ready to reverse themselves even on issues they seem to feel strongly about."[18] But what are the specific components of "cognitive capacity" which become the building blocks of ideology?

One of the cognitive skills indispensable for ideological thought is the ability to think causally. In order for a political ideology to grow, the individual must be able not only to see the inter-relations of social events and personalities, but also to arrange such events and personalities in meaningful causal sequences. Otherwise, few ideas in his repertory will exhibit constraint. Second, the individual must believe that the political world is malleable, for otherwise there is no motivational basis for an activating political ideology. Finally, the person's understanding of events, his scheme of political causation, must be at least partially capable of communication to others. Developed political ideologies, such as liberalism and conservatism, are *shared*. They are based upon principles of causation which have been communicated and understood consensually. To sum up, the individual must be able to reason from cause to effect. The causes of effects in the political world must seem partially and/or potentially under human control, and the principles by which causes and effects are linked must be transmissible.

An examination of the reasoning processes of young children indicates clearly how much learning and maturation must transpire before these requirements can be met. According to Piaget and his followers, the young child is incapable of causal thought as we have described it.[19] Instead, the child reasons pre-causally until the ages of 10–13. What are the characteristics of pre-causal thought? Laurendeau and Pinard have isolated and examined four major forms of this childish reasoning: realism, artificialism, dynamism, and animism.[20]

According to Kohlberg, realism is "the confusion of subjective phenomena with objective things."[21] For example, young children who are asked the origins and spatial placement of such subjective phenomena as dreams report that "the events that occur in the dream have an origin external to the dreamer and also take place in front of him. . . ."[22] The child does not understand that he has created the objects he sees in the dream. The im-

---

[18]Joseph Adelson and Robert P. O'Neil, "The Growth of Political Ideas in Adolescence: The Sense of Community," unpublished, n. d., p. 29.
[19]The most important sources for this aspect of Piaget's thought are Barbel Inhelder and Jean Piaget, *The Growth of Logical Thinking*, trans. Anne Parsons and Stanley Milgram (New York: Basic Books, 1958); and Jean Piaget, *The Language and Thought of the Child* (Cleveland and New York: Meridian Books, 1955). For an extensive review of the pertinent literature and a helpful bibliography, see Monique Laurendeau and Adrien Pinard, *Causal Thinking in the Child* (New York: International Universities Press, 1962), Chaps. 1–4.
[20]*Causal Thinking in the Child.*
[21]Lawrence Kohlberg, "The Development of Children's Orientations Toward a Moral Order: I. Sequence in the Development of Moral Thought," *Vita Humana*, 6 (1963), pp. 11–38, 18.
[22]Laurendeau and Pinard, *Causal Thinking in the Child*, p. 107.

plications of this thought process are important. Because every child has a
somewhat idiosyncratic subjective world, each child also has a different
"real" world. Therefore, children are unable to communicate consensually
enough to develop shared ideologies. Furthermore, because all phenomena
are viewed as objective, the child finds it difficult to realize that some events
need not be imposed upon him. He has no sense of the effects his own
efforts or his own ideas might have on the world. Because it is unalterable
by human effort, the world has no place for the judgments that human
beings might make to change it.

In addition, the child attributes much natural and social phenomena to
artifical and supernatural, hence unalterable, forces. For example, the child
explains that the coming of night is not a natural, but a supernatural process.[23] The child also states that the clouds are pushed by God.[24] Unseen
supernatural forces with human-like personalities manipulate the world.
This childish attribution of causation to supernatural forces functions to
remove many matters of choice from human control and to render the construction of a political ideology virtually impossible. Furthermore, inevitably, complex interactions of events are reduced to short and distorted
sequences. The many subtleties of the transition from day to night are
eliminated by invoking a personalized supernatural actor.

But the child is inconsistent. Laurendeau and Pinard also report that children often consider the movement of inorganic objects to be self-generat-
ing.[25] Why? Because movement or dynamism is taken as a sign of life.
Therefore, when objects change their state, they are either directly pro-
pelled by God or by their own unregulated desires. Causation is either
wholly supernatural or wholly personal. It is never natural or social. Even
some college students mistake the movement of an object for a sign of life.
Dennis found that many college students in his sample believed that the sea
is a living organism because it moves.[26] A belief in the personal autonomy
of objects and individuals except when they are subject to God's will is incompatible with the knowledge that political processes can alter events.

The unifying and summarizing principle of these pre-causal tendencies
may be called *animism*, the tendency for the child to explain all things an-
thropomorphically. As Laurendeau and Pinard explain, the child attributes
some form of life to virtually all phenomena.[27] Even inanimate objects have
unique personalities which are peculiarly free of physical limitations or
laws. Furthermore, his beliefs about the behavior of individuals become the
child's tools for explaining the actions of social institutions. Adelson and
O'Neil note that young children, unable to conceptualize such impersonal
terms as "government" and "society," reduce such abstractions to imagi-

[23] *Ibid.*, p. 161.
[24] *Ibid.*, pp. 188–192.
[25] *Ibid.*, pp. 192–196.
[26] Wayne Dennis, "Animistic Thinking Among College and University Students,"
Scientific Monthly, 76 (April, 1953), pp. 247–249. Other sources cited therein and in
Laurendeau and Pinard are particularly useful on this topic.
[27] Laurendeau and Pinard, *Causal Thinking in the Child*, Chap. 9.

nary persons able to determine their own destinies.[28] In a world in which people and things are either entirely free or entirely subjected to divine control, no intervention based on personal conviction or understanding is possible. There are no natural or social cause-effect linkages. Consequently, there exists no cognitive base on which political ideologies can be constructed.

Pre-causal thought in the child is accompanied by what Piaget calls "egocentrism." As Piaget describes it, childish egocentrism takes two interrelated forms, personal and logical. Personal egocentrism is well illustrated by Piaget's description of childhood argumentation. The younger the child involved in debate, the more likely he is merely to assert and reassert his own position. Rarely does he confront and deal with the views of his opponent. Nor does he attempt to prove his own contentions or to probe his opponent's logic. The child is encased in his own world.[29] Such egocentrism in discussion may be traced to an even earlier tendency. Piaget observes that very young children go through a prolonged period of egocentric play and speech before any habits of cooperation arise. Although several children may be playing in the same area with the same toys, they generally remain relatively unconscious of each other. Nor are they able or disposed to adopt a common play pattern.[30] The expectation of cooperation, of abiding by rules of conduct, and of observing rules of thought is slow in arriving. Childhood play, talk, and debate are variants of a single monologue.

Egocentric logic is defined by Piaget in the following way:

> Egocentric logic is more intuitive, more "syncretistic" than deductive, i.e., its reasoning is not made explicit. The mind leaps from premise to conclusion at a single bound, without stopping on the way. . . . Little value is attached to proving, or even checking propositions. The vision of the whole brings about a state of belief and a feeling of security far more rapidly than if each step in the argument were made explicit. . . . Personal schemas of analogy are made use of. . . . Visual schemas also play an important part.[31]

In short, the child intuits the meaning of things without ever laying bare to others or to himself the principles by which his meanings are derived. It is, therefore, not surprising that he should make the sorts of logical and causal errors which hinder the development of political ideologies. Furthermore, his personal egocentrism prevents him from gaining consensual validation for his logic, faulty though it be. His thought, consequently, remains unexamined, defective, and idiosyncratic.

To be capable of ideological thought the child must surmount egocentrism and pre-causality. He must develop a consensually validated sense of logic and an ability to reason from social cause to social effect. Furthermore, growing ideologically necessitates his recognition that the world of human

[28] Adelson and O'Neil, "The Growth of Political Ideas in Adolescence," pp. 8–9.

[29] Piaget, *The Language and Thought of the Child*, pp. 45–46.

[30] Jean Piaget, *The Moral Judgment of the Child* (New York: Free Press of Glencoe, 1965), p. 45.

[31] Piaget, *The Language and Thought of the Child*, p. 66.

events is contingent on the behavior of men and social forces, neither of which is entirely beyond human control. Beacuse the earliest stages of human thought are not conducive to such ideological development, it seems fair to speculate, accepting the Freudian position on the psychological dominance of earliest modes of thought, that adult political ideologies always rest on an unstable base. We shall explore the implications of this conclusion shortly.

Many of the principles of cognitive development which we have described apply, with some modifications, to the course of moral development. While in the area of cognition the child views the world as given and unalterable by human intervention, in the moral realm he finds it impossible to account for the origins of rules, regulations, or moral standards except by reference to history. When, for example, Piaget asked his youthful subjects to explain the origins of the rules which govern the game of marbles, the children replied that the rules had existed from time immemorial and were simply passed on unchanged from one generation to the next. The children could not imagine the possibility of their or anyone else's changing the rules.[32] It is easy to see what function is performed by attributing all rules and judgments to historical figures or processes. The rules, having weathered the test of time and having been sanctified by parental transmission, need not be questioned. Therefore, there exists no impulse to the formulation of political ideologies.

Because the moral standards which govern the world are given, he who violates them, regardless of motivation, is guilty. Young children evaluate rule-breaking primarily in terms of the objective material effects of violation, rather than in terms of the motivation of the law-breaker or his relation to the law. It is the degree of injury done, not the motivation of the law-breaker or the facts of the case, which determines the extent of punishment. The world is viewed as a sort of moral machine in delicate equilibrium which, if disturbed, must be set right by the proper amount of retribution and expiation. "An eye for an eye" is the principle which insures the moral order of the world.[33]

But how is this tribute to be exacted? Again, we find in the child's answer to this question a method of removing from human agencies the necessity to make a choice and justify the choice one made. Human beings do not exercise retribution; rather, the rules themselves and the objects which they protect become the agents of punishment. The child's credo is "immanent justice," which may be defined as a belief in "the existence of automatic punishments which emanate from things themselves."[34] Piaget, for example, discovered that children explained accidents to people who had earlier violated a rule by attributing the accident to the violation.[35] All

[32] Piaget, *The Moral Judgment of the Child*, pp. 50–65.
[33] It is this tendency on the part of the child which Piaget has labeled "moral realism." *Ibid.*, pp. 109–197.
[34] *Ibid.*, p. 251.
[35] *Ibid.*, pp. 251–263.

disruptions of the law produce their own remedies, much as in classical Greek tragedy the Furies seek out and punish any man who presumes to challenge the natural order. The child is a great *aficionado* of the "deus ex machina."

This view of the moral world, which lifts the burden of choice from the child, is based upon a belief that laws and moral codes are objective.[36] The child conceives that moral regulations are set down clearly and unalterably within the world itself and, further, are understood consensually by all. There can be no conflict of interpretation nor failure of understanding. Therefore, if an individual violates the law he cannot defend himself by citing mitigating or idiosyncratic circumstances. The child has no sense of the relationship between his own mind and the law, nor does he see that rules are the creation of individuals and, therefore, can be modified by individuals.

It may be conjectured that the child's belief in the invariance and immanent justice of the moral order is caused by his total dependence on his parents. The human child is much more dependent on parents for a longer time than are the offspring of other species. In some primitive way, the child may compensate for this vulnerability by proclaiming the ultimate rectitude of those who control him and who are, at the same time, the symbols of history and rules—his parents. This universal tendency may become exaggerated, however. Piaget postulates that the child's natural glorification of history may be reinforced by parental resort to arbitrary commands.[37] I shall have more to say about this problem momentarily.

As maturation proceeds, the child emerges from his early conception of morality. He acquires a more subjective, more contingent view of rules, morality, and transgression. This new position requires him both to investigate the motives of those who do not conform to the law and to vary his judgments accordingly. His early emphasis on punishment is replaced by a consideration of equity. Retribution and expiation give way to distributive justice. By adolescence rules are accepted only in relation to the purposes for which they are intended. For example, the adolescent understands that the rules which govern the game of marbles can be manipulated for the transitory enjoyment of the players.[38] Curiously enough, this transition may be illustrated especially well by the deviant case of psychopaths. Stephenson discovered that adolescent psychopaths, who had obviously been retarded in development, were actually *more* punitive in their judgments of other people's transgressions than were normal adolescents.[39]

Not only does the child develop a relativistic sense of morality, but he

---

[36] *Ibid.*, pp. 121–163.

[37] *Ibid.*, pp. 101–197. For a recent attempt to test this hypothesis in the area of childhood attitudes about political authorities, see Dean Jaros, "Children's Orientations Toward the President: Some Additional Theoretical Considerations and Data," *Jouranl of Politics*, 29 (May, 1967), pp. 368–388.

[38] Piaget, *The Moral Judgment of The Child* p. 83.

[39] Geoffrey M. Stephenson, *The Development of Conscience* (London: Routledge and Kegan Paul, 1966), p. 43.

also gradually internalizes his own moral norms. The apparent inconsistency between these two processes can be dispelled quickly. The child's reliance upon sacred authority or history as the source of morality and rules, coupled with his belief that moral standards are automatically enforced, relieves him of any need to develop a conscience of his own. Conscience, on the other hand, grows only when the child desires an internal compass for the evaluation of a newly complex, contingent world. Indeed, the child's early belief in the external regulation of the moral order actually frees him to indulge in erratic behavior and inconsistent judgment. As Piaget reports, echoing Converse's observations about the political statements of non-ideologues, "It may even happen that one and the same child judges sometimes one way, sometimes the other."[40] Because the world is itself reliable and can substitute its own controls, the child does not need the judgmental consistency which conscience provides him. But once the world is seen as morally contingent and risky, the child must formulate his own rules and be able to defend them against other people's standards. The child thus moves from a "punishment and obedience orientation" to a "morality of individual principles of conscience."[41]

Cognitive and moral development are closely linked. Cognitive growth produces the realization that there are controllable human and social forces which have effects. Neither willful inanimate objects nor an invariant divine order determines the character of events. These discoveries enable the child to recognize the existence of moral variety and situational contingency. In turn, these latter realizations provide the impulse for the development of his own moral standards. On the other hand, the child's new-found desire to internalize his own sense of morality motivates him to inquire into the actual causal structure of events. Before he can make his own judgments about human behavior, he must understand the motivations and social forces which underlie that behavior. Therefore, the development of cognitive skills and the construction of a conscience are reinforcing processes. Laying the groundwork for ideology is all of a piece.[42]

As the citations in this section indicate, much of the theory upon which we have based our description of cognitive and moral development is trace-

---

[40] Piaget, *The Language and Thought of the Child*, p. 91.
[41] Kohlberg, "The Development of Children's Orientations," pp. 13–14.
[42] Parenthetically, it is striking the extent to which the development of the child, as outlined in this theory, resembles historical developments over whole eras. For example, we have talked much about the child's shift from an external, but wholly dictatorial form of morality to an internalized conscience. This shift seems to parallel what many scholars believe to be the difference between late Old Testament Judaism and early Christianity. Many scholars have commented upon the emphasis on legalism and expiation in Old Testament Judaism, and the disintegration of codification thereafter. We have no wish to argue seriously that ontogeny does recapitulate phylogeny. We only wish to indicate the parallelism. The young child's belief in ritualism, supernaturalism, the deus ex machina, etc., remind one, however, of the thought processes of "primitive" people. To develop this argument so as to make it more palatable to the reader would require knowledge and space not available to the author. The general idea seems worth pursuing, however.

able to Jean Piaget.[43] Before leaving this discussion, therefore, it is important to point out briefly some of the shortcomings of the Piagetian stage-developmental approach. A number of criticisms have been leveled at Piaget's theories and, as a result, some important modifications have already been or are in the process of being made.

Students of child development since Piaget have become well aware of his methodological errors. His theories, which he describes as being universally applicable, are now known to suffer from cultural bias.[44] In addition, not only are his samples all Swiss, but they overrepresent the working class.[45] Nor are their sizes sufficient to generate much confidence.

There is also uncertainty about the fate of those stages through which the child has passed. Some authors hold that new stages replace and erase old, while other authors, such as Sullivan,[46] contend that new stages are terraced on old. If this latter conception is true, no stage would ever be entirely surmounted. Earlier stages would simply remain in a latent form, capable of reinstated impact under special conditions. Piaget was himself inconsistent in his formulations on the subject. At some points he implies that early stages crumble entirely under advanced phases of development, while at other times he argues that stages are only statistical tendencies and never disappear entirely.[47] The implications of this ambiguity will concern us shortly.

There is, finally, much uncertainty about the relative importance of genetic and environmental factors in Piaget's developmental scheme. Piaget attempts to recognize the importance of environment. He argues that aging forces the child into increasingly demanding social relationships, and it is these relationships which are the major intervening variables in the developmental process.[48] But he assumes that the social relationships themselves are constant at every level for every child. Such an argument implies that *all*

---

[43] Piaget's immense corpus of work is only now having a major impact in the United States. For an enjoyable introduction to his thought, see David Elkind, "Giant in the Nursery–Jean Piaget," *New York Times Magazine*, May 26, 1968.

[44] See Urie Bronfenbrenner, "The Role of Age, Sex, Class, and Culture in Studies of Moral Development," *Religious Education* (Research Supplement), 62 (July–Aug., 1962), pp. S-3, S-5, S-18. For contrasts between American and English children, see E. M. and M. Eppel, *Adolescents and Morality* (London: Routledge and Kegan Paul, 1966), pp. 157–170. For interesting comparative studies on Senegalese children, see Jerome S. Brunner, *et. al.*, *Studies in Cognitive Growth* (New York: John Wiley and Sons, 1966), Chaps. 11–13. A well-known study which also indicates Piaget's cultural bias is Gustav Jahoda, "Children's Concepts of Nationality: A Critical Study of Piaget's Stages," *Child Development*, 35 (Dec., 1964), pp. 1081–1092.

[45] Bronfenbrenner, "The Role of Age, Sex, Class." For the first empirical study to touch this deficiency, see M. R. Harrower, "Social Status and Moral Development," *British Journal of Educational Psychology*, 5 (1935), pp. 75–95.

[46] For an overview of Sullivan's work, see Patrick Mullahy, ed., *The Contributions of Harry Stack Sullivan* (New York: Hermitage House, 1952), Chaps. 1–2.

[47] For example, Piaget sets only a percentage boundary on thought categories; he also admits that a particular child may evidence thought characteristic of a variety of levels at once. Piaget, *The Moral Judgment of the Child, passim.*

[48] *Ibid.*, Chap. 3.

children, excluding those who have physical and mental defects, should, as adults, manifest similar levels of cognitive and moral development. To accept such a contention would be to undercut the major theoretical problem of this article, the widespread absence of ideology. In fact, of course, adults have widely different patterns of cognition and morality. Therefore, they evidence disparate capacities for ideological thought. Piaget's theory is probably understood best as an ideal type. People must pass through the stages he describes if they are to think ideologically, but most people do not succeed in making the passage. What are the factors which determine whether the process will be completed or not? It is these intervening factors, responsible for inhibiting the maturation process and producing different levels of ideological development, to which we now turn.

III. FACTORS PRODUCING DIFFERENT LEVELS OF IDEOLOGICAL
DEVELOPMENT

The major factors which affect the course of ideological development are of two sorts: those relevant to identification and child-rearing practices, and those involving the many and complex components of morality and cognition. We will investigate each sort in turn.

Of course, both psychological and psychoanalytic theory have long focused on the character of a child's identification with his parents. Theories about the identification process would not be germane to this paper, however, were it not for evidence indicating a link between positive identification and the development of moral and cognitive skills.[49] It now appears that a positive form of identification encourages the growth of political ideology.[50]

Suggestive recent evidence indicating the inter-relationships of identification and ideological development may be found by turning to Keniston's studies of college students. Keniston reports that his alienated and politically apathetic Harvard students felt themselves to be rebelling against their parents and, particularly, struggling to surmount the demands placed on them by their mothers.[51] Elsewhere, Keniston discovers that the major-

[49] See the review and codification of the relevant literature in Robert F. Winch, *Identification and Its Familial Determinants* (Indianapolis: Bobbs-Merrill, 1962).

[50] This formulation should not be taken to imply that identification has an unambiguous meaning. Lazowick, for example, has specified at least three major definitions which seem currently in use: (1) acting as if the subject were the same person as his model; (2) imitating the model; (3) introjecting the model's norms and values. Lionel M. Lazowick, "On the Nature of Identification," *Journal of Abnormal and Social Psychology*, 51 (Sept., 1955), pp. 175–184, 175–176. Bronfenbrenner specifies yet a fourth meaning, i.e., acting in terms of an ideal image of the model rather than on the basis of his actual behavior. Urie Bronfenbrenner, "The Study of Identification through Interpersonal Perception," in Renato Tagiuri and Luigi Petrullo, eds., *Person Perception and Interpersonal Behavior* (Standford: Stanford University Press, 1958), pp. 110–131, 123. Despite their importance for psychology, these definitional ambiguities do not affect the basic argument of this paper.

[51] Kenneth Keniston, *The Uncommitted: Alienated Youth in American Society* (New York: Harcourt, Brace and World, 1965), Chap. 6.

ity of campus activists identify strongly with parental authority.[52] He finds that activists are not only more likely than the other students to respect their parents, but also generally enjoy the support of their parents in their political activities. Lipset and Altbach claim that most campus activists are actually following a line of political activity gratefully in imitation of their parents.[53] Clearly, therefore, close identification with parents, at least for these primarily middle-class students, forges an important link in the chain of ideological development.

We know that the structure of the family affects the likelihood of successful identification. There is considerable evidence which indicates, for example, that the children of husbands and wives who value the same things are more likely than are other children to identify with their parents.[54] This finding is easily interpretable. It is unlikely that there will be much tension in homes where the parents approve of each other. Furthermore, parents who profess the same values will present a fairly consistent picture of themselves to their children, and will also display a single set of ideals for emulation. In short, parents who approve of each other minimize cognitive and moral confusion in their children.

Unfortunately, however, the effects of most family structure characteristics on identification remain obscure. This is true particularly of such factors as father absence.[55] Consensus comes nearest to existing only on the matter of child-rearing patterns as they affect identification.

Within the bounds of psychological theory there have been two major schools of thought about patterns of child rearing in the identification process. One school, populated largely by Freudians, has postulated that identification is the result of a childhood defensive reaction against a highly punitive and physical parental environment. The child, supposedly fearing his severe parents, fantasizes himself retaliating against them. But his retaliation fantasies, because they would bring abnormally severe retribution if acted out, are even more disturbing than the parental environment itself. Therefore, the child tries to repress his rebellion. But his repression can

[52]Kenneth Keniston, *Young Radicals* (New York: Harcourt, Brace and World, 1968), Chap. 2.

[53]Seymour Martin Lipset and Philip G. Altbach. "Student Politics and Higher Education in the United States," in Seymour Martin Lipset, ed., *Student Politics* (New York: Basic Books, 1967), pp. 199–252, 216.

[54]John A. Clausen, "Family Structure, Socialization, and Personality," in Lois W. and Martin L. Hoffman, eds., *Review of Child Development Research*, Vol. 2 (New York: Russell Sage Foundation, 1966), pp. 1–55, 42.

[55]For concise statements of opposing positions, see Winch, *Identification and Its Familial Determinants*, p. 35, and Joan McCord, William McCord, and Emily Thurber, "Some Effects of Paternal Absence on Male Children," in Robert E. Grinder, ed., *Studies in Adolescence* (New York: Macmillan, 1963), pp. 118–133. For studies indicating the possible importance of father absence to both identification and political ideology, see Keniston, *The Uncommitted*, esp. pp. 113–118; and Dean Jaros, Herbert Hirsch, and Frederic J. Fleron, Jr., "The Malevolent Leader: Political Socialization in an American Sub-Culture," *American Political Science Review*, 62 (June, 1968), 564–578, 573.

succeed only if he internalizes the values of his parents. The process ends with the child identifying with the aggressors, his parents.[56]

Anaclitic theories of identification, which comprise the second school, dispute the truth of these assertions. According to the anaclitic theorists, successful identification is most likely to occur in a warm, tightly knit, relatively permissive family atmosphere. Discipline in such a family proceeds primarily through threats to withdraw love rather than through the imposition of physical sanctions. Anaclitic theorists claim that love and succor encourage the child to reflect on his own behavior and internalize those standards which will prevent withdrawal. Also, according to Hoffman, parents who do not punish their child physically provide him with a model of restraint that he is motivated to emulate.[57] The behavior of parents who discipline by physical aggression, however, encourages the child to believe that internal controls are unnecessary. Therefore, physical sanctions actually encourage rebellion. Anaclitic theorists also claim that physical punishment breeds the primitive, expiatory form of morality which we have described, rather than an internalized set of values.

Students of identification also differ over the autonomy-supervison dimension in child rearing. Theorists of defensive identification argue that the imposition of close parental supervision is necessary for the growth of identification. The anaclitic theorist Robert Sears claims, however, that identification is dependent upon parental willingness to grant the child a measure of autonomy to develop his own personality.[58] The child must be expected to adhere to certain standards, but the parent should not remain hovering over him monitoring his behavior and correcting minor faults.

As the debate indicates, interpreting the effects of varying child-rearing patterns on identification has not been easy. Nor has the dialogue been as clear on terms and hypotheses as one might desire. For example, the control relationship between parent and child—as most parents and virtually all children realize—is both multi-dimensional and subtle. A parent who is demanding in one phase of his child's life may be premissive or uninterested entirely in another. Measures of identification and control capable of dealing with these subtleties have been noticeable mainly by their absence. Not surprisingly, therefore, research linking child-rearing practices to identification is not entirely consistent or reliable. However, there seems to be a growing consensus along three dimensions. These dimensions are the mode of punishing children, the warmth of the relationship between parent and child, and the age at which responsible behavior on the part of the child is first expected. Let us investigate these three dimensions as they affect identification, cognitive development, and moral development.

[56] Morton Deutsch and Robert M. Krauss, *Theories in Social Psychology* (New York: Basic Books, 1965), p. 158.

[57] For a review of these theories, see Martin L. Hoffman, "The Role of the Parent in the Child's Moral Growth," *Religious Education* (Research Supplement), 57 (July–Aug., 1962), pp. S-18 through S-33, S-22.

[58] Robert R. Sears, "Identification as a Form of Behavioral Development," in Dale B. Harris, ed., *The Concept of Development* (Minneapolis: University of Minnesota Press, 1957), pp. 149–162, 160.

As Hoffman puts it, summarizing the research on punishment and moral development, "The relatively frequent use of discipline that makes some sort of appeal to the child's inner need seems to foster the development of an internalized moral orientation, especially as reflected in the child's reactions to his own transgressions. The use of coercive measures that openly confront the child with the parent's power, on the other hand, apparently contributes to a moral orientation based on the fear of authority."[59] According to available evidence, the parent who resorts to physical punishment not only provides an aggressive model for his child, but also demonstrates vividly to him the unbridgeable gulf between his own standards and those of the child. Such a parent makes no appeal to the child's own latent moral sense. The use of psychological punishment, such as threatened love-withdrawal, assumes a standard shared equally by the child and his parents. Such a technique accustoms the child to think through and judge the behavior which has disappointed his parents. Physical sanctions also appear to suggest to the child that merely his willingness to absorb pain provides an expiation for wrongdoing. Moral rectitude does not require his own set of values. The child who is, implicitly, treated as an adult temporarily unable to meet shared standards learns to evaluate himself; but the child who is not taken into his parents' confidence and who is punished physically begins to expect society to judge him. An internalized conscience, obviously, is the moral base from which ideological preferences grow. Reliance on external authorities to define what is proper builds no stable moral framework within which political events can be arrayed.

There is also evidence that parental warmth toward children stimulates the growth of a consistent, internalized moral orientation.[60] Of course, an affectionate environment may be viewed partly as an off-shoot of certain discipline techniques, but the warmth of family relationships seems to have its own independent effect. The same principles operating in the punishment dimension seem to obtain here. In addition, however, unlike the children of punitive and distant parents, the children of affectionate parents have good reason to feel conflicted about violating parental standards. The kindness of parents may well seem to demand better repayment. Tensions of this kind may force children to evaluate their own behavior carefully. The habit of self-evaluation is certainly a major requirement for the growth of a stable, internalized moral orientation.

Finally, the time at which responsibility is first expected of the child seems related to the growth of a moral sense. Studies by Grinder[61] and by Whiting and Child[62] show that the child s early assumption of responsibility results in a propensity to feel guilt and to experience remorse after transgression. The principle may be illustrated simply. When, for example, the

[59] Hoffman, "The Role of the Parent," p. S-24.
[60] Ibid, p. S-25.
[61] Robert E. Grinder, "Parental Child-Rearing Practices, Conscience, and Resistance to Temptation of Sixth-Grade Children," Child Development, 33 (Dec., 1962), pp. 803–820.
[62] John W. M. Whiting and Irvin L. Child, Child Training and Personality (New Haven: Yale University Press, 1953), pp. 254–258.

child is given early responsibility for his own toilet and cleanliness, he is, in effect, on notice that he is to be held responsible for an important part of his behavior. This sense of responsibility encourages him to make autonomous decisions and to think for himself.

To sum up, the optimal child-rearing pattern for the growth of conscience appears to combine rapid shouldering of responsibility, the use of psychological discipline, and continuing parental warmth. This pattern is found rarely, with two factors primarily responsible. First, many parents believe that warmth, affection, and "permissiveness" are incompatible with the child's early assumption of responsibilities. They construe permissiveness broadly so as to make it require late and relatively lax training in fundamental areas. Second, many parents who do attempt early toilet training find it difficult to remain affectionate toward their children when errors occur. Their punitive response often sets a continuing pattern. Hence, early training may well become associated with physical punishment, relatively cold parent-child relations, and considerable anxiety on all sides.

We have less evidence about the effects of differing child-rearing styles on the growth of cognitive capabilities than we have of their influence on moral development. However, some experimental findings permit speculation. Solley and Murphy report that punishment by the use of electric shock disrupts the ability of experimental subjects to distinguish between figure and ground.[63] Such findings suggest that large doses of physical punishment may disorient the conceptual apparatus which permits the individual to make the elementary perceptual distinctions necessary for ideological thought. Physical punishment concentrates the subject's mind on only those of his acts which have painful consequences, thereby depriving him of varied sensory stimulation. The subject focuses primarily on his suffering, rather than on the world around him. This sensory deprivation effect may be thought of as a kind of psychological "tunnel vision." As Solley and Murphy indicate, sensory deprivation may become associated with autism, the pathological rejection of environmental stimuli.[64] The autistic person finds the world dull, undifferentiated, and ultimately, unworthy of attention. In short, the excessive use of physical punishment may reduce both the desire and the ability to view the outer world in all its richness. In nonexperimental contexts, such as concentration camps, observers have noted similar effects.[65] The relevance of this discussion both to child rearing and to the growth of ideological thought needs no elaboration.

We referred earlier to the debate over whether child development proceeds via a substitution of entirely new phases for old or by a terracing of new stages over latently powerful older, more "primitive" stages. If we assume that the former process operates, non-adoption of the optimum child-rearing process we have described may fixate the child at a particular

[63]Charles M. Solley and Gardner Murphy, *Development of the Perceptual World* (New York: Basic Books, 1960), p. 274.

[64]*Ibid.*, p. 62.

[65]Bruno Bettleheim, "Individual and Mass Behavior in Extreme Situations," *Journal of Abnormal and Social Psychology*, 38 (1943), pp. 417–452.

stage of development. But if we assume that development proceeds regardless, imposition of punishment or threat may still cause at least temporary regression to a more primitive behavioral stage. In the latter case, we would also expect that an adult whose early development had been disrupted by faulty child rearing would be especially prone to regress under imposition of punishments identical or symbolically equivalent to those he experienced as a child. Experiments on both humans and lower animals provide some interesting illustrations.[66]

Let us examine the fixation effect first. Kleemier reports that rats who have been frustrated by the use of electric shock develop severe response rigidity. Not only do they find it difficult to respond to new demands, but even after shock is removed so as to open up new options, the rats cleave to old behavioral patterns which will not reward them.[67] Frustration induced by severe punishment glues them to a particular developmental level. Comparable behavioral and perceptual rigidity in humans would cut down the range of attention necessary to interpret the political world ideologically.

Frustration, no matter what its source, has its own fixation properties. Maier reports on a variety of experiments which indicate that frustrated rats and humans settle on a few patterns of behavior, often the ones least functional, and remain with them. Rats, for example, resort to "symbol stereotypy," an invariant but unrewarded response to a specific sign.[68] Their behavior becomes almost purely ritualistic. Lawson and Marx show that frustration retards perceptual acuity, problem solving abilities, and learning.[69] In short, both excessive physical punishment and frustration rigidify behavior and retard cognitive development. These effects persist even after the cessation of frustration and physical punishment. They inhibit the growth of an ideological framework responsive and alert to new pieces of information [70]

The psychodynamic process by which fixation occurs may have as its core the experience of anxiety. Sullivan, for one, believes that the onset of anxiety can be traced either to psychological distance from the mother or to excessive punishment. He also claims that anxiety inhibits moral and cog-

---

[66] Some may question this introduction of data drawn from studies conducted on lower animals. I have used this material not because I think it definitive (I would not even argue the point), but precisely because it is illustrative. Were I to attempt a definitive argument on this point, I would naturally rely wholly on studies of humans. It is, however, possible that the same reactions which exhibit themselves in purity with lower animals also occur in humans, but are masked or distorted. We ought not to assume that the responses of lower animals and humans are incomparable. They may be different in expression, but not in substance.

[67] Robert Kleemier, "Fixation and Regression in the Rat," *Psychological Monographs*, 54, No. 4, Whole No. 246 (1942), p. 13.

[68] Norman R. F. Maier, *Frustration: The Study of Behavior Without a Goal* (Ann Arbor: Ann Arbor Paperbacks, 1961), p. 28.

[69] Reed Lawson and Melvin H. Marx, "Frustration: Theory and Experiment," *Genetic Psychology Monographs*, 57 (March, 1958), pp. 393–464, 437.

[70] I do not contend that psychological modes of punishment may not be frustrating. But physical intervention to block desired behavior probably is more frustrating than psychological intervention.

nitive development.[71] Odier describes the close relationship between the experience of anxiety and consequent primitive, magical, and animistic interpretations of events.[72] The obsessive, repetitive, ritualistic thought patterns of anxious people are similar to, though more elaborate than, the early forms of thought in the child as Piaget and his followers have described them.

If we prefer the terracing rather than the substitution theory of development, we can also marshal illustrative evidence showing that frustration, physical punishment, and anxiety may cause behavior to regress, at least temporarily, to a primitive stage. In a famous experiment, Barker, Dembo, and Lewis found that children who were permitted to see but were forcibly prevented from playing a second time with some desirable toys regressed. Specifically, their behavior became disorganized and their physical movements undifferentiated.[73] Barthol and Ku demonstrated that college students reacted to task-induced frustration by returning to their first learned successful task behavior, even when such behavior was no longer appropriate.[74] Adelson and O'Neil discovered that when children became angry or anxious, there was a momentary cognitive regression, expressing itself in a loss of abstractness, and a reversion to personalized modes of discourse."[75] The terracing theory would predict that even persons normally capable of expressing a political ideology would, under stress, regress cognitively and morally, becoming at least temporarily unable to think ideologically. Any such reversion, as Odier points out, is likely to be characterized by special attention to the symbolic aspects of experience rather than to the factual, by a disposition to make absolute, rather than contingent, judgments about events, and by a willingness to rely heavily upon supernatural "signs."[76]

To sum up, the frustrations and anxieties which inadequate child-rearing methods produce may inhibit the identification process and prevent the growth of cognitive and evaluational skills sufficient for the development of political ideology. Furthermore, the imposition of excessive physical punishment and frustration on normally ideological people may induce a regression to less ideological conceptual frameworks. These remarks have obvious

[71] Mullahy, *The Contributions of Harry Stock Sullivan*, p. 34.

[72] Charles Odier, *Anxiety and Magic Thinking*, trans., Marie-Louise Schoelly and Mary Jane Sherfey (New York: International Universities Press, 1956), pp. 52–53. Odier's work is one of the few attempts to bring together Piaget's and Freud's perspectives on human development.

[73] R. F. Barker, T. Dembo, and K. Lewin, "Frustration and Regression: An Experiment with Young Children," *University of Iowa Studies in Child Welfare*, 18 (1941). For a re-analysis of this experiment, see John M. Davis, "A Reinterpretation of the Barker, Dembo, and Lewin Study of Frustration and Regression," *Child Development*, 29 (Dec., 1958), pp. 503–506.

[74] Richard P. Barthol and Nani D. Ku, "Regression Under Stress to First Learned Behavior," *Journal of Abnormal and Social Psychology*, 59 (July, 1959), pp. 134–136.

[75] Adelson and O'Neil, "The Growth of Political Ideas in Adolescence," p. 10.

[76] Odier, *Anxiety and Magic Thinking*, pp. 48–49.

implications for understanding the paranoiac and disorganized behavior of individuals during political crises.[77]

The second class of variables which influences ideological development includes the components of the moral and cognitive dimensions themselves. Two such components are the sense of time and the ability to handle language. To think ideologically requires the capacity to link present trends to preferred future states or past experiences. Therefore, the character of political cognition is partly determined by the experience of time. Although little is known about the development and stability of the consciousness of time, Ames discovered that the younger the child, the less likely he is to have a conception either of past or future.[78] The very young child lives in an eternal present, attaining a sense of future by age three and a sense of past only by age three and a half.[79] The most natural and earliest mode of viewing the world is in the present. Child-rearing patterns which fixate or cause regression might restrict the child to the incomplete experience of time evident in the early months of life. The effects of traumatic events may alter even the adult's consciousness of time.

Nor is the sense of time important only for cognition. Mischel discovered that children who prefer immediate small reinforcements to delayed larger reinforcements, when compared to children with an expanded time orientation, scored extremely low on a scale of social responsibility.[80] Grim, Kohlberg and White claim that ". . . there is substantial evidence relating indexes of moral character to ego-strength factors such as . . . anticipation of future events. . . ."[81]

We would also expect to find in language a second cognitive component relevant to ideological thought. Traditionally, and Ames seconds this conclusion,[82] we have assumed that children first use language concretely and then abstractly. If this were true, we might postulate that the abstract language ability necessary for ideological thought rests on as unstable a developmental base as does the sense of time. However, Roger Brown disputes Ames' position by arguing that, "The child's vocabulary is more immediately determined by the naming practices of adults."[83] In some cases, as Brown shows, language development may proceed from abstract conceptions to more precise differentiations within such conceptions. At

[77]The most spectacular tendency involved is, of course, scapegoating.

[78]Louise Bates Ames, "The Development of the Sense of Time in the Young Child," *Journal of Genetic Psychology*, 68, First Half (March, 1946), pp. 97–125, 110.

[79]*Ibid.*

[80]Walter Mischel, "Preference for Delayed Reinforcement and Social Responsibility," *Journal of Abnormal and Social Psychology*, 62 (Jan., 1961), pp. 1–8.

[81]Paul F. Grim, Lawrence Kohlberg, and Sheldon H. White, "Some Relationships Between Conscience and Attentional Processes," *Journal of Personality and Social Psychology*, 8 (1968), pp. 239–252, 239.

[82]Ames, "The Development of the Sense of Time," p. 115.

[83]Roger Brown, "How Shall a Thing Be Called?" in Robert J. C. Harper, et al., eds., *The Cognitive Process: Readings* (Englewood Cliffs: Prentice-Hall, 1964), pp. 647–655, 651.

present it only seems safe to conclude, with Brown, that "The vocabulary of a child is not a very direct index of his cognitive preferences."[84] Language development may be sufficiently idiosyncratic to defy generalizations about its relation to ideological thought.

While cognitive and moral development depend on a complete sense of time and an ability to abstract, the actual character of cognitive and moral judgments presents its own problems. Let us use as an example the development of morality, about which we have expended so much effort. Piaget assumed that morality was a uni-dimensional quality which could be measured accurately by asking children about their likely behavior in situations which presumably tempted them to violate their sense of rightness. However, verbal responses to hypothetical temptations expose only one aspect of the moral sense. Investigators of moral development have utilized at least three other designs. Some researchers have examined the actual behavior of children in situations where they have been tempted to violate moral injunctions. The earliest and most influential studies of this sort were conducted by Hartshorne and his associates.[85] Other researchers have investigated the extent to which children express guilt after transgression. Yet others have asked children to imagine their likely reactions to hypothetical situations in which they are supposed to have transgressed.

Interestingly enough, MacRae shows that inter-correlations along these four dimensions are far from perfect.[86] Consequently, there is reason to believe that conscience is a multi-dimensional collection of attributes. Complete moral development in a person might be characterized by high correlations between moral dimensions; in fact, high correlations might serve as an operational *definition* of complete moral growth. But such development is hindered by the fact that at least four complex moral dimensions must be mastered and integrated. The child must learn to resist actual temptation, feel remorseful after transgression, resist his own imaginary temptations, and imagine his guilt after fantasized transgressions. Development along these dimensions apparently does not proceed at parallel speeds with identical end-points.

The complexity of cognition and moral judgment raises the chances of cognitive and moral instability. The more capacities to be mastered, the less likely it is that there will be consistency along any single dimension. Evidence confirms the suspicion. The Hartshornes discovered that children who cheated at one time refrained at another, despite the fact that objective

---

[84] *Ibid.*

[85] H. Hartshorne and M. A. May, *Studies in the Nature of Character*, Vol. I (New York: Macmillan, 1928). H. Hartshorne, M. A. May, and J. B. Maller, *Studies in the Nature of Character*, Vol. II (New York: Macmillan, 1929). H. Hartshorne, M. A. May, and F. K. Shuttleworth, *Studies in the Nature of Character*, Vol. III (New York: Macmillan, 1930).

[86] Duncan MacRae, Jr., "A Test of Piaget's Theories of Moral Development," *Journal of Abnormal and Social Psychology*, 49 (Jan., 1954), pp. 14–18. Grinder's assertion that by age 11 the various measures of conscience intercorrelate closely seems to represent a minority position. The evidence simply does not support his argument. Grinder, "Parental Child-Rearing Practices," p. 818.

circumstances had not changed.[87] More recently, Durkin found that the same child judges instances of a single class of reciprocity problems differently with no apparent rule tying the judgments together.[88] These findings parallel exactly Converse's discovery that as one proceeds from more- to less-informed publics, persons judge the same political events and objects differently within relatively short periods.[89] Perhaps the explanation of Converse's finding inheres in the complexity and fluidity of those moral and cognitive skills which underlie political judgment. Converse's finding, in other words, becomes less perplexing when we recognize that, for many, political perceptions are underpinned by unstable moral and cognitive senses.

These remarks are not intended to suggest any inadequacy in the picture of development Piaget and his followers have sketched. All we have meant to stress is that both the multi-dimensionality of moral and cognitive maturation and the rarity of optimal child-rearing techniques make development problematic. It is therefore not surprising to discover that so few individuals develop into political ideologues.

IV. POLITICAL SOCIALIZATION AND THE DEVELOPMENT OF IDEOLOGY

While this paper's focus has been on the developmental roots of political ideology, it should by now be apparent why I feel that the theory it explicates also has applicability to the political socialization literature. Indeed, we have already considered a few findings in the socialization area which are interpretable in terms of the developmental factors we have outlined. More data on political socialization can be integrated into this general framework, thereby providing some conceptual unification for a field which, currently, may well be accused of vulgar empiricism.[90] Let us briefly review some socialization literature which our framework subsumes and illuminates.

Two classes of socialization findings fit into our discussion. One set may be understood primarily by means of the developmental sequence presented in Part II of this paper, the other in terms of the retardation or facilitation factors discussed in Part III.

The developmental sequence helps account not only for the growth of political ideology, but also for the oft-noted "authoritarianism" of the child. We can now see that the child's authoritarian view of politics is only an extension of, first, his natural tendency to idealize history and authority; second, his belief in the inability of humans to alter the world; and third, his conception of justice as a self-regulating, mechanical, expiational pro-

---

[87] As cited in Hoffman, "The Role of the Parent," p. S-29.

[88] Dolores Durkin, "The Specificity of Children's Moral Judgments," *Journal of Genetic Psychology*, 98 (Jan., 1961), pp. 3-13.

[89] Converse, "The Nature of Belief Systems," pp. 238-245.

[90] For a recent article which evidences realization of this problem, see Jack Dennis, "Major Problems of Political Socialization Research," *Midwest Journal of Political Science*, 12 (Feb., 1968), pp. 85-115.

cess. Similarly, the "benevolent leader" syndrome[91] by which the child links himself to the polity may be explained partly by his inability to reason abstractly, to be self-conscious about his thinking, or to relate concrete judgments to general rules. Because the child reasons intuitively and syncretically, he reaches the personal application side of thought very rapidly. Reliance on a benevolent leader is both the outcome and the symbolic representation of a syncretic rather than analytic thought process. The "benevolent leader" syndrome, in other words, is an elliptical and condensed expression[92] of syncretic, personalized, unself-conscious thought. As Adelson, Siegel, and Piaget agree, not until the crucial 11–14 age range do children gain the capacity to reason abstractly and thereby arrange their relationship with the political system on different terms.

The intervening factors which determine the outcome of the developmental process illuminate a second set of socialization findings. We have argued that failures in cognitive and moral development seem uniquely linked to the psychological process of identification. This contention has already permitted us to interpret the perhaps puzzling discovery that student rebels and ideologues are *not*, by and large, also rebels against their parents. This generalization may be extended now to other kinds of political leadership. For example, Malcolm X in his *Autobiography* speaks in glowing and sympathetic terms of his mother, whose tribulations apparently sparked a latent political interest in him.[93] Nor should it be surprising that the children of clergymen seem to be especially prone to political activism.[94] These children, more than others, must incorporate moral norms in order to identify successfully with their parents.

The modalities of intergenerational transmission of party identification— at the heart of much socialization literature[95]—also become more understandable by use of the framework. We can explain why such transmission is easiest in the child's early years, because it is then that the child views the parent as the embodiment of a stable moral order. But we would also predict that when the conditions for identification between parents and children are weakened, the transmission process will similarly be endangered. Jennings and Niemi find, for example, that transmission of party identifica-

[91]For a discussion, see Fred I. Greenstein, *Children and Politics* (New Haven: Yale University Press, 1965), Chap. 3, and the sources cited therein. Also, Robert D. Hess and Judith V. Torney, *The Development of Political Attitudes in Children* (Chicago: Alldine, 1967), Chaps. 2–3; Jaros, Hirsch, and Fleron, "The Malevolent Leader"; and Jaros, "Children's Orientations Toward the President."

[92]These aspects of childish thought seem similar to "dreamwork" in the psychoanalytic theory of dreams.

[93]*The Autobiography of Malcolm X* (New York: Grove Press, 1964), Chap. 1.

[94]The names of Woodrow Wilson, Harriet Beecher Stowe, Martin Luther King, Jr., and Malcolm X come most readily to mind.

[95]See Herbert Hyman, *Political Socialization* (Glencoe: Free Press, 1959), pp. 69–85; Greenstein, *Children and Politics*, Chap. 4; Hess and Torney, *The Development of Political Attitudes in Children*, Chap. 9; Campbell, *et al.*, *The American Voter*, Chap. 6; and M. Kent Jennings and Richard G. Niemi, "The Transmission of Political Values from Parent to Child," *American Political Science Review*, 52 (March, 1968), pp. 169–185, 172–174.

tion from parent to child is considerably less successful today than it appears to have been a generation ago.[96] How can this change be explained? It is no secret that the present generation of American families is more plagued by divorce than were its predecessors. In most cases, divorce results in family disintegration, bitterness, and a breakdown of communication between the generations. Children viewing the break-up of their parents' marriage can seize on more than enough reasons not to identify with those parents. Obviously, divorce is not the only factor at work in weakening the identification process; I have used it merely as an illustration. Those many aspects of contemporary life which are responsible for the celebrated "generation gap" no doubt contribute as well.

Of course, a framework's analytic utility should be judged not only by the existing findings it interprets, but also by the originality of the hypotheses it yields. Does our framework pass this test? Let me indicate three kinds of nonobvious questions which our framework leads us to investigate. I shall start with a relatively low-level hypothesis, move through a middle-range question, and continue on to what might be called a systemically relevant problem.

First, though I have indicated the importance of identification to the acquisition of a political ideology and have specified some factors which affect the identification process, the specification is incomplete. For example, identification might be related to birth order because, as Stephenson points out, ". . . the higher the birth order of the child, the more time will the parents be able to spend with the child."[97] Assuming Stephenson is correct, we would predict that first-born children would be especially likely to become political ideologues. But we should also expand and qualify this hypothesis somewhat. It is proverbial that not only first but also last-born children get heavy doses of parental attention. It is true that for a time the oldest child has exclusive claim to parental interest and, often, to parental hopes, but the last child, normally coming relatively late in the reproduction cycle, often receives a tenderness and warmth not afforded his brothers and sisters. To his parents he may seem nature's going-away present. Therefore, intermediate children may be less likely to identify with parents and, consequently, less likely to become political ideologues.

A middle-range hypothesis takes up the differing and inconsistent moral standards evidenced by most children. We have already noted the relationship of these findings to the adult ideological inconsistencies uncovered by Converse. This parallelism indicates the need for a searching inquiry into the variety of moral standards people employ in their perceptions of political events. Are different standards applied to different classes of events, institutions, or personalities? Are there ways of predicting or describing the

[96] Compare *ibid.* with Hyman, *Political Socialization*, p. 74.

[97] Stephenson, *The Development of Conscience*, p. 112. For evidence indicating the superiority of first-born children over middle children in two other spheres—occupational and educational achievement, see Peter M. Blau and Otis Dudley Duncan, *The American Occupational Structure* (New York: John Wiley and Sons, 1968), pp. 307–308.

Too "human nature" oriented [handwritten annotation in top margin]

standard in use for any particular perception? Until now, most investigations of public opinion have generally assumed, very superficially, that people employ a single judgmental dimension in evaluating politics. Only
Lane's work has described fully the many moral standards applied to politics.[98] Our framework leads us to hypothesize that single moral standards
and judgmental consistency will be applied primarily by people whose
parents were warm to them, accorded them responsibility early, and disci-
plined them psychologically. Other child-rearing patterns will lead to a fragmented view of the political world.

Finally, at the systemic level, we may investigate the intertwining of
moral and cognitive development. I argued that moral and cognitive progress reinforced each other. The need to evaluate the world gives rise to the
desire to uncover the causal patterns *in* the world, and vice versa. I also implied that impairment of development affects cognition and evaluation
equally. But there are certainly *uneven* rates of moral and cognitive development. What might be the outcome if, for some reason, a person's cognitive development proceeded faster and more smoothly than his moral development? Though there is currently no way by which to explain such
aberrant processes, we can at least hypothesize about effects. For example,
we might predict differing occupational patterns for people with different
balances of moral and cognitive abilities. Children whose moral development exceeds their cognitive development might be attracted to occupations where moral questions are central. Such people might enter religious
careers. On the other hand, children whose cognitive capacities outstrip
their moral faculties might be attracted to occupations requiring advanced
cognitive skills but little moral judgment. Might this be true of mathema-
ticians? Finally, what mix of moral and cognitive development will lead a
child to the political life, and might this mix differ from culture to culture?

So much for the organizing and heuristic values of this framework. The
argument developed here has several specific implications for the understanding both of political structures and of ideology—implications which I
wish to highlight in conclusion. Assuming, as I have, that early learning
and conceptualization processes have lasting impacts, the sequence of development favors some political movements and regimes over others.
Specifically, movements of the left rest on a less secure psychological base
than do movements of the right. Left movements, in their call for innovation and their emphasis upon the secular over the sacred and equity over
expiation, appeal to high levels of moral and cognitive development. Movements of the right stress the need to respect authority, tradition, and punitive law. In so doing, they appeal to the earliest inculcated and most "natural" forms of thought. Therefore, more people are capable of reaction than
reform.

For these reasons the revolutionary cycle from reform to reaction, which

[98] Lane, *Political Ideology*. For an excellent empirical description of one kind of
ideological structure, with moral standards at the forefront of the discussion, see
Leonard Berkowitz and Kenneth G. Lutterman, "The Traditionally Socially Responsible Personality," *Public Opinion Quarterly*, 32 (Summer, 1968), pp. 169–186.

Brinton describes in structural terms,[99] may also be understood as a psychological problem. It is difficult for the mass of people to sustain commitments to left movements. Therefore, after such movements have succeeded in redistributing wealth or property, the less ideologically sophisticated adherents become apathetic or even antagonistic. As a consequence, leadership passes from agitators to colorless administrators or ruthless pragmatists. The maxim, "The revolution swallows its own children," is not entirely accurate. Rather, the children of the revolution defect, and can be brought back only by coercion. This formulation need not imply, however, that reactionary movements are invariably successful. Movements of the right in democratic regimes are forestalled both by leaders whose psychological capacities allow them to maintain a commitment to gradual reform, and by the apathy, inconsistency, and material self-interest of mass publics.[100]

We can also understand how difficult it is to meet the psychological requirements for a stable democratic regime.[101] Democracy demands much with its emphasis on openness, flexibility, gradual reform, progress through secular endeavor, and tolerance for those on the margins of society. Most people do not reach a high enough level of moral or cognitive development to maintain a long-run commitment to such a system. Either democracy must support itself by assuring material well-being for most of its citizens[102] or it must extract commitment at the cost of developing in its people a sense of nationalism. Both forms of support may eventually come into conflict with the norms of the system itself. We are led to the conclusion that diverse kinds of democratic commitment, resting as they do on different modes of perception and evaluation, provide considerable potential for fission and fragmentation. As Lasswell argued long ago, insufficient cognitive and moral development constitute continuing threats to democracy.[103]

We have also considered evidence and theory suggesting that individuals may slide between levels of political perception depending upon events.

[99]Crane Brinton, *The Anatomy of Revolution*. (Englewood Cliffs: Prentice-Hall, 1965).

[100]For evidence on these characteristics of mass publics, see Samuel Stouffer, *Communism, Conformity, and Civil Liberties* (Gloucester: Peter Smith, 1963); Herbert McClosky, "Consensus and Ideology in American Politics," Edward C. Dryer and Walter A. Rosenbaum, eds., *Political Opinion and Electoral Behavior* (Belmont, Calif.: Wadsworth, 1966), pp. 236–267; James W. Prothro and C. W. Grigg, "Fundamental Principles of Democracy: Bases of Agreement and Disagreement," *Journal of Politics*, 22 (Spring, 1960), pp. 276–294; Bernard R. Berelson, Paul F. Lazarsfeld, and William H. MacPhee, *Voting* (Chicago: University of Chicago Press, 1954), Chap. 14. For a recent critique, see Peter Bachrach, *The Theory of Democratic Elitism* (Boston: Little, Brown, 1967).

[101]A study which addresses this problem is Harry Eckstein, *A Theory of Stable Democracy* (Princeton: Center of International Studies, 1961).

[102]Seymour Martin Lipset, *Political Man* (Garden City: Anchor Books, 1960), Chap. 2.

[103]Harold D. Lasswell, "Democratic Character," in *The Political Writings of Harold Lasswell* (Glencoe: Free Press, 1951), pp. 465–525. For a recent discussion of these same problems, see Fred I. Greenstein, "Personality and Political Socialization: The Theories of Authoritarian and Democratic Character," *The Annals*, 361 (Sept., 1965), pp. 81–95.

The implications of this discovery are far-reaching, and take two forms. First, we need to identify both the characteristic processes by which people shift and the circumstances which contribute to such movement. Edelman explores the mechanisms by which feared or experienced sanctions can cause regression to less advanced modes of political perception.[104] But political crises of a magnitude sufficient to cause widespread severe regression rarely occur. We should concentrate, therefore, on the process by which less traumatic but more frequent political events induce movement between cognitive and evaluative levels. At the very least, as Converse's discussion demonstrates,[105] there is need for periodic replication of all attitude studies.

Second, we should not ignore the effects of our making attitudinal inconsistency and slippage a primary assumption in the study of politics. Accepting such a premise makes our tasks doubly difficult. Many of our most cherished findings, not only from the "behavioral" sides of political science—such as public opinion and electoral behavior—but also from the more institutional areas of the discipline, become problematic. Still, these retrenchments seem required if the foregoing argument is persuasive.

[104]Murray Edelman, *The Symbolic Uses of Politics* (Urbana: University of Illinois Press, 1964), Chap. 9.
[105]Converse, "The Nature of Belief Systems."

RESPONSE SET BIAS AND POLITICAL SOCIALIZATION RESEARCH[1]

KENNETH L. KOLSON
Hiram College

JUSTIN J. GREEN
University of Iowa

SINCE SO MUCH OF THE LITERATURE IN THE FIELD OF POLITICAL SOCIALIZA-tion deals with the "basic political orientations" of young people,[2] it would seem in order to examine some of the basic assumptions inherent in studies which report children's political attitudes. In particular some attention should be focused upon those assumptions which have implications for the validity of this research.

The investigation of children's "basic political orientations" has normally taken the form of attitude measurement with standard survey items. Although this is a conventional procedure in social science, it is worthy of reiteration that survey research, like all other methods, is not without certain shortcomings.[3] Aside from the many technical kinds of problems involved in this approach, there exists the fundamental problem of the validity[4] of all data gathered by the questionnaire technique. That is to say,

[1] The authors wish to express their appreciation to Dean Jaros, John H. Kessel, Michael Baer, and Thomas Walker, who read and commented upon earlier drafts of this article. The research was undertaken while the authors were Ph.D. candidates at the University of Kentucky.

[2] David Easton and Robert Hess define these "basic political orientations" as "knowledge, values, and attitudes toward the political system." This concept not only permeates their own work, but also the work of their associates and most of the other researchers in the field. At the same time, this research has focused upon children, since it is presumed that the "basic political orientations" are transmitted during youth. In this regard Easton and Hess have noted that "every piece of evidence indicates that the child's political world begins to take shape well before he even enters elementary school and that it undergoes the most rapid change during these years." See either David Easton and Robert Hess, "Youth and the Political System," in S. M. Lipset and L. Lowenthal, eds., *Culture and Social Character* (New York: The Free Press, 1961), pp. 226–251; or "The Child's Political World," *Midwest Journal of Political Science*, 6 (Aug., 1962), pp. 229–246. These basic notions also underlie the research recently reported in David Easton and Jack Dennis, *Children in the Political System: Origins of Political Legitimacy* (New York: McGraw-Hill Book Company, 1969).

[3] For a lively critique of contemporary social science methodology, see Eugene J. Webb, Donald T. Campbell, Richard D. Schwartz, and Lee Sechrest, *Unobtrusive Measures: Nonreactive Research in the Social Sciences* (Chicago: Rand McNally and Company, 1966).

[4] One of the classic discussions of validity is included in Samuel A. Stouffer, Louis Guttman, Edward A. Suchman, Paul F. Lazarsfeld, Shirley A. Star, and John A. Clausen, *Measurement and Prediction* (New York: John Wiley and Sons, 1950), esp. Chap. 2. Stouffer, *et al.*, distinguish between "internal validity" ("the problem of definition") and "external validity" ("the problem of prediction"). The internal validity of a questionnaire item is determined by asking whether the content of the item is ap-

how much information about an attitude, if any, is transmitted by a particular response to a questionnaire item?

Too many researchers have blithely assumed that responses to survey items find their source in the respondent's cognitive processes. Answers are considered nonrandom in origin and as accurate verbalizations of the end product of the respondent's thought process. Are the responses to our questions really indicative of cognitive and attitudinal dimensions,[5] as we say they are? This research note is an attempt to show that such inferences may not always be justified.

SOURCES OF INVALIDITY IN SURVEY RESEARCH

There are problems of several genres which a researcher may encounter when he takes his questionnaire or interview schedule into the real world. Among these are problems associated with the fixed alternative question— the primary data-gathering device of nearly all students of socialization save the unorthodox Piaget and Jahoda.[6] Fixed alternative questions are

---

propriate for the universe of behavior being studied. That is to say, "if one wishes to study opinions about the President, then one asks questions about the President." With regard to the latter kind of validity, Stouffer, *et al.*, write that "a universe has but one 'internal validity,' but *it has many possible 'external validities,'* since it can be used for many prediction purposes." What is the external validity of a questionnaire item which asks for opinions about the President? According to Stouffer, *et al.*, "Opinion of President Truman may have some validity in predicting who will vote for him on election day, a different validity for predicting who will support his program on price control, etc., etc."

According to Stouffer, *et al.*, "to inquire into the 'accuracy' of opinions does not in general make much sense." That is to say, the "opinion" is defined according to how the specific question is answered. There is no other empirical referent. Consequently, we can say that in this paper we are concerned with both internal and external validity. We are charging that if a question is internally invalid, it will also be externally invalid once it is used to predict. That is, we can only predict the existence of an attitude when we are sure that our question is tapping attitudes.

All of the above quotations are from Stouffer, *et al.*, pp. 57–59.

[5] See Theodore Newcomb, Ralph H. Turner, and Philip E. Converse, *Social Psychology* (New York: Holt, Rinehart and Winston, Inc., 1965), esp. Chap. 2. This article treats cognition as being, after Newcomb, *et al.*, the creation of categories which serve to store information in a way that makes it meaningful to the individual. Once stored, the individual can then make use of the information at some later time. Attitudes may be considered simply as "stored cognitions that have some positive or negative association" (p. 40). "From a cognitive point of view," Newcomb and his associates assert, "an attitude represents an organization of valenced cognitions" (p. 40).

[6] Piaget and Jahoda are also among the more prolific writers in this field. The reader is directed to Jean Piaget, *The Moral Judgment of the Child* (New York: The Free Press, 1966). For a smaller dose of Piaget's work see Jean Piaget and Anne-Marie Weil, "The Development in Children of the Idea of the Homeland and Relations with Other Countries," *International Social Science Bulletin*, 3 (July, 1951), pp. 561–578. For a good exposure to Jahoda's work see Gustav Jahoda, "Children's Concepts of Nationality: A Critical Study of Piaget's Stages," *Child Development*, 35 (Nov., 1964), pp. 1081–1092; "The Development of Children's Ideas about Country and Nationality, Part I: The Conceptual Framework," *British Journal of Educational Psychology*, 33 (Feb., 1963), pp. 47–60; and "The Development of Children's Ideas about Country

biased if they fail to offer a set of responses which are "balanced" in the manner of the so-called Likert scale. A useful example of this kind of built-in positive bias is an item used by Easton and Dennis to measure children's affective orientations toward the President. The respondents were offered the following alternatives:

I like him more than anyone.
I like him more than most people.
I like him more than many people.
I like him more than some people.
I like him more than a few people.
I like him less than almost anyone.[7]

Five of the six alternatives offered here are worded in a positive manner. If a child really dislikes the President, he can register this attitude only by selecting the last alternative. And it is interesting to note that this option is not as extreme as the corresponding alternative offered in the positive direction. It is evidently assumed that children *do* like the President, and therefore an attempt is made in this question only to measure the intensity of the presumed attitude without careful preliminary determination of its direction. It could be argued, moreover, that such items should include a "Don't Know" option since, as in the above example, the respondent may be left with the choice of either leaving the question blank or giving a reluctant answer.

Yet another problem accrues from the unallayed trust which researchers often display in the ability of children to answer their questions. Some students of political socialization have exhibited a naive faith in the child's ability to report his own activity accurately. Hess and Torney, for instance, report that fully 62 per cent of the sixth graders in their sample have worn campaign buttons, and that 21.6 per cent of their third graders have "handed out buttons and handbills."[8] Seventh graders, they report, are more participatory than their teachers![9]

In any scientific endeavor it is crucial that inferences be kept within the limits of the data. It has been observed previously that children give positive evaluations of unfamiilar authority figures,[10] yet researchers seem to be unable to resist the temptation of making grandiose inferences from questionnaire data. Easton and Dennis, for example, report that in an open-ended situation children react to the word "government" with such statements as "Government is a good man," and "Government is love."[11] Yet

and Nationality, Part II: National Symbols and Themes," *British Journal of Educational Psychology*, 33 (May, 1963), pp. 143–153.

[7] Easton and Dennis, *Children in the Political System*, p. 179.

[8] Robert D. Hess and Judith V. Torney, *The Development of Political Attitudes in Children* (Chicago: Aldine Publishing Company, 1967), p. 88.

[9] *Ibid.*, p. 87.

[10] See Robert D. Hess and David Easton, "The Child's Changing Image of the President," *Public Opinion Quarterly*, 24 (Winter, 1960), pp. 632–644.

[11] David Easton and Jack Dennis, "The Child's Image of Government," *Annals of the American Academy of Political and Social Science*, 361 (Sept., 1965), pp. 40–57.

these same authors are prepared to make sweeping statements about the ideology of these children:

> the child is likely to be a "conservative collectivist" in that he is not much in favor of extending the scope of government beyond its present limits. He is rather happy with government as it stands and would not give it "more power over the people."[12]

Many other threats to validity in survey research exist, including willful deceit and some others which are probably impossible to overcome. The sources of invalidity which shall occupy our attention in this article are "irrelevant but lawful sources of variance"[13] which are commonly referred to as "response sets." Cronbach, who was one of the first to appreciate the importance of response sets, offers the following definition:

> A response set is defined as any tendency causing a person consistently to give different responses to test items than he would when the same content is presented in a different form.[14]

There are three types of response sets which we will later hypothesize to be sources of invalidity in political socialization research. First is a tendency to respond in a testing situation when the subject is not sure of the proper answer. Since there is usually no penalty for making a mistake, the respondent exhibits a "tendency to gamble."[15] Second, respondents are inclined to choose particular alternatives in preference to others regardless of the content of the question. Cronbach has offered the following description of this bias, which is usually called "acquiescence response set":

> When students are offered two alternatives, as "True" versus "False," "Like" versus "Dislike," "Agree" versus "Disagree," etc., some use one more than the other . . . . The majority of students have an excess number of "Yes" responses on true-false tests. Since response tendencies affect an answer only when the student is to some degree uncertain about the content of the item, acquiescence tends to make false items more valid, and true items less valid.[16]

Finally, we will consider "agreement response set," which is similar but not identical to acquiescence. A tendency to agree with things authoritative, this set is especially likely to be activated when some bias is included in the question. In the case of acquiescence, the inclination is to make a

---

[12] *Ibid.*, p. 53.

[13] Webb, *et al.*, *Unobtrusive Measures*, p. 19.

[14] Lee J. Cronbach, "Response Sets and Test Validity," *Educational and Psychological Measurement*, 6 (1946), p. 476. See also "Further Evidence on Response Sets and Test Design," *Educational and Psychological Measurement*, 10 (1950), pp. 3–31, by the same author.

[15] Of course, there are individual differences in the tendency to gamble, as there are with all response sets. According to Cronbach, "the tendency to 'gamble,' to respond when doubtful, appears to be distributed over a continuum, from the student who answers only when very sure to the one who attempts every item." From Cronbach, "Response Sets and Test Validity," pp. 476–477.

[16] *Ibid.*, pp. 479–480.

certain response regardless of content. Agreement, on the other hand, can be thought of as looking for a behavioral cue in the question, and then responding in accordance with that cue. Couch and Keniston describe these "cue-takers"[17] as "individuals with weak ego controls, who accept impulses without reservation and who 'agree' and easily respond to stimuli exerted on them."[18]

Most of the research on response sets has been directed toward determining the personality factors which account for the variation in their use. But, besides personality traits, it should be clear that the activation of a response set depends to a large extent upon the cognitive state of the individual with regard to the content of the question. Relevant here is a study done by Roper during the early days of survey research.[19] Roper asked essentially the same question concerning United States involvement in World War II in three different ways, and found that biased wording can evoke a significant difference in the response pattern. Cantril's reaction was:

> The most important finding here was that on issues where people were uncertain, it was possible to produce sizable effects by biasing the issue with an interventionist or noninterventionist argument, but where opinion was well crystallized, biasing statements had relatively little effect on the results.[20]

As Peabody has observed, "if the individual has no definite attitudes of either kind, then his response must be based on 'response set' . . . and any inference to attitude content is invalid."[21]

Cognitive dissonance theory[22] offers an explanation for these phenomena. The respondent is receiving information which he cannot place into any of his existing categories, and hence is cognitively uncomfortable. According to the tenets of the theory as formulated by Festinger, the respondent will tend to take any measure which will reduce the discomfort.[23] This may be achieved by evasive tactics, such as opting for a "Don't Know," or by avoiding commitment to an extreme attitudinal position. The behavior of a person in this kind of situation should be closely observed.

[17] Arthur Couch and Kenneth Keniston, "Yeasayers and Naysayers: Agreeing Response Set as a Personality Variable," *Journal of Abnormal and Social Psychology*, 60 (March, 1960), p. 151. For purposes of elucidation, we shall refer to those individuals whom Couch and Keniston call "yeasayers" as "cue-takers."

[18] *Ibid.*, p. 173.

[19] *Fortune Survey*, 23 (April, 1941), p. 102; and 23 (June, 1941), p. 70.

[20] Hadley Cantril, *Gauging Public Opinion* (Princeton: Princeton University Press, 1944), p. 45.

[21] Dean Peabody, "Attitude Content and Agreement Set in Scales of Authoritarianism, Anti-Semitism, and Economic Conservatism," *Journal of Abnormal and Social Psychology*, 63 (July, 1961), p. 1.

[22] The basic source for the theory is Leon Festinger, *The Theory of Cognitive Dissonance* (New York: Harper and Row, 1957).

[23] In other words, there are dissonance-avoidance mechanisms. Festinger says, "A fear of dissonance would lead to a reluctance to take action—a reluctance to commit oneself." See Festinger, *The Theory of Cognitive Dissonance*, p. 31.

Whatever choice he eventually makes is interesting to us, but if he decides to select one of the alternatives from which we usually infer the existence of an attitude, it has important implications for validity.

METHOD

The above discussion suggests the advisability of ascertaining the degree to which political socialization research instruments are measuring what we claim they are measuring. That is, to what extent are our instruments vulnerable to response set bias, and under what circumstances?

This research is based on a questionnaire which was administered to 289 fourth through eighth grade students in the public schools of Fayette County (Lexington), Kentucky. The total sample was divided randomly into three groups, and each group was exposed to a different set of questions concerning the same political objects. For each object three questions were constructed—one biased in a positive direction, one biased negatively, and one unbiased. The questions, in their various forms, were then interspersed among the three groups so that no one group would receive a set of questions which were all biased in the same direction.

An explicit attempt was made to put the subjects in precisely the situation described by Peabody. We asked them to evaluate objects which we assumed they would know very little about—Harold Wilson and the speaker of the House of Representatives. We also offered the respondents a hypothetical name, "Thomas Walker," and for comparative purposes items were included concerning Spiro Agnew and a non-political object, summer school. In each case we asked for an affective response. In this way, it was thought that we could gain some knowledge about the way in which response sets work with children. In light of what we know about response sets, we had some rather specific expectations about what our data would show:

Expectation #1. According to the "tendency to gamble" set, the subjects should tend to respond, even when cognitive and attitudinal substance is totally lacking.

Expectation #2. According to "agreement response set," the subjects should respond in the direction indicated by the cue when a cue is included in the question.

Expectation #3. According to the notion of "acquiescence response set," the subjects will respond in a positive manner when the question is unbiased.

Expectation #4. According to cognitive dissonance theory, we expect that the subjects will, when their responses are not based upon attitudes, behave in such a way as to minimize dissonance.

FINDINGS

Table 1 shows that large proportions of the subjects fulfilled our first expectation by demonstrating the "tendency to gamble." That is, many subjects chose to respond even when they could not possibly have had much pre-existing information about the content of the question. (And in the case of "Thomas Walker," they could have had no previous information). The proportion of "Don't Knows" for the various items ranges from a low of 2.5 per cent to nearly 70 per cent. Such a variation in response rate can be attributed, in part, to the working of cognitive dissonance theory, as set forth above. Ambiguity generates dissonance,[24] and the greater the amount of dissonance generated, the larger the proportion of those who would avoid the issue by opting for the "Don't Know" alternative.[25] Following this line of reasoning it can be understood why there were so few DK's in regard to the summer school items. It is especially interesting that the positively biased summer school item apparently created the most dissonance since it produced substantially more DK's. This is what we would expect according to Festinger's notion that dissonance is generated when an individual is exposed to information which contradicts his currently held attitudes.[26] The item biased in the direction of the children's attitudes (negatively) created the least dissonance, and the contradictory cue created the most. It is interesting also that in the "Thomas Walker" example the *neutral* group opted most often for the "Don't Know" alternative, indicating that a total lack of information and a perceived duty to respond creates the most dissonance when there is no cue included in the question; this is what we would expect. Our first expectation has been confirmed. A sufficient number of subjects responded in order to provide us with, for our purposes, meaningful data. In addition, the pattern of nonresponse is in itself indicative of the manner in which some of the responses were produced.

Our second expectation was that the subjects would respond in the direction indicated by the cue when one is included in the question. A brief glance at the tables and at the chi-square values shows that this proved to be the case. Moreover, it seems that our ability to change the response patterns is directly related to the amount of information which the subject cognitively possesses. In other words, we can induce massive shifts in the evaluation of "Thomas Walker," but we are much less able to do so with "summer school" and with "Spiro Agnew." The summer school item is particularly interesting. We were able to change the response patterns to a

---

[24] Actually, Festinger's conception is that dissonance occurs only after a decision has been made. Strictly speaking, then, ambiguous information in a decision-making situation generates *conflict*, and the eventual decision produces the *dissonance*. We feel, however, that it makes sense to think of pre-decisional dissonance when an individual is exposed to information which does not fit into pre-existing cognitive categories—therefore causing discomfort. In such cases the balance is upset to the extent that the individual must create a new category, revise cognitive elements, or make some other kind of cognitive adjustment. This is entirely different from the decision-making case of a person trying to decide what kind of car to buy—Festinger's favorite example. In short, when a person experiences cognitive discomfort in a decision-making situation, we feel that it is instructive to speak of pre-decisional dissonance, since it implies something more than the usual "conflict" implicit in making a decision.

[25] *Ibid.*

[26] See Festinger's discussion of exposure to information in Chap. 6 of *The Theory of Cognitive Dissonance.*

TABLE 1

Responses to Five Items by Type of Cue in Percentages

Subject and Response Alternative	+	Type of Cue neutral	−	χ^2 [a]
Thomas Walker[b]				
I like him a lot	46.5	8.8	12.0	
I like him pretty much	19.3	24.4	16.6	
I don't like him very much	2.2	7.7	14.8	
I don't like him at all	1.1	2.2	6.4	
Don't Know	30.6	56.6	50.0	
Totals	99.7	99.7	99.8	
	(N=88)	(N=90)	(N=108)	23.12, P<.001
Harold Wilson[c]				
I like him a lot	7.7	10.2	1.1	
I like him pretty much	23.3	22.4	13.6	
I don't like him very much	8.8	7.4	9.0	
I don't like him at all	0.0	2.8	6.8	
Don't Know	60.0	57.0	69.3	
Totals	99.8	99.8	99.8	
	(N=90)	(N=107)	(N=88)	7.86, P<.02
Summer School[d]				
Should have to go to summer school	10.4	2.8	6.4	
Should *not* have to go to summer school	74.4	92.5	90.9	
Don't Know	15.1	4.6	2.5	
Totals	99.9	99.9	99.8	
	(N=86)	(N=107)	(N=77)	6.04, P<.05
Spiro Agnew[e]				
I like him a lot	23.3	9.0	24.1	
I like him pretty much	30.8	31.8	37.8	
I don't like him very much	14.9	18.1	9.8	
I don't like him at all	1.8	3.4	3.2	
Don't Know	28.9	37.5	25.2	
Totals	99.7	99.8	99.6	
	(N=107)	(N=88)	(N=91)	4.75, P<.10
Speaker of the House[f]				
Very good	43.1	29.2	13.4	
Fairly good	36.6	37.0	42.6	
Not very good	4.5	3.3	5.6	
Very bad	0.0	0.0	1.1	
Don't Know	15.5	30.3	37.0	
Totals	99.7	99.8	99.7	
	(N=109)	(N=89)	(N=89)	2.06, P<.5[g]

[a] Don't Know responses were dropped and the categories were collapsed into one positive and one negative category for the purpose of calculating the chi-square statistic. This procedure was followed because our primary interest is in observing the

relative distributions of positive and negative responses, as well as to avoid the problems caused by small cell entries.

[b] Items were as follows: *Positive Cue*—Thomas Walker is an American leader who wants to help the poor people. How do you feel about Mr. Walker? *No Cue*—You've probably heard of Thomas Walker. How do you feel about Mr. Walker? *Negative Cue*—Thomas Walker is a radical socialist leader in America, and many people dislike him. How do you feel about Mr. Walker?

[c] Items were as follows: *Positive Cue*—Harold Wilson, the Prime Minister of England, is a very popular world leader. How do you feel about Mr. Wilson? *No Cue*—You've probably heard of Harold Wilson. How do you feel about Mr. Wilson? *Negative Cue*—Harold Wilson, the Prime Minister of England, is disliked by many people. How do you feel about Mr. Wilson?

[d] Items were as follows: *Positive Cue*—Some of our leaders say that every child should go to school in the summer so that he can learn more. What do you think? *No Cue*—Do you think that children should have to go to school in the summer? *Negative Cue*—Some grown-ups want to make every child go to school in the summertime. What do you think?

[e] Items were as follows: *Positive Cue*—Vice-President Spiro Agnew is a very powerful and important person, and is the President's helper. How do you feel about Mr. Agnew? *No Cue*—You've probably heard of Spiro Agnew. How do you feel about Mr. Agnew? *Negative Cue*—Many people make jokes and laugh about Vice-President Agnew. How do you feel about Mr. Agnew?

[f] Items were as follows: *Positive Cue*—The Speaker of the U.S. House of Representatives is one of our leaders in Washington, and is a very powerful man in our government. What kind of job do you think he has been doing? *No Cue*—What kind of job do you think the Speaker of the U. S. House of Representatives has been doing? *Negative Cue*—Many people are complaining about the way in which the Speaker of the U. S. House of Representatives is doing his job. What kind of job do you think he is doing?

[g] Because nearly all of the cases fall in the positive cells of the table, our chi-square statistic (computed, like the others, by dropping the DK's and collapsing the categories) is highly insignificant. If we do not collapse the categories, however, we get a chi-square of 16.456, which is significant at the .02 level (df=6). This is an indication of the ease with which we were able to change the responses from highly positive to only slightly positive. It is *also* an indication of the reluctance of the respondents to make negative evaluations.

significant degree by biasing the question, even though the cues do not seem to be very strong, and we expect that the children have very real attitudes about this issue. And even though the chi-square value in this case is probably in part an artifact of the small number of cases in the positive cells, we are still able to change the response patterns more than we expected. From this we can only conclude that "agreement response set" is a rather important source of invalidity when the respondent has little cognitive substance.

We should take care not to exclude from our scrutiny one of the most basic and important aspects of these data. That is the overwhelmingly positive direction of nearly all the response patterns. Of course we expected (Expectation #2) positive responses when we biased the question in that direction. And we also expected (Expectation#3) positive responses to unbiased items, due to the acquiescent response set. But we did not expect positive evaluations of objects which were introduced with a negative cue.

In point of fact there were only four instances where the negative evaluations outnumbered the positive. Three of these can be accounted for by the summer school questions, and the fourth case was in response to the negatively biased item about Harold Wilson (interestingly enough, the only foreigner evaluated by the children). With regard to the summer school responses, we would not have expected them to be positive, even when positively cued, and the group which responded to the negatively biased Wilson item was very evenly split. Why is it that a majority of the children consistently expressed positive evaluations of objects about which they previously had no information, and which were described to them in negative terms? Apparently there is a tendency for children (if not adults) to respond in a positive direction once they have decided to "gamble." A negative response is evidently conceived to be a very grave incrimination of the object in question. Consequently, it seems that if a response is given under these circumstances, it will probably be a positive one. Since children seldom have vast cognitive store-houses filled with information, we feel that our data must be interpreted as evidence of the considerable import of acquiescent bias.

DISCUSSION AND SUMMARY

At the beginning of this article we posited the notion that questions designed to tap attitudes often have the effect of activating response sets. We have argued that this is a major source of invalidity, and that the degree to which response sets are activated depends primarily upon the cognitive structure of the respondent.

We put children in dissonance-producing situations by exposing them to ambiguous or biased stimuli in order to observe the effect which response sets have upon their answers. When asked a question about which he has no information, a child's first tendency is to respond, despite his cognitive deficiencies. When a cue is included in the question, and when the respondent has nothing else upon which to base his response, he will turn to the stimulus and extract something that will guide his behavior. In this sense he is exhibiting the "agreement" syndrome.

A third source of invalidity which is especially evident in our data is acquiescent bias. This set is illustrated by the reluctance of the respondents to give a negative evaluation of any object save summer school—even when exposed to a very powerful negative cue. This is one of the most unambiguous findings of our research. Of course the acquiescence response set, like the others, is activated only when the respondent cannot make any cognitive sense out of the question. The summer school item, as well as the "Agnew" item, indicates that the presence of cognitive substance minimizes the effect of bias resulting from each of the three sources of invalidity which we have considered.

We are of the persuasion that Festinger's dissonance formulation provides the best interpretation of the kinds of behavior which we have observed. Although Festinger is concerned primarily with post-decisional dissonance rather than pre-decisional "conflict," he at least implies that an individual will tend to opt for the alternative which promises to produce the least dissonance.[27] Assuming this to be the case, our data clearly suggest that the subjects anticipate less dissonance from a positive response than from a negative response. A basic part of Festinger's theory is that, ". . . just as attitudes influence behavior, behavior can in turn exert an influence toward change in attitudes."[28]

Why should negative attitudes (or potential negative attitudes) produce more dissonance than positive attitudes? It seems reasonable to suggest that, given the innocence and naiveté which we associate with childhood, negative attitudes with little cognitive support are incongruous with the child's view of the world. Although this is really beyond the scope of our inquiry, our data do offer some support for the so-called "vulnerability thesis."[29]

We have tried to demonstrate that a child who has no information about an object can, due to response set, behave in such a way as to delude the researcher into believing that he has detected the presence of a cognitive or attitudinal dimension, or both. Our finding that acquiescent bias seems to be an important source of invalidity when children experience pre-decisional dissonance raises some questions about previous findings of political socialization research. First is the generally positive orientation which children purportedly have toward political leaders and politics in general.[30] Likewise, previous research has shown that children do not reflect the cynical attitudes of many of their elders, nor do they seem to display negative orientations of any kind toward politics.[31] In our experiment we have seen that children are extremely reluctant to make an unfavorable judgment of an object with which they are unfamiliar, and we know that politics are not particularly salient for children. What does it really mean when a child indicates that for him the President is a "benevolent leader?" To what extent do children's responses indicate "covert support" for the system, and to what extent are they simply thoughtless acts of acquiescence? Do these early manifestations of acquiescence foreshadow later patterns of deference to political authority? Cognitively speaking, how much information, and what kind of information, does it take to transform this "support" for authority into cynicism and contempt?

On the basis of our data, we would urge that subsequent research in the

[27] *Ibid.*, Chap. 2.

[28] From the discussion of cognitive dissonance theory in Newcomb, *et al.*, *Social Psychology*, p. 105.

[29] See Sebastian deGrazia, *The Political Community* (Chicago: University of Chicago Press, 1948), Chap. 1.

[30] This is a common finding in the literature. See, for example, Hess and Torney, *Development of Political Attitudes*, Easton and Dennis, *Children in the Political System*, or Fred I. Greenstein, *Children and Politics* (New Haven: Yale University Press, 1965).

[31] See Hess and Torney, *Development of Political Attitudes*, pp. 75–79, and specifically in regard to cynicism, M. Kent Jennings and Richard G. Niemi, "The Transmission of Political Values from Parent to Child," *American Political Science Review*, 62 (March, 1968), pp. 169–184.

area focus on the cognitive content of children vis-a-vis politics, as well as on the relative salience of politics for children. Measurement of affect without a prior consideration of the cognitive dimension apparently produces results which, at best, can be said to have validity problems. That there are many potential contributors to the invalidity of survey data in the field of political socialization does not mean that we should abandon this approach —only that we ought to refine it.

PRE-ADULT ATTITUDES TOWARD LEGAL COMPLIANCE: NOTES TOWARD A THEORY[1]

HARRELL R. RODGERS, JR.
University of Georgia

GEORGE TAYLOR
University of Georgia

S TUDENTS OF POLITICAL SOCIALIZATION HAVE ECHOED THE FINDINGS OF PSY-chologists, that children develop early a disposition to obey the law. Hess and Torney, for example, observe that "norms about the justice of law and necessity for conformity are established firmly at an early age."[2] Dawson and Prewitt call attention to the fact that "children are taught to obey authority and to love their country at the same time and by the same models of behavior, they come to believe that it is good to obey."[3] Merelman points out that the young child's compliance disposition is rooted in a belief that laws are objective, timeless, and unchanging.[4]

To our knowledge, generalizations about the effects of maturation on attitudes toward legal compliance come exclusively from data on elementary school children.[5] Piaget, Merelman, Hess and Torney report that the most important effect of maturation in these early years is to produce a more subjective and complex approach to law.[6] Ideally as the child matures and comes to realize that the world is "morally contingent and risky . . . (he will) formulate his own rules and be able to defend them against other people's standards."[7] Another body of literature concerned with the attitudes of adults toward law and compliance supports these findings of increasing subjectivity. Even though individual attitudes become more

[1] This research was made possible by a grant from the Social Science Research Institute of the University of Georgia. We would like to thank our colleagues Charles Bullock, Robert Clute, Roger Hanson and Brett W. Hawkins for advice and criticism on an earlier draft of this paper.

[2] Robert D. Hess and Judith V. Torney, *The Development of Political Attitudes in Children* (Chicago: Aldine Publishing Co., 1967), p. 215.

[3] Richard E. Dawson and Kenneth Prewitt, *Political Socialization* (Boston: Little, Brown and Company, 1969), p. 211.

[4] Richard M. Merelman, "The Development of Political Ideology: A Framework for the Analysis of Political Socialization," *American Political Science Review*, 63 (Sept., 1969), pp. 750–767.

[5] Most socialization studies have simply ignored compliance and attitudes toward law. The Hess and Torney study is by far the most comprehensive treatment. Easton and Dennis, using the same data that the Hess and Torney study is based on did not center attention on the questions. See *Children and the Political System* (New York: McGraw-Hill Book Co., 1969), *passim*. The sociologist and psychologist who have studied the moral development of children have not been particularly interested in compliance with political authority.

[6] Jean Piaget, *The Moral Judgment of the Child* (New York: The Free Press of Glencoe, 1965), p. 83; Merelman, "The Development of Political Idealogy," pp. 754–757; Hess and Torney, *Development of Political Attitudes*, pp. 50–59.

[7] Merelman, "The Development of Political Ideology," p. 756.

subjective by adulthood, broad support for law and the legal system seems to be stable. For example, Boynton *et al.* asked respondents in a study to react to the statement: "Even though one might strongly disagree with a state law—after it has been passed by the state legislature one ought to obey it." Only three per cent of the total sample disagreed with this statement.[8]

From a number of other studies we know that this finding does not mean that this proportion of the population will always obey laws they disagree with (or even those they agree with); what it tells us is that most adults are aware of, and support, the democratic norm of lawabidingness. There is a considerable difference, however, in what the average adult conceives in the abstract, and how he will act in a specific situation. At least one study has found that if adults are asked how they would react to specific laws, they tend to base their behavior on personal values, such as agreement with the particular law.[9] Such behavior, we could argue, is more representative of most citizens' daily approach to law than their verbalized support of the legal system would lead us to believe.

This does not mean that most citizens indiscriminately go about breaking the law. Our argument is that they are selective lawbreakers. Presumably citizens find the compulsion to obey the law strong, and conform in the great majority of cases. Still, the average citizen, and even public officials, also disobey a good number of laws in their day-to-day endeavors. Obvious examples would include official and public noncompliance with civil rights laws enacted by Congress, and prayer and desegregation decisions enunciated by the United States Supreme Court. In situations of this type the individual breaks the law because he disagrees with it or questions the right of the government to make such a law. This type of action might be called "rule rejection." Most citizens (it would probably be safe to say all) engage in another type of lawbreaking which might be called "rule exception." That is, they generally support many laws that they do not always obey because they decide that it is all right to break the law under certain circumstances that can be rationalized. Thus speeding on a lonely road or adding a few "extra" deductions to one's income tax becomes justifiable behavior to the individual. The extent of these two types of lawbreaking is revealed by the President's Commission on Law Enforcement and Administration of Justice which reported that "an independent survey of 1,700 persons found 91 per cent of the sample admitted they had committed acts for which they might have received jail sentences."[10] This same incidence of lawbreaking is reported in at least two other well-known studies.[11] Laws that collide with prevailing norms are subjected to rule ex-

[8] G. R. Boynton, Samuel C. Patterson, and Ronald Hedlund, "The Structure of Public Support For Legislative Institutions," *Midwest Journal of Political Science,* 12 (May, 1968), p. 173.

[9] Harrell R. Rodgers, Jr., *Community Conflict, Public Opinion and the Law* (Columbus, Ohio: Charles Merrill Publishing Co., 1969), pp. 111–115.

[10] *The Challenge of Crime in a Free Society* (Washington, D. C.: U. S. Government Printing Office, 1967), p. v.

[11] Austin L. Porterfield, *Youth In Trouble* (Fort Worth, Texas: The Leo Potishman

ception and rule rejection on a grand scale. Ring Lardner summed up one such example when he sardonically observed that "Anyhow, prohibition is better than no liquor at all."[12]

By adulthood, then, the simple objective moral world of the child has been transformed into a more complex and personalized entity. In this paper we will try to cast some light on this conversion process and expand the generality of compliance theory by: (1) comparing high school students' attitudes toward law with those of elementary school children; (2) examining the sophistication of high school students' orientations toward legal obedience; and (3) isolating the correlates of compliant and noncompliant attitudes.

The data were gathered from seven high schools in an urban area of South Carolina. A detailed questionnaire, modeled to a large extent on a previous study by Jennings and Niemi, was used.[13] A sample was drawn of 350 students in grades nine through twelve; and 302 usable questioniaires were obtained. Two of the schools are segregated (1 white, 1 black), two are integrated, and three are partially integrated (15 per cent to 35 pet cent mixed). 196 of the respondents are white, and 106 are black. In each section of the paper we report the differences between black and white students.

CHANGES IN ATTITUDES TOWARD LAW

Our data do not allow us to make any broad generalizations about the development of attitudes toward law, but we can examine the relative change in students' attitudes over the school years by comparing our findings about high school students with Hess and Torney's finding about elementary school children. Hess and Torney report that the young child's approach to law and compliance becomes less and less idealistic over the grade school years. For example, in the second grade 83 per cent of the children agree that "all laws are fair."[14] By the eighth grade agreement has dropped to only 54 per cent.[15] Consistent with the trend uncovered by Hess and Torney only 21 per cent of the ninth graders in our sample agreed with this statement. By the twelfth grade agreement had dwindled to only 15 per cent. By the high school years, then, the subjectivity of law is clear to almost all students. There is no significant difference between the black and white students on this question. The black students are more inclined to think that all laws are just, but only 5 or 6 percentage points per grade.

Foundation, 1946), *passim*; and James S. Wallerstein and Clement J. Wyle, "Our Law-Abiding Law-Breakers," *Federal Probation*, 25 (May, 1947), p. 110.

[12] Quoted by Paul A. Freund, "The Civil Rights Movement and Frontiers of Law," in Talcott Parsons and Kenneth B. Clark, eds., *The Negro American* (Boston: Houghton Mifflin Company, 1966), p. 369.

[13] M. Kent Jennings and Richard G. Niemi, "Patterns of Political Learning," *Harvard Educational Review*, 38 (Summer, 1968), pp. 443–467.

[14] Hess and Torney, *The Development of Political Attitudes*, pp. 50–59.

[15] We would like to thank Professor Jack Dennis of the University of Wisconsin for providing us with these data.

Hess and Torney also asked their respondents, "Do people who break laws: (1) always get caught; (2) usually get caught; (3) usually get away; (4) always get away?"[16] Fifty-seven per cent of the second graders believed that lawbreakers always get caught. By the eighth grade this belief had declined to only 16 per cent. In our study we asked the students: "Are lawbreakers always punished?" Seventy-two per cent of the ninth graders said "no." By the twelfth grade dissent had risen to 85 per cent. Presumably attitudes toward the inevitablity of punishment for transgressors change very little after the eighth grade.

The black and white students in our sample differ significantly on this question (p. < .01). The white students are less inclined to believe that lawbreakers are always punished. At the twelfth grade 95 per cent of the white students respond "no," while 79 per cent of the black students give this response. The black students may be more idealistic or more naive than their white peers, or the experiences of their environment may lead them to be more inclined to believe that lawbreakers are always punished.

A TYPOLOGY OF ATTITUDES TOWARD LEGAL OBEDIENCE

To tap the sophistication of the average student's attitudes toward law and compliance we sought to find out both how the student thought he should relate to the law, and what reasons he would give for his behavior. The replies of the respondents indicate the degree of sophistication in their approach to law and the political system. For example, we can determine whether the individual's compliance behavior is based simply on acceptance of, or resignation to, the prescribed rules of the game, or whether the individual has internalized the values of the system as his own. Similarly, we can determine whether socialization to legal compliance is more or less effective when the individual has internalized the values of the system as his own.

We began the questions on attitudes toward compliance by asking the respondents: "Do you think people should always obey laws?" 202 answered "yes," 94 answered "no." If the respondent answered yes, he was asked, "Why would you obey a law you disagreed with?" If he answered "no," he was asked "why not?" Table 1 classifies the reasons the respondents gave for being willing to obey a law they disagreed with. The classification is an adaptation of Kohlberg's typology of moral development.[17] Surprisingly only about a third (those at level 3) of the students responding positively have internalized any standards to guide their compliance behavior. The other two-thirds of the students responding positively base their behavior on punishment avoidance or rule conformity—external standards.

Table 2 classifies the reasons given by 94 respondents for not always being willing to obey the law. Each of the three groups has internalized

---

16 Hess and Torney, *The Development of Political Attitudes*, p. 57.

17 Kohlberg's typology is discussed and evaluated by Eleanor E. Maccoby, "The Development of Moral Values and Behavior in Childhood," in John A. Claussen, ed., *Socialization and Society* (Boston: Little, Brown and Co., 1968), pp. 227–270.

TABLE 1

A Typology of Compliance in Percentages

	All Respondents N=202	Yes Answers	White Yes Answers N=123	Black Yes Answers N=79
Level 1. Pre-Moral Level:				
A. Punishment and obedience orientation (obey rules to avoid punishment).	19	28	29	28
Level 2. Morality of Conventional Rule-Conformity:				
B. Authority-maintaining morality (no choice but to obey, law is law, if society says to obey, one must).	23	33	31	37
Level 3. Morality of Self-Accepted Moral Principles:				
C. Morality of contract and democratically-accepted law (conform to maintain the respect of the impartial spectator judging in terms of community welfare).	22	32	34	29
D. Morality of individual principles by conscience (conform to avoid self-condemnation).	2	3	2	2
No Answer	3	4	4	4
Total	69	100	100	100

values and each is willing to make personal judgments about right and wrong. In a democratic system of government an individual can internalize the values of the system and still refuse to comply with the system on individual decisions. The individual can, in fact, use the values of the system as the basis for his noncompliance. Such a refusal is seen here as grounded in a more complex and internalized antecedent of conformity than fear of punishment or rule conventionality. This is exemplified by 65 per cent of the noncompliers who state that a citizen is not obligated to obey an unjust or inappropriate law. Adding the students at level 3 on Table 1 and the three groups here, we find that only 53 per cent of all the students respond to compliance on the basis of any internalized standards.

Tables 1 and 2 are also broken down by race. In his well-known study of racism in America, Gunnar Myrdal notes that the treatment black Americans have received from the white majority "... prevent[s] the Negro from

TABLE 2

A Typology of Noncompliance in Percentages

	All Respondents N=94	No Answers	White No Answers N=68	Black No Answers N=26
Level 1. Morality of Rule-Conformity Tempered by Personal Judgment:				
A. Extenuating circumstances as justification for rule modification (emergencies might necessitate breaking the law).	5	17	16	19
Level 2. Morality of Self-Accepted Moral Principles:				
B. Obedience based on soundness or agreement with law (not obligated to obey an unjust or inappropriate law).	21	65	62	73
C. Obedience based on individual principles of conscience (a person is morally obligated to break an unjust law).	3	11	13	4
No Answer	2	7	9	4
Total	31	100	100	100

identifying himself with society and the law."[18] If this is true, we might expect to find that the black students are more inclined to believe that laws should not always be obeyed. From the percentage breakdowns in Tables 1 and 2, however, it is easy to see that there is very little difference between black and white responses. To check this further we used discriminant function anaylsis to determine if there were a statistically significant difference between black and white students in terms of degree of compliance.[19] The analysis revealed no statistically significant difference between black and white students in terms of compliance disposition. This does not mean, however, that the predictors of black and white attitudes toward compliance are the same, only that their attitudes do not differ in terms of our classification.

[18] Gunnar Myrdal, *An American Dilemma* (New York: Harper and Brothers, 1944), p. 995. Quoted in Dean Jaros, "Children's Orientations Toward the President: Some Additional Theoretical Considerations and Data," *The Journal of Politics*, 29 (May, 1967), pp. 380–381.
[19] The discriminant function is a multivariate statistical technique that ranks variables according to their ability to discriminate between groups. The technique produces an F value for each variable which indicates whether there is a significant difference between groups on that variable.

TABLE 3

Changes in Attitude Toward Compliance Over the
High School Years in Percentages

Compliance	Grade Level			
	12th	11th	10th	9th
1. Yes, Avoid Punishment	14.1	23.1	23.1	21.5
2. Yes, Rule-Conformity	29.6	30.8	24.2	15.2
3. Yes, Self-Accepted Moral Principles	23.9	7.7	26.4	31.6
4. No, Rule Conformity Tempered by Personal Judgment	2.8	10.3	7.7	3.8
5. No, Self-Accepted Moral Principles	29.6	28.2	18.7	27.8
Total	100	100	100	100
(N)	(71)	(39)	(91)	(79)
	Gamma = 0.0			

Table 3 shows that attitude toward compliance did not differ significantly by grade (freshman, sophomore, etc.). When the sample was divided on race, the analysis still showed no significant differences.

CORRELATES OF COMPLIANCE: TOTAL SAMPLE

Since the socialization literature gives few clues as to the antecedents of compliance, we decided to do an exploratory analysis utilizing multiple regression. Each respondent was asked over 60 questions, including those attitude items usually included in Survey Research Center surveys at the University of Michigan. Single attitude items were combined into indexes of theoretically relevant concepts, most of them familiar to students of political behavior. The indexes were constructed by factor analyzing the variables to check for dimensionality and then each student's score for these several questions was totaled. The indexes were then used as independent variables in the regression analysis.[20] Five major variables constructed were: (1) Police Attitude; (2) Political Trust; (3) Personal Efficacy; (4) Personal Trust; and (5) Political Efficacy.[21]

[20] A good description of this procedure can be found in Oliver Benson, *Political Science Laboratory* (Columbus, Ohio: Charles E. Merrill Publishing Co., 1969), p. 238.

[21] All of these variables except the Police Attitude Score can be found along with a description of the factor analysis technique used to construct them in: Walter F. Murphy and Joseph Tenenhaus, "Public Opinion and the United States Supreme Court: Mapping of Some Prerequisites for Court Legitimation of Regime Changes," *Law and Society Review*, 3 (May, 1968), pp. 380–384. The Police Attitude Score was constructed from the following questions by use of the factor analysis technique described in the above mentioned work (i.e., Kaiser's Varimax solution, with SMC's in the diagonals, orthogonally rotated):
A. Generally speaking, most policemen like to give someone like me a hard time.

These indexes and a number of other variables were all regressed on compliance attitude. Table 4 shows the results for the total sample, and the two major subgroups. Perhaps the most surprising finding for the total group is that the higher the student's grade average[22] the more disposed he is to disobey the law.[23] This finding is consistent, however, with Hess and Torney's finding that "children of high intelligence tend to regard the system in less absolute terms."[24] Table 5 shows that the relationship between grade average and compliance is significant for all three groups, especially the white students. For the total sample, variables 2, 3, and 5 seem to tap a form of support for the political system, its agents, and rules which is associated with compliance.

Some variables that might be expected to be correlated with compliance are not. For example, response to the question "Are all lawbreakers punished?" has no predictive value. Fear of punishment does not significantly account for differences in attitudes toward compliance because neither the compliers or noncompliers are inclined to believe that lawbreakers are always punished. Also, whether the student attended an integrated, partially integrated, or segregated school had no discernible impact on attitude toward compliance.

CORRELATES OF COMPLIANCE: BLACK AND WHITE DIFFERENCES

Earlier we noted that there is no significant difference between the black and white students in terms of compliance disposition. This does not mean, however, that the attitudes of the two groups can be explained by the same antecedents. Therefore, the sample was divided by race, and regression analysis was utilized to determine whether the correlates for each subsample were different from the results obtained for the whole sample.

As Table 4 shows, the correlates for the black students are different in several ways from those of the white students. By far the most significant correlate for the black students is their degree of Political Trust. As Table 6 demonstrates if the black student manifests high or moderate Political Trust, he is significantly more likely to be compliant. However, if the black

---

B. If I need help, I can rely on the police to come to my aid.

C. How honest do you think the police are compared to other men?

D. If I were in trouble with the police, I would feel most confident in being treated fairly by the police.

E. A police officer is only following orders when he is carrying out his duties, and cannot be blamed for what he does.

[22] A beta weight can be thought of as a partial. It shows how much change there is in the dependent variable for each unit of change in an independent variable while holding all other variables constant. See Hubert Blalock, "Causal Inference, Closed Populations, and Measures of Association," *American Political Science Review*, 61 (March, 1967), pp. 130–136.

[23] We have used grade average instead of IQ on the advice of our colleagues in the Department of Education. Standard IQ tests are not used in the state where the data was gathered and many professionals believe the test used to be of little value.

[24] Hess and Torney, *The Development of Political Attitudes*, p. 223.

TABLE 4

Correlates of Compliance Disposition

All Students	
Independent Variables	Beta*
1. Grade Average	− .21
2. Political Trust	.20
3. Police Attitude	.14
4. Personal Trust	.13
5. Laws are Just	.10
* p < .01	R = .41
Black Students	
1. Political Trust	.49
2. Personal Trust	.23
3. Sex	.19
4. Political Efficacy	.14
5. Intent to Continue Education	.12
* p < .01	R = .46
White Students	
1. Grade Average	− .29
2. Laws are Just	.29
3. Police Attitude	.18
4. Family Structure	.14
* p < .01	R = .49

student manifests low Political Trust (alienation)[25] he is slightly more inclined than his similarly inclined white peers to be non-compliant. Our finding that Political Trust has a strong impact on black attitudes toward compliance indicates that Myrdal's thesis (discussed above) is still partially true. The full significance of Political Trust becomes clear when we consider that two variables found to be significantly related to compliance for the black students (grade average, −.14; and Police Attitude, .42) drop out of the equation completely when Political Trust is held constant. Political Trust, then, seems to be an important intervening variable for the black students. Despite either positive or negative attitudes toward the police, or high or low grade average, Political Trust is the principle determinant of compliance disposition for black students. Other important correlates for the black students are Political Efficacy, Personal Trust, and sex. The females are significantly (p < .05) less inclined to break the law than the males. The noncomplying black, then, would most likely be a male who is alienated from the political system.

[25] Joel D. Aberbach has found that the major dimension of political alienation is political trust. See "Alienation and Political Behavior," *American Political Science Review*, 63 (March, 1969), p. 93.

TABLE 5

The Relationship Between Compliance and Grade Average with Race Held Constant (in Percentages)

Compliance Disposition	Grade Average				White Grade Average				Black Grade Average			
	A	B	C	D	A	B	C	D	A	B	C	D
1. Yes, Avoid Punishment	21.9	15.9	23.1	26.3	16.0	15.6	26.6	16.7	42.9	16.7	19.3	42.9
2. Yes, Rule–Conformity	6.3	23.4	27.3	36.8	4.0	22.1	21.9	50.0	14.3	26.7	33.3	14.3
3. Yes, Self-Accepted Moral Principles	15.6	23.4	28.1	26.3	20.0	23.4	28.1	25.0	0.0	23.3	28.1	28.6
4. No, Rule–Conformity Tempered by Personal Judgment	6.3	4.7	5.8	5.3	4.0	5.2	6.3	8.3	14.3	3.3	5.3	0.0
5. No, Self-Accepted Moral Principles	50.0	32.7	15.7	5.3	56.0	33.8	17.2	0.0	28.6	30.0	14.0	14.3
Total	100	100	100	100	100	100	100	100	100	100	100	100
(N)	(32)	(107)	(121)	(19)	(25)	(77)	(64)	(12)	(7)	(30)	(57)	(7)
	Gamma = −.29 p < .01				Gamma = −.33 p < .01				Gamma = −.14 p < .05			

TABLE 6

The Relationship Between Political Trust and Compliance with Race Held
Held Constant (in Percentages)

Compliance Disposition	Political Trust			Black Political Trust			White Political Trust		
	High	Medium	Low	High	Medium	Low	High	Medium	Low
1. Yes, Avoid Punishment	33.3	18.1	15.9	43.8	20.0	13.3	28.6	17.1	17.9
2. Yes, Rule–Conformity	21.6	25.6	21.7	18.8	34.5	23.3	22.9	21.0	20.5
3. Yes, Self-Accepted Moral Principles	31.4	26.9	14.5	31.3	29.1	13.3	31.4	25.7	15.4
4. No, Rule–Conformity Tempered by Personal Judgment	2.0	5.6	8.7	0.0	1.8	13.3	2.9	7.6	5.1
5. No, Self-Accepted Moral Principles	11.8	23.7	39.1	6.3	14.5	36.7	14.3	28.6	41.0
Total	100	100	100	100	100	100	100	100	100
(N)	(51)	(160)	(69)	(16)	(55)	(30)	(35)	(105)	(39)
	Gamma = .26 p < .05			Gamma = .38 p < .01			Gamma = .21 p < .05		

The correlates for the white students are very much like those for the total sample, except that Political and Personal Trust drop out of the equation. It is only for the white students that grade average is an imporant determinant of compliance disposition. Similarly the white students' attitudes toward the police and their perception of the justness of laws are important to their compliance disposition. The typical noncomplier in the white sample, then, is bright and skeptical of the regime's agents (the police), and rules (justness of laws).

We were somewhat intrigued by our findings that perception of the justness of laws is an important correlate for the white students (beta = .29), but not for the black students (beta = .03). Our first guess was that the difference was related to cognitive maturity, but our data (using grade average) do not support this conclusion. Further analysis produced some evidence which seems to indicate that the black and white students view the law from a somewhat different perspective. For example, many of the protocols reveal statements by whites like "Niggers don't have to obey the law." On the part of the blacks we found very few replies of that kind with reference to whites. The difference might be that many white southerners feel that recent laws have worked against them, and many blacks may now consider the law to be an ally (not local law, but national law). Notice that in Table 2, 13 per cent of the white students stated that a person is morally obligated to break an unjust law, while only 3.8 per cent of the black students gave such a response. When any individual is asked in a formal situation to think of noncompliance, he may naturally think of laws he disagrees with. For the white students this most likely would be national laws that conflict with regional and local mores. For the black students, however, there may be few examples of laws left that they find obnoxious. Local and state laws supporting racial discrimination have been undercut, even in the South. Private acts are now the pillars of racism. Consequently, the black students may feel that laws are allies, or, at least, not an issue.

This speculation is supported in part by the answers obtained to a question asking the students in which level of government they had the most and least confidence. The answers reveal that the black and white students order their allegiance to the various levels of government in a very different way which leads us to expect that the actions of the various levels would also be perceived and supported differently by the two groups. Sixty-five per cent (N = 67) of the blacks said they had the most confidence in the national government as opposed to 43 per cent (N = 84) of the whites (difference significant at the .01 level). Similarly, 83 per cent (N = 84) of the blacks said they had the least confidence in state or local government whereas only 65 per cent (N = 122) of the whites gave this answer (difference significant at the 0.1 level).

DISCUSSION AND CONCLUSION

Our analysis has shown that the average student's attitude toward law and compliance becomes increasingly more subjective and less idealistic over the school years. By the high school years the subjective nature of laws is obvious to some 85 per cent of the students. Still, we found a surprisingly large number of students who manifest a very unsophisticated attitudinal approach to compliance late into their teens. Of the 202 students who stated that people should always obey the law, two-thirds (N = 124) based their reasoning on fear of punishment or resignation to external rules. These students have not internalized a set of norms to use in relating to the system even at this late stage of their development. This suggests that a large number of adults perhaps never approach law from a very sophisticated perspective. Merelman's speculations about the reasons that the average citizen never develops a political ideology may apply equally well here. That is, a certain level of moral development and cognitive skill may be required before an individual is psychologically capable of approaching law ideologically.[26]

It is worthy of note that of those students who base their compliance attitudes on internalized values (53 per cent of the total sample), a majority (55 per cent) do not believe that people should always obey the law. We doubt that this means that students who have internalized values engage in "rule exception" any more frequently than their peers. It may mean that they are more inclined to "rule rejection," i.e., more inclined to question the right of the system to make certain laws.

Our exploratory analysis of the antecedents of compliance reveals that above-average cognitive skills (high Grade Average) and political alienation (low Political Trust) are the best correlates of noncompliance for the white and black students, respectively. The more developed the student's cognitive skills the more inclined he is to develop personal standards by which he will judge both his and the system's behavior. Similarly, the more alienated the student from the political system, the less inclined he is to go along with its rules. The main supporters of the legal status quo turn out to be that great mass of citizens who are unburdened either by political alienation or above-average cognitive skills (the silent majority?).

[26] Merelman, "The Development of Political Ideology," p. 753.

POLITICAL RESPONSE TO NEW SKILLS: THE CONFORMING AND THE DEVIANT[1]

DEAN JAROS

University of Kentucky

THE MODERN WORLD IS CURRENTLY UNDERGOING A "PARTICIPATION EX-plosion." As the most rapid and dramatic social change that the world has ever seen progresses, men everywhere expect to be more directly involved in the events and institutions which shape their lives. And, with the wider distribution of the skills and resources necessary to participation, these expectations are being realized. The political implications of this increasing emphasis on participation, however, are not clear. It is quite possible that contemporary change fosters attitudes congruent with the "civic culture" and thus produces increased political participation along the lines of the western liberal democratic model. While this notion is important to students of the "development" of emerging nations, it also merits consideration by scholars of systems that already are modern democracies. The dissemination of new skills and resources in such areas might be expected to raise the overall level of conventional democratic political activity like voting and performing party work. Conforming behavior is increased, while a deviant political response, withdrawal or apathy, is minimized.[2]

On the other hand, contemporary change may make men available for political mobilization; subject participants rather than citizen participants may emerge from the process and something quite unlike liberal pluralism might be the expected end product. The consequences for modern democracies are obvious: new skills and more widely distributed resources may produce not conformity but deviance. Moreover, the deviance in question would not be passive withdrawal as discussed above, but positive behavior perhaps to the point of revolutionary activity.[3]

This paper reports an admittedly exploratory inquiry into the conditions under which these differential responses might be expected in democracies. It approaches the problem from the standpoint of anomie theory. Merton holds that in some societies there is a disjunction between "cultural goals" and the "institutional means" for their attainment. In the U.S., for example, there is "great emphasis on the accumulation of wealth as a success symbol without a corresponding emphasis on using legitimate means to march toward this goal."[4] Thus, in the U.S. there will be a "strain toward anomie" distributed among the members of society according to differential abilities

[1] The author gratefully acknowledges the University of Kentucky Research Foundation for its support of the research on which this article is based.

[2] Gabriel Almond and Sidney Verba, *The Civic Culture* (Princeton: Princeton University Press, 1963).

[3] William Kornhauser, *The Politics of Mass Society* (Glencoe: Free Press, 1959).

[4] Marshall B. Clinard, "The Theoretical Implications of Anomie and Deviant Behavior," in Marshall B. Clinard, ed., *Anomia and Deviant Behavior* (New York: Free Press of Glencoe, 1964), p. 14.

to secure the goals by legitimate means. Those who have access to such means will respond to the pressures to achieve wealth in "normal" patterns (conform). Those who do not (generally located in more disadvantaged classes), but who are still urged to achieve wealth as part of a universal cultural ethic, are more likely to exhibit deviant behavior. Various kinds of deviant adaptations are envisioned, but for present purposes "retreatism" (withdrawal, apathy) on the one hand and the more active "innovation" (use of illegitimate means to secure cultural goals) and "rebellion" (use of new means to achieve new goals) on the other are most interesting.

It is reasonable to think of non-participation in a democracy as a retreatist adaptation to an anomic disjunction. The high rate of electoral non-participation in America has drawn considerable comment over the years as has the relationship of non-participation to perceived inability to affect decisions.[5] The current emphasis on increased participation only emphasizes its heretofore low level. But if there are many retreatists, the critical problem is in the nature of their probable response to new resources and skills. Merton would argue that retreatists have opted for their particular deviant mode of behavior because of pre-existing "internalized prohibitions" against any more positive, change-oriented adaptations. They cannot reject the means which society regards as legitimate. Lacking the resources to achieve societal goals by such means, they have failed as members of the system and opted out.[6] One might deduce that the provision of new resources simply eliminates the cause of failure and thus enables these persons to proceed successfully by legitimate means (conform). If retreatists are of this internalized prohibition type, the participation explosion should produce increased conventional democratic political activity, for strain toward anomie is reduced.

Cloward, however, would argue that retreatists may not have any internalized prohibitions at all. As Merton indicates, failure at conformity may produce deviancy. But suppose that these failures fully reject socially sanctioned means. They may seek to innovate, that is use illegitimate means to approach the societal goals, or they may attempt rebellion. However, the use of such positive deviancy does not guarantee any kind of success. Employing even such new and unsanctioned means as may be available, deviants may fail *again* to achieve anything. Then, only after the second round in this double failure may they retreat and become passive. The retreatists in this case are inactive not because of any inhibitions, but because of lack of resources to pursue conforming behavior successfully *and* lack of resources to pursue active non-conforming behavior successfully.[7] If retreatists are of the double-failure variety, the participation explosion may not presage the decline of anomie at all; it might well in-

[5] The number of authors commenting on non-participation is extremely large. For a summary of their concerns, see Lester Milbrath, *Political Participation* (Chicago: Rand McNally Company, 1966), pp. 142–143.

[6] Robert K. Merton, *Social Theory and Social Structure* (Rev. ed., New York: Free Press of Glencoe, 1957), pp. 153–154.

[7] Richard A. Cloward, "Illegitimate Means, Anomie, and Deviant Behavior," *American Sociological Review*, 24 (April, 1959), pp. 164–176.

volve the translation of resources into the ability to sucessfully pursue positive non-conformity in the form of political innovation or rebellion.

Thus, whether the activation of previously inarticulate segments of the population will result in decreased strain toward anomie and produce "re-integration" with society or in increased ability to employ illegitimate means and greater probability of positive deviant behavor depends upon whether we have "internalized prohibition" retreatists or "double failure" retreatists. It is the specific premise of this paper that the non-participatory masses are divided among these two kinds of individuals. Attempts to upgrade, activate, involve, or provide skills for inactive persons can be expected to have differential effects accordingly.

THE STUDY

It should be noted that embedded in the models of non-participation spelled out above there are principles akin to classical learning theory. In both the Merton and the Cloward formulations, retreatism is approached only after specific kinds of behavior have failed to bring reinforcements. Legitimate acts, and perhaps illegitimate acts, have not been rewarded; these acts thus are not learned and do not become part of the response repertoire. However, if the literature on political socialization tells us anything, it is that political dispositions can be acquired without individuals actually undergoing political experiences. The thrust of this literature is certainly toward a conception of "imitative" learning such as developed by Bandura and Walters.[8] It would be extremely difficult to demonstrate that all politically inactive citizens had actually previously experienced some kind of non-rewarding political activity. In fact, much of the literature suggests that many begin their political lives as inactives and stay that way.[9] People, perhaps while very young, learn the retreatist response. This, however, does not damage the utility of anomie theory in the study of political inactivity. In the course of learning a retreatist response, persons may also learn norms relating to political alternatives—legitimate political acts and illegitimate political acts—also by imitative processes.[10] Since this latter learning may be differential, it is possible to have two distinct kinds of inactives despite the fact that neither kind may have engaged in any kinds of political activity at all.

Though the research reported herein hinges importantly on the ability to distinguish between persons who have rejected legitimate political means and those who have not, this distinction is based on manifestations of extant belief systems rather than records of past behavior.

[8] Albert Bandura and Richard H. Walters, *Social Learning and Personality Development* (New York: Holt, Rinehart and Winston, 1963), esp. Chaps. 1–2.

[9] Stein Rokkan and Angus Campbell, "Citizen Participation in Political Life: Norway and the United States of America," *International Social Science Journal,* 12 (No. 1, 1960), pp. 69–99; David Easton and Jack Dennis, "The Child's Acquisition of Regime Norms: Political Efficacy," *American Political Science Review,* 61 (March, 1967), pp. 25–38.

[10] Richard L. Simpson and H. Max Miller, "Social Status and Anomia," *Social Problems,* 10 (Winter, 1963), pp. 256–263.

Subjects. Subjects were 513 students at eastern Kentucky vocational schools. These represented a complete enumeration of all students at the Pikeville and Hazard institutions in the spring of 1968, as well as a complete enumeration of new admissions to the Pikeville school in the fall of 1968. Eastern Kentucky was chosen as the theater for research in order to assure some variance on the means acceptance-rejection dimension. While the overwhelming majority of citizens in politically placid America have not rejected legitimate political means, many eastern Kentucky residents are overtly anti-political and can hardly be said to have internalized prohibitions. Rejection of and hostility toward political authority, especially federal authority, has long characterized the region. Also, the propensity to use violent means for the achievement of ends has drawn much comment.[11]

Variously advanced vocational education students were chosen in order to provide variance on the independent, "new skills" variable. Although the purpose of these schools is hardly overtly political, it is clear that they are designed to counter the withdrawal of a disadvantaged people and to induce and enable them to enter conventional modes of activity (i.e., conform). It is reasonable to assume that some of the skills acquired in these schools' programs (both occupational and social) would be translated into political resources and that these resources might be variously employed. Subjects had no training (the new admissions), one year of training, or two years of training. This three-fold classification characterizes the independent variable.[12]

Instrumentation. A multi-purpose paper and pencil questionnaire was administered to these students by their regular vocational education instructors. Several standard instruments and modes of soliciting data were

---

[11] The cultural tradition of negativism necessary to produce this variance is well reflected in the sample. Though additional evidence could be marshalled, comparisons of the Kentucky subjects with those studied elsewhere in the United States on anomia and political efficacy are instructive.

	Kentucky subjects mean values (N=531)	Comparative data
Anomia[a]	3.46	2.59
Political efficacy[b]	2.41	1.99

[a] Anomia scores range from 0 (non-anomic) to 7 (most anomic). The comparative data are from Aiken, et al., p. 68 (see note 13 below) and refer to a group of displaced Detroit factory workers (N=260). No variances were reported, so tests for significance of difference are not given.

[b] Efficacy scores range from 0 (most efficacious) to 4 (least efficacious). The comparative data are from Angus Campbell, et. al., *The American Voter* (New York: John Wiley and Sons, 1960), p. 105 and refer to a national sample (N=1764). Absence of variance data prevents testing the significance of the difference.

---

[12] These subjects are highly homogeneous along most other variables. Since they are essentially identical in race, class, religion, urbanity, age, and career prospects, no attempt is made to impose controls on any of the reported findings.

employed to provide demographic information, data on normal political participation like voting and registration, and intention to perform normal political acts. Specifically, these involved close adherence to the items of the Survey Research Center's interview schedules.

Propensity to perform or support illegitimate political acts (i.e., positive political deviancy) was measured by two items which rely on face validity: 1) "If a leader were making some really big changes in politics which he thought were right, but found out that he would have to deny some people their legal rights, he should stop." 2) "If a candidate were trying to clean up politics but was defeated in an election, it might be all right for him to use force to take power." Responses were permitted along a five point continuum from strongly agree to strongly disagree.

The strain toward anomie was measured by the Index of Anomia set forth by Aiken, Sheppard and Ferman,[13] a device similar to Srole's well known scale.[14] Political efficacy was measured by the Survey Research Center's four-item instrument. It is reassuring to note that these measures demonstrate acceptable coefficients of reliability even on this subculturally atypical population (.84 and .88 respectively).

The question of acceptance or rejection of legitimate means for the attainment of social goals was approached obliquely. Two themes which run most prominently through the literature of anomie were investigated: the notion of success through individual effort and the idea of despair of one's condition.

Consistently with this literature[15] we argue that persons who see *personal improvement* as a chief social concern are least likely to have rejected prevailing social mores. On the other hand, persons with more collectivist orientations have probably reached the point at which they have considered or are willing to consider unconventional means of attainment. Specifically, our respondents were classified as societal improvers, group improvers, or individual improvers according to the following item:

> Many people see a need for some kind of improvement or betterment in the world. Read the following statements about different ways of making things better and tell which you feel is the *most* true. (Choose only one) 1) Our whole country is sick and needs to be improved. Every person and every group in the nation is at fault, and we must all work to make the whole society better. 2) Society as a whole is fine. The basic problem today is that some groups of people do not do as well as they should. I just feel that some Americans are not being allowed to get what is justly theirs nor do what they want. If some groups had more influence, everything would be all right. 3) We don't have to worry about society and we don't have to

---

[13] Michael Aiken, Louis A. Ferman and Harold L. Sheppard, *Economic Failure, Alienation, and Extremism* (Ann Arbor: University of Michigan Press, 1968), p. 67.

[14] Leo Srole, "Social Integration and Certain Corollaries: An Exploratory Study," *American Sociological Review*, 21 (Dec., 1956), pp. 709–716.

[15] Robert A. Nisbet, *The Quest for Community* (New York: Oxford University Press, 1953), pp. 93–97; James F. Short, Jr., "Gang Delinquency and Anomie," in Clinard, ed., *Anomia and Deviant Behavior*, pp. 75–79.

worry about groups. They are doing fine. It is the individual that needs betterment. The important thing is for me to improve myself.

This device must be treated cautiously on at least two accounts: first, it is subject to all of the difficulties of reliability and validity that attend single-item measurement; and second, there is clearly more to the notion of "rejection of institutional means for attaining societal goals" than can be measured by such an item. It is quite possible for means rejections to take place along quite different dimensions while many legitimate means presently in use in America are quite collective in character.

The idea of despair is also critical to anomie theory.[16] There can be no doubt that anomics are despairing. The more despairing man, we argue, is willing to consider a wider range of alternatives and therefore has a greater propensity to perform illegitimate political acts.

Despair is measured by simply inquiring, in conjunction with the query on the type of human improvement envisioned, what the probability of actual progress is: "How much chance is there that the kind of improvement you choose will actually happen in the near future?" 1) much, 2) some, 3)little, 4) none.

FINDINGS

Our fundamental operating principle is that education or training provides skills that are translatable into propensities to perform political acts. If our reasoning (and previously reported research) have been correct, we should find that our more educated subjects display higher levels of political behavior, whether the behavior in question be legitimate or illegitimate.

We expect that positive relationships will exist between training on the one hand and registration and presidential voting on the other for those respondents who are individually oriented toward improvement and those who are optimistic about improvement. Since this would represent a movement away from the deviant behavior of retreatism toward the conforming behavior of activity, we would expect it to be accompanied by an increase in feeling of efficacy and decrease in feelings of anomie. Persons who are "group" or "society" oriented toward improvement, or who are pessimistic toward improvement are not expected to increase these normal activities with training—we expect them to be activated along other dimensions. If anything, with the increased saliency of other activities, the propensity to perform these acts may decline. For these persons, unlike individualists, training should not affect feelings of anomie or of efficacy. Tables 1 and 2 report these data.

The differential effect of training in producing increased rates of normal political activity is quite striking. Only among persons whom we define to have not rejected societally sanctioned means(the individualists and the optimists) is training a stimulus towards this kind of activity. Moreover,

[16] Dorothy L. Meier and Wendell Bell, "Anomia and Differential Access to The Achievement of Life Goals," *American Sociological Review*, 24 (April, 1959), pp. 189–202.

TABLE 1[a]

Effect of Training on "Normal" Political Activity with Means
Acceptance-Rejection Controlled

| | Kind of Improvement Preferred | | | Probability of Improvement | | | |
	Individ- ual	Group	Society	Much	Some	Little	None
Relationship between training and registration	.51	—.07	.10	.47	.20	—.03	—.28
Relationship between training and presidential vote	.42	.04	—.18	.49	.26	—.43	—.28

[a] All correlation coefficients in this and subsequent tables are Goodman and Kruskal *Gammas*. Dichotomous data on participation are regarded as ordinal. To have voted or registered is more active than not to have done so.

there is at least some tendency for individualists (if not optimists) who are exposed to training to demonstrate a decline in feelings of anomie and increases in feelings of efficacy. The hypotheses that these kinds of subjects would react to training-derived skills by a decline in anomie and a move from retreatism to conformity is at least partly confirmed.

On the other hand, training, as predicted, generally has little effect on the normal political activity of our rejective subjects. Notable, perhaps, is a slight tendency for this kind of behavior to be shunned among those with

TABLE 2

Effect of Training on Anomie and Political Efficacy, With Means
Acceptance-Rejection Controlled

| | Kind of Improvement Preferred | | | Probability of Improvement | | | |
	Individ- ual	Group	Society	Much	Some	Little	None
Relationship between training and political efficacy	.16	.05	.00	.01	.09	—.02	—.01
Relationship between training and anomie	—.22	—.09	—.03	—.04	—.03	—.19	—.10

TABLE 3

Effect of Training on Positive Political Deviancy, with Means
Acceptance-Rejection Controlled

| | Kind of Improvement Preferred | | | Probability of Improvement | | | |
	Individual	Group	Society	Much	Some	Little	None
Relationship between training and willingness to support forceful takeover	−.07	−.08	−.11	−.35	−.06	.05	.39
Relationship between training and willingness to see rights denied	− .01	.13	.19	.01	.02	.21	.56

training. The general lack of impact is duplicated in the miniscule effect which training has on efficacy and anomie levels of the rejective subjects.

What of positive forms of deviant political behavior? Since the rejective subjects are not moved toward conformity by training and their feelings of anomie remain, our suspicion that they may translate their training-derived skills into positive deviancy is increased. Table 3 examines this proposition directly.

Again the evidence is convincing. Though the suggestion that collectivists translate their training skills into positive deviancy is relatively weak, the contrast between the optimistic and despairing in this regard is pronounced. The despairing clearly declare themselves more likely to support extreme political moves when they are trained. Generally, training does not affect the propensity of optimists or individualists to support positive deviancy, except for one instance in which it produces a decrease.[17]

[17] It is interesting to note that if means acceptance-rejection is not controlled, the relationship between training and political behavior, "normal" or deviating, is largely obscured. The suggestive nature of our approach is thus underscored.

Relationships Between
Vocational Training and Political Behaviors and Expressions

Registration	Participation 1968 primary	Participation 1968 Presidential Election	Support for Denial of Rights	Support for Force to Take Power
.23	−.08	.10	−.09	−.10

DISCUSSION

The question of the direction that increased participation in democracies may take appears to have a two-fold answer. Anomie theory suggests that new political skills may be translated into increased "normal" democratic activity or into deviant forms depending upon the nature of the inactive people who receive the skills. They may be "internalized prohibition" retreatists (who have not rejected socially sanctioned means) or "double failure" retreatists (who, by contrast, are quite rejective of such methods).

We showed that both kinds of retreatist empirically exist, and that they exhibit differential responses to stimuli to action. For the former, training appears to be translated into legitimate means and increased propensities to perform "normal" political activity, while at the same time decreasing feelings of anomie. For the latter, training does little to eliminate the strain toward anomie; it merely provides the skills necessary to move to another deviant response.

The implications are twofold: first, the utility of anomie theory for the explanation of various kinds of mass political behavior should be more thoroughly explored. If it can aid in explaining the occurrence of one form of deviant behavior as opposed to another—or for that matter conformity as opposed to deviancy—it will prove invaluable. The present results are offered as a suggestion that it can. Many potentially fruitful questions are raised. For example, what kinds of conditions make for the creation of an inhibited retreatist rather than a rejective one? Second, from a practical application point of view, one cannot help speculating on the implications of programs (now quite numerous) to involve and activate previously non-participant segments of the population in community life. Exactly what are the effects of providing skills and resources? The fact that they may be differential, even within an apparently quite homogeneous group, should give the policy-maker pause. Nonparticipation, after all, can give way to at least two kinds of behavior; conforming activity or more active deviancy.

SOCIAL DETERMINISM AND RATIONALITY AS BASES OF PARTY IDENTIFICATION[*]

ARTHUR S. GOLDBERG
University of Rochester

I N *THE RESPONSIBLE ELECTORATE*, V. O. KEY URGED UPON US "THE PERVERSE AND unorthodox argument . . . that voters are not fools."[1] He challenged the notion that the voting act is the deterministic resultant of psychological and sociological vectors. He believed that the evidence supported the view of the voter as a reasonably rational fellow. The present article offers a corollary to Key's "unorthodox argument." It suggests that certain sociological determinants, specifically group norms regarding party identification, may, upon examination, prove to be rational guides to action. For the voter who is a reasonably rational fellow, it will be argued, these group norms may seem rather sensible.

I. THE CONCEPT OF RATIONALITY

Before proceeding to the analysis of data, some discussion of the notion of rationality seems in order. The usage subscribed to in the present analysis derives from contemporary game theory.[2] Put most simply, being rational in a decision situation consists in examining the alternatives with which one is confronted, estimating and evaluating the likely consequences of each, and selecting that alternative which yields the most attractive set of expectations. Formally, this process entails making calculations of the following type as a basis for the decision:

$$E(Va_1) = P(o_1 \mid a_1)V(o_1)$$
$$+ P(o_2 \mid a_1)V(o_2) + P(o_3 \mid a_1)V(o_3)$$
$$E(Va_2) = P(o_1 \mid a_2)V(o_1)$$
$$+ P(o_2 \mid a_2)V(o_2) + P(o_3 \mid a_2)V(o_3)$$

where:

$E(Va_j)$ = expected value of alternative i.
$P(o_j \mid a_i)$ = probability of outcome j given that alternative i is chosen.
$V(o_j)$ = value of outcome j to the decision maker.

Having made such calculations, one then chooses the alternative with the greatest expected value. All individuals are assumed to act so as to *try* to maximize expected value. In this sense, all are equally rational. However,

[*]Reprinted by permission of the author and publisher, from Arthur S. Goldberg, "Social Determinism and Rationality as Bases of Party Identification," *American Political Science Review*, 63 (March, 1969), pp. 5–25.
[1]V. O. Key, Jr. *The Responsible Electorate* (Cambridge, Mass.: The Belknap Press of Harvard University Press, 1966), p. 7.
[2]See R. Duncan Luce and Howard Raiffa, *Games and Decisions* (New York: John Wiley and Sons, 1957), Chap. 2.

there is room for error in these calculations. Individuals may, therefore, vary in their effective rationality.

There are several sources of error. The relevant probabilities are not necessarily known, and may have to be estimated; the quality and cost of information thus affect the accuracy of the calculations. The calculations themselves are not cost free, being far more costly for some than for others. However, one component of these calculations is not admissible within the theory as a source of error, i.e., the values assigned to outcomes. The placing by an actor of a very high value for him upon having a Catholic for Predident, or upon obtaining an outcome which will aggravate his brother-in-law, or upon thwarting some target group cannot be adjudged within the theory. Therefore, in the analysis that follows, terms such as "more rational" and "less rational" refer in all cases to effective rationality, i.e., to the accuracy of the expected value calculations. No set of values is being judged against some exogenous criterion of "rational correctness."

However, the analysis is heavily dependent upon an assumption about effective rationality. Specifically, the assumption is made that, *ceteris paribus*, effective rationality, i.e., the accuracy of one's expected value calculations, increases as a function of education. Education is assumed to lower information costs, e.g., by improving one's ability to read and comprehend such information sources as the *New York Times*, and thus to improve the accuracy of one's estimates of relevent probabilities. Education is also assumed to act upon innate intelligence so as to develop it toward its full potential. Thus, errors in the performance of the calculations ought to be reduced. In brief, education is assumed to facilitate accurate perceptions of means-ends relationships and to facilitate appreciation of the import of such relationships for one's own goals.[3]

Of late, there has been emerging from the voting literature a model of the voter as rational maximizer of expected utility.[4] The analysis of empirical evidence in the context of this model is still quite rare, but by no means non-existent. Current intellectual investments in the model, and the very nature of its logical qualities, suggest that it will increasingly become a central concept in the discipline.[5] In its application, the political scientist is, of course, primarily interested in the substance of the expected value cal-

---

[3]One may regard education, from this point of view, as a capital investment oriented toward long-run reduction of information and calculation costs. For these notions on rationality and education, I am indebted to Peter C. Ordeshook, from whose work on a general rationality model of electoral behavior they are derived.

[4]The seminal work here has been Anthony Downs, *An Economic Theory of Democracy* (New York: Harper & Row, 1957). For critical appraisals, see Donald E. Stokes, "Spatial Models of Party Competition," *American Political Science Review* 57 (1963), pp. 368–377; and Philip E. Converse, "The Problem of Party-Distances in Models of Voting Change," in M. Kent Jennings and L. Harmon Zeigler, eds., *The Electoral Process* (Englewood Cliffs: Prentice-Hall, 1966), Chap. 9.

[5]See, for example, James M. Buchanan and Gordon M. Tullock, *The Calculus of Consent* (Ann Arbor: The University of Michigan Press, 1962); Otto A. Davis and Melvin Hinich, "A Mathematical Model of Policy Formation in a Democratic Society," *Mathematical Applications in Political Science, II*. Arnold Foundation Monographs XVI. (Dallas: Arnold Foundation, Southern Methodist University,

culations. One is particularly concerned with ascertaining which factors are heavily weighted in the calculations. Are they policy outputs and promises as in the Downs model,[6] non-policy-based anxieties as in some psychological findings,[7] desires for symbolic gratifications,[8] or what? What is the distribution of dominant factors across the electorate? Key was persuaded that policy counted heavily. (In fact, he seemed willing to regard behavior as rational only where this was the case—a usage different from that in the present analysis.) The present article, while not directly addressed to this question, is substantially related to it. The question at issue here is whether group political norms are seen as effective means to their desired ends by those best equipped to make the judgment.

II. A CONFLICT OF MODELS?

One of the most powerful determinants of voting behavior isolated to date appears to be the self-identification of the voter with a particular party. Empirical findings to this effect are legion.[9] Moreover, there is a substantial empirically-based literature, which indicates that an individual develops a party identification quite early in life, during childhood, in fact. This identification is well-established before the individual has any knowledge of either the policy history of the party with which he identifies, or of the implications of that history for his own interests. Essentially, the acquisition process appears to consist in imitative and affective conditioning to the parental partisan preference.[10] Once acquired the identification proves to be remarkably stable, with some 70 to 80 per cent of those voters who know their paternal party identifications reporting the same identifications for themselves.[11]

1966), pp. 175–208; and William H. Riker and Peter C. Ordeshook, "A Theory of the Calculus of Voting," *American Political Science Review*, 62 (March, 1968), pp. 25–42.

[6] Downs, *An Economic Theory of Democracy*.

[7] For example, in Eugene Burdick and Arthur J. Brodbeck, eds., *American Voting Behavior* (Glencoe: Free Press, 1959), see Arthur J. Brodbeck, "The Problem of Irrationality and Neuroticism Underlying Political Choice," Franz Alexander, "Emotional Factors in Voting Behavior," and Richard E. Renneker, "Some Psychodynamic Aspects of Voting Behavior."

[8] See Murray Edelman, *The Symbolic Uses of Politics* (Urbana: University of Illinois Press, 1964).

[9] See, for example, Bernard R. Berelson, Paul F. Lazarsfeld, and William N. Mc-Phee, *Voting* (Chicago: The University of Chicago Press, 1954), Chaps. 9–10; Angus Campbell, Philip E. Converse, Warren E. Miller, and Donald E. Stokes, "Party Loyalty and the Likelihood of Deviating Elections," *Journal of Politics*, 24 (1962), pp. 689–702.

[10] See Herbert H. Hyman, *Political Socialization* (Glencoe: Free Press, 1959), Chaps. 2–3; David Easton and Robert D. Hess, "The Child's Political World," *Midwest Journal of Politics*, 6 (1962), pp. 229–246; and Fred I. Greenstein, *Children and Politics* (New Haven: Yale University Press, 1965), Chap. 4. An overview of the socialization processes involved is provided in Robert E. Lane and David O. Sears, *Public Opinion* (Englewood Cliffs: Prentice-Hall, 1964).

[11] Cf. Campbell, *et. al*, "Party Loyalty," p. 147; see also Philip E. Converse and Georges Dupeux, "Politicization of the Electorate in France and the United States," *Public Opinion Quarterly*, 26 (1962), p. 14.

How well does the notion of the rational voter comport with the evidence cited which suggests that a party identification, established in childhood and seemingly quite resistant to change, is a major determinant of voting behavior? Having no wish to build straw men, let me immediately point out that there is not necessarily an incompatibility here. If one admits the possibility that the imitatively and affectively conditioned party identification learned in childhood might prove a rationally sound guide to action when examined in adulthood, a possible basis for reconciliation is available. This is the possibility which will be explored in the present analysis.

While the evidence to be examined sheds light on the question at hand, some of that evidence was initially analyzed for a different purpose. An appreciation of the meaning of the evidence requires that a somewhat circuitous route be taken in examining it. Some forebearance is therefore sought from the reader in the initial stages of the analysis. In return, assurance is given that the initial data presented, while somewhat removed from the main question, are themselves of substantive import, and lead to a sharp focus upon the main question, namely, rationality and social determinism as bases of party identification.

III. BACKGROUND OF THE INVESTIGATION

The original topic of inquiry was defection from parental party identification. In seeking to account for this relatively infrequent phenomenon, some unanticipated findings were encountered. After a bit of retroductively-oriented contemplation, it became possible to "make sense" out of these findings. Quite simply, they made sense if the norms proffered by the parent were substantively rational for the self-interest of the offspring, i.e., increased his effective rationality. Since an explanation can be found for almost any set of findings, the discovery of an explanation was not, in itself, taken as proof of the validity of the explanation. Instead, several deductions were made, based upon the foundations of this explanation. Upon investigation, these deductions were found to be supported by the data, and, as a result, the reader is burdened with the present article. At the outset one must dwell a bit upon the original inquiry in order to appreciate the nature of the unanticipated findings.

Since the object of that inquiry—defection from parental party preference—occurs rather infrequently, some care was used in conceptualizing the independent variables in order that they might more readily be operationalized in productive ways. One of the major variables initially under consideration was social mobility. The usual reasoning applied: it was assumed that such mobility put the individual into a new social environment, the norms of which might be different from those of his parents. The resultant pressures of his adult environment might produce a shift on his part toward the norms of the new environment, and thus an abandonment of the parental party preference. A bit of additional thought on this matter, however, revealed that the logically implicit variable was not necessarily social mobility, but a strain between the parental partisan norm and the norm of the adult social environs. Moreover, there was an additional path to such strain, beyond that provided by social mobility. Specifically, it is logically possible for such strain to develop when the parental norms are atypical in their social environs and the individual remains in those environs in adulthood. Thus, the individual whose father is an Irish blue-collar worker, and a Republican in an urban Democratic neighborhood and who is himself a blue-collar worker in that neighborhood, may be under as much strain as he would have been had his father been a Democrat while he himself became a physician and moved to the suburbs. It was not too difficult to devise a technique for measuring this hypothetical strain, however caused.

The technique used was to develop an "expected value" of the respondent's being a Republican, based upon his sociological characteristics.[12] In order to do this the respondent's party identification (Coded Republican = 1, Democrat = 0) was regressed upon five of his sociological characteristics in a multiple regression analysis.[13] The expected value thus generated is effectively an estimate of the probability that an individual with a given set of sociological characteristics is a Republican. One can compare this value with the father's party identification (Coded Republican = 1, Democrat = 0) and see how close the respondent's probability of being a Republican is to his father's actual state of being one. The absolute difference is a measure of strain between partisan norms of the respondent's adult environment, and the partisan preference of his father.[14] This concept will be referred to as

[12] The reader should note, at this point, that in the operation to be described, statistical averages of a national sample were used as representations of felt environmental norms. This dubious procedure will be discussed at a later point in the analysis (see pp. 244, below). Particular sociological characteristics were chosen with a view toward reducing the discrepancies between such averages and felt norms and with a concern for minimizing multicollinearities. The specific characteristics utilized were: religion, self-rating on class, size of community, region (South, non-South), and race (white, non-white).

[13] In all cases, nominal data were converted to dummy variables and treated as prescribed in Daniel B. Suits, "The Use of Dummy Variables in Regression Equations," *Journal of the American Statistical Association* 52 (1957), pp. 548-551.

[14] The reader's attention is called to the fact that paternal partisan preference is ascertained on the basis of respondent's recall. Work by M. Kent Jennings and Richard G. Niemi suggests something of the magnitude of the error thus induced. From the point of view of correlation, Niemi finds a Kendall's tau of 0.60 between party identification claimed by the respondent's father and that ascribed to the father by the respondent. See Richard G. Niemi, "A Methodological Study of Political Socialization in the Family," Ph.D dissertation, University of Michigan, 1967), pp. 113-115, 128. A further analysis of this data by this writer with the cooperation of Professor Niemi indicates that 78.4 per cent of the students correctly identify their fathers in the broad categories of Democrat, Independent, Republican. The 21.6 per cent of incorrect identifications are about evenly split between incorrect assignment with regard to the category of Independent (10.6 per cent) and assignment to incorrect partisanship (11.0 per cent).

Insofar as there is any systematic bias in the errors, it seems to operate in a manner not seriously debilitating to the present analysis. Respondents appear to be biased toward perceiving their patents as having a partisanship which is "normal" for people of like social characteristics. Thus where parents are identified as having a sociologically deviant identification, the ascribed identification is apt to be correct. This is rather important as such identification proves of central concern in the present analysis. See Niemi, "A Methodological Study of Political Socialization," pp. 126-128.

TABLE 1

Defection as a Function of Intergenerational Strain[a]

	Score on Strain											
	0.0	0.1	0.2	0.3	0.4	0.5	0.6	0.7	0.8	0.9	1.0	Total
Defection	4	1	22	51	67	46	51	17	2	—	1	262
Loyalty	7	11	109	234	135	73	55	25	2	—	2	653
Total	11	12	131	285	202	119	106	42	4	0	3	915
% Defecting	36.4	8.3	16.8	17.9	33.2	38.7	48.0	40.5	50.0	—	33.3	28.6
$\tau_b = 5.5\%$												

[a] $p < .05$ in this and other tables, unless otherwise indicated.

"intergenerational strain." Recapitulating: intergenerational strain is operationalized as the absolute difference between the father's party identification (Coded Republican = 1, Democrat = 0) and the respondent's regression-generated probability of being a Republican, given his sociological characteristics.

Given this perhaps elaborate operational procedure, one may well ask, does intergenerational strain account for much defection from the parental norm? The data are presented in Table I and again in Figure 1. That the hypothesized relationship is borne out by the data is fairly obvious. Since the frequencies associated with the scores 0.0 and 0.1, as well as with the

FIGURE 1.

Defection as a Function of Intergenerational Strain.

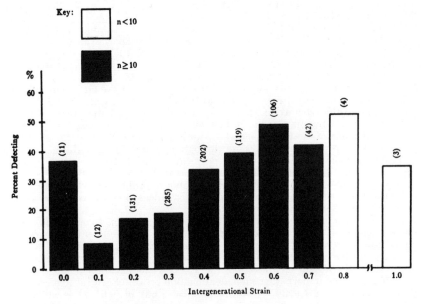

scores 0.8–1.0, are quite small, interest centers on the scores between and inclusive of 0.2 and 0.7. Here the hypothesized relationship does hold, although the relationship is S-shaped rather than linear. Whether much of the defection is thereby explained is another question. As against the standard of 100 per cent of the variance, clearly not much is accounted for. Even using an asymmetric measure of association, Goodman and Kruskal's tau, designed to take advantage of the expectation that there is more information in the independent variable about the dependent variable than vice versa, errors in assignment on the dependent variable are reduced only by about 5.5 per cent.[15] On the other hand, as against other single variable accomplishments with regard to this dependent variable, 5.5 per cent is not trivially small.[16] This finding was, in itself, neither dramatic nor surprising. However, it was in the process of exploring the origins of intergenerational strain that a rather surprising finding did emerge, which in turn proved to be an opening wedge into the inquiry with which the present article is concerned.

In the interest of neatness, if nothing else, it seemed desirable to see how much of strain derived from social mobility on the part of the respondent, and how much of it derived from parents who had party identifications which were sociologically atypical. It was not anticipated that these deviant parental identifications would account for much strain, but some method had to be devised for measuring this "deviance" in order to put the question to rest.

Fortunately a measure of such deviance was readily at hand. The residual in a regression analysis is theoretically a measure of the extent to which an element differs in its dependent variable value from the average of other elements having the identical values on the independent variable(s). Thus, a multiple regression analysis in which the respondent's father's sociological characteristics were the independent variables and in which the father's party identification was the dependent variable would yield residuals well suited to the present task. Indeed, just such a regression was run, and the absolute values of the residuals thus generated were used to measure the extent of sociological deviance in paternal party identification.[17] It may be of

[15] See Hubert M. Blalock, Jr., *Social Statistics* (New York: McGraw-Hill Book Company, 1960), pp. 232–234.

[16] About the best that has been done along these lines with a single variable is the 7.29 per cent of the variance in level of voter stability explained by family reinforcement, in Herbert McClosky and Harold E. Dahlgren, "Primary Group Influence on Party Loyalty," *American Political Science Review*, 53 (1959), p. 774.

[17] Clearly some qualms arise in using the residuals of a linear regression analysis in which the dependent variable was dichotomous. One worries about saturation effects, etc. [See Arthur S. Goldberg, *Econometric Theory* (New York: John Wiley and Sons, 1964), pp. 248–251.] In the actual event, visible saturation effects were infrequent (less than 1 per cent of the cases had predicted values less than zero or greater than one). Moreover, the dichotomous nature of the dependent variable offered certain advantages. First, there is only one possible way to obtain each non-zero value of the residual. Second, there are only two points at which the residuals can be zero, namely, where the predicted and actual values are zero and where the predicted and actual values are one. These polar points become, in effect, the

some comfort to note that those parents who had the highest residuals, 0.847 and 0.718, were intuitively quite deviant, being on the one hand white, working-class, Catholic, Northern, urban, Republicans, and on the other white, middle-class, Protestant, Northern, rural, Democrats. Similarly, those with the smallest residuals, 0.000 and 0.282, were what one would tend to regard as "pure" types, being white, working-class, Catholic, Southern, urban Democrats, and white, middle-class, Protestant, Northern, rural Republicans. Withal, there are some *caveats*, beyond those concerned with statistical propriety, which should be observed. Statistical deviance from a sample norm and social deviance from a felt group norm are not identical, and yet the present study treats them as though they were. The most statistically deviant case in the national sample—the white, working-class, Catholic, Northern, urban Republican—can be found feeling not the least bit deviant and under no social pressures, in, for example, the city of New Haven, Connecticut.[18] Yet such errors of measurement, as they might affect the present study, would of necessity do so in a conservative way, biasing the outcomes *against* the findings which proved to be of interest. Thus, if such findings emerged, they did so in spite of and not because of the weakness in the operational measure.

How much, then, of intergenerational strain results from sociologically deviant paternal party identification? The r^2 between the two variables is 0.58. That is to say, 58 per cent of the variance in one is explainable in terms of the other. Thus, there is a substantial covariation between the two. One can say more than this, however, after examining the pattern of the relationship. This pattern is revealed in Table 2, wherein the variables are each dichotomized, with the attendant loss of information, and yet still yield a tau of 53.9 per cent. Most particularly, one should note in this table that 80.6 per cent of high intergenerational strain seems to result from highly deviant paternal party identification.

Given so strong a relationship between intergenerational strain and sociological deviance in paternal party identification, it certainly seemed advisable to inquire into the effect of such deviance on the relationship between intergenerational strain and defection. This effect is set forth in Table 3 and is quite noteworthy. In the universe comprised solely of those whose paternal party identification is sociologically normal, i.e., where strain results only from social mobility, there is no significant relationship between differences in strain and rate of defection. In the universe comprised solely of those whose paternal party identification was sociologically deviant, there is a significant relationship between strain and defection. In the light of Table 2 one might be inclined to impute all of the high strain in this

---

"normal" points for their respective segments of the distribution (this division occurring at that value of X which yields a predicted value of y of 0.5). Thus, by comparing any two cases on the basis of the absolute values of their residuals, one can say which is closer to his respective "normal" point. It is on this basis that sociological deviance in paternal party identification was measured.

[18] See Robert A. Dahl, *Who Governs?* (New Haven: Yale University Press, 1961), Chapter 5, esp. Table 5.4, p. 60.

TABLE 2

Intergenerational Strain as a Function of
Deviance in Paternal Party Identification

	Score on Deviance[a]			
	High	Low	Total	% High Deviance
High Strain[a]	221	53	274	80.6
Low Strain	49	592	641	7.6
Total	270	645	915	29.6
% High Strain	81.9	8.2	29.9	
τ_b = 53.9%				

[a] High implies >0.500.
Low implies <0.500.
No respondent scored 0.500.

TABLE 3

Defection as a Function of Intergenerational Strain
Controlling for Deviation of Paternal Party Identification

(a) Given normal paternal party identification:

	Score on Strain		
	High	Low	
Defection	14	130	144
Loyalty	39	462	501
	53	592	645
% Defecting	26.4	22.0	22.4
$p > 0.05$			
τ_b = 0.2%			

(b) Given deviant paternal party identification:

	Score on Strain		
	High	Low	
Defection	103	15	118
Loyalty	118	34	152
	221	49	270
% Defecting	46.6	30.6	43.7
$p < 0.05$			
τ_b = 1.7%			

TABLE 4

Defection as a Function of Intergenerational
Occupational Status Mobility Given Deviant Paternal
Party Identification and High Intergenerational Strain[a]

	Intergenerational Occupational Status Mobility		
	Upward	None	Downward
% Defecting	48.0	43.4	49.4
(N)	(77)	(67)	(75)

[a]Two of the 221 respondents in this category provided no information on occupational status mobility. The total N here is therefore 219 as against the 221 in the relevant column of Table 3 (b).

group to the deviant nature of the paternal party identification. However, this assumption is not altogether warranted. Therefore, some direct evidence was sought in the data regarding social mobility. Fortunately this was available in the form of information about intergenerational occupational-status mobility. Therefore, the "high strain" category of Table 3 (b) was examined in terms of the relationship between occupational status mobility and defection. As can be seen in Table 4, there does not appear to be any significant relationship. Thus, on the bases of Tables 3 and 4, social mobility does not appear to be a significant factor in explaining defection from paternal party identification.

This finding concurs with that of Campbell, *et al.*, in their slightly different analysis of the same body of data.[19] However, it does seem to fly in the face of the current lore in the discipline. For example, Henry W. Riecken, in a survey of the literature dealing with primary groups and party affiliation, argues that:

> Upward mobility ... signals not only alienation from parental values, but the likelihood that political preference will shift from Democratic to Republican since the upward mobile person will be moving into predominantly Republican affiliations in primary groups.[20]

He goes on to cite the works of Berelson, Lazarsfeld, and McPhee, of Maccoby, *et al.*, and of McClosky and Dahlgren in evidence.[21]

[19]Campbell, *et al.*, "Party Loyalty," pp. 458–459.
[20]Henry W. Riecken, "Primary Groups and Political Party Choice," in Burdick and Brodbeck, *American Voting Behavior*, p. 167.
[21]*Ibid.*, pp. 167–168. The relevant works are: Berelson, Lazarsfeld, and McPhee, *Voting*; Eleanor E. Maccoby, Richard E. Matthews, and Anton S. Morton, "Youth and Political Change," *Public Opinion Quarterly*, 18 (195?), pp. 23–29; McClosky and Dahlgren, "Primary Group Influence on Party Loyalty." An intimation of the findings of the present study may be seen in Philip E. Converse. "The Nature of Belief Systems in Mass Publics," in David E. Apter, ed., *Ideology and Discontent* (London: Collier-Macmillan Limited, Free Press of Glencoe, 1964), pp. 231–233.

Surely such apparently conflicting conclusions about the role of social mobility in accounting for intergenerational changes in party identification deserve serious treatment. However, since the material to this point is very much by way of preface, such as extended digression here seems ill-advised. Therefore a consideration of the works cited, as they bear upon this problem, is provided as an appendix to the present article. At this point, let it suffice to note that the assertion made in the present study, i.e., that social mobility is not a significant factor in explaining defection, is compatible with the assertion that social mobility, when it occurs, tends to produce defection. All that is required for this compatibility is that either there be relatively little social mobility or that the tendency toward defection induced by social mobility be rather weak. In the actual event, it appears that both conditions exist. For a fuller discussion, the reader is referred to the Appendix.

Presented with the substantial relationship between intergenerational strain and deviance in paternal party identification, as well as with the vitiating effect of such deviance when used as a control on the original relationship between strain and defection, one was naturally curious as to the direct relationship between sociological deviance in paternal party identification and defection from paternal party identification on the part of the offspring. The data are presented in Table 5 and in Figure 2. The relationship is somewhat stronger than the original one between intergenerational strain and defection ($\tau = 6.4$ per cent in the present case as against 5.5 per cent in the earlier case). However, interest in the relationship derives not from its magnitude which is, after all, still quite modest, but from the fact that this phenomenon of sociologically deviant paternal party identification appears to be a more important source of intergenerational defection than does social mobility on the part of the offspring. Sociological deviance in paternal party identification thus assumes a heretofore unanticipated importance, and is perhaps deserving of serious recognition in future analyses.[22]

[22] At this point, it may be worth noting that this concept (sociological deviance) helps to clarify at least one peculiar finding in the existing literature. In *The American Voter*, Campbell, *et. al.*, after noting that the direction of intergenerational social mobility, as measured by occupational status differences, did not seem to be associated with shifts toward the Republican or Democratic identification go on to note, on pp. 458–459, note 15, that: "Upward mobile people are slightly more likely to have shifted from Democrat to Republican identification, than those people whose status has moved downward, *but both types of changers* are more likely to have moved toward the Republican Party than away from it (emphasis added)."

However, this appears to be a consequence of the operation of sociological deviance in paternal party identification, because when analysis is confined to those respondents whose fathers were normally identified, the findings are more in line with what one might traditonally have expected. Upward mobile offspring of Democrats are more apt to become Republicans than are downward mobile offspring of Democrats. Conversely, downward mobile offspring of Republicans are more apt to become Democrats than are upward mobile offsprings of Republicans. Moreover, contrary to the SRC suggestion, the downward mobile progeny of normal Republicans are more likely to become Democrats than are such progency of normal Demo-

TABLE 5

Defection as a Function of Deviance of Paternal Party Identification

	Score on Deviance											
	0.0	0.1	0.2	0.3	0.4	0.5	0.6	0.7	0.8	0.9	1.0	Total
Defection	6	17	48	48	25	36	40	35	5	1	1	262
Loyalty	3	67	198	158	75	39	58	40	14	1	0	653
Total	9	84	246	206	100	75	98	75	19	2	1	915
% Defection	66.7	20.2	19.5	23.3	25.0	48.0	40.6	46.6	26.2	50.0	100.0	28.6
τ_b = 6.4%												

In the present analysis, this new variable, however intrinsically interesting, does not of itself shed light on the central problem of concern. This, the reader may recall, is the potential conflict between the rational voter model and the evidence for social determinism in the establishment of party identification. That sociological deviance in paternal party identification would produce defection among offspring who remained in the same social environs was anticipated under the general social determinism model: only the relatively high incidence of such cases was unanticipated. However, when a relatively routine control was applied to the relationship between deviant paternal party identification and defection, several findings emerged which appeared quite germane to the central concern of this inquiry.

IV. THE PRECIPITANT OF THE PRESENT INQUIRY

Pursuant to relatively standard operating procedure, respondent's education was applied as a control to the relationship between deviance in paternal party identification and defection from that identification on the part of the respondent. There was, at that point in the analysis, no genuine theoretical expectation as to the effect of this control. It did, however, produce a rather unexpected finding. The control revealed that the better educated

---

crats to·become Republicans. Finally, where occupational status has not changed between generations, the Republicans have lost more than the Democrats—a finding compatible with the history of the Republican Party over the past thirty years.

Defection as a Function of Occupational Status Mobility:
Given Normal Paternal Party Identification

	Upward	None	Downward
Father Democrat			
% Defecting	26.4	12.3	18.0
N	(167)	(114)	(122)
Father Republican			
% Defecting	24.5	22.2	29.0
N	(94)	(72)	(76)

FIGURE 2.

Defection as a Function of Deviance of Paternal Party Identification.

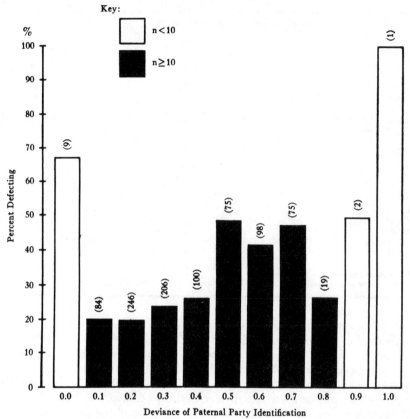

respondents were more likely to defect from deviant paternal party identification than were the less well educated, and, conversely, the better
educated respondents were less likely than the poorly educated to defect
from normal paternal party identification.

As indicated earlier in Table 5, errors in assignment on the dependent
variable (defection from paternal party identification) are reduced by 6.4
per cent by a knowledge of the extent to which paternal party identification
was sociologically deviant.[23] When one controls for education (dichotomizing the sample at the median), the τ_b is increased to 11.3 per cent in the
universe of the better educated, whereas, in the universe of the poorly edu-

[23]Strictly speaking, the reduction is calculated against a null model which is based
upon random assignment in proportions prescribed by the distribution on the dependent variable. For clarification, the reader is again referred to Blalock, *Social
Statistics*.

TABLE 6

Defection as a Function of Deviance of Paternal Party Identification,
Controlling for Education[a]

(a) Given high education level on the part of the respondent:

Score on Deviance

	0.0	0.1	0.2	0.3	0.4	0.5	0.6	0.7	0.8	0.9	1.0	Total
Defection	3	12	27	22	13	19	24	20	1	—	1	142
Loyalty	1	42	125	100	45	16	28	16	5	—	0	378
Total	4	54	152	122	58	35	52	36	6	0	1	520
% Defecting	75.0	20.2	17.7	18.0	22.4	54.3	46.1	55.5	16.7	—	100.0	27.3

$\tau_b = 11.3\%$

(b) Given low education level on the part of the respondent:

Score on Deviance

	0.0	0.1	0.2	0.3	0.4	0.5	0.6	0.7	0.8	0.9	1.0	Total
Defection	3	5	21	26	12	17	16	15	4	1	—	120
Loyalty	2	25	73	58	30	23	30	24	9	1	—	275
Total	5	30	94	84	42	40	46	39	13	2	0	395
% Defecting	60.0	16.7	22.4	31.0	28.6	42.5	34.8	38.5	30.8	50.0	—	30.4

$\tau_b = 3.4\%$

[a]Dichotomization of education level:
low = none through some high school; high = more than some high school.

cated it is reduced to 3.4 per cent. (These results may be seen in the data presented in Table 6, and in Figure 3.) Education appears to sensitize one to the fact of deviance in paternal party identification where such deviance is or has been present. Moreover, where the father has been normally identified, education of the offspring enhances the likelihood of filial loyalty. Perhaps this may be more clearly seen in the percentages in Table 7, despite the loss of information entailed in dichotomization of the independent variable. Most likely to defect are the well-educated offspring of fathers with sociologically deviant party identifications; the defection rate here being 50.0 per cent. Least likely to defect (19.7 per cent) are the well-educated offspring of normally identified fathers. Among poorly educated respondents, those whose paternal party identifications were deviant are more likely to defect than are those whose paternal party identifications were normal (37.9 per cent as against 26.2 per cent). However, poorly educated respondents whose paternal party identifications were deviant, are less likely to defect than are well-educated respondents with similar paternal antecedents (37.9 per cent as against 50.0 per cent). Finally, the poorly educated offspring of normally identified fathers are more likely to defect than the well-educated offspring of normally identified fathers (26.2 per cent as against 19.7 per cent).

None of these differences in per cent defecting are very likely to be due to chance. Of the four comparisons made, and on the basis of two-tailed tests, only one has a probability of occurrence by chance greater than 0.05.

FIGURE 3.

Impact of Education on Defection as a Function of Paternal Deviance.

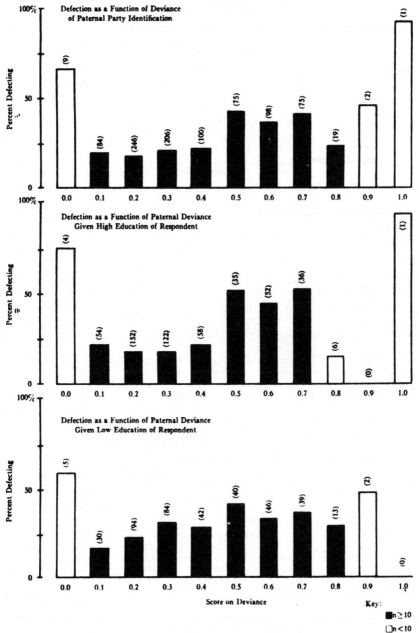

TABLE 7

Defection as a Function of Deviance in Paternal Party Identification
Controlling for Respondent's Level of Education

		Per Cent Defecting (N = 915)	
		Education	
		High	Low
Paternal Party Identification[a]	Deviant	50.0 (130)	37.9 (140)
	Normal	19.7 (390)	26.2 (255)

[a]Deviant: abs value of residual > 0.5
(see above, p. 243).
Normal: abs value of residual < 0.5.

The difference in question is that between the defection rates of poorly educated as against well-educated respondents with normally identified fathers (26.2 per cent as against 19.7 per cent). Even here the probability of occurrence by chance is only 0.0525. These findings, then, seem to warrant serious attention.[24] Assuming for the moment that they are not a function of measurement error—a problem which will be discussed later—under

[24]Lest the reader be apprehensive that the findings in Table 6 reflect *only* the impact of education on offspring of sociologically deviant Democratic identifiers, through the ensuring that such offspring will be in a Republican environment, a further breakdown is presented below.

Defection as a Function of Deviance in Paternal Party Identification,
Controlling for Respondent's Level of Education:
By Partisanship of Father

		Per Cent Defecting			
		Father Democrat		Father Republican	
		High Edu.	Low Edu.	High Edu.	Low Edu.
Paternal Party Identification	Deviant	56.8 (74)	38.7 (62)	41.1 (56)	37.2 (78)
	Normal	18.7 (235)	23.5 (170)	21.2 (155)	31.8 (85)

Two points are particularly worth noting in this breakdown. First, the pattern found in Table 7 holds, regardless of paternal party preference. Second, normally identified Democratic parents also help to insure the political loyalty of their children by furthering their educations.

what theoretical scheme do they make sense? Or put somewhat differently, under what set of assumptions would one expect these results?

V. EXPLANATIONS

There are at least two sets of assumptions under which one would expect these results. One of these, the "brainwashing" model, entails only one assumption, namely, that the educational system of the country "brainwashes" people into believing in their group norms. This model will not be treated seriously in the present study. It is mentioned because it is a logical alternative to the model which will be offered, and because none of the tests performed on the latter in this study are capable of discriminating between the two models. Thus, should any reader wish to dwell upon the matter to the extent of conceiving of a discriminating test, a service would be rendered.

The model which will be treated seriously, the "rationality" model, consists of the general utility maximization model plus three assumptions. These are: (1) that group-based norms regarding party identification produce effective rationality with regard to the goals of the group; (2) that the individual in the group shares the goals of the group; (3) that education increases rationality in the special senses of lowering information costs and developing innate intelligence toward its full potential.[25] Under this set of assumptions, one would expect the well-educated respondents to be better able than the poorly educated respondents to accurately judge the effectiveness of the parental party identification as a guide for the implemention of their own goals. One would also expect, from this set of assumptions, that the sociologically normal identification would be more efficacious than deviant identifications for the accomplishment of the respondents' goals. The well-educated being more readily able to see this than the poorly educated, one would expect defection rates in the following rank order, from highest to lowest: paternal party identification sociologically deviant and respondent well-educated; paternal party identification deviant and respondent poorly educated; paternal party identification normal and respondent poorly educated; paternal party identification normal and respondent well-educated. Thus, these assumptions lead to a set of expectations congruent with the empirical findings; i.e., they provide an explanation for the findings. Of course, an explanation's discovery is not to be taken as proof of its validity. Therefore, attention is shifted to testing, by way of empirical evidence, deductions derived from these explanatory assumptions.

VI. EDUCATION, DEFECTION, AND RATIONALITY

Before proceeding with a description of these deductions, their testing, and the results thereof, a few words are very much in order regarding the direct impact of education in intergenerational defection. Insofar as there was, prior to the explanatory assumptions suggested above, any expectation with regard to this impact, it was that probability of defection would increase with respondent's level of education. This expectation was derived

[25] See note 3, above.

from the work of Maccoby, Mathews, and Morton who found that in Cambridge, Massachusetts, education was positively correlated with defection.[26] Upon application of Goodman and Kruskal's tau to their findings, one finds that a knowledge of education yields a reduction in assignment errors on defection of 4.5 per cent. Thus a similar relationship was expected in the present body of data. However, this did not prove to be the case; a very weak relationship was found, which did not prove significant at the .05 level. The data are presented in Table 8.

TABLE 8

Defection as a Function of Educational Level[a]

	0	1	2	3	4	5	6	7	8	—	Total
Defection	0	29	42	49	5	58	31	28	19	1	262
Loyalty	2	74	90	109	14	146	63	86	66	3	653
Total	2	103	132	158	19	204	94	114	85	4	915
% Defecting	0.0	28.2	31.8	31.0	26.3	28.4	33.0	24.6	22.4	25.0	28.6

$p > .05$

$\tau_b = 1.0\%$

[a]The code for educational level is as follows:
0 = none
1 = some grade school
2 = completed grade school
3 = some high school
4 = some high school & other non-college
5 = completed high school
6 = completed high school & other non-college
7 = some college
8 = completed college
— = not ascertained
Note: Those for whom educational level was not ascertained constitute a violation of the rule that only those about whom full information was available—albeit an inadvertent violation. Where these four enter into calculations, and that is only when education is dichotomized, they are treated as though well educated.

The discrepancy between the findings of the Maccoby, *et al.*, study and the present one may reflect differences in sample bases or in operational procedures. Direct comparisons between the two studies are not quite legitimate, since the operationalization of the dependent variable, defection, was accomplished in substantially different ways. This operation in the present study entails only the establishment of whether or not the respondent continues to identify himself with the party with which he believes his father to have associated himself. Maccoby, *et al.*, on the other hand, have built an index which takes into account the respondent's party identification and current vote preference, and the relationship of these preferences to those of both of his parents.[27]

[26]Maccoby, Matthews, and Morton, "Youth and Political Change."
[27]The problem raised by such as index is that it is difficult, probably impossible, to ascertain which permutation of the components is reflected in a particular instance of a given value of the index, yet it is by no means clear that a given value of the index has the same theoretical relationship to the independent variables, regardless of the permutation of components upon which it is based.

More important for present purposes than their empirical finding, is the rationale which Maccoby, *et al.*, offer for it.

> Presumably, in the course of obtaining an education, the young person is exposed to a wider variety of points of view and more information, so that he is able to make political choices on the basis of "rational" considerations rather than simply on the basis of family tradition (or revolt against family tradition).[28]

Although there is some ambiguity in their explanation—exposure to more points of view and more information could lead to increased defection, even without any increase in the rationality of political choice—the idea that education might produce more rational choice is certainly intriguing, as well as compatible with the assumptions offered in the present study. However, to argue that an increase in rationality—however one wishes to define it—must produce an increase in defection from the traditional primary-group party identification is to argue that the latter is irrational. Doubtless this is not the authors' intent. A more tenable line of argument would be that an increase in rationality produces an increase in defection from traditional identifications in some direct proportion to the extent to which those identifications are irrational. Such a line of argument is readily supported by the present empirical findings relating defection to sociological deviance in party identification with respondent's education as a catalyst in the relationship.

VII. TESTING THE EXPLANATION

It now remains to inquire into the tests of the "rationality" model. The reader may recall that in addition to the general utility maximization model, this approach assumes that group-based norms regarding party identification are rational and that education facilitates utility maximization by reducing information and calculation costs. If education has this catalytic effect, sensitizing the respondent to the irrationality in paternal deviance from group norms of party identification, it ought to be the case that the proportion of defection which occurs during the high school and college years is greater among respondents whose fathers have sociologically deviant party identifications than where those identifications are normal. If sociological norms are rational, and if education sensitizes one to this rationality, then it ought to be possible to predict party identification from sociological characteristics with greater accuracy for well educated than for poorly educated people. Finally, if the better educated, to a greater extent than the poorly educated, do use sociological referents in maintenance of their party identifications, this should be reflected in differences between these two groups in the strength of association between sociological characteristics and partisan attitudes. It was against these deductions that the "rationality" model was tested by way of their goodness of fit with available evidence.

[28] Maccoby, Matthews, and Morton, "Youth and Political Change," p. 38.

In order to test the first deduction, i.e., that the high school and college years account for a greater proportion of the defection which occurs where paternal party identification was deviant than of the defection which occurs when such identification was normal, it was necessary to establish the respondent's age at the time of defection. This had to be done in an indirect way and a certain problem of inference developed. The body of data being analyzed permitted one to establish the respondent's recollection of his father's party affiliation, the respondent's own present party identification, whether or not the respondent had ever identified himself with a party other than the one with which he was currently identified, if so, when he had assumed his current identification, and his age. From these data one could establish whether the respondent had a party identification different from that of his father. If so, the respondent was classified as a defector and became of interest for present purposes. His age at defection was established on the bases of the year in which he had assumed his current identification and of his age in 1956. However, more than half of those who did not identify with the same party as that with which they identified their fathers, claimed *never* to have identified themselves as supporters of a party other than their current one.

The work of Greenstein and others suggests a substantial recall error here, perhaps because of respondents' confining themselves to their adult years in tracing their histories of party identification.[29] The data are presented in Table 9. The grouping of the data in the table into five-year blocs

TABLE 9

Age at Time of Defection as a Function of Deviance in
Paternal Party Identification

| | | Frequency Distributions | | | | | | | |
| | | | | | | Age at Defection | | | |
		0-4	5-9	10-14	15-19	20-24	25-29	30-34	35-39
Paternal Party	Deviant	72	0	8	8	7	8	3	4
Identification	Normal	68	2	13	9	8	18	4	11

		40-44	45-49	50-54	55-59	60-64	65+		Total
Paternal Party	Deviant	0	6	0	2	0	0		118
Identification	Normal	6	1	3	0	0	1		141

was done for convenience, but the reader should bear in mind that those classified as defecting between birth and the end of the fourth year are actually those who claim never to have identified with the father's party.

An examination of the table reveals that the high school and college years (ages 15–24) account for 15/118ths or 12.7 per cent of the defection which occurs where paternal party identification was sociologically deviant, and

[29] See note 10, above.

16/144ths or 11.1 per cent of the defection where such identification was normal. Although the difference in proportions is in the expected direction, the difference is so small as to have a very high probability of occurrence by chance. At this point, those respondents who claim *never* to have identified with the paternal party become a source of concern. If one assumes (and it is a rather arbitrary assumption) that these respondents mean *never during their adult years*, then one may possibly infer that their defections occurred between the ages of 15 and 24. If these people are included in the previous analysis, then the high school and college years account for 87/-118ths or 73.7 per cent of the defection which occurs where paternal party identification was sociologically deviant as against 85/144ths or 59.0 per cent of the defection where such identification was normal. This difference in proportions is not only significant at the .05 level, but has a probability of occurrence by chance of only 0.0132. However, despite this, the rather arbitrary assumption made with regard to those responding "never," requires one to conclude that at best the deduction being tested was not refuted by the data. To say that it was supported by the data would be unwarranted.

The next deduction to be tested was somewhat more straightforward, and the results were also rather more straightforward. If the sociological norms of party identification are rational, and if education enables one more readily to perceive this rationality, then one ought to be able to predict party identification from sociological characteristics with greater accuracy for the better educated half of the sample than for the less well educated half. With the sample thus divided at the median level of education into two groups, a linear multiple regression was run in each group in which respondent's party identification was regressed upon his religion, self-identification as working or middle class, community size (farm, town, metropolis), region (South, non-South), and race. In the better educated half of the sample, these characteristics accounted for 26 per cent of the variance in party identification, whereas among the less-well-educated half of the sample only 7 per cent of the variance was accounted for by these characteristics. Thus one can safely say that the data here support the deduction, in that sociological characteristics account for very nearly four times more of the variance in party identification among the well-educated than in the case among the poorly educated. This was the strongest single finding supportive of the explanatory model, but the third deduction remained to be tested in order to shed light upon the cognitive processes involved. While sociological characteristics appeared to be rational guides to action, was this reflected in the attitudes of the respondents? Inquiry was made into this via the relationship between partisan attitudes and sociological characteristics.

Ascertaining the extent to which partisan attitudes reflect sociological characteristics was something of a problem. Had each of these been a single variable, the problem would have been relatively simple, lending itself to analysis by way of correlations. In the actual event, partisan attitudes consisted of four variables, and sociological characteristics were five separate variables.[30] The approach taken was to ask to what extent predictions of party identification based upon sociological characteristics lead to the same set of expectations as those generated by basing such predictions upon partisan attitudes. This approach was implemented by using the two sets of predicted values generated by regressions of party identification upon sociological characteristics and partisan attitudes respectively. Each of these sets of predicted values was then dichotomized at 0.500. Within each set, those with predicted values greater than 0.500 were classified as "expected Republicans," and those with predicted values less than 0.500 were classified as "expected Democrats." These two sets of expectations regarding party identification—one set based upon sociological characteristics and the other set based upon partisan attitudes—were then cross-tabulated and the Goodman and Kruskal tau measure of association used to establish how much information expectations based upon sociological characteristics contained about expectations based upon partisan attitudes.[31] This entire procedure was implemented separately in each of the two educational groups. The results are presented in Table 10.

As can be seen in Table 10, there is very nearly five times as much information about the dependent variable in the independent variable among the well-educated as among the poorly educated. (Goodman and Kruskal's tau is 11.0 per cent in the former instance and no more than 2.4 per cent in the latter instance.) Thus, the findings support the idea that sociological considerations are a more salient referent for the formation of partisan attitudes among the well-educated than among the poorly educated, and hence, they support the explanatory model being offered. However, given that even among the well-educated, the tau is only 11 per cent, it seems clear that sociological considerations, as herein measured, are only a part of the total set of rational considerations.

VIII. SUMMARY, CAVEATS, AND CONCLUSIONS

The inquiry began with the discovery of two rather unanticipated relationships in the data. First, the evidence suggested that sociological deviance in party identification on the part of the respondent's father was an important source of intergenerational defection in party identification. Moreover, and of central importance here, it was discovered that this relationship was stronger among the better educated than among the less-well-educated respondents. An explanation was generated for the second finding. This explanation consisted in the utility maximization model plus three assumptions: (1) that group-based norms regarding party identification produce effective rationality with regard to the goals of the group; (2) that the individual in the group shares the goals of the group; (3) that

[30] For operational procedures see: Arthur S. Goldberg, "Discerning a Causal Pattern Among Data on Voting Behavior," *American Political Science Review*, 60 (Dec., 1966), p. 922.

[31] Cf. Blalock, *Social Statistics*.

TABLE 10

Prediction of Party Identification from Sociological Characteristics
and from Partisan Attitudes

Given high education:

Prediction Based Upon
Sociological Characteristics

		Republican	Democratic	Total
Prediction Based Upon Partisan Attitudes	Rep.	122	63	185
	Dem.	63	143	206
	Total	185	206	391

τ_b = 11.0%

Given low education:

Prediction Based Upon
Sociological Characteristics

		Republican	Democratic	Total
Prediction Based Upon Partisan Attitudes	Rep.	53	48	101
	Dem.	60	119	179
	Total	113	167	280

τ_b = 2.4%

education increases rationality in the special sense of reducing the costs of information and of calculation. This approach explained the findings in that, under the assumption of the approach, one would expect the well-educated to perceive more accurately than the poorly educated the expected utility associated with paternal party identification. One would expect, under these assumptions, that sociologically deviant party identification would have a lower expected utility than sociologically normal party identification. The findings, then, become anticipated results under the assumptions of the explanatory model.

The explanatory model was then tested by testing deductions made from it against available data. Three deductions were made and tested: first, that the proportion of defection occurring during the high school and college years would be greater where paternal party identification had been sociologically deviant than where it had been sociologically normal; second that one would be able to predict party identification on the basis of sociological characteristics with greater accuracy for the better educated than for the less-well-educated halves of the population; finally, that attitudes toward each of the two parties would reflect sociological characteristics to a greater extent among the well-educated than among the poorly educated halves of the population. As tested, all of these deductions were sustained by the data. However, the strengths of association and differences in proportions involved in the testing, while always in the predicted direction, and while in all cases, save one, statistically significant at the 0.05 level, are nonetheless small enough to preclude seriously considering the inquiry closed.

As the matter now stands, the present analysis seems to suggest that there is a rational component to sociological norms of party identification, but that there are most probably other rational considerations as well. In the absence of such additional considerations, the validity of the rationality model can only be defended by attributing *all* of the unexplained variance in each of the tests to measure error. Both an extension of the model to include other rational considerations, and a reduction in measurement error seem apt prescriptions for further research in this area.

At least three modifications should be made in the model. First, and perhaps most obviously, the model should take account of the fact that there are many routes—other than education—to the reduction of information costs. Occupational roles, leisure time activity, location in formal and informal communication networks, all produce an effect upon information costs beyond that accomplished by education. Second, the model should be made dynamic. That is, it should be able to take into account the fact that policy outputs through time entail shifts in the relative advantages or deprivations to various components of the electorate, and that rational group norms would change accordingly. Finally, as a model of human dynamics, provision ought to be made for the time lag involved in learning that an old norm is no longer functional. One might go further and recognize that there are very likely two time lags, during the first of which opinion leaders learn that the old norm is no longer desirable and during the second of which the new prescription offered by these leaders are being considered and tested by their followers.[32] Indeed, one might even wish to distinguish between opinion leaders and followers by the factors which receive heavy utility weightings in their respective calculations. For opinion leaders, policy considerations might be taken to outweigh considerations of interpersonal affect. For followers, on the other hand, affective consideration might receive priority. Certainly, other modification may prove warranted, but these ought to provide at least a beginning.

Serious efforts are also required in the matter of reducing measurement error. In the earlier discussion of measuring "deviance" in paternal party identification it was noted that the present study treats a statistical norm as a felt norm and that these two are not necessarily equivalent. There are at

[32] Cf. William N. McPhee, *Formal Theories of Mass Behavior* (London: Collier-Macmillan Ltd., Free Press of Glencoe, 1963), Chap. 2. See also William N. McPhee and William A. Glaser, *Public Opinion and Congressional Elections* (New York: Free Press of Glencoe, 1962), esp. pp. 139–151.

least two solutions to the reduction of this aspect of measurement error. For purposes of testing the model, recourse ought to be had once again to community, or perhaps even sub-community studies. Here one could not only more accurately measure norms, but could trace information flows much more readily than with national samples. On the other hand, for inferring national parameters, the simulation approach of Pool, Abelson, and Popkin seems more appropriate.[33] However, the problems of the simulation approach are formidable, most particularly if one recognizes the dynamics operative in the system being approximated by the simulation. It may be recalled that the authors of the Simulmatics Project used "common sense, social science theory, and similar guides" and thus expressed their "best judgment on how different types of voters would respond to a campaign focused on the religious issue."[34] These judgments were assessed against the extent to which they led to correct results when applied in the equations of the model.[35] However, as the authors themselves point out, the inference of national parameters in a complex model entails many difficulties, most especially if the dependent variable is dichotomous. No single trial can genuinely test the estimated parameters, even if the model is assumed correct, in as much as many permutations of the parameters would produce the same results.[36] Many deductions, entailing other than dichotomous outcomes, must be tested in many trials, before one can reasonably begin to believe the estimates of the parameters. However, if these parameters themselves are in flux, the problem becomes substantially more complicated, to say the least.

An even more formidable source of measurement error inheres in the identification of salient group norms. As social scientists, investigators are almost certain to be middle-class people. As political scientists, they are apt to be atypically preoccupied with policy outputs. How likely, then, are such investigators to design a questionnaire which captures the salient events used by a slum dweller in his rational calculus. Even with regard to middle-class norms, there are substantial areas of ignorance. What statistically based inference can one make from the 1956 election data about middle-class values which will explain the Eisenhower victory and the Republican Congressional defeat in that election?[37] The problem of mapping and weighting preferences in the electorate is still rather far from solved. Thus, one can expect tests of the model to be contaminated by measurement error for some time to come.

Despite all these qualms, the present study strongly suggests that there is a rational component to party identifications rooted in group norms. At least in retrospect, the notion is an obvious one. If one considers the origins of

[33] Ithiel de Sola Pool, Robert P. Abelson, and Samuel L. Popkin, *Candidates, Issues, and Strategies* (Cambridge, Masachusetts: The M.I.T. Press, 1964).

[34] *Ibid.*, pp. 54–56.

[35] *Ibid.*, pp. 56–57.

[36] *Ibid.*, pp. 102–106.

[37] Despite Key's laudable efforts in this direction in *The Responsible Electorate* (see, for example, pp. 79–89 of that work), I suggest that the question remains open.

group norms, one expects that at their inception they were rational means to group ends. It may not then be surprising to find that they continue to be rational guides to action, even when learned on primarily affective bases. It might not be untoward, then, for research to be addressed to a world of rational voters seeking to reduce information costs by following group norms, which have in the past seemed effective, with due allowance made in the analytical model for the learning and adaptative processes incumbent upon the voter in attempting to cope with a changing political environment, as well as with his sundry immediate and perhaps more pressing responsibilities.

APPENDIX: AN EVALUATION OF SOME OF THE LITERATURE ON SOCIAL MOBILITY AND INTERGENERATION DEFECTION

Let us examine the literature which Riecken cites regarding the impact of social mobility on partisanship. The first piece of evidence cited in this connection is *Voting*, which presents a chart entitled "The Child's Correspondence with the Father's Vote Is Affected by His Relative Status in the World."[38] Table A1, below, is abstracted from that chart (see Figure A1) and presents information on the impact of upward mobility on the offspring of Democratic fathers. The tau produced by this array is 0.5 per cent and $p > .05$. Thus, as presented in *Voting*, the impact of social mobility on voting behavior is at best very small, as illustrated in Table A1.

Maccoby, Matthew, and Morton in their article "Youth and Political Change" are also interested in the relationship between social mobility and partisan preference.[39] However, their central concern is with the

TABLE A1.

Intergenerational Defection from Democratic Paternal Voting Preference
as a Function of Occupational Mobility[a]

	Child's Occupation		
	Higher than Father	Same as or Lower than Father	Total
Defection	28	41	69
Loyalty	33	63	96
Total	61	104	165
% Defecting	45.9%	39.4%	41.8%
$p > .05$			
$\tau_b = 0.5\%$			

[a]Abstracted from Chart 39 in Bernard R. Berelson, Paul F. Lazarsfeld, and William N. McPhee, *Voting* (Chicago: University of Chicago Press, 1954), p. 91.

[38]Berelson, Lazarsfeld, and McPhee, *Voting*, p. 91.
[39]Maccoby, Matthews, and Morton, "Youth and Political Change."

FIGURE A1.

The Child's Correspondence with the Father's Vote Is
Affected by His Relative Status in the World [a]

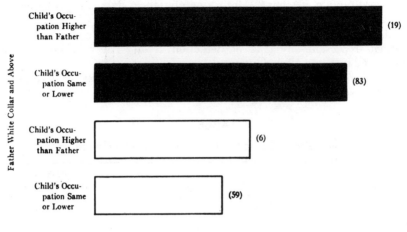

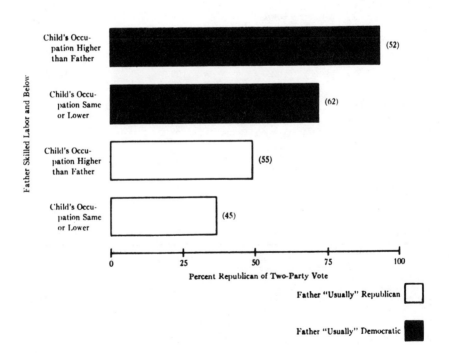

[a] Berelson, Lazarsfeld, and McPhee, *Voting.*

phenomenon of adaptation to group norms. Their data do seem to support the contention that upward-mobile persons tend to manifest the norms of the social strata into which they are moving to a greater extent than downward-mobile persons.[40] Unfortunately, their data are presented in such a way that it is impossible to know the relevant rates of intergenerational defection, or, for that matter, the extent to which the percentage differentials represent any kind of defection at all. The relevant table is reproduced as Table A2, below.

The most directly relevant and, in many ways, the most substantial set of findings supporting social mobility as a major factor in intergenerational

TABLE A2

Social Mobility Related to Choice of Party and Candidate[a]

Party Preference	Upward Mobile	Non-Mobile, in Class Where Upward Mobiles Originated[b]	Non-Mobile, in Class to Which Upward Mobiles Moved[b]
Republican definitely	18%	8%	21%
Republican leanings	5	—	—
Independent	9	18	28
Democratic leanings	12	1	8
Democratic definitely	56	73	43
	100%	100%	100%
Number of cases	82	73	73
Candidate choice			
Eisenhower	48%	28%	37%
Stevenson	52	72	63
	100%	100%	100%
Number of cases	82	72	72
Republican definitely	28%	21%	11%
Republican leanings	3	—	—
Independent	8	28	17
Democratic leanings	4	8	3
Democratic definitely	57	43	69
	100%	100%	100%
Number of cases	75	73	73
Candidate choice			
Eisenhower	46%	38%	27%
Stevenson	54	62	73
	100%	100%	100%
Number of cases	74	72	72

[a]Students are excluded from this table, since their mobility is still undetermined.

[b]For purposes of comparison, the non-mobile cases have been weighted to cancel out differences between them and the mobiles in socio-economic status. That is, for the first comparison, the non-mobiles have been weighted so as to have the same SES distribution as the mobile people at their point of origin. For the second comparison, the non-mobiles have been weighted so as to have the same distribution as the mobiles have in their destination class.

Source: Eleanor E. Maccoby, Richard E. Mathews, and Anton A. Morton, "Youth and Political Change," *Public Opinion Quarterly*, 18 (1954–1955), p. 35.

[40] *Ibid.*, pp. 33–36.

TABLE A3

Relation Between Voter Stability, Family Preferences, and Social Distance[a]

Family Preference Is Republican

Respondent's Preference Is	Favorable (Rep)	Respondent's Social Mobility is: Neutral (%'s Down)	Antagonistic (Dem)
Republican	84.6	60.8	42.1
Democratic	15.4	39.1	57.9
Sample size	39	23	19
Mean Stability score*	4.90	3.91	3.32

Family Preference Is Democratic

Respondent's Preference Is	Favorable (Dem)	Respondent's Social Mobility is: Neutral (%'s Down)	Antagonistic (Rep)
Democratic	84.3	62.9	50.0
Republican	15.5	37.0	50.0
Sample size	32	27	12
Mean Stability score*	5.25	4.04	3.50

*The Mean Stability score is computed on a 6-point scale in which 6.0 represents highest party stability in the same direction as the family preference, and 1.0 represents highest stability in the direction of the party opposed by th family.

[a]Herbert McClosky and Harold E. Dahlgren, "Primary Group Influence on Party Loyalty," *American Political Science Review*, 53 (1959), p. 769.

defection is that produced by McClosky and Dahlgren.[41] The relevant table from their article is presented as Table A3, below. Among those whose family preference is Republican, the relationship between respondent's social mobility and his party preference yields a tau of 13.5 percent ($p < .01$); among those whose family preference is Democratic, the same relationship yields a tau of 8.6 per cent ($p < .05$). In comparison with the strengths of association developed in the present study, these are sufficiently large to warrant a reconsideration of the assertion that social mobility is not a significant factor in accounting for intergenerational defection. Yet, a careful examination of Table A3 reveals that McClosky and Dahlgren are utilizing the term social mobility in a rather unusual way. They do

[41]McClosky and Dahlgren, "Primary Group Influence on Party Loyalty."

not use the trichotomy "upward-none-downward," but rather a trichotomy "favorable-neutral-antagonistic" to describe their categories of social mobility. An examination of the marginals strongly suggests that these are *not* equivalents. For example, if where the parental preference was Democratic, "antagonistic" is taken to mean upward mobility, then only 17 per cent of the offspring of Democratic parents have been upwardly mobile. Moreover, if "antagonistic" is taken to mean upward mobility in this case, then "favorable" ought to mean downward mobility; on this basis 45 per cent of the offspring of Democratic parents have been downwardly mobile. Since recent studies suggest the upward mobility in the United States runs at about 40 per cent and downward mobility at about 25 per cent,[42] and since in the present study, about 40 per cent of the offspring of Democratic fathers are upwardly mobile, as compared with about 30 per cent of such offspring who are downwardly mobile, it seems most unlikely that "favorable-antagonistic" is in any sense a direct analogue to "upward-downward" or "downward-upward." Rather, it would seem that McClosky and Dahlgren have included in the "favorable" and/or "neutral" categories a good deal of upward mobility for offspring of Democrats, and have done the same regarding downward mobility for offspring of Republicans. Thus, for them the upward mobility from unskilled to semi-skilled labor would not be regarded as unfavorable to the persistence of Democratic Party preference. This is not necessarily ill-advised, in fact it seems quite sound for their purposes—the measurement of support provided by current milieu for parental party preference. However, in such an approach mobility itself is not the explanatory factor. It is neither the fact of mobility itself nor the size of the increment which is important, but rather the thresholds which are crossed. Thus, a high rate of upward social mobility would not necessarily produce a steady flow to the Republican Party. Such a flow could be expected only if the mobility occurred across certain critical points, e.g., skilled labor to administrative occupational categories. The McClosky and Dahlgren findings are sound, but their invocation in support of the contention that "upward mobility signals . . . the likelihood that political preference will shift from Democratic to Republican" is a bit misleading, for it is true only with regard to such mobility across certain thresholds. Thus, the literature which Reicken cites does not preclude the acceptance of the findings on social mobility and defection presented in the present study.

[42] Elton F. Jackson and Harry J. Crockett, Jr., "Occupational Mobility in the United States: A Point Estimate and Trend Comparison," *American Sociological Review*, 29 (1964), pp. 5–15.

"DARK AREAS OF IGNORANCE" REVISITED: CURRENT KNOWLEDGE ABOUT ASIAN AFFAIRS[1]

DON D. SMITH

Florida State University

A GENERATION AGO, KRIESBERG LOOKED AT THE ROLE OF AMERICAN PUBLIC opinion in foreign affairs, and at the part played by the mass media in formulating that public opinion. At that time he observed that only a small minority of the American electorate could be considered knowledgeable about foreign affairs.[2] Other observers of that period concurred with this pessimistic evaluation, finding American public opinion about foreign affairs to be characterized by "dark areas of ignorance."[3]

Our contemporary period is a time in which increasing attention and importance is given to the opinions and attitudes of the general public. Particularly whetted by the advent of survey research techniques, high speed means of tabulation and analysis, and immediate dissemination of the results through the mass media, this period in American society can truly be considered as the "age of public opinion." The opinions of the general public are avidly sought and publicized on many important and complex issues, included in which are many issues of foreign affairs. Further, there is increasing acknowledgment that these opinions are being listened to, in varying ways and to differing degrees, by policy-makers at many levels of government. Just this past year, for example, we have witnessed the President of the United States pointing to the results of a national public opinion survey as substantiation of his foreign policy in Vietnam.[4]

The exposure patterns of the American public to political information have been revolutionized in the generation since Kriesberg made his pessimistic evaluation. Television, in particular, with its capability of bringing foreign events visually to the public, and its 97 per cent saturation of American households, has radically altered the accessibility of information about foreign affairs to the general public. The frequent assumption is that actual utilization of these media innovations has enabled the public to

[1] I am indebted to Dr. Charles M. Grigg, Director of the Florida State University Institute for Social Research, for assistance in obtaining the resources for this study. I also acknowledge the helpful assistance of the Roper Public Opinion Research Center, Opinion Research Corporation, and the Columbia Broadcasting System.

[2] Martin Kriesberg, "Dark Areas of Ignorance" in Lester Markel, ed., *Public Opinion and Foreign Policy* (New York: Harper & Bros., 1949), pp. 49–64.

[3] Kriesberg, "Dark Areas of Ignorance."

[4] Associated Press reports of November 4, 1969, state that President Nixon sent each U. S. Congressman a copy of the Gallup Poll survey which found that 77 per cent of the American public endorsed his stand on Vietnam. For a discussion of public opinion and policy-making, see Douglas Cater, *The Fourth Branch of Government* (New York: Vintage Books, 1959).

achieve and maintain a level of knowledge about foreign affairs that is commensurate with the significance currently attached to its opinions about these affairs.

THIS STUDY

This research examines the question: How informed is the current American public about Asian affairs, an aspect of foreign affairs that currently affects American life so prominently? The focus is on the public's knowledge of easily known, verifiable "facts"[5] commonly used in every-day discourse, rather than items of information subject to interpretation. This focus includes: (a) awareness of politically significant events, (b) identification of prominent political figures, (c) knowledge of politically important locations, and (d) knowledge of terms and facts relevant to important issues in Asian affairs.

The data for this study consist of all the information on file in the Roper Public Opinion Research Center relevant to the issue of the public's knowledge of Asian affairs, plus the results of other studies gleaned from numerous other sources. The examination of these data has emphasized surveys which used (1) nationally representative samples of American adults, (usually) 21 years of age and over, (2) indices of knowledge that are not esoteric, (3) questions which elicit actual knowledge rather than the respondent's self-evaluation of their knowledge, and (4) a reasonable latitude of response in evaluating replies as "correct" or "incorrect."[6] All data, of course, are subject to the time the particular survey was taken.

FINDINGS

Public opinion polls chart daily the ebb and flow of American opinion on the significant and very complex issue of the war in Vietnam. How informed are Americans of this aspect of Asian affairs which affects us so directly and which has become a major element in many of our domestic social problems as well? In a 1966 multiple-choice test of a national cross-section of the American population 18 years of age and over, an average score of 46 (on a 100 point scale) was achieved on 10 questions dealing with Vietnam. On the basis of this national sample, 28 per cent of the American public had a reasonably correct idea of the number of American troops in Vietnam (another 29 per cent were off by as much as 300,000 troops), 45 per cent did not know any country which was giving refuge to Viet Cong and North Vietnamese troops, and 43 per cent could not pick out the nearby country which permitted U.S. air bases within its borders. Sixty-nine per cent of these Americans were under the very mistaken im-

[5] The term "fact" is used in this research to refer to items of political information that are demonstrably and non-controversially "true." For example, "The Pueblo is a U. S. Naval ship seized by the North Koreans."

[6] As an example of the wide latitude permitted in this examination, the following responses were all considered "reasonably correct" responses to what is meant by "balancing the federal budget": (a) Making income equal expenses, (b) paying off debts, (c) keeping agencies within their allowance, (d) getting budget on steady basis, and (e) getting money into the treasury.

pression that Premier Ky had been elected to that position by a South Vietnamese Parliament, a point which indicates a significant lack of knowledge of the complex situation which characterizes South Vietnamese politics and which contributes so significantly to our difficulties there (CBS: Jan., 1967).[7] When asked as late as July, 1967, less than half of the American people knew who Ky was (AIPO: July, 1967).

Many Americans clearly misperceive the magnitude of the Vietnam war. When queried in 1967, again with multiple-choice questions, on the strength of our troop commitment in South Vietnam (at a time when our troop strength in that country was being publicized at 450,000), 34 per cent of the public was knowledgeable enough to indicate the correct number to be somewhere between 300,000 and 600,000 troops. One-fourth of the public felt that our troop commitment at that time was less than half its actual figure (AIPO: July, 1967). The public's misconception of the magnitude of that war is further suggested in the finding that at a time when official sources were publicizing the number of Americans killed in the war at 11,600, 20 per cent of the American public had a reasonably correct grasp of that situation.[8] Although perhaps not essential to an understanding of the Vietnamese situation, it is nonetheless disconcerting that 31 per cent of the American public thinks that South Vietnam is a country with less than 5 million people. Considering any answer between 5 million and 23 million to be reasonably correct, we find that only 14 per cent have any such idea of the population size (AIPO: July, 1967). While most Americans (97 per cent) had heard of the war in Vietnam by 1966 (Patchen found in 1964 that 25 per cent had not yet heard anything about the war),[9] 64 per cent of the American public had not heard of the labels of "hawk" or "dove" in association with positions about that war (AIPO: March, 1966). Even when the meaning of such labels is explained to them, many Americans' perceptions of the ideological positions of various national figures on this issue are very vague and often quite erroneous. For example, one-third of those Americans who consider themselves to be "doves" (by the definitions supplied to them by the interviewer), perceive Ronald Reagan to be a "dove;" one-fourth of them perceive George Wallace to hold a similar position (AIPO: Jan., 1968).

In 1966, with armed conflict openly prevailing in Communist China, and widely reported in the Western press, 53 per cent of the American people had it exactly backwards; they thought the Chinese Red Guards were trying to overthrow Mao Tse-tung (CBS: Jan., 1967). Indeed, by 1964, Patchen reported that 28 per cent of the American people were still un-

[7] The abbreviations used in the citations of this report refer to the following organizations: Columbia Broadcasting System, Opinion Research Corporation, and the American Institute for Public Opinion. The Columbia Broadcasting System was the sponsoring organization for data collected on Vietnam by Opinion Research Corporation in November, 1966.

[8] This is considering any answer between 9,000 and 14,000 as a reasonably correct response.

[9] Martin Patchen, *The American Public's View of U. S. Policy toward China* (New York: Council for Foreign Relations, 1964).

TABLE 1[a]

Percentage of Replies to "Who Is Head of the Communist Party in China?"
(1966)

| | | Multiple-Choice Alternatives | | | |
	Weighted N	Mao Tse-tung	Ho Chi Minh	Chiang Kai-shek	
Total Sample	1894	58	19	23	100
Sex:					
Male	879	64	20	16	100
Female	1015	54	17	29	100
Age:					
18–29	484	50	25	25	100
30–39	353	58	19	23	100
40–49	368	67	15	18	100
50 & over	679	60	16	24	100
Education:					
8th grade & under	429	45	20	35	100
High School	1023	57	19	24	100
College	427	77	15	8	100
Region:					
Northeast	455	60	22	18	100
Northcentral	568	58	14	28	100
South	563	51	22	27	100
West	308	71	16	13	100
Informed on News:					
Above average	287	74	11	15	100
Average	804	62	19	19	100
Below average	728	50	21	29	100

[a] These data have been supplied through the courtesy of Opinion Research Corporation and the Columbia Broadcasting System.

aware that mainland China had a Communist government, and an additional 29 per cent did not know of the existence of an alternative Chinese government on Formosa; only 54 per cent of the public had even heard or read of Mao Tse-tung.[10] And, as with South Vietnam, Americans display little recognition of China's population size, a factor which does play a role in China's actions in foreign affairs. When considering any answer between 500 million and 1 billion (on a multiple-choice question) as a reasonably fair grasp of the fact that China has a huge population, only 20 per cent of the American public exhibits this awareness (AIPO: Feb., 1965).

How informed is the "more informed" segment of our population about this aspect of our foreign affairs? Table 1 illustrates some of the trends obtained in our examination of these survey studies. That table shows the responses of a national sample to the multiple-choice question, "Who is head of the Communist Party in China?" Fifty-eight per cent of the public

[10] *Ibid.*

correctly identified Mao Tse-tung as the leader, with 23 per cent opting for Chiang Kai-shek and 19 per cent for Ho Chi Minh. Typical of the results on most of the foreign affairs issues examined in this study, more males are correct than females (46 per cent of the American women missed that question), and the number of correct responses increases with age and education. The higher percentage of correct responses from those people in the western region of the United States is characteristic of the patterns found on other indices of knowledge about Asian affairs. It is a sobering acknowledgement, however, that of those individuals who consider themselves "above average" in their knowledge of the news, 26 per cent still miss the correct alternative, and that of those who have had some college education, 23 per cent miss the correct response to that question (CBS: Jan., 1967). Some indication of just how closely this educated public follows the analysis and interpretation of foreign affairs in the mass media may be found in the results that 37 per cent of those Americans who hold college degrees can not come close to an identification of Walter Lippmann, 56 per cent can not identify David Lawrence, and 46 per cent of these college graduates can not reasonably identify Joseph Alsop (AIPO: July, 1963).

Just as important as the American public's current knowledge about foreign affairs is the question of whether or not the level of that knowledge has been changing. It is difficult to make exact time comparisons on foreign affairs; such events are frequently episodic, with little continuous exposure on the same issue over an extended period of time. Recognizing these limitations, the following comparisons can be made. In 1950, a year of war in Asia for the United States, 66 per cent of the American public could correctly identify the U.S. Secretary of State (AIPO: Dec., 1950). Sixteen years later, in 1966, another war year in Asia for the United States, the figure was approximately the same—65 per cent (AIPO: March, 1966). A citizen's national political representatives frequently have significant bearing on international affairs; yet, we find that when asked in 1945, 35 per cent of the public knew the names of both the U.S. Senators from their state, 22 per cent knew the name of one, and 43 per cent could identify neither (AIPO: Jan., 1945). Twenty-two years later, in 1967, the results are again about the same; 34 per cent identified both of the Senators from their state, 25 per cent knew the name of one, and 41 per cent could identify neither (CBS: Nov., 1967).

The Congressman from their district doesn't fare much better; in 1947, 38 per cent could reasonably identify him (AIPO: Aug., 1947), 37 per cent could do so in 1957 (AIPO: June, 1957), and 40 per cent could do so in 1965 (AIPO: Oct., 1965). A prominent writer on foreign affairs, Walter Lippmann, was correctly identified in May, 1945, by 40 per cent of the public (AIPO: May, 1945), and by 32 per cent in 1963 (AIPO: July, 1963). Despite the wide publicity, there has been little change in the percentage of Americans who correctly grasp the magnitude of the Vietnam war (when measured by reasonable knowledge of how many American troops are in Vietnam): 28 per cent had a reasonably correct notion in 1966 (CBS: Jan., 1967), 35 per cent could do so in 1967 (AIPO: July, 1967). In 1965,

20 per cent of the public had a reasonably correct idea of the magnitude of China's population; in 1952, using any figure between 300 million and 700 million as a reasonably correct estimate of its purported 500 million population at that time, a corresponding figure of 24 per cent was obtained (AIPO: Feb., 1952).

DISCUSSION

The data reported in this study would suggest that the American public can still be considered poorly informed about foreign affairs. Obviously, there are factors which need to be considered other than just the amount of information an individual has. Different people do different things with the same information, for example. Nevertheless, accurate information itself is a necessary requisite to informed opinion and attitude formation.

No indictment of the American people is warranted by the results of this examination. Understandably, the general layman, with many competing pressures on his time and interests, would find it difficult to keep well-informed, even if he desired to do so. On these grounds, some observers have resigned us to the status quo, and have suggested that we concentrate our efforts instead on the training of policy and opinion elites.[11] Aside from this rather easy surrender of one of the most basic tenets of our democratic philosophy, it should be noted that no concerted, deliberate effort has ever really been made to encourage the general public to adopt the stance and responsibilities commensurate with the leadership role played by our nation in foreign affairs. The efforts that have been made in this direction have continued to transmit the same information in much the same way as we have always done (albeit along different media channels), with little attempt to create motivational interest in the subject matter itself.

Despite our communication research findings that people of differing life situations have differing accessibilities to international news, and expose themselves, for differing reasons, to different media which cover different things in different ways, there has been little social research into alternative ways of presenting news of foreign affairs in a more enticing way for the general public. Consequently, it is really no surprise that "dark areas of ignorance" about foreign affairs still characterize our population. The same kind of people who expose themselves to information about foreign affairs today are the same kind of people who exposed themselves a generation ago when Kriesberg made his observations; interest in, and knowledge about, foreign affairs have seemingly made little inroad into the psychological field of the remaining bulk of the population.

[11] See Gabriel Almond, *The American People and Foreign Policy* (New York: Harcourt, Brace and Co., 1950).

THE DISTRIBUTION OF POLITICAL
KNOWLEDGE IN THE UNITED STATES*

NORVAL D. GLENN
The University of Texas at Austin

T HE PRECEDING PAPER BY DON D. SMITH MAKES IT CLEAR THAT AS RECENTLY AS 1966–1967 the American public was not well informed about Asian affairs, and it shows that most people did not know the name of their Congressman and could not identify such prominent columnists and writers on political affairs as Walter Lippman and Joseph Alsop. Other recent data on knowledge of domestic political issues and personalities also reveal widespread ignorance. For instance, in 1967, when possible federal legislation on open housing was being widely discussed in the media, 42 per cent of the respondents to a Gallup poll did not know the meaning of the term "open housing." In the same year, only 28 per cent of the respondents to another Gallup poll knew who would represent their district in the State Senate the following year, and only 24 per cent could name their representative in the State Legislature or Assembly. In 1966, only 19 per cent of a national sample said they knew what their Congressman thought about Vietnam; 19 per cent said they knew what he thought about civil rights, and only 14 per cent said they knew his stand on strikes and labor problems. In 1970, only 21 per cent of a Gallup sample knew how their Congressman had voted on any major bills during the year. More than a third of these respondents admitted they did not even know whether their Congressman was a Democrat or a Republican.

The evidence could be multiplied, but these data are sufficient to establish that a large proportion of the American public can not, or recently could not, intelligently vote or participate in the democratic process. My purpose here is not merely to establish this fact but to help explain it and to help explain the lack of any apparent considerable increase of political knowledge in recent years.[1] This lack of a greater increase is especially puzzling, because, as Smith points out, opportunities to learn of political issues from the media have increased. Furthermore, since political knowledge varies with amount of education, one might well have expected the steep increase in median years of school completed by the adult U.S. population in recent years to have brought about at least a moderate increase in political knowledge.

I shall seek clues as to the bases of the widespread political ignorance by examining its distribution among the categories of the population coded on each Gallup data deck. Of course, the differences among these categories can only suggest the reasons for the ignorance but, hopefully, the clues

---

*Written for this volume.
[1]The only evidence for an increase which I have found is shown in Table 1, and as I point out below, much of this apparent increase may well have resulted from sampling variability.

they provide will stimulate research that will result in more nearly conclusive evidence.

THE DATA

One of the most useful kinds of political knowledge for my purpose is knowledge of the name of one's Congressman (see Table 1). Data on this knowledge were gathered periodically by Gallup polls from 1942 to 1970, and the pattern of its distribution among categories of the population has remained rather stable and is generally similar to the pattern of distribution of the other kinds of political knowledge that have been investigated by the polls.

The differences among the categories in 1966 and in 1970 are shown in Table 1. Not surprisingly, males, whites, and persons at the higher levels

TABLE 1

**Percentage of Gallup Poll Respondents Who Knew the Name of
Their Congressman, by Categories of the Population,
1966 and 1970**

	1966	1970
Total Sample	46	53
Sex		
Men	54	60
Women	40	46
Race		
White	49	54
Non-white	25	38
Education		
College	68	65
High School	47	54
Grade School	31	38
Occupation		
Professional and Business	60	61
White-Collar	57	57
Farmers	49	62
Manual	36	43
Age		
21–29	37	44
30–49	47	55
50 and over	50	54
Religion		
Protestant	48	53
Catholic	41	56
Politics		
Republican	61	56
Democrat	40	51
Independent	46	52

TABLE 1 (continued)

	1966	1970
Region		
East	43	49
Midwest	43	55
South	47	55
West	56	52
Income		
$15,000 and over	67	68
$10,000–14,999	59	59
$7,000–9,999	51	54
$5,000–6,999	39	43
$3,000–4,999	39	47
Under $3,000	38	36
Community Size		
1,000,000 and over	36	44
500,000–999,999	49	57
50,000–499,999	50	55
2,500–49,999	54	60
Under 2,500, rural	46	51

Sources: Gallup Political Index, Aug., 1966, p. 10, and *Gallup Opinion Index*, Oct., 1970, p. 10.

of education, income, and occupation were more knowledgeable than the other respondents, and these differences need no elaborate explanation. Education should certainly enhance political awareness, and differences in the amount, quality, and effects of education may to a large extent account for the differences by race, occupation, and income. Occupation and income make a difference when amount of education is held constant, but this may be largely because low-education persons with high incomes and in high-status occupations often associate with well-educated persons and are often self-educated to a high degree. The differential political knowledge of males and females probably results largely from differential socialization and from the fact that the major activities and responsibilities of males are typically more obviously and directly related to political issues. Even the relative recency of female enfranchisement may still be of some importance.

Of more interest are the less commonly known differences, those that could not be predicted by what the layman would call "common sense." Two of these stand out—the differences by age and by community size. Young adults had less knowledge than middle-aged or elderly persons, and residents of very large and very small communities had less knowledge than residents of intermediate-size cities. Evidence that these differences were not restricted to knowledge of the name of the Congressman is given in Tables 2 through 6.

TABLE 2

Percentage of Gallup Poll Respondents Who Knew Certain
Political Facts, by Age

	Age		
	21–29	30–49	50 and over
Name of state senator (1967)	17	30	31
Name of representative in state legislature or assembly (1967)	14	26	28
Name of mayor (1967)	57	72	73
Name of county clerk (1967)	18	30	32
The difference between the positions of Robert Kennedy and Lyndon Johnson on Vietnam (1967)	50	49	45
Meaning of term "open housing" (1967)	52	61	59
Whether congressman was Democrat or Republican (1970)	54	63	64
How congressman voted on any bills during the year (1970)	16	23	21
MEAN	35	44	44

Sources: Gallup Opinion Index, Feb., 1967, April, 1967, and Oct., 1970.

In Table 3, the data on political knowledge by age from Gallup Survey 732 are presented with controls for sex and color and with the responses at each age level standardized to the same educational distribution. This standardization is useful because it reveals the differences that would have existed if the younger respondents had not had considerably more education on the average than the older respondents. Without the standardization, middle-aged persons consistently had more knowledge than young adults and tended to have more than the oldest respondents. However, the standardization generally produced a positive monotonic relationship between age and knowledge, and it appreciably increased the difference between the young adults and the people at both of the older age levels.

These differences in political knowledge by age are consistent with the relatively low voter turnout and reported political interest of young adults in the United States, which have been discussed in detail in previous publications.[2] From the cross-sectional data alone, one can not tell whether the lower knowledge at the younger ages has resulted from the older adults having become more knowledgeable since they were young or from "generational" differences in political knowledge. If the generational explanation is correct, present young adults are less knowledgeable than

[2] E. g., see Norval D. Glenn and Michael Grimes, "Aging, Voting, and Political Interest," *American Sociological Review*, 33 (Aug., 1968), pp. 563–575; and John Crittenden, "Aging and Political Participation," *Western Political Quarterly*, 16 (June, 1963), pp. 323–331.

TABLE 3

Percentage of Gallup Poll Respondents (Whites Only) Who Knew Certain Facts
About Their Congressman, by Age and Sex, 1966

Age	His Name	What He Thought About Vietnam	Civil Rights	Strikes and Labor Problems
Males				
		Raw Percentages		
21–39	48	23	21	20
40–59	64	32	28	28
60 and over	59	26	28	21
		Education-Adjusted Percentages*		
21–39	37	15	14	14
40–59	64	32	28	28
60 and over	67	37	40	29
Females				
		Raw Percentages		
21–39	37	8	11	5
40–59	41	16	18	11
60 and over	51	19	13	11
		Education-Adjusted Percentages*		
21–39	30	6	7	3
40–59	41	16	18	11
60 and over	57	23	14	11

*Standardized to the educational distribution of respondents aged 40–59.
Source: Gallup Survey 732.

present middle-aged and elderly persons were when they were young
adults, and the former probably will not become more knowledgeable as
they grow older. However, if the low level of political knowledge and the
low voter turnout of young adults have common bases (and they probably
do), the generational explanation is not correct, because longitudinal data
show that in recent years voter turnout has increased among persons who
have matured toward and into middle age.[3] That is, low voter turnout,
and probably low political knowledge, are characteristic of young adulthood and not of any particular generation.

If young adults in the United States characteristically pay little attention to political issues and personalities, the reasons are less than obvious.
They have completed more years of school on the average than their
elders, and because they have longer life expectancy, they have more at
stake in the long-term outcomes of political processes. One might well expect, therefore, that they would be the most politically active, attentive,
and knowledgeable segment of the population.

The fact that they are not is probably due in at least some measure to
the many distractions in young adulthood that tend to draw attention

[3] Glenn and Grimes, "Aging and Voting."

away from political issues. A large proportion of the "significant life events," such as completion of formal education, marriage, beginning a career, and the bearing of children, are often concentrated in the first decade of adulthood, and these are very absorbing of time and attention. Pressing personal concerns, it is reasonable to assume, will be given priority over abstract political issues that have no immediate, direct, and obvious impact upon the individual.

Another probable reason for the lesser political knowledge of young adults is their greater geographic mobility. It is reasonable to expect long-standing residents of an area who do not plan to move to take more interest in local politics than the more transient residents, and therefore it is hardly surprising that young adults know less about their Congressman and about local political personalities than the older, less mobile persons.[4] However, the young adults were also less knowledgeable in 1967 about open housing (Table 2), which was a national political issue, and Smith shows in his Table 1 that they were less able than older adults to name the head of the Communist Party in China. Mobility *per se* can not explain either of these differences, although the lack of a high rate of home ownership among young adults might explain their apparent lack of concern about open housing.[5] Young respondents had an unusually high level of knowledge of the positions of Robert Kennedy and Lyndon Johnson on Vietnam in 1967 (Table 2), but this probably grew less out of the national scope of the issue than out of its relevance to the personal interests of draft-age males and their wives and girl friends.

Knowledge of both local political figures and national issues generally varied in a curvilinear fashion with community size (Table 4). However, an exception was in knowledge of the name of the mayor, on which the residents of the largest communities ranked highest, probably because the mayor of a large city is a more prominent figure, and receives more coverage by the media, than the mayor of a small or intermediate-size city. The reverse is true of the county clerk, who may be a prominent figure in a small county seat but who is greatly overshadowed by other officeholders and political figures in a county which contains a large city.

The relatively low political knowledge of residents of small towns and rural areas is hardly surprising, since they had not completed as many years of school on the average as the other respondents, and more of them had low incomes and were in low-prestige occupations.[6] They had relatively little political knowledge even with education held constant (data

---

[4] For data on mobility by age, see *ibid.*, Table 2.

[5] Data in my files from The University of Michigan *Survey of Consumer Finances* show much lower rates of home ownership among young adults than among older persons.

[6] See Leo Schnore, "Some Correlates of Urban Size. A Replication," *American Journal of Sociology*, 69 (Sept., 1963), pp. 185–193. The data in Table 6 show that among white males in the high-status occupations, differences in political knowledge between the smallest and the intermediate-size communities were not great.

TABLE 4

Percentage of Gallup Poll Respondents Who Knew Certain
Political Facts, by Community Size

	Community Size				
	Under 2,500, Rural	2,500– 49,999	50,000– 499,999	500,000– 999,999	1,000,000 and over
Name of state senator (1967)	31	42	22	23	23
Name of representative in state legislature or assembly (1967)	26	43	16	17	18
Name of mayor (1967)	55	74	76	74	84
Name of county clerk (1967)	44	49	20	11	8
The difference between the positions of Robert Kennedy and Lyndon Johnson on Vietnam (1967)	43	45	52	50	45
Meaning of term "open housing" (1967)	43	56	70	64	58
Whether congressman was Democrat or Republican (1970)	59	68	62	62	60
How congressman voted on any bills during the year (1970)	19	26	23	19	21
MEAN	40	50	43	40	40

Sources: Gallup Opinion Index, Feb., 1967, April, 1967, and Oct., 1970.

not shown), probably because their education was of poorer quality on the average, and because political awareness is affected by the education and political awareness of one's associates as well as by one's own education. According to one stereotype, rural and small-town people tend to be preoccupied with events and people in their own communities and to pay relatively little attention to the outside world. It is assumed that the urbanites' greater geographic mobility, diversity, and participation in activities and organizations that transcend community boundaries tend to give them a more cosmopolitan outlook. The data presented here are consistent with this stereotype, although they do not prove that it is categorically correct.

The relatively low political knowledge in the largest cities is harder to explain. The residents of these communities do not rank lower in amount of

education, income, or occupational prestige than the residents of intermediate-size cities.[7] Nor are they more mobile, according to the most
commonly used census indicators of geographic mobility.[8] They do have
a higher percentage of foreign-born persons, but the difference was only
about five percentage points in 1960 and was probably less in 1966–1970.
Therefore, even a complete lack of political knowledge among the foreign-
born could not account for the differences in knowledge by community
size.[9] There was also a greater percentage of blacks in the larger cities, but
again the difference was not great enough to account for much of the
variation in political knowledge. Non-whites are excluded from the data in
Table 5, but the pronounced curvilinearity remains.

Again, as with young adults, greater distraction from political issues may
be part of the explanation. Life in the largest cities is presumably faster-
paced, and more stimuli may impinge upon the individual and compete
for his attention. If the widespread stereotype of life in the large cities is

TABLE 5

Percentage of Gallup Poll Respondents (Whites Only) Who Knew Certain Facts
About Their Congressman, by Community Size and Sex, 1966

Community Size	His Name	What He Thought About Vietnam	Civil Rights	Strikes and Labor Problems
Males				
1,000,000 and over	39	20	22	16
500,000–999,999	57	31	24	32
50,000–499,999	63	37	33	33
2,500–49,999	68	27	26	23
Under 2,500, rural	59	23	24	17
RANGE	29	17	11	17
Females				
1,000,000 and over	38	14	14	7
500,000–999,999	44	15	13	3
50,000–499,999	47	17	19	18
2,500–49,999	44	8	10	6
Under 2,500, rural	37	14	13	7
RANGE	10	9	9	15

Source: Gallup Survey 732.

[7] Schnore, "Some Correlates of Urban Size."

[8] For instance, the percentage of persons five years old and older who did not live
in the same county in 1960 as in 1955 was 13.8 for the urbanized areas whose central
cities had at least 1,000,000 residents in 1960, whereas it was 17.8 for the urbanized
areas whose central cities had 500,000–999,999 residents and was 17.5 for the country as a whole.

[9] And the foreign-born may well not have been any less knowledgeable than
native-born persons.

correct, competition tends to be more intense there, and therefore pursuing personal ambitions may typically absorb more time and attention. Furthermore, life is in some ways more difficult in the largest cities; getting to and from work is harder, noise and crowding typically are greater,[10] and one consequence may be fewer alert hours off the job when one is inclined to read about, contemplate, and discuss political issues. And an abundance of types of entertainment, commercial and otherwise, are available to absorb non-working time.

Most of these possible reasons for less political knowledge in the largest cities should be more operative with males than with females who are not employed outside the home, and indeed the differences in political knowl-

TABLE 6

Percentage of Gallup Poll Respondents (White Males Only) Who Knew Certain Facts About Their Congressman, by Community Size and Occupation, 1966

Community Size	His Name	What He Thought About Vietnam	Civil Rights	Strikes and Labor Problems
Businessmen and Professionals				
1,000,000 and over	59	32	22	29
500,000–999,999	83	52	24	50
50,000–499,999	78	38	27	39
2,500–49,999	79	41	32	27
Under 2,500, rural	73	42	39	27
RANGE	24	20	17	23
Clerical and Sales Workers				
1,000,000 and over	31	29	27	4
500,000–999,999	62	35	41	35
50,000–499,999	64	43	59	59
2,500–49,999	91	30	30	30
Under 2,500, rural	84	44	51	33
RANGE	60	15	32	55
Manual Workers*				
1,000,000 and over	24	11	21	13
500,000–999,999	36	18	15	21
50,000–499,999	52	34	30	23
2,500–49,999	66	24	23	20
Under 2,500, rural	57	12	14	14
RANGE	42	23	16	10

*Excluding farm laborers.
Source: Gallup Survey 732.

[10]Gallup polls have consistently shown that a smaller percentage of persons in the largest cities than in the intermediate-size communities report that they are "very happy" and that they are satisfied with such aspects of their lives as their income, jobs, and housing.

edge between the largest and the intermediate-size communities were considerably and consistently greater with males than with females (Table 5). Although there was a rather pronounced curvilinear pattern with both sexes, females employed outside the home may have accounted for most of the variation by community size among females.

Among the white males, the differences in political knowledge between the largest and the intermediate-size cities averaged higher at each of three broad occupational levels than when no controls for occupation were applied (Table 6). Most of the differences in knowledge about the Congressman were greatest with the clerical and sales workers, among whom the faster-paced, noisier, and more crowded life in the largest cities may have its greatest impact.

Smith cities evidence that the level of political knowledge in the country did not increase measurably from the 1940s to the mid-1960s, and the apparent increase of seven points from 1966 to 1970 in the percentage of Gallup respondents who knew the name of their Congressman (Table 1) is not evidence for a general increase in political knowledge in the late 1970s. Although all of this apparent increase is not likely to have resulted from sampling variability ($p < .05$), the increase in the total population may well have been less than seven percentage points. And, of course, other kinds of political knowledge may not have risen with the ability to name one's Congressman.

Some of the recent changes in the distribution of the adult population among the categories shown in Table 1 should have tended to increase the overall level of political knowledge. These include the increase in the proportion of people at the higher levels of education, income, and occupational prestige and the decrease in the proportion residing in rural areas and small towns. At least one change, an increase in the proportion in the 21-29 age range,[11] has tended to lower political knowledge in the total adult population. However, it seems that the net influence of all of these changes should have been toward greater knowledge. Since in fact there was little increase, at least through the mid-1960s, the net influence of these changes must have been offset by opposing influences.

At the risk of overworking it, I again invoke the "distraction" explanation. If the impressions of journalists and "armchair" social scientists can be trusted, the "pace of life" in the country has accelerated in recent years and decades.[12] Possibly this change, and almost certainly the greater saturation of the population by the mass media, have increased the number and variety of stimuli that impinge upon the individual. Thus, while Smith is correct in asserting that the media have made political information more readily available, they have also provided a super-abundance of other stimuli to distract from the political ones.

In his provocative best-selling book, *Future Shock*, Alvin Toffler argues that modern man increasingly tends to suffer from "over-stimulation,"

---

[11]This change has occurred only since the mid-1950s.
[12]See especially Alvin Toffler, *Future Shock* (New York: Random House, 1970), Chap. 3.

from a surfeit of exposure to facts, ideas, images, and the like.[13] This over-stimulation can, according to Toffler, have various adverse psychological and physiological consequences. Therefore, the individual tries to cope with the surfeit of stimuli by blocking out some of them—no doubt usually the least urgent and titillating ones, such as reports of the more common-place and banal political activities.

It is not my purpose here to exhaust the probable reasons for the con-tinuing prevalence of political ignorance in the United States; there are several I have not mentioned. For instance, as the society becomes more complex, the individual may see less relationship between most political issues and processes and his personal interests, needs, and endeavors. Polit-ical personalities and events may seem more remote and impersonal. And the feeling that the individual is largely unable to affect political outcomes may have increased, or at least it is still prevalent.

CONCLUSION

Certainly the "distraction thesis," which I have emphasized here, should not be relied upon as a one-factor explanation for the low level of political knowledge. However, it appears to deserve more than the incidental, casual treatment it has received, when mentioned at all, in most discus-sions of political participation, interest, and knowledge.

If my emphasis upon it is warranted, what are the implications for po-litical knowledge and democratic processes in the future? Is there no hope that an informed, politically alert electorate can develop unless the dis-tractions are lessened—unless significant life events are distributed more evenly through the adult stages of the life cycle, unless the tenor of life is changed in the largest cities or their populations redistributed into smaller communities, and unless the barrage of stimuli upon the indivi-dual is moderated? I think the answer is no, although the prospects for a considerable increase in political knowledge in the near future hardly seem bright. Hopes that such an increase will inevitably result from in-creased affluence, levels of education, and leisure time are, I think, not well founded.[14] However, perhaps political information could be made to compete more effectively against other stimuli for the attention of the electorate, although making it more appealing, as Smith recommends, would not be easy. And perhaps it is unlikely that those persons, groups, and agencies capable of accomplishing that difficult task will be motivated to make the effort.

[13]Chap. 16. Toffler also implies that geographic mobility has increased, and if it had, that change would have tended to lessen knowledge of local political figures and issues. In fact, however, the rate of geographic mobility, in the sense of chang-ing place of residence, apparently did not change appreciably from the late 1940s to the late 1960s, the period considered by Smith. See Donald Bogue, *Principles of Demography* (New York: John Wiley and Sons, 1969), Table 19.3.

[14]The belief that leisure time has increased appreciably in recent decades has been challenged. See Sebastian deGrazia, *Of Time, Work and Leisure* (New York: Twentieth-Century Fund, 1962). Perhaps a real and substantial increase in leisure time (which may not be forthcoming) would increase political knowledge to an im-portant extent.

PART III

Political Attitudes: The Problem of Consistency

INTRODUCTION

As students of political attitudes, both sociologists and political scientists have often observed a notable lack of consistency in the attitudes expressed by individuals toward political objects, figures, situations, or events. It is not unusual, for example, to discover citizens who profess a strong belief in freedom of speech yet strongly oppose allowing any person to deliver an address against churches and religion.[1] The frequency with which individual citizens have been found to hold contradictory, or at least contrasting, views has led sociologists and political scientists to investigate the sources of attitudinal consistency or inconsistency in an effort to explain the phenomenon.

There are actually two aspects of attitudinal consistency of concern to the social scientist. The first is the apparent inconsistency in attitudes so often uncovered by research. Because researchers *expect* to find personal attitudes coherently organized in a logical fashion, they are sometimes overly impressed when persons under investigation do not see the world as the researcher would have predicted. In short, an investigator may think he has uncovered inconsistency in attitudes which in fact may simply be a case of the investigator's inability "to see the logic of the other's thought processes, that is, one's explanation of why he believes as he does may not be comprehensible to the other."[2] Much of what passes for observed attitudinal inconsistency is an artifact of the attitude measurement process itself. Smith and Hyman, for example, asked interviewers to code tape-recorded interviews and found a clear distortion traceable to the interviewers' expectations that respondents have "consistent personality structures."[3] Our concern with attitudinal consistency may thus stem from our failure to verify our expectations rather than from the presence or absence of consistency as such.

There is, however, a second side to the consistency problem and it stems from the nature of attitudes themselves. This aspect of attitudinal consistency is related to what social psychologists have described as three classes of measurable characteristics of attitudes: the cognitive, affective, and conative.[4] The cognitive component refers to the informational content of a person's attitudes—his beliefs, understandings, stereotypes, and factual knowledge—and to his expectations of what he will find in contemporary and future situations because of those beliefs. The affective pertains to how an individual feels about the referent of an attitude and evaluates the characteristics he perceives in the attitude object. The affective

[1]Samuel A. Stouffer, *Communism, Conformity, and Civil Liberties* (New York: John Wiley and Sons, Science Editions, 1966), pp. 26–57.

[2]Steven R. Brown, "Consistency and the Persistency of Ideology: Some Experimental Results," *Public Opinion Quarterly*, 34 (Spring, 1970), pp. 60–68.

[3]H. Smith and H. Hyman, "The Biasing Effect of Interviewer Expectations on Survey Results," *Public Opinion Quarterly*, 14 (1950), pp. 491–506.

[4]The dimensions and functions of political attitudes are described succinctly in M. Brewster Smith, "The Personal Setting of Public Opinions: A Study of Attitudes Toward Russia," *Public Opinion Quarterly*, 11 (1947), pp. 507–523.

component varies in direction (whether the feeling is positive or negative, warm or cool, etc.) and intensity (whether the feeling is strong or weak). Finally, the conative, or expressive, component describes what a person will do about the object, person, event, or situation that constitutes the attitude referent; that is, what *action* the person favors or opposes and how he expresses his views—by verbal opinions, voting, protest, violence, or whatever.

When a person's beliefs, feelings, and expressions are congruent with one another, he displays attitudinal consistency. Frequently, however, these three components are not consistent. An example on the most superficial level is the citizen who believes in the good intentions of the President of the United States and expects great accomplishments, yet he differs with the President on every major pronouncement; finally, the citizen compounds the puzzle offered by contrasting beliefs and feelings by voting for the incumbent's re-election. Or, single attitudinal components may differ over two or more objects. Hence, for instance, a person respects the political views of a friend, yet finds intolerable the views of a candidate endorsed by his friend. Unless he is willing to live with the inconsistency, presumably he will resolve it, perhaps responding differently to the friend or revising his attitude toward the candidate. The range of potential inconsistency is thus fairly large: a person may be inconsistent in his cognitive beliefs, affective evaluations, or conative expressions about an attitude object or objects; moreover, he may experience consistency between beliefs and feelings but have inconsistent expressions, between beliefs and expressions but with inconsistent feelings, between feelings and expressions with inconsistent beliefs, or experience inconsistency across cognitive, affective, and conative dimensions.

Concern with problems of consistency generally carries with it the assumption that persons experiencing attitudinal inconsistency will consciously or unconsciously attempt to re-establish consistency by changing one or more attitudinal elements. Just as there are a variety of sources of attitudinal inconsistency there are a variety of explanations for how people re-establish congruency in the face of seeming contradictions. The selections in Part III illustrate two principal lines of theory and research into the consistency problem—inquiries into *status* consistency and *cognitive* consistency.

Persons occupy different positions, or statuses, in the social structure; each status is distinguished from, and at the same time related to, other positions in the social structure by its rights and obligations. When a person's statuses are related in such fashion that his attitudes in one status reinforce attitudes associated with others, he is said to be characterized by status crystallization, or status consistency (as, for example, when education, income, and occupation contribute to congruent attitudes and consistent responses from others). If, however, differing status positions give rise to incongruent attitudes (as for a chaplain in the army or an unemployed Ph.D.), we speak of status inconsistency. Status inconsistency appears frequently when there is tension between a person's ascribed and

achieved status position, that is, between the status he has inherited in society and that he has achieved through his abilities, skills, and accomplishments; for instance, female physicians occupy what in many societies is a
lower sex status (ascribed) than their elevated professional status (achieved).

Cognitive consistency refers to the congruency in a persons's beliefs,
expectations, information, and other cognitions about an object, other person, situation, or event. Cognitive consistency theories (dissonance, balance, and other variants) assume that an individual with inconsistent cognitions will experience discomfort or tension that motivates him to reduce
the dissonance by modifying one or more of his cognitions.

Status-consistency and cognitive-consistency approaches reflect two different perspectives from which to regard the consistency-in-political attitudes problem—the former emphasizing a social perspective has been especially popular among sociologists while the latter is oriented toward a
more psychological point of view. Yet the two perspectives are compatible
as the opening selection in Part III, "Continuities in Theories of Status
Consistency and Cognitive Dissonance," illustrates. In this essay James A.
Geschwender demonstrates that cognitive dissonance theory provides a valuable device for explaining the consequences of status inconsistency. In the
process he reviews and integrates three theories of motivation from social
psychology into a dissonance perspective—the Theory of Social Certitude,
the Principle of Expectancy Congruence, and the Theory of Distributive
Justice. Geschwender's contribution is a particularly useful review of the
major research into status crystallization, especially as status inconsistency
is related to social mobility, political ideology, social isolation, attitudes
toward social change, psychosomatic problems, and prejudice. He develops
a schematic presentation that succinctly summarizes the various ways that
status inconsistents potentially cope with cognitive dissonance.

The following selection, "Status Inconsistency, Militancy, and Black
Identification Among Black Veterans," by Theodore Chiricos, Michael A.
Pearson, and James M. Fendrich, exemplifies the relevance of the status-
inconsistency approach for understanding a problem of growing urgency
in contemporary America. The authors focus upon a randomly selected
sample of 199 black veterans released from military service in the 1960s and
residing in Jacksonville, Florida, in 1968. Black veterans, they reason, are
undergoing status inconsistency; briefly, their military experience provided
opportunities to achieve a social status inconsistent with that normally
associated with being black in America. How black veterans returning to
the urban ghetto cope with that inconsistency forms the substance of the
authors' analysis. This selection highlights the differences in findings when
contrasting measures of status inconsistency are employed. Using objective
measures the researchers found no statistically significant relationship between status inconsistency and two coping strategies—black militancy
and black identification; however, using subjective measures of the black
veterans' perceived inconsistency, important relationships were established.

The two subsequent selections in Part II deal with the relationship between status discrepancies and the clusters of political attitudes conven-

tionally associated with ideological stances. Right-wing extremism is one such stance and it is explored by Larry L. Hunt and Robert C. Cushing in their contribution, "Status Discrepancy, Interpersonal Attachment, and Right-Wing Extremism." As with the authors of the first two selections in Part III, Hunt and Cushing draw heavily upon the literature of status inconsistency in hypothesizing about the possible relationship between status discrepancy and extremism; however, they contrast that approach with a theory of political cross-pressures generated by studies of voting behavior. They note that whereas status inconsistency models usually assume that inconsistency itself produces stresses that make individuals vulnerable to extreme political appeals for social change, cross-pressure models suggest that an individual's membership in many categorical social groups generates pressures that moderate his political attitudes and lessen the likelihood of extremism. The substance of their investigation achieves partial reconciliation of these contrasting models by introducing the phenomenon of "interpersonal attachment" as a mediating variable. They explore the impact of such mediation upon attitudes toward the John Birch Society among respondents in the 1968 election study of the Survey Research Center, University of Michigan. D. Stanley Eitzen also utilizes data from the Survey Research Center—the 1964 election study—but his focus is the relationship between status inconsistency and liberalism-conservatism. In "Social Class, Status Inconsistency, and Political Attitudes" Eitzen argues that in exploring any relationship between status and political attitudes it is wise to incorporate measures of social class as well as status consistency. Doing so in charting attitudes toward social welfare, civil rights, and internationalism in 1964, Eitzen concludes that when social class is included in the analysis, it may be a better predictor of political attitudes than status consistency.

Whereas many social scientists favor the status-inconsistency orientation in researching and explaining political attitudes, the perspective supplied by cognitive consistency and related theories is not ingored. John P. Robinson's "Balance Theory and Vietnam-Related Attitudes" is a case in point. For students of political attitudes Robinson's article is worthy of close scrutiny for two reasons. First, Robinson provides a concise, easily grasped description of the nature of balance theory in attitude studies. Second, relying on data from recent studies by the Survey Research Center, principally the 1968 survey, Robinson compares the attitudes toward groups opposed to the war (especially attitudes toward anti-war demonstrators at the 1968 Chicago Democratic National Convention). In general, Robinson's findings cast doubt upon the utility of balance theory in explaining political attitudes: he reveals relatively low correlations between attitudes toward the Vietnam war and attitudes toward protesting groups; moreover, the balance model seems more appropriate for explaining attitudes of the better educated than those with lesser degrees of formal education.

Attitudes pertaining to black veterans, political extremism, ideological issues, and the Vietnam war were of critical salience to many Americans in the 1960s and the early years of this decade. The same can be said with respect to the problem investigated by sociologist Robert B. Smith in the final selection of Part III, "The Vietnam War and Student Militancy." Smith explores a consistency in the relationship between student attitudes toward the Vietnam war and their militant stance taken in demonstrations on college campuses. His data are based upon questionnaires completed in 1968–1969 by a sample ($N = 348$) of the student body at the University of California at Santa Barbara. The author reveals that at the time of the interview, sampled college students were substantially more disaffected from the war than was the general American public. This student disaffection was manifested in rising numbers of campus protests that appeared only tangentially to be about the war. A growing shift from non-violence to violence was associated with a perception of increasing military violence in Vietnam, the seeming unresponsiveness of the university to student demands, police "harassment" for smoking marijuana, and the militants' desire for social justice and new domestic priorities. Although de-escalation of the Vietnam conflict will certainly decrease campus turmoil in the immediate future, Smith contends that there will be no quick end to the rebellion of the younger generation. That rebellion, he asserts, stems from a delegitimation of authority in America (a legitimacy crisis spawned in part by the Vietnam war) that may reappear in a variety of forms in the 1970s.

CONTINUITIES IN THEORIES OF STATUS CONSISTENCY AND COGNITIVE DISSONANCE*

JAMES A. GESCHWENDER
*State University of
New York at Binghampton*

T
HE CONCEPT OF STATUS CONSISTENCY (STATUS CRYSTALLIZATION OR STATUS congruence) is gradually assuming greater prominence in the literature of social stratification. Its major weakness lies in its use as a structural characteristic predicting behavioral consequences without an explicitly stated social-psychological theory of motivation to account for these predictions. Three such theories have been proposed. They are Homans' Theory of Distributive Justice,[1] Zaleznik's Theory of Social Certitude,[2] and Sampson's Principle of Expectancy Congruence.[3]

The last-named is an attempt to explain the findings of status consistency research within the framework of Festinger's Theory of Cognitive Dissonance.[4] Sampson's approach is similar to that of Zaleznik but has the advantage of being more general. However, it is still incomplete as it does not adequately explain all consequences of status inconsistency. It is suggested herein that the Theory of Distributive Justice can bridge this gap if it can be integrated into a dissonance framework. Two attempts to do this have been made.[5] However, they represent mere beginnings as they are limited as to degree of specification and detailed analysis. The present paper hopes to complete the task and to spell out in some detail further implications of the combined theory.

The strategy of attack will be to briefly describe the Theory of Social Certitude and the Principle of Expectancy Congruence, to relate them to each other, and to evaluate this combination. The Theory of Distributive Justice will then be described and integrated into dissonance theory. This combination will subsequently be evaluated as to its ability to explain the em-

*Reprinted with permission of the author and publisher, from James A. Geschwender, "Continuities in Theories of Status Consistency and Cognitive Dissonance," *Social Forces*, 41 (December, 1967), pp. 160-171.
[1] George C. Homans, *Social Behavior: Its Elementary Forms* (New York: Harcourt, Brace and Co., 1961).
[2] A. Zaleznik, C. R. Christenson, and F. J. Roethlisberger, in collaboration with George C. Homans, *The Motivation, Productivity, and Satisfaction of Workers* (Cambridge: Harvard University Press, 1958), pp. 56–66.
[3] Edward E. Sampson, "Status Congruence and Cognitive Consistency," *Sociometry*, 26 (June, 1963), pp. 146–162.
[4] Leon Festinger, *A Theory of Cognitive Dissonance* (Evanston, Illinois: Row, Peterson and Co., 1957).
[5] James A. Geschwender, "Explorations in the Theory of Social Movements and Revolutions," unpublished manuscript; and C. Norman Alexander, Jr. and Richard L. Simpson, "Balance Theory and Distributive Justice," *Sociological Inquiry*, 34 (Spring, 1964), pp. 182–192.

pirical findings of status consistency and further theoretical implications will be derived.

SOCIAL CERTITUDE AND EXPECTANCY CONGRUENCE

The essence of the Theory of Social Certitude is the assumption that each status position carries with it a set of behavioral expectations regarding both the behavior of the occupant of said position and the behavior of all persons with whom he interacts. Each individual occupies several positions and possesses several sets of behavioral expectations which may either reinforce or contradict one another.

The status consistent possesses sets of behavioral expectations which either reinforce or are consistent with one another. A condition of social certitude exists and social relations are fluid and satisfying. The status inconsistent possesses sets of expectations which conflict with one another. A condition of social certitude does not exist. Anxiety is produced for all concerned and social relations are hampered and unsatisfying. This sets in motion forces tending toward the creation of status consistency.

The Principle of Expectancy Congruence and the Theory of Social Certitude have much in common. The major difference between them is that the former is stated within the framework of the more general dissonance theory while the latter stands alone. Sampson bases his analysis upon the following assumption:

> Let us make the assumption that one aspect of each position—or set of positions—along a given status dimension consists of certain expectations for the behavior of the occupant of that position. Thus, for example, a person ranking high in education may meaningfully be said to have certain expectations held by others and by himself for his behavior. A similar parallel between rank position and expectation can be drawn for other dimensions along which persons can be ranked.[6]

From this point, the analysis is identical to that proposed by Zaleznik. Incongruent expectations are a problem for everyone and interfere with interaction. Congruent expectations simplify interaction. Thus, there is a pressure on all participants to create and maintain a congruence of expectations. This is why status inconsistency is an undesirable state which produces pressure toward changing the situation.

EVALUATION OF SOCIAL CERTITUDE AND EXPECTANCY CONGRUENCE

The Principle of Expectancy Congruence has the advantage of being derivable from a more general theory of motivation. This makes it more attractive than the Theory of Social Certitude as it may be more easily related to findings in other areas. However, the ultimate test of any theory is how well it explains empirical findings. It is at this point that the principle breaks down.

Research has demonstrated a relationship between status inconsistency

---

[6] Sampson, "Status Congruence," p. 153.

and tendencies toward social isolation, mobility striving, political liberalism, psychosomatic symptoms of stress, and preference for changes in the social order or actual attempts to bring about these changes. This research will be discussed below. Some of these findings are explainable within an expectancy congruence approach and some are not.

The frustrations and anxieties produced by a lack of expectancy congruence might easily produce psychological symptoms of stress. They might interfere with social interaction and produce a tendency for inconsistents to withdraw into social isolation. They might also produce mobility strivings to achieve a state of expectancy congruence. However, this approach does not do a very good job of explaining the status inconsistent's preference for a change in the social order and predisposition for participation in social movements. Actually, mobility strivings are only partially explained. This approach does not supply us with any means of predicting which response to inconsistency a status inconsistent will be likely to select. An expanded theory which integrates the Theory of Distributive Justice into dissonance theory might perform this function.

THE THEORY OF DISTRIBUTIVE JUSTICE

An author can usually state his own ideas better than someone else can summarize or paraphrase them. Thus, it is best to quote Homans' description of his theory:

> A man in an exchange relation with another will expect that the rewards of each man will be proportional to his costs—the greater the investments, the greater the profits.... Finally, when each man is being rewarded by some third party, he will expect the third party, in the distribution of rewards, to maintain the relation between the two of them.... The more to a man's disadvantage the rule of distributive justice fails of realization, the more likely he is to display the emotional behavior we call anger.... Men are rewarded by the attainment of justice, especially when just conditions are rewarding in other ways. For instance, I am more likely to demand justice when justice would bring me more money than when it would bring me less.... Not only do men display anger, or less predominantly, guilt when distributive justice fails in one way or the other, but they also learn to do something about it. They learn to avoid activities that get them into unjust exchanges; they learn to emit activities that are rewarded by the attainment of justice.[7]

Homans suggested that certain status dimensions could be viewed as investments into a social situation while others could be viewed as rewards received from that situation. The four dimensions that Lenski utilized in his analysis of status consistency may be classified according to this framework. Education and ethnicity may be seen as investment dimensions. There are universalistic norms in American society which lead one to expect that he will be rewarded in terms of his level of education. There are also particularistic norms which lead one to expect that he will be rewarded in terms of

[7] Homans, *Social Behavior*, pp. 332-333.

his ethnic status. Thus, education may be classified as an achieved investment and ethnicity as an ascribed investment.

Occupation and income may be viewed as reward dimensions. Income
is clearly a reward as it determines one's standard of living. Occupation
may also be seen as a type of reward. Some occupations are preferable to
others in terms of the amount of physical labor demanded by them, the
cleanliness of the work, and the amount of individual autonomy allowed.
Thus, occupation may be classified as a social reward and income as a material reward.

Using these definitions, it could be concluded that a state of distributive
justice exists when individuals who possess greater investments (higher education and/or ethnicity) also possess greater rewards (higher occupation and/or income). Those persons whose investments are higher than rewards (level of occupation and/or income below level of education and/or
ethnicity) will experience a felt injustice and feel anger. It is reasonable to
assume that this anger may be directed against the society which fails to
maintain distributive justice and may lead to behavior designed to change
society in order to eliminate this inequity.

Those persons whose investments are lower than their rewards (education and/or ethnicity below level of occupation and/or income) would experience a felt injustice and feel guilt. It may be assumed that individuals
who are over-rewarded will not attempt to reduce guilt feelings by lowering their reward level. It is more likely that they will develop a political
philosophy which, if implemented, would ameliorate the consequences of
being short-changed for those who are under-rewarded. They might also
develop a philosophy which defines ascribed investments as irrelevant to
rewards. In short, they may become political liberals. If educational investment is the low dimension, they may either attempt to raise their level of
education to one consistent with rewards received or else develop a definition of education as being "ivory tower" and impractical, which would
lead to anti-intellectualism. It is to be noted that the Theory of Distributive
Justice is not equipped to handle an explanation of the consequences of
either investment (education–ethnicity) or reward (occupation-income) inconsistencies.

RELATION OF DISTRIBUTIVE JUSTICE TO DISSONANCE THEORY

It is possible to incorporate the Theory of Distributive Justice into dissonance theory with the addition of a few assumptions. We may assume that
every individual includes within his cognitive set cognitions concerning
his status level in the educational, occupational, ethnic, and income hierarchies. We may assume that he possesses cognitions defining education as
an achieved investment, ethnicity as an ascribed investment, occupation as
a social reward, and income as a material reward. We may also assume that
he possesses cognitions which define the proper relation that should hold
between investment and reward dimensions. This definition of the proper
relation between investments and rewards would be based upon the individual's perception of that relation which normally exists in society.

Thus, experiencing a state of felt injustice is reduced to experiencing cognitive dissonance resulting from inconsistency among simultaneously held cognitions. The empirical consequences of felt injustice may be seen as behavioral attempts to reduce dissonance.

This may be combined with Sampson's assumption that each status position carries with it expectations regarding behavior that should be forthcoming from, or directed toward, the occupant of that position. Congruent sets of expectations facilitate the development of satisfying patterns of social interaction and incongruent sets of expectations impede this development. Thus, status inconsistency leads to the development of cognitive dissonance, and attempts to cope with this inconsistency represent behavioral attempts to reduce dissonance. Other behavioral responses may be non-coping responses indicating an inability to reduce dissonance. Dissonance theory, thus expanded, may enable us to explain the empirical consequences of status inconsistency which have been observed and to predict others not yet observed.

EVALUATION IN RELATION TO FINDINGS

The research literature has demonstrated six different types of responses to status inconsistency. These are enhanced mobility striving, withdrawal into social isolation, psychosomatic symptoms of stress, political liberalism, preference for and attempts to change the social order, and prejudice. The findings in each of these areas of research will be considered separately and in relation to the foregoing theoretical approach.

Mobility Striving. Benoit-Smullyan proposed the existence of a status-equilibration process.[8] He stated that individuals are ranked or have status on three major dimensions: the economic, political, and prestige hierarchies. These types of status are analytically distinguishable and often empirically independent, but there is a tendency for one to be transformed into the others through a status equilibration process.

Implicit in Benoit-Smullyan's analysis is the assumption that possession of discrepant statuses in different hierarchies creates strain for individuals and causes them to follow a course of action designed to bring their statuses into line with one another. This assumption was not tested. Fenchel, *et al.*, did attempt to test this hypothesis with an undergraduate population at CCNY.[9] They had the students rate themselves as to their general standing in five potential reference groups and as to where they would like to stand. The difference between the two ratings was taken as an index of status striving. The hypothesis was supported as the students did tend to strive for a common ranking in all reference groups.

Homans re-interpreted one of his earlier studies into a framework which lends support to the equilibration hypothesis.[10] This was a study of female

[8] Emile Benoit-Smullyan, "Status, Status Types, and Status Interrelations," *American Sociological Review*, 9 (April, 1944), pp. 151–161.

[9] Gerd H. Fenchel, Jack H. Monderer, and Eugene H. Hartley, "Subjective Status and the Equilibration Hypothesis," *Journal of Abnormal and Social Psychology*, 46 (Oct., 1951), pp. 476–479.

[10] Homans, *Social Behavior*, pp. 237–242.

clerical workers and involved two categories of jobs—cash posters and ledger clerks. The line of promotion was from cash poster to ledger clerk. The general evaluation was that the position of ledger clerk was a better job, carried more responsibility, and conveyed more status. However, the same salary was paid to both positions. Ledger clerks protested, demanding that they be paid more than the cash posters as would befit their more important jobs. They were status inconsistent because their material rewards were not comparable to their occupational status. They were attempting to reduce dissonance by raising their lower-ranking status to a level consistent with their higher-ranking one.

The literature does not deal with variations in response by pattern of status inconsistency. However, it does yield implications for it. It suggests that persons experiencing dissonance resulting from status inconsistency may attempt to reduce this dissonance by altering their ranking on one or more of the dimensions of status. This would not be equally possible for all types of inconsistents. Persons who are low ethnically but high on the other dimensions could not normally be expected to alter their ethnic status through individual mobility. But a person who is high in education and low in occupation and/or income might hope to reduce dissonance through hard work, individual effort, and mobility on the occupational and/or income dimensions. More will be said about this below.

Political Liberalism. Lenski studied the relationship between status inconsistency and political liberalism.[11] A sample of persons were asked their views toward a government-sponsored health insurance program, price controls, and a general extension of governmental powers. Their responses were classified along a continuum of liberalism. The more liberal responses were found to be associated with low status consistency. Democratic voting was taken to be an indication of relative liberalism and was found to be associated with low status consistency.[12]

Both of these associations held when general status levels were controlled. Certain patterns of inconsistency were more closely associated with liberalism than others. A person of low ethnic status and high income, occupational, or educational status tended to be more liberal than the reverse combinations. Individuals with low educational and high occupational statuses tended to be more politically liberal than did those with the opposite combination. An inconsistent with high occupational and low income status was more likely to be liberal than was the reverse combination. In

[11] Gerhard E. Lenski, "Status Crystallization: A Non-Vertical Dimension of Social Status," *American Sociological Review*, 19 (Aug., 1954), pp. 405–413.

[12] Kenkel's retest of this hypothesis produced results which did not support it. See William F. Kenkel, "The Relationship Between Status Consistency and Politico-Economic Attitudes," *American Sociological Review*, 26 (June, 1961), pp. 365–368. However, this retest was severely criticized. See Gerhard E. Lenski, "Comments on Kenkel's Communication," *American Sociological Review*, 26 (June, 1961), pp. 368–369. Lenski maintained that Kenkel erred in using different indices of status. His lack of results may have resulted from not using those that Lenski believed had a central place in American society. For the purposes of the present analysis, it will be useful to assume that Lenski's criticisms are correct.

fact, the high income–low occupation inconsistent was less likely to be liberal than were consistents.

Lenski's findings have been interpreted as indicating that status inconsistents may be prone to engage in social movements designed to bring about major changes in society. This may be erroneous. The particular items that Lenski used to measure political liberalism appear to be more closely related to a mild reformist perspective as might be incorporated into a welfare state or great society philosophy rather than the type of outlook that would motivate a person to join a social movement with more sweeping aims.

These findings suggest that a person who experiences dissonance resulting from status inconsistency may try to reduce his dissonance through the development of a liberal political outlook. The relationship of particular types of inconsistents to political liberalism is suggestive. Inconsistents with low educational and high occupational statuses and inconsistents with low ethnic and high occupational or income statuses are types of inconsistents categorized above as over-rewarded. Their investment dimensions are lower than their reward dimensions. They would be expected to feel guilt. Their attempts to reduce dissonance might be expected to take the form of attempting to ameliorate the consequences for others of their getting more than their share, and to develop a belief that ethnicity should not be related to rewards. Both of these are indications of political liberalism.

The inconsistent with low ethnicity but a high educational status represents a different type. He has brought his achieved investment to a level higher than his ascribed investment. In this sense, he is a success. One might expect that, in this sample, this type of inconsistent is also high on reward dimensions. This is based on the fact that inconsistents with high education and low occupation are lower on the liberalism scale. Thus, they may also be over-rewarded and react as the others described above. However, I would suggest that we reserve judgment of this type of inconsistent. It might be necessary to know his position on reward dimensions before making any predictions about him. Similarly, we should reserve decision on the two types of reward inconsistents (high income–low occupation and high occupation–low income). It is difficult to draw any conclusions regarding the relative importance of income and occupation as types of rewards.

Social Isolation. Lenski also studied the relationship between status inconsistency and tendencies toward social isolation.[13] He found that status inconsistents were less likely than status consistents to interact with neighbors and fellow workers outside of business hours, to be members of voluntary associations, to be regular participants in those voluntary associations in which they were members, and less likely to report sociable motives (non-economic reasons) for those voluntary ties that they had. No attempt was made to analyze the relation between types of inconsistency and tendency toward social isolation.

[13]Gerhard E. Lenski, "Social Participation and Status Crystallization," *American Sociological Review*, 21 (Aug., 1956), pp. 458–464.

Homans provided data which suggest that this tendency toward social isolation may not always be voluntary.[14] He found that the status inconsistent members of a work group were high on initiating interaction for others but were low on the receipt of interaction from others. Generally the interaction that they initiated took the form of horseplay or joking. Homans suggested that joking may be the reaction of the inconsistent to the insecurities in the situation, while the reaction of others is a tendency to avoid the inconsistent.

These results are explainable with the assumptions that Sampson makes in his Principle of Expectancy Congruence. Status inconsistency creates a situation in which there exist conflicting sets of behavioral expectations. This interferes with the development of fluid tension-free interaction. Thus, interaction becomes unpleasant and tends to be broken off. It may be possible that the earliest stage of this process is found in other persons avoiding the inconsistent and in the inconsistent resorting to joking. Withdrawal on the part of the inconsistent may represent the final acceptance on his part of the impossibility of creating satisfying patterns of interaction. Suicide is the most extreme form of withdrawal, and Gibbs and Martin found a relationship between status inconsistency and propensity toward suicide.[15]

Preference for Social Change. Lenski postulated that status inconsistents might be prone to react against society by participating as leaders in social movements and that a society with widespread status inconsistencies was unstable and generated pressures toward change.[16] However, he never empirically tested this proposition. Benoit-Smullyan made a similar suggestion when he stated, "There are historical grounds for supposing that when legal, customary, or other barriers seriously hamper the equilibrating tendency, social tensions of revolutionary magnitude may be generated."[17] He cited as evidence the fact that support for the Nazi Party came from large classes of persons who became impoverished but retained their former prestige statuses.

[14]George C. Homans, *Sentiments and Activities* (Glencoe: Free Press, 1962), p. 100.

[15]Jack P. Gibbs and Walter T. Martin, "Status Integration and Suicide," *American Sociological Review*, 23 (April, 1958), pp. 140–147. For other research documenting the fact that status inconsistency interferes with the development of free communications and satisfying interaction see Stuart Adams, "Status Congruency as a Variable in Small Group Performance," *Social Forces*, 32 (Oct., 1953), pp. 16–22; Ralph V. Exline and Robert C. Ziller, "Status Congruence and Interpersonal Conflict in Decision-Making Groups," *Human Relations*, 12 (April, 1959), pp. 147–162; and Arlene C. Brandon, "Status Congruence and Expectations," *Sociometry*, 28 (Sept., 1965), pp. 272–288.

[16]Lenski, "Status Crystallization," p. 412.

[17]Benoit-Smullyan, "Status Interrelations," p. 160. For supporting documentation, see also William Kornhauser, *The Politics of Mass Society* (Glencoe: Free Press, 1959), p. 181. Lipset cites unpublished research by Robert Sokol which found a relationship between perceived status discrepancy and support of McCarthy, but patterns of discrepancy were not discussed. See Seymour M. Lipset, "Three Decades of the Radical Right," in Daniel Bell, *The Radical Right* (New York: Anchor Books, 1955), p. 403.

There are other historical examples of status inconsistents who have supported social movements. Frazier noted that Negro support for organizations like the Urban League and the NAACP tends to come from middleclass Negroes.[18] Lipset pointed out that urban middle-class leaders in the CCF tended to come from minority groups, while the urban middle-class leaders in the Liberal and Conservative Parties tended to come from the Anglo-Saxon majority group.[19] Michaels noted that middle-class Jews were quite prominent in European Socialist parties.[20] These last three examples are all of status inconsistents whose ethnic status was lower than their occupational status. It is worth noting at this point that the examples show low ethnicity–high occupation inconsistents supporting leftist movements and high occupation-low income inconsistents supporting rightist movements.

Ringer and Sills found a high proportion of status inconsistents among political extremists in Iran. They were over-represented among the extremists on the revolutionary left and the nationalistic right.[21] The inconsistents were of a high educational level and only a moderate economic status. The degree of inconsistency was sharpest for the revolutionary left. Both types of extremists were anti-colonialist and this common antagonism to vestiges of colonialism may have been more important in attracting adherents than their left–right differences. These data show a tendency for underrewarded inconsistents with a high level of education to take an extremist position in reacting against the social order. The data regarding the NAACP, CCF, and Jewish socialists show over-rewarded inconsistents with a low ethnic status taking a more moderate reformist position when reacting against the social order.

Goffman related status inconsistency to preferences for change in power distributions within society.[22] Status inconsistency was measured using the educational, occupational, and income hierarchies. Preference for change was measured by asking respondents to check their perceptions of the amount of influence in the conduct of national affairs presently held by, and the amount of influence that they prefer be held by, state governments, big business, labor unions, businesses that were not big, and the national government. Status inconsistents exhibited a greater preference for change than did status consistents. This relation held with general status levels controlled. No attempt was made to analyze differences between status types. It is not possible to discuss the left–right direction of these preferences for change without knowing more detail about the responses than Goffman provided.

[18] E. Franklin Frazier, *Black Bourgeoisie* (Glencoe: Free Press, 1959), pp. 98–104.
[19] Seymour M. Lipset, *Agrarian Socialism* (Berkeley: University of California Press, 1950), p. 191.
[20] Robert Michels, *Political Parties*, trans. Eden and Cedar Paul (New York: Dover Publications, 1959), pp. 260–261.
[21] Benjamin B. Ringer and David L. Sills, "Political Extremists in Iran," *Public Opinion Quarterly*, 16 (Winter, 1953), pp. 689–701.
[22] Irwin W. Goffman, "Status Consistency and Preference for Change in Power Distribution," *American Sociological Review*, 22 (June, 1957), pp. 275–288.

These findings suggest that there is reason to believe that status inconsistents may attempt to reduce dissonance by reacting against the social order, or at least by expressing a preference for a change in the present distribution of power within society. They further suggest that under-rewarded inconsistents are more likely than over-rewarded inconsistents to take an extreme reaction against the social order. This is predictable from the assumptions incorporated into dissonance theory from the Theory of Distributive Justice. Homans states that anger is a stronger emotion than guilt. The angry (under-rewarded) inconsistent would be expected to experience a sharper form of dissonance and a more extreme reaction than would guilty (over-rewarded) inconsistents.

Psychosomatic Symptoms. Elton Jackson studied the relationship between status inconsistency and the exhibition of psychosomatic symptoms.[23] Consistency was measured in terms of the ethnic, educational, and occupational status dimensions. He found a significant relationship between status inconsistency and the exhibition of psychosomatic symptoms. He also found a significant difference between types of inconsistents.

Jackson noted that two types of inconsistents (high ethnicity combined with either low occupation or low education) had high rates of psychosomatic symptoms, while the opposite types (low ethnicity combined with high education or high occupation) did not have symptom rates which differed from that of status consistents. He noted that Lenski had found the two types of status inconsistents with high symptom rates to exhibit only a slight tendency toward political liberalism and the two types with low symptom rates to exhibit strong tendencies toward political liberalism. He suggested that the important determinant is the relationship between achieved and ascribed ranks. Those with high ascribed and low achieved ranks are likely to see themselves as failures and to develop high psychosomatic symptom rates. Persons with low ascribed and high achieved ranks are likely to see themselves as successes—they have made it despite their ethnic handicap. Thus, they will direct their response to stress outward. This will take a political form for many.

The major difficulty with this interpretation of political and psychosomatic responses as alternative ways of reacting to inconsistency is that it does not seem to apply equally well to all types of inconsistents. Jackson included in his table, but did not discuss, psychosomatic symptom rates and tendencies toward political liberalism for high occupation–low education and high education–low occupation inconsistents. Both types of inconsistents have symptom rates higher than consistents and also exhibit a stronger tendency toward political liberalism. The one possible support for viewing

[23]Elton F. Jackson, "Status Consistency and Symptoms of Stress," *American Sociological Review*, 27 (August, 1962), pp. 469–480. Dunham has also found that persons with high education and low occupation exhibit a tendency toward both schizophrenia and psychopathies, though he raises questions regarding the causal direction. See H. Warren Dunham, Patricia Phillips, and Barbara Srinivasan, "A Research Note on Diagnosed Mental Illness and Social Class," *American Sociological Review*, 31 (April, 1966), pp. 223–227.

political and physical reactions as alternative responses comes from the fact that the symptom rates for these two types of inconsistents are lower than those with high physical, low political responses and their tendency toward political liberalism is less than those with high political, low physical responses. Possibly these results show a tendency for some persons experiencing this type of inconsistency to react physically and others to react politically.

Jackson advanced one other tentative proposition that bears examination. He found male inconsistents with high occupation and low educational statuses to have a symptom rate much higher than did status consistents. Those males who had high educational and low occupational statuses exhibited a symptom rate lower than that of status consistents. He suggests that mobility opportunities might explain this. The latter type of inconsistent is likely to see the possibility of future mobility bringing about consistency, while the former type cannot look forward to this possibility. More mobility would simply cause greater inconsistency. Jackson indicated elsewhere the existence of the relation of mobility possibilities and age.[24] Younger inconsistents, who had status profiles which could become consistent through mobility, had lower levels of psychosomatic symptoms than older inconsistents with similar profiles. This could indicate that with advanced age mobility would be defined as less likely and persons would give up striving and develop physical responses.

Jackson's major contribution came in demonstrating that failure to reduce dissonance through either mobility or political reactions might force one to attempt to live with dissonance. Dissonance is tension-producing and, in the absence of dissonance-reducing behavioral attempts, might easily produce a physical response leading to psychosomatic symptoms.

Prejudice. There is currently very little research relating status inconsistency to prejudice.[25] However, we can draw indirect inferences regarding this relationship if we accept membership in the Ku Klux Klan as an indication of racial prejudice. Vander Zanden has pulled together the names and occupations of 153 members of the Klan.[26] Ninety-eight of these were

[24]Elton F. Jackson, "Status Consistency, Vertical Mobility, and Symptoms of Stress," unpublished Ph.D. dissertation, University of Michigan, 1960, p. 95.

[25]See Donald J. Treiman, "Status Discrepancy and Prejudice," *American Journal of Sociology*, 71 (May, 1966), pp. 651–664. Treiman attempted to evaluate the relative utility of a status consistency and an additive hypothesis for the explanation of prejudice. He concluded that the additive hypothesis was adequate for the explanation of prejudice without making the complex assumptions involved in a status consistency hypothesis. His treatment is unsatisfactory for three reasons. First, he limited himself to a consideration of education—income inconsistents. Second, he used family income rather than individual income. This does not give an individual status profile as one does not know how many people contribute to total family income. Third, and most important, he used a system of classification which produced some "inconsistents" which could be more accurately classified as consistents. This does not mean that his findings are necessarily wrong—merely that they are questionable.

[26]James W. Vander Zanden, *Race Relations in Transition* (New York: Random House, 1965), pp. 42–43.

found in occupations (skilled labor, marginal businessmen, and marginal white-collar occupations) which are the occupations in which Negroes are making the greatest inroads.[27] The rest are transportation workers, semi-skilled or unskilled laborers. These are occupations in which whites have been receiving competition from Negroes for many years. It is reasonable to assume that in the South, the status attributed to an occupation declines with increases in the proportion of Negroes. Thus, KKK members are status inconsistent because their occupational status fails to come up to their high ethnic status.

If membership in the KKK is not accepted as a valid indication of racial prejudice, it certainly is an indication of willingness to express and/or act out hostility toward members of a racial minority. Thus, we can see that under-rewarded status inconsistents may attempt to reduce dissonance by directing hostility against members of a minority group.

DISCUSSION

It would appear that all research findings to date dealing with conse-quences of status inconsistency can be explained within the framework of an expanded version of dissonance theory. This would require combining the initial premises of the theory with Sampson's assumptions and a series of assumptions derived from the Theory of Distributive Justice. A brief statement of the assumptions would go as follows:

1. All persons hold sets of cognitions which include some that are reality-based, some which are definitional, and some that are normative. Reality-based cognitions describe the existing state of affairs while normative cognitions describe the state of affairs which should exist.

2. Any set of cognitions may stand in a relation of dissonance, conso-nance, or irrelevance depending upon the internal relations which hold among reality-based and normative cognitions. If the conjunction of a reality-based and a normative cognition implies another reality-based cognition in the set then a state of consonance exists. If this conjunction implies the negation of another reality-based cognition in the set then a state of dissonance exists. If this conjunction implies neither another reality-based cognition nor the negation of one in the set then a state of irrelevance exists.

3. Reality-based cognitions will include perceptions of one's status in the educational, occupational, income, and ethnic hierarchies. They will also include perceptions of behavior expected from, and expected to be directed toward, the occupants of positions in each of these hierarchies. Definitional cognitions will include the definition of ethnicity as an ascribed investment, education as an achieved investment, occupation as a social reward, and income as a material reward. Normative cognitions will include beliefs re-

---

[27] For a description of these inroads see James A. Geschwender, "Social Structure and the Negro Revolt: An Examination of Some Hypotheses," *Social Forces*, 43 (Dec., 1964), pp. 248–256; James A. Geschwender, "Desegregation, the Educated Negro, and the Future of Social Protest in the South," *Sociological Inquiry*, 35 (Winter, 1965), pp. 58–68.

garding the proper relation that should exist among the various status positions. Particularly, they will include the belief that rewards received should be proportional to investments. Possession of a higher level of ascribed investments than achieved investments will be defined as failure. The reverse combination will be defined as success.

4. Dissonance is an upsetting state and will produce tension for the individual. This tension will lead to an attempt to reduce dissonance by altering cognitions, adding new cognitions or deleting old ones. Attempts to alter reality-based cognitions will involve attempting to change the real world. Attempts to alter normative cognitions will involve attempts to change evaluations of the real world and will take place within the cognitive system.

5. Status inconsistents whose rewards received are less than believed to be proper for their investments will feel anger and inconsistents whose rewards exceed investments will feel guilt. Anger is a sharper form of dissonance than guilt. The perception of failure produces a sharper form of dissonance than the perception of success. The intensity of dissonance-reducing behavior will be directly proportional to the sharpness of dissonance.

6. Dissonance-reducing attempts will take the form of coping responses, attempts to change the real world, when possible. When coping responses are not possible, dissonance-reducing attempts will take the form of attempting to withdraw from interaction. When neither changing the real world nor withdrawal from it is possible, dissonance will remain and the tension will be manifested in psychosomatic symptoms.

7. Dissonance-reducing attempts will move from the simple to the complex. That is, the simplest types of alterations in reality that would reduce dissonance will be attempted first. If these attempts are unsuccessful, a shift will be made to increasingly complex attempts. The simplest form of altering reality is to attempt to change one's own status through individual mobility. Downward mobility would create sharper dissonance by causing a comparison with rewards received in the past, and therefore believed possible, and rewards currently received. Thus, only upward mobility would be a dissonance-reducing move. The next most simple form of altering reality is to strike out against individuals and categories of individuals (e.g., prejudice and discrimination). The most complex form of attempting to change reality is attempting to alter society. The simplest form of withdrawal is social isolation, and the most complex form of withdrawal is suicide.

These assumptions enable us to make deductions for each of the patterns of inconsistency which would explain the empirical findings to date. These patterns are presented in Table 1.

Under-rewarded status inconsistents whose high-investment dimension is ethnicity would feel sharp dissonance (anger). Mobility might possibly be a way of reducing dissonance depending on their level of education. If it is possible, it will be attempted first. If it is not possible, or if it is unsuccessful, attempts to reduce dissonance will shift to attacking categories of persons. It would be expected that this type of inconsistent would be highly prejudiced and would engage in discrimination. Any attempt to change the society would likely take the form of trying to create a state of affairs in which ethnicity has increased importance—a racist social movement. If none of these attempts is successful, then one would expect a tendency toward social isolation and a high level of psychosomatic symptoms.

Under-rewarded inconsistents whose high-investment dimension is education would experience sharp dissonance (anger). Mobility for them is possible and will be attempted as a means of reducing dissonance. If mobility attempts are unsuccessful or blocked (e.g., if they are minority group members) then the individual will shift to more complex forms of dissonance reduction. Prejudice and discrimination may develop but could hardly result in changing reality if they were directed against members of the majority group. Thus one would be prone to attempt to change society and this attempt would take a more extreme form (social movements or revolution). A requirement for participating in social movements and revolutions is the belief that one has the power to be successful. If this is lacking, or the change attempt fails, then the inconsistent would be forced into social isolation and/or exhibition of psychosomatic symptoms.

Over-rewarded status inconsistents whose low-investment dimension is ethnicity will not be able to reduce dissonance through mobility. They may develop anti-majority group prejudices but this will do them little good. Thus, they will be forced to attempt to reduce dissonance by changing society. Their mild state of dissonance (guilt) will produce a moderate change response such as political liberalism or participation in a moderate reform social movement. It is doubtful if they will be forced into social isolation or exhibition of psychosomatic symptoms, as they will be able to define themselves as successes for overcoming their ethnic handicap.

Over-rewarded inconsistents whose low-investment dimension is education will probably not be able to reduce dissonance through individual mobility, nor would they benefit by attacking other categories of people through prejudice. Thus, it is likely that they would start their dissonance-reducing attempts at the level of societal alteration. Their mild state of dissonance (guilt) would lead to a moderate response such as political liberalism. It is possible that this would fail and force them into social isolation, but the mild degree of dissonance might make it unlikely that they would develop psychosomatic symptoms to any great extent.

Investment inconsistents could not be considered as either over- or under-rewarded. Those with ethnicity as the higher dimension are failures and those with ethnicity as the lower dimension are successes. Failures would not be able to expect mobility. They would probably develop hostility toward minority groups, and might be prone to join racist social movements. If these dissonance-reducing attempts fail, they would be forced into social isolation and be prone to display psychosomatic symptoms. The successes could not expect social mobility and would not gain from attacking categories of persons. Their mild dissonance might lead them into attempts to reduce dissonance by moderate attempts at social change such as developing a liberal political philosophy or supporting moderate reform movements.

TABLE 1

Status Consistency Pattern and Reactions to Dissonance

Responses	Under-Rewarded Inconsistents				Over-Rewarded Inconsistents			
	High Ethnicity		High Education		Low Ethnicity		Low Education	
	Low Occupation	Low Income	Low Occupation	Low Income	High Occupation	High Income	High Occupation	High Income
Emotional reaction Mobility possibility	Anger Possible, depends upon level of education		Anger Possible, depends upon age		Guilt Not possible		Guilt Unlikely	
Prejudice	If no mobility, then high prejudice and discrimination likely		If no mobility, then possible prejudice against majority or minority groups (unlikely to aid in coping)		May develop anti-majority prejudice (unlikely to help cope) or prejudice against other minorities		May develop prejudice, but this is unlikely to aid in coping	
Social change attempt	If neither mobility nor prejudice proves adequate, then possibly joins a racist social movement		If other coping responses fail (as is likely), then prone to join extremist social movements—providing perception of adequate power		If prejudice fails to reduce dissonance, then moderate change response such as liberalism or moderate reform social movement		Moderate change response such as political liberalism or participation in moderate reform social movement possible	
Social isolation	If coping responses fail, then tendency to withdraw into social isolation		If coping responses fail, then tendency to withdraw into social isolation		Doubtful, even if coping responses fail		Doubtful, even if coping responses fail	
Symptoms of stress	If coping responses fail and withdrawal impossible, then symptoms likely		If coping responses fail and withdrawal impossible, then symptoms likely		Doubtful, even if coping responses fail		Doubtful, even if coping responses fail	

Row grouping (left margin labels): COPING RESPONSES (Emotional reaction / Mobility possibility, Prejudice, Social change attempt); NON-COPING (Social isolation, Symptoms of stress)

Table 1 (cont'd.)

Responses	Investment Inconsistents		Reward Inconsistents	
	High Ethnicity / Low Education	High Education / Low Ethnicity	High Occupation / Low Income	High Income / Low Occupation
Emotional reaction Mobility possibility	Definition as failure Unlikely	Definition as success Not possible	Ambiguity Unlikely, but depends upon age	Ambiguity Not possible
Prejudice	Prejudice and discrimination highly probable	May develop antimajority prejudice (unlikely to help cope) or prejudice against other minorities	Possible, but probably not aid in coping	Possible, but probably not aid in coping
Social change attempt	Prone to join racist social movements	Moderate change response such as political liberalism or participation in reform social movement likely	No prediction. Data show tendency toward both political liberalism and extremist movements	No prediction. Data show no tendency toward liberalism
Social isolation	If coping responses fail, tendency toward social isolation	Doubtful, even if coping responses fail	Tendency toward social isolation quite probable	Tendency toward social isolation quite probable
Symptoms of stress	If coping responses fail, and isolation impossible, symptoms likely	Doubtful, even if coping responses fail	If social isolation not possible, symptoms quite probable	If social isolation not possible, symptoms quite probable

COPING RESPONSES (Emotional reaction, Prejudice, Social change attempt)

NON-COPING (Social isolation, Symptoms of stress)

If these attempts are unsuccessful, it is unlikely that they would exhibit strong psychosomatic symptoms though they may be forced into social isolation.

Reward inconsistents could not be defined as over- or under-rewarded, successes or failures, without knowledge of their investment dimensions. The only prediction one could make about them is that they would exhibit a tendency toward social isolation and possibly the exhibition of psychosomatic symptoms. However, one might expect that high occupation–low income inconsistents would also have a high level of education and be prone to act like other under-rewarded–high education inconsistents.

CONCLUSIONS

Sampson made a major contribution to the development of a motivational theory which would explain the behavioral consequences resulting from status inconsistency. He did this by placing reactions to status inconsistency within a cognitive dissonance framework through the addition of an expectancy congruence assumption. The present paper attempts to develop this further by adding a set of assumptions derived from the Theory of Distributive Justice. The task is hardly finished. Considerable refinement of these assumptions and empirical testing of derived propositions is required. Nevertheless, it is hoped that the present paper is a step in the right direction.

STATUS INCONSISTENCY, MILITANCY AND BLACK IDENTIFICATION AMONG BLACK VETERANS[1]

THEODORE G. CHIRICOS
Florida State University

MICHAEL A. PEARSON
Florida State University

JAMES M. FENDRICH
Florida State University

A S OUR NATION SLOWLY DISENGAGES FROM ITS VIETNAMESE COMMITment,[2] it will encounter many transitional problems that undoubtedly develop near the end of most wars. Given the unprecedented number of black soldiers serving combat roles in its armies however, the United States faces a situation that is unique in its history of war-making. This nation must consider the response of battle trained black veterans to a black community that is potentially volatile and to a larger society that is admittedly racist.[3] Indeed, with approximately 400,000 black soldiers assuming civilian status and with an apparent drop in first term reenlistment rates for blacks,[4] the black veteran will certainly have a major impact on the future of black-white relations in America.

The veteran returning to the black community in America is likely to encounter two aspects of black American culture that are more ubiquitous today than when he volunteered or was drafted into the military. He encounters an expanding black consciousness which may border on separatism, and a heightened demand for immediate and radical social change. In the pursuit of either, the role of the black veteran could be pivotal. As noted by Whitney Young,[5] that role could range from "full participation" in society—with a rejection of militancy, separatism and violence—to the

---

[1] A previous draft of this paper was presented at the Southern Sociological Society meetings in New Orleans, April, 1969. The research was supported, in part, by a Florida State University Research Council grant #20–036.

[2] As the final draft of this paper is being prepared, the U. S. military is in the midst of its "temporary" incursion into Cambodia (May, 1970). Presumably this action will not—so we are promised—impede Nixon's undisclosed timetable for "withdrawal" from Vietnam.

[3] That the American society is "racist" in character was one of the principal conclusions of: The National Advisory Commission on Civil Disorders, *Report of the National Advisory Commission on Civil Disorders* (New York: New York Times Press, 1968).

[4] Daniel Llorens, "Why Negroes Re-Enlist," *Ebony* (Aug., 1968), pp. 92–97.

[5] Whitney Young, "When the Negroes in Vietnam Come Home," *Harpers* (June, 1967), pp. 63–69.

use of guerilla warfare skills in militant attempts to realize a full measure of the rights being "defended" in Vietnam.

The rationale by which black veterans may be expected to endorse or participate in militant attempts at social change is suggested by status inconsistency theory. The logic of status inconsistency theory is briefly summarized here: (1) an individual may represent disparate positions on several status dimensions; (2) the perception of these inconsistencies may create tensions and "strains toward consistency" within the individual; and (3) attempts may be made to reduce the tension so produced, through various "coping responses" such as upward mobility, attempts to change the social order, or the seeking of social isolation.

As an "independent variable" status inconsistency has been linked with a number of coping responses, including: preference for change in power distribution, political liberalism, political extremism, preference for social change, and attempts to change the social order.[6] Recently, Geschwender refined this link by hypothesizing relationships between specific *patterns* of inconsistency and specific coping responses.[7] For example, it was suggested that individuals whose ethnic (ascribed) status was lower than their achieved status characteristics (education, occupation) would find it difficult to obtain consistency through upward mobility. Given the difficulty of changing one's ethnic status, Geschwender hypothesized that "low-ethnic" inconsistents would ". . . be forced to attempt to reduce their dissonance by changing society."[8] Geschwender also hypothesized that "under-rewarded" status inconsistents (i.e., high education, low occupational status, low income) could be expected to join "extremist social movements," in an effort to achieve a redistribution of societal rewards.[9]

Our research seeks a partial empirical test of Geschwender's recent hypotheses, as well as a partial test of more general status inconsistency theory. Our objective is to examine several patterns of status inconsistency among black veterans, and two "extreme coping responses," which we have termed "black militancy" and "black identification." The analysis involves both objective and subjective measures of inconsistency. The relevance of "perceived," or subjective inconsistency is suggested by an underlying assumption of consistency research, which notes that coping responses may be attempted by status inconsistents who perceive their inconsistency. The

---

[6] See, for example: Gerhard Lenski, "Status Crystallization: A Nonvertical Dimension of Social Status," *American Sociological Review*, 19 (Aug., 1954), pp. 405–413; William F. Kenkel, "The Relationship Between Status Consistency and Politico-Economic Attitudes," *American Sociological Review*, 21 (June, 1956), pp. 365–368; Irwin Goffman, "Status Consistency and Preference for Change in Power Distribution," *American Sociological Review*, 22 (June, 1957), pp. 275–281; Dennis Kelly and William Chambliss, "Status Consistency and Political Attitudes," *American Sociological Review*, 31 (June, 1967), pp. 375–381; Gary Rush, "Status Consistency and Right-Wing Extremism," *American Sociological Review*, 32 (Feb., 1968), pp. 86–92.

[7] James A. Geschwender, "Continuities in Theories of Status Consistency and Cognitive Dissonance," *Social Forces*, 41 (Dec., 1967), pp. 160–171.

[8] *Ibid.*, p. 171.

[9] *Ibid.*, p. 170.

coping responses can be viewed as a reaction to "tensions" generated by the perception of inconsistency.[10]

The specific coping responses that we examine are basic to the fiber of contemporary black culture, and they represent rather extreme alternatives to the existing social order. For our purposes, the coping response of *black militancy* refers to support for black leaders and organizations whose attempts to advance black people are generally beyond the bounds of traditional reformist politics. These leaders and organizations have rejected traditional black reform efforts and have advocated, in their rhetoric and action, the restructuring of American society.

The second coping response, or dependent variable—which we term *black identification*—reflects a desire to supplant traditional white definitions and values with alternatives that are principally or exclusively black. In effect, black identification connotes a social psychological separation of blacks from whites—a kind of black consciousness. Through black identification, blackness becomes a central part of one's belief system, in a process that is similar to the development of parochial interests among other minority groups.

RESEARCH HYPOTHESES

The earliest empirical tests of consistency theory were those of Lenski[11] and Kenkel,[12] each of whom examined the relationship between inconsistency and certain political attitudes reflecting a desire for social change. While their findings were somewhat contradictory, both employed measures of consistency that were based upon objective indices of status characteristics. Our initial hypothesis derives from the approach of these two:

Hypothesis 1: Among black veterans, objectively defined status inconsistents will express greater militancy and black identification than status consistents.

Subsequent contributions by Mitchell,[13] Bloombaum,[14] and Kelly and Chambliss,[15] included the suggestion that *perceived* inconsistency may have greater behavioral and attitudinal consequences than objectively defined inconsistency. This subjective component has proved useful in recent

[10] Geschwender (1967) has suggested that three assumptions underlie the theory of status inconsistency: (1) The individual is cognizant of the inconsistency in his status; (2) Inconsistency results in an "upsetting" state and produces tension for the individual; (3) The individual will attempt to reduce the tension through various "coping responses" such as upward mobility, attempts to change the social order, or social isolation.

[11] Lenski, "Status Crystallization"; Gerhard Lenski, "Social Participation and Status Crystallization," *American Sociological Review*, 21 (Aug., 1956), pp. 458–464.

[12] Kenkel, "The Relationship Between Status Consistency," pp. 365–368.

[13] J. D. Mitchell, "Methodological Notes on a Theory of Status Crystallization," *Public Opinion Quarterly*, 18 (Summer, 1964), pp. 315–325.

[14] Milton Bloombaum, "Mobility Dimension in Status Consistency," *Sociology and Social Research*, 48 (April, 1964), pp. 340–347.

[15] Kelly and Chambliss, "Status Consistency and Political Attitudes," pp. 375–381.

consistency theory and research, and provides the basis for our second research hypothesis:

Hypothesis 2: Among black veterans, those who *perceive* their own status inconsistencies will express greater militancy and black identification than those who perceive their statuses to be consistent.

In addition, the status inconsistency literature has dealt with patterns or *types* of inconsistency. The relevance of "low-ethnic" and "under-rewarded" inconsistency patterns—as discussed by Geschwender—was noted above. The remaining hypotheses involve these types of inconsistency and the coping responses of militancy and black identification.

Hypothesis 3: Among black veterans, those with objectively defined high SES, may be considered "low-ethnic" inconsistents, and therefore will express greater militancy and black identification than status consistents.

Hypothesis 4: Among black veterans, *subjectively* defined "low-ethnic" status inconsistents will express greater militancy and black identification than status consistents.

Hypothesis 5: Among black veterans, those who perceive their status to be "under-rewarded" will express greater militancy and black identification than those who view their status as consistent or "over-rewarded."

DATA COLLECTION

Data were gathered through interviews with 199 randomly selected black veterans, who had been released from military service since January 1, 1963, and were residing in the Jacksonville, Florida, urban area in the fall of 1968.[16] Because anticipated cooperation of federal agencies was not available, names and addresses of black veterans were obtained from several sources: (1) a census enumeration of 80 city blocks, randomly selected from predominantly black areas of the city; (2) seven local agencies which kept information on veterans and race; and (3) several "snowball" techniques.[17] These various sources yielded a total of 945 names and addresses, which was reduced to a sampling frame of 772 after duplicates and individuals with incomplete addresses were eliminated. From this number, a total of 256 valid names and addresses of veterans were randomly chosen, 199 (77.7 per cent) of which were interviewed.[18]

[16] The cut-off point of 1963 was used primarily to take into account the time factor necessary for utilization and participation in various veterans' programs by at least part of our sample.

[17] The "snowball" techniques involved sending postcards to the first 400 names and addresses, acquiring additional names after the interviews, and asking potential interviewers if they knew the names and addresses of additional veterans.

[18] It was hoped that the response rate would be higher, but the veterans were extremely mobile and difficult to contact. Of those veterans on the sampling list who were

Twenty-three black veterans who were attending local colleges were employed as interviewers. The interviewers participated in the census enumeration, a pre-test of the interview schedule, and the final interview process in the fall of 1968.

OPERATIONAL DEFINITIONS

Socioeconomic status (SES) and an objective measure of status inconsistency are computed for each black veteran from income, education and occupation data obtained in the interview. The reported education, income,[19] and occupation of a veteran are assigned nationally standardized scores developed by Nam and Powers.[20] A veteran's SES is represented in our analysis by the arithmetic mean of these three standardized scores. A procedure similar to Lenski's[21] is used to operationalize objective measures of status inconsistency. However, the aforementioned *nationally* standardized[22] scores for income, education and occupation are used, whereas Lenki used scores standardized for his own sample. A score of 100 represents perfect consistency among income, education and occupation; lower scores represent degrees of inconsistency.

Perception of inconsistency is ascertained with data generated by the following questions asked of each veteran: "Where do you suppose that the majority of Americans would rank you on the basis of your race, your income, your education, your job?" "Where would you rank *yourself* in terms of your race, your income, your education, your job?" For each status dimension, both "self" and "other" rated, a seven-point forced choice Likert set of responses was used, ranging from "very low" to "very high."

The perceived ratings by *others* are used to compute an *other-rated inconsistency* score which focuses upon the relative evaluation of the black veteran's racial status. That is, a veteran's "other-rated" income, education and occupation scores are subtracted from his "other-rated" race score. Veterans with lower scores apparently perceive that "the majority of Americans" ascribe very low value to their black ethnicity, and may be considered other-rated, *low-ethnic status inconsistents*.

The hypothesized coping response of *black militancy* is operationally defined by the veteran's assessment of four militant black leaders, and five militant black organizations. The leaders and organizations include: Stokely Carmichael, H. Rap Brown, Malcolm X, Floyd McKissick, the

---

not interviewed, four were dead; three were females; eight were released from the Armed Forces before 1963; one was white; seven had re-enlisted; two were themselves, interviewers; fifteen had incorrect addresses; twenty-eight had moved without leaving a forwarding addrss; twenty-five could not be reached after two call-backs; two questionnaires were invalidated; and two refused to be interviewed.

[19] Education was collected as "last year of school completed"; Income was collected as "present personal monthly income."

[20] Charles B. Nam and Mary Powers, "Changes in the Relative Status Level of Workers in the United States, 1950–1960," *Social Forces,* 47 (Dec., 1968), pp. 158–170.

[21] Lenski, "Status Crystallization," pp. 405–413.

[22] Nam and Powers, "Changes in the Relative Status Level."

Congress of Racial Equality, the Student Non-Violent Coordinating Committee, Deacons for Defense and Justice, Black Muslims, and the Black Panthers. Veterans were asked to rate the "effectiveness" of these leaders and organizations[23] on a five-point Likert scale ranging from "excellent" to "poor."

Black identification is the second hypothesized coping response, or dependent variable, and is measured with an eight item Likert scale. Veterans were asked to indicate the direction and intensity of their feelings with regard to issues involving black independence, identity and consciousness. The issues included: Afro hairstyles, African history in school curricula, dating only black women, buying only from black merchants, black administration of neighborhood schools, preferential hiring of blacks by black employers, lack of sympathy for unfortunate whites, and identification of oneself first as a black man and second as an American. Likert scales for both militancy and black identification are internally consistent.

ANALYSIS

The data are analyzed in 3×3 tables. Scores for the dependent variables are divided into "High," "Medium" and "Low," on the basis of an approximate 25 per cent, 50 per cent, 25 per cent distribution.[24] Chi-square is used to test the null hypothesis of no relationship among the research variables.

Hypothesis 1 is based upon traditional inconsistency theory, as implemented by Lenski[25] and Kenkel,[26] among others. We expected the coping responses of militancy and black identification to be more common for *objectively* defined status *inconsistents* than for consistents. Table 1 reports the relationship between objectively measured status inconsistency, black militancy and black identification. Analysis is limited to 151 cases because complete objective data for income, education, and occupation were unavailable for 48 veterans. Contrary to expectations, no significant relationship is found between objective status inconsistency and the two hypothesized coping responses. Indeed, there appears a tendency for *both* consistents and inconsistents to be rated "low" on scales of militancy and black identification. Higher scores on the two scales also appear with about the same relative frequency among status consistents and inconsistents.

[23] This procedure for measuring militancy has been used by a number of researchers. See, for example, *Supplemental Studies For The National Advisory Commision on Civil Disorders* (1968); or William Brink and Louis Harris, *The Negro Revolution in America* (New York: Simon and Schuster, 1964).

[24] Scores on the *independent* variables were also trichotomized into High, Medium and Low on the basis of an approximate 25 per cent, 50 per cent, 25 per cent distribution. The one exception to a 3 x 3 format is found in Table 5, wherein types of perceived inconsistency are divided into two categories: under-rewarded and those who are consistent or over-rewarded. It should be emphasized, with regard to the dependent variable of black identification, that all black veterans identified with black values to some extent. Thus, a so-called "low" black identification still represents some endorsement of black values.

[25] Lenski, "Status Crystallization," pp. 405–413.

[26] Kenkel, "The Relationship Between Status Consistency," pp. 365–368.

TABLE 1

Objective Status Inconsistency: Militancy and Black Identification in Percentages

Status Inconsistency	Militancy					Black Identification				
	High	Medium	Low	Total	(N)	Strong	Medium	Low	Total	(N)
Sharply Inconsistent (1–70)	21.4	50.0	28.6	100.0	(42)	21.4	47.6	31.0	100.0	(42)
Moderately Inconsistent (71–86)	18.2	57.1	24.7	100.0	(77)	23.4	55.9	20.7	100.0	(77)
Consistent (87–100)	21.9	37.5	40.6	100.0	(32)	15.6	53.2	31.2	100.0	(32)
Total	19.9	51.0	29.1	100.0	(151)	21.2	53.0	25.8	100.0	(151)

$X^2 = 3.928$ $p < .50$ $X^2 = 2.541$ $p < .70$

TABLE 2

Self-Rated Status Inconsistency: Militancy and Black Identification in Percentages

Self-Rated Status Inconsistency	Militancy					Black Identification				
	High	Medium	Low	Total	(N)	Strong	Medium	Low	Total	(N)
Sharply Inconsistent (1–50)	36.4	54.5	9.1	100.0	(44)	4.5	72.7	22.8	100.0	(44)
Moderately Inconsistent (51–80)	21.2	53.8	25.0	100.0	(104)	22.1	54.8	23.1	100.0	(104)
Consistent (81–100)	18.8	37.5	43.7	100.0	(48)	35.4	31.3	33.3	100.0	(48)
Total	24.0	50.0	26.0	100.0	(196)	21.4	53.1	25.5	100.0	(196)

$X^2 = 16.384$ $p < .01$ $X^2 = 19.356$ $p < .01$

Our second hypothesis builds upon the suggestion that preceived inconsistency may be of greater consequence than objectively measured inconsistency. Table 2 presents the relationship between militancy, black identification and perceived inconsistency; the latter being measured with *self-ratings* of status characteristics. The most frequent pattern of self-rated *inconsistency* is one in which the black veteran rated his race-ethnicity high in relation to his income, education and occupation. Perceived *consistency* usually occurred when all four status characteristics were rated relatively high.

As expected, self-defined status inconsistents show a marked tendency toward strongly militant responses, while those with consistent statuses are more likely to be low on the militancy scale. The null hypothesis of no relationship is rejected at the .01 level of significance. However, self-rated inconsistents fail to show the expected tendency toward strong black identification. Indeed, when comparing consistents with inconsistents (both categories being of roughly equivalent size) a strong black identification appears far more likely for *consistents* than inconsistents. Again, X^2 is significant at .01. These two significant though contradictory findings suggest: (1) that perceived inconsistency may, indeed, be more relevant than objectively defined inconsistency, and (2) the coping responses of black militancy and black identification may be differentially related to status inconsistency. Both of these suggestions are examined further in the subsequent analyses.

As noted earlier, Geschwender hypothesized that *low-ethnic* status inconsistents may ". . . be forced to attempt to reduce their dissonance by changing society."[27] To the extent that our indices of militancy and black identification represent attempts by blacks to alter the status quo, hypotheses three and four seek a limited test of Geschwender's assumptions regarding low-ethnic inconsistency.

Given that the entire sample of black veterans may be considered "low" on the ethnic status dimension, *higher* SES black veterans may be "objectively" termed low-ethnic inconsistents. Thus, it was hypothesized that veterans with a relatively "high" objective SES would—as low-ethnic inconsistents—exhibit greater degrees of militancy and black identification than low SES blacks who would not be ethnic inconsistent.

However, as indicated by the data in Table 3, objectively defined SES bears no significant relationship to the coping responses of militancy and black identification. The null hypothesis of no relationship is accepted for both dependent variables.[28]

The relationship between low-ethnic inconsistency and our dependent variables was further examined in Table 4 by taking into account the veteran's own status perceptions. It was expected that militancy and black identification would be stronger for those who perceived that "the majority

[27] Geschwender, "Continuities in Theories," p. 171.
[28] Neither income, occupation or education—considered *separately*—was significantly related to level of militancy or black-identification.

TABLE 3
Socioeconomic Status: Militancy and Black Identification in Percentages

Socioeconomic Status	Militancy					Black Identification				
	High	Medium	Low	Total	(N)	Strong	Medium	Low	Total	(N)
High (64–100)	25.6	38.5	35.9	100.0	(39)	20.5	51.3	28.2	100.0	(39)
Medium (46–63)	16.4	56.2	27.4	100.0	(73)	23.3	52.0	24.7	100.0	(73)
Low (1–45)	20.5	53.9	25.6	100.0	(39)	17.9	56.4	25.6	99.9	(39)
Total	19.9	51.0	29.1	100.0	(151)	21.2	53.0	25.8	100.0	(151)

$X^2 = 3.592$ $p < .50$ $X^2 = .600$ $p < .98$

TABLE 4
Other-Rated Ethnic Inconsistency: Militancy and Black Identification in Percentages

Ethnic Inconsistency Types	Militancy					Black Identification				
	High	Medium	Low	Total	(N)	Strong	Medium	Low	Total	(N)
Low-Ethnic										
Inconsistent[a] (1–21)	24.5	54.7	20.8	100.0	(53)	28.3	54.7	17.0	100.0	(53)
Consistent (22–27)	16.7	45.5	37.8	100.0	(90)	23.3	43.3	33.3	99.9	(90)
High-Ethnic										
Inconsistent[b] (28–38)	35.8	52.8	11.3	99.9	(53)	11.3	67.9	20.8	100.0	(53)
Total	24.0	50.0	26.0	100.0	(196)	21.4	53.1	25.5	100.0	(196)

$X^2 = 15.550$ $p < .01$ $X^2 = 11.827$ $p < .02$

a Race perceived as being rated lower than Income, Education and Occupation.
b Race higher than Income, Education and Occupation.

of Americans" evaluated their racial status component lower than their other status components. Veterans with such perceptions were considered other-rated, low-ethnic status inconsistent.

As before, (see Table 2 above) black militancy and black identification appear related, though differentially to the measures of *perceived* inconsistency. Black identification, as hypothesized, is somewhat stronger for other-rated *low-ethnic* status inconsistents. The null hypothesis of no relationship is rejected at the .02 level of confidence. However, contrary to expectations, black militancy appears strongest for those veterans who perceive their other-rated status to be *high-ethnic*. This latter finding, which is statistically significant at the .01 level of confidence, runs counter to the expectations raised by Geschwender, with regard to low-ethnic status inconsistency. Still, it is important to note again that perceived inconsistency appears related, though differentially, to the coping responses of militancy and black identification.

The final hypothesis—again suggested by Geschwender—indicates an expected relationship between *types* of inconsistency and the dependent variables. The logic by which "under-rewarded" inconsistency may be linked to certain coping responses is given by Geschwender.

> Underrewarded inconsistents whose high investment dimension is education, would experience sharp dissonance (anger). Mobility for them is possible and will be attempted as a means of reducing dissonance. If mobility attempts are unsuccessful or blocked (e.g. if they are minority group members) then the individual will shift to more complex forms of dissonance reduction [such as joining "extremist movements"].[29]

On the basis of self-ratings, veterans were classified as either *under-rewarded, consistent,* or *over-rewarded.*[30] However, only 9 veterans were considered over-rewarded, and for analytical purposes, these veterans are combined with those classified as status consistent in Table 5.

Contrary to expectations, black veterans who are self-defined, under-rewarded inconsistents, appear no more likely to give strong support to militant leaders and organizations than those veterans who are over-rewarded or status consistent. A low X^2 value allows us to accept the null hypothesis of no relationship with some confidence. However, there does appear to be a slight—though non-significant—relationship between subjective types of inconsistency and black identification. Those black veterans who are under-rewarded by their own definition, appear *less likely* to endorse statements of strong black identification. In fact, strong black identification seems twice as likely for status consistents and over-rewarded

[29] Geschwender, "Continuities in Theories," p. 169.

[30] The question of "under-rewarded inconsistency" was also examined using *objective* status measures, exclusive of any objective rating of race-ethnicity. That is, an under-rewarded inconsistent was one whose income or occupation was appreciably lower than his education rating. When veterans were classed as under-rewarded, status consistent and over-rewarded, no relationship could be found between objectively defined types of inconsistency and the dependent variables of militancy and black identification.

TABLE 5

Subjective Types of Status Inconsistency: Militancy and Black Identification in Percentages

Status Consistency	Militancy					Black Identification				
	High	Medium	Low	Total	(N)	Strong	Medium	Low	Total	(N)
Under-rewarded	22.2	50.0	27.8	100.0	(126)	15.1	58.7	26.2	100.0	(126)
Consistent and Over-rewarded	27.1	50.0	22.9	100.0	(70)	32.9	42.8	24.3	100.0	(70)
Total	24.0	50.0	26.0	100.0	(196)	21.4	53.1	25.5	100.0	(196)

$X^2 = 0.874$ $p < .80$ $X^2 = 4.826$ $p < .10$

inconsistents than for under-rewarded inconsistents. Still, the relatively low X^2 value will not permit more than tentative conclusions at this point.

SUMMARY AND DISCUSSION

The status inconsistency literature suggests that liberal or extreme attitudes, preference for change in the distribution of power, and attempts to change the social order may be characteristic of the following: (1) status inconsistents; (2) under-rewarded status inconsistents; and (3) low-ethnic status inconsistents. Thus, the rationale of status inconsistency theory may be useful in accounting for militancy and black identification among black veterans who are returning to potentially explosive black communities. Our research first examined *objective* measures of status inconsistencies for our sample, and found no statistically significant relationship between them and the dependent variables: militancy and black identification.

The finding of no statistically significant relationship between *objective* measures of inconsistency, and the dependent variables, lends support to the earlier negative findings of Kenkel[31] and Kelly and Chambliss.[32] However, our data do not allow categorical rejection of objectively defined inconsistency as a potentially useful independent variable. It is possible that several methodological shortcomings could have contributed to the negative findings and the rejection of hypotheses which involved objective measures of inconsistency.

In this regard, Jackson and Curtis[33] have suggested that homogeneous populations are a basic problem in status consistency research: "Sharp status inconsistency, like extreme mobility, is relatively rare. . . ." One problem with our sample may have been its relative homogeneity. That is, because of its limited size and specific composition, a sample of veterans does not possess sufficient variability in status characteristics to generate meaningful differences in objective status inconsistency. We may have contributed to this homogeneity by excluding veterans for whom objective data were incomplete. Initial inspection of data for the 48 veterans who were excluded, suggests that many of these veterans may be sharply status inconsistent. For example, 26 of those excluded were unemployed, and 12 were full-time students, not in the labor force.

Nevertheless, our data do suggest that *perceptions* of status inconsistency may be differentially related to the coping responses of militancy and black identification. That *perceived* inconsistencies should exhibit some relevance for these coping responses is not unexpected in light of earlier suggestions by Kelly and Chambliss,[34] Mitchell[35] and Bloombaum.[36] That

[31] Kenkel, 'The Relationship Between Status Consistency," pp. 365–368.

[32] Kelly and Chambliss, "Status Consistency and Political Attitudes," pp. 375–381.

[33] Elton Jackson and Richard Curtis, "Conceptualization and Measurement in the Study of Social Stratification," in Hubert M. Blalock, Jr. and Ann B. Blalock, eds., *Methodology in Social Research* (New York: McGraw Hill, 1968), pp. 112–149.

[34] Kelly and Chambliss, "Status Consistency and Political Attitudes," pp. 375–381.

[35] Mitchell, "Methodological Notes," pp. 315–325.

[36] Bloombaum, "Mobility Dimension in Status Consistency," pp. 340–347.

these coping responses should appear differentially related to perceptions of inconsistency suggests that two distinct though related dimensions of black response to status inconsistency may exist.

From the data presented earlier, a very tentative typology can be drawn with regard to black militancy and status inconsistency for our sample of veterans. The strongest support for militant leaders and organizations appears to be characteristic of: (1) the black veteran who perceives his own status to be inconsistent[37] (Table 2); or (2) the black veteran who perceives that society evaluates his income, education and occupation lower than its evaluation of his race, (i.e. "high-ethnic inconsistent"— Table 4).

At the same time, and in contrast with the foregoing, black identification appears strongest for: (1) the black veteran who perceives or rates his own status as consistent[38] (Tables 2 and 5); or (2) perceives that society evaluates his racial status component *lower* than his income, education and occupation, (i.e. "low-ethnic inconsistent"—Table 4). Tentative explanations of these differential relationships are offered here.

From our data, it may be inferred that black-identification as a coping response is most characteristic of black veterans who perceive that their *racial status* component is relatively *under-valued* by society. Such a perception seems more likely to occur among blacks with somewhat higher levels of income, education and occupation, than for lower status blacks.

Due to the ascribed character of the racial status component, individual upward mobility has, traditionally, been ruled out as a workable coping response for low-ethnic inconsistents. In this regard, Geschwender noted that:

> ... persons experiencing dissonance resulting from status inconsistency may attempt to reduce this dissonance by altering their ranking on one or more of the dimensions of status. Persons who are low ethnically but high on the other dimensions could not normally be expected to alter their ethnic status through individual mobility.[39]

However, this observation overlooks the very real possibility of "perceptual upward mobility." That is, perceived consistency may be accomplished for those blacks who have re-defined the value of black ethnicity. We would argue that those veterans who have a strong black-identification are, in effect, asserting the primacy of blackness, and rejecting society's relative *under-valuation* of their ethnic status.[40] This, we suggest, may be the principal function of black identification for *higher* SES blacks, or at least for those blacks who believe that society undervalues their black ethnicity.

---

[37] The most common pattern of self-rated inconsistency was one in which the black veteran rated his *race-ethnicity high* in relation to his income, education and occupation.

[38] The most common pattern of self-rated consistency was one in which the black veteran rated his four status characteristics uniformly high.

[39] Geschwender, "Continuities in Theories," p. 164.

[40] In this regard, see, for example: St. Claire Drake, "The Social and Economic Status of the Negro in the United States," *Daedalus*, 94 (Fall, 1965), pp. 771–814.

This identification may achieve a perceptual consistency that has been denied to blacks by traditional white values. In brief, black identification allows for a state of *perceptual status consistency* by raising the low-ethnic status dimension to the levels represented by the veteran's income, education and occupation.

The notion that perceptual status consistency may be achieved for black veterans through a re-evaluation of black ethnicity, is supported by the fact that black identification appears more common among veterans whose *self-rated* status is *consistent* than among those whose self-ratings are inconsistent (Tables 2 and 5). It appears that for some blacks—those who perceive their ethnic status component to be undervalued—the task of self-rating one's status provides still another opportunity to achieve perceptual consistency. These individuals may be expected to rate their own ethnic status at least as high as their self-ratings for income, education and occupation thereby achieving perceptual status consistency.

If this interpretation is correct, then high self-evaluation of race, and the process of black identification may simply be two different indices of the same phenomenon. Both may represent the traditional "strain toward consistency." However, due to the ascribed nature of the inconsistent status dimension—low ethnicity—consistency may be achieved *only* on a subjective or perceptual level. For some blacks, this coping response may be all that is necessary to achieve consistency.

While black-identification may, and apparently does occur with some frequency among lower-status blacks (Table 3), its function among these veterans may *not* be that of providing a coping response to achieve consistency. In fact, to the extent that lower-status blacks *do* perceptually raise their ethnic-status, or increase their black identification, they may "achieve" a state of high-ethnic inconsistency as described by Geschwender.[41] Given the fact that the lowest of values have been traditionally ascribed to black ethnicity as a status investment, the pattern of high-ethnic inconsistency has generally not been considered possible for blacks. However, with a burgeoning of black pride, consciousness and identification, it seems reasonable for lower status black men to *perceive* themselves as high-ethnic status inconsistents.

With regard to this pattern of inconsistency, Geschwender observed that:

> . . . status inconsistents whose high investment dimension is ethnicity would feel sharp dissonance (anger). Mobility might possibly be a way of reducing dissonance depending upon their level of education. . . . If it is not possible, or if it is unsuccessful, attempts to reduce dissonance will shift to attacking categories of persons. It would be expected that this type of inconsistent would be highly prejudiced and would engage in discrimination. Any attempt to change the society would likely take the form of trying to

---

[41] Geschwender, in "Continuities in Theories," p. 169, discusses "status inconsistents whose high investment dimension is ethnicity." However, that discussion does not anticipate the possibility of high-ethnic inconsistency among blacks whose ethnic status is traditionally ascribed the lowest of relative values.

create a state of affairs in which ethnicity has increased importance—a racist social movement.[42]

Thus, assuming that (1) black-identification fosters a perceptual state of high-ethnic inconsistency; and (2) that many blacks have despaired of traditional avenues of upward mobility, then Geschwender's conditions for "angry" and possibly "racist" coping responses may be met for lower status blacks in America. Our data for black veterans provide partial support for the hypothesized relationship between high-ethnic inconsistency and attempts to change society through support of "racist social movements." The strongest support for militant leaders and organizations among black veterans seems to come from those who perceive their own status to be inconsistent (Table 2) and those who are high-ethnic inconsistent (Table 4).

In summary, we offer the very tentative suggestion[43] that some forms of militancy may be characteristic of blacks—particularly lower status blacks —who have placed a high positive value upon black identity. Within the rationale of status inconsistency theory, the process of affirming black identity may be an important first step in the development of strongly militant attitudes. In a very real sense, black identification and the rejection of traditional white values, could serve to jolt the Negro out of his customarily passive role as ascribed by white *and* Negro tradition. Having rejected the notion of blackness as something to be ashamed of, and having substituted pride in black identity, the possibility of perceiving one's society as unjust rather than oneself as undeserving, clearly exists. Perhaps it is in this context that the black American is moving out of his "place" and into militant subcultures that are demanding a piece of the promised action.

[42] *Ibid.*, p. 169.
[43] These suggestions can be taken as tentative hypotheses that may be apropriate for future empirical testing.

STATUS DISCREPANCY, INTERPERSONAL ATTACHMENT AND RIGHT-WING EXTREMISM

LARRY L. HUNT

University of Maryland

ROBERT G. CUSHING

University of Texas at Austin

T HE RELATIONSHIP BETWEEN DIFFERENT PATTERNS OF STATUS DISCREPANCY and right-wing politics constitute the substantive focus of this research.[1] Specifically, the concern is with the effects of discrepancy among the status dimensions of occupation, education, income, and racial-ethnic background on attitudes towards the John Birch Society, a right-wing political organization which enjoyed considerable public attention in the 1960's.

Although Lenski's research suggests that most types of status discrepancy lead to liberal political orientations,[2] there is some evidence of a link between discrepancy and right-wing orientations.[3] In addition to the empirical evidence, it is theoretically relevant to assume that the nature of the status dilemma rather than the structural condition of discrepancy *per se* may determine the direction of the political response. Whether some discrepancy patterns or profiles dispose individuals to hold favorable at-

---

[1] Concepts such as "status inconsistency," "status crytallization," "status congruence," and "cross-pressures," are associated with particular traditions in the literature. We use the label of "status discrepancy" as a more neutral designation for the conflicting structural properties common to each concept.

[2] Gerhard E. Lenski, "Status Crystallization: A Non-vertical Dimension of Status," *American Sociological Review*, 21 (Aug., 1954), pp. 458–464; Lenski, *Power and Privilege: A Theory of Social Stratification* (New York: McGraw-Hill, 1966); and Lenski, "Status Inconsistency and the Vote: A Four Nation Test," *American Sociological Review*, 32 (April, 1967), pp. 298–301. Lenski suggests that the direction of the response, left-wing versus right-wing politics, is largely a function of the political alternatives available. "One might . . . hypothesize a high frequency of extreme right-wing voting when voters are offered this alternative, but this alternative has not really been available to voters in national elections in the four English-speaking democracies included in this study," "Status Inconsistency," p. 299n.

[3] Benjamin B. Ringer and D. L. Sills, "Political Extremists in Iran: A Secondary Analysis of Communication Data," *Public Opinion Quarterly*, 16 (Winter, 1952–1953), pp. 689–701; Seymour M. Lipset, "Social Stratification and 'Right-wing' Extremism," *British Journal of Sociology*, 10 (Dec., 1959), pp. 1–38; Lipset, "Three Decades of the Radical Right: Coughlinites, McCarthyites, and Birchers," pp. 373–446 in Daniel Bell, ed., *The Radical Right* (Garden City, N.Y.: Anchor Books, 1964); Martin Trow, "Small Businessmen, Political Tolerance, and Support for McCarthy," *American Journal of Sociology*, 64 (Nov., 1958), pp. 270–281; and Gary B. Rush, "Status Consistency and Right-Wing Extremism," *American Sociological Review*, 32 (Feb., 1967), pp. 86–92.

titudes towards right-wing groups such as the John Birch Society is the first question we seek to answer.

A second theoretical basis for anticipating a variety of political responses to status discrepancy arises from an examination of the "status inconsistency" and the "cross-pressures" literature. Further, there has been increasing recognition that the expectations for political behavior generated by a status inconsistency model are clearly different from those derived from a cross-pressures model.[4] Investigators working with the concept of status inconsistency have generally assumed that inconsistency generates stress for individuals and increases their vulnerability to political appeals advocating social change. By contrast, the tradition developing out of the work of Lazarsfeld and Berelson suggests that discrepancies among the individual's categorical memberships generate cross-pressures, a type of structurally generated strain which serves to moderate the individual's politically relevant responses.[5] Manifesting itself in delay of voting decision, non-voting, less partisanship, apathy, and tolerance for opposing political views, the moderating effect of cross-pressures is assumed to lead to flexibility within the political system making for a more stable social order.

Thus, the two models suggest different consequences of status discrepancy for political behavior. The apparent conflict may be reconciled by examining the structural and non-structural conditions from which the models make predictions. The common theme in both traditions is that individuals may be marginal men because of their linkages to disparate parts of the social order. The fact that different adaptations are expected suggests that predicting the outcome to status discrepancy cannot rest entirely upon the structural condition of discrepancy itself.[6]

[4] Nicholas J. Demerath, *Social Class in American Protestantism* (Chicago: Rand McNally, 1965); Donald Trieman, "Status Discrepancy and Prejudice," *American Journal of Sociology*, 71 (May, 1966), pp. 651–664; and David R. Segal, "Status Inconsistency, Cross Pressures, and American Political Behavior," *American Sociological Review*, 34 (June, 1969), pp. 352–359.

[5] Paul R. Lazarsfeld, Bernard Berelson, and Hazel Gaudet, *The People's Choice* (New York: Duell, Sloan and Pearce, 1944); Bernard Berelson, Paul F. Lazarsfeld, and William McPhee, *Voting* (Chicago: University of Chicago Press, 1954); and Lipset, "Three Decades."

[6] Elton F. Jackson, "Status Consistency and Symptoms of Stress," *American Sociological Review*, 27 (Aug., 1962), pp. 469–480; Seymour Parker, "Comment on 'Status Consistency and Stress'," *American Sociological Review*, 28 (Feb., 1963), pp. 131–132; Walter T. Martin, "Socially Induced Stress: Some Converging Theories," *Pacific Sociological Review*, 8 (Spring, 1965), pp. 63–69; Bruce P. Dohrenwend, "Social Status and Psychological Disorder," *American Sociological Review*, 31 (Feb., 1966), pp. 14–35; James A. Geschwender, "Status Inconsistency, Social Isolation, and Individual Unrest," *Social Forces*, 46 (June, 1968), pp. 477–483; Richard L. Meile and Philip N. Haesse, "Social Status, Status Incongruence and Symptoms of Stress," *Journal of Health and Social Behavior*, 10 (Sept., 1969), pp. 237–244. The effects of the cross-pressures and status inconsistency models can be assessed via the different statistical models implied in the two positions. (Trieman, "Status Discrepancy.") The cross-pressures model may be represented by a linear, additive statistical model in which each structural property is assumed to have an independent effect. Thus, the response predicted would reflect an "averaging" of the tendencies

In an attempt to resolve the apparent conflict between the cross-pressures and status inconsistency models, we have limited our focus to the
interpersonal factor of attachment. We suggest that in addition to assuming
some type of discrepant structural context, the cross-pressures model presupposes an "attached" individual who remains implicated in solidary
groupings and, because of his attachments, honors the competing claims
of his structural properties so that his political responses tend towards
moderation. On the other hand, the status inconsistency model assumes an
individual who is "unattached" or alienated from others in his interpersonal
environment. The status inconsistent, lacking attachments to solidary
groupings which might diminish his stress and frustrations, is likely to be
available for the pursuit of political goals entailing fundamental change in
the social order.

The cross-pressure and status inconsistency models predict political
extremism and political moderation in exactly the opposite status profiles
when interpersonal attachment is taken into consideration. The cross-
pressures model predicts extremism when status rankings are consistent
and when the individual is highly attached. When status discrepancy exists
and when the individual is highly attached, political moderation is expected. When the individual is not attached, the effect of homogeneity of
contacts (isolation from cross-pressures) on extremism and of cross-pressures on moderation are expected to be weakened. The status inconsistency
model comes close to predicting interpersonal *de*tachment as a consequence of status discrepancy with political extremism as one potential
result.

Assuming that both models are descriptive of some of the realities of
political behavior, our strategy has been to seek to examine the effects of
both structural and interpersonal variables which shape political attitudes.
Thus, in addition to defining specific patterns of status discrepancy, we
have attempted to examine discrepancy within different conditions of interpersonal attachment. Whether specification of this non-structural condition permits the clarification of the differences between the cross-pressures
and status inconsistency models is the major concern of this research.

METHOD

The sample. The empirical base of the research was a secondary analysis
of data obtained in the 1964 Election Study (S 473) conducted by the
Survey Research Center of the University of Michigan. The complete study
consisted of a series of pre-election and post-election interviews (N =

---

implied by each structural property. The status inconsistency model postulates a linear,
non-additive statistical model in that it assumes the presence of statistical interaction
between structural variables. "Inconsistency effects" are indicated when the additive
model fails to account for the observed values for the discrepant status profile while
accounting for the observed values for the consistent status profiles. Significant depar-
tures from the additive model for the specified status profiles are assumed to reflect the
presence of stress and behavioral outcomes not predictable in terms of the independent
effects of the status ranks.

1,571) gathering information of the respondents' socioeconomic characteristics, political attitudes and political behavior.[7] The respondents constituted a representative cross-section of voting-age citizens living in private
households within the 48 contiguous states.[8]

The dependent variable. The dependent variable consisted of an index
of the respondents' attitudes towards the John Birch Society. Attitudes
were recorded on the Survey Research Center's feeling thermometer. Each
respondent was asked to report a number ranging from zero (indicating a
very cold or unfavorable attitude) to ninety-nine (indicating a very warm
or favorable attitude) which would most accurately reflect his attitude
towards the Society. The specific question regarding the JBS was preceded
by the general statement that "there are many organizations in America
that try to get the government or the American people to see things more
their way." After listing other organizations such as the NAACP and KKK,
the interviewer asked if the respondent had ever heard of the JBS. The
1,143 of 1,450 respondents who had knowledge of the JBS were then asked
"Where would you put the John Birch Society on the thermometer?"

Attachment. A dichotomized general index of attachment was constructed from three items dealing with the respondent's general attitude
towards others in his interpersonal environment.[9] Ideally, we would have
preferred measures of the respondent's linkage to specific groups. Unfortunately, no such measure was available.

The status dimensions. In order to facilitate identifying consistent and

---

[7] Much of the data included in this research was obtained from the 1,450 respondents who were reinterviewed in the post-election investigation. The actual number of
cases used in each of our analyses was always substantially smaller due to incomplete
data, particularly in regard to ethnic background information. Over 250 respondents
were not classifiable in terms of racial-ethnic background and were eliminated from
the analyses including this dimension. Other cases which could not be clearly classified on any of the status dimensions, attachment, or the dependent variable were eliminated from the analysis.

[8] The sampling design involved the random selection of dwelling units after previous
delimitation of the total population by area. The entire nation was divided into 95
strata on the basis of population density and geographic location. Within each strata,
a primary sampling unit (typically a county) was randomly selected. Within each primary sampling unit, blocks were randomly selected, except for cities over 50,000 in
which case the area was stratified on the basis of average rental values and number of
dwelling units per block. Within the selected blocks, dwelling units were selected
randomly according to the sampling rate of two units per block. Within each dwelling,
one adult of voting age was interviewed.

[9] The three items were:
1. "Generally speaking, would you say that most people can be trusted or that you
can't be too careful in dealing with people?"
2. "Would you say that most of the time people try to be helpful or that they are mostly
just looking out for themselves?"
3. "Do you think most people would try to take advantage of you if they got a chance
or would they try to be fair?"
As would be expected, responses on the three items were highly interrelated (62 per
cent responded the same way on all three items), which provides some support for
the reliability of the dimension measured.

discrepant status profiles, the four status dimensions were trichotomized as follows:

(1) The dividing points for *income* were $4,000 and $7,500 based upon the annual income of the head of household. This resulted in the assignment of high rank to 28 per cent, medium rank to 38 per cent, and low rank to 34 per cent of the respondents.

(2) *Occupations* were coded by the Survey Research Center into eleven general categories. Our high rank included the professional and technical, and self-employed businessmen, managers, and officials categories (28 per cent of the respondents). The medium rank included the clerical and sales, skilled workers, protective workers, and farm managers categories (35 per cent of the respondents). The low rank included the semi-skilled, operative and kindred workers, service workers (exclusive of "protective services"), unskilled laborers, and farm operators (exclusive of "farm managers") categories (37 per cent of the respondents). Respondents not classifiable in terms of these categories (for example, some students, some unemployed, and housewives) were not included in the analyses.

(3) High rank on *education* was assigned to respondents who reported at least "some college" as their highest level of educational attainment (25 per cent of the respondents). Criteria for assignment of ranks to the remaining cases varied according to the age of the respondent. Following the suggestions of Lenski and Jackson that older persons would not be expected to have had as much formal schooling as younger ones and would therefore not be treated in terms of the same status criteria applied to more youthful respondents, categories of under 40 and over 40 were established.[10] For the under 40 category, medium rank was assigned if the respondent had completed high school, otherwise low rank as assigned. For respondents over 40, medium rank was assigned to those having any high school and low rank to those reporting no high school training. These procedures resulted in the assignment of high rank to 25 per cent, medium rank to 41 per cent, and low rank to 34 per cent of the respondents.

(4) Low rank on *racial-ethnic background* was assigned to all respondents identified by the interviewer as non-white (Negro, Oriental, Mexican, and so forth). For whites, native-born Americans were classified as follows: high rank was assigned to those reporting ethnic ties with Anglo-Saxon countries; medium rank to those of Northwest European extraction; and low rank to all other types of ethnic background. Respondents who were foreign born were assigned according to the above pattern but were categorically "demoted" one rank. Lastly, low rank was assigned to respondents who identified themselves as Jewish in religious affiliation with other ethnic characteristics being ignored. These procedures resulted in the assignment of high rank to 30 per cent, medium rank to 43 per cent, and low rank to 27 per cent of the respondents.

Procedure. In order to create status profiles differing in degree and type

---

[10] Gerhard E. Lenski, "Status Crystallization"; Elton F. Jackson, "Status Consistency," pp. 469–480.

FIGURE 1

Typology of Status Profiles[a]

Education	Income High	Medium	Low
High	H-H consistency	Moderate I/E discrepancy	Extreme E/I discrepancy
Medium	Moderate I/E discrepancy	M-M consistency	Moderate E/I discrepancy
Low	Extreme I/E discrepancy	Moderate I/E discrepancy	L-L consistency

[a] Education and income are used as examples. Similar profiles can be constructed by pairing any of the four status dimensions.

of status discrepancy, our procedure was to cross-classify status dimensions taking two at a time.[11] Figure 1 illustrates the typology of profiles created by this procedure. The next step was to compute mean scores on the dependent variable which permits comparison among the profiles with reference to their support or rejection of the JBS.

The task of operationally defining status discrepancy is relatively straightforward compared with the task of assessing its precise effects. The problem of insuring that spurious "discrepancy effects" are not imputed to the data is demanding and intricate. Despite numerous attempts to investigate the phenomena of status discrepancy, there presently exists no basis for inferring the presence of discrepancy or inconsistency effects which has received general acceptance.[12] Lenski has recently proposed

[11] Although we would have preferred to be able to control for the effects of all four status dimensions simultaneously, our interest in examining structural and interpersonal variables forced us to analyze political attitudes controlling for only two status variables at a time. For example, in the occuupation by income analysis, we have cross-classified respondents on these dimensions without controlling for their education or racial-ethnic ranks. As can be seen by examining the number of cases available for these analyses, especially when the interpersonal variable of attachment is controlled, further cross-tabulation on status dimensions would have been impossible.

[12] For a perspective on the problems of identifying inconsistency effects and of distinguishing these from status effects see Robert E. Mitchell, "Methodological Notes on a Theory of Status Crystallization," *Public Opinion Quarterly*, 28 (Summer, 1964), pp. 315–325; Gerhard E. Lenski, "Comment," *Public Opinion Quarterly*, 28 (Summer, 1964), pp. 326–330; Elton F. Jackson and Peter J. Burke, "Status and Symptoms of Stress: Additive and Interactive Effects," *American Sociological Review*, 30 (Aug., 1965), pp. 556–564; Martin D. Hyman, "Determining the Effects of Status Inconsistency," *Public Opinion Quarterly*, 30 (Spring, 1966), pp. 120–129; Hubert M. Blalock, "Theory Building and the Statistical Concept of Interaction," *American Sociological Review*, 30 (June, 1965), pp. 374–380; "Tests of Status Inconsistency Theory: A Note of Caution," *Pacific Sociological Review*, 10 (Fall, 1967), pp. 69–74; "Status Incon-

that interaction effects which an additive statistical model cannot describe may be interpreted as reflecting "inconsistency effects."[13] Jackson and Burke and Trieman have followed this suggestion by attempting to develop an additive statistical model for use as a point of reference to examine observed values characteristic of status inconsistents.[14] Their procedure involves converting the separate ranks on status dimensions into dummy variables and performing a regression analysis using separate ranks on each dimension as predictor variables. Since dummy regression represents the best current strategy for attempting to establish the presence of effects attributable to status discrepancy, the procedure was adopted in this research.

Expectations. Our initial concern in examining the data was to examine observed levels of support and deviations from an additive model within status profiles ignoring attachment level. After noting the patterns displayed by a structural level of analysis, our attention shifted to the interpersonal level of analysis to see if interpersonal attachment improved specification of the responses predicted by the cross-pressures and status-inconsistency models. We obviously expected to discover linkages between status discrepancy and distinctive attitudes towards the John Birch Society. We anticipated that such linkages would possibly emerge only when both structural and interpersonal variables are analyzed simultaneously.

Substantively, prior research has suggested that status discrepancies involving low racial-ethnic status and higher achieved status and the pattern where education is higher than income are especially likely to generate liberal political orientations.[15] Thus, we expected to observe the lowest level of support and negative deviations for these profiles. For all other discrepant profiles we elected to explore the possibility that status discrepancy would result in support for the John Birch Society. Operationally,

---

sistency and Interaction: Some Alternative Models," *American Journal of Sociology*, 73, (Nov., 1967), pp. 305–315; "The Identification Problem and Theory Building: The Case of Status Inconsistency," *American Sociological Review*, 31 (Feb., 1966), pp. 52–61; "Status Inconsistency, Social Mobility, Status Integration and Structural Effects," *American Sociological Review*," 32 (Oct., 1967), pp. 790–801; Elton F. Jackson and Richard F. Curtis, "Conceptualization and Measurement in the Study of Social Stratification," in Hubert M. Blalock and Ann B. Blalock, eds., *Methodology in Social Research* (New York: McGraw-Hill, 1968), pp. 112–154.

[13] Gerhard E. Lenski, "Comment."

[14] Elton F. Jackson and Peter J. Burke, "Status and Symptoms of Stress," pp. 556–564; and Donald Trieman, "Status Discrepancy," 1966.

[15] In addition to Lenski's work, see Irwin W. Goffman, "Status Consistency and Preference for Change in Power Distribution," *American Sociological Review*, 22 (June, 1957), pp. 275–281. However, the following failed to uncover a relationship between status discrepancy and political behavior. William F. Kenkel, "The Relationship Between Status Consistency and Political-Economic Attitudes," *American Sociological Review*, 21 (June, 1956), pp. 365–368; K. Dennis Kelly and William J. Chambliss, "Status Consistency and Political Attitudes," *American Sociological Review*, 21 (June, 1966), pp. 375–382.

we expected high observed means and positive deviations from an additive model.

When controlling for the interpersonal variable of attachment we were attempting to identify non-structural conditions under which status discrepancy results in distinct types of political responses, that is, moderation versus more definite support of right-wing extremism. Thus, we expected status discrepancy in the condition of high attachment to lead to low levels of support for the John Birch Society and higher support levels in the low attachment condition.[16] Not only should observed support levels vary for the discrepant profiles by attachment level, but (assuming Trieman's suggestion that cross-pressures effects imply an additive statistical model and status inconsistency effects a nonadditive one is correct) high attachment should be the locus of additive effects and low attachment the context for marked deviations from an additive model.

FINDINGS

The average support for the John Birch Society on the feeling thermometer is definitely on the cool side for all status profiles in the structural level of analysis.[17] Given the Society's extreme political views, the lack of widespread support is not surprising. The strategic questions for the present research are (1) whether certain types of status discrepancy are linked with more or less acceptance and/or rejection of the John Birch Society than expected on the basis of the additive effects of status properties and (2) whether controlling for the interpersonal variable of attachment specifies the locus of the effects predicted by the cross-pressures and status inconsistency models.

Turning first to the parts of Tables 2 and 3 containing the results of the structural level of analysis, the data strongly suggest that some types of discrepancy produce distinctive attitudes towards the John Birch Society. In most modes of analysis there are interesting effects in at least one of the discrepant profiles. The most striking pattern is the marked rejection where achieved status is higher than rank on the ascribed racial-ethnic dimension as evidenced by the lowest levels of support in the tables and the generally large negative deviations from an additive model. Rejection is also marked in the high education, low income profile. Thus, our expectations that

[16] This general expectation does not hold for discrepant profiles where racial-ethnic rank is low or for the high education-low income profile. Since we anticipate rejection of the John Birch Society in these profiles, the expectations relative to moderation and increasing support by high and low attachment are not directly relevant. To test the implications of the two models for these profiles would require a measure of left-wing extremism.

[17] Note that the tables include only four of the nine status profiles used in each mode of analysis. Because of the imprecision of the indexes used and the fact that, paralleling Jackson and Burke's findings, moderate discrepancy reveals no interesting or readily interpretable associations, only the high-high and low-low consistents and the two extreme discrepancy profiles are presented. It is in these profiles that one would expect to find, as we did, the most revealing patterns of relationship.

TABLE 1

Associations Among Predictor Variables (ϕ^2, N's in parentheses)

	Education	Occupation	Income	Racial-ethnic	Attach-ment
Education	1.00	.43*	.31*	.02	.06*
		(369)	(364)	(230)	(364)
Occupation		1.00	.48*	.02*	.06*
			(434)	(268)	(434)
Income			1.00	.01	.03*
				(270)	(434)
Racial-ethnic				1.00	.07*
					(369)
Attachment					1.00

* P<.05.

"liberal" political orientations would be linked with these types of status discrepancy have been fulfilled.

Evidence for a relationship between discrepancy and right-wing orientations is observed only in the Occupation by Income analysis where both types of extreme discrepancy (high income-low occupation and low income-high occupation) show comparatively high levels of support. Apparently, these profiles are the loci of different types of status dilemmas than experienced by the high achieved-low ascribed and high education-low income types of discrepancy.

That different patterns of discrepancy produce different types of strain and directionality of political response is especially clear when the high occupation-low income and high education-low income types are compared. Both types have in common the low income rank yet the former leads to acceptance, the latter generates rejection. Neither pattern can be accounted for by examining the effects of high occupation or high education alone. Hence, not only does status discrepancy have effects that a unidimensional analysis of vertical status would conceal, but different patterns of discrepancy produce markedly different types of political orientation.

Finally, although not anticipated, there appears to be evidence that some deviations occur in status consistent profiles. This pattern and its meaning will become clearer after moving to the interpersonal level of analysis.

Inspection of the profiles in Tables 2 and 3, containing the results of the interpersonal level of analysis, suggests that controlling for attachment leads to more precise identification of the contexts of the status discrepant's acceptance or rejection of the John Birch Society. Substantively, the low observed means and large negative deviations are specific to status discrepants with high attachment. With respect to support, although the high income-low occupation type accepts the John Birch Society to an equal degree in both attachment conditions, the high occupation-low income

TABLE 2

Observed Levels of Support for the John Birch Society and Deviations from an Additive Model for Status Profiles Based Upon Occupation, Education, and Income Ranks by Two Levels of Analysis

Status Profile	Structural			Level of Analysis Interpersonal						Diff. between Obs. Ȳ's, High & Low Attachment[c]
				High Attachment			Low Attachment			
	Obs. Ȳ[a]	Dev.[b]	N	Obs. Ȳ[a]	Dev.	N	Obs. Ȳ	Dev.	N	
O by I										
Hi Hi	24.23	−2.06	198	23.46	−.84	157	27.17	−6.34**	41	−.317
Hi Lo	35.14	5.64*	49	25.88	−.03	33	54.25	17.04**	16	−28.37**
Lo Hi	36.78	5.88**	50	35.68	4.77*	28	38.18	6.41*	22	−2.50
Lo Lo	33.69	−.42	137	31.62	−.90	74	36.11	.64	63	−4.49
E by I										
Hi Hi	26.00	.21	159	25.60	1.24	124	27.43	−2.90	35	−1.77
Hi Lo	23.57	−5.45**	47	18.17	−8.18**	30	33.12	−.75	17	−14.95**
Lo Hi	31.74	1.38	34	32.95	3.02	20	30.00	−1.94	14	2.95
Lo Lo	34.96	1.37	124	34.75	3.37*	61	35.16	−.32	63	−.41
E by O										
Hi Hi	25.85	−1.18	184	23.47	−1.62	144	34.45	.00	40	−10.98**
Hi Lo	30.15	−1.94	34	29.57	−2.03	23	31.36	−2.73	11	−1.97
Lo Hi	28.04	−2.02	28	26.18	−2.28	17	30.91	−3.91	11	−4.73
Lo Lo	37.11	1.99	123	40.07	5.11*	60	34.29	−.16	63	5.88

* p < .10.
** p < .05.
[a] Observed mean.
[b] Deviation of expected (regression) mean from the observed mean.
[c] Two-tailed t-test used to test significance of the difference.

TABLE 3

Observed Levels of Support for the John Birch Society and Deviations from an Additive Model for Status Profiles Based Upon Occupation, Education, Income and Racial-Ethnic Ranks by Two Levels of Analysis

| Status Profile | Structural | | | Level of Analysis — Interpersonal | | | | | | Diff. between Obs. Ȳ's, High & Low Attachment[c] |
| | | | | High Attachment | | | Low Attachment | | | |
	Obs. Ȳ[a]	Dev.[b]	N	Obs. Ȳ[a]	Dev.	N	Obs. Ȳ	Dev.	N	
R by O										
Hi Hi	31.82	1.19	82	30.75	1.86	65	35.88	−2.54	17	−5.13
Hi Lo	28.40	−5.73**	47	26.32	−6.47**	34	33.85	−4.23	13	−7.53*
Lo Hi	20.28	−4.96**	68	17.36	−5.54**	55	32.62	.99	13	−15.26**
Lo Lo	34.23	5.49**	71	34.72	7.92**	36	33.71	2.42	35	1.01
R by E										
Hi Hi	32.35	2.92	80	30.16	2.50	62	39.44	3.08	18	−9.28*
Hi Lo	29.08	−2.18	38	25.40	−3.35	25	36.15	.62	13	−10.75*
Lo Hi	19.90	−4.28*	61	16.56	−5.04**	48	32.23	1.50	13	−15.67**
Lo Lo	28.73	2.72	51	28.54	5.85*	24	28.89	−1.01	27	−.35
R by I										
Hi Hi	30.44	1.11	79	28.85	1.75	61	35.83	−1.65	18	−6.98
Hi Lo	33.41	.74	57	29.23	−1.10	38	41.84	4.61	19	−12.52**
Lo Hi	22.21	−2.10	68	17.55	−3.66	51	36.18	4.16	17	−18.63**
Lo Lo	28.62	.89	66	25.45	.92	33	31.79	.02	33	−6.34

* p<.10.
** p<.05.
[a] Observed Mean.
[b] Deviation of expected (regression) mean from observed mean.
[c] Two-tailed t-test used to test significance of difference.

type's acceptance is clearly linked with low attachment. Further, introducing attachment into the analysis yields even more evidence that nonadditive effects occur in consistent status profiles.

Deviations for the consistent profiles plus the occurrence of large deviations in the high attachment condition make it apparent that some of the assumptions which guided the formation of our original expectations are incorrect. Examining the locus of deviations from the additive models, it is clear that the attachment measure does not identify interpersonal conditions which clearly separate additive and nonadditive effects. Thus, assuming that the cross-pressures and status inconsistency models can be represented by the statistical models we have used, this research has not been able to demonstrate the conditions under which these models hold.

Returning to an examination of observed means, however, the data suggest that the attempt to identify interpersonal contexts where status discrepancy has different political consequences in a substantive sense was somewhat more successful. Comparing support in the profiles by attachment level reveals that nearly all the large differences between means occur in profiles which are discrepant. Although there is a contextual shift towards higher support in most profiles, the dramatic shifts toward higher or lower support are largely linked with status discrepancy. This suggests that the attachment measure does identify non-structural conditions under which different types of adaptation to similar structural discrepancies occur. Noting that the shifts follow the substantive implications of the two models, we find that the variable of attachment is relevant to substantively differentiating cross-pressure and status inconsistency effects. The interest in the structural conditions that generate interpersonal attachment is a secondary problem for the present research. From either the status inconsistency model or the cross-pressures model, we may postulate an uneasiness on the part of the status discrepant individual in his interpersonal relations. Such an expectation suggests an inverse relationship between the interpersonal attachment index and the status discrepancy. The expectation is not supported by an analysis of the frequencies reported in Table 2 and 3. Perhaps the factors that directly affect interpersonal attachment, such as whether or not the respondent is married, lives alone, has friends or relatives in the neighborhood, and so forth, are not closely related to status discrepancy. Considering the direct relationship between the various status dimensions and interpersonal attachment level (see Table 1), a more likely possibility is that low attachment is a reflection of a world outlook shaped by status deprivation. To examine this possibility more thoroughly, interpersonal attachment was transformed into a dummy criterion variable and analyzed via the dummy regression procedure using the various status dimensions as predictors.[18] In all cases, the degree of interpersonal attachment is clearly predictable from an additive model.

[18] See J. Johnston, *Econometric Methods* (New York: McGraw-Hill, 1963) pp. 221–230, for the mathematical model. The expected value for the criterion may be interpreted as the probability that a given individual is attached or as the expected proportion of cases in a given status profile that are attached.

CONCLUSIONS

Before attempting to place any final interpretations on the data or form conclusions about the substantive and theoretical issues originally raised by this research, we must first call attention to a methodological dilemma. A "problem" is posed by the large deviations in *consistent* profiles which was firmly established as a result of controlling for the variable of attachment. Recognizing that deviations may be methodological artifacts or reflect substantively meaningful effects, how do we decide when and where to assign substantive meaning to the deviations observed?

The most obvious "explanation" for the large deviations in consistent profiles is that our failure to control for the effects of all status dimensions simultaneously has led to the classification of respondents who are discrepants in other modes of analysis as consistent. Thus, the effects attributed to consistents might be actually due to discrepants on other status dimensions. This appears to be the case in the Education by Occupation analysis where the low-low profile includes a number of cases who are high on the income dimension. However, in all other cases, no apparent pattern whereby consistents might be clearly identified as discrepants in other modes of analysis could be discerned. Hence the problem remains for the other profiles. It is possible that the dummy variable regression procedure does not control for the separate effects of status ranks in a manner which permits an automatic equating of statistical interaction and discrepancy effects. Which deviations are substantively meaningful and which are artifacts thus remains a problem. Unfortunately, we have no solution and can only interject a cautionary note into the present discussion. Obviously, suggestions for solving the identification dilemma are welcome—and needed.

Returning to the more clearly theoretical issues raised in this research, we may ask first what kinds of interpretations may be made of the specific linkages found between structurally defined discrepancy profiles and political attitudes. Assuming that conservative forms of political expression are understandable as rear-guard responses to technical, political, and social changes which have led to increasing complexity in economic affairs and centralization of political authority, the status dilemmas which lead to support or rejection of the JBS are probably related to the way status discrepants are affected by the changing shape of American society; whether their marginality is decreased or increased by recent changes.

The John Birch Society's clearly identifiable preference for the pre-New Deal era is probably not shared by the ACH/ASC status discrepant. His status dilemmas are generated by the persistence of customary ascription processes which deny many equality of opportunity. Although this status type has been somewhat successful relative to achievement criteria, his low racial-ethnic status continues to be an important source of his social identity and contributes to problematical experiences in his interaction with others. The "celebration" of the American experience and reverence for the good old days so prevalent on the political right serves only as a reminder of a troubled past and not as a meaningful rallying point. It is not that the ACH/ASC discrepant is unmoved by the ideologies of the right. His experiences move him towards rejection of an ideology which, if widely accepted, would probably result in an aggravation of his status problems, not an alleviation of them. A continuation of New Deal reforms for traditional social inequalities is likely to be favored by the ACH/ASC discrepant.

In a related vein, the status discrepant whose educational rank is high and income low is not likely to be attracted to the JBS. Although the E/I discrepant is ambivalent relative to the present social order which fails to recognize his "essential worth" by appropriate financial rewards, his status dilemmas would not be resolved by the political goals of the JBS. His low income predisposes him to favor attempts to redistribute wealth, not return to the heyday of finance capitalism. His high education may dispose him to identify with the intellectual community which is often subject to attack from the political right and to reject extremist movements which tend to be politically intolerant and/or not strongly committed to civil liberties. Thus, the E/I discrepant is likely to be favorably disposed towards the recent structural changes in American society and seek continuation of the political reforms begun during the New Deal Era.

Acceptance of the John Birch Society, though not dramatically present in our data, seems to be linked with status discrepancies where people are potentially threatened or displaced by the increasing complexity and centralization of national life. The I/O type of discrepancy represents a conjunction of relatively high income and few occupational skills. This status discrepant is likely to be threatened by the general movement towards rationalization of production and distribution systems which increasingly call for greater technical skills as a means of gaining or maintaining high income reward levels. This type thus lacks a firm base for sustained economic rewards. Similarly, the O/I types of discrepancy represent a social type similar to supporters of McCarthyism observed by Trow in the early fifties.[19] Those whose occupational status has traditionally been a prestigious and functional part of local community, such as small businessmen, are increasingly on marginal terms economically and especially vulnerable to displacement by modern merchandizing and distribution techniques. Although the cultural system still pays lip service to the ideal of the small, independent entrepreneur, the scale and complexity of national life seems generally destructive of such roles and identities. Thus, the I/O and O/I types of discrepancy which have revealed tendencies to be somewhat favorably disposed towards the John Birch Society are probably responding positively towards a group which seems to be challenging, either directly or symbolically, the drift away from a relatively secure past towards a social order which increases their own marginality.

Concerning, finally, the attempt to reconcile the CP and SI models, it is clear that we were only partially successful in identifying conditions under which the different adaptations implied by the models occur. While the

---

[19] Martin Trow, "Small Businessmen."

observed levels of support for the JBS vary by high and low attachment as expected, and this control identifies effects relatively specific to status discrepant profiles, the attachment measure does not identify non-structural conditions under which additive and non-additive outcomes are observed. It is probable that investigations will have to specify more precisely the particular patterns of commitments and attachments of individuals to their solidary groups and reference groups than was possible in this research.

Although the CP and SI models are not entirely reconciled, controlling for the interpersonal variable of attachment does show there is considerable variance in political response associated with patterns of status discrepancy. This variance suggests that an important residue of the research is the conclusion that further research on status discrepancy can profit from the specifications of non-structural concomitants and consequences of status discrepancy which mediate and shape attitudinal and behavioral outcomes. Political orientations are not automatic outcomes of structural properties but are shaped in a social process which is directly mediated by interpersonal relationships.

In sum, certain types of status discrepancy appear to be predisposed by distinct status dilemmas rather than discrepancy *per se* to either support or reject right-wing politics as exemplified in the John Birch Society. Our attempt to uncover linkages between discrepancy and right-wing orientations was a limited success, but the main drift of the substantive findings suggests that the recurrent association between status discrepancy and political liberalism is probably both theoretically and empirically sound. On the other hand, the variety of response and the limited evidence of support for the JBS suggests that status discrepancy is not a unitary phenomenon having only liberal consequences. Further, controlling for attachment level suggests that identifying the consequences of status discrepancy entails, in part, specifying the conditions under which distinct status dilemmas are experienced. Future research on status discrepancy can not only profit from keeping separate the different patterns of discrepancy but also from specifying non-structural correlates which heighten or possibly resolve the status dilemmas implied by the structural condition of discrepancy.

SOCIAL CLASS, STATUS INCONSISTENCY AND POLITICAL ATTITUDES[1]

D. STANLEY EITZEN

University of Kansas

ALTHOUGH HE WAS NOT THE FIRST TO FOCUS ON THE MULTIDIMENSION-
ality of social status, Lenski can be credited with giving impetus
to empirical studies of the social and political consequences of holding differential status ranks.[2] In particular, he elaborated the possibility
of a consistency dimension of status which is, by definition, non-vertical.[3]
Basing his methodology on this assumption, he isolated consistents from
inconsistents and compared them on political attitudes and voting behavior. He found status inconsistents to be more inclined toward the
Democratic party and toward a liberal stance on social welfare items than
were status consistents. Lenski and others have suggested that this finding
may represent a more general tendency for inconsistents to adopt extreme
stances, either to the left or right.[4] This was verified in later research
by Rush, who found status inconsistents were disproportionately "right-
wing extremist."[5]

The findings of Lenski, Rush and others run counter to the widely accepted generalizations that social class and political attitudes are linearly
related.[6] The omission of social class from the analysis had led to a good
deal of criticism of status inconsistency studies.[7] By focusing on the degree

[1] I am indebted to Kenneth C. W. Kammeyer, Gary M. Maranell, and Marston M.
McCluggage who read earlier versions of this paper and offered useful criticisms. The
data utilized in this study were from the 1964 Election Study conducted by the Survey Research Center, University of Michigan. These data were made available by the
Inter-University Consortium for Political Research.

[2] Gerhard E. Lenski, "Status Crystallization: A Non-Vertical Dimension of Social
Status," *American Sociological Review*, 19 (Aug., 1954), pp. 405–413.

[3] Lenski's method assigned scores to individuals according to the degree to which
they are crystallized in status. This technique has the effect of nullifying social class
distinctions since consistently upper status persons are classified together with persons
consistently low in their status attributes.

[4] Cf. Gerhard E. Lenski, "Social Participation and Status Crystallization," *American
Sociological Review*, 21 (Aug., 1956), p. 459; Benjamin B. Ringer and David L. Sills,
"Political Extremists in Iran," *Public Opinion Quarterly*, 16 (Winter, 1952–53), p. 694;
and Seymour M. Lipset and Reinhard Bendix, *Social Mobility in Industrial Society*
(Berkeley: University of California Press, 1960), pp. 64ff.

[5] Gary B. Rush, "Status Consistency and Right-Wing Extremism," *American Sociological Review*, 32 (Feb., 1967), pp. 86–92.

[6] Cf. Seymour Martin Lipset, *Political Man: The Social Bases of Politics* (Garden
City: Doubleday Anchor Books, 1963), p. 92; K. Dennis Kelly and William J. Cham-
bliss, "Status Consistency and Political Attitudes," *American Sociological Review*, 31
(June, 1966), p. 380; and V. O. Key, Jr., *Public Opinion and American Democracy*
(New York: Alfred A. Knopf, 1961), pp. 123–150.

[7] Cf. N. J. Demerath III and Alan Orenstein, "Status Consistency and Vertical
Status: Interaction or Additivity," (mimeographed), 1964; Robert E. Mitchell, "Methodological Notes on a Theory of Status Crystallization," *Public Opinion Quarterly*,

to which individuals deviate from status consistency, persons may be classified together who differ dramatically in social class. Should one expect persons with uniformly high status ranks to have the same attitudes and/or behaviors as persons with uniformly low ranks? Traditional status crystallization studies make this assumption implicitly by combining these categories together under the rubric "status consistents," despite the evidence that high status persons differ substantially from low status persons on many characteristics.

The purpose of this study was to demonstrate that in the realm of political attitudes social class is a more meaningful variable than status inconsistency. If, as the literature suggests, political attitudes are linearly related to social class, then the grouping of persons with uniformily high status ranks and the persons with uniformly low status ranks into one category called "status consistents" should nullify such a relationship.[8] We would expect to find persons with uniformly high status attributes to be significantly different in their political attitudes from persons with uniformly low ranks. It was also expected that status inconsistents as a category would be approximately midway between these two status consistent categories on each political attitude dimension.

METHOD

The three status variables most commonly used in status inconsistency studies—education, occupational prestige, and income[9]—were selected for investigation. For the first two variables, the data for family heads were used, which is in keeping with Lenski's procedures.[10] The data for income, on the other hand, were for "family income."

Since the focus of this study was on status inconsistency, it was necessary to characterize some of the individuals in the sample as "high" and

---

28 (Summer, 1964), pp. 315–325; Martin D. Hyman, "Determining the Effects of Status Inconsistency," *Public Opinion Quarterly,* 30 (Spring, 1966), pp. 120–129; and Hubert M. Blalock, Jr., "Status Inconsistency, Social Mobility, Status Integration and Structural Effects," *American Sociological Review,* 32 (Oct., 1967), pp. 790–801.

[8] This argument is also relevant for the category "status inconsistents." High-low inconsistents, for example, should differ in political attitudes from low-high inconsistents. To combine them into one gross category will have the effect of averaging their opposite effects upon the dependent variable. The focus of status inconsistency studies, then, should be the comparison of types of inconsistency, as Lenski has noted. Cf. Gerhard E. Lenski, "Comment on Kenkel's Communication," *American Sociological Review,* 21 (June, 1956), pp. 368–369.

[9] The ascribed status dimension of ethnicity, admittedly a most relevant variable in determining political attitudes, is omitted in the present study because it introduces many problems in research when used as a variable. Such research is destined to confusion because ethnicity is not unidimensional. Moreover, the researcher is faced with the problem of whom to include as ethnics—the foreign born, second generation immigrants, religious groups, racial groups, or others? Finally ethnic group membership is more salient for some groups than for others. All these problems preclude the use of ethnicity unless one operationalizes the concept very carefully and has a very special sample.

[10] Lenski, "Status Crystallization," p. 407.

others as "low" on each status dimension. The simplest classification is achieved by dichotomizing the frequency distribution for each status variable. This oversimplifies and distorts the findings, however, since many cases near the center of the distribution and characterized as "high" will be quite similar to many classified as "low." To minimize this disadvantage it seemed reasonable to make the cutting points at about the upper 40 per cent and the lower 40 per cent on each status hierarchy. This omitted the middle 20 per cent on each status variable but still allowed for enough cases to make statistical analyses. The rationale for these cutting points was to have clearly defined "high" and "low" categories on each status variable. This objective was also achieved by omitting certain ambiguous categories from the sample.

The data presented in this paper were taken from the 1964 Election Study by the Survey Research Center, University of Michigan—a collection of data from a cross-section of voting-age citizens living in the 48 contiguous states. Interviews were conducted with 1571 persons prior to the 1964 election and 1450 (92 per cent) of the original sample were re-interviewed after the election. Since some of the data essential to the present study were found only in the post-election sample, the analyses omit those persons not re-interviewed.

Each of the individuals in the sample was classified as "high" status, middle status or ambiguous, and "low" status on each of the three variables. The cutting points were made as close as possible to the arbitrary upper 40 per cent-lower 40 per cent standards (see Table 1).

The omission of those persons of middle or ambiguous status from each status hierarchy excluded 829 individuals from the sample of 1450 (57 per cent).

The basic assumption of the present study was that persons with uniformly high status ranks have significantly different political attitudes than persons with uniformly low ranks. The working sample of 621 was found to include 214 (34 per cent) "high" consistents (i.e., those persons consistently high in their status attributes), 203 (33 per cent) inconsistents and 204 (23 per cent) "low" consistents. These three categories approximate a three-class hierarchy since inconsistents fit logically between the "high" and "low" consistents including as they do, those persons with some high and some low status characteristics.[11]

The dependent variables used in this research were three dimensions of liberalism-conservatism: social welfare, civil rights, and internationalism. Nineteen items were selected from the 1964 Election Study which seemed logically to fit among these dimensions. Two techniques, cluster analysis and Guttman scaling were employed to determine if the items clustered together into three distinct scales and whether the resulting scales were legitimate. Both techniques confirmed scalability in each case.[12]

[11] This three-class hierarchy is not meant to be interpreted descriptively since an important segment of the representative sample has been excluded from the analysis.
[12] The reader is reminded that the questions utilized in the present study to construct three scales of liberalism-conservatism were taken from those designed by the Survey

TABLE 1

The Distribution of the Sample on Each of the Three Status Variables

Status	Education Category	N	Per Cent	Occupation Category	N	Per Cent	Income Category	N	Per Cent
High	Doctorate	24	1.7	Professional	162	11.2	$15,000+	98	6.8
	Masters	29	2.0	Businessmen	254	17.5	10,000–14,999	194	13.4
	BA	133	9.2	Clerical & sales	168	11.6	7,500–9,999	220	15.2
	Some college	191	13.2						
	12 plus non-college	129	8.9						
Subtotals		506	35.0		584	40.3		512	35.4
Middle or	12 grades	265	18.3	Skilled	226	15.6	6,000–7,499	201	13.9
	9–11 non-college training	59	4.1	Protective	28	1.9	5,000–5,999	161	11.1
Ambiguous	DK, no answer	23	1.6	Farmers	100	6.9	DK, no answer	50	3.5
				Students	10	.7			
				No answer	25	1.7			
Subtotals		347	24.0		389	26.8		412	28.5
Low	9–11	206	14.2	Semi-skilled	232	16.0	4,000–4,999	126	8.7
	8	194	13.4	Housewives	69	4.8	3,000–3,999	129	8.9
	1–7	184	12.7	Unskilled	138	9.5	2,000–2,999	112	7.7
	None	13	.9	Unemployed	38	2.6	under 2,000	159	11.0
Subtotals		597	41.2		477	32.9		526	36.3
Totals		1450	100.2		1450	100.0		1450	100.2

For each of these items, the answers were coded to reflect the strength of opinions (i.e., to what degree did the respondent have his mind made up on the issue) with Likert-type scale responses. The Likert scores were summed for each individual on each scale. The lower the score, the greater the liberalism.

THE FINDINGS

In order to demonstrate the importance, indeed the necessity, of incorporating social class into the analysis, the findings were compared when social class was included and excluded on each of the three dimensions of liberalism-conservatism.

Part B of Table 2 is the same as Part A except that the status consistent category is separated into "high" and "low" consistents. The data in Part A show that status inconsistents do not differ significantly from status consistents on any of the three dimensions of political attitudes. When the status consistent category is divided into consistent "highs" and "lows," however, the data show that the two categories are significantly different on each dimension of liberalism-conservatism.[13]

Research Center for another purpose—the determination of the degree to which individuals held pro- and anti-government attitudes. The questions selected are presented below in abbreviated form.
Social Welfare (the CR for this scale is 91.8 and the CS is 68.4)
    1. Do you favor or oppose medicare?
    2. Do you favor governmental aid to insure minimal living standards?
    3. Do you favor or oppose federal aid to education?
    4. Do you feel the federal government is too powerful or not too strong?
    5. Do you favor or oppose the government ownership of power plants?
Civil Rights (the CR for this scale is 93.0 and the CS is 61.6)
    1. Do you favor residential integration or do you feel that white people have the right to keep Negroes out of their neighborhoods?
    2. Are you in favor of desegration, strict segregation, or something in between?
    3. Are you for or against school integration?
    4. Do you favor or oppose integrated public accommodations?
    5. Do you favor governmental insistence on equal job opportunities?
Internationalism (the CR for this scale is 92.5 and the CS is 68.8)
    1. Do you favor talking to the Communists or are you against this?
    2. Should we give foreign aid?
    3. Do you favor or oppose trade with Communist countries?
    4. Some people feel that we must do something to get the Communist government out of Cuba. Others feel that it is up to the Cuban people to handle their own affairs. Have you been interested enough in this to favor one side over the other?
  [13] The comparison of the Q value for Part A and the Gamma value for Part B and the quite different Chi-square values for each show clearly that consistent "highs" differ significantly from consistent "lows." Moreover, the means for the two categories differ significantly for each political attitude dimension (P<.01):

	Means	
	Consistent "highs"	Consistent "lows"
Social Welfare	17.27	12.91
Civil Rights	13.61	15.56
Internationalism	9.76	10.73

TABLE 2

Percentage of Liberal and Conservative Respondents on Each of Three
Dimensions of Political Attitudes by Type of Consistency

Type of Consistency	Social Welfare			Civil Rights[a]			Internationalism		
	Cons.[b]	Libs.	Total	Cons.	Libs.	Total	Cons.	Libs.	Total
A. Consistents	53 (222)	47 (196)	100	50 (168)	50 (171)	100	44 (184)	56 (234)	100
Inconsistents	57 (115)	43 (88)	100	50 (94)	50 (95)	100	44 (83)	59 (120)	100
	$X^2=.69$; P<.50; Q=−.07			$X^2=.001$; P<.99; Q=.004			$X^2=.32$; P<.70; Q=.05		
B. "High" Consistents	70 (149)	30 (65)	100	43 (85)	57 (114)	100	37 (79)	63 (135)	100
Inconsistents	57 (115)	43 (88)	100	50 (94)	50 (95)	100	41 (83)	59 (120)	100
"Low" Consistents	36 (73)	64 (131)	100	59 (83)	41 (57)	100	51 (104)	49 (100)	100
	$X^2=48.89$; P<.001 Gamma = .44			$X^2=9.03$; P<.02 Gamma = −.17			$X^2=8.90$; P<.02 Gamma = −.19		

a All nonwhites are excluded from the civil rights data (N=93) since they will be liberals and are overly represented in the consistent "low" category.
b The median is used for each political attitude dimension to determine liberals and conservatives.

The comparison of Parts A and B in Table 2, then, indicates that combining the consistent categories as Lenski and Rush have done nullifies a relationship that is present. Moreover, the data in Part B show in each case that status inconsistents as a category are found midway between the consistent "highs" and "lows." Since status inconsistents are by definition persons with some high and some low status characteristics, we would expect them to be in between the consistent "highs" and "lows" if social class had significant effects upon political attitude. The data, then, offer support for the assumption that when social class is included in the analysis, status inconsistents will be more moderate in political attitudes than status consistents.

How are the present findings to be reconciled with the studies of Lenski, Rush, and others who have found status inconsistents to be more "extremist" than status consistents? There are at least two possible explanations for the difference in the findings. In the first place, the methodology used in the present study does not replicate Lenski's technique. It is possible that the use of Lenski's technique would have included or excluded different persons from those included or excluded in either category in the present study. The middle consistents, for example, were omitted in our analysis. By leaving middle consistents in on variables linearly related to status, as Lenski did, there would be some pulling toward the middle for the total consistent category, thereby accounting for consistents being more moderate than inconsistents.

Secondly, there are significant differences in the samples from which the data were drawn. The 1964 Election Study data were secured from a national sample. Lenski used a sample of Dettroit residents, while Rush used a sample of residents from Springfield-Eugene, Oregon. In Rush's case, mail-back responses were used, resulting in a sample over-represented by high status persons.

SUMMARY

The major purpose of this study was to test empirically the notion prevalent in the literature that status inconsistents are more "extremist" in their political attitudes than are status consistents. To summarize, it was found, first of all, that there is a relationship between social class and political attitudes. This implies that status crystallization studies employing a dependent variable which has been found to relate to social class should incorporate class into the analysis. The findings of this study indicate that to neglect this consideration nullifies a relationship that is present.

Secondly, when social class is included in the analysis, status inconsistents are found midway between "high" consistents and "low" consistents on three dimensions of liberalism-conservatism. This finding raises some doubts as to the findings and methods of Lenski and Rush who found inconsistents to be more liberal and conservative, respectively, when compared to consistents.

Finally, the findings suggest that social class is a better predictor of political attitudes than status consistency. This is consistent with the conclusion of Kelly and Chambliss that social class membership appears to be a far better explanatory concept than status consistency. They say, "Concepts like status consistency, status congruency, status crystallization, and status integration unquestionably have a more sophisticated sound to them than social class. But if we sacrifice substantive usefulness for sophisticated appearance then our contribution will be meager indeed."[14]

Although the conclusions of the present study support those of Kelly and Chambliss, they do not deny the viability of the concept status inconsistency. It is entirely possible that particular forms of status inconsistency may indeed predispose individuals toward a more extreme position than that found for either "high" consistents or "low" consistents. Consequently, the category "status inconsistent" itself may be too gross. This was suggested by Lenski in his rebuttal to Kenkel when he stated that status crystallization studies should begin to concentrate on the systematic examination of the consequences of each of the various patterns of status inconsistency.[15] The theoretical merit of status inconsistency is likely to lie in these kinds of comparisons—not in the comparison of status consistents with inconsistents.

[14] Kelly and Chambliss, "Status Consistency and Political Attitudes," p. 382.
[15] Lenski, "Comment on Kenkel's Communication," pp. 368–369.

BALANCE THEORY AND VIETNAM-RELATED ATTITUDES[1]

JOHN P. ROBINSON
University of Michigan

ERHAPS THE OUTSTANDING DEVELOPMENT IN THE STUDY OF SOCIAL ATTI-tudes in the last 20 years has been cognitive consistency or "balance" theory.[2] An abundant body of laboratory evidence[3] and political observation[4] would lead us to depend heavily on consistency models in explaining the nebulous workings of public opinion. Moreover, these models have been found to be highly predictive in the few field studies in which they have been applied to political phenomena.[5]

An example may illustrate the persuasiveness of the basic model. Suppose you and a close friend have a disagreement concerning what our government should do about the Vietnam War, you feeling that the United States should unilaterally withdraw, your friend feeling that the United States has to keep troops there. Pictorially, we can represent the state of opinion as follows:

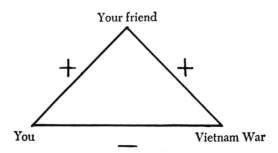

[1] Revision of paper presented at the annual meetings of the American Psychological Association, Washington, D.C., September, 1969. Certain portions of the analysis of the public attitudes toward Vietnam are covered more fully in John Robinson and Solomon Jacobson, "American Public Opinion about Vietnam," in Walter Isard, ed., *Vietnam: Some Basic Issues and Alternatives* (Cambridge, Mass.: Schenkman, 1969).

[2] An exhaustive review of the features of each of the various consistency theories proposed by Heider, Osgood, Cartwright and Harary, Festinger, and others is provided in Charles Insko, *Theories of Attitude Change* (New York: Appleton-Century-Crofts, 1968).

[3] See, for example, Milton Rosenberg *et al.*, eds., *Attitude Organization and Change: An Analysis of Consistency among Attitude Components* (New Haven: Yale University Press, 1960).

[4] Robert Lane and David Sears devote a pivotal chapter in their introductory text, *Public Opinion* (Englewood Cliffs: Prentice-Hall, 1964), to the pervasive role of consistency theories in describing the interplay between public opinion and the political process.

[5] For example, Don Smith, "Cognitive Consistency and the Perception of Others' Opinions," *Public Opinion Quarterly*, 32 (Spring, 1968), pp. 1–15.

In order for this "unbalanced" or inconsistent set of opinions to be resolved into a balanced state, one of the signs on the three sides of the above triangle has to change. Thus, balance can be attained by your coming to view the Vietnam war positively:

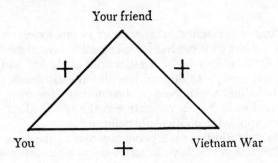

or you can discontinue your friendship:

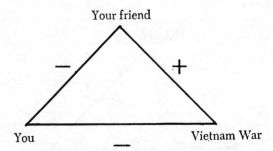

or you can perceive that your friend really is opposed to war (or would be if he were properly informed).

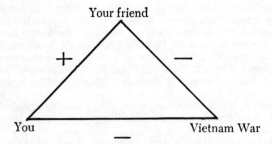

There are, of course, more elaborate cognitive mechanisms by which people form and change opinions, but the existing research evidence indicates that unbalanced attitude states tend to be rather uncommon in most attitude situations.

THE CONTEXT OF VIETNAM-RELATED ATTITUDES

In this paper we shall examine the degree of balance that exists in public opinion about Vietnam as a function of opinions of a particular "reference group"—members of the Vietnam protest movement. Here we assume for analysis purposes that only two balanced states (the other two balanced states require protestors to be viewed as favoring the war) prevail:

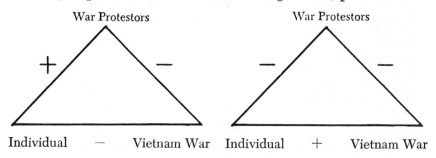

Thus to have a consistent set of opinions according to the model, an individual must either be (a) against the war and view war protestors positively or (b) for the war and view war protestors negatively. The individual is thus defined as having inconsistent opinions if he (a) is against the war and against the war protestors or (b) is for the war and for war protestors.

An index of the degree of balance across a group of individuals would be provided by the magnitude of correlation between opinions toward Vietnam and opinions toward protestors. The opinion data that were collected in this study are treated as measured on an ordinal scale, and so Kendall's tau-beta[6] is used as a measure of correlation. The attitude data were collected as part of the Survey Research Center's 1968 election study, the latest of a series of biennial investigations of voting behavior in the United States public. A nationwide probability sample of adults 21 years of age and older was interviewed both prior to and after the 1968 election.

The Vietnam opinion question that has been used by the Survey Research Center is concerned with policy options about the war, and is presented in Table 1 along with distribution of public responses to the question obtained from four national surveys conducted between 1964 and 1968. While the 1968 sample indicated the highest approval of withdrawal it can be seen this was still a minority position[7] that had shown negligible

[6] Leo Goodman and William Kruskal, "Measures of Association for Cross-Classifications," *Journal of the American Statistical Association,* 49 (Dec., 1954), pp. 732–734.

[7] Presentation of the question to advanced undergraduate students at the University of Michigan in 1967 and 1968 resulted in a distribution of replies that reflected the tone of vocal anti-war sentiment encountered in the mass media. Almost half (45 per cent) of these students chose the "pull out" option. This, however, should not be considered representative of how all college students felt. Evidence that students (and professors) in less prestigious colleges shared more hawkish views has been reviewed in Robinson and Jacobson, "American Public Opinion about Vietnam."

TABLE 1

Distribution of Public Opinion on Vietnam
(in percentages of those taking an attitude position on Vietnam)

Which of the following do you think we should do now in Vietnam?	Nov. 64 (N=928)	Nov. 66 (N=1046)	Oct. 67 (N=1148)	Oct. 68 (N=1362)
Pull out of Vietnam entirely	13	11	15	22
Keep our soldiers there but try to end the fighting	34	45	38	41
Take a stronger stand even if it means invading North Vietnam	43	44	47	37
Total	100	100	100	100

change in previous surveys (the 1968 change perhaps being due to the initiation of peace negotiations which indicated the unlikelihood of clear-cut victory).

Feelings about Vietnam War protestors were obtained by having this group rated on a "feeling the thermometer" along with other political and social groupings. The extremes on the scale ranged between 00 (coldest possible feeling) and 100 (warmest possible), with 50 being used as a neutral point. Protestors received by far the coldest reception of any group rated, 36 per cent of the national sample rating them at zero, another 35 per cent below the neutral point of 50, 13 per cent at this neutral point, with just 16 per cent registering any warm feelings toward protestors.[8] By comparison, the group receiving the next coolest reception was "Liberals," less than 5 per cent of the sample rating them at zero.[9]

The 16 per cent figure for persons feeling warm toward protestors is only slightly less than the 22 per cent of the population who expressed the desire to withdraw from Vietnam in Table 1. However, the correspondence between holders of these two attitude positions in correlational terms is not as close as these percentage figures might indicate. In fact, the correlation of .23 obtained between the two attitudes seems strikingly low in view of the strong record of previous successful research with the balance model.

Nevertheless, absolute judgments as to goodness-of-fit are difficult to make because we lack comparable data on correlation coefficients obtained

[8] The overwhelming negative feeling toward protestors, however, had little carry-over to the group from which they arose—college students. Less than 1 per cent of the sample rated "college students" at zero and less than 10 per cent gave them any negative ratings (this 10 per cent however were considerably more hostile to war protestors, so some carry-over does exist).

[9] One must return to the 1964 Survey Research Center election study to find two groups who were received only slightly less favorably than war protestors—Black Muslims and the Ku Klux Klan.

in previous balance studies. Furthermore defenders of balance theory will rightly claim that there are plausible reasons why the model does not work more effectively for these data, such as the likelihood that many members of the public simply do not mentally join together the two attitudes as the balance model requires. Thus the man in the street can find many reasons besides the war to reject war protestors—because large numbers of protestors wear beards, take drugs, desecrate the flag, or openly espouse other forms of threats to his way of life.

A more important discovery, therefore, is that the degree of correlation between attitude toward the war and attitudes toward protestors varies significantly with respondents' level of education. An initial clue to the differential effects of education emerged from the finding that while amount of education correlates negatively with feelings that the U.S. should pull out of Vietnam, it correlates positively with warm feelings toward war protestors. Put another way, compared to better-educated citizens the less-educated are more in favor of pulling out of Vietnam while feeling less warmly to war protestors. This discrepancy is dramatically reflected in the consistent rise in correlation between the two attitudes as a function of education:

Did not finish high school	.17
High school graduate	.22
Some college	.36
College graduate	.45

The amount of variance in attitudes toward war protestors that is explained by variations in attitudes toward the Vietnam War is over six times as high among college graduates as among persons who did not finish high school.

It appears that this latter group's attitudes are much more affected by the types of "unbalanced" attitude processes described in the preceding paragraph. The less-educated are more favorable toward pulling out of Vietnam (probably, as Patchen[10] argues, because of their basic isolationism), while at the same time rejecting the professed deviants who constituted the core of the protest movement and who represented such an overt threat to the existing American value system.[11] While the balance model cannot really be expected to apply to such mental processes, the fact that it is so inappropriate with this set of attitudes should alert us against indiscriminately applying the balance model to portray the formation of opinion in all segments of the public.

---

[10] Martin Patchen, "Social Class and Dimensions of Foreign Policy Attitudes," *Social Science Quarterly*, 50 (Dec., 1970), pp. 649–667.

[11] In this connection, it is well to remember Samuel Stouffer's *Communism, Conformity, and Civil Liberties* (Garden City, N. Y.: Doubleday, 1955), finding strong intolerance of persons perceived as deviant among the less-educated segments of the public 15 years ago.

ATTITUDES TOWARD THE CHICAGO DEMONSTRATIONS

The previous results have implications for other attitude areas, and we shall conclude by exploring public reaction to one other Vietnam-related issue. The clash between Chicago police and the largely anti-war contingent of demonstrators at the Chicago Democratic National Convention undoubtedly served as a most visible and concrete embodiment of the differing values of this movement and the rest of the public. Not unexpectedly, of those with an opinion about events in Chicago, the proportion feeling that the police used too much force—25 per cent—was only slightly larger than the proportions wanting to pull out of Vietnam or feeling positive toward war protestors (all three groups also being smaller than the 33 per cent feeling that the police did not use *enough* force with the demonstrators). The social correlates of attitudes toward events in Chicago have been examined extensively in a separate article.[12]

Of the two attitudes that we have already explored in this paper, attitudes toward protestors emerges as a somewhat better correlate of Chicago attitudes than Vietnam attitudes, the two correlations being .28 and .18 respectively. This can be seen more directly in Table 2, where variations in the proportion feeling that the Chicago police used too much force are examined as a function of attitudes on the two issues. Again the strength of correlation increases with advanced educational level (although not as cleanly) in line with our main findings about the relation between attitudes toward protestors and Vietnam:

	Chicago-Protestors	Chicago-Vietnam
Did not finish high school	.22	.15
High school graduate	.19	.10
Some college	.26	.34
College graduate	.37	.28

The attitudes of two interesting social groupings—black people and youth—examined at the outside edges of Table 2 indicate that education is only one factor (although the major factor) that yields differential correlational patterns. It can be seen for black people—who were three times as likely as whites to say the Chicago police used too much force—neither Vietnam War nor protestor attitudes provided much explanatory power in their Chicago attitudes. On the other hand, for the under 30 generation both attitudes provided greater explanatory power than for older people, but especially for those with more radical attitudes (namely the 85 per cent figure for those under 30 feeling extremely warmly toward protestors and the 67 per cent figure for those under 30 desiring to pull out of Vietnam). It is likely therefore that background factors besides

[12] John P. Robinson, "Public Reaction to Political Protest: Chicago 1968," *Public Opinion Quarterly*, 34 (Spring 1970), pp. 1–9. Briefly it was found that race, education, age, and the above attitude variables explained far larger amounts of variance in Chicago attitudes than preferences for political candidates (that is, between supporters of Eugene McCarthy and supporters of Ronald Reagan).

TABLE 2

Percentages Thinking Police Used Too Much Force as a Function of Attitudes
Toward Vietnam War and Toward Vietnam War Protestors
(of Those Taking an Attitude Position on Chicago)

Feeling toward protestors	What should we do now in Vietnam?					
	Pull out troops	Keep soldiers there	Take stronger stand	Total per cent	Blacks only	Under 30 only
Extremely warm (N = 67)	67	67	33	61	77	85
Warm (N = 170)	56	60	33	54	87	62
Neutral (N = 202)	28	38	29	33	52	57
Cold (N = 521)	24	28	16	23	57	28
Extremely cold (N = 540)	15	19	8	12	50	12
Total Per Cent (N)	35 (246)	30 (425)	14 (334)	25		
Blacks only (N = 134)	63	64	63		64	
Under 30 (N = 231)	67	43	14			34

educational level can be employed profitably to isolate further segments
of the public in which the balance model is differentially appropriate as a
descriptor of public opinion processes.

In a more general context, these findings may have behavioral implications for the recent "hard-hat" demonstrations, which have been interpreted as support of this country's Vietnam war policies among the less-
educated segment of our society. If our data apply to participants in these
demonstrations, their behavior is more likely grounded in anti-protestor
sentiment than in support for the war.

THE VIETNAM WAR AND STUDENT MILITANCY[1]

ROBERT B. SMITH

University of California, Santa Barbara

THIS PAPER SEEKS TO CLARIFY HOW DISAFFECTION FROM THE VIETNAM war affects aggressive student militancy against university administrators. On the basis of their recent analysis of chronologies of student protests, the Urban Research Corporation concluded that the Vietnam war is not a major cause of campus unrest, because the war was an issue in only 2 per cent of the student protests occurring between January and June, 1969.[2] This survey analysis contradicts their interpretation, indicating that disaffection from the war is a major determinant of student militancy even in protests that are unrelated explicitly to the war.[3]

This analysis is based primarily on a survey of undergraduates at the University of California at Santa Barbara (UCSB) during the 1968–1969 academic year.[4] At the time of the survey, there were 12,619 students enrolled; 86 per cent were undergraduates.[5] About 95 per cent of the undergraduates were residents of California prior to their admission; at least 93 per cent are white; about 80 per cent come from white collar and professional families; and 70 per cent have fathers with at least some college education.

The attitudes and behavior of these students are of interest because, unlike the students at Berkeley, Chicago, or Columbia, these students were noted for their surfboarding, sun bathing, and conservative political apathy. But only a year after this survey was taken, many of these same students were actively confronting police both on campus and in Isla Vista, the student community adjacent to the campus, during several months of in-

[1] This report is a revision of a paper presented at the annual meeting of the American Sociological Association, September, 1970. The author is indebted to Richard Flacks, Morris Friedell, and Milton Mankoff for their helpful comments. Generous grants of computer time were provided by the National Institute of Mental Health and the Computer Center of the University of California, Santa Barbara.

[2] John Naisbitt, *Student Protests, 1969 Summary* (Chicago: Urban Research Corporation, 1970).

[3] The impact of the war on student anti-war protests has been described in other studies. See Allen H. Barton, "The Columbia Crisis," *Public Opinion Quarterly*, 49 (Fall, 1968), pp. 333–351; Richard Flacks, "Who Protests: The Social Basis of the Student Movement," in Julian Foster and Durward Long, eds., *Protest* (New York: Morrow, 1970), pp. 134–157; Edward E. Sampson, "Student Activism and the Decade of Protest," *Journal of Social Issues*, 23 (July, 1967), pp. 1–33; and Jerome Skolnick, *The Politics of Protest* (New York: Simon and Schuster, 1969), pp. 27–124.

[4] This survey was carried out as part of an introductory research methods course. The students in the course designed the questionnaire under the direction of the teaching assistant, Byron Eckerson.

[5] These statistics were reported by the Office of Analytical Studies, University of California, Santa Barbara, in their fall, 1968, report.

tensive protest behavior. In these protests, the Isla Vista branch of the Bank of America was destroyed by fire, a student was killed by the police, and about 900 students, faculty, and Isla Vista residents were arrested.

A systematic sample was drawn from the UCSB student directory, and 655 questionnaires were given out in December, 1968, during "dead week," the week before final exams. By January, 1969, 287 were returned to ballot boxes located in various places both on and off campus. The anonymity of the respondents was protected by having them detach from the questionnaire an extra sheet which had their name on it. This sheet was collected separately and destroyed immediately after noting that the respondent had returned his questionnaire. During the spring quarter, just after the Berkeley "People's Park" protests in which a bystander was killed by the police, there was a follow-up contact for 61 randomly selected non-respondents. These people were given a second questionnaire which contained additional questions about the Berkeley protests. The resulting sample of 348 students represents a reasonably satisfactory response rate of 53 per cent.[6] Comparison of early and late returns does not show any large differences or any important trends. In general, there are no important differences between the marginal distributions of sex, grade in school, major, and attitude about the war (a key opinion) for the returned sample and the undergraduate population.[7] Estimates of population characteristics may be off by 5 or 10 per cent due to bias, but the relationships between the variables and the magnitudes of their effects, which are our main concern, should be approximately correct.

THE PIVOTAL INDEPENDENT VARIABLE

Disaffection is defined as the absence or withdrawal of affection or loyalty, as disagreement, discontent or disloyalty, especially toward a government. It also connotes alienation, estrangement, and dislike.[8] In this report, disaffection from the Vietnam war is gauged by the Gallup poll (AIPO) item used to assess whether a person is a "dove" or a "hawk." That is, whether he wants the war in Vietnam de-escalated or escalated. Table 1 presents the exact wording of the question and response distributions for the samples of UCSB students and the American public. The marginals indicate that at the time of this survey, the UCSB students were considerably more disaffected than the public.

[6] This is about the same response rate as that reported by Barton, "The Columbia Crisis," p. 335.

[7] In this sample about 74 per cent say they are doves on Vietnam. In a student referendum in November, 1969, El Gaucho, the UCSB student newspaper, reported that 76 per cent of the students who voted desired an immediate and total withdrawal of all troops from Vietnam. In this same referendum, 86 per cent of the voters stated that politics is playing too large a role in the governing of the University. On a very similar item, 85 per cent of the survey respondents felt that the autonomy of the University is threatened by politics. These small differences between the survey respondents and the student voters indicate that the survey sample is representative of the UCSB undergraduates.

[8] The American College Dictionary (New York: Random House, 1948), p. 343.

TABLE 1

Disaffection from the Vietnam War: UCSB Students and the American Public

"People are called 'hawks' if they want to step up our military effort in Vietnam. They are called 'doves' if they want to reduce our military effort in Vietnam. How would you describe yourself—as a 'hawk' or a 'dove'?"

	Hawk	Per Cent Dove	No Opinion	Total
UCSB Students (Dec., 1968)	12	74	14	100 (N=348)
Public (AIPO) (Oct., 1968)	44	42	14	100 (N=approx. 1,500)

Because disaffection from the war is the pivotal independent variable, we must insure that the above item fulfills the two usual criteria for validating an index comprised of a single item.[9]

First, the question has face validity. It directly gauges sentiment about the war. Moreover, it is reasonable to assume that the doves, those who disagree most with the government's Vietnam policy, would be disaffected from this policy.

Second, the question is externally valid (it predicts responses to other items that are related to, or are alternative measures of, the concept the question purports to measure). The numerous comparisons of Table 2 are strong evidence for the external validity of the dove-hawk item. These comparisons indicate that doves are more likely than hawks to (1) disagree with government policies on important issues, including the war in Vietnam, drug policy, and conservative administration in general, (2) have disrespect for laws and institutions, including the use of existing channels of communication and authority to make their wants known, narcotics laws, and conventional career plans (after graduation most plan to go to graduate school, to participate in Vista and the Peace Corps, or to travel, rather than to get a job, to go into the military, or to become a housewife), and (3) give evidence of alienation and estrangement (they are more likely to feel lonely, worry about personal and world problems, and use drugs other than marijuana—pep pills, LSD, and other psychedelic drugs).

Given the above correlates of disaffection, there is no doubt that students who are doves are disaffected not only from the war, but also from many other aspects of conventional American society. It would be reasonable to predict that these disaffected students would express their general dis-

---

[9] For an excellent discussion of criteria for validity, see Gary T. Marx, *Protest and Prejudice* (New York: Harper & Row, 1967), pp. 45–68. Since only one item is used to gauge disaffection, the internal consistency of this index is not a concern.

TABLE 2

External Validation of the Dove-Hawk Index of
Disaffection Among UCSB Students

Dimensions of Disaffection	Doves (N=42)	Per Cent Hawks (N=258)	Difference
Disagreement with Government Policies			
Vietnam war a mistake	89	30	59
Radical or Liberal	60	18	42
No restrictions on marijuana	75	48	27
Free availability of drugs	30	15	15
Disrespect for Laws and Institutions			
(delegitimation of authority)			
Protestors need not always use existing channels of communication and authority	20	3	17
Leniency for protestors who use non violent civil disobedience	51	33	18
Smoked marijuana at least once thereby breaking a law	57	24	33
Less conventional career plans	67	46	21
Alienation and Estrangement			
Feels lonely	60	47	13
Worries about personal and world problems	69	35	34
Tried pep pills	32	18	14
Tried LSD and other psychedelic drugs	25	9	16

content in militancy, specifically against the university, which is so much
a part of their lives.

THE PIVOTAL DEPENDENT VARIABLE

Student militancy against university administrators is defined as a readiness to aggressively press demands for changes in the structure of the university. In this report, it was gauged by asking students to agree or disagree
with the following statement: "When existing channels of communication
prove inadequate or unsatisfactory, students should then directly confront administrators with their grievances, even if this entails civil disobedience in some form or other." The militant students are the 68 per
cent who agree with this statement. The students who disapprove of these
tactics (29 per cent) we shall call conservative.[10] Three per cent had no
opinion.

[10] For an excellent survey analysis of militant and conservative students at the
University of California, Berkeley, see Robert H. Somers, "The Mainsprings of the
Rebellion: A Survey of Berkeley Students in November 1964," in Seymour Martin
Lipset and Sheldon S. Wolin, eds., *The Berkeley Student Revolt* (Garden City, N. J.:
Anchor Books, 1965), pp. 530–557. Somers classified about 30 per cent of the Berk-

At the time of this survey, militancy connoted a willingness to use force-ful, but nonviolent tactics. Several facts suggest this, and at the same time are strong evidence for the external validity of the item. First, there is a high association (Gamma is .635) between the militancy item and an item about leniency for participants in nonviolent protests (in which there is no damage to property, and no people are hurt). Second, only 8 per cent of the militant students say they are radical, and it would be the radical students who would be most likely to support violence as a tactic.[11] Third, until a year after this survey was taken, violent protests were very infre-quent at UCSB. Finally, there are strong relationships between militancy and support for nonviolent, but forceful, protests.

Table 3 presents the reactions of militant and conservative UCSB stu-dents to three protests against University administrators. The first was staged by the Black Student Union to protest institutional racism at UCSB and to press for the creation of a Black Studies department. In this protest, 16 black students took over the campus computer center for most of the day of October 14, 1968. There was no damage to property and the blacks withdrew after the administration met many of their demands. Although a few white students and faculty were vocal in their opposition to the blacks' tactics, the vast majority of the students supported the Black Stu-dent Union, with the militant students being more supportive than the conservatives (see Table 3).[12]

The second protest was a response to the death of James Rector, a by-stander shot by the police during the Berkeley "People's Park" confronta-tion on May 15, 1969. At UCSB, the Berkeley Solidarity demonstrations began on Thursday, May 22, with a rally. On Friday the Chancellor can-celled classes at 3:00 P.M. for a University Convocation at the athletic field. After the speeches there was a call for a two day strike on Monday and Tuesday. On these days most classes were either cancelled, poorly at-tended, or devoted to discussing the events at Berkeley and means for achieving constructive social change. On Tuesday, there also was a peace-ful march on Santa Barbara to explain student views on the Berkeley situation, as well as to increase rapport between the students and the community. As might be expected, the militant students, to a greater extent than conservatives, supported these demonstrations (see Table 3).[13]

---

eley students as militant during the Free Speech Movement. These students supported both the goals and the tactics of the demonstrators.

[11] Data from a later survey about the burning of the Bank of America corroborate this assertion. Students who support the Radical Union are more likely to agree that when grievances pile high, violence may be the only effective response (49 per cent difference), are less likely to totally reject violence as a means of political dissent (41 per cent difference), are more likely to agree that violent tactics do not subtract from the just goals of protests (42 per cent difference), and to agree that legitimate chan-nels of protest are not effective (43 per cent difference).

[12] This description of the BSU sit-in is based on my own observations of the events, and on newspaper reports in *El Gaucho,* the UCSB student newspaper, and in the *Santa Barbara News-Press.*

[13] The description of the events at Berkeley was gleaned from a careful reading of

TABLE 3

Student Militancy and Support for Forceful, Nonviolent Protests
Against University Administrators

UCSB Student Protests	Militant (N=237)	Per Cent Conservative (N=101)	Difference
Black Student Union Protest (October 2–17, 1968)			
BSU sit-in justifiable	80	40	40
Favored take over of computer center	85	50	35
Favored Chancellor's handling of the matter	74	53	21
Berkeley Solidarity Protest (May 22–27, 1969)			
Favored protesting excessive use of force by police	93	50	43
Favored student strike	64	15	49
Participated in 2 or more activities	69	23	46
Bill Allen Controversy[a] (January 20–February 12, 1970)			
Administration was unresponsive to petition signed by 7,776 students	84	33	51
Allen was right in trying to change anthropology department's decision to fire him	88	40	48
Allen was right to encourage rallies and demonstrations to protest his being fired	69	7	62
Student representatives should vote in department faculty meetings	86	39	47
Student representatives should vote in the academic senate	88	43	45

[a] Data from a survey about the burning of the Isla Vista Bank of America (March, 1970).

The third protest, the Bill Allen controversy, became very visible during the winter quarter of the next academic year when by January 23, 1970, 7,776 students, faculty and staff had signed a petition asking for an open hearing for William Allen, an assistant professor in the UCSB anthropology department. The preceding spring Allen had been notified that his contract would be terminated at the end of the 1969–1970 academic year. His supporters felt that Allen had complied with the major requirements for advancement, that he was a good teacher and a productive scholar; and that

reports in the New York Times, the Santa Barbara News-Press, and El Gaucho. The description of the events at UCSB is based on my own observations.

he was being fired unjustly for his radical political beliefs and his permissive life style. But on January 26 the Acting Chancellor said no to the petitioning students. He stressed that Allen was not fired capriciously, that Allen's political beliefs were not a factor, and that even though students were being asked to participate at all levels of campus activities, in academic personnel matters the decisions would be made by professional peers and the administration.

This decision touched off several weeks of intensive protests sponsored by the Radical Union and the 7,776 signers of the petition, the Black Student Union, and the Santa Barbara chapter of the New University Conference, an organization of radical professors. All three parties in the coalition wanted an open hearing for Allen and maximum student participation in the governance of the University. These demands were enforced by aggressive nonviolent tactics. During this controversy there were daily rallies near the administration building which was sealed off for several days, the faculty club was taken over for half a day, there were several student strikes, and several massive face-to-face confrontations between the police and the students took place in which the police used restraint and the demonstrators remained nonviolent.

In contrast to the sit-in at the computer center the year before, the administration and the police were strict. Nineteen students and leaders of the demonstration, many of whom had publicly advocated nonviolence during the protests, were arrested by the police and punished by the administration. In negotiations with the students, the Acting Chancellor and the academic senate would not compromise on the various issues. Their position was supported by the Chancellor upon his return to campus on February 8. In his statement of February 11, he reaffirmed the decisions made during his absence, but he did promise more student participation in the future and encouraged the formation of undergraduate organizations in each department.[14]

On February 25, two weeks after the end of the Allen controversy, and after a speech by William Kunstler, UCSB students and others burned down the nearby Isla Vista branch of the Bank of America. Soon after this violent protest took place, an extensive survey of the students' political attitudes and behavior, which included several questions about the Allen controversy, was undertaken.[15]

---

[14] This description of the Allen controversy is based on my own observations and notes, on a careful analysis of the events reported in *El Gaucho* and on newpaper reports in the *New York Times* and in the *Santa Barbara News-Press*. For a more detailed description of the Allen controversy, see Robert B. Smith, "Campus Protests and the Vietnam War," in Marvin Wolfgang and James F. Short, Jr., *Collective Violence* (Chicago: Aldine Brooks, forthcoming).

[15] The survey was administered to a random sample of 36 small classes and discussion sections of large classes during dead week of the winter quarter, about two weeks after the bank burning. The teachers usually permitted the questionnaires to be passed out in class, but seldom permitted the students to use class time to fill out the questionnaire. The classes were contacted at subsequent meetings and the filled out ques-

The survey indicates that the students solidly supported the Allen protests. About 63 per cent of the students thought the administration was unresponsive to the petition signed by 7,776 for an open hearing, 67 per cent thought Allen was right to try to change the decision to fire him, and 54 per cent of those with an opinion thought Allen was right to encourage rallies and demonstrations in his behalf. With respect to student participation in the governance of the University, 69 per cent wanted student representatives to be able to vote in the academic senate and 66 per cent wanted representatives to vote in department meetings.

Table 3 above reports the differences between militant and conservative students on these items. In general, the militants are more favorable to Allen and want more student participation. These comparisons, along with the others in Table 3, serve to validate the militancy item. It is important to emphasize that the war in Vietnam was not an issue in any of these protests. But, as we shall see later, disaffection from this war is a major determinant of student militancy.

THE TEST VARIABLES

In this subsequent analysis of the effect of Vietnam disaffection on student militancy, the effects of six other explanatory variables will be quantified and controlled:

Attitudes about black power. Attitudes about black power were gauged by the following direct question: *"Black Power* strikes different chords in different people. What is your reaction?" About 55 per cent reacted favorably. The direct nature of this question insures its face validity; the following correlates suggest its external validity. Respondents favorable to black power were more likely to read books by black authors (17 per cent difference), were activated by Martin Luther King's death (25 per cent difference), thought the BSU sit-in was justifiable (28 per cent difference), and supported this takeover (44 per cent difference).[16]

Complaints about the university. In the 1968–1969 student survey there are questions about the numerous complaints that were then foci of dis-

---

tionnaires collected. About two-thirds of the questionnaires (497) were returned. A detailed comparison of sample and population characteristics is not yet available, but a preliminary analysis suggests that this sample is at least as accurate as the 1968–1969 survey.

[16] For documentation of the importance of support for civil rights and demands for social justice as an explanation for student militancy, see the following sources: Robert H. Somers, "Mainsprings of the Rebellion," p. 532; Seymour Martin Lipset and Philip G. Altbach, "Student Politics and Higher Education in the United States," in Seymour Martin Lipset, ed., *Student Politics* (New York: Basic Books, 1967), pp. 201–202; Edward E. Sampson, "Student Activism and the Decade of Protest," pp. 25–26; Allen Barton, "The Columbia Crisis," pp. 349–350; Jeanne H. Block, Norma Haan and M. Brewster Smith, "Activism and Apathy in Contemporary Adolescents," in James F. Adams, ed., *Understanding Adolescence* (Boston: Allyn and Bacon, Inc., 1968), pp. 198–231; and Daniel Bell, "Quo Warranto," *Public Interest*, 19 (Spring, 1970), pp. 53–68.

content—complaints about courses and professors, noise in Isla Vista, "slum" housing, restrictive rules and regulations, and so forth. Only two of these complaints are consistently linked to student militancy: complaints about restrictive housing regulations (no pets allowed, no visitors after certain hours, no musical instruments, and the like); and complaints about irrelevant courses. Only 16 per cent of the students had complaints about restrictive regulations (43 per cent did not complain and 41 per cent had no regulations), but 76 per cent complained about irrelevant courses. These two items were combined to form a complaints index by simply counting the number of complaints. The resulting index was dichotomized by grouping together the 79 per cent with one or two complaints versus the remaining 21 per cent with none.

This simple index fulfills the usual criteria for validity. First of all, the two items have face validity; they directly gauge complaints. Secondly, the index is internally consistent, since both items are similarly related to militancy and are intercorrelated. Finally, the index is externally valid. Students who had complaints tallied by the index also complained about other matters. They were more likely to report that their living accommodations hinder studying (13 per cent difference), that regulations hinder their social life (14 per cent difference), that they don't enjoy most of their courses (25 per cent difference), and that only a few of their professors are good teachers (16 per cent difference).

Social statuses predisposing toward militancy. The students were asked to report their religious preference by checking Protestant, Catholic, Jewish, agnostic, or other. Inspection of the relationships between these categories and student militancy suggests that those who are not Protestant are more militant. Consequently, religion was dichotomized into *non-Protestant* (Catholic, Jewish, agnostic, atheist and other) which comprises 60 per cent of the students, and *Protestant*, which comprises the remaining 40 per cent. Of the 60 per cent who are non-Protestant, about 40 per cent said they are atheists, agnostics, or other.[17]

The students were asked to note their father's primary occupation. Their responses were coded into four categories: professional (and businessman), white collar, blue collar, and other. Inspection of the relationships between these categories and student militancy suggests that children from the more affluent professional (and business) families are more militant. Consequently, father's occupation was dichotomized into *professional* (including businessman) and *non-professional* (white collar, blue collar, and other). About 37 per cent have professional fathers.[18]

---

[17] For documentation about the role of religion in student militancy, see Richard Flacks, "The Liberated Generation," *Journal of Social Issues*, 23 (July, 1967), pp. 52–75; Robert H. Somers, "Mainsprings of the Rebellion," pp. 547–548; and Seymour Martin Lipset and Philip G. Altbach, "Student Politics and Higher Education," pp. 220–221.

[18] For documentation of the effect of father's occupation on militancy, see Richard Flacks, "The Liberated Generation," p. 65; Lipset and Altbach, "Student Politics and

The male students are more militant than the females. Consequently, student's sex is included as a test variable.[19]

Predisposition toward militancy. In order to control simultaneously for the effects of attitudes about black power, complaints about the University, and the three social statuses, it is necessary, because of the small sample size, to combine the latter three attributes into an index of predisposition toward militancy. This has been done by simply counting the number of statuses predisposing a student toward militancy. The resulting index ranges from a score of zero (Protestant, non-professional father, female) to three (non-Protestant, professional father, male). The index was dichotomized by inspecting the relationships between the index scores and student militancy and by taking into consideration the natural inflections in the data. As a result, students with either zero or one predisposing status were grouped together as *low predisposition* toward militancy, and those with two or three as *high predisposition*. About 58 per cent had a low predisposition; the remaining 42 per cent, a high predisposition.[20]

PROCEDURE

To measure the independent effects of Vietnam disaffection and other determinants of student militancy, we employ the method of multivariate analysis developed by Coleman.[21] His continuous time, discrete space, stochastic model for multivariate analysis defines three types of parameters: the substantive effect parameters (a_i's), the random shock toward the positive category of the dependent attribute (r), and the random shock toward the negative category of the independent attribute(s).[22]

Higher Education," pp. 217–222; and Richard Flacks, "The Revolt of the Young Intelligentsia," in Norman Miller and Rod Aya, *Revolution Reconsidered* (New York: Free Press, 1970). Data at UCSB from the survey about the bank burning indicate that there is little difference in militancy between students from professional or managerial families. About 86 per cent of the students from professional families are militant compared to 81 per cent from managerial families. Blue collar, engineering, and white collar (clerical) fathers' occupations are associated with low militancy.

[19] The finding that the male students are more militant than the females is consistent with past research on voting which has found men to be more politicized than women. I have not found any studies of student activists in which male-female differences in militancy have been noted. For the voting studies, see Bernard Berelson, Paul F. Lazarsfeld, and William N. McPhee, *Voting* (Chicago: University of Chicago Press, 1954), Appendix A.

[20] For a similar index of political predisposition, see Paul F. Lazarsfeld, Bernard Berelson, and Hazel Gaudet, *The People's Choice* (New York: Columbia University Press, Second Edition, 1948).

[21] James S. Coleman, *Introduction to Mathematical Sociology* (New York: Free Press, 1964).

[22] In this application of Coleman's method the effect parameters are identical to those that would be obtained from a dummy-variable regression analysis of this data. This is so because all of the variables have been dichotomized and Boyle's weighting procedure has been used. See Richard Boyle, "Causal Theory and Statistical Measures of Effect: A Convergence," *American Sociological Review*, 21 (Dec., 1966), pp. 843–851. For the same reasons, the parameters are very similar to those that would be

The sum of these latter two parameters is called the total random shocks. The total random shocks of Coleman's model provide a measure of unexplained variation in the dependent attribute somewhat analogous to "unexplained variance" in traditional regression analysis.[23]

The causal effect of the explanatory variables is measured only if the causal ordering of the variables is correct.[24] In order to establish a correct causal ordering and to interpret the findings, the elaboration principles and procedures developed by Lazarsfeld and Hyman have been applied.[25] Quite simply, the pivotal independent variable, Vietnam disaffection, and the test variables are either antecedent in time, antecedent in structure, or more general concepts than the specific pivotal dependent variable, student militancy.[26] Consequently, it is more plausible to assume that these variables affect militancy than to assume the opposite. Whenever possible, the effects of the explanatory variables will be interpreted, that is, the reasons underlying these effects will be studied.[27]

SOCIAL BASES OF VIETNAM DISAFFECTION

Before the pivotal analysis of Vietnam disaffection and student militancy is presented, the social bases of disaffection from the war will be examined, along with some important correlates of student militancy.

Recent research on the social bases of disaffection from the Vietnam war has been based on national cross-sections of the adult population.[28] Typically, these studies report that attitudes about the war do not decisively follow the usual lines of political cleavage in America. As Converse and Schuman state:

> Although attitudes toward the Vietnam war have consistently shown less distinct differences among various standard groups of the population than

---

obtained by calculating partial dyx's using Somers' procedure. See Robert H. Somers, "Simple Measures of Association for the Triple Dichotomy," *Journal of the Royal Statistical Society* (Series A, 127), pp. 409–415.

[23] The total random shocks quantify how much variation in the dependent attribute remains to be explained. For an insightful analysis of the meaning of random shocks, see J. Michael Polich, "The Coleman-Boyle Techniques and Multiple Regression Analysis (Unpublished Senior Honors Thesis, Dartmouth College, June 5, 1967).

[24] Coleman, *Introduction to Mathematical Sociology*, Chap. 3.

[25] See Herbert Hyman, *Survey Design and Analysis* (Glencoe: Free Press, 1955), and Paul F. Lazarsfeld, "Evidence and Inference in Social Research," in Daniel Lerner, ed., *Evidence and Inference* (Glencoe: Free Press, 1959).

[26] These principles are explicitated by Paul F. Lazarsfeld in his introducton to Herbert H. Hyman's *Survey Design and Analysis*.

[27] For examples of interpretations, see *Ibid.*, Chap. 7.

[28] For examples of research on this topic, see Sidney Verba, *et al.*, "Public Opinion and the War in Vietnam," *American Political Science Review*, 61 (June, 1967), pp. 317–333; Philip E. Converse, *et al.*, "Continuity and Change in American Politics: Parties and Issues in the 1968 Campaign," *American Political Science Review*, 63 (Dec., 1969), pp. 1083–1105; and Robert B. Smith, "Rebellion and Repression and the Vietnam War," *The Annals of the American Academy of Political and Social Science* (Fall, 1970), pp. 156–167.

TABLE 4

Social Background and Disaffection

	Effect on Disaffection	Effect, Control War Mistake	Effect, Control Black Power	Effect, Control Both Variables
Social Statuses				
Non Protestant religion or no affiliation	+.121	+.049	+.085	+.022
Minority ethnicity	+.123	+.106	+.068	+.061
Professional father	+.022	—	—	—
Father with some college	+.044	—	—	—
Males	+.020	—	—	—
Academic Statuses				
Letters and Science	+.242	+.157	+.238	+.178
"Good Student" (B or higher G.PA.)	—.060	—	—	—
Upperclassman	+.017	—	—	—

is true of many other political attitudes, two exceptions stand out. They are race and sex. Blacks and women have shown more disenchantment with the involvement in Vietnam than white males over the entire period when relevant samplings have been made. . . .

Another pattern, not quite as distinct, is a positive association between education and support for the nation's involvement in Vietnam. Respondents classed as "college-educated" register disproportionately among those who are most "hard-line," or least negative, about the Vietnam war.[29]

A similar, but not identical, pattern of indistinct differences between social background and Vietnam attitude characterizes the college students at UCSB. Table 4 (column 1) shows that only two social statuses—non-Protestant religion and minority ethnicity—have statistically significant zero-order effects. Father's occupation, father's education, and student's sex are unrelated to disaffection. Differences in academic major do have large effects. Letters and Science majors are more disaffected than students majoring in the performing arts, engineering, or physical education.

Finding of no effect associated with being an upperclassman, coupled with the earlier lack of relationship between student's sex and disaffection, suggests that differences in eligibility for the draft are not major determinants of differences in disaffection.[30] Quite clearly, men are more eligible for the draft than women, and upperclassmen are more threatened by the draft than freshmen or sophomores. But the zero-order effects of these variables are negligible and so are the effects when the two variables

[29] Philip E. Converse and Howard Schuman, "Silent Majorities and the Vietnam War," *Scientific American*, 222 (June, 1970), pp. 17–25.
[30] For corroborating evidence, see Barton, "The Columbia Crisis," pp. 348–349.

are simultaneously controlled. When this is done, the independent effects of these variables are both .017. They have no effect. This suggests that students at UCSB do not oppose the war merely because they might be drafted. For most students, disaffection from war is linked to the perception that American intervention in Vietnam is a catastrophic mistake, and, for some, to demands for social justic and new domestic priorities.[31]

Table 4 also clarifies the manner in which religion, ethnicity, and academic major affect disaffection. These variables are interpreted by the intervening variables (1) evaluating our involvement in Vietnam as a mistake, and (2) supporting black power. The first interpretive variable is related to perceptions of the government's ineffectiveness and to subsequent delegitimation of authority. It is measured by the standard Gallup poll (AIPO) Vietnam mistake item: "In view of the developments since we entered the fighting in Vietnam, do you think the U.S. made a mistake sending troops to fight in Vietnam?" Seventy per cent of the students evaluated our involvement as a mistake in December, 1968, compared with only 54 per cent of an October, 1968 Gallup sample. The second interpretive variable is linked to demands for social justice and for a greater emphasis on domestic priorities, as measured by the black power question described earlier. When the mistake item is controlled, the effect of non-Protestant religion is reduced by almost two-thirds, and the effect of academic major by about two-fifths. But when the black power item is controlled, these effects are reduced to a lesser degree, suggesting that for the majority of white students perceptions of governmental ineffectiveness and delegitimation more directly interpret the effects of social background than do demands for social justice and new domestic priorities.

The opposite pattern characterizes the minority students. For these students, when attitudes about black power are controlled, the zero-order minority ethnicity effect on disaffection is reduced by one-half. But when attitudes about the war are controlled, this effect is hardly reduced at all. This suggests that for the minority students, demands for social justice and new domestic priorities more directly interpret their disaffection than do perceptions of governmental ineffectiveness and delegitimation. For neither the minority nor majority students do social background variables (except academic major) directly affect disaffection.

The indirect linkages between social background and disaffection are made even more explicit by the causal diagram presented in Figure 1. This diagram synthesizes three separate multivariate analyses of the causes of: (1) support for black power, (2) evaluating the war as a mistake, and (3) disaffection from the war. In these applications, the Coleman effect parameters have been standardized and are identical to path coefficients.[32]

[31] *Ibid.*, pp. 349–350.

[32] In Figure 1, the Coleman effect parameters are identical to path coefficients since each coefficient has been standardized by multiplying it by the ratio of the standard deviations of the independent and dependent variables. This enables the zero-order relationship (measured by Phi) between any two variables to be decomposed into

FIGURE 1

Causes of Disaffection

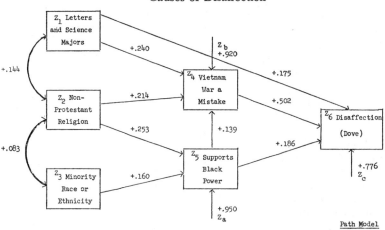

Path Model

(1) $z_5 = +.253z_2 + .160z_3 + .950z_a$

(2) $z_4 = +.240z_1 + .214z_2 + .139z_5 + .920z_b$

(3) $z_6 = +.175z_1 + .502z_4 + .186z_5 + .776z_c$

The diagram clearly shows that for the UCSB students religion and ethnicity do not directly affect disaffection but operate via the two intervening variables. Academic major affects disaffection indirectly via its effect on the "Vietnam is a mistake" variable, but it also has a direct effect on disaffection. Through disaffection it eventually affects student militancy.

THE MILITANCY SYNDROME

Militancy is a pivotal characteristic that distinguishes one student from another. Early studies of militant students found them to be idealistic, intellectual young people committed to social change via nonviolent tactics.[33] Now they are sometimes characterized as unstable personality

---

direct and indirect effects. For more information about the path analysis of attributes, see Raymond Boudon, "A New Look at Correlation Analysis," in Hubert M. Blalock and Ann B. Blalock, *Methodology in Social Research* (New York: McGraw-Hill, 1968), pp. 216–220. The sizes of the direct and indirect effects of the three status variables on disaffection are as follows:

	Phi	Direct Effects	Indirect Effects
Letters and Science Majors	.321	.176	.145
Non-Protestant Religion	.226	.000	.226
Minority Ethnicity	.068	.000	.068

[33] See Somers, "Mainsprings of the Rebellion"; Lipset and Altbach, "Student Politics and Higher Education"; Block, Haan, and Smith, "Activism and Apathy in Contemporary Adolescents"; and Kenneth Keniston, "Notes on Young Radicals," *Change in Higher Education*, 1 (Nov.–Dec., 1969), pp. 25–33.

TABLE 5

Political and Social Attitudes
of Militant and Conservative Students[a]

Political and Social Attitudes	Militant	Per Cent Conservative	Difference	Per Cent of Total
New Left Politics				
Radical or Liberal	81	33	48	60
Supports Radical Union	41	0	41	19
America is an imperialist nation	84	44	40	58
Capitalism is largely responsible for the ills of American society	67	24	43	52
Vietnam war a mistake	95	76	19	84
Social Problems Orientation				
Supports civil rights	74	26	48	51
Supports black power	68	17	51	41
Supports chicano power	72	20	52	34
Supports ecological action	98	76	22	87

[a] Data from a survey about the burning of the Isla Vista branch of the Bank of America (March, 1970).

types ready to use deceit and violence to gain their ends.[34] In order to help clarify what the militant students are like today, some behavioral and attitudinal correlates of UCSB militants will be described. This militancy syndrome has three aspects: (1) political and social attitudes, (2) life style, and (3) support for violent dissent.

Political and social attitudes. Table 5 reports the political and social attitudes of militant and conservative UCSB students. Like militant students studied earlier, those at UCSB tend to support the New Left. What is surprising in these data, however, is the extent to which these beliefs are also held by the conservative students. Similarly, idealism, as indicated by concern for underprivileged minorities and social problems, is much stronger among militants, but not uncommon among conservatives.

Life style. Compared to the descriptions in the earlier studies, the life style of today's UCSB militants appears to differ from those described in earlier studies. First, the militants are neither more nor less intellectual than the conservative students, as evidenced by data presented in Table 6.[35]

A second difference between the earlier student activists and today's UCSB militants is the involvement of the latter in the "new sensibility" of

[34] Bell, "Quo Warranto," pp. 65–66.
[35] The earlier studies that found the activists to be more intellectual are Somers, "Mainsprings of the Rebellion," p. 544, and Flacks, "Liberated Generation," pp. 69–70.

TABLE 6

Life Style of Militancy

Life Style	Militant	Per Cent Conservative	Difference	Effect, Control Disaffection
Not Intellectual				
Good grades (B or more)	35	41	− 6	−.01
Conscientious student	71	75	− 5	−.08
Plans for graduate school	70	69	+ 1	+.03
The New Sensibility				
Has smoked marijuana	61	21	+40	+.40
Has tried pep pills	38	8	+26	+.26
Has tried LSD	26	3	+23	+.26
Approves of pre-marital sex	78	50	+28	+.26
Interested in the New Consciousness[a]	62	38	+24	+.18
No Personal Problems				
Unsatisfactory social life	12	25	−13	−.13
Feels lonely	58	57	+ 1	0
Often worries	69	65	+ 4	−.02
Worries about gossip	33	38	− 5	−.06
Worries about personal and world problems	56	52	+ 4	−.04

[a] Data from a survey about the burning of the Isla Vista branch of the Bank of America (March, 1970).

American society.[36] The new sensibility is a form of cultural radicalism which dictates that all realms of experience must be opened and explored.[37] Table 6 shows that the militant students are definitely involved in the radical culture of the new sensibility. They are more likely to have tried marijuana, pep pills, and LSD. They approve of pre-marital sex and are interested in the New Consciousness, a program of confrontation and sensitivity training groups.

Earlier in this paper (in Table 2) similar correlates between disaffection and drug usage were reported. But disaffection from the Vietnam war does not explain the relationship between militancy and the new sensibility. When disaffection is controlled (last column, Table 6), these effects of militancy are unchanged. These data suggest that the new sensibility is an intrinsic part of the new militancy.[38]

[36] For an earlier study of the new sensibility at UCSB, see Edward A. Suchman, "The 'Hang Loose' Ethic and the Spirit of Drug Use," Journal of Health and Social Behavior, 9 (June, 1968), pp. 146–155. Some of the data used from this study in later tables were reported in the pre-publication draft of Suchman's paper and not in the published version.

[37] Bell, "Quo Warranto," p. 60.

[38] Marijuana smoking is a key aspect of the new sensibility. This is a serious problem because it implies a violation of a law, not because of the psychological conse-

The militants' search for experience and subsequent drug usage does not imply that they are unstable personality types or neurotic. Indeed, the militants report fewer personal problems than the conservative students. The data in Table 6 indicate that when disaffection is controlled, the militants are less likely to report an unsatisfactory social life, that they often worry, that gossip bothers them, or that they are burdened with personal or world problems. These findings do not support the idea that variables of personality or mental health explain the militants' new readiness to use violent tactics in campus protests.

Violence. During the 1969–1970 academic year, after the Allen controversy, many militant students at UCSB began to support and to participate in violent protests in Isla Vista. These demonstrations were directed against the police, the realty companies, and the Bank of America branch. On February 25, 1970, after a speech by William Kunstler about the Chicago conspiracy trial and after an arbitrary and forcible arrest of a former student who was carrying a bottle of wine, the students went on a rampage. Some of the thousand demonstrators stoned the police, driving them out of the business area, destroyed a patrol car, vandalized all of the realty companies, and burned down the Isla Vista branch of the Bank of America.[39] The precise causes of support for the burning of the bank cannot be analyzed in this report, but it is possible to describe the new relationship between student militancy and support for violent tactics, and the causes of the shift from nonviolence to violence.

Table 7 reports the relevant data. Support for violence is divided into three dimensions: (1) perceptions of the ineffectiveness of nonviolence, (2) tolerance for violent dissent, and (3) support for the burning of the Isla Vista branch of the Bank of America. Each of these dimensions is gauged by two items. The table reports the per cent of the students who agree with each item, the zero-order effect of militancy on each item, and the reduction in the zero-order militancy effect when various antecedent test variables are individually controlled. Here a large reduction in the

---

quences for the user. The data indicate that there is no association between using marijuana and the indicators of personal problems used in Table 6. The effects are below:

Unsatisfactory social life	—.051
Feels lonely	+.041
Often worries	—.030
Worries about gossip	—.114
Worries about personal and world problems	+.073
Average of effects	—.016

[39] This description of the bank burning is based on my own observations, discussions with students and colleagues, news reports from the UCSB radio station, a chronology of events prepared by *El Gaucho,* and newspaper reports in the *New York Times* and the *Santa Barbara News-Press.* For interesting discussions of these events, see Richard Flacks and Milton Mankoff, "Revolt in Santa Barbara: Why They Burned the Bank," *The Nation* (March 23, 1970), and Winthrop Griffith, "The Isla Vista War—Campus Violence in a Class by Itself," *New York Times Magazine* (August 30, 1970).

TABLE 7

Violence and Militancy[a]

Aspects of Violent Dissent	Reduction in Zero-Order Militancy Effect Caused by:							
	Zero-order Military Effect	Military Violence in Vietnam	Unresponsiveness of UCSB Administration and Academic Senate	Police too Eager to Arrest for Marijuana	Demands for Social Justice (pro Black Power)	Hearing Kunstler's Speech	America Is an Imperialist Nation	Capitalism Causes Ills of American Society
Ineffectiveness of Nonviolence								
Aggressive students cannot bring about changes in the University by working through legitimate channels (46 per cent agree)	.453	-.124	-.177	-.119	-.101	-.035	.000	-.043
Legitimate channels of protest—petitions and the like—are not effective means for bringing about change. (50 per cent agree)	.382	-.093	-.112	-.074	-.044	-.053	-.010	-.067
Tolerance for Violent Dissent								
When grievances pile high and most leaders represent established authority, then violence may be only effective response (47 per cent agree)	.500	-.174	-.120	-.153	-.128	-.050	-.090	-.065
Americans should not completely and totally reject violence as a means of political dissent (42 per cent agree)	.484	-.188	-.130	-.117	-.132	-.055	-.058	-.034
Support for the Burning of the Bank of America								
Forgetting about rational considerations, the burning of the bank was emotionally satisfying (30 per cent agree)	.376	-.155	-.140	-.130	-.144	-.061	-.076	-.074
Would not help put fire out, even if there was no danger from the police, the demonstrators, or the fire (53 per cent agree)	.451	-.162	-.170	-.123	-.130	-.065	-.095	-.064
Average Reduction in Militancy Effect	—	-.149	-.141	-.119	-.113	-.053	-.055	-.058

[a]Data from a survey about the burning of the Isla Vista branch of the Bank of America (March, 1970) (N=497).

zero-order effect means that the test variable explains a large part of the original relationship between militancy and violence.[40] In other words, a test variable causes a shift from nonviolence to violence if the relationship between militancy and support for violence is reduced when the test variable is controlled. This principle of elaboration enables us to discern which of the numerous hypothetical explanatory variables in fact cause militant students to become violent.

First, the data indicate that many of the students are prone to support violence (Table 7). Similarly, almost half of the students have tolerance for violent dissent. Active support for the bank burning is small: only 10 per cent approve of the destruction, and 8 per cent say it is a tactically wise way to protest grievances, but passive support (Table 7) is high.

Secondly, the data suggest that the previously nonviolent militant students now support violent tactics. They believe nonviolence is ineffective (the average of the two effects is .418), they have tolerance for violent dissent (the average of the two effects is .490), and they also passively support the bank burning (the average of the two effects is .414).

Finally, the data report that these zero-order effects are substantially reduced by four of the seven test factors. The test variables that explain the shift from nonviolence to violence are (in order of their explanatory power): (1) agreeing that the military violence in Vietnam is worse than the violence of protestors in America (−.149 average reduction in the militancy effect); (2) the unresponsiveness of the administration and academic senate to student requests for participation in the governance of the University (−.141 average reduction); (3) the perception that the police are too eager to arrest students for smoking marijuana (−.119 average reduction); and (4) demands for social justice and new domestic priorities as indicated by support for black power (−.113 average reduction).

The three test variables that do not explain the shift to violence are "outside agitators" and the two indicators of New Left beliefs. Hearing Kunstler's speech reduces the militancy-violence linkage at least: it has the smallest explanatory power of the seven variables (−.051 average reduction). Moreover, the explanatory power of each of the two New Left beliefs is only slightly larger (−.055 average reduction for "America is imperialist" and −.058 for "capitalism causes the ills of American society").

These data suggest that campus violence will not be reduced by barring controversial speakers from campuses or by demanding ideological conformity from teachers. If anything, restrictions on free speech and academic freedom in the name of law and order will undoubtedly cause more campus disorders than they prevent.[41]

---

[40] Lazarsfeld, "Evidence and Inference in Social Research," pp. 129–131.

[41] Restrictions on free speech and academic freedom were largely responsible for the Free Speech Movement at Berkeley. See almost any chapter in Lipset and Wolin, *The Berkeley Student Revolt.*

STUDENT MILITANCY AND THE VIETNAM WAR

Disaffection with the Vietnam war is a primary root cause of student militancy. When disaffection is high, campus protests are frequent, whether or not the protests are manifestly about the war or war-related issues. In the past, protests at UCSB were virtually devoid of violence, but recently both the demonstrators and the police have been ready to resort to violence.

Aggregate trends. Table 8 documents these trends in disaffection from the war, campus protests, and repression of protest at UCSB during the last three academic years. Disaffection from the Vietnam war, gauged by the number of students who are doves, has increased from 56 per cent in 1967–1968 to 87 per cent in 1969–1970. The trends of two important correlates of disaffection show similar increases. The number of students who evaluate the war as a mistake has increased by 33 per cent; and the number who smoke marijuana (thereby breaking a law) has increased by 45 per cent.[42]

This disaffection expresses itself in campus protests that are increasingly issueless and violent, and only tangentially about the war in Vietnam, the major cause of the discontent. During the 1967–1968 academic year, *El Gaucho,* the student newspaper, reported 22 student protests at UCSB.[43] Of these, 11 (50 per cent) were explicitly about the war in Vietnam or other war-related issues. Confrontation and violent tactics were not used in any of these protests, which consisted of non-disruptive sit-ins, teach-ins, picket lines, rallies, marches, and petitions.

In contrast, during 1969–1970 *El Gaucho* reported 114 protests, eight (7 per cent) of which were explicitly about the war or war-related issues.[44] Seventy-five per cent of the reported protests were nonviolent and non-forceful, a decrease of 25 per cent. This decrease is compensated for by increases in forceful but nonviolent (confrontation) protests (13 per cent shift) and by violent protests (12 per cent shift). In these violent protests, students burned a bank, vandalized realty offices, attacked policemen, threw fire bombs, and broke windows.

Data from University records corroborate the trend toward violence. Fire bomb threats have increased from one during 1967–1968 to 128 during this past academic year. Similarly, the number of windows broken in campus buildings has increased from none to about 50.

[42] This tremendous increase in marijuana smoking may be a consequence of disaffection from the war. Like most usage of drugs, marijuana smoking may be a form of retreatism, in this case in response to the anomie engendered by the war. See the discussion below and Robert K. Merton, "Social Structure and Anomie," in *Social Theory and Social Structure* (Glencoe: The Free Press, 1957), Chap. 4.

[43] The coding of the *El Gaucho* reports was done by Sandy Rhone, an undergraduate student in the UCSB sociology department. In 1967–1968, there were reports of six non-forceful sit-ins, five teach-ins, two picket lines, seven rallies, one march, and one petition.

[44] During 1969–1970, the detailed breakdown of reported protest events is as follows: *Non-forceful, nonviolent*—three sit-ins, one trash-in, five boycotts, four picket lines, 36 rallies, 20 marches, and 17 petitions; *forceful, nonviolent*—eight strikes, seven disruptions; *violent events*—four severe violence to property events, two fire bombings, three vandalisms, and four window-breaking events.

TABLE 8

Disaffection, Campus Protests, and Punitive Actions
(University of California, Santa Barbara, 1967–1970)[a]

| | Percent | | | |
	1967–1968	1968–1969	1969–1970	Trend
Disaffection and Correlates				
Dove	56	74	87	+31
Vietnam war a mistake	51	70	84	+33
Smoked marijuana at least once thereby breaking a law	21	47	66	+45
Campus Protests Reported in El Gaucho				
Antiwar or war related	50	6	7	−43
Nonviolent, non-forceful	100	90	75	−25
Nonviolent, forceful	0	6	13	+13
Violent	0	4	12	+12
Total Number of reported protests	(22)	(48)	(114)	(+92)
Indicators of Turmoil from University Records				
Fire bomb threats	(1)	(6)	(128)	(+127)
Broken windows	(0)	(2)	(50)	(+50)
Punitive Actions Reported in El Gaucho				
By the University administration	(0)	(0)	(6)	(+6)
By the police	(0)	(14)	(43)	(+43)

[a] The disaffection of the students in 1967–1968 was gauged by data from Edward Suchman's survey of UCSB undergraduates. See Edward Suchman, "The 'Hang-Loose' Ethic and the Spirit of Drug Use," *Journal of Health and Social Behavior*, 9 (June, 1968), pp. 146–155. The 1969–1970 disaffection data are from the survey about the burning of the Bank of America branch in Isla Vista (March, 1970). The number of fire bomb threats was gleaned from UCSB fire department records. The number of broken windows was estimated by the UCSB chief of police. The events coded from *El Gaucho* in 1969–1970 do not include Isla Vista III and therefore are very conservative estimates of police repressions.

As might be expected, there has been a parallel increase in administration and police punitiveness. During 1967–1968, *El Gaucho* reported no punitive actions by either the administration or the police. In 1969–1970, there were reports of six punitive actions by the administration and 43 by police, sheriff's deputies, and the national guard.[45] Demonstrators and others were subjected to curfews, beatings, arrests, threats of violence, tear gassings, thrown rocks, and gunshot wounds; one student was killed.

[45] During 1969–1970, the reported academic and police punishments were as follows: six academic suspension events, one killing by the police, seven threat of guns events, eight beating events, 24 arrest events, one harassment event, two curfew events. These data exclude Isla Vista III and are conservative estimates of police repressions.

TABLE 9

Disaffection Affects Militancy, Control Black Power, Complaints,
and Social Background (1968–1969)

Variables	Effects When Status Is Non-Protestant Religion	Effects When Status Is Professional Father	Effects When Status Is Male	Effects When Status Is Ad Hoc Index	Average of Affects
Doves	.187	.211	.222	.162	.195
Black Power	.283	.280	.263	.284	.277
Complaints	.088	.096	.118	.102	.101
Status Variable	.083	.118	.150	.142	.123
Random Shock toward Militancy	.155	.237	.182	.182	.189
Random Shock toward Conservatism	.132	.058	.065	.128	.096

Individual correlations. The relationship between disaffection and campus protests documented by these aggregate trends also holds true for individual students. Students who are doves are considerably more militant than hawks (76 per cent compared with 38 per cent); the zero-order effect is .383. That is, disaffection from the war affects student militancy.

The underlying model is quite simple. The events of the Vietnam war and our Indochina policy produce severe strains for students who are doves. This engenders disaffection from the war which is expressed in militancy and in campus protests that often are not explicitly about the war.

This mechanism also can be conceptualized sociologically as anomic in character, in the Mertonian sense.[46] The doves strongly hold a goal, namely, to *end* the war in Vietnam. But their access to this goal is restricted: the war drags on. Many disaffected doves adapt to this situation by rebellion. They reject societal goals and means and live in a youth counter-culture that is anti-war, anti-establishment, and involved in the new sensibility.

Before accepting this explanation of the linkage between the Vietnam war and campus protests, it is necessary to demonstrate that the pivotal relationship between disaffection and militancy is not spurious.[47] Table 9 reports the required evidence—the effect parameters for four multivariate analyses that corroborate the causal relationship between disaffection and militancy. In each of these analyses, three antecedent test variables are simultaneously controlled. These are: (1) demands for social justice and and new domestic priorities indicated by support for black power, (2) complaints about the University, and (3) a variable of social status. In the first

[46] Merton, *Social Theory and Social Structure*, Chap. 4.
[47] Lazarsfeld, "Evidence and Inference in Social Research," pp. 129–132.

analysis the social status is religion; in the second, father's occupation; then, student's sex; and, finally, an index of predisposition toward militancy comprised of the three statuses.

The last column in Table 9 presents averages of the effects across the four analyses. In these data from the 1968–1969 survey, disaffection from the war consistently has the second largest direct effect on student militancy. The average of its effects is .195. Consequently, the relationship between disaffection and militancy is not likely to be spurious. Only the effect of the closely related variable, "support for black power," is larger. Its average effect is .277.[48] Taken together, disaffection from the war and demands for social justice and new domestic priorities account for about half of the variation in student militancy. The random shocks are further reduced by the effects of the other test variables. The average of the effects of complaints about the University is .101, and the average for the predisposing status variables is .123. In sum, disaffection from the war and the test variables explain 70 per cent of the variation in student militancy. The average of the total random shocks is only .285.

SUMMARY AND IMPLICATIONS

This survey analysis has shown that disaffection from the Vietnam war is a pivotal determinant of student dissent even in campus protests that do not explicitly concern the war. At present, about 87 per cent of the UCSB undergraduates are disaffected from the war and from other important aspects of American society. These students disagree with governmental policies on the salient issues of Vietnam, liberalism, and drugs; they evaluate governmental and university authority as illegitimate, and they suffer from feelings of alienation and estrangement. Their disaffection stems from their belief that the war is a catastrophic mistake and from their idealism—they desire social justice for blacks and other oppressed minorities, and new domestic priorities to achieve this.

The students express their disaffection in militancy and in subsequent campus protests that are increasingly only tangentially about the war, the primary source of their disaffection. At UCSB, about two-thirds of the students are now militant. These militant students have certain characteristics in common with the student activists described earlier by other social scien-

---

[48] During the 1968–1969 academic year, black power was a very salient issue on campus because it was the first year of the E.O.P. which brought 200 new black students to campus. This probably accounts for the larger effect of this variable.

During 1969–1970, disaffection is clearly the major determinant of militancy. When disaffection from the war, support for black power, and complaints about the unresponsiveness of the University are simultaneously controlled, the effects on militancy are as follows:

a_1 = disaffection from the war   =.465
a_2 = support for black power   =.187
a_3 = unresponsiveness of university   =.223
r = random shock toward militancy   =.168
s = random shock toward conservatism   =.000 (−.043)

tists. But they also differ from these students in several important ways. They are similar to the earlier activists in their commitment to New Left politics, idealism, and concern for social problems. They are differentiated from these students by their lack of an intellectual orientation, by their involvement in the new sensibilities of marijuana, sex, and sensitivity training, and by their new readiness to support violent tactics. About half of the students now think nonviolence is ineffective and will support violent protests under certain circumstances. These percentages are considerably higher for the militant students.

Four variables apparently explain the militants' shift from nonviolence to violence. These are: (1) the military violence in Vietnam, (2) the unresponsiveness of the University, (3) police harassment for smoking marijuana, and (4) the militants' desire for social justice and new domestic priorities. It appears that New Left beliefs and "outside agitators" do not explain this shift to violence.

The frequency of campus protests is closely related to disaffection from the Vietnam war. When disaffection is high, campus protests are frequent. This is true even when the protests are not manifestly about the war or war-related issues. These aggregate relationships between disaffection and protest also hold true for individual students. Students who are disaffected are considerably more militant. This relationship is true even when a range of other test variables that independently affect militancy are simultaneously controlled. Taken together, disaffection from the war and the test varibles explain about 70 per cent of the variation in student militancy.

At UCSB disaffection from the war provides the most powerful explanation for the change in student militancy and campus protests. This is true because the level of disaffection has increased tremendously over the last three academic years, while the levels of the test variables and the political and social characteristics of the faculty and students, except for a shift to the left, have remained constant.[49] These are the parameters of the system. It is the change in the level of disaffection that has caused the change in the frequency of campus protests and the decline in the quality of intellectual life.

An end to the war in Vietnam will undoubtedly decrease campus turmoil, but it probably will not end the rebellion of the younger generation. For many, the war has pointed out the unresponsiveness and ineffectiveness of the American political and social institutions, and this has caused a delegitimation of authority.[50]

[49] The evidence for the stability of the social characteristics of the UCSB students and faculty, and the merits of various alternative explanations of campus protests are presented in Robert B. Smith, "Campus Protests and the Vietnam War."

[50] For a clear statement of the effectiveness-legitimacy hypothesis, see Seymour Martin Lipset, *Political Man* (Garden City, N.Y.: Doubleday and Co., 1960), pp. 77–96. This hypothesis can explain why students rebel in other countries where the war in Vietnam is not an issue. In these other rebellions, the sources of the ineffectiveness and delegitimation are different (for example, in South America the military elites might be a problem; in France, the economic structure might have been the issue, etc.); but the consequences are the same—student protests.

PART IV
The Distribution
of Attitudes and Opinions

INTRODUCTION

Many behavioral scientists employ the concepts of "attitudes" and "opinions" interchangeably. At least for purposes of descriptive simplicity, however, it is useful to think of an opinion as the expressive element in an attitude; this perspective squares with the discussion of attitude characteristics in Parts I and III and will be of assistance in Part V. In speaking of political opinions, therefore, we refer to the expressions of predispositions on matters pertaining to the regulation of conflict in society through the creation and allocation of benefits and deprivations. Although there are no strict boundaries, *attitudes* are relatively enduring, inclusive, diffuse, and often vague predilections disposing persons to behave in certain ways under certain conditions; *opinions*, in contrast, refer to short-run, topical, and specific judgments about public affairs based upon personal beliefs and feelings.[1]

The distribution of political attitudes and opinions among persons in a polity takes diverse forms. Generally, however, it is possible to demarcate three major patterns of distribution. First, if one regards political opinions as the verbalized expressions of people concerning a political object, person, or issue, a simple counting of alternative views—pro, con, and neutral—reveals a statistical pattern of identifiable clusters. If most persons cluster about a single point of view, the pattern is one of consensus (of course, it is possible to encounter a situation in which relatively few persons express any opinion at all, a uniform pattern of indifference[2]); if persons are divided into pro and con clusters, there is a discernible conflict; if persons vary in the intensity of their opinions (hence dividing into several groupings), the pattern is pluralist and reflects the prospect for conflict if intensities differ sharply, or a moderate situation if no opinions are voiced strongly. Students of political attitudes and opinions label these three statistical distributions as *unimodal, bimodal,* and *multimodal* respectively. By concentrating on these statistical distributions, political sociologists have inquired into the social correlates of selected opinions, opinion conflict and consensus, and the linkage between mass opinions and public policies.

Second, it is possible to identify opinions with specific groups and categories of groups in society. The views of the John Birch Society, Americans for Democratic Action, American Medical Association, Baptists, Catholics, and others provide illustrative cases. This is not to say that every member of a given group shares the same viewpoint; in fact, group cohesion may sometimes be minimal. It is to say, however, that group leaders take stands on political issues, endeavor to identify their members with those opinions, and exert group influence in politics. In focusing on this variety of distribution, sociologists and political scientists have raised questions about the

---

[1] This distinction between attitudes and opinions is spelled out in Bernard Berelson and Gary A. Steiner, *Human Behavior: An Inventory of Scientific Findings* (New York: Harcourt, Brace and World, 1964), p. 558.

[2] V. O. Key, Jr., *Public Opinion and American Democracy* (New York: Alfred A. Knopf, 1961), pp. 27–76.

relationships of leaders and followers, how group leaders are recruited, and how group members are mobilized.

Finally, there are times when no statistical pattern in opinions seems apparent and no clear-cut group stands emerge. Yet, policy-makers gauge an unspoken consensus or "mood" of the public's interest or disinterest in certain questions, how they feel, and to what extent they will support, permit, or oppose certain decisions. Thus, both America's isolationist foreign policies in the 1920s and 30s and interventionist actions in the 1950s and 60s were partly based on the reading of the public mood of Americans. Researching the existence and empirical content of such consensus has been a major task of students of political attitudes in the last two decades.[3]

The studies reported in Part IV illustrate but a few of the research questions implied by focusing upon statistical clusters, groups, and moods as distributive patterns of political attitudes and opinions. Regardless of the type of social distribution political opinions take, the pattern has its origins in the ways individuals order, or distribute, personal attitudes. But political scientists, as contrasted with other social scientists, have engaged in relatively little research endeavoring to link attitudinal orderings by individuals with opinion distributions in society at large. One exception is Samuel A. Kirkpatrick whose research interests have led him to pose questions about the relationship between attitudinal consistency on the personal level and opinion conflict and consensus in society. An example of the fruits of his investigations serves as the opening selection of Part IV, Kirkpatrick's article on "Political Attitudes and Behavior: Some Consequences of Attitudinal Ordering." Basing his inquiry on data generated by the 1964 election study of the Survey Research Center, Kirkpatrick provides an analysis that is instructive in two principal respects. First he clearly demonstrates how the distribution of political attitudes and opinions is intertwined with a concern emphasized in Part III of this anthology, the consistency problem. The author explains and operationalizes a model of cognitive consistency borrowed from social psychology by measuring the consistency-inconsistency of respondents in direction of total partisan affect, in cognitions of parties and candidates, and in expectations of the outcome of the 1964 election. Second, finding that the American population exhibits a high degree of consistency between cognitive and affective elements of attitudes as they pertain to political objects, Kirkpatrick proceeds to spell out the ramifications for political interest, partisan intensity, voting decisions, and participation in political affairs.

The distribution of political attitudes and opinions frequently varies from one social segment to another. It is the task of public officials in a democracy to inform themselves of what different elements of society believe and feel on issues, note conflicting opinions, and either reconcile them or choose between them in making policy decisions. On highly vola-

---

[3]Gabriel A. Almond, *The American People and Foreign Policy* (New York: Frederick A. Praeger, 1960), pp. 69–135.

tile issues the perception of constituents' opinions and the resolution of conflict are very difficult. The essay by Harlan Hahn and Joe R. Feagin, "Rank and File Versus Congressional Perceptions of Ghetto Riots," illustrates the disparities that develop between opinions of governed and governors. The authors are concerned with contrasting perceptions of black and white rank-and-file citizens of Detroit (as sampled in 1967) with Congressional perceptions of the causes of, and cures for, riots in urban ghettos. They reveal that black residents attribute riots to underlying social conditions and suggest economic reforms, social policies, and anti-discrimination as methods of prevention; however, white members of the rank and file blame agitators and criminals for riots and urge more effective law enforcement by police to prevent ghetto disturbances. Congressional perceptions, as revealed by a survey of U.S. Senators and Representatives in the summer of 1967, coincide more closely with those of white citizens than with views of black urbanites.

Contrasts between the opinions of black and white Americans regarding different political objects and in a different setting are explored by Dennis S. Ippolito and Martin L. Levin in "Public Regardingness, Race, and Social Class: The Case of a Rapid Transit Referendum." Ippolito and Levin explore the question of whether or not middle-class blacks share with middle-class whites a hypothesized "public regarding" orientation to community affairs, that is, if they emphasize community interest rather than narrower ethnic interests and if they respond to politics in terms of class rather than racial values. Their findings are based on a survey of 1,321 registered voters in the Atlanta metropolitan area regarding their attitudes toward construction and financing of a proposed rapid transit system. Employing controls for race, education, and occupation, the authors found marked differences in the opinion patterns of blacks and whites which suggest public regardingness orientations among the latter but that blacks appraised the transit proposal on the basis of their more generalized assessments of governmental performance in the area.

The selections by Hahn and Feagin and by Ippolito and Levin provide useful insights into the patterns of opinions of both urban whites and blacks regarding specific issues—ghetto riots in the one instance and urban transportation in the other. John M. Orbell in "The Impact of Metropolitan Residence on Social and Political Orientations" is concerned with a slightly different problem. As the title of his essay suggests, his focus is on not only the views of urban residents but on the effects of urban residence on political attitudes and opinions. His study illustrates how both aggregate and survey data may be combined in examining political orientations. Using tract data from the 1960 census in Columbus, Ohio, Orbell is able to define the urban character of areas of residence for persons he surveyed in 1966. His findings suggest that urbanism is related to the sense of personal morale of respondents (being lower in urban areas than in less densely populated suburban areas) but not related to their sense of political efficacy. The morale of blacks and whites in central cities was found to differ, with blacks exhibiting higher morale than whites. Levels of education also appeared as related to morale; the morale of the lesser educated was affected by moving from one locale to another in the urban area. Orbell's study suggests that sociologists and political scientists should look more closely at the impact of environment upon the acquisition and expression of political attitudes, especially at the differences in personal susceptibility for environmental influences.

The studies in Part IV introduced thus far are concerned with statistical distributions of political opinions, particularly with reference to domestic issues. In "The 'Mood Theory': A Study of Public Opinion and Foreign Policy" William R. Caspary utilizes statistical data to test a theory regarding opinion consensus on matters of foreign affairs. Caspary is interested in examining the empirical evidence for what has become a classical theory in political science, the "mood theory" of interest in and support for particular foreign policies by the American public. The author outlines the content of the mood theory and employing data generated by surveys of the National Opinion Research Center for various years, explores popular support among Americans for overseas involvement, their expressed interest in foreign affairs, and the character of the attentive public. He concludes that the mood theory—which attributes unstable support for foreign policy commitments to low and unstable levels of attention paid by Americans to foreign affairs—should be replaced by an alternative interpretation accounting for the strong and stable "permissive mood" of Americans toward international involvements.

The distribution of American opinions pertaining to foreign policy issues is also the focus of another article in Part IV, "Social Class and Foreign Policy Attitudes" by Martin Patchen. Of particular interest to Patchen are the opinions of members of the lower class respecting policies America should take toward other nations. In his analysis he incorporates data from a 1964 national survey relating opinions about Communist China and Vietnam to a variety of social and personal characteristics—education, sex, level of information, region, age, and political affiliation. Patchen's findings lead him to conclude that, contrary to interpretations derived from previous research, lower-class people are not consistently more conciliatory on foreign policy issues than are those of higher social classes. If any attitude can be said to characterize the lower class, it is one of non-involvement in foreign affairs.

The final selection in Part IV deals with the problem of the extent to which orientations of certain groups are reflected in electoral politics. In "Religion and the Rise of the Radical White: The Case of Southern Wallace Support in 1968" Anthony M. Orum explores the links between George Wallace's Independent Party, an example of radical politics in the American context, and religious attitudes. The study is based upon interviews with white residents of a major Southern metropolitan community. Interviews were directed at identifying respondents' religious affiliations, acceptance or rejection of major tenets of fundamentalism, and degree of religious involvement. Orum found that, controlling for socioeconomic status, Wallace received a disproportionate share of support from Baptists and fundamentalists. Frequent churchgoers, however, were less likely to vote for Wallace than those not so highly involved. The pattern of Wallace support suggests that the candidate had a special attraction for those estranged from politics, intolerant of political differences, and opposed to racial integration.

POLITICAL ATTITUDES AND BEHAVIOR: SOME CONSEQUENCES OF ATTITUDINAL ORDERING[*]

SAMUEL A. KIRKPATRICK
University of Oklahoma

P OLITICAL SCIENCE HAS ACCUMULATED A BODY OF KNOWLEDGE ABOUT FACTORS influencing political behavior without paying serious attention to intrapersonal attitudinal structures and their impact. Most research treats the impact of attitudes on vote direction and levels of participation and involvement without considering the importance of the way in which these attitudes toward political objects are ordered. The focus for this paper is the way in which attitudes (cognitions and affects) are ordered along a consistency-inconsistency continuum and the attitudinal and behavioral consequences of such alignments. Utilizing a national sample it is suggested that unusually high levels of attitudinal balance are evident in the American electorate and that individuals characterized by unbalanced states evidence higher degrees of attitudinal intensity, a tendency for delay in the voting decision, and a predisposition for various forms of political interest and participation.

CONSISTENCY CONCEPTS IN THE SOCIAL SCIENCES

The role of perception and the attitudinal consequences of the perception of political objects has been of some concern to scholars of public opinion and the political process. However, political science has failed to develop a coherent body of knowledge about intrapersonal processes in the perception of political objects and the impact that these processes may have on the political system. Political pundits, normative theorists, and empirically oriented behavioralists have attempted to evaluate the individual as political man and as rational man in the context of an ongoing political system. A body of prescriptions, proscriptions, guesses, and crude measures has developed by which we make generalizations of individual capacities in the political sphere. The following is an attempt to refine these measures and guesses in search for knowledge about the way in which the individual (modal) organizes his perceptual-attitudinal structure and its impact on his political behavior and attitudinal intensity.

Normative political philosophers have been interested in rationality[1] (a

[*]Reprinted by permission of the author and publisher, from Samuel A. Kirkpatrick, "Political Attitudes and Behavior: Some Consequences of Attitudinal Ordering," *Midwest Journal of Political Science*, 14 (Feb., 1970), pp. 1–24. I wish to acknowledge the earlier draft comments of Lawrence K. Pettit of the American Council on Education and Bernard C. Hennessy of Pennsylvania State University. An earlier version of this paper was presented at the annual meeting of the Midwest Political Science Association, Ann Arbor, Michigan, April 24–26, 1969.

[1]For comprehensive statements see Bernard Berelson, "Democratic Theory and

component of consistency[2]); empirical political scientists have offered restatements and modifications of rationality assumptions based on survey research;[3] and theory has been constructed from these generalizations.[4] Social psychologists have focused on the assumption that the individual strives toward a state of consistency between attitude objects which he perceives in the environment, and if a state of inconsistency exists, cognitive reorganization will occur to reduce it. This approach has utilized balance models,[5] congruity approaches,[6] and dissonance theory.[7] Although these represent a related set of theories, there are theoretical and methodological distinctions

---

Public Opinion," *Public Opinion Quarterly*, 16 (1952), pp. 313–330; Henry Mayo, *An Introduction to Democratic Theory* (New York: Oxford University Press, 1960); William T. Bluhm, *Theories of the Political System* (Englewood Cliffs: Prentice Hall, 1965); and Richard E. Ashcraft, "Political Rationality and Democratic Values," a paper presented at the annual meeting of the Western Political Science Association, Tucson, Arizona, March 17, 1967.

[2] Don D. Smith, "Cognitive Consistency and the Perception of Others' Opinion," *Public Opinion Quarterly*, 32 (1968), pp. 1–15; William A. Scott, "Rationality and Non-Rationality of International Attitudes," *Journal of Conflict Resolution*, 2 (1958), pp. 8–16; and R. B. Zajonc, "Balance, Congruity, and Dissonance," *Public Opinion Quarterly*, 24 (1960), pp. 280–296.

[3] Especially the interdisciplinary endeavors of Bernard Berelson, Paul F. Lazarsfeld, and William N. McPhee, *Voting* (Chicago: University of Chicago Press, 1954); Berelson, "Democratic Theory and Public Opinion"; Eugene Burdick, "Political Theory and the Voting Studies," in Eugene Burdick and Arthur Brodbeck, eds., *American Voting Behavior*, (Glencoe: Free Press, 1959), pp. 136–149; J. Plamenatz and G. Sartori, "Electoral Studies and Democratic Theory," *Political Studies*, 6 (1958), pp. 1–75; V. O. Key, Jr., *The Responsible Electorate* (Cambridge: Harvard University Press, 1966); and Hugh A. Bone and Austin Ranney, *Politics and Voters* (New York: McGraw-Hill, 1963).

[4] Robert A. Dahl, *A Preface to Democratic Theory* (Chicago: University of Chicago Press, 1956); Harry Eckstein, *A Theory of Stable Democracy* (Princeton: Princeton University, Center of International Studies, 1961); Charles Lindblom, *The Intelligence and Democracy* (New York: Free Press, 1965); Gabriel A. Almond and Sidney Verba, *The Civic Culture* (Boston: Little, Brown & Co., 1965); Philip E. Converse, "The Nature of Belief Systems in Mass Publics," in David E. Apter, ed., *Ideology and Discontent* (New York: Free Press, 1964), pp. 206–262; and Gabriel A. Almond, *The American People and Foreign Policy* (New York: Frederick A. Praeger, 2nd ed., 1960).

[5] Fritz Heider, "Attitudes and Cognitive Organization," *Journal of Psychology*, 21 (1946), pp. 107–112. Important explications have been developed by Dorwin Cartwright and Frank Harary, "Structural Balance: A Generalization of Heider's Theory," *Psychological Review*, 63 (1956), pp. 277–293; Julian O. Morrissette, "An Experimental Study of the Theory of Structural Balance," *Human Relations*, 11 (1958), pp. 239–254; and Milton J. Rosenberg and Robert Abelson, "An Analysis of Cognitive Balancing," in Carl I. Hovland and Milton J. Rosenberg, eds., *Attitude Organization and Change* (New Haven: Yale University Press, 1960), pp. 112–163.

[6] Charles E. Osgood and Percy H. Tannenbaum, "The Principle of Congruity in the Prediction of Attitude Change," *Psychological Review*, 62 (1965), pp. 42–55.

[7] Leon A. Festinger, *A Theory of Cognitive Dissonance* (Stanford: Stanford University Press, 1957); and Jack W. Brehm and Arthur R. Cohen, *Explorations in Cognitive Dissonance* (New York: John Wiley and Sons, 1962).

between them.[8] The theoretical framework for the following analysis borrows heavily from the concept of structural balance. As it was originally formulated by Heider, the scheme contains an individual viewer (P), another person (O), plus an impersonal entity (X), with a focus on how P, O, and X are organized in P's cognitive structure. These elements of the model are linked by "relations" which are either positive, negative, or null. More specifically, two types of information are included: affect or feelings, and cognitions or cognitive unit information. Therefore, "attitude" becomes the aspect of the cognitive unit that is a focal point for the balance principle. Generally, the theory deals with "the perception of social objects such as persons, ideas, and concepts."[9] Analytical attention is given to the perceiver (who, below, is "outside" the attitude object triads) and to the relationships between the objects of perception. In the following analysis, these objects are treated broadly as persons, events, issues, groups, and combinations of feelings, beliefs, or expectations associated with them. McGuire has reiterated the underlying hypothesis as follows: "The person tends to behave in ways that minimize the internal inconsistency among his interpersonal relations, among his intrapersonal cognitions, or among his beliefs, feelings, and actions."[10]

Although consistency concepts have been found to have high predictive power,[11] plus the advantages of generality and applicability to a large number of psychological problems,[12] the applications have occurred almost exclusively in the laboratory of the experimental social psychologist and in the context of attitude change. This focus has left questions unanswered about the impact of attitude orderings at one point in time. In spite of the criticisms leveled at researchers for an experimental bias,[13] and the claimed advantages of survey research (defined populations, natural settings, and generalizability), only a few attempts have been made at applying various aspects of balance-related theory to political data (and most of these are

---

[8] Congruity is frequently viewed as a special case of balance, but finer distinctions are made about dissonance. See Samuel A. Kirkpatrick, "Social-Psychological Approaches to the Study of Political Phenomena," a paper presented at the annual meeting of the Rocky Mountain Social Science Association, Lubbock, Texas, May 2–3, 1969.

[9] Robert B. Zajonc, "Cognitive Theories in Social Psychology," in Gardner Lindzey and Elliot Aronson, eds., *Handbook of Social Psychology* (Reading, Mass.: Addison-Wesley Publishing Company, 2nd ed., 1968), vol. I, p. 339.

[10] William J. McGuire, "The Current Status of Cognitive Consistency Theories," in Shel Feldman, ed., *Cognitive Consistency: Motivational Antecedents and Behavioral Consequents* (New York: Academic Press, 1966), p. 1.

[11] Festinger, *A Theory of Cognitive Dissonance*, p. 1.

[12] Brehm and Cohen, *Explorations in Cognitive Dissonance*, p. vii.

[13] Carl I. Hovland, "Reconciling Conflicting Results Derived from Experimental and Survey Studies of Attitude Change," *American Psychologist*, 14 (1959), pp. 8–17; Karl E. Weick, "Promise and Limitations of Laboratory Experiments in the Development of Attitude Change Theory," in Carolyn W. Sherif and Muzafer Sherif, eds., *Attitude, Ego-Involvement and Change* (New York: John Wiley and Sons, 1967), pp. 51–75; and Bertram L. Koslin, "Laboratory Experiments and Attitude Theory," in Sherif and Sherif, *Attitude, Ego-Involvement and Change*, pp. 76–87.

found in unpublished sources). Lewis Froman has tried to develop a theory of relationships between definitions, values, and beliefs, and consistencies in values and beliefs about five political institutions based on responses from university students.[14] National Opinion Research Center data on value judgments of foreign policy have been analyzed to determine whether policy actions follow from basic value orientations and to test the rational quality of the public's views on foreign policy.[15] Other survey designs have measured congruencies between attitudes about the candidates and the political parties;[16] social cross-pressures and degrees of consistency on socio-political issues;[17] the impact of a mass communications campaign on consistencies in issue and party affect;[18] the relationship between attitude objects (candidate, party, religion) and the vote in the context of balance models;[19] the association between "logical consistency" in responses to questions about the country's problems and opinion leadership and political participation;[20] and incongruities in foreign affairs opinions.[21]

For the most part, the above attempts have failed to treat the specifics of balance theory (e.g., cognitive-affective distinctions); they have been based on either small, homogeneous samples or various parts of diverse samples; very specialized and diverse views of consistency have been adopted; and attitude objects have been defined narrowly (e.g., institutions,[22] issues[23]) without relevance to complexes of attitudes.

INDEX CONSTRUCTION

Social psychologists have hypothesized a strain toward consistency as a characteristic of human behavior, as well as a determinant of various forms of behavior. Zajonc comments that "it is significant that, although Heider drew upon Gestalt theory, he clearly recognized that cognitive inconsistency may have not only cognitive and attitudinal consequences, but 'behavioral' consequences as well."[24] Political scientists have been some-

[14]"Cognitive Consistency of Political Values and Beliefs," Ph.D. dissertation, Northwestern University, 1960.

[15]Leonard S. Stein, "Consistency of Public Opinion on Foreign Policy," Ph.D. dissertation, University of Chicago, 1962.

[16]Peter W. Sperlich, "Cross-Pressure and Conflict in Political Behavior," Ph.D. dissertation, University of Michigan, 1966.

[17]Roy T. Bowles, "The Social Sources of Opinion Consistency," Ph.D. dissertation, University of Oregon, 1965.

[18]William N. McPhee, Bo Anderson, and Harry Milholland, "Attitude Consistency," in W. N. McPhee and W. A. Glaser, eds., Public Opinion and Congressional Elections (New York: Free Press, 1962), pp. 78–120.

[19]Denis Sullivan, "Psychological Balance and Reactions to the Presidential Nominations in 1960," in M. Kent Jennings and L. Harmon Zeigler, eds. The Electoral Process (Englewood Cliffs: Prentice-Hall, 1966), pp. 238–264.

[20]John Kessel, "Cognitive Dimensions and Political Activity," Public Opinion Quarterly, 29 (1965), pp. 377–389.

[21]Scott, "Rationality and Non-Rationality of International Attitudes."

[22]Froman, "Cognitive Consistency of Political Values and Beliefs."

[23]Samuel A. Kirkpatrick, "Issue Orientation and Voter Choice in 1964," Social Science Quarterly, 49 (1968), pp. 87–102.

[24]"Cognitive Theories in Social Psychology," p. 341.

what concerned with "cognitive maps," yet they have neglected the concept of balance as an analytic and predictive tool. The experimental focus has been on induced discrepancies and syllogistic reasoning, and field research has focused primarily on issue consistencies to the point of avoiding other objects in the environment. The present research effort is an attempt to discover to what extent the theory has broader implications for political behavior. Objects are expanded to a treatment of candidates, issues, party identification, party affect, levels of conceptualization, political preferences, political expectations, knowledge, and various forms of political behavior. The data are from a sample of the national population,[25] there is an attempt to operationally separate affect and cognition, and attitude objects are treated as complexes of variables (multi-points in graph theory) with binary relations between them (e.g., likes-dislikes). The "attitudinal map" of respondents is conceptualized as a pattern of consistency and inconsistency relationships with regard to perceived political objects in the environment. In order to establish attitudinal map variables, a number of attitudinal responses were used to derive several indices of consistency-inconsistency.

1. *Total Partisan Affect–Party Identification–Political Preference Index (AIP).* The first balance model represents the direction of total partisan affect (for all indices the direction is either Democratic or Republican), party identification, political preference in 1964, and the extent to which these three attitudinal elements are consistent or inconsistent. In order to derive a level of consistency for each respondent on this index and any of the following indices, it was first necessary to measure the direction of affect (feeling) for each of the three elements.

The direction of total partisan affect[26] was estimated from a large number of unstructured (open-ended) questions asked the respondent about the parties and candidates. For example: What do you like about the Democratic Party? (five possible responses for each of these questions); What don't you like about the Republican Party? What do you like about Johnson? What don't you like about Johnson? What do you like about Goldwater? and What don't you like about Goldwater? Note that a single respondent could have as many as forty possible responses. These responses were summed for each individual (N = 1,571) to yield an attitude toward each party and candidate, then combined to get one attitude toward parties and one attitude toward candidates, and the latter were summed to yield a total partisan attitude. The following symbolic representations indicate the steps involved in this process.[27]

[25] The data from the 1964 election study utilized here were made available by the Inter-University Consortium for Political Research. The data were originally collected by the Survey Research Center of the University of Michigan. Neither source bears any responsibility for the index construction or interpretation presented here.

[26] The index is a summary of cognitive unit information as well as affect.

[27] From "Construction of Don Stokes' Six-Predictor Master Code Indexes," Memorandum, University of Michigan, Survey Research Center, May 22, 1967.

Number of Pro-Democratic Party Responses (S_1)
Number of Anti-Democratic Party Responses (S_2)
Number of Pro-Republican Party Responses (S_3)
Number of Anti-Republican Party Responses (S_4)
Number of Pro-Democratic Candidate Responses (S_5)
Number of Anti-Democratic Candidate Responses (S_6)
Number of Pro-Republican Candidate Responses (S_7)
Number of Anti-Republican Candidate Responses (S_8)
Attitude toward the Democratic Party ($S_9 = S_1 - S_2 + 5$)
Attitude toward the Republican Party ($S_{10} = S_4 - S_3 + 5$)
Attitude toward the Democratic Candidate ($S_{11} = S_5 - S_6 + 5$)
Attitude toward the Republican Candidate ($S_{12} = S_8 - S_7 + 5$)
Combined Attitude toward the Parties ($S_{13} = S_9 + S_{10}$)
Combined Attitude toward the Candidates ($S_{14} = S_{11} + S_{12}$)
Total Partisan Attitude ($S_{15} = S_{13} + S_{14}$)

The direction of party identification was derived from a structured Survey Research Center (SRC) question, as was the respondent's candidate preference in 1964. Any affect other than Democratic (D) or Republican (R) was treated as "no affect"; therefore, if a respondent had no affect on any two of these three elements, he was dropped from the sample for purposes of this index. However, if a respondent had only one "no affect" he was judged to be consistent or inconsistent on the basis of the direction of the remaining two affects. For example, a respondent with a Republican total partisan affect, Republican Party identification, and a preference for Goldwater was scored as totally consistent (TC), as was a respondent with two Republican affects and no affect (0) on a third variable. An inconsistent (i.e., not totally consistent, NTC) respondent had a combination of Republican and Democratic responses.

Graph theoretic terms explain the index derivation more vividly.[28] Points in graph theory represent an affective, cognitive, or conative component, or a combination of these components (e.g., an attitude). Lines connecting points in a triad (three elements) denote the existence of a logical or rational relationship between points (attitudes) in the real world. A simple linear graph model for all of the indices, given three elements, can be represented as a triad of points:

[28]Graph theory is a branch of mathematics and is more general than indicated here. Joseph Berger, *et al.*, *Types of Formalization in Small Group Research* (Boston: Houghton Mifflin Company, 1961); Frank Harary, Robert Norman, and Dorwin Cartwright, *Structural Models: An Introduction to the Theory of Directed*

In order to make such a model attitudinally specific, the points can be identified as to their type, i.e., type of attitude. For example, point A = total partisan affect, point I = party identification, and point P = political preference:

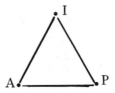

Internally, each respondent has an affective direction which he associates with the attitudinal points; therefore, let each point have a subscript which denotes Republican affect (r), Democratic affect (d), or no affect (o):

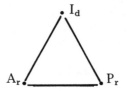

From the triads we can derive symbolic formulae (ordered sets) to indicate which combinations (cycles) or attitudes will be consistent (TC) or inconsistent (NTC). For example, in Table 1, the A_rI_r bond represents a linkage of Republican total partisan affect and Republican Party identification. It can be used as a guide to the way in which most indices were derived.

2. *Directional Conceptualization Index (CON)*.   This consistency-inconsistency index measures the degree to which a respondent is consistently Democratic or Republican in his references to the parties and candidates, i.e., how consistent he is within the overall partisan index used to tap overall affect in the AIP index. It is a measure of the congruence between the levels of conceptualization that he used to evaluate the parties and candidates, that is, a measure of consistency in preference when preference is explained subjectively by different levels of conceptualization. These levels of conceptualization are similar to those derived in *The American Voter*.[29] From the unstructured questions about the parties and candidates, the SRC staff has developed an index of partisanship in Johnson references, an index of partisanship in Goldwater references, and indices of partisanship in references to groups, domestic issues, foreign issues, and the parties as mana-

---

Graphs (New York: John Wiley and Sons, 1965); and John G. Kemeny and J. Laurie Snell, *Mathematical Models in the Social Sciences* (Waltham: Blaisdell Publishing Company, 1962), pp. 95–108.
   [29] Angus Campbell, *et al.*, *The American Voter* (New York: John Wiley and Sons, Inc., 1960), Chapter 10.

TABLE 1

Symbolic Representation of the Total Partisan Affect-Party Identification-Political Preference Index

Affective Direction on: Total Partisan Affect	Party Identification	Political Preference	Symbolic Representation of Structural Balance
R	R	R	$\{(A_r,I_r),\ (I_r,P_r),\ (P_r,A_r)\}$ = TC
D	D	D	$\{(A_d,I_d),\ (I_d,P_d),\ (P_d,A_d)\}$ = TC
R	R	O	$\{(A_r,I_r),\ (I_r,P_o),\ (P_o,A_r)\}$ = TC
R	O	R	$\{(A_r,I_o),\ (I_o,P_r),\ (P_r,A_r)\}$ = TC
O	R	R	$\{(A_o,I_r),\ (I_r,P_r),\ (P_r,A_o)\}$ = TC
D	D	O	$\{(A_d,I_d),\ (I_d,P_o),\ (P_o,A_d)\}$ = TC
D	O	D	$\{(A_d,I_o),\ (I_o,P_d),\ (P_d,A_d)\}$ = TC
O	D	D	$\{(A_o,I_d),\ (I_d,P_d),\ (P_d,A_o)\}$ = TC
R	R	D	$\{(A_r,I_r),\ (I_r,P_d),\ (P_d,A_r)\}$ = NTC
R	D	R	$\{(A_r,I_d),\ (I_d,P_r),\ (P_r,A_r)\}$ = NTC
D	R	R	$\{(A_d,I_r),\ (I_r,P_r),\ (P_r,A_d)\}$ = NTC
D	D	R	$\{(A_d,I_d),\ (I_d,P_r),\ (P_r,A_d)\}$ = NTC
D	R	D	$\{(A_d,I_r),\ (I_r,P_d),\ (P_d,A_d)\}$ = NTC
R	D	D	$\{(A_r,I_d),\ (I_d,P_d),\ (P_d,A_r)\}$ = NTC
R	D	O	$\{(A_r,I_d),\ (I_d,P_o),\ (P_o,A_r)\}$ = NTC
D	O	R	$\{(A_d,I_o),\ (I_o,P_r),\ (P_r,A_d)\}$ = NTC
O	R	D	$\{(A_o,I_r),\ (I_r,P_d),\ (P_d,A_o)\}$ = NTC
D	R	O	$\{(A_d,I_r),\ (I_r,P_o),\ (P_o,A_d)\}$ = NTC
R	O	D	$\{(A_r,I_o),\ (I_o,P_d),\ (P_d,A_r)\}$ = NTC
O	D	R	$\{(A_o,I_d),\ (I_d,P_r),\ (P_r,A_o)\}$ = NTC

gers of government. Each respondent has a Democratic or Republican affect (or no affect) on each of these levels of conceptualization. Therefore, in terms of graph theory, we have a six-point graph (six attitudinal categories) with an affect associated with each point or attitude. To represent this symbolically, as in the AIP index, would require 729 ordered sets. If a respondent has six Republican affects or fewer than six Republican affects with a combination of no affects, he is consistently Republican. The same holds for Democratic affect. Any combination of Republican and Democratic affect is scored as a state of imbalance.

3. *Expectation—Preference Index (EP)*. This index measures consistency-inconsistency in terms of congruencies between a cognitively oriented expectation of who is likely to win the 1964 presidential election and an affect oriented preference for a candidate (i.e., how the respondent expects to vote). Unlike the other indices, only two attitudinal elements are involved. If the respondent expects Johnson to win and prefers Johnson, or if he expects Goldwater to win and prefers Goldwater, he is consistent.[30] Other combinations are inconsistent and the existence of any "no affect" eliminates the respondent.

[30] Due to the logical connotations of balance theory, this index is not unlike aspects of dissonance theory. See Bernard C. Hennessy, *Public Opinion* (Belmont: Wadsworth Publishing Co., 1965), p. 324.

THE PREVALENCE OF ATTITUDINAL CONSISTENCY

Table 2 indicates the total levels of consistency and inconsistency in the 1964 sample of the national population as measured by three indices. All of these indices exhibit higher levels of consistency than inconsistency and most of them are well above any even probability level. However, one disclaimer must be made about the bias toward higher consistency levels. In order to measure these psychological-attitudinal levels, an individual must give a sufficient number of responses so that his affect or cognition can be measured. That is, it is possible that some respondents who fail to indicate an affect or cognition on the questions used to formulate the indices do so on the basis of inconsistency avoidance. Although it is impossible to measure this bias, its movement in the direction of greater consistency is likely. Festinger contends that "a fear of dissonance would lead to a reluctance to take action—a reluctance to commit oneself."[31]

TABLE 2

The Existence of Consistency-Inconsistency in 1964

Index of Consistency	Level of Consistency-Inconsistency		Total N[a]
	Per Cent Consistent	Per Cent Inconsistent	
Total Partisan Affect–Party Identification–			
Political Preference (AIP)	86	14	1,538
Directional Conceptualization (CON)	64	36	1,521
Expectation-Preference (EP)	81	19	1,087

[a]Deviance from a total N of 1,571 is caused by omissions due to failures to respond or the existence of "no affects" in certain indices.

Using the Total Partisan Affect–Party Identification–Political Preference Index (AIP) as a criterion, Table 2 indicates that 86 per cent of the population is consistent. This means that these respondents are consistent in the direction of their total partisan affect as measured by the index, their political party identification, and their political preference for a candidate in 1964. Some of these respondents are consistently Republican (24 per cent), but most are consistently Democratic (62 per cent). This finding represents, to some extent, the gross level of party identifiers in the electorate. Among all the indices, this one produces the highest consistency level. It is felt that this is representative of the most typical and vocal identifications and attitudes among the population. That is, the high total number of responses (N = 1,538) indicates that the universe responds overwhelmingly on the items composing the scale. Most Americans have at least some degree of general feeling toward the political parties and candidates, and many have distinct party identifications as well as political preferences. Nearly the entire population exhibits an affect on at least two of these attitude objects.

[31] *A Theory of Cognitive Dissonance*, p. 31.

More importantly, those who exhibit attitudes do so coherently along a Democratic-Republican continuum.

The Directional Conceptualization Index (CON) attempts to measure a related kind of consistency: consistencies in responses toward the parties and candidates, that is, consistencies within one of the elements (Total Partisan Affect) in the AIP Index. The attitudes toward the parties and candidates were separated in content based on levels of conceptualization (e.g., the parties as managers of government) and a directional affect (Democratic or Republican) was obtained for each of these levels. Table 2 indicates that 64 per cent of the sample is able to arrange responses toward parties and candidates along a consistently Republican (15 per cent) or a consistently Democratic (49 per cent) continuum. These individuals can at least respond in a consistent fashion to questions which tap their attitude on any two levels of conceptualization. The percentage is substantially less than that displayed by the other indices, a probable reflection of the demand placed on the respondent and his difficulty in conceptualizing political objects on even these rather crude conceptual levels. In comparison with the other indices, the 36 per cent who are inconsistent exhibit difficulty in making their evaluations of candidates and parties congruent.

The levels of consistency displayed by the Expectation-Preference Index (EP) are high (81 per cent) and indicate a strong capability for individuals to align their expectations with their political candidate preferences. This index measures a cognitive element (expectation of which candidate is going to win the election) a well as an affective element (which candidate the individual prefers). The measure is remote from any indications of rationality or logical syllogism, but it does give an indication of psychological forces that tend to make an individual's expectations congruent with his preferences. That is, for those respondents included in the measure there is a strain toward cognitive-affective consistency at one point in time.

Political scientists have focused on psychological and behavioral frailties (e.g., the lack of ideology, knowledge, rationality, and objectivity) of members of the electorate. Social psychologists have focused on the individual, but not the individual as a political man, and concluded that there is a tendency for the individual to reduce states of imbalance. In general, each of the balance models indicates that relatively high levels of various forms of attitudinal consistency are prevalent in the population. The American electorate exhibits a strain toward consistency similar to that postulated in social-psychological cognitive consistency theories. Nevertheless, there are sufficiently high levels of attitudinal inconsistency to warrant an examination of the behavioral consequences of these levels. The rates of inconsistency indicate that there may be a segment of the population which fails to resolve structural imbalance or which seeks cognitive tension. It has been postulated that in certain circumstances, the organism may seek inconsistency and exacerbate levels of inconsistency in order to maximize satisfaction derived from the ultimate tension reduction. Furthermore, the respondent may seek inconsistency in order to hide more serious conflicts which are irresolvable through action (e.g., a passive person may seek cognitive excitement[32]). Research in political science has indicated that many citizens are able to tolerate high amounts of conflict,[33] that some people enjoy the tension of risk taking,[34] and that many respondents can hold inconsistent beliefs without trying to reconcile them.[35]

ATTITUDINAL AND BEHAVIORAL CONSEQUENCES: STATISTICAL SUMMARY

In an attempt to measure the consequences of attitude orderings, three clusters of dependent variables were selected for cross tabulation with the three indices: issue and partisan intensity; the time for deciding how one is going to vote; and political interest, participation, and efficacy.[36] Table 3 indicates the significance level and direction of relationship for each of the indices.

The table evidences a general lack of significant relationships for the AIP model, yet most of the issue intensity measures relate negatively to consistency. That is, the more consistent a respondent is in his ordering of partisan affect, party identification, and political preference, the less intense he is in his stand on domestic issues. However, intensity of party identification moves in the opposite direction. Seven of eleven political interest variables show no discernible relationship to attitudinal configurations; however, the direction for the decision time variables is clear. The time at which an individual makes up his mind about an important decision is a crucial element in the test of structural balance. The body of cognitive consistency theory postulates that an individual subject to inconsistency delays his decision under the influence of conflicting psychological demands. The decision time for vote direction meets this test: most consistents make up their minds before or during the political conventions, whereas inconsistent respondents decide how they are going to vote during the post-convention campaign.

A clearer pattern of relationships is evident when consistency is measured by congruence in party direction when expressed as levels of conceptualization. Inconsistency is related to high issue intensity; however, as with the AIP Index, consistent respondents display higher degrees of intensity about their party identification. The time at which an individual decides how he is

---

[32] Albert Pepitone, "Some Conceptual and Empirical Problems of Consistency Models," in Feldman, ed., *Cognitive Consistency*, pp. 257–297.

[33] Robert Lane, *Political Ideology* (New York: Free Press, 1962), pp. 30–31.

[34] R. B. Zajonc, "Balance, Congruity and Dissonance," p. 295.

[35] Robert Dahl, *Who Governs?* (New Haven: Yale University Press, 1961), p. 319.

[36] Although the independent variables are complex indices, the advantages of parsimonious indices on the dependent variables were avoided for both theoretical and methodological reasons. For example, theoretically, there are important differences (information, personal interaction, and involvement) between various participation variables in the context of balance theory. A serious methodological problem which constrains such index construction is the reduction of N, particularly for issue intensity and specific forms of participation. These problems became evident in a Candidate-Party-Issue index discussed in Kirkpatrick, "Social-Psychological Approaches to the Study of Political Phenomena."

TABLE 3

Attitudinal and Behavioral Consequences of Consistency-Inconsistency[a]

Consequences	Significance Level and Direction of Relationship for:		
	AIP	CON	EP
Issue Intensity for:			
General power of the federal government	.89 0	.00*–	.00*–
Aid to education	.34 –	.00*–	.00*–
Medicare	.84 0	.06 0	.14 –
Government responsibility for living standards	.24 –	.63 0	.00*–
Government ownership of power plants	.30 –	.00*–	.00*–
Equal job opportunities	.52 –	.20 –	.81 0
School integration	.53 –	.23 0	.45 –
Integrated public accommodations	.21 –	.38 –	.90 0
Intensity of Partisan Identification	.00*+	.00*+	.25 +
Decision Time for Making up Mind About Vote Direction	.00*+	.00*+	.00*+
Political Interest and Participation:			
Interest in the campaign (asked before election)	.90 0	.00*–	.00*–
Attention paid to the campaign (post-election)	.64 +	.16 –	.00*–
Expect to vote	.95 0	.05*–	.20 –
Turnout	.91 0	.27 –	.11 –
Mass media usage	.47 0	.00*–	.06 –
Talking to others to influence them	.68 0	.03*–	.00*–
Attending political meetings	.60 0	.37 0	.01*–
Political club membership	.53 0	.66 0	.02*–
Using a button or bumper sticker	.00*+	.02*+	.03*–
Giving money	.30 +	.22 –	.00*–
Political involvement index	.01*+	.28 0	.13 –
Political Efficacy	.88 0	.06 –	.02*–

[a]See Appendix for coding procedures and table interpretation.

going to vote is also significantly related to levels of consistency: there is substantial evidence that individuals with conflicting affects will delay this decision. When most of the behavioral variables are examined, it can be seen that inconsistency is associated with political interest and action. For example, respondents with incongruous attitudes are more interested in the campaign and election, they are more likely to expect to vote and to actually vote, they use more forms of the mass media than do consistents, and they talk to others to influence them about the election. The only relationship which is contrary to the above set is that for participation involving a campaign button or bumper sticker. There is nothing inherent in the CON Index or the participation measure to give clues to this divergent relationship.

Table 3 also indicates that an individual who is inconsistent in his expectation of who is going to win the election and his preference for a candidate is most likely to take an intense stand on all but two of the measured domestic issues. In congruence with the other indices, the EP Index relates consistency to high partisan intensity, although it fails to meet the .05 probability level. The time for making up one's mind about how he is going to vote continues to be a strong variable in its association with consonance. In the face of structural imbalance, the above respondents also tend to take greater interest in the campaign, participate more, and express a higher degree of political efficacy about their influence on government.

ISSUE AND PARTISAN INTENSITY

Although the AIP measure fails to evidence significant relationships, the indices all indicate that inconsistent respondents tend to be more intense in the stands they take on domestic issues. The AIP and CON indices are based on a foundation of similar variables: attitudes (open-ended) toward the parties and candidates are used by CON, and AIP includes these same attitudes plus structured responses to questions about party identification and candidate choice. They exhibit a pattern of relationships which is similar, yet less powerful in their predictive force than the EP Index. The Directional Conceptualization Index relates consistency to lower intensity in a more statistically significant fashion than does the AIP Index, and the Expectation-Preference Index evidences more significant relationships than either the AIP or CON Index. Through the use of these indices, there is evidence to suggest the following: there is a tendency for respondents with mixed direction (combinations of Democratic and Republican) on their total affect toward parties and candidates, their party identification, and their preference for a candidate in 1964, to be more intense about domestic issues; respondents with mixed directions on their total affect toward parties and candidates (internally, according to Republican or Democratic affects attached to various levels of conceptualization) are more intense about domestic issues (strongly agree and strongly disagree); and individuals who prefer one candidate but expect another to win take more intense stands on issues.

The relationship between consistency and intensity of partisan identification is more stable than the relationships with issue intensity. According to all three indices, consistent respondents are more intense in their party identification. Although there is partisan identification bias in the measures (especially AIP), it appears that the fine distinction which inconsistent respondents make between elements in any consistency-inconsistency triad translate into more intense feelings about issues. Issues require these fine distinctions whereas intense party identification is a more prevalent and stable affect,[37] based on past partisan ties, and susceptible to strong feeling

[37] McPhee, Anderson, and Milholland, "Attitude Consistency," views partisanship as a stable element which has the potential to increase consistency. Also see Converse, "The Nature of Belief Systems in Mass Publics."

by respondents with broader (stereotypical and habitual) perceptual categories.

DECISION TIME ABOUT VOTE DIRECTION

The pattern of association which exists for the relationships between balance-imbalance and time of voter decision is stable across the indices: the indices indicate a strong (and significant) positive association between consistency and an early decision on vote direction. Any incongruence between the elements of attitudinal triads (or dyads in the case of the EP Index) leads to a delay in the vote decision. For example, a respondent who has mixed affects (Democratic-Republican) toward the parties and candidates will tend to delay his decision, as will a respondent who prefers one candidate but expects another to win.

This is not the first instance in which a type of conflict situation related to a delay in decision time. Although Lazarsfeld, Berelson, and Gaudet focused on social (versus attitudinal) cross-pressures and inconsistencies, they found that cross-pressured individuals arrive at a decision late:

> In the first place, it was difficult for them to make up their minds simply because they had good reasons for voting for both candidates. Sometimes such reasons were so completely balanced that the decision had to be referred to a third factor for settlement. The doubt as to which was the better course—to vote Republican or to vote Democratic—combined with the process of self-argument caused the delay in the final vote decision for such people. . . . In the second place, some of the people subject to cross-pressures delayed their final vote decision because they were waiting for events to resolve the conflicting pressures.[38]

Cross-pressures theory posits the existence of conflicts between or among determinants of behavior and its existence leads to avoidance, withdrawal and fluctuation. Although cross-pressures theory and cognitive balance theory share the same basic concerns, the focus for balance theory is the resolution of conflict rather than avoidance and withdrawal. Cross-pressures theory has been used in political science largely in a social rather than psychological-attitudinal context. It was recently tested in an attitudinal context[39] (most similar to the CON Index) and the focus was on one measure of consistency-inconsistency (conflict) which considered fewer relevant factors than those incorporated here, yet the measure enabled the author to tap centrality and magnitude of dissonance. It was found that conflict is not the exclusive motivational principle of human behavior; that there are delays in decision time for cross-pressured respondents at high centrality (based on number of responses), more so than at medium or low centrality; and that there is a decrease in the rate of early decisions as magnitude of dissonance increases. That is, centrality acts as a separate and stronger factor than does tension reduction, and delays in decision time occur when the

---

[38] Paul F. Lazarsfeld, Bernard Berelson, and Hazel Gaudet, *The People's Choice* (New York: Columbia University Press, 1948), pp. 60–61.

[39] Sperlich, "Cross-Pressure and Conflict in Political Behavior," p. 130. This is clearly a departure from early cross-pressures theory.

conflict has attained some strength. These findings are not unlike those presented here, yet the measures cannot tap centrality and magnitude. Furthermore, if there is any centrality bias to the data, it occurs in the direction of high centrality. That is, the elimination of "no affect" responses increases the chance that respondents will be highly central. This may be an explanation for the extraordinary strength of relationships between inconsistency and decision delays.

The data support the contentions of cross-pressures theory which postulate avoidance of decision (conflict) under strain. More importantly, they support cognitive balance theory. The psychological-attitudinal focus of the data and the similar focus for balance theory increase its conceptual importance over cross-pressures theory. Incongruent affects and cognitions about political objects produce psychological tensions which are sufficient to cause a delay in making a decision about vote direction.

POLITICAL INTEREST AND PARTICIPATION

Although the AIP Index lacks some degree of predictive ability, the remaining indices (CON and EP) relate inconsistency to high participation and interest. This is one area in which the possible interpretations according to cross-pressures theory and balance theory are in conflict. According to cross-pressures theory, inconsistency and conflict stimulate withdrawal, avoidance, and reluctance. However, these data suggest modification of this inference. Cognitive consistency theory's emphasis on dissonance resolution is not necessarily congruent with cross-pressures theory's emphasis on withdrawal. For example, a way that an individual can solve his inconsistency between his political expectations and political preferences is to actively seek to alter one of these elements. According to the Expectation-Preference Index, a person who is inconsistent over whom he wants to win and who he thinks will win is very likely to be an active participant. He may participate in order to change his expectation of who is going to win so that a state of consistency can be achieved.[40] Although the short-term effects of the 1964 election seem to be operating, as evidenced by lower participation scores for the inconsistents who expect Goldwater to win but prefer Johnson,[41] there is no clear evidence about motivations beyond the strain toward consistency. For example, on all but two dependent variables (meetings and club membership), the $E_d P_r$ link evidences the highest possible relationship to participation. There is evidence of an interactive effect between expectation and preference and their impact on the dependent variables. That is, the Republican (r) affect seems to play a more positive role vis-à-vis participation when it is combined with a Democratic cognition rather than a Republican cognition.

Except for the interaction effects, a similar pattern of relationships exists for the Directional Conceptualization Index. Given that an individual's

[40] Related panel data support the ease of changing a cognitive component over an affect. Samuel A. Kirkpatrick, "Attitudinal Consistency and Political Behavior," Ph.D. dissertation, The Pennsylvania State University, 1968, Chap. 5.

[41] Generalizations about this cell are difficult because only 7 per cent of the inconsistents were located here.

affect toward parties and candidates (as tapped from unstructured questions) is the most relevant set of variables for his behavior,[42] any internal inconsistency in that set of variables will stimulate action. Although it was not measured directly in this index, it has been shown in a similar context[43] that inconsistent respondents have higher levels of centrality (based on the quantity of responses rather than the quality of responses) and therefore higher activation.

More specifically, the EP Index indicates that individuals who are inconsistent in their preferences and expectations tend to engage in social interaction as measured by political club membership, political meeting attendance, and talking to others. There is supporting evidence to suggest that the existence of imbalance leads to the seeking of social support and the initiation of communications.[44] Festinger comments that "the existence of dissonance in a person leads to a process of social communication by which he attempts to reduce the dissonance."[45] Therefore, there is reason to believe that an individual who prefers one candidate but expects another to win will seek social support to reduce his inconsistency. This social and political group support is in line with his desire to alter his expectation of who is going to win in order to make it congruent with his preference. A more conclusive answer could be given if data were available on the type of meeting he went to or the type of group he joined. This could then be related to his preferences and expectations to see if, for example, an individual who favored Goldwater, but expected Johnson to win, joined a Republican group.

On both the EP and CON Index, inconsistency is related to mass media usage. This should mean that inconsistents seek more information to resolve their unbalanced state. Although this may be the case, the mass media picture is rather complex. Festinger comments that: "If little or no dissonance exists, there would be no motivation (considering this source of motivation alone) to seek out new and additional information."[46] Yet there may also be no motivation to avoid new information. If a respondent is inconsistent he may seek out information which will introduce consonances, or he may avoid information which will increase the existing inconsistency. That is, inconsistency may mean attention or non-attention depending on the content of the information.[47]

[42] Kirkpatrick, "Issue Orientation and Voter Choice in 1964," p. 99.

[43] Sperlich, "Cross-Pressure and Conflict in Political Behavior," p. 130.

[44] Dick H. Baxter, "Interpersonal Contact and Exposure to Mass Media During a Presidential Campaign," Ph.D. dissertation, Columbia University, 1951. A more recent study of political data in this theoretical context is Fred W. Grupp, "Personal Satisfactions Derived From Membership in the Birch Society," a paper presented at the annual meeting of the Southwestern Political Science Association, Houston, Texas, April 3–5, 1969).

[45] A Theory of Cognitive Dissonance, p. 204.

[46] Ibid., p. 127.

[47] Although a content analysis of newspapers read might be helpful, a recent review of selective exposure research supports the inconclusive nature of hypotheses on information seeking and avoidance. David O. Sears and Jonathan L. Freedman, "Selective Exposure to Information: A Critical Review," Public Opinion Quarterly, 31 (1967), pp. 194–214.

Although some research has found a positive relationship between consistency and involvement, this research has either focused on social cross-pressures or it has defined consistency in a different manner. For example, Stein has found that individuals with conflicting or ambiguous opinions on some issues are likely to take only weak action. However, this discovery was made in the context of consistency defined in a more syllogistic (versus psychological) sense as "logical common sense-ness about goals."[48] In a similar context, Lane has found that involvement tends to be associated with greater stability of political attitudes over time, greater consistency in electoral preferences, and greater resistance to conflicting social pressures.[49]

Research has also indicated that the individual strives to confirm expectations: "The events that confirm expectancies are consonant, sought out."[50] The data presented here fail to support this finding because expectancies are accompanied by preferences. That is, the disconfirmation of expectancies may be a motivating factor in human behavior where one's preferences are inconsistent with one's expectancies. Although the exact means of tension reduction cannot be measured without time series data, related sets of longitudinal data have indicated a tendency to change cognitive components (e. g., expectation) before affective ones (e. g., preference). This implies that there is an attempt to change the environment by changing the situation (the fact that the preferred candidate is an underdog) to which the cognitive element corresponds. Although this may be a difficult task, Festinger supports the possibility: "Changing the environment itself in order to reduce dissonance is more feasible when the social environment is in question than when the physical environment is involved."[51] The political environment *is* one which is susceptible to change.

THE INDIVIDUAL IN THE POLITY

Characteristics of individual attitudinal structures do not exist in a state of intrapersonal isolation. After discussing the relationships between individual structures and the consequences of them, there remains a question of relevance for the polity. Man, with his cognitive-affective maps, lives in a total system where the mind and the environment interact. Herbert Hyman has commented that "cognitive processes underly [sic] political participation and party orientation and give meaning to these aspects of political behavior."[52]

The American population exhibits a high degree of consistency between cognitive and affective elements (as measured here) when these elements represent political objects in the real world. Furthermore, related research indicates there is clear strain toward consistency after states of inconsistency have been encountered. When man is viewed as part of a total system of ac-

[48]"Consistency of Public Opinion on Foreign Policy," p. 14.
[49]Robert E. Lane, *Political Life* (New York: Free Press, 1959), Chap. 10.
[50]Brehm and Cohen, *Explorations in Cognitive Dissonance*, p. 178.
[51]*A Theory of Cognitive Dissonance*, p. 20.
[52]*Political Socialization* (Glencoe: Free Press, 1959), p. 20.

tion, the goal of the strain toward inconsistency becomes an inner harmony with oneself and with the environment.[53]

Except for situations of incomplete knowledge, rationality implies cognitive consistency.[54] As an element of rationality, consistency between attitudes toward political objects exists at high levels in the population. The authors of *Voting* have contended that political preferences are not reasoned preferences.[55] Because the present research does not focus on vote direction, it does not attempt to judge this conclusion. However, preferences tend to be in line with sets of affects and expectations. The data presented in this paper support the findings of a small sample of respondents which were based on consistencies between party identification and candidate choice.[56] This early study by Lipset, *et al.*, measured the most likely set of congruent attitudes (party and candidate). Although less likely sets of congruent attitudes have been included here, high rates of consistency have been found.

Nevertheless, there are inconsistents, some of whom fail to resolve inconsistency. For these individuals, psychic pleasure does not seem to be the crucial motivating force: The Benthamite calculus may not be relevant for all goals. For some, delayed gratification may be more important than immediate gratification. The higher an individual's education and self-acceptance, the greater the ability to tolerate ambiguity and to delay states of congruity.[57] Individuals who do not change their attitudinal structures in the face of unbalanced states over time possess infra-threshold intensity. That is, they have not met the threshold of intolerance for inconsistency. As has been suggested earlier, some individuals may actively seek states of imbalance (e.g., the internally passive). External pressures may force man to behave in ways inconsistent with his principles, and he may be presented with new information which is incongruous with previous beliefs.

Those writers critical of restatements of democratic theory are interested in the psychic satisfactions of man (e.g., Wolin[58]). Attitudinal balance is not unrelated to this gratification. Man can attain a form of psychic satisfaction through the strain toward consistency. For example, inconsistents who participate in order to reach a state of consistency may do so on the basis of a type of psychic gratification (yet consistency may be a secondary and instrumental goal to participation). If this inconsistency and the reduction of psychic tension is functional for participatory democracy described nor-

[53] Prescott Lecky, *Self-Consistency: A Theory of Personality* (New York: Island Press, 1945), p. 119.

[54] Scott, "Rationality and Non-Rationality of International Attitudes," p. 11; and Zajonc, "Balance, Congruity and Dissonance," p. 280.

[55] Berelson, Lazarsfeld, and McPhee, *Voting*, p. 311.

[56] Seymour M. Lipset, *et al.*, "The Psychology of Voting: An Analysis of Political Behavior," in Gardner Lindzey, ed., *Handbook of Social Psychology* (Reading, Mass.: Addison-Wesley Publishing Company, 1954), pp. 1124–1175.

[57] Kirkpatrick, "Attitudinal Consistency and Political Behavior," p. 108 ff.

[58] Sheldon Wolin, *Politics and Vision* (Boston: Little, Brown & Co., 1960), Chap. 10.

matively, research on the inner man vis-à-vis his political world can assist in the bridge building that is necessary between empirical research and normative theory. Although complex multivariate techniques will give us a more complete picture of politically active man, it is suggested that there are conceptual and empirical foundations for the phenomenon of "ordering" and that we must begin to build a theory about the role of inconsistent attitude states, subsequent decision delays, and the pursuit of active or passive support in the attainment of congruent states. Despite the exploratory nature of the above findings, the relationship between any environmental socio-political homeostasis and man's inner homeostasis remains a fruitful research endeavor.

APPENDIX: KEY FOR THE INTERPRETATION OF TABULAR ANALYSIS

Dependent Variables (coding). Issue Intensity: high, low, no interest; Intensity of Partisan Identification: strong, not very strong, independent but leaning toward one party, independent, apolitical; Decision Time for Making Up Mind about Vote Direction: knew all along, pre-convention, during convention, during campaign, within two weeks of election day, election day; Interest in the Campaign: (before election) very much, somewhat, not much; Attention Paid to the Campaign: very much, fairly, slightly, no interest; Expect to Vote: yes, probably yes, questionable, probably no, no; Turnout: yes or no; Mass Media Usage: none through use of four forms of media; Talking to Others to Influence Them: yes or no; Attending Political Meetings: yes or no; Political Club Membership: yes or no; Using a Campaign Button or Bumper Sticker: yes or no; Giving Money: yes or no; Political Involvement Index: (based on whether the respondent cares who wins the election and whether he is interested in the campaign) 1 (high) to 8 (low); Political Efficacy Index: (based on the following statements: "People like me don't have any say about what the government does." "Voting is the only way that people like me can have a say about how the government runs things." "Sometimes politics and government seem so complicated that a person like me can't really understand what's going on." "I don't think public officials care very much what people like me think.") very low, moderate, high, very high.

Probability. Due to the low level of measurement necessarily assumed by most of the variables, significance level was determined by Chi-Square tests, with the Yates Correction Factor for 2 × 2 tables. ° = significant at the .05 level. Exact probabilities have been rounded to two decimal places.

Direction of Relationship. + = the positive association of consistency with "high" issue intensity, "high" intensity of partisan identification, an early vote decision, "high" participation and interest, and "high" efficacy. − = a negative association between consistency and the above levels of the dependent variables. 0 = no discernible relationship.

RANK-AND-FILE VERSUS CONGRESSIONAL PERCEPTIONS OF GHETTO RIOTS[1]

HARLAN HAHN

University of California, Riverside

JOE R. FEAGIN

The University of Texas at Austin

THE NUMEROUS GHETTO RIOTS WHICH ERUPTED IN THE SIXTIES RAISED anew the critical issue of the ability of democratic institutions to respond to the needs of a deprived and disaffected minority. As yet, the disorders have not become an organized movement to overturn the existing political structure. The characteristic features of the riots, their confinement to ghetto neighborhoods, the lack of specific targets other than local merchants and police, the relative absence of conflict between black and white civilians, the absence of wide support in the general population, have distinguished them from more violent forms of political upheaval such as revolutions.

While the ghetto riots did not represent an organized attempt to wrest control from existing political authorities, few would argue that they lacked a political purpose. After centuries of frustrating experience with the traditional avenues of political expression, many black Americans displayed their dissatisfaction by adopting a type of protest that could not be ignored. Evidence of dissatisfaction with traditional political mechanisms can be found in the famous Kerner Report, which concluded that the "ineffectiveness of the political structure and grievance mechanisms" was a major complaint in many ghettos. Furthermore, the rioters themselves, according to 1967 Newark and Detroit surveys, were more disaffected with the government and more convinced that anger against politicians was a major cause of the riot than were non-involved ghetto residents; yet these same rioters were actually better informed on political matters than were the non-involved.[2] After the failure of other avenues for expressing dissent, such as voting, petitioning government officials, and nonviolent demonstrations, rioting may well have become a desperate method of communicating ghetto frustration to the outside public.[3]

If one can indeed perceive the riots as a form of political protest, then an important question arises: What were the political effects of the riots? A

---

[1] The authors wish to express their appreciation to Congressional Quarterly, Inc., for permission to re-analyze and incorporate some of their data in this paper and to the University of Michigan for the support which made the Detroit survey possible.

[2] *Report of the National Advisory Commission on Civil Disorders* (Washington, D.C.: Government Printing Office, 1968), pp. 76–82.

[3] Since this was originally written, other analysts have emphasized the political implications of the ghetto revolts. See Jerome H. Skolnick, *The Politics of Protest* (New York: Simon and Schuster, 1969).

comprehensive answer to this broad question would doubtless fill several volumes. The main purpose of this paper is to examine one particular segment of the governmental process, the U.S. Congress, to determine its response to the 1964–1967 ghetto riots; this will be done by contrasting Congressional perceptions with the perspectives of black and white rank-and file citizens. Specifically, differences in perspectives on the causes of, and cures for, ghetto riots will be examined.

THE DATA

Data for this study were obtained primarily from two sources: (1) a survey conducted by the senior author of the black residents of Detroit's Twelfth Street area shortly after the 1967 riot there; (2) a unique survey of U. S. Senators and Representatives conducted by Congressional Quarterly, Inc., in the summer of 1967. The Detroit data will be supplemented, where appropriate, with data from similar post-riot surveys in other black ghettos, particularly the Bedford-Stuyvesant ghetto of New York City (1964).[4] The Detroit survey data were obtained from a modified probability sample of black ghetto residents interviewed by professional black interviewers; the Congressional data were obtained from a mail questionnaire survey that yielded replies from about half of all Senators and Representatives, almost all of whom were white.

RANK-AND-FILE VIEWS ON RIOT CAUSES

A convincing argument might be made that the persons in the best position to assess the causes of urban violence were the residents of the ghetto areas in which riots have erupted. The perspectives of Detroit's Twelfth Street ghetto residents, after the 1967 riot there, can be seen in Table 1. The overwhelming majority (86 per cent) of these black respondents singled out discrimination and deprivation as the main "reasons" for the riot, as key factors in the generation of ghetto tensions lying behind riots. Hostility toward the police and discontent over police brutality ranked second in their list of causes. Only one in seven mentioned criminals or delinquents; and a very small fraction cited agitators or militants as main reasons for the trouble.[5] Of the socioeconomic conditions which

---

[4] For a description of the Bedford-Stuyvesant sample, see Joe R. Feagin, "Social Sources of Support for Violence and Nonviolence in a Negro Ghetto," *Social Problems*, 15 (Spring, 1968), pp. 432–441. The sampling procedure in the Detroit survey was as follows: All blocks in the Twelfth Street neighborhood were stratified on the basis of a socioeconomic status index derived from the value of owner-occupied dwelling units, mean rent, and substandard units (according to the 1960 housing census). Respondents were selected randomly within each stratum; quota assignments in each block were based on age and race. The Detroit sample included 270 Negroes and 37 whites, roughly proportionate to the racial characteristics of the neighborhood; only the data for the black respondents are discussed in this paper.

[5] The "miscellaneous" category in the Detroit study also included 5 per cent of the respondents who cited complaints against government officials as a primary reason for the riots.

TABLE 1

Ghetto Resident Evaluations of Riot Causes[a]
(Detroit, 1967)

	Percentage of Respondents (N = 270)
Precipitating incident (Raid on "blind pig" social club)	8
Reaction to other riots; related to other riots	3
Hostility to police; police brutality	24
Protest discrimination: deprivation	86
Animosity toward whites; revenge	12
Agitation, organized by militants	8
Delinquents, criminals, hoodlums	15
Miscellaneous and vague responses	22
Don't know	14

[a] Question: "What were the two or three main reasons for the trouble?"

have spawned violence, these Detroit respondents emphasized employment problems as the most important; when they were asked whether unemployment, bad housing, or poor police practices was "most likely to produce trouble," more than 60 per cent chose unemployment as the principle cause of civil disorders.

These findings have been confirmed by other surveys of rank-and-file ghetto residents made in riot areas. In a 1964 Bedford-Stuyvesant survey a similar ranking of riot causes was found. A majority viewed the riot there as a protest against the police, discrimination, or deprivation; only a handful saw the activities of agitators or delinquents as the "real cause" of the riot.[6] A Kraft poll after the 1965 Watts riot found that over half of the blacks interviewed mentioned economic problems; one fifth, racial humiliation; one quarter, prior police actions; one sixth, present police actions, as the "real cause" of the violence in Watts. Again, only a small percentage (8 per cent) referred to hoodlums or agitators.[7] The importance of longstanding ghetto complaints was made clear in a UCLA survey, also based on interviews with Watts ghetto residents after the riot there. The survey found that two-thirds of the Watts residents said that long-term grievances,

[6] Joe R. Feagin and Paul B. Sheatsley, "Ghetto Resident Appraisals of a Riot," *Public Opinion Quarterly*, 32 (Fall, 1968), p. 354.

[7] John F. Kraft, Inc., "The Attitudes of Negroes in Various Cities" in *Federal Role in Urban Affairs*, Part 6, Hearings before the Subcommittee on Executive Reorganization of the Committee on Government Operations, U. S. Senate, 89th Congress, 2nd Session, September 1, 1966, pp. 1387–1388.

such as economic deprivation and mistreatment by whites, caused the riot; only one in ten cited criminals, agitators, or extremists.[8]

The pattern of responses found in the riot area surveys was borne out by a much more extensive survey of ghetto residents in 15 major cities, including non-riot cities, conducted by the University of Michigan Survey Research Center.[9] Early in 1968, nearly 3,000 black ghetto residents were asked about the purpose and causes of urban riots. A majority viewed the disorders as "mainly a protest by Negroes against unfair conditions." When asked specifically about the main cause of the disturbances, the respondents emphasized discrimination (49 per cent), unemployment (23 per cent), and bad housing (23 per cent). Only one in ten cited "looters or other undesirables," while one in twenty mentioned militants or radicals as a main cause.[10]

The attitudes of ghetto residents whose lives have been touched by riots provide a sharp contrast to the prevailing opinions of rank-and-file white Americans. In a nationwide poll conducted shortly after the 1967 riots, Harris asked white adults to specify in their own words the "two or three main reasons" for the disorders. By far the most frequent replies fell into the category of "outside agitation." While 45 per cent of the whites interviewed spontaneously cited agitators, much smaller proportions mentioned such things as prejudice (16 per cent) and poverty (14 per cent), ranking a poor second and third, respectively, on the white list of causes.[11] Moreover, in the 1968 University of Michigan survey, 3,000 white urbanites in 15 major cities were asked a question about the main cause of ghetto riots. Leading the list of causes cited by white males in that sample were "looters and other undesirables" (34 per cent) and "black power or other radicals" (26 per cent).[12]

Even many of the predominantly white occupational groups in daily contact with black urbanites seem inclined to blame riots primarily on agitators, militants, or criminals. One important survey of three such groups with extensive ghetto contacts found that samples of policemen (75 per

[8] T. M. Tomlinson and David O. Sears, *Negro Attitudes Toward the Riot* (Los Angeles: UCLA Institute of Government and Public Affairs, 1967), p. 13.

[9] Angus Campbell and Howard Schuman, "Racial Attitudes in Fifteen American Cities" in *Supplemental Studies for the National Advisory Commission on Civil Disorders* (Washington, D.C.: Government Printing Office, 1968), pp. 47–48. These percentages are for the Negro males in the sample, since total figures are not presented; however, the pattern for females is quite similar.

[10] One study of black participants in the Newark and Detroit riots concluded similarly that: "The survey data support the blocked-opportunity theory. One is led to conclude that the continued exclusion of Negroes from American economic and social life is the fundamental cause of riots." Nathan S. Caplan and Jeffrey M. Paige, "A Study of Ghetto Rioters," *Scientific American*, 219 (Aug., 1968), p. 21.

[11] The proportion of Negroes spontaneously citing agitation as a main cause was only 10 per cent. *Newsweek*, Aug. 21, 1967, pp. 18–19.

[12] Campbell and Schuman, "Racial Attitudes," p. 48. These percentages are for males in the white sample, since total figures are not presented. The pattern for white females is roughly similar, although they place greater emphasis on discrimination.

cent white), merchants (70 per cent white), and employers (100 per cent white) placed the greatest emphasis on "criminal elements" and "nationalists and militants" in assessing the main reasons for urban disorders. They also tended, more so than the predominantly black occupational groups also interviewed, to play down the importance of police brutality in their appraisals of theories of riot causation. In contrast, the predominantly black occupational groups interviewed in the same project (educators, social workers, political workers) were more sympathetic to the rank-and-file Negro point of view. Overwhelming majorities of these occupational groups attributed the riots to "unheard Negro complaints;" deviants, whether criminals or militants, received relatively little emphasis in their evaluations of riot causes.[13]

Agitators, especially "Communist" and "outside" agitators, criminals, delinquents, and hoodlums—these are the main reason that riots have occurred, as seen by large proportions of the white population.[14] Conditions in the ghetto are spontaneously mentioned less frequently. Rank-and file black Americans, assessing the same riots, have a substantially different ranking of causes, with conditions of discrimination and deprivation leading their lists, and with agitators and delinquents ranking near the bottom. Thus, recent opinion surveys dealing with riots provide clear evidence of the black-white polarization of rank-and-file perspectives in American society.[15]

CONGRESSIONAL PERSPECTIVES ON RIOT CAUSES

Such a polarization of public attitudes poses a serious dilemma for Congressmen and other public officials. Which of the publics, the blacks or the whites, are they to listen to? With which view should they agree? Large-scale urban disorders obviously cannot be overlooked. For most Congressmen, the white community within which they were socialized has long been a primary reference group in regard to racial matters. Given this, one would expect the orientation of a predominantly white Congress to follow that of the white public. Yet, if the disorders have been a successful means of communicating ghetto problems to white leaders, one might expect the attitudes of Congressmen to parallel the sentiments of black ghetto residents.

An unusual opportunity to examine legislative perceptions of urban riot causes was provided by a Congressional Quarterly poll of Senators and Representatives, who were asked, "What importance would you attribute to the following factors mentioned by various persons as playing

---

[13] Peter H. Rossi, et al., "Between White and Black: The Faces of American Institutions in the Ghetto" in *Supplemental Studies for the National Advisory Commission on Civil Disorders* (Washington, D.C.: Government Printing Office, 1968), pp. 96–97.

[14] For a brief explanation of the American tendency to view causes of social crises in individualistic terms, see Feagin and Sheatsley, "Ghetto Resident Appraisals," p. 362.

[15] Compare David O. Sears and T. M. Tomlinson, "Riot Ideology in Los Angeles: A Study of Negro Attitudes," *Social Science Quarterly*, 49 (Dec., 1968), pp. 485–503.

a significant role in the build-up to the riots?" Table 2 records the percentage of Congressmen, by region and party, that viewed each of the 13
factors as being "of great importance" as a cause of riots.[16]

The causes in the table are listed in rank order of the importance attached to them by the Congressmen. The cause most frequently cited as of
great importance was "joblessness and idleness, especially among young
Negroes." Unfortunately, the phrasing of this item joined the term "idleness" with the somewhat different notion of "joblessness." Two different
perceptions of the job situation were probably present in the replies: (1)
an individualistic view that regarded self-generated lack of initiative or motivation as primary, and (2) an alternative perspective that emphasized
structurally-generated unemployment. That an individualistic perspective
lay behind many Congressional comments seems likely, since this item received more emphasis than other statements that placed the blame un-
equivocally on social conditions or white indifference.

The tendency of Congressmen to rely upon social stereotypes and to
reflect the views of the white constituency was illustrated most dramatically by the second and third ranked causes. More than half of the
southern Democrats and Republicans, as well as a third of the northern
Democrats, stressed a "lack of responsibility among Negroes"; and nearly
half of all the Congressmen believed that "outside Negro agitators" were
of great importance in the build-up of the riots. This general emphasis
corresponded with the prevailing opinions of rank-and-file white Americans who, in the surveys cited previously, have most often blamed irresponsible agitators and criminal elements for ghetto riots. This is in stark
contrast to the de-emphasis which such theories of riot causation have
received among rank-and-file black Americans. For example, only 8 per
cent of our Detroit sample cited "agitation" as a main cause of the riot
there, while just 15 per cent mentioned "delinquents" or "criminals." This
conspicuous lack of emphasis on agitators and criminals has been characteristic of other post-riot surveys of black ghetto residents.

These Congressmen also exhibited a strong tendency to blame the riots
on political institutions other than the federal government itself. The public
agencies that drew the most criticism were "state and local governments,"
cited by 41 per cent for their "neglect of social and economic problems."
Causes that reflected adversely upon Congress such as "insufficient federal
aid" were rated rather low on the list. Significantly, the factor that was
selected *least* often by members of Congress was "Negro resentment

---

[16] Unlike the ghetto surveys, the CQ poll did not use open-ended questions. Percentages are based on the number of Congressmen responding to a given fixed-response
item, a number which varies; inclusion of "no answer" Congressmen reduces the percentages somewhat but does not significantly alter the ranking. Proportions of Congressmen replying "of some importance" or "insignificant" have been omitted from the
tables but can be calculated by subtracting the tabulated figures from 100 per cent.
The raw numbers from which the percentages were calculated were taken from *Congressional Quarterly Weekly Report*, No. 36, Sept. 8, 1967, p. 1738.

TABLE 2

Congressional Evaluations of Riot Causes (1967)[a]

	N	Percentage Replying "Of Great Importance"[b]			
		All Congressmen	Northern Democrats	Southern Democrats	Republicans
Joblessness and idleness, especially among young Negroes	(259)	68	87	54	62
Lack of responsibility among Negroes	(257)	47	33	55	55
Outside Negro agitators	(259)	46	17	62	59
Neglect of social and economic problems by state and local governments	(241)	41	69	31	27
Irresponsible news media coverage of riots	(254)	39	33	55	36
Supreme Court crime decisions	(256)	33	5	56	41
Poor administration of existing federal programs in these areas	(254)	31	18	23	43
Poor police-community relations	(252)	27	44	28	15
White indifference to Negro needs	(254)	26	51	21	10
Insufficient federal aid in such areas as education, job training, anti-poverty, housing, etc.	(250)	26	58	12	8
Irresponsible training techniques in Community Action Programs	(237)	22	13	25	28
Communist agitation	(241)	20	8	38	20
Negro resentment against Congressional inaction or restrictions on Great Society legislation and House exclusion of Adam Clayton Powell	(248)	5	7	6	4

[a] Data presented with permission of Congressional Quarterly, Inc.

[b] Question: "What importance would you attribute to the following factors mentioned by various persons as playing a significant role in the build-up to the riots?"

against Congressional inaction or restrictions on Great Society legislation." Only one Congressman in 20 felt this factor was of great importance as an underlying cause of the riots.

Congressional evaluations of certain causes varied significantly by party and region. The three causes most frequently cited by northern Democrats —joblessness and idleness among young Negroes, neglect of social and economic problems by state and local governments, and insufficient federal aid—were more or less related to social and economic conditions affecting ghetto residents. These causative factors were given much less emphasis by southern Democrats. Southerners placed the greatest emphasis on outside Negro agitators, Supreme Court crime decisions, irresponsible news media coverage, and a lack of responsibility among Negroes. Republican Congressmen most frequently considered joblessness and idleness, outside Negro agitators, and a lack of responsibility among Negroes as causes of great importance. A cause that would be regarded as very significant by ghetto residents—white indifference to Negro needs—was viewed as of great importance by half of the northern Democrats, but by only one fifth of the southern Democrats, and by only one tenth of the Republicans.

RANK-AND-FILE VIEWS ON RIOT PREVENTION

Given the divergent views of black ghetto residents and the predominantly white Congressional sample on the causal factors in the development of ghetto riots, one might well predict differing perspectives on riot prevention. Although numerous ghetto residents have volunteered the response that riots were difficult to avoid, many have not hesitated to suggest possible remedies for riots. The post-riot survey in Detroit posed the question as follows: "Before it started, did you think the trouble could have been avoided or did you feel it had to happen sooner or later anyway?" Fifty-eight per cent of the Detroit respondents initially said that the riot was bound to happen sooner or later, while 27 per cent felt that it

TABLE 3

Ghetto Resident Remedies for Riots (Detroit, 1967)[a]

	Percentage of Respondents (N = 270)
Improve police practices	22
More discussions, negotiations with white leaders	2
Give black people equal rights	27
End job discrimination	15
Improve housing in the area	8
Provide more education, social welfare services	11
Keep criminals, looters at home	17
Could not have been avoided under the circumstances	20
Miscellaneous	11
Don't know	14

[a] See text for questions.

could have been avoided. In follow-up questions, persons in the Twelfth Street area sample were asked why it had to happen, or how it could have been avoided.

Responses to both open-ended questions from the Detroit survey have been combined in Table 3, which reports the proportion of respondents in Detroit that suggested, explicitly or implicitly, various remedies for the riots.[17] It can be seen from examining the table that many people who initially replied that the riot had to happen later touched on possible remedies that might be developed to prevent future urban disorders. The largest proportion of respondents gave answers such as "give black people equal rights." Most stressed the need to improve ghetto conditions and/or to end discrimination as the major means of avoiding the riot, while over one fifth stressed the need for improved police practices. Less than one fifth of these ghetto residents suggested tougher social control measures in regard to deviants and criminals.

Other post-riot surveys have found ghetto residents stressing the need to eradicate oppressive ghetto conditions in order to prevent riots, a logical recommendation given the theories of riot causation which they support. The aforementioned 1964 Bedford-Stuyvesant survey asked "How do you think the trouble could have been avoided?" Articulate in their replies, the largest proportion placed the responsibility for riot prevention directly on the white establishment. Most emphasized the need to alleviate ghetto conditions, to improve police practices, to eliminate discrimination, and to increase black-white communication as the primary means of avoiding disorders. Proposals to suppress local ghetto residents, including juvenile delinquents and criminals, were mentioned by a very small minority (8 per cent). Moreover, few respondents were fatalistic; the overwhelming majority felt that "had certain persons acted differently or had certain intolerable conditions been altered, there would not have been a riot."[18]

A survey after the Watts riot in Los Angeles produced a similar ranking of riot avoidance suggestions. A Kraft poll asked black residents of the area about actions that could have prevented the riot there. In reply, nearly one third focused on police brutality and malpractice issues, one third mentioned the need for increased economic assistance, and one third called for an end to racial discrimination. Again, relatively small proportions mentioned tougher law enforcement (16 per cent) or the need for greater respect for the law (10 per cent).[19] Moreover, this focus on underlying social and economic conditions was also found in the extensive University of Michigan survey of ghetto residents in 15 major cities. Inspecting their data on proposals to reduce the likelihood of riots, the researchers note

---

[17] Those who said that the Detroit riot was inevitable because "it had happened in other cities" and those who guessed "it was planned" have been classified among those who felt the riot "could not have been avoided under the circumstances."

[18] Feagin and Sheatsley, "Ghetto Resident Appraisals," p. 360.

[19] Kraft, "The Attitudes of Negroes," p. 1401.

that over half of the black urbanites spontaneously recommended the "improvement of social and economic conditions as the first solution, with more and better jobs the most frequently offered specific recommendation."[20]

Although the riots represented intense demands for social and political reforms, they failed to yield the desired response from most rank-and-file white Americans. In their fifteen-city survey Campbell and Schuman found that whites assigned top priority to more police control as the "most important thing the city government . . . could do to keep a disturbance like the one in Detroit from breaking out here." Social and economic reforms received less emphasis in the spontaneous white replies to this open-ended question.[21] Lack of spontaneous and enthusiastic support for social and economic reform was apparently based on white failure to recognize the intensity of Negro feelings about ghetto problems. For example, Campbell and Schuman report some data indicating that, when you specifically call it to their attention and talk in terms of long-term goals, a majority of whites will give some support to "trying harder" to improve the conditions of black urbanites, though many will still couple that with tighter police control. Campbell and Schuman make the interesting suggestion that the fundamental difference between rank-and-file blacks and whites may be more one of "salience and focus of attention" than of absolute opposition on the part of whites.[22]

This ability to play down the significance of ghetto conditions and the need for immediate far-reaching reforms was also reflected in the Rossi study of the perspectives of three predominantly white occupational groups with extensive ghetto contacts. In reply to a question, "How well are Negroes treated in (your city)?" three quarters of the police interviewed denied the existence of racial discrimination; similar proportions of the merchants and employers interviewed also denied the existence of racial inequality in their cities.[23] Given these views of white "experts" on the ghetto, it is not surprising that rank-and-file whites do not emphasize the need for crash programs to deal with discrimination and ghetto conditions. The polarization between white and black citizens on these issues, therefore, raised the problem of whether or not Congressmen would exclusively represent the white constituency in framing solutions and enacting legislation to avoid further violence.

[20] Campbell and Schuman, "Racial Attitudes," p. 48.

[21] Only the first responses are tabulated. *Ibid.*

[22] *Ibid.*, p. 37. These data suggest that there is, at least potentially, significant white support for concrete social and economic reforms, should these be emphasized and implemented by progressive political leaders. The failure to implement the necessary reforms in the midst of racial crisis would seem due more to the failure of political leadership than to any other single factor. Compare the argument in Skolnick, *Politics of Protest*, pp. 208–209.

[23] Rossi, *et al.*, "Between White and Black," p. 88. In contrast, overwhelming majorities of the social service groups interviewed in the same study (but 50 per cent or more Negro in composition) acknowledged the existence of racial discrimination.

CONGRESSIONAL PERSPECTIVES ON RIOT PREVENTION

Table 4 presents Congressional evaluations of ten proposals to prevent the recurrence of rioting. While the largest proportion yielded to the propensity to delegate vague responsibilities to state and local officials, thereby again transferring responsibility from the federal level to other governmental levels, sizeable proportions also stressed a moralistic reliance on "traditional church and family values" as well as a program of "private sector involvement." Majorities felt "greater penalties for rioters" and "larger, better-paid police forces" to be of great importance in preventing riots. "Greater expenditures for police anti-riot training" were frequently emphasized. Significantly, suggestions for expanded federal economic programs, such as a "Marshall plan" for the cities and "increased federal aid," ranked near the bottom of the list. Most Congressmen were apparently willing to rely heavily on traditional social control mechanisms to prevent future riots, particularly the reassertion of traditional moral and religious values and tougher police action. There was less emphasis on remedies focusing on ghetto conditions; where such remedies received substantial support they seemed to be vaguely-defined local government programs or private plans rather than massive efforts by the federal government to deal with urban problems.

Although northern Democrats were more likely than other legislators to stress economic assistance, particularly an urban "Marshall Plan," many of them shared the sentiments of their colleagues from the South and from the opposition party regarding traditional moral values, as well as law enforcement tactics. However, legislation designed to void Supreme Court crime decisions received little support among northern Democrats. As reflected in this survey, the general mood of Congress seemed to represent a desire to avoid major social reform or—at best—to escape the responsibility for preventing future riots by delegating it to other public and private agencies.

CONCLUSION

Riots in black ghettos have so far produced few major disruptions in traditional political procedures or perceptions. The grievances of ghetto citizens who have experienced violence have been clearly and powerfully expressed. Black urbanites interviewed after the critical riots in Detroit, Watts, and elsewhere have attributed the disorders to underlying social and economic conditions; moreover, they have placed a predominant emphasis on anti-discrimination and economic assistance programs as specific governmental remedies to prevent future disturbances.

Despite the fact that these ghetto revolts demonstrated extensive dissatisfaction, they have failed to stimulate significant new attempts by the outside white society to understand ghetto problems or to undertake large-scale ameliorative action. In fact, the violence seems to have promoted a growing polarization between rank-and-file white and black Americans. Unlike most of their black counterparts, white citizens have reacted to the

TABLE 4

Congressional Evaluations of Remedies for Riots (1967)[a]

| | N | Percentage Replying "Of Great Importance"[b] | | | |
		All Congressmen	Northern Democrats	Southern Democrats	Republicans
Greater state and local efforts (unspecified)	(257)	74	86	66	68
Emphasis on traditional church and family values	(254)	73	54	85	80
Private sector involvement through such devices as public low-income area development corporations	(235)	66	69	44	74
Greater penalties for rioters and those who incite to rioting	(249)	61	44	77	65
Larger, better-paid police forces	(263)	54	49	64	52
Greater expenditures for police anti-riot training	(258)	42	43	38	43
Legislation to avoid Supreme Court decisions relating to arrest, interrogation of prisoners, etc.	(252)	33	7	46	47
A massive "Marshall Plan" for the cities using federal funds	(239)	26	60	14	4
Gun control legislation	(243)	23	49	18	6
Increased federal aid for urban problems . . . through block grants to the states	(231)	17	11	6	27

[a] By permission of Congressional Quarterly, Inc.

[b] Question: "What importance would you attach to each of the following proposals to prevent recurrences of the rioting?"

disorders by blaming them primarily on militants, agitators, and criminals and by emphasizing increased police control measures to avert them in the future.

The conflicting perspectives of black and white voters have posed an important dilemma for elected representatives. Congressmen might have adopted the perspective of black urbanites on discrimination and the oppressive character of ghetto conditions, supporting the remedial recommendations of those directly affected by such conditions; yet, to adequately represent the views of the white majority, they might have felt compelled to take a diametrically opposite position. Although northern Democrats were more sensitive to socioeconomic problems than other legislators, the prevailing Congressional views on riot causes and remedies seemed closer to that of the white community than to that of black ghettos. Prevailing Congressional sentiment contained a pronounced individualistic and moralistic strain that placed an emphasis on Negro idleness, lack of responsibility, and agitators in assessing the causes of riots, and that pinned hopes for the future on a renewed emphasis on traditional moral values, plus a heavy dose of tougher law enforcement and a vaguely-conceived program of private sector involvement in low-income areas. A minority of the Congressmen emphasized the pervasive role of white indifference and discrimination in laying the groundwork for riots and stressed their own (federal) responsibility for grappling with ghetto conditions with tools equal to the task, such as a massive "Marshal Plan" for the cities.

The polarization not only between black and white Americans at the grass roots level but also between ghetto residents and influential policymakers hints at a bleak prospect for the future. The perennial problem of a visible and disaffected minority within a system of representation based upon majoritarian principles has been raised in a radical new form; and it apparently has been resolved again in favor of the majority. Even in the face of extreme threats to the societal fabric, the majority of Congressmen have continued to neglect the sentiments of black ghetto residents and to provide almost exclusive representation for the white community.

PUBLIC-REGARDINGNESS, RACE, AND SOCIAL CLASS: THE CASE OF A RAPID TRANSIT REFERENDUM

DENNIS S. IPPOLITO
Emory University

MARTIN L. LEVIN
Emory University

I N THEIR STUDY OF NEGRO POLITICAL PARTICIPATION, MATTHEWS AND Prothro echoed the widely held notion that "Perhaps when the Negro middle class becomes fairly large, it tends to become more isolated from other Negroes, more preoccupied with the middle class round of life, less identified with the black masses. A sharpening of class cleavages within the Negro community may lead to some loss of political effectiveness."[1] A crucial implication of this hypothesis is that changes in life style among blacks can be expected to affect their political orientations.[2]

There are, of course, numerous factors which can be considered as political orientations. These include party identification, candidate support, policy attitudes, and the like. One of the more interesting manifestations of a broad political orientation, however, is what Banfield and Wilson have characterized as the "political ethos" of the Anglo-Saxon Protestant middle class.[3] According to Banfield and Wilson, this ethos or style is denoted by an "emphasis upon the obligation of the individual to participate in public affairs and to seek the good of the 'community as a whole.'...."[4] Distinguished from this is the "ethnic" style of politics which emphasizes self-interest and which takes "no account of the community."[5]

Thus, if the black middle class is indeed moving away from its group of origin and undergoing a political reorientation toward white middle class values, one might expect to find middle class blacks and whites taking similar positions on policy issues which are stated in terms of community interest. In other words, where issues of this type are involved, middle class blacks should exhibit a tendency to respond more in terms of their class position than in terms of their race. As Banfield and Wilson state:

[1] Donald R. Matthews and James W. Prothro, *Negroes and the New Southern Politics* (New York: Harcourt, Brace, and World, 1966), pp. 121–122.

[2] For an extended examination of this hypothesis, see Dennis S. Ippolito, William S. Donaldson, and Lewis Bowman, "Political Orientations Among Negroes and Whites," *Social Science Quarterly*, 49 (Dec., 1968), pp. 548–556. This study concluded, however, that "Negroes in the middle- and upper-income and education categories are substantially closer to Negroes in the low-income and education levels than they are to whites with comparable incomes and education" (p. 556).

[3] Edward C. Banfield and James Q. Wilson, *City Politics* (New York: Vintage Books, 1963), Chap. 3.

[4] *Ibid.*, p. 41.

[5] *Ibid.*

One would expect that as the "newer" ethnic groups become assimilated to the middle class, they would become assimilated to the Anglo-Saxon Protestant political ethos as well, and that their interest in ethnic politics would decline accordingly.[6]

At the same time, there is the effect which discrimination or rejection may have upon such political reorientation. Lopreato has argued that "The likelihood of retaining political links with the class of origin (avoiding re-socialization) increases with the degree of status discrepancies, namely, rejection."[7] Thus, the black middle class can be viewed as operating under conflicting pressures. Insofar as social mobility may lead to a loss of iden-tification with the class of origin, some lessening of political cohesion with-in the black community can be expected. On the other hand, the relation-ship of the black middle class to the larger white society is still character-ized by discrimination and outright rejection which may tend to reinforce such cohesion.

A recent survey of the attitudes of registered voters on an issue of com-munity interest, a prospective rapid transit system, provides an opportu-nity to explore empirically some of the factors involved in the relationship between race, social class, and political attitudes. This survey was designed to study the failure of the expenditure referendum for the transit system, and it might be noted that Wilson and Banfield have argued that such referenda are particularly useful tests of "public-regardingness," since vot-ing which is not in accord with one's narrow self-interest on such matters is presumably "based upon some conception of the 'public interest'."[8]

METHODOLOGY AND LOCALE

The survey was conducted in the City of Atlanta, Fulton County, and DeKalb County, Georgia, in the spring of 1969.[9] In November 1968, a ref-erendum was held in these jurisdictions on funding construction of a rapid transit system for the Atlanta metropolitan area. The proposal was de-feated in each of the jurisdictions, albeit by differing margins.[10] The sur-

---

[6] *Ibid.*, p. 42.

[7] Joseph Lopreato, "Upward Social Mobility and Political Orientation," *American Sociological Review*, 32 (Aug., 1967), p. 592.

[8] James Q. Wilson and Edward C. Banfield, "Public-Regardingness as a Value Prem-ise in Voting Behavior," *American Political Science Review*, 58 (Dec., 1964), p. 876. In their usage, "public-regardingness" corresponds to the political ethos of the white middle class noted above. For an interesting examination of the Wilson and Banfield thesis, see Robert L. Lineberry and Edmund P. Fowler, "Reformism and Public Policies in American Cities," *American Political Science Review*, 61 (Sept., 1967), pp. 701–716.

[9] The authors acknowledge the support of the Institute of Public Administration (New York) and the Urban Mass Transportation Authority, U.S. Department of Trans-portation, who provided funding for the survey, and the assistance of Professors Lewis Bowman, Jack Hopkins, and William Pendleton, all of Emory University, who partici-pated in the larger study from which these data are drawn.

[10] Official returns (excluding absentee ballots) showed 43.6 per cent of the Atlanta voters, 37.9 per cent of the Fulton County voters, and 48.9 per cent of the DeKalb County voters voted for the rapid transit proposal.

vey gathered data on the attitudes of registered voters toward the rapid transit proposal—or, as it was widely referred to, the MARTA proposal.[11]

Using a two-stage stratified sampling procedure, personal interviews were conducted with a sample drawn from the official lists of registered voters. Of the 1400 interviews originally contemplated, 1321 were completed, with all respondents interviewed by members of their own races.[12]

FINDINGS

In row 1 of Table 1, the relationship between education, race, and attitude toward the MARTA proposal on election day is presented by jurisdiction.[13] Strong differences appear by education among the whites, with the better educated voter more likely to be favorable to the MARTA proposal. Among blacks, however, no difference by education appears, contrary to what might be expected on the basis of the Matthews-Prothro and Banfield-Wilson arguments.

It is interesting to observe, however, the consequences of introducing as a test variable a measure of the respondent's confidence in local government's ability to solve public problems.[14] As a rough indicator of the respondent's degree of disaffection from local government, it is reasonable to expect this variable to affect the voter's willingness to support innovative local programs, especially those involving large, capital expenditures. However, as shown in rows 2 and 3 of Table 1, while educational differences among whites maintain their effect after the introduction of this test variable, striking differences emerge among blacks.

For whites, both education and attitude toward potential governmental success have an independent effect upon attitudes toward the MARTA proposal. This can be seen quite clearly by examining the weighted meas-

[11] MARTA is the Metropolitan Atlanta Rapid Transit Authority, the statutory body which presented the rapid transit proposal to the voters.

[12] The sample closely mirrored the voting results. The overall percentage favoring MARTA in the actual election was 44 per cent, as opposed to 47 per cent for the sample.

[13] Recalled attitude toward the MARTA proposal on election day has been used in this study even though recall data on the respondents' votes are also available. Attitude was used rather than vote so that the number of respondents in each table after cross-tabulations were made would be increased. In the total sample, 108 persons did not have a definite attitude position relating to MARTA. Of the remainder, 131 did not vote on the proposal but expressed an attitude pro or con. However, of the 1,213 expressing an opinion, only 17 reported voting contrary to their opinion. It should also be noted that the tables are divided into two jurisdictions—Fulton County (including the City of Atlanta) and DeKalb County.

[14] Respondents were first asked to list the major public problem which they thought affected the Atlanta area. They were then asked whether they expected local government to be "very successful," "somewhat successful," "not very successful," or "not successful at all" in solving the problems which they had mentioned. In this paper, "successful" expectations include the "very successful" and "somewhat successful" responses; "unsuccessful" expectations include the "not very successful" and "not successful at all" categories. This variable, then, is an attempt at ascertaining the respondent's attitudes toward government in terms of those governmental responsibilities which the respondent perceives as important.

TABLE 1

Support for MARTA by Race,[a] Education,[b] Occupation, and Attitudes
Toward Governmental Success

| | Per Cent Favoring MARTA | | | | | |
	DeKalb Whites[c]		Fulton Whites		Fulton Blacks	
	Low Ed-ucation	High Ed-ucation	Low Ed-ucation	High Ed-ucation	Low Ed-ucation	High Ed-ucation
Total Sample by Education	44 (194)	62 (342)	42 (184)	62 (191)	39 (127)	37 (51)
Expectation of Governmental Success (by Education)						
Successful	47 (104)	68 (210)	46 (119)	63 (114)	41 (82)	54 (28)
Unsuccessful	41 (90)	53 (132)	34 (65)	60 (77)	33 (45)	17 (23)
Expectation of Governmental Success (by Occupation)	Blue Collar	White Collar	Blue Collar	White Collar	Blue Collar	White Collar
Successful	50 (36)	65 (162)	41 (41)	53 (113)	32 (44)	48 (23)
Unsuccessful	29 (42)	53 (116)	38 (21)	54 (70)	33 (21)	23 (22)

[a] The N's in this table include only those voters for whom the relevant data were complete.

[b] Low education is defined as high school graduate or less. High education is formal education beyond high school.

[c] The number of blacks located in DeKalb County was too small for analysis.

ures of effect for each variable.[15] Thus, for Fulton and DeKalb whites, education explains 20.5 and 17.1 per cent of the variation in MARTA attitudes respectively, while the governmental success variable explains only 7.3 and 11.7 per cent of the variation in each instance.[16] When the educa-

[15] The "measure of effect" employed here was developed by James S. Coleman and designed to be used with attribute data. Basically, it provides a measure of the percentage of variation in a dichotomous dependent variable which can be attributed to each of the independent variables. To account for differences in the size of the bases in the cross-tabulation, a weighted measure of effect was also developed which weights the contribution of each observed percentage difference in the calculations of the effect measure by the inverse of its variance. This procedure was used here. For a complete description of the technique see: James S. Coleman, *Introduction to Mathematical Sociology* (New York: The Free Press, 1964), pp. 189–210.

[16] All of these measures are significantly different from zero at the one per cent level with the exception of the measure of effect of governmental success for Fulton whites which is not significantly different from zero.

tional variable is replaced by occupation, the same pattern of effects obtains. For occupation, the weighted measures of effect are 19.8 per cent for DeKalb whites and 13.4 per cent for Fulton whites. For governmental success, the respective values are 14.1 and 0.0 per cent.[17]

However, the pattern of these independent effects upon MARTA attitudes does not hold for the blacks. Among blacks, the important difference is that while the direction of the effects for the governmental success variable is the same as that among whites, not only do differences in MARTA attitudes by educational level occur where none appeared in the zero-order relation, but the direction of these differences is not consistent with that observed among whites. In particular, among the blacks the highly educated who indicated confidence about local government success showed the highest support for MARTA, while those highly educated blacks who reported little or no confidence in local government exhibited the lowest level of support.[18] An identical pattern is observed when education is replaced by occupation.[19]

SUMMARY

The findings presented here are suggestive in several ways. First, among lower class whites and blacks, support for a measure such as the MARTA proposal is affected by broader attitudes regarding governmental performance. When future governmental performance is assessed positively, support for the immediate proposal is greater than when governmental performance is assessed negatively. However, while the effect of such assessments is discernible, it is generally less than striking.

Second, among middle class whites, support for the MARTA proposal is higher than among lower class whites regardless of expectations about government. These expectations do affect the degree of support among middle class whites, but, once again, the extent of the effect is not overwhelming.

Third, the support of middle class blacks for the MARTA proposal is

[17] For DeKalb whites, the measures are both significant at the one per cent level. For Fulton whites, only the measure for occupation is significant but at the five per cent level.

[18] This particular data configuration has been referred to as the "intensifier phenomenon." According to Coleman, it was first identified by Professor Paul Lazarsfeld in a seminar at Columbia University's Bureau of Applied Social Research. Coleman, *Introduction to Mathematical Sociology*, p. 224. A review of the major findings of this seminar may be found in Edward A. Suchman and Herbert Menzel, "The Interplay of Demographic and Psychological Variables in the Analysis of Voting Surveys," in Paul F. Lazarsfeld and Morris Rosenberg, eds., *The Language of Social Research* (Glencoe, Illinois: The Free Press, 1955), pp. 148–155. In developing his measures of effect, Coleman emphasized the fact that his measures are apt to prove misleading if employed on intensifier attributes. Instead, Coleman suggested as a rough measure of the intensifier effect an index which might be termed the "amplification factor." Coleman, *Introduction to Mathematical Sociology*, pp. 228–229. For the data with education, this value is 8.98; i.e., high education amplified the effect of confidence in government upon MARTA attitudes approximately 9 times.

[19] The value of the amplification factor for white-collar occupation among the blacks is 34.8.

less than the support among middle class whites, but most important, the effect of expectations about governmental success is particularly pronounced among middle class blacks. It appears, then, that the political behavior of middle class blacks is affected by generalized attitudes toward governmental success to an extent which is greater than that characterizing any of the other sub-groups.

Given the publicity which transportation problems receive in the Atlanta area, an issue such as the MARTA proposal is inevitably associated (whether or not the proposal is adequate) with community progress and the public interest. The middle class whites in the study apparently responded to this cue, which lends support to the Banfield-Wilson hypothesis as far as whites are concerned. Among middle class blacks, however, a similar response was manifested primarily among those whose generalized attitudes toward government were positive.

In terms of public policy, it seems that the Matthews-Prothro hypothesis regarding black political orientations may be overdrawn. There is apparently a significant segment of the black middle class which is disaffected about governmental performance and which will, therefore, display political orientations quite similar to those of lower class blacks. This suggestion is consistent with Lopreato's notions concerning status discrepancy and rejection in relation to the maintenance of political attachments between certain middle class and lower class persons. Further, the Banfield-Wilson concept of public-regardingness is perhaps somewhat irrelevant when applied to the black community, since it applies primarily to those middle class blacks who display positive assessments relating to governmental performance.

It is also questionable whether or not white middle class support for various "good-government" or community interest proposals not directly tied to self-interest constitutes "public-regardingness." These types of proposals do serve the white community.[20] Political and social stability, governmental efficiency, and the like are, after all, quite important to the white middle class community.

As the black community becomes still more assertive politically, however, it can be expected to increase its demands for tangible policy benefits. This, likely, will be the case with proposals such as rapid transit. For some middle class blacks, support perhaps can be obtained through appeals to community interest. For other middle class blacks, however, benefits to the black community will have to be made particularly apparent if their disaffection is to be countered and their political support is to be forthcoming.

[20] Wilson and Banfield appear to recognize this when they speak of "self-interest narrowly conceived . . . ." Wilson and Banfield, "Public-Regardingness as a Value Premise," p. 885.

THE IMPACT OF METROPOLITAN RESIDENCE ON SOCIAL AND POLITICAL ORIENTATIONS[1]

JOHN M. ORBELL

University of Oregon

ESPITE THE GREAT INCREASE IN SCHOLARLY ATTENTION PAID TO "THE urban crisis" recently, we still have scant knowledge about the impact of residence in different parts of the city on fundamental social orientations. This is an odd gap since much criticism of the metropolis is based on the assumption that different kinds of areas do affect people in various ways. This paper attempts to fill part of that gap. It studies the impact of residence in different kinds of areas on feelings of personal morale and political efficacy.

The paper is frankly exploratory. Personal morale is chosen as one dependent variable because of long-standing theories relating it to urban residence; political efficacy is chosen as another because, while not unrelated, it is a narrower orientation than morale. The first objective is to isolate the effects of urban differences on these two orientations. The second, a more important objective, but one that cannot be completely fulfilled, is to develop and test theory about the processes relating the orientations to place of residence.

EXISTING THEORY AND DATA

There are two main ideas about *why* place of residence might be expected to affect such basic social orientations as these. The first can be called the structural perspective and has its roots in the social psychology of Cooley and Mead. It views attitudes toward self as derivative from attitudes of others, and concludes that when the individual lacks close social relations with others he will also lack clear attitudinal and behavioral cues. The result is a confused state of mind and anomia—or, in the term preferred here, personal demoralization.[2]

Wirth made the classic statement of how such social psychological processes relate to the specific circumstances of city life.[3] He began with

[1] This is a revised version of a paper originally presented to the 1969 Annual Meeting of the American Political Science Association. The author wishes to thank the National Science Foundation and the Graduate School of the University of Oregon for financial assistance. He also wishes to thank Pat Rutherford and Jim Smith for coding assistance; Stuart Macdonald, Frances Shocket, Warren Dixon and Rich Norling for assistance in data collection and analysis at various stages. Kevin Cox of the Geography Department, The Ohio State University, provided valuable help with the aggregate data in the early stages of the study, and Robert Agger, James Davies, and Joe Allman critically read an earlier draft. Of course, responsibility for the paper is the author's own.

[2] This paper attempts to stay clear of the conceptual and operational confusion revolving around the concepts of alienation and anomia; the term personal demoralization is being used because it has a relatively clear intuitive meaning and does not bring with it the conceptual baggage of the other terms.

[3] Louis Wirth, "Urbanism as a Way of Life," *American Journal of Sociology*, 44 (July, 1938), pp. 8–20.

"a limited number of identifying characteristics of a city" from which he hoped to develop a systematic theory of urbanism. The main variable was density of population; large numbers of people living in a small space resulted in fluid and unstable social relations which, in turn, were the direct cause of anomia.

This formulation paid little attention to variations within metropolitan areas, being more concerned with the differences between cities and rural areas. Subsequent empirical analysis of social relationships in urban areas has tended to disconfirm the central proposition that people living in them lack stable ties with others; family linkages seem particularly important, but there is no shortage of other kinds of friendships either.[4] Wirth has been criticized for generalizing from too limited observations of transitional immigrant areas in Chicago, but his paper remains important because of its recognition that theorizing about "urbanism" must proceed on several levels at the same time. It should specify varying characteristics of urban *areas*; it should specify individual-level psychological processes; and it should proceed to the individual-level consequences of these phenomena. A theory of metropolitan behavior clearly must specify distinctively metropolitan independent variables before it examines behavior, but comparatively few studies of the contemporary metropolis have done this.

The second idea does not depend on the supposed different patterns of interaction in different areas, but rather—in a direct and unmediated way —on exposure to the physical and social conditions that exist in them. Some reform oriented literature (rather optimistically) pays particular attention to the physical environment which is more capable of being manipulated than the social environment. For example:

> With the immense technology available to us, the vast resources at our disposal, and the accumulation of centuries of knowledge, we should be able to make our cities into places which are a joy to behold and a pleasure to experience. Much so-called mental illness and antisocial behavior should abate when these solutions to environmental problems are forthcoming.[5]

Other writing, however, emphasizes the social environment, "the totality of human relations into which an individual enters in his lifetime . . . the all pervasive human environment."[6] Children and adults absorb the cultural values which surround them and respond to the demands of the situa-

---

[4] See especially William Foote Whyte, *Street Corner Society* (Chicago: University of Chicago Press, 1942, 2nd ed., 1955); Harold L. Wilensky, "A Second Look at the Traditional View of Urbanism," in Harold L. Wilensky and Charles N. Lebeaux, *Industrial Society and Social Welfare* (New York: The Free Press, 1965), pp. 121–133; Morris A. Axelrod, "Urban Structure and Social Participation," *American Sociological Review*, 21 (Feb., 1956), pp. 13–18; Robert C. Angell, "The Moral Integration of American Cities," *American Journal of Sociology*, 57 (July, 1951), pp. 1–40; Dorothy L. Meier and Wendell Bell, "Anomia and Differential Access to the Achievement of Life Goals," *American Sociological Review*, 24 (April, 1959), pp. 189–202.

[5] Leo Levy and Harold M. Visotsky, "An Analysis from the Perspective of Mental Health," in Henry J. Schmandt and Warner Bloomberg, Jr., eds., *The Quality of Urban Life* (Beverly Hills, Calif.: Sage Publications, 1969), pp. 247–255.

[6] Hans Blumenfeld, "Criteria for Judging the Quality of the Urban Environment," in Schmandt and Bloomberg, *Quality of Urban Life*, p. 140.

tion. In central areas, particularly the ghetto, crime and violence are significant aspects of the situation and corresponding social attitudes are learned.

Published data on the matter are fragmentary and confusing. To this author's knowledge, only one paper has systematically related variations in urban *areas* to personal demoralization and none has done so for political efficacy. In 1957 Bell showed that anomie (measured by the Srole items) varied significantly with the status of areas when individual status was taken into account; men living in low status areas were more anomic than men living in high status areas.[7] He took four census tracts ranked differently on the Shevky and Bell index of "urbanism" and compared the mean responses of individuals in the areas. This was not the main concern of his paper and he did not explore the processes by which the individual was influenced, but the study did bring "metropolitan" variables and individual variables together in the same analysis.[8]

Apart from this, fragmentary evidence must be pieced together from studies conducted in a particular area or suburb. Mental illness is a somewhat related dependent variable but the one-area approach does not let us draw conclusions about the causal impact of the area variable; studies in central areas have shown high rates of illness, but so have studies in the suburbs.[9] The "suburban critique" literature has emphasized the blandness, conformity, status-seeking, and anxiety said to be associated with suburbia; seldom, however, is there any attempt to distinguish an *effect* of suburban residence from the fact that many bland, status-seeking, anxious people chose to live there.[10]

In the fifties much critical attention was focused on the suburb; in the sixties racial crisis has turned attention to the central areas. Systematic comparative studies have not been forthcoming largely because of a failure to adopt analytic techniques that will permit them.

THE STUDY DESIGN

The study uses a combination of individual and aggregate data; the in-

---

[7] Wendell Bell, "Anomie, Social Isolation, and the Class Structure," *Sociometry*, 20 (June, 1957), pp. 105–116.

[8] Other studies by Bell and his collaborators have done the same, but for dependent variables other than those examined in the present study, see, especially, Wendell Bell and Marion D. Boat, "Urban Neighborhoods and Informal Social Relations," *American Journal of Sociology*, 62 (Jan., 1957), 291–298.

[9] On the central areas and ghettos, see Leo T. Srole, T. A. C. Rennie, and T. S. Langer, *Midtown Manhattan* (New York: McGraw Hill, 1962). On the suburbs, see Richard E. Gordon and Katherine N. Gordon, "Psychiatric Problems of a Rapidly Growing Suburb," *A.M.A. Archives of Neurology and Psychiatry*, 79 (May, 1959), pp. 543–548.

[10] Most importantly, see: William H. Whyte, Jr., *The Organization Man* (New York: Simon and Schuster, 1956), David Riesman, *et al.*, *The Lonely Crowd* (New Haven: Yale University Press, 1950); David Riesman, "The Suburban Dislocation," *The Annals*, 314 (Fall, 1957), pp. 123–246; David Riesman, "Flight and Search in the New Suburbs," in David Riesman, *Abundance, For What?* (Garden City: Doubleday, 1964), pp. 258–269.

dividual data are from a survey of Columbus, Ohio, in 1966,[11] and the aggregate data are based on census tract returns from the 1960 census. A single area variable is used in this study. It is the product of a factor analysis across 18 census tract variables and was clearly identifiable as an "urban-suburban" dimension.[12]

[11] The best available sample frame was the Columbus City Directory which proved a reasonably reliable listing of households. Individuals were sampled from households by a respondent-selection key detailed in Charles H. Backstrom and Gerald Hursh, *Survey Research* (Evanston: Northwestern University Press, 1963), pp. 50–59. Interviews were conducted by graduate students and advanced undergraduate majors in political science. Extensive telephone checking revealed complete reliability of the interviewers. Somewhat over 83 per cent of the interviews attempted were completed. The total N in the sample was 604.

[12] A standard factor analysis was performed and a three-factor solution was obtained. After verimax rotation the single factor explaining the largest amount of the variation was the urbanism factor. The variables loaded on this factor, and the loadings (> .5) are as follows:

Per cent Negro	+
Per cent white collar	—
Per cent dwellings owner-occupied	—
Per cent married	—
Median school years	—
Median income	—
Houses built since 1950	—
Occupational-sex ratio	+

Variables included in the factor analysis, but not loaded on the urbanism factor, are as follows:

Median age of men

Median age of women

College enrolled as per cent of total enrolled in educational institutions

Sex ratio

Those living in same house in 1960 and 1950 as per cent of all persons five years and over

Those who lived elsewhere in central city of this SMSA in 1955 as per cent of all persons five years and over

Those living elsewhere in SMSA in 1955 as per cent of all persons five years and over

Those who lived outside SMSA in 1955 as per cent of all persons five years and over

Those living elsewhere in North and West in 1955 as per cent of all persons five years and over

Those living in South in 1955 as per cent of all persons five years and over

Distance from CBD

The factor scores were normalized and coded as one-half standard deviation units.

The city of Columbus includes (in the SMSA) about 750,000 people who live in the usual range of metropolitan districts. The city has fewer ethnic enclaves than (say) Cleveland, but has several very wealthy all-white areas comparable with the most wealthy suburbs in the United States. The general pattern of status increasing with distance from the central core holds with the single major exception of one high-status suburb adjacent to the ghetto; this area has a disproportionate number of Jews living in it. The ghetto is characteristic of most ghettos in American cities, and there are several "zones of contact" where blacks are moving in and whites moving out. For an analysis of racial attitudes among whites of different status living in different kinds of areas in this city, see John M. Orbell and Kenneth Sherrill, "Racial Attitudes and the

Respondents were assigned the urbanism factor score for the tract in which they lived. It thus became possible to relate their individual-level answers to survey questions to aggregate-level characteristics of their residential environment. This combination of data avoids the weaknesses of aggregate analysis and, at the same time, recognizes that survey respondents are not socially isolated atoms. In Coleman's terms, we are no longer limited to "within-individual" analysis but can relate individual responses to variables external to the individual.[13] Respondents were also asked for the address at which they had lived "for any length of time" and the urbanism score for that tract was also coded, thereby making it possible to take into account the impact of at least one other context to which the individual was once exposed.[14] In the present analysis it will be possible to measure the relative impact of present and past place of residence on the dependent orientations. A modified version of Srole's anomia scale is used to measure "personal demoralization" and an index of political efficacy based on a number of standard items is used for the second attitudinal variable.[15]

Metropolitan Context: A Structural Analysis," *Public Opinion Quarterly* (Spring, 1969), pp. 46–54.

[13] James Coleman, "Relational Analysis: The Study of Social Organizations with Survey Methods," *Human Organization,* 17 (1958–1959), pp. 28–36.

[14] The problem of measurement error, of course, comes up in both of the urbanism indices, but it is most acute for past urbanism. The interviews were conducted in the winter and spring of 1966, and the census data on which the "present" values were based were drawn from the 1960 census. The time lag no doubt involved changes in residential patterns that mean the structure of the area some respondents lived in at the time of the interview was different from what it was when the census was taken. Little can be done but admit this possibility. For the "past" scores the possibility was that the move took place some time *before* the data were collected. To cope with this, at least to some extent, the rule was adopted that if the respondent said he had moved before January 1, 1956, his urbanism score was coded from the 1950 census; if he moved after that date the 1960 census was used. The factor analysis of the 1950 data revealed essentially the same loadings as did the 1960 data, and the same coding procedures were used.

[15] The following are the questions used in the demoralization scale:
1. There's not much use people like me voting because all the candidates are usually against what I want. (20.7 per cent pos.)
2. The Government has little effect on the really important things that happen. (33.6 per cent pos.)
3. Sometimes, I think people ought not bring children into the World, the way things look for the future. (37.4 per cent pos.)
4. Nowadays a person has to live pretty much for today and let tomorrow take care of itself. (50.9 per cent pos.)
5. In spite of what some people say, the condition of the average man is getting worse, not better. (58.2 per cent pos.)
6. These days a person doesn't really know whom he can count on. (76.1 per cent pos.)
   The responses were dichotomized so that only a *strong agree* was considered a positive one. The coefficient of reproducibility is .90. The following quesitons were asked for political efficacy:
1. Some people we've interviewed have said that they find local politics too complex to follow easily, but others say they don't have this problem. How about you? Do you find local politics too complex to be easy to follow, or not too complex to follow?
2. Suppose a regulation were being considered by the Columbus City government that

THE ANALYTIC MODEL

The data on which this study is based let us proceed in the manner of the developing literature on "contextual analysis." As Blalock has pointed out, contextual analysis is "not a substantive theory at all but rather a 'meta-theory' suggesting how variables might be expected to combine."[16] Its distinguishing characteristic is the use of individual-level and group-level measures in the same data-set. Most contextual analyses have involved fairly small interpersonal groups such as work groups but there are some important exceptions.[17]

A "group" effect exists when variation in the dependent variable is associated with variation in the group variable (in this case, an area variable; strictly speaking) independently of individual characteristics. An "individual" effect exists when the dependent variable is associated with individual characteristics independently of the group ones.

Education and race are the two individual variables used in this analysis. Education is used initially in order to help isolate the effect of the area variable from the effect of individual characteristics correlated with it; there is ample literature showing that education is related to both personal demoralization and political efficacy, and highly educated individuals are concentrated disproportionately in the suburban areas.

However, there are good reasons to hypothesize an interaction between education and urbanism for both dependent variables. High education

---

you considered unjust or harmful. What do you think you could do? (The *number* of possibilities was coded)

3. If you made an effort to change this regulation, how likely is it that you would succeed?

4. How likely is it that you would make an effort to change this regulation?

Since the questions did not meet the criteria for an acceptable Guttman scale, a simple index measuring number of efficacious responses was constructed.

[16] H. M. Blalock, "Status Inconsistency, Social Mobility, Status Integration, and Structural Effects," *American Sociological Review*, 32 (Oct., 1967), pp. 790–801.

[17] In sociology, see: Peter M. Blau, "Structural Effects," *American Sociological Review*, 25 (April, 1960), pp. 178–193; James A. Davis, Joe L. Spaeth, and Carolyn Huson, "A Technique for Analyzing the Effects of Group Composition," *American Sociological Review*, 26 (April, 1961), 215–225; Ernest Q. Campbell and C. Norman Alexander, "Structural Effects and Interpersonal Relationships," *American Journal of Sociology*, 71 (Nov., 1965), pp. 284–289; and Arnold S. Tannenbaum and Jerald G. Bachman, "Structural versus Individual Effects," *American Journal of Sociology*, 69 (May, 1964), pp. 585–595. For contextual analysis using larger aggreate units, see: Tapani Valkonan, "Individual and Structural Effects in Ecological Research," paper presented to the Symposium on Quantitative Ecological Analysis in the Social Sciences, Evian, France, September, 1966; David R. Segal and Marshall W. Meyer, "Levels of Political Orientation: A Contribution to the Theories of Mass Society," in Mattei Dogan and Stein Rokkan, *Quantitative Ecological Research* (Cambridge: M.I.T. Press, 1969), pp. 217–232. Two important examples in the political science literature that also use counties as the aggregation unit are: Warren E. Miller, "One Party Politics and the Voter," *American Political Science Review*, 50 (Sept., 1956), pp. 707–725; and Robert D. Putnam, "Political Attitudes and the Local Community," *American Political Science Review*, 60 (Sept., 1966), pp. 640–654. In geography see especially Kevin R. Cox, "The Spatial Structuring of Information Flow and Partisan Attitudes," Dogan and Rokkan, *Quantitative Ecological Research*, pp. 157–185.

does at least two relevant things: first, it provides the individual with internal resources that seem likely to make him less susceptible to whatever impact the context might have; second, it gives him a wider range of interests and correspondingly wider life space which has the same effect.

> Not only do their [the professional and managerial classes] prime interests
> and personal contacts transcend their residential environment, but they also
> enjoy a large measure of mobility, geographical as well as social and occu-
> pational, and greater opportunity of choice. Cosmopolitan in outlook and
> well-equipped by education and resources for the competitive life of modern
> urban society, they have neither the insecurity of the lower middle-class
> white nor the localist bias of the suburban tract dweller. Their investment
> in the neighborhod is negligible, their interest in it as a potential community
> is minimal.[18]

With this in mind, and also Bell's findings regarding anomia and the metropolitan context, we can formulate the following hypotheses: (1) When education is held constant, there will be a positive association between urbanism and personal demoralization (that is, demoralization will be higher in central areas). (2) When education is held constant, there will be a negative association between urbanism and political efficacy. (3) The association between the two attitudinal measures and urbanism will be stronger in both cases among the low educated sub-set.

The first three hypotheses refer to the white population only; since there are literally no blacks living in the great majority of suburban census tracts, there is no point in relating their attitudes to variations in urbanism. However, we can compare them with whites living in other central areas. There is no *prima face* reason why the assumptions underlying the first three hypotheses should not apply to blacks as well as whites; we can argue that the generally lower education of the black population increases the effect of the area variable *in aggregate terms*, but that the individual-level processes are the same. This leads to: (4) When education is held constant, there will be no difference between the demoralization and efficacy scores of whites and blacks living in the central areas.

These hypotheses approach the question of processes by manipulating individual-level variables. Education and race are important because they have implications for the way individuals relate to their residential areas. Nevertheless, a more complete statement of how residential areas come to have their effect would require the exploration of a wider range of dependent orientations and also greater specification of the circumstances in various areas. The hypotheses are based on the assumption that both orientations are affected in the same way by the area variable, but evidence to the contrary would be suggestive since one has to do with general life orientations and the other with the substantially narrower area of politics.

Unfortunately, the data-set does not let us distinguish between aspects

---

[18] Henry J. Schmandt and John C. Goldbach, "The Urban Paradox," in Schmandt and Bloomberg, *Quality of Urban Life*, p. 481.

of the physical environment and aspects of the social environment; dimensions of each are loaded on the urbanism factor. Separation of these, and also greater specification of the role played by interaction patterns in different areas, will have to await more detailed study. Using the data for past place of residence, however, it is possible to elaborate on the causal assumptions contained in the above hypotheses. If it is actually *living* in an area that affects people by changing their attitudes—and not say, selection *into* the area of people already possessing those attitudes—then it should be possible to separate the effects of past place of residence from the effects of present place of residence. Therefore: (5) When the effects of present place of residence are taken into account, past place of residence will have no effect on either orientation.

THE FINDINGS

In most of this analysis urbanism has been broken down into three categories: "urban" or central areas, "mixed," and "suburban" areas. Urban areas are those more than one-half of a standard deviation unit below the mean urbanism value (for census tracts, not individuals), suburban areas are those more than one-half unit above, and the mixed areas are the remainder.

Table 1 provides data relevant to hypotheses one and three, insofar as demoralization is concerned. Education has been dichotomized with "low" being less than a high school graduate. As can be seen, the size of the individual effect depends on the area variable: in suburban areas the high and low educated sets are identical while in mixed areas the difference increases to 15 percentage points and in urban areas to 21 percentage points. Neither of these differences quite reach the .05 level of significance (mixed areas: $X^2 = 3.64$; $P = < .10$; suburban areas: $X^2 = 2.3$; $P = < .20$), but, in view of their general trend, they are worth noticing.

The table also shows a between-area difference within both education categories, and, as predicted, that this difference is greater among the low-educated population (high educated: $X^2 = 8.5$; $P = < .02$; low educated: $X^2 = 10.7$; $P = < .01$). This can also be reflected by the correlation between urbanism and demoralization for the two sub-sets. Using all seven categories of demoralization, and with urbanism broken down into eight

TABLE 1
Per Cent "High" in Personal Demoralization by Urbanism,
with Education Constant (Whites only)[a]

	Suburb	Urbanism Mixed	Urban
Low Education	25.0	40.0	64.5
	(28)	(45)	(31)
High Education	24.2	25.0	43.1
	(178)	(128)	(58)

[a] "High" demoralization includes those respondents falling in the three highest categories of the seven-category scale.

one-half standard deviation units, the product moment correlation for the low educated population is .331 and for the high educated it is .158.

The difference in correlation coefficients cannot properly be taken as a difference in susceptibility—which implies a causal relationship—until other variables have been taken into account. The obvious possibilities are income and occupation. These are both strongly associated with the urbanism index (indeed their aggregate equivalents are important components of that index) and have been related in the literature to the dependent variable. Home ownership and age are also associated with urbanism, and there are intuitive grounds for expecting them to be related to demoralization; however, the latter is not supported by the data, and they have been ignored in the present analysis.[19] When the relationship between urbanism and demoralization is partialled for income and occupation[20] the value remains about the same for the low educated but falls to insignificant levels for the high educated. The correlational data are summarized in Table 2; it seems justifiable to conclude, at least for the low educated population, that there is a causal relationship between area of residence and personal demoralization.

Hypotheses one, two, and three held similar expectations for political efficacy as for personal demoralization, but findings to the contrary are presented in Table 3. There is some suggestion that, among the low educated sub-set, political efficacy increases as the area becomes more suburban, but the trend in the data is not statistically significant. In all areas it is the individual-level variable (education) that makes the difference; we can conclude that, among whites, the metropolitan social context has no in-

---

[19] The correlations with urbanism are .283 and .164 respectively. That home ownership is not *more* strongly associated with urbanism when the aggregate equivalent (per cent homes owner-occupied) is a major component of that variable derives, of course, from the fact that one is an individual measure and the other a summary term for an aggregate. Similar findings with respect to age and demoralization have been reported by Frederic Templeton, "Alienation and Political Participation; Some Research Findings," *Public Opinion Quarterly*, 30 (Summer, 1966), p. 253 and Marvin Olsen, "Alienation and Political Opinions," *Public Opinion Quarterly*, 29 (Summer, 1965), p. 204.

[20] Income was coded in the following categories:

01 under $ 1,000	02 to $1,999	03 to $ 2,999
04 to $ 3,999	05 to $4,999	06 to $ 5,999
07 to $ 7,499	08 to $9,999	09 to $14,999
10 above $15,000		

Occupation was measured by the Duncan index of occupational status. For details of its construction, see: Otis Dudley Duncan, "A Socioeconomic Index for All Occupations," in Albert J. Reiss, Jr., with Otis Dudley Duncan, Paul K. Hatt and Cecil North, *Occupations and Social Status* (Glencoe: The Free Press, 1961), p. 109. Notice that the partials are computed from the zero-order correlations based on the available data for each pair. This means, strictly, that the cases involved are not always exactly the same. The alternative was to compute the partials only from those cases for which all variables were measured. Where two or more variables are partialled simultaneously this could result ni considerable loss of cases and consequent instability of estimates. We prefer the (plausible) assumption that the missing data are distributed randomly.

TABLE 2

The Correlations between Urbanism and Demoralization,
with Education Constant

	Zero-order	Partialling Income and Occupation
Low Education (N:118)	.331	.326
High Education (N:484)	.158	.091

fluence on feelings that one can influence broad political processes. Of course, that central areas have *in the aggregate* more people likely to feel they are unable to influence things is of some significance for the governance of the metropolis.

Hypothesis four predicts that whites and blacks in central areas will be comparable once the effects of education are taken into account. Significantly, this expectation was not borne out. Table 4 shows the relationship between education and demoralization for whites and blacks living in the central areas, and Table 5 shows equivalent data for efficacy. While the difference in demoralization between education categories is about the same (19 percentage points) for whites and blacks in these areas, absolute levels of demoralization are lower for blacks. The difference between the races does not reach statistical significance in either case, but the trend is noteworthy.

TABLE 3

Per Cent "Low" in Political Efficacy by Urbanism,
with Education Constant (Whites only)[a]

	Suburb	Urbanism Mixed	Urban
Low Education	60.7	66.6	74.2
	(28)	(45)	(31)
High Education	45.3	43.6	37.7
	(161)	(112)	(53)

[a] "Low" political efficacy includes all those in the lowest three categories of a five-item index.

TABLE 4

Per Cent "High" in Personal Demoralization by Race, with Education Constant
(Only those respondents living in the central urban areas)

	Black	White
Low Education	50.0	64.5
	(38)	(31)
High Education	30.4	43.1
	(23)	(58)

TABLE 5

Per Cent "Low" in Political Efficacy by Race, with Education Constant
(Only those respondents living in the central urban areas)

	Black	White
Low Education	40.6	74.2
	(32)	(31)
High Education	47.8	37.7
	(23)	(53)

However, there is a significant difference between low educated blacks and whites in the case of political efficacy; blacks are substantially more efficacious than whites ($X^2 = 6.63$; P < .02). Low educated whites with their low levels of efficacy, are the exception in these areas since there is no significant difference between blacks in either education category and high educated whites. Of course, neither these findings nor the findings on demoralization can be attributed in a causal way to place of residence since there is no variation in that—at least in terms of the present measure of urbanism. They are important, though, because of the sharp differences they identify between the black residents of the ghetto and the white residents of the areas close by. Contrary to many current impressions, the blacks appear to be higher in morale and higher in efficacy than many of their close white neighbors. And one cannot project from the relationship, among whites, between urbanism and personal morale to the morale of blacks living in ghetto areas.

Hypothesis 5, dealing with the effects of mobility, suggests an immediacy of the area effect; it is where one lives *now* that is important, not where one lived in the past. Since the previous data show a considerable area effect only for the personal morale of the low educated sub-set, the hypothesis is only tested for that orientation and that population. Table 6 shows the product moment correlations among present urbanism, past urbanism, and personal demoralization for the low educated. As previously, all seven scale items are used, and both urbanism measures are coded in eight one-half standard deviation units.

The first thing to notice is that the correlation between past urbanism and demoralization is lower than that between present urbanism and de-

TABLE 6

Correlations among Present Urbanism, Past Urbanism, and
Demoralization (Low educated population only)

	Past Urbanism	Present Urbanism
Past Urbanism	—	—
Present Urbanism	.368	—
Demoralization	.181	.368

moralization; in itself, this supports the hypothesis. But as we might expect, there is a moderate correlation between past and present urbanism scores, suggesting a tendency for people to move between like areas. When the correlation between past urbanism and demoralization is partialled for present urbanism it falls from the zero-order, .181 to .064. On the other hand, when the correlation between present urbanism and demoralization is partialled for past urbanism it only falls from .311 to .307. We can conclude that the place in which people presently live tends to obliterate the effect of the place in which they have lived previously.

SUMMARY AND SPECULATIONS

The findings of this paper can be summarized as follows:
1. Residence in central areas increases the personal demoralization of low educated whites and residence in suburban areas decreases it.
2. Mobility from one kind of area to another influences the morale of this population: it is where one presently lives that matters, not where one has lived in the past.
3. Residential area has no influence on feelings of political efficacy; this must be explained solely by individual variables such as education.
4. The findings about the relationship between area and demoralization for whites cannot be projected to blacks: although the ghetto is physically similar to some surrounding white areas, blacks living in the ghetto have higher morale than whites living close by.

The analysis identifies three foci of particular theoretical interest. First, what are the *area* conditions likely to promote particular attitudes? Second, what are the *individual* processes that influence the learning of such attitudes? Third, what kind of *attitudes* and *behaviors* are most likely to be influenced? The data provide more speculative opportunities than they do hard conclusions, but the speculations are testable with the use of more elaborate contextual data than employed here.

From the perspective of remedial action-taking, area conditions are often more easy to manipulate than the individual characteristics that influence whether or not (or to what extent) people are susceptible to their local context. As mentioned earlier, Wirth argued that the transient nature of personal contacts in urban areas was important, but from other research on such areas this seems a misrepresentation since there is no particular shortage of close ties there. One plausible explanation for the present findings involves a relatively direct response to the physical environment: decaying buildings and the lack of open space lower the morale of people living in such areas and where the opposite prevails they simply feel better.

If the physical conditions are important, the data on blacks from this study suggest that, at best, the relationship is not a simple one. Of course, we can argue that the urban contexts of whites and blacks are significantly different: the presence of blacks has been shown to affect the racial hostility of whites living in the central areas,[21] and perhaps this also reduces

---

[21] John M. Orbell and Kenneth S. Sherrill, "Racial Attitudes and the Metropolitan

white morale. But a different view might focus on why black morale is *so high* despite exposure to the same—or perhaps much worse—physical conditions, instead of asking why white morale is *so low.* Several possible explanations suggest themselves—most interestingly that supportive interaction patterns in the ghetto, and community values there, might act as a buffer against an otherwise destructive environment. This speculation, if correct, is significant in view of the present discussion about the relative merits of maintaining the ghetto, albeit with major changes in its political and economic structure, or dispersing blacks in some urban melting pot. Considerable attention has been paid to the breakdown of social relations in the ghetto; this speculation suggests that the situation there might be characterized by more interaction than in some white areas.[22]

Although Wirth's view of urbanism has been found deficient at several key points, its strength *as theory* resides in its specification of social psychological processes linking individuals to characteristics of their urban environment. In a very provocative recent paper, Milgram has suggested the outline of an alternate view specifying different social psychological processes, and the present data—although by no means a test of his hypotheses—appear consistent with that view. Milgram begins, like Wirth, with the observation that urban areas contain large numbers of diverse people in close contact with each other.[23] The social psychological concepts he develops are *overload* and the adaptations it requires. Overload ". . . refers to a system's inability to process inputs from the environment because there are too many inputs for the system to cope with, or because successive inputs come so fast that input A cannot be processed when input B is presented."[24] These continuous "encounters with overload" influence role performance, the evolution of social norms, cognitive functioning, and the use of facilities. Adaptations include allocating less time to each input, developing principles of selection, restricting boundaries of social transactions, the use of filtering devices that permit only superficial in-

---

Context: A Structural Analysis," *Public Opinion Quarterly,* 33 (Spring, 1969), pp. 46–54.

[22] Some recent research has shown that "pessimism" (operationalized by a similar scale to that used here for "personal demoralization") tended to increase among blacks as an aftermath of the assassination of Martin Luther King. See Philip Meyer, "Aftermath of Martyrdom: Negro Militancy and Martin Luther King," *Public Opinion Quarterly,* 33 (Summer, 1969), pp. 160–173. This tendency was greatest among the higher educated. Another study has shown that affect toward various political objects became more negative among blacks as a consequence of the same event. See C. Richard Hofstetter, "Political Disengagement and the Death of Martin Luther King," *Public Opinion Quarterly,* 33 (Summer, 1969) pp. 174–179. Since the present data were collected before the recent wave of uprisings and before the assassination of King, it is quite possible that the patterns reported here have changed. Meyer reports an *increase* in political efficacy after King's death, and some impressionistic reports suggest the uprisings might have had the same effect. If this is the case, the present data show that the base line before these events was quite high.

[23] Stanley Milgram, "The Experience of Living in Cities," *Science,* 167 (13 March, 1970), pp. 1461–1468.

[24] *Ibid.*

volvement with others, and the interposition of institutions between the individual and the social world.[25]

The disengagement all of these imply (disengagement from the majority of daily contacts, not necessarily the absence of supportive friendships) is a necessary consequence of inability to process the excessive inputs of the urban environment; given human limits, in this view, life in urban areas might be impossible without them. Other authors have discussed more pathological consequences of the same basic urban conditions. Carstairs, for example, has drawn together findings that imply a relationship between overcrowding and attempted suicide, crimes of violence, alienation, despair, and various neurotic symptoms.[26] Statistics on population growth make his conclusions particularly relevant:

> . . . overpopulation only aggravates the widespread threat to social stability presented by masses of our population who are basically unsure of their personal future, who have lost confidence in their chance of ever attaining a secure place in the community.[27]

The present data, showing that personal morale is lower in urban areas than the less densely populated suburban areas, also suggest the need for elaboration of such models to take account of variations in individual *susceptibility* to urban conditions. One's morale (and, we can hypothesize, the other behaviors discussed by Milgram and Carstairs) is more likely to be influenced by area conditions when one has a "local" orientation as opposed to a "cosmopolitan" orientation, restricted mobility options (that is to say, limited life space), and perhaps when one lacks the internal resources to deal effectively with factors in the environment; these inferences are consistent with the interaction between urbanism and education.

The socialization literature also suggests that one is more likely to be susceptible if one happens to be a child. Children are more susceptible to most learning experiences than adults,[28] and the potential seems especially great when family values and objective environmental conditions act in the same direction. Children living in urban areas are exposed to the same

[25] *Ibid.*

[26] George M. Carstairs, "Overcrowding and Human Aggression," National Commission on the Causes and Prevention of Violence, *Violence in America,* (New York: New American Library, 1969), pp. 730–742. Carstairs draws on evidence from animal studies as well as studies on humans. A study of lemmings by Howard S. Deevey draws conclusions that are also relevant to humans in cities. The problem Deevey seeks to answer is why lemmings engage in their four-yearly suicidal behavior. He concludes that overcrowding—not cyclical interaction between the mammals and their predators —is the basic condition. "Pathological togetherness" produced by very high reproduction rates produces the physiological condition *stress* and its mental counterpart *anxiety.* Deevey traces the physical processes that end in such behaviors as continual fighting, irrational behavior (such as wandering around on the surface in the daytime), and, in general, neurotic symptoms. See Howard S. Deevey, "The Hare and the Haruspex: A Cautionary Tale," *Yale Review,* 49 (Dec., 1959), pp. 161–179.

[27] Carstairs, *Ibid.*

[28] For a useful development of this theme, see Orville G. Brim, Jr., "Socialization Through the Life Cycle," in Orville G. Brim and Stanton Wheeler, *Socialization After Childhood* (New York: John Wiley & Sons, Inc., 1965).

circumstances that lower the morale of their parents, and, in addition, are likely to learn such values from their parents in the normal course of growing up. One of the most frequent reasons people give for wanting to move from the city to the suburbs is that "things will be better for the children in the suburbs";[29] the present data emphasize the social urgency of such moves.

[29] See, for example, Wendell Bell, "Familism and Suburbanization: One Test of the Social Choice Hypothesis," *Rural Sociology*, 21 (Sept.–Dec., 1956), pp. 276–283, and Peter Rossi, *Why Families Move* (Glencoe: The Free Press, 1955).

THE "MOOD THEORY": A STUDY OF PUBLIC OPINION AND FOREIGN POLICY*

WILLIAM R. CASPARY°°
Washington University, St. Louis

T HIS PAPER IS CONCERNED WITH ASSESSING THE STABILITY OF THE AMERICAN public's attention to foreign affairs, and the relationship of this to public support of international programs and commitments. In particular, the paper presents an empirical investigation of the evidence for the "mood theory" proposed by Gabriel Almond as one element of his classic study, *The American People and Foreign Policy*.

The mood theory contends, first of all, that attention to or interest in foreign policy is generally low and subject to major fluctuations in times of crisis.

> The characteristic response to questions of foreign policy is one of indifference. A foreign policy crisis, short of the immediate threat of war, may transform indifference to vague apprehension, to fatalism, to anger; but the reaction is still a mood.[1]

On the basis of this premise about attention, Almond predicts that the *public* will not provide stable support for international commitments undertaken by the U.S. government.

> Because of the superficial character of American attitudes toward world politics . . . a temporary Russian tactical withdrawal may produce strong tendencies toward demobilization and the reassertion of the primacy of private and domestic values.[2]

°Reprinted by permission of the author and publisher, from William R. Caspary, "The Mood Theory: A Study of Public Opinion and Foreign Policy," *American Political Science Review*, 64 (June, 1970), pp. 536–547.
°°This research is a segment of a larger project on public reaction to international events (see also William R. Caspary, "United States Public Opinion During the Onset of the Cold War," *Peace Research Society (International), Papers*, 9 (1968), pp. 25–46; and "Dimensions of Attitudes on International Conflict," *Peace Research Society (International), Papers*, 13 (1970, forthcoming). This research has been partially supported by grants from Northwestern University and Washington University. Survey data of the National Opinion Research Center (NORC), and the American Institute of Public Opinion (AIPO), was obtained from the Roper Public Opinion Research Center. Supplementary survey data was provided by the library of NORC. The author gratefully acknowledges the help he received from these sources and from individuals associated with these institutions.
It may interest the reader that, during the more than four years that have elapsed since this article was first written in substantially the present form, my own interests have shifted considerably. If one is passionately concerned as I am with the injustice of the U.S. globalist—or, if you will, imperialist—foreign policy, research of the sort presented here seems a rather sterile exercise. My current work is devoted to a study of the economic, ideological, and bureaucratic sources of American interventionism in the undeveloped world.

[1] Gabriel A. Almond, *The American People and Foreign Policy* (New York: Frederick A. Praeger, 1960), p. 53.
[2] *Ibid.*, p. 55. See also pp. 60, 80, 99, 106.

The acceptance of this view by scholars is evidenced by its presentation in important textbooks and treatises.[3] As far as I have been able to determine it has not been challenged.

The empirical investigation in this paper considers evidence on both of these variables—attention = interest, and support for foreign policy commitments.

It should be remembered that Almond warned against over-reaction to the Soviet threat as well as the tendency to demobilize. Discussion in this paper of popular support for American foreign policy should not be taken as indicating the author's support for the "globalism," the "Pax Americana" strategy that characterizes that policy today.

I. STABILITY OF POPULAR SUPPORT FOR OVERSEAS INVOLVEMENT

In marked contrast to the mood theory is a result we have obtained from national public opinion poll data gathered by the National Opinion Research Center (NORC). This result is the remarkable stability of strong pop-

FIGURE 1.

Percent supporting an active part in world affairs for the U.S., over time.

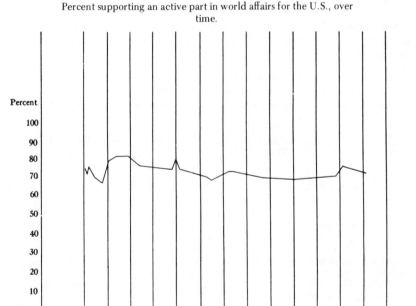

[3]See, for example, James N. Rosenau, *Public Opinion and Foreign Policy* (New York: Random House, 1961), pp. 35–37; Martin C. Needler, *Understanding Foreign Policy* (New York: Holt, Rinehart and Winston, 1966), p. 23; Edgar S. Furniss, Jr., and Richard C. Snyder, *An Introduction to American Foreign Policy* (New York: Rinehart, 1955;, p. 198; Bernard C. Cohen, *The Political Process and Foreign Policy* (Princeton: Princeton University Press, 1957;, p. 55.

ular support for an active U.S. role in world affairs. Trend data on the item: "Do you think it will be best for the future of the country if we take an active part in world affairs, or if we stay out of world affairs?" are shown in Figure 1. The average percentage favoring an active part is 71 per cent. The standard deviation of the points from the average is only 1.8 per cent, less than the expected sampling error. This remarkable stability occurred over a time of violent change in world affairs from war to peace and demobilization, through the onset of the Cold War and the shock of the Korean struggle. The popular commitment to an active U.S. role, however, did not appear to waver.

Some of these data were available when Almond wrote. His evaluation of this item on an active part in world affairs, however, stressed that it is an "emotionally loaded question" which evokes responses that misrepresent the amount of concern Americans have for foreign affairs. Nevertheless, I find that the respondent's answers to this question is an excellent predictor to his response on a wide range of policy questions involving international commitments. The tests of this relationship are shown in Table 1. Across 47 different tests, the average value of gamma is .50.

In the light of the strong association between the stable internationalism indicator and specific policies, it is not surprising to find that support for individual policies is also fairly stable (see Figure 2). Support for military aid to Europe was followed in NORC polls over an eight-year period. The support which fluctuated around 50 per cent of the sample during the late forties gave way to slightly higher, but equally stable support after the

FIGURE 2.

Percent supporting internationalist policies, over time.

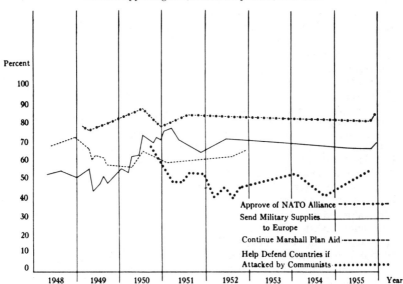

TABLE 1

Association Between Support for an Active U.S. Role in
World Affairs and Specific International Policy Commitments

Survey Number	Policy	Gamma
124, Korea worth fighting		.58
Talks fail: pull out, hold line, attack		-.48
Defend other countries if Communists attack		-.61
127, Too many sacrifices for defense		-.39
137, Aid, as cut, is too much, right, not enough		-.35
Do more to help Indochina		.48
105, U.S. was right to send troops to Korea		.64
If Communists attack other countries, help defend		.74
Continue Marshall aid		.50
Approve NATO agreement		.66
Send military supplies to Europe now		.50
Send troops to Europe now		.39
Too many sacrifices for defense		-.39
Send military supplies to Asian countries threatened by Communists		.28
U.S. has gone too far with the problems of the world		-.76
094, Send military supplies to Europe now		.50
Continue Marshall aid		.53
Marshall aid is too much		-.38
As cut by Truman, Marshall aid is too much		-.44
Stop Communists from spreading in Asia		.53
Important for U.S. to cooperate with Arab countries		.35
Important for U.S. to cooperate with France		.47
Important for U.S. to cooperate with Greece		.47
Important for U.S. to cooperate with Israel		.33
Important for U.S. to cooperate with India		.42
Important for U.S. to obtain Middle East oil		.42
Important for U.S. to stop spread of communism in the world		.48
091, Continue Marshall aid		.58
Marshall aid too much		.51
Aid really helps U.S.		.64
Aid has been stopping communism		.42
Countries would go Communist without aid		.26
Aid is getting Europe on its feet		.22
They could get along without aid		-.58
Use U.S. troops to stop Communist attack in Europe		.57
Use U.S. troops to stop Communist attack in South America		.37
Use U.S. troops to stop Communist attack in India		.49
Send military supplies to Europe		.34
Stop communism in Asia		.58
Real concern for England's finances		.62
078, Satisfied with Marshall Plan		.46
Continue Marshall Plan next year		.73
Spending too much on Marshall Plan		-.54
Send military supplies to Europe now		.44
Keep occupation troops in Germany		.74
Keep occupation troops in Japan		.68
Keep occupation troops in Korea		.65

Korean war. Though data were collected for shorter periods, the results for Marshall Plan aid, military aid to Europe, support for NATO, and willingness to intervene militarily against a Communist attack also show impressive stability.

To a certain extent, Almond's interpretation allows for these findings. He formulates the concept of "permissive mood" to characterize the passive acceptance by the public of internationalist policies formulated and urged by its offical leaders.[4] He sees this permissive mood as a particular characteristic of the Cold War situation in which the threat of the Soviet Union at least temporarily forces Americans to accept international commitments. Almond repeatedly warns, however, that this is a mood response and not an intellectually structured one. The mood may change if the international environment does. "The undertow of withdrawal is still powerful."[5]

The question is whether Almond would have anticipated the amount of stability that our data indicate. Suppose we give a more precise formulation of Almond's analysis as follows: the percentage of people supporting international commitments will vary directly with the percentage perceiving a given level of threat from the Soviet Union. To test this, we will use as an indicator of perceived threat, the expectation of war. This indicator has several things to recommend it. It correlates strongly with various other items on expectations of Russian behavior, and trend data is available which is sensitive to changes in Soviet behavior and pronouncements.

Comparison between the trends in expectation of war and in support for an active U.S. role is shown in Figure 3. As we have already seen, support for an active role scarcely fluctuates. Expectation of war, on the other hand, shows fluctuations up to 50 per cent. Clearly a direct ratio between the two variables does not hold.

A weaker formulation that is also consistent with Almond's analysis that support for an active role should remain steady at some high level as long as perceived threat is above some threshold value. In this formulation, support for an active part would decline sharply if perceived threat fell below the threshold. From 1947 through 1953, the period covered by our data, more than 47 per cent of the population expected war within ten years. But in November, 1946, when NORC first asked about expectation of war, only 28 per cent thought it likely within ten years. If the question had been asked in the immediate postwar lull, the figure would probably have been even lower. Nonetheless, support for an active part remained steady around 70 per cent at these times.

In any event, the threshold formulation has weaknesses on theoretical grounds. The aggregate results with which we are dealing come from summing over individuals who are likely to exhibit different thresholds and to perceive different amounts of threat at a given time. A slight easing in Soviet pressures would probably mean that all individuals would perceive slightly less threat. If Almond is correct that the commitment is only a re-

---

[4] Almond, *The American People and Foreign Policy*, p. 88.
[5] *Ibid.*, p. 85.

FIGURE 3.

Internationalism and perceived threat, over time.

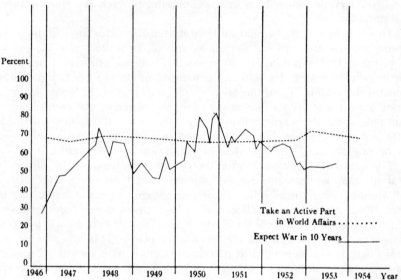

sponse to threat, some individuals would cross their personal thresholds and no longer feel compelled to support an active U.S. role.

II. MENTION OF INTERNATIONAL PROBLEMS AS AN INDICATOR OF "ATTENTION" OR "INTEREST"

Almond's pessimistic expectation of unstable commitments is based on his belief that the characteristic response of Americans to foreign policy issues is indifference. His data lead him to see "(1) the extreme dependence of public interest in foreign affairs on dramatic and overtly threatening events; (2) the extraordinary pull of domestic and private affairs even in periods of international crisis."[6] This conclusion is based upon trend data on one questionnaire item.

> On of the most interesting accumulations of evidence on this general question of the focus of public attention is a series of Gallup polls which has been conducted since 1935. On more than twenty occasions during the fifteen-year period the American Institute of Public Opinion has asked a sample of the public: "What do you regard as the most important problem before the American people today? . . . The form of this question has the advantage of registering spontaneous responses. In the multiple-choice or 'yes-no' type of question one can never be sure that the respondent draws a clear distinction between what really is on his mind and what he thinks ought to be on his mind. The undirected response is a more reliable indication of the real degree and extent of spontaneous interest in foreign policy problems.[7]

[6] *Ibid.*, p. 72.   [7] *Ibid.*, p. 71.

This question was coded for whether the respondent mentioned an international problem or a domestic one. The percentage of the sample mentioning international problems over the years, as reported by Almond, is shown
in Figure 4.[8] If this item is indeed an indicator of attention to or interest

FIGURE 4.

Percent mentioning international problems as most
important, over time.

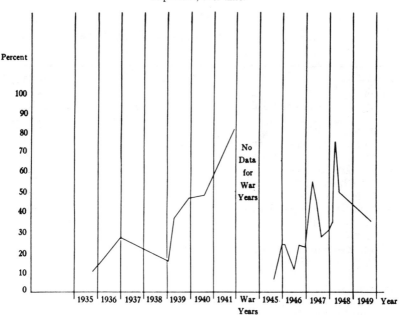

in foreign affairs, then it is plain that there have been dramatic fluctuations
in interest and/or attention. It is also clear, as Almond elaborates in his
book, that the peaks of the trend line come at times of international crisis
such as the Communist coup in Czechoslovakia and the Italian elections of
1948. Similarly the troughs of the curve show preoccupation with domestic
concerns such as economic reconversion in the wake of World War II.

But is the mention of an international problem really an indicator of interest or attention? It would seem on the face of it that this is so, but surprisingly enough this response shows rather weak association with the respondent's judgment of how interested he is in China (gamma = .157), the
United Nations (gamma = .141), and England's financial crisis (gamma =
.146). It may be that, as Almond says, the open-ended question is a more
trustworthy indicator since it does not structure the replies or favor a partic-

[8] *Ibid.*, p. 73.

ular alternative. On the other hand, one would expect a somewhat stronger association between the two.

To test this further, let us look at another indicator of attention—whether the respondent says he has heard or read of a particular foreign policy issue or international event. This item was frequently used and we have a total of 12 tests of association between it and mention of an international problem. These are shown in Table 2. Although the association is quite weak (gamma

TABLE 2

Association Between Mention of International
Problems and Awareness of Issues

Survey Number and Date	Heard or Read	Gamma	Per Cent Who Did Not Hear or Read
078, June 29, 1948			
	Reorganization of Berlin (and have opinion)	.22	60
084, January 26, 1949			
	Tito-Stalin split	.08	53
	Indonesia dispute	.11	48
	Truman's inaugural speech	.04	40
510, January 9, 1953			
	H-bomb	.12	20
	Universal military training	.00	40
596, March 4, 1958			
	Foreign aid bill	.07	43
628, May 24, 1960			
	U-2 incident	.26	6
631, July 14, 1960			
	U.S.-Cuba relations	.26	17
648, July 25, 1961			
	Berlin dispute	.27	13
663, September 18, 1962			
	Our troubles with Cuba	.65	6
664, October 17, 1962			
	The Peace Corps	.24	28
	Berlin dispute	.39	11

less than .13) for five of these, the rest show stronger association. In all but one of these cases it turns out that the attention items cut the population into a large group aware of some important event and a small group that is unaware. It appears that only the people at the bottom of the attention scale differ significantly from the rest in their tendency to mention international problems. I shall discuss the significance of this finding in Section III.

The question about hearing or reading of an event, like the one about interest, may tempt the respondent to give a false report in order to gain the interviewer's approval. The respondent cannot, however, falsify replies to requests for factual information. Five such questions have appeared on surveys along with the item on the most important problem facing the country. The results of tests of association between these two variables are shown in Table 3. Three of the tests show very weak association (gamma less than .09). Of the other two, one uses an indicator that discriminates a small group at the bottom of the attention scale. Finally, some additional

TABLE 3

Association Between Mention of International Problems and Factual Knowledge and Other Indicators of Attentiveness

Survey Number and Date	Indicator or Attentiveness	Gamma	Per Cent Don't Know or Wrong Answer
066, April, 1947	Know that the U.S. has joined an organization for world peace	.26	36
084, January 26, 1949	Know who is Secretary of State	.03	40
078, June 29, 1948	Know if fighting still going on in Palestine	.08	51
	Know if some Jewish groups are opposed to the Jewish government in Palestine	.09	66
648, July 25, 1961	Know what a geiger counter is	.25	29
066, April, 1947	Belong to organization in which foreign affairs are discussed	.09	
078, June 29, 1948	Report some impression of the Greek government (favorable or unfavorable)	-.05	
	Report some impression of the Chinese government (favorable or unfavorable)	-.11	
084, January 26, 1949	Believe that a citizen can influence his government by writing letters, or taking miscellaneous other actions; or don't know, or believe citizens can't or shouldn't have influence	.13	

TABLE 4

Association (Gamma) Among Indicators of Attention to or Interest in World Affairs

	Heard or Read	Interest	Factual Knowledge	Active Part	Well Informed	Belong to Organization
Heard or read of event, person, program, etc.	098: .64 084: .81 664: .79					
Interested in event, issue, person, etc.	088: .70 .44 .51 077: .34 .37 .12 .21	091: .73 .56 .58 088: .65 .64 .57 054: .60 .40 .65 077: .75 .58 .69 .48 .59 .70 082: .72 .67 .70 .75 .74 .83 083: .16 .51 .77				
Factual knowledge of event, person, etc.	084: .67 .70	648: .69 054: .31 .53 .31				
Want U.S. to take an active part in world affairs	094: .54 078: .44	091: .48 .43 .37	127: .57			
Consider self well informed about event, person, etc.		688: .51 .34 .35 .18 .53				
Belong to organization in which world affairs are discussed			066: .36 079: .78 .71 .73 .77 .74 .81			

Note: Number in italic is identification number of survey.

miscellaneous indicators of attention were used. The results are shown in Table 3. All the associations were weak (gamma less than .14).

The result of these tests (with two minor exceptions) appears to be that for all but the very least attentive respondents an increase in mention of international problems is not likely to be associated with an increase in attentiveness. Though there might have been reason to doubt this negative result on the basis of any one of these indicators, the consistent findings across all of them strengthen that interpretation.

As a further check on the validity of the various attention indicators we constructed a matrix of intercorrelations among them as shown in Table 4. Some of the cells of the matrix are fuller than others because on many surveys not all of the various kinds of indices occurred together. We see in this matrix that all but three of the tests of association show gamma greater than .30 and that most of them are quite strong (gamma greater than .50). This suggests that there is a single dimension of attention which is tapped more or less by all of these items. Structured and unstructured questions, reports of interest and factual knowledge, and actual behavior such as membership in organizations where foreign affairs are discussed all seem to be loaded on this dimension. Do trend data exist on these other attention indicators that compares in frequency with the most-important-problem data. The best that is available is four occurrences of the item, "How much in-

FIGURE 5.

Interest in the U.N. and mention of international problems, over time.

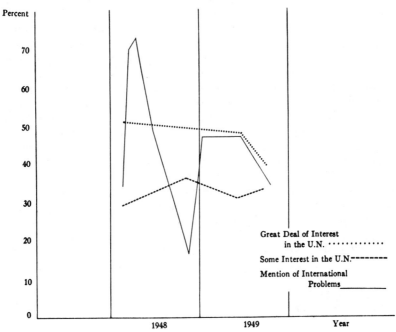

terest do you take in the United Nations Organization?" A comparison between this item and the mention of international problems as most important is shown in Figure 5. It is fortunate that the National Opinion Research Center poll which showed no change in interest in the U.N. at the end of 1958 was taken within a few days of the Gallup poll which registered a striking decline of mention of international problems. This indicates stability of attention to international affairs at a time when domestic events appear to have been exerting a great pull on people's attention. Thus we have not only cast doubt on the evidence from which Almond inferred instability, we have found evidence to the contrary.

III. RATE OF MENTION OF INTERNATIONAL PROBLEMS BY THE MOST
ATTENTIVE RESPONDENTS

We have seen that the mention of international problems does not seem to be associated with this attention dimension, except to the extent that those very low on attention mention international problems somewhat less. Almond, on the contrary, singles out the *most* attentive group as the one that should be different! He expects that stable attention will be characteristic of only those individuals whose attitudes show "intellectual structure" and factual content.[9] To meet this criterion, an individual must "have explicit evaluations of the relative costs and efficiency of alternative means of maximizing the value position of [his] country."[10]

Have we actually shown that this top attention group is not more likely to mention international problems? That would be demonstrated only if the attention tests we have used are finely enough calibrated to discriminate between this group and the others. Almond does not give a clear operational procedure for isolating this "attentive public," but Rosenau estimates on the basis of circulation figures for quality media that the attentive public is "no larger than ten percent of the population and possibly much smaller."[11] Roper gives a similar estimate.[12]

A few of the attention indicators we have used discriminate a top group on the order of 10 per cent of the population or less, but show weak association with mention of international problems. To check this result, scales were constructed by taking the sum of the scores on two or three separate items. In no case is the top attention group sharply distinguishable from the neighboring ones in frequency of mention of international problems.

If the attentive public indeed has a stronger and more stable tendency to mention international events this difference should show up most at times when the overall percentage of people mentioning international events is low. At times of relative international calm, or at times when domestic events pre-empt attention, only the attentive public would continue to have its eye focused on international problems and mention them to the inter-

[9] *Ibid.*, p. 56.
[10] *Ibid.*
[11] Rosenau, *Public Opinion and Foreign Policy*, p. 40.
[12] Quoted by Rosenau, *ibid.*

viewer. The lowest level reached in mention of international problems was 28 percent (AIPO Survey No. 596, March, 1958.)[13] The degree of association between mention of international problems and one indicator of attention (heard or read of foreign aid bill) was still quite low (gamma = .07, see Table 2). For all other surveys on which attention measures were available the per cent mentioning international problems was 37 per cent or over, and for all but three it was greater than 50 per cent.

IV. INTERPRETATION OF THE WEAKNESS OF MENTION OF INTER-NATIONAL PROBLEMS AS AN INDICATOR OF ATTENTION

It would appear, then, that a strong case has been made against using the mention of international problems as most important as an indicator of attention. The reader may wonder why such a major effort was mounted in this paper on behalf of the negative result of contesting the validity of a single indicator. There are several reasons: (a) the indicator has been widely used: in addition to Almond's work and the many citations of it, Smith, and Deutsch and Merritt, have made important empirical studies which rely upon this indicator;[14] (b) a major proposition about the instability of American foreign policy attitudes based on this indicator may now be called into question; (c) we may be at a stage in the development of this area of inquiry at which it is appropriate to turn from sweeping and imaginative theory construction to the more mundane task of rigorous testing of individual indicators and propositions; (d) we have striven by using a variety of indicators and techniques to make the most of a data pool not designed to produce answers to this particular question. What would be desired, of course, would be an elite sample as well as a general population sample, and a battery of interest and attention measures. Given such data we conceivably could still find that the "most-important-problem" indicator proved to discriminate between the general public and a much smaller elite group on the order of less than 1 per cent of the population. Even for such a elite, however, there are reasons to suspect that this measure will not be a valid measure of attentiveness.

(a) This indicator is a measure of primacy of attention, not of strength of attention. An individual who is inattentive to both international and domestic problems might be slightly less inattentive to international ones and mention one of these as most important. Conversely an individual strongly interested in politics may be slightly more interested in domestic than international issues and mention a domestic one to the interviewer.

(b) The use of the word "today" (or "now" in some variants) may do a

---

[13] A slightly different interpretation of these marginals from AIPO Survey No. 596, item 2, has appeared in an article by Deutsch and Merritt. See appendix for details.

[14] Paul A. Smith, "Opinions, Publics, and World Affairs in the United States," *Western Political Quarterly*, 14 (1961), 698-714; Karl W. Deutsch and Richard L. Merritt, "Effects of Events on National and International Images," in Herbert C. Kelman, ed., *International Behavior* (New York: Holt, Rinehart and Winston, 1965).

great deal to structure the responses by focusing upon immediate problems and crises rather than broad, long term issues. The crisis dominated aspect of public responses which Almond found[15] may be purely an artifact of this wording. Though this interpretation cannot be tested with available data, it is not hard to see how it would be tested in the future. One could simply substitute the phrase, "over the next ten years" for "today."

(c) Mention of international problems as most important is also uncorrelated with indicators of isolationism. Thus there must be substantial numbers of people whose responses were coded as international who are of isolationist persuasion. When they mention international problems it may be with the thought of how best to withdraw from them. If the isolationists tend to be less attentive than the rest of the population, then their presence would lower the attention score for the group that mentions international

TABLE 5

Variation in Attention with Internationalism Within Mention-International-Problems-Group

Measure of Attention	Mention International Problems			Mention Domestic Problem		
	Military Aid to Greece			Military Aid to Greece		
	Approve	Disapprove	Total	Approve	Disapprove	Total
Acheson named	47%	34%	40%	41%	39%	40%
Aware of change	22	27	25	23	24	23
Not aware of or don't know	31	39	35	36	37	37
	100	100	100	100	100	100
Heard or read of Tito-Stalin dispute	59	50	54	49	38	44
Didn't hear or read	41	50	46	51	62	56
	100	100	100	100	100	100
Heard or read of Indonesia conflict	64	56	59	54	43	49
Didn't hear or read	36	44	41	36	57	51
	100	100	100	100	100	100
	n=246	322	567			

	Send Military Supplies to Europe Now			Send Military Supplies to Europe Now		
	Approve	Disapprove	Total	Approve	Disapprove	Total
Acheson named	47	31	40	40	35	38
Aware of change	23	27	25	24	22	23
Not aware of change	30	42	35	36	43	39
	100	100	100	100	100	100
Heard or read of Tito-Stalin dispute	61	41	53	43	49	46
Didn't hear or read	39	59	47	57	51	54
	100	100	100	100	100	100
Heard or read of Indonesia conflict	62	51	57	50	52	51
Didn't hear or read	38	49	43	50	48	49
	100	100	100	100	100	100

[15] Almond, The American People and Foreign Policy, p. 72 (see quote, above, p. 444, note 6).

problems. Evidence that this does happen is shown in Table 5. The variation within the four major cells of the table is greater than the variation between them.

V. CONCLUSION

The mood theory was summarized at the start of this paper as having a premise—generally low and unstable attention to foreign affairs—and a conclusion—unstable support for foreign policy commitments. Empirical evidence has been presented in these pages to show that both the premise and the conclusion are false.

On the basis of these findings I suggest the following alternative interpretation: that American public opinion is characterized by a *strong* and *stable* "permissive mood" toward international involvements. Although I have not included any data analysis on current opinion it is tempting to speculate that the support by the long-suffering American public of ten years of fighting—and four years of heavy combat—in Vietnam is an indication of the existence of a permissive mood. It also indicates that such a mood provides a blank check for foreign policy adventures, not just a responsible support for international organization, genuine foreign assistance, and basic defense measures. Almond by no means ignored this line of thought—indeed the notion of permissive mood is his own and he stressed its dangers. There is no indication, however, that he anticipated the strength or stability of commitment to American foreign policy that our data suggest. He appears to have been heavily influenced (as have a number of other commentators) by evidence which we have demonstrated on closer examination to be of dubious validity. Finally it should be noted that we have dealt here with only one element of the rich array of theory and findings in Almond's classic work.

APPENDIX

TABLE A1

Interpretation of Responses on "Most Important Problem," AIPO Survey 596, March 1958

AIPO Code[a]	Per Cent Responding[b]	Gallup Press[c] Release	Deutsch and[d] Merritt	This Paper
"11 Peace; prevention of war; keeping out of war; fear of war, etc.	8			
12 Foreign affairs; international problems, general	4			
13 Relations with Russia (general)	2	"keeping the peace 17%"	"foreign policy interest 17%"	
14 Threat of Russia, threat of Communism; communism	3			
15 World Economic problems	0			
16 Foreign aid, general	1			international problems 28%
17 Problems of Space (general)	0			
18 Arms race—atomic bombs, missiles	3			
19 Rockets, missiles—space problems	4			
21 Problems of the Atomic age (general)	1			
29 Miscellaneous International Problems				
31 National Security; preparedness, national defense; defense program"	3	"national defense 3%"		
Total	29			
"32 Clean Government; honest leaders, etc.				
33 Balancing the budget	63			domestic problems 63%
34 Taxes (etc., 35–52; other domestic problems)"				

[a]Obtained from Roper Public Opinion Research Center.

[b]Tabulated from survey cards.

[c]"'Unemployment' Named No. 1 Worry for First Time Since '37," *Public Opinion News Service*, for release March 23, 1958, American Institute of Public Opinion.

[d]Karl W. Deutsch and Richard L. Merritt, "Effects of Events on National and International Images," in Herbert G. Kelman, ed., *International Behavior* (New York: Holt, Rinehart and Winston, 1965, p. 161). (Note: an error in the text of the Deutsch and Merritt article states that the survey took place in May but their information clearly identifies it as number 596 which was done in March, 1958.

SOCIAL CLASS AND DIMENSIONS OF FOREIGN POLICY ATTITUDES[1]

MARTIN PATCHEN
Purdue University

IN A RECENT ARTICLE, HAMILTON HAS PRESENTED EVIDENCE THAT LOWER class people were more likely than others to oppose "tough" military initiatives in Korea and Vietnam.[2] He interprets these data to indicate that low status groups are " 'moderate' and conciliatory" on these foreign policy issues and that their foreign policy attitudes are inconsistent with Lipset's description of working class authoritarianism.[3]

The purpose of this paper is to summarize and comment upon other evidence relevant to the issues Hamilton has discussed—especially evidence from another national survey of public attitudes concerning U.S. policy in Vietnam and toward China. On the basis of the evidence reviewed, some conclusions will be drawn about the relation between social class, foreign policy attitudes, and authoritarianism which differ from those of Hamilton. The issues considered will also lead to a consideration of the basic dimensions underlying attitudes on foreign affairs.

THE SPRING 1964 S.R.C. STUDY

First, I will summarize some of the results of a representative national survey, based on a sample of 1,501 Americans, conducted by the Survey Research Center of the University of Michigan in the spring (May-June) of 1964. One section of that survey, directed by this writer,[4] concerned public perceptions of Communist China, attitudes about U.S. policy towards Communist China, and attitudes concerning U.S. policy in Vietnam. The original report of the survey showed the association between opinion on these issues and a variety of social and personal characteristics (education, sex, level of information, region, age and political affiliation).[5] However, in this paper I will focus on the relation between opinions and social class—looking at education, income, and occupation as components of social class, with particular attention to education.[6]

---

[1] Helpful comments on an earlier version of this paper were made by Alvin Richman.

[2] R. Hamilton, "A Research Note on the Mass Support for 'Tough' Military Initiatives," *American Sociological Review*, 33 (June, 1968), pp. 439–445.

[3] S. M. Lipset, "Democracy and Working Class Authoritarianism," *American Sociological Review*, 24 (Aug., 1959), pp. 482–502; S. M. Lipset, *Political Man* (New York: Doubleday, 1960).

[4] The study was under the general direction of Angus Campbell. It was sponsored by the Council on Foreign Relations, a private, non-partisan organization.

[5] M. Patchen, "The American Public's View of U.S. Policy Toward China," Appendix to A. T. Steele, *The American Public and China* (New York: McGraw-Hill, 1966).

[6] The data on the relation of foreign policy opinions expressed in this survey to income and occupation are presented here for the first time. The data for this additional analysis were made available by the Inter-University Consortium for Political Research.

ATTITUDES TOWARD DEALING WITH CHINA

General Attitudes. Those persons (43 per cent of the total sample) whose previous answers indicated that they were aware of the existence of both the Communist government and the Nationalist government on Formosa were asked this open-ended question:

> Some people say we should deal with Chiang Kai-shek's Nationalist government on Formosa as the government of all China, and have nothing to do with Communist China. Other people say we should support the Nationalists as the government of Formosa but should deal with the Communists as the government of the rest of China. Do you have an opinion about this or not? (If yes: How do you feel about this?)

Support for dealing with Communist China by education, family income, and occupation of the head of the household[7] (not necessarily that of the respondent), is shown in Table 1. In general, support for dealing with Communist China increased substantially as education increased.[8] Similarly, support for dealing with the Communist government was greatest among those whose family incomes were $15,000 and over while opposition to dealing with Communist China was greatest among those with family incomes under $5,000. (However, between the two extreme income groups, variations in income were not appreciably related to support for dealing with Communist China.)

Comparing various occupational categories, the ratio of general support to non-support for relations with Communist China was highest among clerical workers and was fairly high among the two highest status categories (professional and technical; managers, officials, and proprietors). Intermediate in support for relations with China, with about equal percentages in favor and opposed, were those in sales occupations, craftsmen and foremen, operatives, and laborers and service workers. Greatest general opposition to dealing with Communist China was expressed by people in farm occupations.

Taken together, the data concerning education, income, and occupation are generally consistent in showing those in lower class positions to have been more opposed to the general idea of dealing with Communist China than were those at the upper class levels of our society.[9] Other evidence from the study indicates that such opposition reflects feelings of hostility

---

This part of the analysis was performed with the assistance of The Institute for the Study of Social Change, Purdue University.

[7] Interviews were conducted almost exclusively with heads of households and with the wives of heads of households.

[8] More detailed tables, not shown here, show that higher education remains associated with general willingness to deal with Communist China when those in separate age categories are examined separately.

[9] While opposition to "having anything to do with" Communist China increased as education decreased, those with less schooling were not appreciably more likely than others to favor American support for a Nationalist attack on Communist China. Support for such a policy was fairly uniformly low (from 8 to 14 per cent) within all educational strata. Explicit opposition to American support for such an attack did rise slowly (from 54 to 69 per cent) as respondents' education increased from grade school to college completion, but this difference is relatively small and reflects pri-

TABLE 1

General Support for Dealing with Communist China, for Persons of Different Education, Family Income, and Occupation of Family Head[a]

	Deal Only With Nation- alists	Deal With Com- mu- nists Too	Other An- swers[b]	No Opin- ion	No An- swer	Total Per- cent
By Education						
Grade School (N=90)	30	21	14	30	5	100
Some High School (N=70)	40	20	9	27	4	100
Completed High School (N=235)	22	31	16	25	6	100
Some College (N=114)	21	43	10	19	7	100
College Degree (N=140)	23	48	11	11	7	100
By Family Income						
Under 5,000 (N=162)	28	26	13	26	7	100
5,000–7,499 (N=149)	28	35	11	21	5	100
7,500–9,999 (N=141)	22	38	13	23	4	100
10,000–14,999 (N=131)	27	35	17	16	5	100
15,000 and over (N=69)	19	42	7	25	7	100
By Occupation of Family Head						
Professional and Technical (N=148)	26	40	13	16	5	100
Managers, Officials, Proprietors (N=121)	19	36	9	28	8	100
Sales (N=42)	24	24	14	33	5	100
Clerical (N=48)	23	48	8	17	4	100
Craftsmen and Foremen (N=89)	24	30	18	20	8	100
Operatives (N=76)	28	28	17	22	5	100
Laborers and Service Workers (N=37)	27	30	5	38	0	100
Farmers and Farm Managers (N=34)	41	12	15	26	6	100
Total Sample (N=652)	25	34	13	22	6	100

[a] Only persons who were aware of the existence of both Chinese governments are included in the table. Those whose education, income, or occupation could not be ascertained are included in total sample. Persons in a variety of occupations coded as "miscellaneous" are not included in occupational breakdown.

[b] See Patchen, "The American Public's View," p. 266, for a further breakdown of these other answers.

and distrust toward Communist China.[10] Of those (at all status levels) who opposed dealing with Communist China, most gave reasons which indicate hostility or distrust, including the belief that we should oppose Communist governments, attribution of aggressive intentions to Communist

---

marily a larger proportion of "no opinion" answers among those with less education, rather than a larger proportion favoring support of an attack.

[10] Patchen, "The American Public's View," p. 270.

China, perception of negative or dangerous qualities of the Chinese people or leaders, and the opinion that dealing with Communist China means giving in to them. Since support for having "nothing to do with" Communist China was more frequent among lower status persons, it appears that negative attitudes (hostility, distrust) toward Communist China were stronger at the bottom of the social class spectrum.[11]

Reaction to Specific Contacts. After respondents had expressed their opinions about general U.S. policy toward China, a number of questions were asked to assess willingness to support specific co-operative initiatives toward Communist China. The interviewer said, "Now the President of the United States might decide that it was in our best interest to take certain new actions with regard to Communist China. For each thing I mention, would you tell me how you would feel about it if the President suggested that action?" Five possible actions were mentioned: encouraging visits between Americans and Chinese: exchanging ambassadors; talking over problems of Asia; selling things like wheat; and letting Communist China join the United Nations.

The data indicate that, although there was no consistent relation between social class components and support for an exchange of ambassadors with Communist China, there was a consistent tendency for those of higher class to approve of the four other possible contacts more than did those of lower class. These relationships are strongest with respect to support for visits between Americans and Communist Chinese and for selling things like wheat to Communist China. The data concerning these two types of contacts are presented in Table 2.

The percentage of persons willing to approve these contacts rose substantially as education increased[12] and similarly, rose as family income increased. Occupational level of the household head was not consistently related to support for these conciliatory initiatives, although there was a slight tendency for those of upper occupational status (or their spouses) to be more willing to endorse the proposal for inter-nation visits than are those from families headed by persons of lower occupational status.

In general, the data of Table 2, especially those concerning education and income, indicate that more willingness to have specific friendly contacts with Communist China was found among those of higher social class than among those of lower social class. These data are consistent with the

---

[11] While the reasons for opposition to a policy of dealing with Communist China were not tabulated separately for those of different educational levels, a reading of many interviews indicated that lower class respondents were at least as likely as others, if not more so, to explain their opposition to dealing with China on grounds indicating hostility to China rather than on more legalistic arguments or in terms of positive feelings toward the Nationalists.

[12] Inspection of more detailed tables, not shown here, shows that when age is controlled, there remains an association between higher education and support for contacts with China among younger age groups (18–24, 25–34, 35–44) but that the association is less consistent among older age groups.

data of Table 1 which suggest the same conclusion with respect to a more general attitude toward dealing with Communist China.

ATTITUDES CONCERNING U.S. POLICY IN VIETNAM

Whereas higher social class was associated with an apparently conciliatory, non-militant attitude toward Communist China, social class had an *opposite* relation to opinions about U.S. policy in Vietnam.

All those people who said that they had heard about the fighting in Vietnam (74 per cent of the total sample)[13] were asked their opinion concerning each of "a number of things the United States might do about the situation in Vietnam."[14] The possible U.S. actions mentioned, one at a time, were: (1) "the United States getting out of the Vietnam war completely"; (2) "our continuing to give arms and training to South Vietnam troops fighting against the Communist rebels"; (3) "using American forces in Vietnam if the Communist rebels are winning, even if this means our risking war with Communist China";[15] (4) "trying to make some compromise agreement with Communist China on this—like making all Vietnam neutral." It should be noted that each respondent could agree or disagree with each possible policy independently, rather than trying to choose among them.

Concerning the idea of American withdrawal from the Vietnam war, those of higher social class—especially with respect to education and family income, but also with respect to occupation of family head—were more likely than those of lower class to oppose withdrawal (see Table 3).[16]

Concerning the United States continuing to give arms and training to South Vietnam troops (aside from "advisors," this was the actual extent of U.S. involvement at the time), those of higher social class—especially with respect to education—were most likely to favor this policy while, among those of lower social class, support was not as strong. However, large majorities at every educational, income, and occupational level supported the "aid" policy and the differences among class levels were not great.

Opinion about using American troops, which had not yet been sent to Vietnam in large numbers, was much more sharply divided (41 per cent in favor, 42 per cent opposed for the total sample). Support for using Ameri-

---

[13] At the time of the survey (spring 1964), the war had not yet come to dominate the attention of most Americans, as it did later, but events and battles in Vietnam were often baner headline news.

[14] For each possible action, respondents were presented the following alternatives printed on a card: strongly in favor of it; in favor of it but not very strongly; against it, but not very strongly; strongly against it; no opinion on this.

[15] This item was phrased in this fashion both because of the general focus of the study on U.S.-China relations and because there was much discussion in the media at this time of China's possible involvement in the war or in a settlement.

[16] Better educated people, especially college graduates, were more likely than others to oppose withdrawal even when age was controlled (in more detailed tables, not shown). The relation between more education and opposition to withdrawal was particularly marked among the younger age groups.

TABLE 2

Support of Two Hypothetical Presidential Suggestions for Closer Relations
With Communist China, for Persons of Different Education,
Family Income, and Occupation of Family Head[a]

A. "Suppose the President suggested visits between Americans and people from Communist China—like newspapermen from each country visiting the other?"

	In favor	Against	No Opinion	No Answer	Total Percent
By Education					
Grade School (N=183)	59	24	17	0	100
Some High School (N=148)	62	19	19	0	100
Finished High School (N=415)	79	12	8	1	100
Some College (N=169)	76	17	5	2	100
College Degree (N=162)	82	14	4	0	100
By Family Income					
Under 3,000 (N=152)	53	25	19	3	100
3,000–4,999 (N=160)	69	20	10	1	100
5,000–7,499 (N=274)	75	13	11	1	100
7,500–9,999 (N=215)	78	14	7	1	100
10,000–14,999 (N=201)	76	15	8	1	100
15,000 and over (N=87)	82	11	7	0	100
By Occupation of Family Head					
Professional and Technical (N=201)	76	15	8	1	100
Managers, Officials, Proprietors (N=178)	77	15	7	1	100
Sales (N=63)	76	11	13	0	100
Clerical (N=84)	79	13	5	3	100
Craftsmen and Foremen (N=162)	70	19	11	0	100
Operatives (N=152)	66	18	15	1	100
Laborers (N=45)	73	20	7	0	100
Service Workers (N=41)	63	17	20	0	100
Farmers and Farm Managers (N=56)	66	18	16	0	100
Total Sample (N=1088)	73	16	10	1	100

B. "Suppose the President suggested selling things like wheat to Communist China?"

	In favor	Against	No Opinion	No Answer	Total Percent
By Education					
Grade School (N=183)	41	50	8	1	100
Some High School (N=148)	38	49	12	1	100
Finished High School (N=415)	41	46	12	1	100
Some College (N=169)	43	48	7	2	100
College Degree (N=162)	54	43	3	0	100
By Family Income					
Under 3,000 (N=152)	31	54	12	3	100
3,000–4,999 (N=160)	45	45	9	1	100
5,000–7,499 (N=274)	40	47	12	1	100
7,500–9,999 (N=215)	47	48	5	0	100

TABLE 2 (Continued)

	In favor	Against	No Opinion	No Answer	Total Percent
10,000–14,999 (N=201)	47	44	9	0	100
15,000 and over (N=87)	51	40	9	0	100
By Occupation of Family Head					
Professional and Technical (N=201)	49	43	7	1	100
Managers, Officials, Proprietors (N=178)	47	44	7	2	100
Sales (N=63)	41	54	5	0	100
Clerical (N=84)	51	35	11	3	100
Craftsmen and Foremen (N=162)	40	48	12	0	100
Operatives (N=152)	34	53	11	2	100
Laborers (N=45)	47	42	11	0	100
Service Workers (N=41)	34	51	15	0	100
Farmers and Farm Managers (N=56)	48	41	11	0	100
Total Sample (N=1088)	43	47	9	1	100

[a] Only persons who were aware that mainland China has a Communist government were asked these questions. Those whose education, income, or occupation could not be ascertained are included in the total sample. Persons in a variety of occupations coded as "miscellaneous" are not included in occupational breakdown.

can troops was strongest among those with a college degree. As one moves down the educational ladder, the support found for use of American troops decreases.[17] (See Table 3-B.)

However, for the two other indicators of social class—family income and occupation of family head—there is no consistent relation between social status level and support for sending troops to Vietnam.

Support for the final policy option mentioned—trying for a compromise agreement, like making all Vietnam neutral—is greatest among those with the least education[18] and at the lowest occupational levels. However, as shown by Table 3-C, there was no consistent relation between income and support for a compromise.

Among those in various occupational groups (and their wives), support for a compromise was greatest among farmers, laborers and service workers, with craftsmen and foremen, clerical workers, and operatives all showing substantial margins of support for this policy. Opposition to a compromise agreement was strongest among those in sales jobs, with op-

[17] When age was controlled, there was no appreciable relation between education and support for using U.S. troops in the two youngest age groups (18–24, 25–34) but some positive relation between education and support in most of the older age categories.

[18] The association between more education and opposition to a compromise settlement holds generally for all age groups, except the 45–54 group.

TABLE 3

Support for Several Possible Policies in Vietnam (1964), for Persons of Different
Education, Family Income, and Occupation of Family Head[a]

A. "Getting out of the Vietnam war completely."	In favor	Against	No Opinion	No Answer	Total Percent
By Education					
Grade School (N=201)	34	38	24	4	100
Some High School (N=155)	31	43	25	1	100
Completed High					
School (N=428)	28	55	16	1	100
Some College (N=170)	24	55	19	2	100
College Degree (N=161)	19	75	5	1	100
By Family Income					
Under 3,000 (N=161)	30	38	27	5	100
3,000–4,999 (N=167)	27	47	25	1	100
5,000–7,499 (N=280)	29	55	15	1	100
7,500–9,999 (N=232)	28	57	14	1	100
10,000–14,999 (N=202)	24	61	13	2	100
15,000 and over (N=86)	28	55	16	1	100
By Occupation of Family Head					
Professional and					
Technical (N=206)	24	66	9	1	100
Managers, Officials,					
Proprietors (N=180)	23	57	18	2	100
Sales (N=64)	27	58	15	0	100
Clerical (N=83)	33	45	21	1	100
Craftsmen and					
Foremen (N=178)	32	47	20	2	100
Operatives (N=160)	24	53	21	2	100
Laborers (N=43)	35	51	12	2	100
Service Workers (N=53)	38	23	37	2	100
Farmers and Farm					
Managers (N=54)	35	37	24	4	100
Total Sample (N=1127)	28	53	18	1	100

B. "Continuing to give arms and training to South Vietnam troops fighting the Communist rebels"					
By Education					
Grade School (N=201)	61	15	21	3	100
Some High School (N=155)	71	10	17	2	100
Completed High					
School (N=128)	76	13	10	1	100
Some College (N=170)	82	9	8	1	100
College Degree (N=161)	86	11	2	1	100
By Family Income					
Under 3,000 (N=161)	58	15	21	6	100
3,000–4,999 (N=167)	75	10	14	1	100
5,000–7,499 (N=280)	77	10	12	1	100
7,500–9,999 (N=232)	77	13	9	1	100
10,000–14,999 (N=202)	84	9	5	2	100
15,000 and over (N=86)	73	15	12	0	100

TABLE 3 (Continued)

	In favor	Against	No Opinion	No Answer	Total Percent
By Occupation of Family Head					
Professional and Technical (N=206)	81	12	6	1	100
Managers, Officials, Proprietors (N=180)	78	11	9	2	100
Sales (N=64)	81	8	11	0	100
Clerical (N=83)	75	11	13	1	100
Craftsmen and Foremen (N=178)	71	13	15	1	100
Operatives (N=160)	74	9	14	3	100
Laborers (N=43)	70	16	12	2	100
Service Workers (N=53)	59	11	28	2	100
Farmers and Farm Managers (N=54)	70	19	9	2	100
Total Sample (N=1127)	75	12	11	2	100

C. "Using American Forces in Vietnam if the Communist rebels are winning, even if this means our risking war with Communist China."

	In favor	Against	No Opinion	No Answer	Total Percent
By Education					
Grade School (N=201)	33	41	22	4	100
Some High School (N=155)	35	44	19	2	100
Completed High School (N=428)	41	42	16	1	100
Some College (N=170)	40	43	16	1	100
College Degree (N=161)	53	37	9	1	100
By Family Income					
Under 3,000 (N=161)	32	37	25	6	100
3,000–4,999 (N=167)	44	40	15	1	100
5,000–7,499 (N=280)	40	40	19	1	100
7,500–9,999 (N=232)	41	44	15	0	100
10,000–14,999 (N=202)	45	43	11	1	100
15,000 and over (N=86)	37	51	12	0	100
By Occupation of Family Head					
Professional and Technical (N=206)	42	44	14	0	100
Managers, Officials, Proprietors (N=180)	37	44	17	2	100
Sales (N=64)	48	34	18	0	100
Clerical (N=83)	36	48	15	1	100
Craftsmen and Foremen (N=178)	41	40	18	1	100
Operatives (N=160)	43	35	19	3	100
Laborers (N=43)	37	42	19	2	100
Service Workers (N=53)	21	47	30	2	100
Farmers and Farm Managers (N=54)	41	44	13	2	100
Total Sample (N=1127)	41	42	16	1	100

D. "Trying to make some compromise agreement with Communist China on this—like making all Vietnam neutral?"

TABLE 3 (Continued)

	In favor	Against	No Opinion	No Answer	Total Percent
By Education					
Grade School (N=201)	44	20	32	4	100
Some High School (N=155)	46	24	28	2	100
Completed High School (N=428)	51	25	23	1	100
Some College (N=170)	42	38	19	1	100
College Degree (N=161)	39	47	14	0	100
By Family Income					
Under 3,000 (N=161)	39	23	32	6	100
3,000–4,999 (N=167)	43	28	28	1	100
5,000–7,499 (N=280)	50	26	23	1	100
7,500–14,999 (N=202)	51	28	20	1	100
15,000 and over (N=86)	48	34	18	0	100
By Occupation of Family Head					
Professional and Technical (N=206)	45	38	17	0	100
Managers, Officials, Proprietors (N=180)	44	32	23	1	100
Sales (N= 64)	28	36	36	0	100
Clerical (N=83)	53	27	18	2	100
Craftsmen and Foremen (N=178)	52	25	22	1	100
Operatives (N=160)	48	25	24	3	100
Laborers (N=43)	51	19	28	2	100
Service Workers (N=53)	43	13	40	4	100
Farmers and Farm Managers (N=54)	65	17	16	2	100
Total Sample (N=1127)	46	29	23	2	100

[a] Only persons who said they had heard about the fighting in Vietnam are included in the table. Those whose education, income, or occupation could not be ascertained are included in the total sample. Persons in a variety of occupations coded as "miscellaneous" are not included in occupational breakdown.

position from the professional-technical and the manager-proprietor-official groups also relatively strong.

Over-all the data of Table 3 generally support the conclusion that lower class people were more likely than higher class people to favor a complete American withdrawal from the Vietnam war and to support a compromise agreement, like making Vietnam neutral, to end the war. Moreover, those at lower educational levels were less likely to favor the use of American troops in the war than were those with most education.[19]

[19] The relation between education and support of militant involvement does not appear to have changed after the U.S. became fully involved in the war. A Gallup Poll of May 22, 1966, at a time of internal squabbling among the South Vietnamese, found that 28 per cent of the college educated, 15 per cent of those with high school education, and only 10 per cent of those with grade school education were willing to have the U.S. "continue the war by itself."

OPINIONS CONCERNING CHINA AND VIETNAM: AN APPARENT PARADOX

Thus far we have seen that lower social class was associated with un-willingness for co-operative dealings with Communist China but with a non-militant attitude toward the war in Vietnam. Higher social class was, conversely, associated with willingness for co-operative contact with Com-munist China but also with support of involvement and militant policies in Vietnam.

However, it is also true that willingness for co-operative dealings with Communist China was positively associated with non-militant attitudes concerning Vietnam policy. For the sample as a whole and within each educational stratum, those who opposed dealing with the Communist gov-ernment of mainland China were more likely to favor the use of American forces in Vietnam and to oppose a compromise settlement than were those who favored dealing with Communist China. Conversely, the more favor-able the reaction to possible co-operative initiatives toward Communist China, the more likely was opposition to use of American forces and sup-port of a compromise agreement in Vietnam.[20] (Differences in attitude to-ward dealing with China were not associated with attitudes toward with-drawal from, or giving military aid to, South Vietnam.)

At first encounter, the results showing that willingness for co-operative relations with China tends to go along with non-militancy in Vietnam ap-pear inconsistent with the previous findings—i.e., that the stratum which was most willing to have co-operative dealings with China (those of higher social class) was also most militant with respect to Vietnam policy. The situation is clarified by inspection of Figure 1 which shows the relationship between willingness for contact with China and willingness to compromise in Vietnam, separately for each educational segment. (Education is used here as the indicator of social class.) This figure shows that within each educational segment, there is a positive association between willingness for co-operative contact with Communist China and willingness to com-promise in Vietnam. However, the general level of willingness to compro-mise in Vietnam (indicated by the height of its line on the graph) is *higher* among those with lesser education than it is for other groups. At the same time, the general level of willingness for contact with China (indicated by the proportion of persons falling toward the right side of the graph) is *lower* for those with less education than it is for other groups. A similar graph (not shown), using willingness to use American troops as the cri-terion of "militancy" in Vietnam, shows a generally similar picture.

Note that Figure 1 shows how it is possible for lower class persons as a category to be both less conciliatory with regard to dealing with Com-munist China and more conciliatory with regard to the Vietnam war, even though, for individuals, being conciliatory in one's China attitudes tends to go with being conciliatory in one's Vietnam attitudes.

It may be noted too that, although this part of the discussion has been restricted to the relation between education and certain foreign policy

[20] Patchen, "The American Public's View," pp. 302–306.

FIGURE 1

Reactions to the Idea of a Compromise Agreement in Vietnam as Related
to Willingness to Follow Presidential Suggestions for Contact with
China, for Persons of Different Educational Levels[a,b]

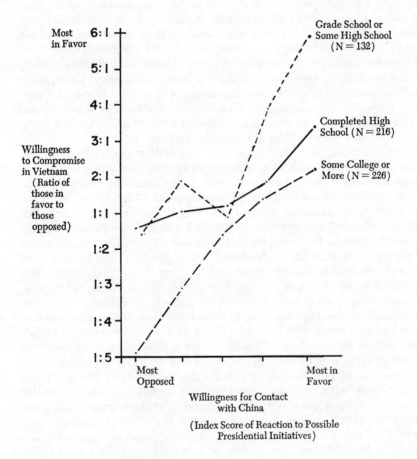

a For each education category, the percentage of persons who fall at each point
along its graph-line, going from left to right, is as follows: Grade school or some high
school: 22, 20, 24, 23, 11; Completed high school: 12, 22, 23, 29, 15; Some College
or more: 13, 21, 24, 20, 22.
b This figure is based on data for persons who gave an opinion about all five possible presidential initiatives and about a compromise agreement in Vietnam.

attitudes, a similar pattern of results was found with respect to the re-lation between age and foreign policy attitudes. Thus, younger persons were more likely than older persons to favor co-operative contacts with Communist China but also to favor militant policies in Vietnam.[21] A graph-ing of the relation between attitudes toward contact with China and atti-tudes toward policy in Vietnam (especially use of U.S. troops), separately for different age groups, yields a picture similar to that shown for educa-tional categories in Figure 1.[22]

CLASS, MILITANCY AND WILLINGNESS FOR INVOLVEMENT

How can we explain the pattern of results which has been found? First, the association found within each educational stratum between opposition to co-operative initiatives toward China and opposition to compromise in Vietnam appears to indicate that these policies have something in com-mon. Apparently, both policies are seen as conciliatory or "soft" and op-position to both reflects an orientation of "toughness" or militancy in deal-ing with certain foreign countries.

On the question of whether the foreign policy attitudes of lower class persons fall toward one end of this militancy dimension, evidence is mixed. The data reviewed by Hamilton and those summarized here show that lower class persons were less likely to favor escalating the wars in Korea and Vietnam and more likely to favor compromise. Thus, lower-status persons (more than others) preferred to "keep on trying to get a peaceful settlement" in Korea rather than to "take a stronger stand and bomb Manchuria and China,"[23] preferred to "keep our soldiers in Vietnam but try to end the fighting" rather than "take a stronger stand even if it means invading North Vietnam,"[24] and favored "some compromise agreement" in Vietnam (Table 3). However, the data reviewed here also show lower class persons to be more opposed to co-operative initiatives toward Com-munist China.

The inconsistent association in these data between social class and sup-port for conciliatory foreign policies appears to be found more generally. For example, Eckhardt[25] and his associates found a significant association in one sample between lower socioeconomic level and militarism while Modigliani[26] found in another sample that the percentage favoring more conciliatory policies was higher at low educational levels than among the college educated. Reviewing some studies that bear on the relation be-tween social class and preference for conciliatory versus tough foreign policy positions, Rosenberg concludes that, "Compared to the data on sex

[21] As noted above, however, the relationships between education and attitudes concerning China and Vietnam are not "washed out" when age is controlled.

[22] Patchen, "The American Public's View," p. 308.

[23] Hamilton, "A Research Note," pp. 440–441.

[24] Ibid., p. 443.

[25] W. Eckhardt, et al., "Militarism in Our Culture Today," paper presented at annual meeting of American Psychological Association (Chicago: Sept., 1965).

[26] A. Modigliani, "Facts, Beliefs, and Baloney about the Cold War Public," Council for Correspondence Newsletter, No. 24 (Jan.–Feb., 1963), pp. 50–56.

and religion . . . the social class variable seems to be less clearly and less strongly related to attitudes on Cold-War issues."[27]

However, the data presented above suggest that the dimension of toughness versus conciliation is not the only one on which different social classes may be compared. The tendency of those of lower education to support both a policy of cold-shouldering China and a compromise agreement in Vietnam suggests that there is something these policies have in common which is appealing to lower class persons. It seems very likely that this common element is that of noninvolvement in foreign activities. Such an interpretation is consistent with much other data which show lower class persons to be more likely to favor noninvolvement by the U.S. in foreign "entanglements."

We have already noted that data from the study reported here shows that support for "The United States getting out of the Vietnam war completely" rose as one goes *down* the social class ladder. Other public opinion studies reviewed by Almond[28] have found lower class Americans to be more isolationist and nationalistic than other segments of the population and more likely than others to oppose policies—e.g., support of world organizations and foreign aid—which involve the U.S. in world affairs. The other recent data which Hamilton presents also indicate greater support for noninvolvement among lower class persons.[29] If his tables are examined with respect to the proportion of those expressing an opinion who favored alternative policies, they show that those with less education and income were somewhat more likely than others to favor pulling out of Korea entirely in 1952 and that those with lower education, income, and occupational status were more likely than others to favor pulling out of Vietnam entirely in the fall of 1964.

It appears consistent with available information, then, to explain the pattern of results found in our 1964 study by assuming that attitudes about policy toward China and Vietnam reflected two basic orientations: (a) involvement-noninvolvement and (b) militancy-non-militancy. If this is correct, the association found within each educational stratum between approval of friendly initiatives toward China and approval of a compromise settlement in Vietnam may be seen as reflecting a basic orientation toward non-militant or conciliatory actions. On the other hand, the tendency of lower class persons as a category to favor both a policy of non-contact with China and a policy of a compromise settlement (or immediate withdrawal) from Vietnam may be seen as reflecting a stronger orientation in this stratum toward noninvolvement in foreign affairs.

It may be noted that because certain groups are likely to favor a particular policy primarily because of its position on the involvement dimension

[27] M. Rosenberg, "Images in Relation to the Policy Process: American Public Opinion on Cold War Issues," in H. Kelman, ed., *International Behavior* (New York: Holt, Rinehart and Winston, 1965).

[28] G. Almond, *The American People and Foreign Policy* (New York: Harcourt, Brace, 1950).

[29] Hamilton, "A Research Note," pp. 440, 443.

and other groups are likely to favor it primarily because of its position on the militancy dimension, strange bedfellows are apt to be found, Thus, for example, the proposal of a compromise to end the war in Vietnam was undoubtedly favored both by those lower class persons who are nationalistic isolationists and by those middle class "peace" advocates who are conciliatory and internationalistic in their foreign policy views. It may be noted too that the policy preferences which tend to be favored by lower class persons in the data that Hamilton and I present all fall toward the noninvolvement end of the involvement dimension but vary considerably on the militancy dimension. This suggests that the push for noninvolvement is a stronger force among lower class persons than is any disposition toward militancy.

CLASS AND AUTHORITARIANISM

If this interpretation of the attitudes of lower class persons is correct, what implications does it have for the idea that the foreign policy attitudes of lower class persons reflect authoritarianism? First, it should be noted that the wish to keep isolated from out-groups is quite consistent with the ideological syndrome which has been labelled authoritarianism. The original studies of authoritarianism showed this ideology (considered to be a measure of basic personality) to be closely related to, and indeed useful as a predictor of, ethnocentrism.[30] One of the possible manifestations of ethnocentrism is, of course, an attempt to stay aloof from foreigners, or isolationism. Consistent with this point, several studies have found scores on the usual measure of authoritarianism (the F scale) to be associated with isolationism.[31] Also, Lipset suggests that "the underlying factors which predispose individuals toward support of extremist movements under certain conditions may result in total withdrawal from political activity and concern under other conditions."[32] If this is true for domestic politics, it may also be true for international affairs—that is, authoritarians may alternate between support for isolation and preference for extreme (perhaps military) or over-simple solutions. Thus, if the typical foreign policy attitudes of lower class persons were a reflection of authoritarianism, we should not have been surprised to find them (more than others) favoring a pull-out from Korea and from Vietnam, (as the evidence summarized above indicates they did) as well as favoring non-involvement in other world affairs.

But if a preference for noninvolvement in foreign affairs is consistent with an authoritarian orientation to the world, the preference for conciliatory methods (compromise, negotiation) over military methods is not. The basic picture of the authoritarian is that of one who is basically hos-

---

[30] T. W. Adorno, et al., The Authoritarian Personality (New York: Harper, 1950).

[31] M. Janowitz and D. Marvick, "Authoritarianism and Political Behavior," Public Opinion Quarterly, 17 (Summer, 1953), pp. 185–201; R. E. Lane, "Political Personality and Electoral Choice," American Political Science Review, 49 (March, 1955), pp. 173–190.

[32] Lipset, Political Man, p. 121.

tile and aggressive in his orientation toward out-groups.[33] Consistent with this point, scores on the authoritarianism (F) scale have been found to correlate with preference for aggressive foreign policies in at least five separate studies summarized by Eckhardt.[34] The fact that available evidence, as summarized above, shows an inconsistent relationship between class and aggressive attitudes suggests that, although lower class persons are generally more authoritarian,[35] their foreign policy attitudes are affected most strongly by factors other than their authoritarianism.

What other factors, then, may be responsible for the pattern of foreign policy attitudes shown by lower class persons—which as we have noted, is characterized most consistently by a preference for non-involvement? The answer is undoubtedly connected with the lower level of information about foreign affairs which lower class persons possess.[36] Less information has at least two effects. First, it means that one cannot understand well the possible implications for the U.S. of various foreign events and activities. Secondly, as Putney and Middleton suggest, those who are better informed are likely to digest not only information but also the policy biases of the government and the media.[37] They are more "in" the society and therefore more influenced by the prevailing norm (at least as it existed in 1964 and before) that involvement by the U.S. in foreign affairs is necessary and beneficial.[38] It may be also, as Almond suggests, that "a greater tendency toward apathy and withdrawal in the personal sense among the lower classes may produce a bias in the direction of political withdrawal or isolation."[39] Finally, the greater fatalism and pessimism of lower class persons concerning world affairs may contribute to their propensity to favor noninvolvement.[40]

ATTITUDE DIMENSIONS

In addition to their implications for understanding the relationship between social class and foreign policy attitudes, the data presented here have implications for our understanding of the basic dimensions under-

[33] Adorno, *et al.*, *The Authoritarian Personality;* G. W. Allport, *The Nature of Prejudice* (Reading, Mass.: Addison-Wesley, 1954).

[34] W. Eckhardt, "War in the Minds of Men," paper presented at annual meeting of the Canadian Peace Research and Education Association (Ottawa: May, 1967).

[35] Lipset, *Political Man,* Chap. 4.

[36] For illustrative material about the relation between social class and foreign policy information, see J. Robinson's *Public Information About World Affairs* (Ann Arbor: Survey Research Center, 1967). Robinson also presents evidence indicating that lower class persons have less interest in foreign affairs than do others; see his article "World Affairs Information and Mass Media Exposure," *Journalism Quarterly,* 44 (Spring, 1967), pp. 23–30.

[37] S. Putney and R. Middleton, "Student Acceptance or Rejection of War," *American Sociological Review,* 27 (Oct., 1962), pp. 655–666.

[38] It should be noted that if norms among the "elite" about the wisdom of involvement change (as may be happening to some extent today), this could reduce, nullify, or even reverse the relation between social class and preference for non-involvement.

[39] Almond, *The American People,* p. 126.

[40] *Ibid.;* S. Withey, "Supplementary Tables from a Study of Public Reactions to Current International Tensions" (Ann Arbor: Survey Research Center, May 1962).

lying attitudes on specific foreign policy issues. I have suggested that postulating the existence of at least two basic attitude dimensions—orientations toward involvement and toward militancy—helps to make sense of the pattern of results obtained in our 1964 China-Vietnam study. Postulating even as few as these two dimensions permits one to explain patterns of specific attitudes better than the use of the single aggression-conciliation dimension considered by Hamilton or the single dimension of nationalism-internationalism discussed by Levinson.[41]

However, while the dimension of involvement-non-involvement appears to be a clear and fundamental one,[42] the dimension of militancy-non-militancy appears to need some additional specification. A potentially fruitful suggestion for such specification comes from the work of a number of scholars who have studied the basic dimensions underlying interaction in dyads.[43] Their work suggests that the basic orientations underlying social interaction may be described by the dimensions of (1) love (friendliness)-affective neutrality-hostility and (2) dominance-autonomy-submissiveness. Although caution is clearly required when applying evidence dealing with personal orientations to the domain of orientations toward foreign countries, there is evidence that the two types of orientations are not unrelated.[44] Thus, it does seem a tenable hypothesis that what we have called militancy in this paper is a combination of an orientation toward dominance and an orientation toward hostility in dealing wth foreign countries. Non-militancy may reflect some combination of willingness to yield (or compromise) and friendliness.

Specification of "toughness" and "softness" in terms of orientations toward dominance and toward friendliness clarifies the somewhat vague concept of toughness or militancy and permits us to distinguish between specific foreign policy attitudes which might all be called tough but which may differ in important respects. Consider, for example, the two possible policies of (a) taking some retaliatory action against North Korea for seizure of the U.S. ship *Pueblo*; and (b) insisting that the U.S. keep control of some important NATO decisions. Though both might be considered militant or tough, the first probably reflects hostility more than it does an attempt to dominate while the second represents an attempt to dominate

[41] D. J. Levinson, "Authoritarian Personality and Foreign Policy," *Journal of Conflict Resolution*, 1 (March, 1957), pp. 37–47.

[42] The amount of interaction is a basic aspect of a social relationship. Thus, Newcomb, Turner, and Converse in *Social Psychology* (New York: Holt, Rinehart and Winston, 1965) discuss frequency of communications as a basic aspect of role relationships and Lundberg in *Foundations of Sociology* (New York: MacMillan, 1939) argues that all social behavior is restatable in terms of the kinds and degrees of communication.

[43] See, for example, R. Longabaugh, "The Structure of Interpersonal Behavior," *Sociometry*, 29 (Dec., 1966), pp. 441–460; and T. Kemper, "The Two Fundamental Dimensions of Social Interaction: A Theoretical Statement," paper given at the annual meetings of the American Sociological Association (San Francisco: September, 1969).

[44] W. A. Scott presents evidence of a positive association between orientations towards interpersonal relations and orientations toward dealings with foreign nations in "International Ideology and Interpersonal Ideology," *Public Opinion Quarterly*, 15 (Summer, 1951), pp. 217–224.

rather than express hostility. Since there is probably a positive association between orientations toward dominance and toward hostility, people who approve of one of these policies would be likely to approve the other (assuming that the involvement dimension was not salient). However, those persons who had a basic orientation toward hostile actions but not to dominant actions and those persons who were oriented toward U.S. dominance but not to hostility would be likely to approve one of these actions but not the other.

Our discussion suggests, then, that a specific policy may be approved or rejected in terms of its position on three basic dimensions: (1) the degree to which it represents involvement with another nation; (2) the degree to which it reflects friendliness or hostility toward the other nation; and (3) the degree to which it reflects dominance or equality or submissiveness vis-à-vis the other nation.[45] (This does not assume that most persons consciously evaluate policies in these terms—only that their policy preferences are guided by these more or less conscious orientations.)

It may be possible to predict the attitudes of people toward a given action by assessing (a) their sentiments concerning each action dimension (involvement, friendliness, dominance) as it applies to a given nation or set of nations; (b) the saliency of each of these dimensions to them; and (c) their perception of the location of the particular action being evaluated with respect to each of the three action dimensions.

It may be noted also that possible policies are often stated—both by politicians and by public opinion surveyors—in a way which does not indicate clearly where the action would fall on all three of the dimensions discussed. For example, the alternative "keep on trying to get a peaceful settlement" of the Korean war (question cited by Hamilton) may be reacted to differently, depending on whether the settlement is one that favors us (dominant) or which favors the other side (submissive). Or a policy of giving aid to the government of Bolivia may elicit different reactions depending on whether it is seen in terms of this action involving the U.S. in a civil war. Another potential use of this analysis, therefore, is to direct our attention to basic aspects of foreign policy actions which, it seems likely, have to be specified in order to elicit reliable opinions about any action.[46]

[45] A different set of basic factors underlying foreign policy attitudes has been proposed by Eckhardt ("War in the Minds of Men"), based on a study by his own group in Des Moines and on a study of Canadians' attitudes by Laulicht. However, the factors extracted in these studies are based on responses not only to items concerning foreign affairs but also to those concerning a wide variety of other matters including background characteristics, "don't know" responses, domestic "welfarism," religious orthodoxy, and mental health. The nature of the domain which the factors represent is, therefore, somewhat amorphous.

[46] Of course, other factors also need to be considered in determining whether one is attaining reliable opinions. See P. Converse's paper "The Nature of Belief Systems in Mass Publics," in D. Apter, ed., *Ideology and Discontent* (New York: Free Press, 1964) for a discussion of related issues.

SUMMARY

The relationship between social class, authoritarianism, and foreign policy attitudes has been re-examined in the light of evidence from a national survey and other studies. These data indicate that, contrary to the suggestion of Hamilton's recent paper, lower class people are not consistently more conciliatory on foreign policy issues than are those of higher social class. The attitudes of lower class people appear to be more consistently characterized by a preference for noninvolvement in foreign affairs. Such a preference for isolation from foreigners is congruent with the ideology which has been called authoritarianism. However, the preference for conciliatory over aggressive foreign policy actions which lower class persons sometimes show is not congruent with authoritarianism. This suggests that, although lower class persons may be more authoritarian, their foreign policy attitudes are determined mainly by other factors. The data reviewed suggest also that foreign policy attitudes can be understood best not in terms of a single orientation toward conciliation versus militancy but in terms of several basic orientations. It may prove useful to characterize specific foreign policy positions in terms of their position on the dimensions of (1) involvement-noninvolvement; (2) dominance-submissiveness; and (3) friendliness-hostility.

RELIGION AND THE RISE OF THE RADICAL WHITE: THE CASE OF SOUTHERN WALLACE SUPPORT IN 1968[1]

ANTHONY M. ORUM

University of Illinois at Urbana

T HAT RELIGION AND RADICAL POLITICS CAN BE COMPATIBLE PURSUITS IN American society is a notion which has stirred considerable controversy. On the one hand, there are those who take their cue mainly from American experience with left-wing movements and argue that the transvaluational and other-worldly nature of many religious groups, especially sectarian ones, are completely antithetic to the acceptance of a radical program for change. Support for their contention comes partly from the observation that American society, as compared with European countries, has been notable for her simultaneous abundance of sectarian religious groups and paucity of radical political movements. "As sects have continued to emerge here, radicalism has been anemic and without appreciable lower class support."[2] Additional substantiation is found in evidence about the behavior of individual American citizens, ranging from indications that partisan support of the Democrats is associated with religious inactivity and estrangement to signs that, among Negroes, civil rights militancy is negatively associated with religious involvement.[3]

On the other hand, almost equally compelling evidence upholds the claim that certain religious orientations and radical political stances can be suitable bedfellows in America, at least partly because of the similar world views held by participants in both activities. Support for this argument comes from activities in the contemporary era like the civil rights movement in which there has been a seemingly heavy concentration of white clergymen.[4] Additional evidence comes from the other end of the political spectrum as well. Commenting on the apparent fascination of religious fundamentalists with right-wing politics in America, Roy notes that:

They see the issue in theological terms. One is God, who leads the legions

[1] I wish to express my thanks to the Emory University Faculty Research Committee which provided the funds to permit me to collect the data for this project. I also would like to thank the University of Illinois Research Board for a small grant that allowed me to complete the processing and analysis of these data. Gerald S. Strom provided invaluable technical assistance on the preparation of the data for this paper.

[2] Charles Y. Glock and Rodney Stark, *Religion and Society in Tension* (Chicago: Rand McNally and Co., 1965), p. 216.

[3] Glock and Stark, *Religion and Society in Tension*, chap. 2, and Gary T. Marx, "Religion: Opiate or Inspiration of Civil Rights Militancy Among Negroes?" *American Sociological Review*, 32 (Feb., 1967), pp. 64–72.

[4] On this point, see, for instance, Charles S. McCoy, "The Churches and Protest Movements for Racial Justice," in Robert Lee and Martin E. Marty, eds., *Religion and Social Conflict* (New York: Oxford University Press, 1964), pp. 37–54.

of good. The other is Satan ... who is the father of Communism ... spreading modernism and disbelief across our land.[5]

This tie between fundamentalism and right-wing politics, proponents point out, is epitomized in such groups as Fred Schwarz's Christian Anti-Communism Crusade which, as its name implies, wages a fight against Communism in the name of Christian principles.

In the present paper, we shall explore the links between a recent illustration of radical politics in the United States, George Wallace's American Independent Party movement, and religion. As a result of this analysis, we hope to shed some further light on the continuing controversy surrounding the issue of the compatibility of religion and radical politics as well as some of the specific religious underpinnings of the Wallace candidacy.

THE WALLACE MOVEMENT AND ITS SUPPORT

While it is almost a foregone conclusion that the Wallace movement represented a case of radical politics in America, it is useful for us to briefly review a few of the things which made this movement radical. George Wallace was the first major third party candidate since Henry Wallace ran for President 20 years earlier. Further, George Wallace's various political stands resembled those of certain radical political groups in America, in particular, right-wing extremist organizations. In a fashion similar to many of these groups, Wallace came out strongly in opposition to the spread of Communism and forcible racial integration in the United States. He, likewise, identified himself, and his American Independent Party, with the good-old-time American values and beliefs—banners at his rallies, for instance, read "Stand Up For America." Perhaps the only stand which genuinely distinguished his movement from contemporary right-wing groups was his support of measures to expand social and economic welfare programs. And finally, because its policies were similar to those of radical right organizations in America, Wallace's American Independent Party was apparently able to attract the aid, financial and otherwise, of many people who belonged or were sympathetic to the goals of right-wing organizations.[6]

It should surprise no one to learn that the Wallace campaign also gained the support of a particular segment of the religious community in America. One analysis of the nature of Wallace's electoral strength suggests that he drew a disproportionate number of voters from members of

[5] Ralph Lord Roy, "Conflict from the Communist Left and the Radical Right," in Lee and Marty, eds., Religion and Social Conflict, p. 66. For the other works that present a similar point of view, the reader is advised to examine the following: David Danzig, "The Radical Right and the Rise of the Fundamentalist Minority," 33 (April, 1962), pp. 291–298; Benton Johnson, "On Church and Sect," American Sociological Review, 28 (Aug., 1963), pp. 539–549; Seymour Martin Lipset, "Religion and Politics in the American Past and Present," in Lee and Marty, eds., Religion and Social Conflict, pp. 68–126; and Ralph Lord Roy, Apostles of Discord. A Study of Organized Bigotry and Disruption on the Fringes of Protestantism (Boston: Beacon Press, 1953).

[6] Seymour Martin Lipset and Earl Raab, "The Wallace Whitelash," Trans-action, 7 (Dec., 1969), pp. 23–24.

one of the more sectlike denominations of the Protestant faith, Baptists. Using data gathered by the Gallup Poll immediately after the election, Lipset and Raab discovered that 16 per cent of the Baptists in the North, and 45 per cent in the South, voted for Wallace. Both figures represent proportions considerably higher than those for any other Protestant denominations or, for that matter, any other religious groups.[7]

Nevertheless, as straight forward as the religious foundations of the Wallace vote in 1968 appear to be, analysis of the impact of religion on political behavior is far too complex a process to be abandoned with simple cross-tabulations of voting and religious affiliation. For example, as many studies of religion reveal, members of the more sectlike religious groups such as the Baptists are disproportionately located in the lower socioeconomic strata.[8] And inasmuch as the Wallace support also seemed to come heavily from members of the lower socioeconomic strata, one naturally wonders if religious affiliation would still distinguish between Wallace voters and Nixon and Humphrey supporters when the effects of socioeconomic differences are removed. Unfortunately, neither Lipset and Raab nor other published evidence considers this matter.[9]

Thus, in addition to our more general concern in this paper, we shall try to clarify the relationship between religion and support for Wallace by examining this relationship with appropriate statistical controls for contaminating influences. Moreover, we shall seek to clarify the impact of religion on the Wallace movement by looking at two related dimensions of religious behavior, religious fundamentalism and religious involvement.

DATA

The data to be analyzed in this paper consist of information collected by means of a sample survey of voting and related political patterns among white residents of the Atlantic Standard Metropolitan Statistical Area soon after the presidential election in November, 1968. We initially established a target of 320 interviews. Because of the anticipated losses due to such problems as sparsely populated blocks, refusals, and others noted below, we actually identified a total of 700 possible households within the metropolitan area. In the course of the interviewing, an additional 500 households were identified because of the high rate of refusals, a problem encountered by many survey researchers at the time of this election.

Within the City of Atlanta, and DeKalb and Fulton Counties, we were able to employ a two-stage probability design in selecting households. Census tracts and then blocks were chosen with probabilities proportionate to size. Once the blocks had been identified, a maximum of seven

---

[7] Lipset and Raab, "The Wallace Whitelash," p. 28.

[8] N. J. Demerath III, *Social Class in American Protestantism* (Chicago: Rand McNally & Company, 1965), p. 2.

[9] Lipset and Raab, "The Wallace Whitelash," and Philip E. Converse, Warren E. Miller, Jerrold G. Rusk, and Arthur C. Wolfe, "Continuity and Change in American Politics: Parties and Issues in the 1968 Election," *American Political Science Review*, 63 (Dec., 1969), pp. 1083–1105.

households was selected within each block. For the remaining areas of the SMSA—Cobb, Clayton and Gwinnett Counties—maps were used in identifying households. Each sample area was chosen by using a random pair of Cartesian coordinates. Since these areas generally were larger than city blocks, and as a means of minimizing labor and costs, the street nearest to the sample point was chosen as the place at which to begin the random selection of households. Households were listed in a clockwise direction, but, unlike the listing of city blocks, a random sample of only four households was selected in an area.

Several restrictions were placed on the selection of respondents within households. First, as a means of achieving an approximate reflection of the sex ratio in the population, interviewers were advised to interview equal numbers of men and women. Second, since the study only dealt with the political patterns among white residents, black residents were not interviewed. Third, in order to insure a sufficient number of voters for the analysis, we gave interviewers two additional guidelines. With the aid of a screening question, interviewers were instructed to reject all people who were under voting age. A second screening question was employed in selecting voters and nonvoters. Voters were somewhat over-represented in the final sample, comprising about three-quarters of the people interviewed rather than the two-thirds which they normally represent in presidential elections.

After discarding several questionnaires which could not be used, the final sample consisted of 317 cases. The subsequent analyses here, however, are based on fewer than 317 cases since we excluded the 77 respondents who were nonvoters, the 23 who were not members of the Protestant faith, and the ten who failed to answer the questions about their religious beliefs, or voting.

RELIGIOUS INDICATORS

Included on the questionnaire administered to the sample of respondents in the Atlanta SMSA were questions about three separate dimensions of religion. The first, and most common one, simply asked the respondent to identify his religious affiliation. If he was a Protestant, the respondent then was asked to indicate the denomination to which he belonged. Inasmuch as there is so small a concentration of Catholics and Jews in the South, we shall confine our attention in this analysis solely to variations among Protestant denominations.

A second religious measure was designed to uncover the degree to which a respondent accepted or rejected the major tenets of fundamentalism. Our measure of the fundamentalist dimension, consisting of four items, was adapted from a scale devised by Lamar.[10] A Guttman scale was created

[10] Ralph E. Lamar, "Fundamentalism and Selected Social Factors in the Southern Appalachian Region," unpublished M.S. thesis, University of Kentucky, 1962. The four items included in our scale, along with the responses which designated the individual as fundamentalist, were:

from responses to the four items with a coefficient of reproducibility of .912, and a coefficient of scalability of .735.

A third dimension of religious behavior that we tapped was degree of religious involvement, using the respondent's frequency of attendance at church services as a measure. Although this is a commonly used measure, some recent research and discussion suggests that it signifies *only one kind* of religious involvement, representing a more public form of worship than something like personal prayer, for example. Hand-in-hand with this distinction goes the fact that the frequency of public worship varies directly with social class, while the frequency of private worship varies inversely with class.[11] When we examine the impact of church attendance on the Wallace vote, we suggest that the reader bear these facts in mind.

FINDINGS

Religion, Fundamentalism and Wallace Support. Our examination of the religious basis of the Wallace vote in 1968 begins with a look at the relationship between religious affiliation and voting for Wallace. As the reader can observe in Table 1, the strength of Wallace's support was greatest among the Baptists and weakest among the Episcopalians. The particular percentage figures correspond almost exactly with the results uncovered by the Gallup poll in the entire South. The poll found that Wallace received 45, 35, and 14 per cent of the vote from Baptists, Methodists, and Presbyterians, respectively, who lived in the South.[12]

Do you thing gambling is always wrong, sometimes wrong, or never wrong? (Always)

Do you think drinking is always wrong, sometimes wrong, or never wrong? (Always)

Do you think card playing is always wrong, sometimes wrong, or never wrong? (Always)

Here are four statements about the Bible. Which is closest to your own view? (Number 1)

The Bible is God's Word and all it says is true.	(1)
The Bible was written by men inspired by God but it contains some human errors.	(2)
The Bible is a good book because it was written by wise men but God had nothing to do with it.	(3)
The Bible was written by men who lived so long ago that it is worth very little today.	(4)

[11] N. J. Demerath, *Social Class in American Protestantism*, esp. chap. 1; Yoshio Fukuyama, "The Major Dimensions of Church Membership," *Review of Religious Research*, 2 (1961), pp. 154–161; Charles W. Estus and Michael A. Overington, "The Meaning and End of Religiosity," *American Journal of Sociology*, 75 (March, 1970), pp. 760–778; Erich Goode, "Social Class and Church Participation," *American Journal of Sociology*, 72 (July, 1966), pp. 102–111; Erich Goode, "Some Critical Observations on the Church-Sect Dimensions," *Journal for the Scientific Study of Religion*, 6 (Spring, 1967), pp. 69–77; Erich Goode, "Further Reflections on the Church-Sect Dimension," *Journal for the Scientific Study of Religion*, 6 (Fall, 1967), pp. 272–273; Erich Goode, "Class Styles of Religious Sociation," *British Journal of Sociology*, 19 (March, 1968), pp. 1–16; and Gerhard Lenski, *The Religious Factor* (Garden City, N.Y.: Doubleday & Co., 1963), pp. 22–24, *passim*.

[12] See Lipset and Raab, "The Wallace Whitelash."

TABLE 1

Religion by Vote

Religion	Nixon	Voting Wallace	Humphrey	Total Per cent	N
Baptist	39	52	9	100	112
Methodist	37	40	24	101	38
Presbyterian	44	16	41	101	32
Episcopalian	62	6	31	99	16
Total					198

$X^2 = 32.65$ $P < .001$

Inasmuch as Wallace's strength comes disproportionately from denominations like the Baptists, among whom there are many people who hold a fundamentalist religious orientation, these data appear to support the claim of Roy and others that a fundamentalist religious orientation is a primary mechanism accounting for a person like Wallace's appeal to different religious groups.[13] As a means of testing this hypothesis, we examined the impact of religious affiliation on the vote, controlling for fundamentalist orientation. These data are presented in Table 2. If we compare the row percentages, we find that people who score high on fundamentalism are more apt to vote for Wallace. Among the Methodists, for example, Wallace received 46 per cent of the vote of people high on fundamentalism compared with only 36 per cent among people low on fundamentalism. Yet, religious affiliation also continues to differentiate the strength of Wallace's appeal. In other words, the fundamentalist orientation *supplements* the

TABLE 2

Religion, Fundamentalism, and Voting
(Per Cent Voting for Wallace)

Religion	Fundamentalism Low	High
Baptist	43	61
	(56)	(56)
Methodist	36	46
	(25)	(13)
Presbyterian	12	[17]
	(41)	(6)ᵃ

Religion by voting, controlling for fundamentalism: $X^2 = 15.15$, P < .01
Fundamentalism by voting, controlling for religion: $X^2 = 4.05$, ns
ᵃ Percentages in brackets are based on fewer than eight cases.

[13] DeJong and Ford, "Religious Fundamentalism and Denominational Preference," p. 28.

effect of religious affiliation rather than removing it.[14] If the reader examines the results of the tests of significance, he will find that with religious preference controlled, religious fundamentalism does not have a statistically significant impact on the voting. Nonetheless, the consistency of fundamentalism's effect on the voting—namely that, in every case, those who were higher on fundamentalism were more apt to vote for Wallace —is strongly suggestive of its substantive importance.

Religion, Fundamentalism, Socioeconomic Status, and Wallace Support. To show the links of religious affiliation and fundamentalism with the Wallace vote in 1968 is by no means to prove the existence of any kind of causal relationship between religion and the Wallace vote. In particular, one could easily argue that the ties are simply an artifact of the effect of social class on the voting in this election. On the one hand, there already is a fair amount of evidence indicating that the ordering of the religious groups in terms of Wallace's strength exactly parallels the ranking of these groups in terms of the concentration of people from the lower class, the largest proportion being found among the Baptists and the smallest among the Episcopalians.[15] At the same time, all the available information also shows that members of the lower class were much more apt to have supported Wallace than members of the middle or upper classes. We found, for instance, that 64 per cent of the people with only a primary school education voted for Wallace compared with 15 per cent of those people who were college graduates.

In order to see whether social class does provide a bridge, as it were, between religion and the voting, we inspected the relationships among religious affiliation, fundamentalism, and the voting, controlling for an indicator of socioeconomic status, the respondent's education.[16] These data

[14] One might well suppose that the relationship uncovered here between fundamentalism and voting for Wallace is an artifact of other factors intervening between fundamentalism and the voting. In particular, it could be argued that fundamentalists are more apt to support Wallace because they tend to be older than the non-fundamentalists. An examination of the association between fundamentalism and voting, controlling for age, reveals this to be an unwarranted conclusion.

Fundamentalism, Age, and Voting
(Per Cent Voting for Wallace)

		Fundamentalism	
Age	Low	Medium	High
Under 40	23	44	59
	(53)	(32)	(17)
40 and Over	16	43	59
	(38)	(30)	(29)

[15] N. J. Demerath, *Social Class in American Protestantism*, p. 2.

[16] At the outset, it is wise to dispense with any questions that might exist about using education as a measure of socioeconomic status. First of all, education is a generally acceptable—although by no means the only—measure of socioeconomic status. Duncan, for instance, concludes that education and income can be used to predict the rank order of occupations in terms of an occupational socioeconomic status index. See the

are presented in Table 3. As a means of conserving the numbers of cases, we controlled education, separately, for religious affiliation and fundamentalism. We find that, on the whole, the effect of religious affiliation on the Wallace voting is the same as that found in the absence of a control for education. The only deviation appears among people whose educational level is a high school diploma or less, where we find that Methodists were more likely than Baptists to have voted for Wallace. With only one exception, we also find that fundamentalism continues to exert its same influence on the Wallace vote when education is held constant, those lower on the scale being more apt to support Wallace than those higher on the scale. In short, we can conclude that although the introduction of education seems to reduce, or at least confuse, the effect of both religious variables, these variables still exert an impact on the voting for Wallace which is independent of any influence of socioeconomic status. (Incidentally, the reader should observe that education has an influence on the voting which is independent of religion. This confirms numerous other analyses of the joint effects of religion and education, among which is a recent illustration in the case of voting for a Southern gubernatorial candidate, Lester Maddox, whose political positions resemble those of Wallace.) [17]

discussion in Peter M. Blau and Otis Dudley Duncan, *The American Occupational Structure* (New York: John Wiley & Sons, Inc., 1967), chap. 4.

Secondly, we found that in our particular sample education possessed relatively high correlations with the other two commonly used measures of socioeconomic status: occupation of the chief wage earner and family income. In the former case, the Gamma coefficient of association registered +.5995, in the latter case, +.4373. Moreover, both of these variables produced the same basic results in terms of the relationships reported here as the use of education.

Finally, it might be thought that the association between age and education would tend to modify the effect of fundamentalism on the voting for Wallace, at least partly because the relationship between the voting for Wallace and education could simply be an artifact of age. We have already shown above that the link between fundamentalism and the Wallace vote is not due to age, and the table below, involving education, age, and voting, also reveals that age has virtually no effect on the link between education and the voting. Indeed, age has little impact at all on the voting for Wallace, a finding borne out in other studies of the Wallace voting. Lipset and Raab, for instance, report that 37 per cent of the Southern residents who were in the age group of 26 to 29 voted for Wallace, compared with 33 per cent of those who were 50 or older. See, Lipset and Raab, "The Wallace Whitelash," p. 28.

Education, Age, and Voting
(Per Cent Voting for Wallace)

| | Age | |
Education	Under 40	40 and Over
Some College or More	22	19
	(68)	(43)
High School or Less	62	54
	(34)	(53)

[17] Anthony M. Orum and Edward W. McCranie, "Class, Tradition and Partisan Alignments in a Southern Urban Electorate," *Journal of Politics*, 32 (Feb., 1970), pp. 156–176.

TABLE 3

Religion, Fundamentalism, Education, and Voting
(Per Cent Voting for Wallace)

	Education	
	High School or Less	Some College or More
Religion		
Baptist	55	45
	(74)	(38)
Methodist	65	19
	(17)	(21)
Presbyterian and		
Episcopalians	18	11
	(11)	(37)
Fundamentalism		
High	61	44
	(49)	(16)
Medium	56	17
	(46)	(30)
Low	29	17
	(21)	(76)

Religion by voting, controlling for education: $X^2 = 18.86, P < .001$
Education by voting, controlling for religion: $X^2 = 9.83, P < .05$
Fundamentalism by voting, controlling for education: $X^2 = 13.66, P < .01$
Education by voting, controlling for fundamentalism: $X^2 = 14.14, P < .01$

Religion, Fundamentalism, Church Attendance, and Wallace Support.
There are, at least, three separate arguments about the possible effect of
religious involvement on the relationship between religion and voting. The
first, suggested by Lenski, among others, claims that religious involvement
will simply produce a greater conformity to the norms of behavior for the
members of a particular religious group.[18] Thus, according to this argument, one would anticipate that the Baptists and fundamentalists who are
frequent churchgoers will be more likely to support Wallace than those
who are infrequent churchgoers.

A second hypothesis, originally profferred by Johnson, takes a somewhat
more subtle view of the effect of church attendance on the association of
religion with politics.[19] Johnson argues that although members of such
higher status Protestant churches as the Presbyterians are predisposed by
economic interests to be conservative in politics, hence Republicans, the
ministers of these congregations tend to be liberal by virtue of their education. Thus, frequent attendance among the parishioners of such groups
should result in lower, rather than higher, rates of political conservatism.

[18] Lenski, *The Religious Factor,* p. 174.
[19] Benton Johnson, "Ascetic Protestantism and Political Preference," *Public Opinion
Quarterly,* 26 (Spring, 1962), pp. 35–46, and Benton Johnson, "Ascetic Protestantism
and Political Preference in the Deep South," *American Journal of Sociology,* 69 (Jan.,
1964), pp. 359–366.

At the same time, Johnson claims that the reverse kind of effect occurs among members of lower status groups like the Baptists who are predisposed to be economic liberals and support the Democratic party. The ministers of these groups tend to be conservative and, thus, frequent attendance should result in higher, not lower, rates of political conservatism and attachment to the Republican banner. Translated into the present context, we would thus expect that frequent attendance among the Presbyterians would produce less support for Wallace than infrequent attendance, whereas frequent attendance among the Baptists would result in greater Wallace voting.

A third kind of argument concerning the impact of religious involvement on religion and politics, suggested by the work of Goode, simply views attendance at church as somewhat akin to attendance at any other kind of organization, religious or otherwise.[20] The meaning attributed to church attendance by this argument tends to be more associational than religious, more public than private, and receives indirect support from the fact that parishioners of high socioeconomic status are likely to attend church more frequently than those of low socioeconomic status. The real thrust of this hypothesis, in short, is that differences in socioeconomic status among religious groups must be removed in order to determine whether church attendance has any impact on the voting apart from its purely associational kind of impact.

Table 4 presents the information necessary to examine these several hypotheses. Separate analysis of the results for religious affiliation and fundamentalism, alike, became a particular necessity here inasmuch as we had to hold constant socioeconomic status differences. Also, in order to achieve comparability with the Johnson hypothesis, we eliminated the Episcopalians from consideration. Looking first at the relationships involving religious fundamentalism, we find support for the Johnson hypothesis among those people who were low in educational attainment. Within this group, one can observe that frequent church attendance produced a lower Wallace vote among those people who were low on fundamentalism, whereas the opposite pattern obtained among those people who were high on fundamentalism. However, inspection of the impact of attendance on fundamentalism and voting among people high in educational attainment reveals that in *each* instance, those people who were frequent churchgoers were less apt to vote for Wallace.

In the second part of Table 4, we see that the pattern among people with low educational attainment is less clear, with church attendance making virtually no difference in the impact of religion on the voting. By contrast, in two of three instances, the least religiously involved among people high in educational attainment are more apt to vote for Wallace.

Although these findings by no means produce any clear tendencies, on balance, they seem to indicate that parishioners who were least actively involved in church worship were more apt to support Wallace, especially among the highly educated. They provide no support at all for Lenski's

[20] Goode, "Social Class and Church Participation."

TABLE 4

Religion, Fundamentalism, Education, Church Attendance, and Voting
(Per Cent Voting for Wallace)

| | | Church Attendance | | | |
| | | Once a month or less | | Two or three times a month or more | |
Education	Fundamentalism				
High School Graduate or Less	High	54	(11)	63	(38)
	Medium	56	(18)	56	(27)
	Low	50	(8)	8	(12)
Some College or More	High	[100]ᵃ	(3)	31	(13)
	Medium	[29]ᵃ	(7)	14	(22)
	Low	26	(34)	10	(40)
Education	Religion				
High School Graduate or Less	Baptist	54	(24)	55	(49)
	Methodist	62	(8)	66	(9)
	Presbyterian	[25]ᵃ	(4)	[20]ᵃ	(5)
Some College or More	Baptist	62	(16)	32	(22)
	Methodist	[20]ᵃ	(5)	19	(16)
	Presbyterian	[29]ᵃ	(5)	6	(16)

ᵃ Percentages in brackets are based on fewer than eight cases.

hypothesis about the likelihood that church attendance will produce greater conformity to religious norms that are manifest in political differences. These results also suggest that people who supported Wallace were less well integrated into society, being marginal to many of its activities. In the next section, we shall examine certain data that will help to clarify this matter.

Who Were Wallace's Religious Adherents? Some Social and Political Correlates. During the 1968 election campaign, Wallace aimed many of his appeals for support at those groups in America who were especially dissatisfied with the political system. He introduced and repeatedly raised issues ranging from discontent with integration to unhappiness with the federal government as a whole. Not too surprisingly, one finds in the published analyses of the Wallace vote that, among other things, his supporters were people who were estranged from and cynical towards the political community in the United States.[21] Yet, in this paper, we seem to have uncovered an independent and powerful religious element in the Wallace support. Obviously, we must raise the question, did those segments of the religious community who provided strong support for Wallace, namely the Baptists and fundamentalists, possess the kind of dissatisfactions that

[21] Converse, *et al.,* "Continuity and Change," p. 1101.

would predispose them, as a group, to be attracted to the Wallace camp?

In order to answer this question, we looked at some of the more important social and political characteristics associated both with religious affiliation and fundamentalism. These data are presented in Table 5. Turn-

TABLE 5

Religion, Fundamentalism, and Some Social and Political Characteristics

Religion	Fundamentalism	Per Cent High on Political Alienation[a]	Per Cent Belonging to No or One Organization	Per Cent Low on Political Tolerance[b]	Percent High on Integration Scale[c]
Baptist	High	70	54	67	10
	Low	67	47	44	30
Methodist	High	50	44	65	0
	Low	48	29	64	33
Presbyterian and Episcopalian	High	44	22	57	14
	Low	54	30	17	58

[a] This scale possessed a coefficient of reproducibility of .9425 and a coefficient of scalability of .7722. It was created from the following items:

It doesn't matter which party wins elections, the interests of the little man don't count. (Strongly agree, slightly agree).

Local officials soon lose touch with the people who elected them. (Strongly agree, slightly agree, neutral).

If people knew what was really going on in high places, it would blow the lid off things. (Strongly agree, slightly agree, neutral).

These items were taken from a scale designed to measure political alienation and developed by Thompson and Horton. See Wayne E. Thompson and John E. Horton, "Political Alienation As a Force in Political Action," *Social Forces*, 38 (March, 1960), pp. 190–195.

[b] This scale possessed a coefficient of reproducibility of .9471 and a coefficient of scalability of .8339. It was created from the following items:

In peacetime, do you think the Socialist Party should be allowed to publish newspapers in this country? (Yes).

Do you think newspapers should be allowed to criticize our form of government? (Yes).

Do you think members of the Communist Party in this country should be allowed to speak out on radio? (Yes).

These questions first were used, then developed into a scale, by Martin A. Trow. See Martin A. Trow, "Small Businessmen, Political Tolerance, and Support for McCarthy," reprinted in Lewis Coser, ed., *Political Sociology: Selected Essays* (New York: Harper & Row, 1966), pp. 181–203.

[c] This scale possessed a coefficient of reproducibility of .9167 and a coefficient of scalability of .6515. It was made up from the following questions:

White people have a right to keep Negroes out of their neighborhoods if they want to, and Negroes should respect that right (Disagree strongly).

Negroes shouldn't push themselves where they're not wanted. (Disagree strongly).

Do you think Negroes should have as good a chance as white people to get any kind of job, or do you think white people should have the first chance at any kind of job? (Negroes should have as good a chance).

ing first to examine our indices of political estrangement, the political alienation scale and the number of organizational memberships, we find that in most instances those religious groups that tended to provide Wallace with his greatest vote also manifested a higher degree of political estrangement. For instance, 54 per cent of the Baptists who were high on the fundamentalism scale belonged to one or no organizations compared with only 30 per cent of the Presbyterians and Episcopalians who scored low on fundamentalism. Parenthetically, these results coincide with our finding above that, regardless of religious affiliation or degree of fundamentalism, those people who attended church infrequently tended to be more likely to vote for Wallace than frequent churchgoers. The same type of pattern is found with respect to our measure of political tolerance. Sixty-seven per cent of the Baptists who were high on fundamentalism were intolerant of differences in political points of view compared with only 17 per cent of the Presbyterians who were low on fundamentalism. And lastly, we find a parallel pattern with regard to favoring integration efforts. Only 10 per cent of the Baptists high on fundamentalism were in favor of racial integration compared with 58 per cent of the Presbyterians and Episcopalians low on fundamentalism.

In summary, we can conclude from this examination that the link between religion and the Wallace vote seems to be at least partly due to the unusual concentration of feelings of political estrangement and intolerance within the segments of the religious commuity which tended to support Wallace.

SUMMARY AND DISCUSSION

In this article, we have looked at the religious characteristics of people in a Southern metropolitan area who supported former Alabama Governor George Wallace in the 1968 presidential race. Our results show that Wallace appealed to a very definite and clear segment of the religious community. In particular, we found that Wallace's appeal was strongest among the Baptists and weakest among the Episcopalians, a result that confirms other evidence on the 1968 presidential vote. We also found that religious fundamentalism affected the voting independently of religious affiliation,

---

Generally speaking, do you think there should be separate sections for Negroes in streetcars and buses? (No).

Do you think Negroes should be able to use the same parks, restaurants, and hotels as white people? (Yes).

Do you think white students and Negro students should go to the same schools, or to separate schools? (Same schools).

How strongly would you object if a member of your family wanted to bring a Negro friend home to dinner—very strongly, somewhat strongly, or not at all? (Not at all).

Do you think there should be laws against marriages between Negroes and whites? (No).

These items were taken from a survey conducted by the National Opinion Research Center in 1963, some of the results of which are reported in Paul B. Sheatsley, "White Attitudes Toward the Negro," *Daedalus*, 95 (Winter, 1966), pp. 217–238.

fundamentalists being more likely than non-fundamentalists to support Wallace. Moreover, both religious affiliation and religious fundamentalism continued to be associated with disproportionate support for Wallace even when the socioeconomic status differences among voters were held constant. Turning to religious involvement, we discovered that those parishioners who were highly involved in church worship, the frequent churchgoers, were less apt to vote for Wallace than those not so highly involved, the infrequent churchgoers, especially among people who were highly educated. Along somewhat similar lines, our analysis suggested that the link between religion and voting for Wallace may have been partly due to the fact that the Baptists and fundamentalists were more apt to possess a cluster of attitudes and feelings for which Wallace had a special attraction; namely, a feeling of estrangement from politics, an attitude of intolerance towards political differences, and a view hostile to racial integration.

These results, of course, support the thesis outlined at the beginning of this paper, that religion and radical politics can be pursued simultaneously in America while casting strong doubts on the countervailing point of view. One must recognize, however, that the former argument takes its evidence from the American experience with right-wing extremist groups, whereas the latter one is based especially on the American experience with left-wing politics. We would suggest, in fact, that the prevailing forms of religious radicalism in the United States and left-wing political movements are antithetic to one another because they make completely opposing demands on individuals. As Johnson and others argue, many of the smaller Protestant sects and sectlike denominations such as the Baptists are presently the bearers of the kind of ascetic and individualistic traditions which formerly characterized groups like the Congregationalists and Presbyterians in America.[22] This spirit of individual self-reliance runs directly counter to the spirit of left-wing radical movements in this country which, on the whole, promotes ideas of humanitarian reform in the name of a collective, cooperative enterprise. In contrast, of course, the beliefs of certain religious sects in America and those of right-wing political groups converge more than they differ. For instance, one of the central positions of groups like the John Birch Society and George Wallace's American Independent Party is the support of individual rights and the condemnation of such collective bodies as the federal government.

The particular bearing of fundamentalism on right-wing politics in this country may also be partly accounted for by the coincidence of some of the beliefs of fundamentalists with those of right-wing political radicals. For one thing, fundamentalists, as compared with the modernists, have assumed the role of primary carriers of the ascetic Protestant traditions in America. But, in addition, the fundamentalists hold a view of the past which converges with one held by right-wing political radicals. Funda-

---

[22] Johnson, "On Church and Sect." See also David Moberg, *The Church as a Social Institution: The Sociology of American Religion* (Englewood Cliffs, N.J.: Prentice-Hall, Inc., 1962), pp. 144–146, *passim*.

mentalists are generally unwilling to admit of scientific advances and change, whereas the modernists are inclined to adapt their religious beliefs to accord with scientific evidence. Fundamentalists, likewise, tend to accept the Bible as the Word of God, while modernists view it as an historical document, subject to some degree of error. In other words, the fundamentalists hold a view of change, especially in the realm of science, which lends itself extremely easily to a right-wing orientation in politics. Both uphold the sanctity of tradition, one of ascetic Protestantism, the other of American individualism.

The number of Baptists and members of small Protestant sects in the United States, together with the number of fundamentalists in other groups, represents a substantial figure. As we have seen, this segment of the religious community in the United States possesses both the religious and political inclinations to support candidates of a right-wing persuasion. Whether the sentiments of this group will be mobilized in the future to support the candidacy of George Wallace remains in doubt, but there is no question at all that this bloc of voters could have a very decided effect on the outcome of future political contests that feature right-wing candidates.

PART V

Attitudes and Opinions as Independent Variables: Social and Behavioral Consequences

INTRODUCTION

Political scientists and sociologists alike generally accept the view that attitudes are hypothetical constructs denoting variables that mediate between a person's experiences with his environment and responses to that environment. They are hypothetical in the sense that attitudes are not observed directly, but inferred from the types of indirect measurement described in Part I. They are mediators since they stand between the various stimuli impinging upon a person and his alternative ways of behaving. This perspective on the character of attitudes has led to two general emphases in research concerning political attitudes and opinions. In the first researchers investigate attitudes as dependent variables, that is, as products of political socialization, status inconsistency, cognitive activity, and other processes. The selections in Parts II, III, and IV of this anthology illustrate this research emphasis. However, acting as mediators, the predispositions which are dependent in their existence upon various formation processes become influences upon personal and social behavior. In this capacity they are no longer merely dependent variables, but act as independent factors with social and behavioral consequences.

The focus on political attitudes as independent variables raises questions regarding the linkage between personal predispositions and behavior, questions explored in the selections contained in Part V. A principal concern is the extent to which political behavior can be said to reflect attitudes on which it supposedly is based; put another way, what is the correspondence between attitudes and behavior? In a definitional sense, at least, there is close correspondence. If attitudes are regarded as having cognitive, affective, and conative dimensions, their conative aspects are invested with a behavioral element (for, as noted in Part III, the conative dimension refers to what a person will do about a political object, person, event, or situation). Yet, what one will do—as inferred from his expressed opinions— and what he actually does may differ markedly. The problem is not merely that expressed opinions may be conscious deceptions. Rather, the problem is that expressed opinions frequently take the form of what Swedish sociologist Ulf Himmelstrand designates as symbolic acts instead of referent acts.[1] A referent act is one in which a person's verbal attitudes constitute ways of learning about an object, manipulating it, and perhaps consuming it. Thus the referent function of the attitude is to assist the individual to appraise objects in his environment and take actions respecting them. Symbolic acts, however, are verbal statements about an object that enable an individual to express his inner anxieties, tensions, and energies without actually behaving toward the object beyond verbalizing about it. With referent acts, gratification comes from manipulation of the objects about which an opinion is expressed; in symbolic acts, the expression constitutes its own reward.[2] Thus, Mr. Citizen reports to a pollster

---

[1]Ulf Himmelstrand, "Verbal Attitudes and Behavior: A Paradigm for the Study of Message Transmission and Transformation," *Public Opinion Quarterly*, 24 (1960), pp. 224–250.

[2]M. Brewster Smith, "Personality in Politics" in Smith, *Social Psychology and Human Values* (Chicago: Aldine Publishing Company, 1969), pp. 14–32.

that he will vote for candidate A for mayor, then remains away from the polling booth altogether.

The discrepancies between attitudes and behavior make it easy to conclude that political attitudes are poor predictors of political action and, hence, explanations for political behavior must be sought elsewhere. This question of the correspondence of attitudes and behavior constitutes the concern of Howard J. Ehrlich in, "Attitudes, Behavior, and the Intervening Variables." Ehrlich cites a number of studies in which attitudes have been poor predictors of behavior. He points out that in many instances the attitude-behavior inconsistency results from inadequate measurement or conceptualization. Assuming, however, that methodological and conceptual errors are not the source of the discrepancy, Ehrlich poses a basic question: "Under what conditions, and to what degree, are attitudes of a given type related to behavior of a given type?" He suggests a research strategy for examining the variables that intervene between attitudes and behavior that will assist both sociologists and political scientists in answering that question and in improving the predictive power of attitudes.

One of the variables that can intervene between personal attitudes and behavior, and thus account for seeming inconsistency, is the amount and type of information received about a political object. A political campaign, for example, generates information about parties, issues, and candidates that intervenes between a voter's party loyalties and his vote decision. The extent to which party loyalty is an effective predictor of voting behavior is thus dependent in part on perceptions of available information. The relationship between party identification, political information, and voting decisions is explored by Warren A. Dixon in "Party Identification and the Party Vote: A Suggested Model." Dixon posits that the strength of a voter's partisan attitudes influences the amount of information he will be exposed to in that campaign. But, the amount of information available and whether it differs from or reinforces information he already possesses, helps to shape his voting decision. Dixon constructs a model describing the relationship and derives five propositions that assist us to understand the complexities in the attitude-behavior matrix.

The congruence between attitudes and voting behavior is also explored by Howard D. Hamilton in "Voting Behavior in Open Housing Referenda." Hamilton uses data from open housing referenda studies in Detroit, Michigan, Toledo, Ohio, Berkeley, California, and the state of California. Using all four studies he is able to describe the relationship of age, religious preference, occupation, home ownership, education, and partisanship to the vote. From the Toledo study he is able to relate selected attitudinal patterns—authoritarianism, alienation, and efficacy—to the vote. His analysis indicates that authoritarianism and alienation have an affinity with prejudice in voting and that income, education, and social status are positively associated with tolerance in open housing referenda. He observes, however, that a few of the hypotheses concerning the consistencies of social position, attitudes, and voting behavior require revision. Hamilton's contribution serves as a good example of what can be gained in the study of political attitudes by comparing the relationship of attitudes and behavior in a variety of settings. The social setting is itself a variable intervening between attitudes and behavior and the "independent" effects of attitudes on behavior can be revealed only by efforts to control for the influence of differing situations.

To the extent that attitudes and opinions act as independent variables, their social and behavior consequences change as attitudes and opinions shift. The "Political Impact of Shifting Attitudes" is the focus of the essay by Harlan Hahn. Hahn notes that in an election campaign one might classify voters into four types on the basis of their attitudes: *Consistents* staunchly hold to the same position throughout; *Converts* switch positions; *Ambivalents* shift from certainty to uncertainty or vice versa; and *Indecisives* remain undecided throughout. To identify the presence of such voter types Hahn conducted a panel survey in Detroit in 1965–1966; shortly after the mayoralty election in 1965 he interviewed 596 persons and then interviewed 406 of the same respondents after the mid-term elections of 1966. Hahn found major differences between Consistents and Indecisives; the former exhibited the highest rate of continual participation in the elections, appeared active, alert, and interested, and may have exerted the greatest impact upon electoral outcome; the latter were uninvolved and liable to vote "incorrectly." Converts were more likely to participate than Ambivalents and were somewhat more influential in shaping electoral outcomes.

The preceding selections in Part V are concerned with relationships between popular attitudes and mass voting behavior. The remaining two selections have a different focus—the relationship between popular attitudes and the behavior of public officials. In democratic theory it is generally assumed that popular attitudes should have a direct bearing on political policies. The extent to which such a relationship does in fact exist is the problem investigated by Warren E. Miller and Donald E. Stokes in the selection "Constituency Influence in Congress." Their study draws upon interviews conducted at the time of the 1958 congressional elections with incumbent congressmen and their opponents (if any), the constituents in 116 congressional districts, and the roll-call votes of the interviewed congressmen. The interviews with constituents and congressmen covered the policy areas of civil rights, social welfare, and foreign policy. Miller and Stokes are thus able to measure the congruence between four sets of variables: (1) the attitudes of constituents, (2) the congressmen's perceptions of their constituents' attitudes, (3) the congressmen's attitudes, and (4) the congressmen's policy voting behavior. Relying upon correlations between these variables the authors conclude that "the Representative's roll-call behavior is strongly influenced by his own policy preferences and by his perception of preferences held by the constituency" but his perceptions of constituency opinions are frequently based upon "imperfect information." Hence, popular attitudes are frequently poor predictors of the actions of governing officials.

The difficulties in achieving a close correspondence between the popular "will" and official action are explored in more detail by the final selection of Part V. In "Congressional Responsibility and the Organization of Constituency Attitudes" David R. Segal and Thomas S. Smith reveal at least one way in which popular attitudes do guide policy-makers. Utilizing the same data as Miller and Stokes, Segal and Smith suggest a principal reason why public officials rarely perceive accurately the policy preferences of constituents; that is, political attitudes in the mass electorate are simply too diffuse and general to provide cues for congressional behavior in specific policy areas. Instead legislators rely on the positions their constituents have taken in the past with regard to the *general* scope of governmental activity and expenditures. To the extent that officials do take into account general conceptions of the public will, therefore, popular attitudes serve as independent influences on public policy-making.

In retrospect, the selections in Part V reinforce the generally held view that attitudes and opinions may, for some purposes, be treated as independent variables despite their clear dependencies for formation upon socialization processes, social structures, and individual personalities. The attitude-behavior relationship is less certain than problematic and less linear than reciprocal. Yet it can be urged with considerable legitimacy, and it is the burden of this anthology to do so, that one core for the understanding of political behavior must be the study of antecedent political attitudes and opinions.

ATTITUDES, BEHAVIOR, AND THE INTERVENING VARIABLES[*]

HOWARD J. EHRLICH
University of Iowa

S TUDIES ON THE RELATION OF ATTITUDES AND BEHAVIOR HAVE ALMOST CONSIS-
tently resulted in the conclusion that attitudes are a poor predictor of
behavior. The majority of these studies have taken ethnic attitudes
as the predictor and some mode of intergroup behavior as the predictand.
The summary statement here has usually been of the form that prejudice is
a poor predictor of discrimination.[1]

It is clear that many social scientists concerned with the study of prejudice and intergroup behavior have taken the prevailing interpretations of
the evidence of attitude-behavior inconsistency as a premise toward the
conclusion that attitude theory has proven inadequate. In his presidential
address to the Society for the Study of Social Problems, Deutscher asserts
that "no matter what one's theoretical orientation may be, he has no reason
to expect to find congruence between attitudes and actions and every reason
to expect to find discrepancies between them."[2] DeFleur and Westie, for
another example, declare a *necessary* inconsistency between verbal scale
scores and other overt actions, pointing to "social constraints" or situational
norms as the crucial determinants of behavior. Consistency between at-

[*]Reprinted with permission of the author and publisher, from Howard Ehrlich,
"Attitudes, Behavior, and the Intervening Variables," *American Sociologist*, 4
(Feb., 1969), pp. 29–34.
[1]D. W. Bray, "The Prediction of Behavior from Two Attitude Scales," *Journal of
Abnormal Psychology*, 45 (1950), pp. 64–84; W. Brookover and J. Holland, "An In-
quiry into the Meaning of Minority Group Attitude Expression," *American Socio-
logical Review*, 17 (1952), pp. 196–202; M. L. DeFleur and F. R. Westie, "Verbal
Attitudes and Overt Acts: An Experiment on the Salience of Attitudes," *American
Sociological Review*, 23 (1958), pp. 667–673; J. Fishman, "Some Social and Psy-
chological Determinants of Intergroup Relations in Changing Neighborhoods: An
Introduction to the Bridgeview Study," *Social Forces*, 40 (1961), pp. 42–51; L. M.
Killian, "The Adjustment of Southern White Migrants to Northern Urban Norms,"
Social Forces, 32 (1953), pp. 66–69; B. C. Kutner, *et al.*, "Verbal Attitudes and
Overt Behavior Involving Racial Prejudice," *Journal of Abnormal and Social Psy-
chology*, 47 (1952), pp. 649–652; R. T. LaPiere, "Attitudes vs. Actions," *Social
Forces*, 43 (1934), pp. 230–237; L. S. Linn, "Verbal Attitudes and Overt Behavior:
A Study of Racial Discrimination," *Social Forces*, 43 (1965), pp. 353–364; J. P.
Lohman and D. C. Reitzes, "Note on Race Relations in Mass Society," *American
Journal of Sociology*, 58 (1952), pp. 240–246; M. Malof and A. Lott, "Ethnocen-
trism and the Acceptance of Negro Support in a Group Situation," *Journal of Ab-
normal and Social Psychology*, 65 (1962), pp. 254–258; R. D. Minard, "Race Re-
lationships in the Pocahontas Coal Field," *Journal of Social Issues*, 8 (1952), pp.
29–44; G. Nettler and E. H. Golding, "The Measurement of Attitudes Toward the
Japanese in America," *American Journal of Sociology*, 52 (1946), pp. 31–39; G. H.
Saenger and E. Gilbert, "Customer Reactions to the Integration of Negro Sales
Personnel," *Public Opinion Quarterly*, 4 (1950), pp. 57–76.
[2]I. Deutscher, "Words and Deeds: Social Science and Social Policy," *Social Problems*, 13 (Winter, 1966), p. 247.

titudes and behavior occurs, they argue, "if the normative processes of the groups within which [people] are interacting are consistent."[3]

It is the thesis of this paper that the evidence for inconsistency may be rejected on both methodological and conceptual grounds, and that there is no necessary incompatibility between a theory of attitudes and theories of interpersonal or intergroup behavior. It is my intent, first, to present briefly the major arguments against interpretations of inconsistency, and then to provide a paradigm for the analysis of the attitude-behavior relation. I shall limit my examples to the study of prejudice and intergroup behavior.

METHODOLOGICAL ARGUMENTS

From a methodological standpoint it can be argued that attitude measurement, particularly in the domain of prejudice, has been demonstrated to be seriously imprecise and unreliable. Rosenthal, in his review of experimenter error, summarized the effects of the real and perceived ethnicity of experimenters on test and questionnaire performance.[4] From this evidence, it is apparent that the ethnic identity of the researcher significantly biases respondent behavior. Ehrlich[5] and Ehrlich and Rinehart[6] have demonstrated that forced-response formats in prejudice scales overstate the degree of prejudice and distort the manifest content of ethnic-group imagery. Fendrich provides a direct test of the effects of the measurement process on predicting intergroup behavior, concluding: "Verbal attitudes can be either consistent or inconsistent with overt behavior, depending upon the way respondents define the attitude measurement situation."[7]

Measurement errors may also be examined in the operations through which the behaviors to be predicted and explained in the attitude-behavior paradigm are measured or assessed. While the operations for attitude-scale construction are relatively well standardized, the operations for observing and recording behavior, particularly in natural settings, are generally unstandardized and problem-specific. Further, while the items of attitude scales are presumably a representative set of statements from the attitude domain studied, most behavioral units selected for study have been chosen on a non-systematic or *ad hoc* basis. It would seem plausible, therefore, to attribute some degree of recorded inconsistency to these less rigorous measures of overt actions in intergroup situations.

It may be, further, that our basic strategy has been wrong. We have generally measured attitudes toward a class of people, but made predictions

[3]M. L. DeFleur and F. R. Westie, "Attitude as a Scientific Concept," *Social Forces*, 42 (1963), p. 28.

[4]R. Rosenthal, *Experimenter Effects in Behavioral Research* (New York: Appleton-Century-Crofts, 1966).

[5]H. J. Ehrlich, "Instrument Error and the Study of Prejudice," *Social Forces*, 43 (1964), pp. 197–206.

[6]H. J. Ehrlich and J. W. Rinehart, "A Brief Report on the Methodology of Stereotype Research," *Social Forces*, 43 (1965), pp. 564–575.

[7]J. M. Fendrich, "A Study of the Association Among Verbal Attitudes, Commitment and Overt Behavior in Different Experiment Situations," *Social Forces*, 45 (1967), p. 355.

about a person's behavior toward a specific member of that class.[8] Certainly a low order of correct predictions may be taken as a special case of the fallacy of ecological correlation (i.e., predicting unit behavior from a knowledge of aggregate relations). Perhaps, more appropriately, we should consider the alternatives: either we measure an attitude toward a specific person and then predict a subject's behavior toward that person, or we measure attitudes toward a class of people and predict a subject's behavior to some (perhaps phenomenologically) representative sample of that class.

On the basis of even these brief and limited methodological arguments, the evidence from past research must be re-examined. The conclusion that verbal attitude expressions are inconsistent with other overt behaviors must be suspended. In reviewing the conceptual arguments, I shall try to show that the conclusion is untenable.

CONCEPTUAL ARGUMENTS

The conceptual arguments that may be adduced to invalidate interpretations of inconsistency need not be tied to a specific theory of attitudes. The strategy of this presentation is based on the assumption that the most cogent arguments are those which can be easily stated in the language of the current, prevailing attitude theories.

In almost all current theories, attitudes are construed as having a componential structure. Not all the components of an attitude imply behavior. It follows from this that without a direct assessment of the "action potential" of an attitude component, the researcher's inference about the subject's behavior, or intentions, may be phenomenologically naive. This possibility is illustrated in a study by Kay,[9] who demonstrated that 36 per cent of a sample of presumably anti-Jewish items, drawn from the Levinson-Sanford scale of anti-Semitism, were judged by naive subjects as friendly or directionally unclear. Predictions of anti-Jewish behavior from these items would probably have displayed high error.

To adopt the argument that not all attitude components imply behavior, it is not necessary to endorse a multi-dimensional strategy of attitude-theory construction. The argument, from the standpoint of a uni-dimensional theory, simply becomes: not all attitudes imply behavior. Whatever the other outcomes of these theoretical strategies, they agree in their fundamental statements concerning the relation of attitudes and behavior. Fishbein, a leading uni-dimensional theorist, states his position clearly:

> Because attitude is a hypothetical variable abstracted from the *totality* of an individual's beliefs, behavioral intentions, and actions, toward a given object . . . any given belief, behavioral intention, or behavior, therefore, may be uncorrelated or even negatively correlated with his attitude. Thus, rather than viewing specific beliefs or classes of beliefs and specific behavioral intentions or types of behavioral intentions as part of attitude, these phenomena must

[8] M. Fishbein, "The Relationships Between Beliefs, Attitudes, and Behavior," in S. Feldman, ed., *Cognitive Consistency* (New York: Academic Press, 1966).

[9] L. W. Kay, "Frame of Reference in 'Pro' and 'Anti' Evaluation of Test Items," *Journal of Social Psychology*, 25 (1947), pp. 63–68.

be studied as variables in their own right, that, like attitudes, may or may not function as determinants of a specific behavior.[10]

Different scaling models and measurement procedures differentially assess the behaviorally directive components of attitudes. The current major scaling models focus primarily on two attitude components, usually direction and intensity; only the procedure of summated ratings considers both dimensions simultaneously. Where an attitude scale is focused on a single component and where that component has a low action potential, successful prediction should be highly unlikely. Tittle and Hill provide some confirming evidence.[11] Aside from formal scaling, the two major procedures for measuring prejudice—the stereotype check list and the social-distance questionnaire—similarly tap only a single attitude component. The check list assesses only the salience (typicality) of a stereotype, and that usually in a categorical manner, while social distance measures provide a report solely of behavioral intentions, usually abstracted from situational reference. Only where these components entail a high directiveness for behavior should a high congruence with behavior be expected.

It may be argued further that the determination of the structure of an attitude at any point in time requires the determination of the inter-relations of the components that constitute the attitude. An attitude can be defined as well formed when all of its components achieve some balance and that balanced state persists over time. If this conceptualization is adequate, it follows that reliable predictions of behavior can occur only from well-formed attitudes, or, in the absence of a well-formed attitude, only when the predicted behavior is close in time to the attitude measurement. Even then, it may be the case that the measurement process per se can change the state of a poorly balanced attitude.

Not only does a single attitude comprise several components, but a single attitude object may implicate many attitudes. Predictions of behavior that do not account for all (or at least the major) attitudes evoked by an object will probably be wrong. In a variation on this argument, Rokeach has contended that at least two attitudes are required to make a correct prediction of behavior.

> . . . an attitude may be focused either on an object or on a situation. In the first instance we have in mind an attitude-object, which may be concrete or abstract, involving a person, a group, an institution, or an issue. In the second instance the attitude is focused on a specific situation, an event, or an activity. To say that a person has an enduring attitude toward a given object is to say that this attitude will, when activated, somehow determine his behavior toward the attitude-object across situations; conversely, to say that a person has an enduring attitude toward a given situation is to say that this attitude will,

[10]Fishbein, "The Relationships Between Beliefs, Attitudes, and Behavior," p. 213.

[11]C. R. Tittle and R. J. Hill, "Attitude Measurement and Prediction of Behavior: An Evaluation of Conditions and Measurement Techniques," *Sociometry*, 30 (1967), pp. 199–213.

when activated, determine his behavior toward the situation, across attitude-objects.[12]

It may be that the reported inconsistency between attitude and behavior is a partial result of our naiveté in phenomenological analysis, i.e., our inability to ascertain the intentional meaning of an actor's verbal and nonverbal acts. Without denying the crudities of phenomenological analysis in contemporary social psychology, the fundamental problem may be that our presumed observations of inconsistencies derive from our failure to specify the criteria for judging a consistent or inconsistent response. Campbell provides a graphic illustration of the problem of assessing consistency:

> On an arithmetic test of four items, the child who gets only two items correct is not necessarily regarded as less consistent than the child who gets all right or all wrong. If he gets the two easiest right and the two hardest wrong, he is equally consistent. On intelligence we today think in terms of a continuum, and can conceive of consistent mediocrity. . . . We can regard honesty as something people have in degree, rather than an all-or-none trait. A person of intermediate degree can be just as consistent as a person of extreme position, and his attitude can be determined from his behavior just as well. . . . For intelligence and honesty, we have achieved dimensionality in our thinking. For more emotion-laden topics, such as standing up for civil rights, we have not. If a university president protects a pacifist professor but fires an atheist, we call him inconsistent. If he protects a pacifist and an atheist, but fires a Communist, we accuse him of backing down under pressure. Conceptually, we have the notion of a total non-defendant of professors' rights and a total defender of professors' rights, and lack any concept of genuine mediocrity which would in consistency produce defense in a situation of low threshold and firing in another situation with a higher threshold value.[13]

The assessment of consistency is initially contingent on the conditions of adequate measurement and the stability of an attitude. Assuming these conditions, it is then necessary to enumerate the set of obligatory and optional behaviors that comprise the attitude domain. Presumably, this is a highly limited set of behaviors, or at least the obligatory behaviors form a highly limited subset. The number of observations required for a sample of this set or subset of behaviors will doubtless be fixed by the degree to which these behaviors are scalar. The extent to which an individual's verbal and nonverbal behaviors may achieve some level of consistency will then depend upon quasi-logical (probably social-psychological) criteria of contradiction. Such criteria, implicit in everyday behavior, have yet to be made explicit.

[12] M. Rokeach, "Attitude Change and Behavioral Change," *Public Opinion Quarterly*, 30 (1967), p. 530.

[13] D. T. Campbell, "Social Attitudes and Other Acquired Behavioral Dispositions," in S. Koch, ed., *Psychology: A Study of a Science*, Vol. 6 (New York: McGraw-Hill, 1961), p. 160.

STRATEGY FOR RESEARCH: THE INTERVENING VARIABLES

The search for a more appropriate research strategy must begin with the understanding that the simple question of the consistency of attitudes and behavior is misleading. The correct representation of the problem should take the form: under what conditions, and to what degree, are attitudes of a given type related to behaviors of a given type? My intent in this section, then, is to identify the social and psychological conditions that intervene between attitudes and behavior. As a matter of intellectual strategy, I shall limit myself here to those variables most directly related to attitude theory. Elsewhere I have attempted to identify the relevant variables of social structure in considering the analogous problem of the relation of role expectations to role behavior.[14] Current alternatives may be reviewed in Fishbein[15] and Himmelstrand.[16]

Clarity. For consistency to occur there has to be a clear way for an attitude to be expressed in behavior. For some attitudes and for some behaviors, the relationship may not be clear. This indeterminacy could appear under a number of possible conditions, the importance of which we shall probably have to ferret out through intensive descriptive research. Williams, in discussing the characteristics of behavior in unclear interracial situations, provides a prospectus for research:

> The unfamiliar situation is, by definition, initially one of uncertainty, which is another way of saying that it induces some degree of insecurity. Past experience does not suffice as a guide, and old norms may not lead to the usual results. New situations are likely, therefore, to instigate heightened alertness —including a generalized vigilance toward cues that may indicate what action will lead to what consequences. Under the circumstances of uncertainty and sharpened attentiveness, the individual who first acts with an appearance of decisiveness and confidence is likely to have marked influence. It can and does often happen that the people in leadership positions are themselves confused; for them the situation is not even structured enough to suggest where to turn for clarification. We saw that, in consequence, action on the part of any other participant became disproportionately important in determining their definitions. Confused participants sought indices of how others defined the situation. Since the crucial question in many of these situations was whether or not membership in a particular racial category (Negro) precluded membership in other groups or categories, the first action to be taken by a white was often interpreted by all as an index of acceptance or rejection.[17]

Expressibility. Some attitudes may be clearly expressible only in verbal behavior. Extremely radical, highly unconventional, or strongly anti-social attitudes may in fact have their primary expression in verbal behaviors or in

---

[14] J. J. Preiss and H. J. Ehrlich, *An Examination of Role Theory* (Lincoln: University of Nebraska Press, 1966), Chap. 9.

[15] Fishbein, "The Relationships Between Beliefs, Attitudes, and Behavior."

[16] U. Himmelstrand, "Verbal Attitudes and Behavior: A Paradigm for the Study of Message Transmission," *Public Opinion Quarterly*, 24 (1960), pp. 224–250.

[17] R. M. Williams, *Strangers Next Door* (Englewood Cliffs: Prentice-Hall, 1964), p. 329.

fantasy. Some attitudes may have their expression in sublimated behavior. Attitudes about matters which a person defines, or which are socially defined, as highly intimate may also have their primary expressions in verbal and fantasy behavior. Other expressions may be deliberately concealed from observation.

Disclosure. Related to expressibility is the willingness of a person to disclose his attitude. Under many circumstances, the failure to disclose one's attitude may be neither an attitude-consistent nor an attitude-inconsistent act. In the case of attitudes toward oneself, their disclosure or concealment has indicated such a regular pattern of occurrence that the conditions of disclosure could represent an important class of variables for more general consideration. The research stimulated by Jourard[18] has confirmed that people vary in their characteristic level of disclosure of self-attitudes. It has also been established, particularly from the work of Altman and Haythorn,[19] that these individual differences are responsive to controlled situational variation both for the number of self-attitude statements disclosed and for their depth of intimacy. Following from this, Graeven[20] has demonstrated that for thirteen different categories of self-attitude statements and for levels of intimacy associated with each of these categories, all subjects—regardless of their characteristic level of disclosure—reciprocated by category and intimacy the disclosures made by another person. This limited research suggests that reciprocity in the verbal and nonverbal expression of attitudes may be a standard interpersonal tactic as well as a more generalized norm of interpersonal behavior. Thus, it may be hypothesized that attitudes expressible in interpersonal situations may not be disclosed either because others do not express their attitudes, or because the actor fails to perceive them. Further, the "race-belief" and the "attitude similarity" hypotheses of Rokeach[21] and Byrne[22] suggest an obverse to the disclosure hypothesis: Attitudes expressible in interpersonal situations may not be disclosed when the actor perceives his attitudes as contrary to the attitudes of others in the situation. These disclosure hypotheses will no doubt have to be qualified by considerations of the duration of the situation, among other situational properties.

Perspective and the Definition of the Act. The indeterminate status of the attitude-behavior relation may also be a consequence of perspective. An act consistent from the standpoint of the actor may appear to the observer to be inconsistent. This becomes particularly problematic when an actor deliberately chooses not to act, or when the outcome of an act is contrary to what the actor intended.

[18] S. M. Jourard, *The Transparent Self* (Princeton: D. Van Nostrand, 1964).

[19] I. Altman and W. W. Haythorn, "Interpersonal Exchange in Isolation," *Sociometry*, 28 (1965), pp. 411–426.

[20] D. B. Graven, *Reciprocal Self-Disclosure in a Dyadic Situation* (Ames: University of Iowa, 1967).

[21] Rokeach, "Attitude Change and Behavioral Change."

[22] D. Byrne, "Interpersonal Attraction and Attitude Similarity," *Journal of Abnormal and Social Psychology*, 62 (1961), pp. 713–715.

Perhaps the most confounding problem of the matter of intent as related to the outcome of an act is that of the social definition of an act. Regardless of the actor's intent, both the scientist as an observer and the actor as an observer of himself must cope with the prevailing social definition. Where the disparity between a personal and social construction of an act is very great, it seems likely that over time an actor may come to question or even redefine his own behavior. The presumed seriousness of this problem has led some social scientists to take the position that a motivational theory must necessarily be a theory of rationalization of behavior:

> The aspect of motive which this conception grasps is its intrinsically social character. A satisfactory or adequate motive is one that satisfied the questioners of an act or program, whether it be the other's or the actor's. As a word, a motive tends to be one which is to the actor and to the other members of a situation an unquestioned answer to questions concerning social and lingual conduct. A stable motive is an ultimate in justificatory conversation. The words which in a type situation will fulfill this function are circumscribed by the vocabulary of motives acceptable for such situations. Motives are accepted justifications for present, future, or past programs or acts.[23]

As a theory of motivation, the conspectus of Mills is seriously defective. Nevertheless, the systematic study of vocabularies of motives should lead to a more sophisticated understanding of intentional behavior and self-report. This uniquely sociological perspective furthermore points to three parameters of self-report requiring serious consideration: the strength of prevailing definitions of social acts, the disparity between personal and social definitions of social acts, and the time between an act and the actor's report of his intent, or vice versa.

The sociology of motivational analysis leads us to still another consideration. The same act over time and in different social contexts changes its meaning, i.e., its social definition. Attitude-consistent behavior at one time may be perceived as inconsistent at another time. Yesterday's radical may be today's impediment to progress, though neither his attitudes nor behavior have changed in consistency. Morton Deutsch, who calls this the problem of "unrecognized locomotion," describes it:

> To the extent that we do not take cognizance of how changes beyond our control affect our positions in relation to our goals, we are likely to behave in ways which are either inconsistent or irrelevant to our purposes. The incorrect assessment of present position is likely to lead to a faulty perception of the direction to one's goal.[24]

Finally, informal evidence indicates that people sometimes intentionally act in an attitude-inconsistent manner. Such behavior, which may be an important condition for attitude change, may have its basis in either per-

---

[23] C. W. Mills, "Situated Actions and Vocabularies of Motive," *American Sociological Review*, 5 (1940), pp. 906–907.

[24] M. Deutsch, "The Directions of Behavior: A Field-Theorectical Approach to the Understanding of Inconsistencies," *Journal of Social Issues*, 5 (1949), p. 49.

sonal curiosity or an attempt to achieve novelty in an unstimulating environment. Inconsistent behavior may also be a primary means by which individuals test themselves and others.

Learning. The discussion so far has focused on the condition of clarity in the relation of attitudes to behavior, where the strategic problems become the determination of an attitude's expressibility and the nexus of intention to act. It is now appropriate to introduce the three assumptions hidden in this discussion. The first of these is the learning assumption. Even where a clear and expressible relation exists between an attitude and behavior, it is not necessary to assume that an actor knows how to behave in a consistent manner. The major determinant of attitude-discrepant behavior may be that an actor has not learned how to express his attitude in action competently. One determinant of the adequacy of such learning may be the level of direct or vicarious experience of the actor, if any, in such behavior situations. Under this condition of no or poor learning, inaction, inappropriate behavior, and sometimes ineffective behavior are defined by the observer as inconsistent acts. Certainly, learning how to behave in a manner consistent with one's attitudes is a primary objective of socialization at all stages of the life cycle.

Accessibility. The second of the assumptions implicit in discussions of attitude-consistent behavior is the assumption of opportunity and access. Knowing how to behave in an appropriate manner is insufficient if the opportunity, access, or perceived access to the opportunity is non-existent. For example, the study of ethnic intermarriage reveals that the best predictor of intermarriage is the opportunity to intermarry. For Negro-white marriages, for instance, opportunity is partly defined by the proportion of eligible mates, the degree of residential segregation, and the degree of status congruence.[25]

Competence. Even knowing what is consistent and having the opportunity to engage in attitude-consistent behavior is only one necessary condition for such behavior. Not only must an actor learn what comprises appropriate behavior, but he must learn how to use his skills and muster his personal resources in order for his actions to be effective. Thus, the third assumption implicit in most past discussions has been an assumption of skill and resource. Patently, individuals vary in the skills they have developed and in the resources they can mobilize for behavior in any given situation. Inferences about behavior, therefore, must take into account such individual differences. An ostensibly inconsistent act may indicate only the actor's deficient skill, his lack of resources, or his inability to organize his resources for effective behavior. It is possible that inferences about behavior and consistency may be biased in the direction of more skillful individuals by the fact that they may emit more behaviors, and/or perform them more confidently and more effectively.

The research strategies indicated so far are of substantial consequence in

[25] D. M. Heer, "Negro-White Marriage in the United States," *Journal of Marriage and the Family*, 28 (1966), pp. 262–273.

establishing the attitude-behavior relation. Two widely discussed problems of crucial importance remain: the problem of situational analysis and the problem of multiple-attitude analysis.

Situational Analysis.   In the absence of any well-established guidelines for such analysis, it seems reasonable to consider as separate problems those concerned with the structural, primarily physical, characteristics of situations and those concerned with the social dimensions. The focus of structural analysis is, first, the study of the properties of situations and their interrelationships, and second, the study of the relation of these properties to behavior. Barker and his associates[26] have developed an extensive language and research operations for structural analysis, but these have not yet had application to the kinds of problems that concern us here. Hall[27] has provided systematic procedures for assessing the effects of space on interpersonal behavior, and Sommer[28] has recently reviewed this developing literature. For the social dimensions of situations, the most well-developed schemes now exist for the analysis of role behavior[29] and for the analysis of interaction processes.[30] Although the significance of role playing and role enactment for attitude change has been clearly demonstrated,[31] attitude theorists have generally ignored role and related theories (and role theorists have generally ignored attitude variables).

Situational characteristics are often given theoretical consideration only if they are *perceived* by the actor, and sometimes they are considered only in terms of the actor's *attitudes* toward them. This strategy may be misleading. It remains to be demonstrated that the actor does, in fact, perceive and have an attitude toward situational properties and that such attitudes are of meaningful behavioral relevance. While many situational variables are invariably perceived, other situational variables of behavioral importance, particularly the structural characteristics, are probably seldom perceived. Whatever the strategy of situational analysis in attitude research, the warrant for its priority should be clear. In the classic formulation of Lewin: behavior is a function of the person and his environment.

Multiple Attitudes.   A strategy for research on multiple attitudes is based on the assumptions that for some situations and objects more than

[26] R. G. Barker and H. F. Wright, *Midwest and Its Children* (New York: Harper & Row, 1955); R. G. Barker, ed., *The Stream of Behavior* (New York: Appleton-Century-Crofts, 1963).

[27] E. T. Hall, *The Hidden Dimension* (Garden City: Doubleday, 1966); and "A System of Notation of Proxemic Behavior," *American Anthropologist*, 65 (1963), pp. 1003–1026.

[28] R. Sommer, "Small Group Ecology," *Psychological Bulletin*, 67 (1967), pp. 145–152.

[29] B. J. Biddle and E. J. Thomas, eds., *Role Theory: Concepts and Research* (New York: John Wiley and Sons, 1966); Preiss and Ehrlich, *An Examination of Role Theory.*

[30] E. F. Borgatta and B. Crowther, *A Workbook for the Study of Social Interaction Processes* (Chicago: Rand McNally and Company, 1965).

[31] T. R. Sarbin, "Role Theoretical Interpretation of Psychological Change," in P. Worchel and D. Byrne, eds., *Personality Change* (New York: John Wiley and Sons, 1964), pp. 176–219.

one attitude will be evoked and that the behavioral strength of a set of attitudes may be formally determined. The research of Bayton, McAllister, and Hamer,[32] for example, has indicated that attitudes toward social class appear almost as important as race attitudes in determining the stereotypes assigned to Negroes. Triandis[33] has demonstrated that the expression of behavioral intentions varies across the class, sex, ethnicity, occupation, and belief similarity of the attitude object. For example, behavior toward a Negro female physician may be primarily directed by one's attitudes toward Negroes, toward females, toward physicians, toward any two of these characteristics, or toward all three simultaneously. The development of a calculus of attitudes across attitude objects and situations should seriously be considered as an item of high research priority.

CONCLUDING REMARKS

The intervening variables presented here were specifically limited to those directly related to current attitude theories. I began by indicating that not all attitudes are behaviorally expressible, or at least clearly expressible, in interpersonal behavior. Some attitudes are deliberately not expressed in behavior, and I suggested that we examine the interpersonal conditions under which people are willing or unwilling to disclose their attitudes.

The exact behavior that complements a specific attitude is not always clear, and the presumed clarity of an act is itself a consequence of the perspective from which it is evaluated as well as the time that intervenes between act and evaluation. Knowledge of how to act consistently has to be learned, and not all actors will be able to use their knowledge with equal competence. Beyond these conditions, it still remains to be demonstrated that the actor has the opportunity to act appropriately. Finally, I indicated that the actor's failure to act in a manner consistent with a given attitude could be a direct result of other situational constraints or a result of conflict with other relevant attitudes that are more important to the behaviors under analysis.

The specific effects that each of these intervening variables has on behavior remains to be determined. There should be no doubt, however, that the study of these variables and the relation of attitudes to behavior is of strategic significance in the development of social psychology. The question I raised about this relation, in beginning our examination of the intervening variables, is a major instance of the classic problem of social psychology. Under what conditions, how, and to what degree do aspects of social structure and aspects of personality determine interpersonal behavior?

[32] J. A. Bayton, et al., "Race-Class Stereotypes," *Journal of Negro Education*, 25 (Winter, 1956), pp. 75–78.

[33] H. C. Trinandis, "Toward an Analysis of the Components of Interpersonal Attitudes," in C. W. Sherif and M. Sherif, eds., *Attitude, Ego-Involvement, and Change* (New York: John Wiley and Sons, 1967).

PARTY IDENTIFICATION AND THE PARTY VOTE: A SUGGESTED MODEL

WARREN A. DIXON

Texas A&M University

RESEARCH ON AMERICAN POLITICAL BEHAVIOR HAS IMPRESSIVELY DOCU-mented the electorate's low level of political information. To the dismay of some social commentators, many American voters not only know little about political issues and candidates, but apparently they have little inclination to become better informed.[1] In contrast, however, to this low level of political information and interest, the saliency and stability of the voters' party affiliation or identification is impressive on both the systemic and individual level of analysis.[2]

First, the electorate's loyalty to the two-party system during the twentieth century has been truly emphatic.[3] Second, the overwhelming majority of American voters are able to (a) identify with one of the two major parties and (b) to vote in line with their party identifications.[4] This behavior is especially striking when it is compared to the behavior of other national electorates.[5]

---

[1] Converse has made the intriguing observation that 20-25 per cent of his respondents randomly guessed as to the relationship among ideological labels, the meanings of these labels, and party labels. Philip E. Converse, "The Nature of Belief Systems in Mass Publics," in David E. Apter, ed., *Ideology and Discontent* (New York: Free Press, 1964), pp. 206–261.

[2] Although the terms "party identification" and "party affiliation" will be used synonymously in this paper, there is an empirical and theoretical distinction. Unlike affiliation, identification is a psychological construct. To put it another way, identification refers to an attitudinal dimension, while affiliation is more precisely a form of behavior. It will be assumed, however, that there is complete congruency between a voter's party identification and party affiliation. It will be assumed, for example, that a voter who considers himself to be a strong (weak) Republican (Democrat) is registered—if he is registered at all—as a Republican (Democrat). The degree of congruency between party identification and affiliation is, of course, an empirical question.

[3] See, however, Walter Dean Burnham, "The Changing Shape of the American Political Universe," *American Political Science Review*, 59 (March, 1965), pp. 7–28 and Jack Dennis, "Support for the Party System by the Mass Public," *American Political Science Review*, 60 (Sept., 1966), pp. 600–615 for some evidence that this commitment may be weakening.

[4] It should be noted, however, that the relationship between party identification and *presidential* voting is less clear. There have been three landslide presidential victories since 1952 and two extremely close ones. This variation in the winning candidates' margins indicate substantial shifting in the electorate's voting patterns. Yet the proportional breakdown of voters by the respective partisan labels has remained virtually unchanged over the past two decades. Thus, it would appear that the presidential vote is more influenced by "short term" variables than underlying partisan attitudes. See Philip E. Converse, *et al.*, "Continuity and Change in American Politics: Parties and Issues in the 1968 Election," *American Political Science Review*, 63 (Dec., 1969), pp. 1083–1105.

[5] Converse and Dupeux discovered that of those individuals who did not refuse to answer the question, less than 45 per cent of the French repondents could classify

Given this high durability and saliency of party identification on the part of the American voters—yet their comparatively low level of political information and interest—an intriguing theoretical problem is presented. How do we account *within one explanatory framework* for these seemingly contradictory behaviors?

It can be suggested that party identification functions as a rational cost-reducing mechanism for the electorate. Ultimately, voting is a decisional process which requires the acquisition and evaluation of information. Yet the acquisition and processing of relevant political information is not a costless process. Thus, as Downs has suggested, voters utilize their political ideology in order to reduce the "cost of becoming informed about specific issues."[6] In an uncertain world, voters have neither the resources nor the inclination to make politics their avocation.

Without seriously violating Downs' formulation, *party identification* can be substituted for ideology in a "rational" model of political behavior.[7] Reformulated, party identification is the primary device which enables the voter to reduce the cost of acquiring and evaluating political information. Rather than deliberating on each separate issue and candidate, the voter short-cuts this costly process and relies on party identification to resolve the competing claims. To put it another way, party identification "averages out" the numerous cost and benefit calculations required in rational decision-making.

More specifically, if voting is conceptualized as a decisional process, the individual voter's party identification serves four basic functions. It:

(a) selectively censors incoming political information;
(b) organizes politically relevant information into a meaningful pattern;
(c) resolves cognitive and emotive dissonance caused by incongruent perceptions of the political environment; and
(d) reduces the necessity by the voter of evaluating synoptically each candidate or issue.

All of these propositions are, of course, subject to empirical testing, and an entire range of experimental and survey research findings would be appropriate in evaluating their validity. For example, we know that people utilize a series of perceptual mechanisms in order to filter informational

---

themselves by party label. Philip E. Converse and Georges Dupeux, "Politicization of the Electorate in France and the United States," in Angus Campbell, *et al.*, *Elections and the Political Order* (New York: John Wiley, 1966), pp. 269–291.

[6] Anthony Downs, *An Economic Theory of Democracy* (New York: Harper and Row, 1957), p. 99.

[7] For examples of the renewed interest by political scientists in the "rational" model of the political man, see Michael J. Shapiro, "Rational Political Man: A Synthesis of Economic and Social-Psychological Perspectives," *American Political Science Review*, 63 (Dec., 1969), pp. 1106–1119; John C. Harsanyi, "Rational-Choice Models of Political Behavior vs. Functionalist and Conformist Theories," *World Politics*, 21 (July, 1969), pp. 513–538; and Arthur S. Goldberg, "Social Determinism and Rationality as Bases of Party Identification," *American Political Science Review*, 63 (March, 1969), pp. 5–25.

stimuli.[8] Furthermore, there are indications that individuals not only re-solve incongruencies between attitudes and behavior, but also between conflicting beliefs in order to achieve cognitive balance or consistency.[9] Finally, the evidence that "independent" voters are less involved in the political process, less politically informed, and less stable in their voting patterns could be interpreted as suggesting what happens to a voter in the absence of a party identification.[10]

While it perhaps reverses the normal procedure, the general proposition that party identification functions as a rational cost-reducing mechanism can also be tested by accounting for the behavior of those individuals whose vote *cannot* be predicted from their party identification. In an im-portant sense one explains the normal by accounting for deviation. That is, implicit in any explanation of a phenomenon is a converse one that ex-plains why the phenomenon did not occur in some other way.

A SUGGESTED MODEL

For purposes of this model, the correlation between party identification and party vote will be conceptualized as being a perfectly positive one (i.e., if we know the individual's party identification, we know the partisan direction of the individual's vote). In every election, however, we know that there are deviations from this model.[11] Two intervening variables can be postulated in order to account partially for why there is not a perfect correlation. First, there is the concept of "congruency of stored political information" and, second, the concept of the "direction of the partisan in-formation flow."[12]

Briefly, the congruency of stored political information is a summary perceptual variable. It measures the voter's perception of the correspond-ence between his political party's programs and his own system of pre-

[8] Joseph T. Klapper, *The Effects of Mass Communication* (New York: Free Press, 1960), pp. 12–52. For a critical review of the "selective exposure" literature, see David O. Sears and Jonathan L. Freedman, "Selective Exposure to Information: A Critical Review," *Public Opinion Quarterly*, 31 (Summer, 1967), pp. 194–213. Finally, for a review of some of the older important experimental research, see Carl I. Hovland, *et al.*, *Communication and Persuasion* (New Haven: Yale University Press, 1953).

[9] For the basic theoretical formulations, see Fritz Heider, *The Psychology of Inter-personal Relations* (New York: John Wiley, 1958) and Leon Festinger, *A Theory of Cognitive Dissonance* (Stanford: Stanford University Press, 1957).

[10] Angus Campbell and Warren E. Miller, "The Motivational Basis of Straight and Split Ticket Voting," *American Political Science Review*, 51 (June, 1957), pp. 293–312; and Angus Campbell, *et al.*, *The American Voter* (New York: John Wiley, abridged edition, 1964), pp. 67–85.

[11] For a recent effort to account for deviations, see Richard W. Boyd, "Presidential Elections: An Explanation of Voting Defection," *American Political Science Review*, 63 (June, 1969), pp. 498–514.

[12] The terms "stored political information" and "information flow" are derived from Philip E. Converse, "Information Flow and Stability of Partisan Attitudes," in Camp-bell, *et al.*, *Elections and the Political Order*, pp. 136–157. While somewhat similar in meanings, there are, nonetheless, significant differences between the two sets of vari-ables. Converse's "stored political information" is measured by the amount of the voter's *accurate* political information, while his "information flow" is measured by the amount of political information created by the electoral process.

ferred policy outcomes. If the voter agrees with the full range of his party's programs and actions, there is a high congruency of stored political information. While on the other hand, if he disagrees with most of the programs, there is a low congruency. Since different policy issues have variable levels of importance for different voters, we should be careful not to assume (a) equal saliency or (b) equal weighting of all issues in the voter's calculation of congruency. For example, some voters may consider symbolic issues to be more important than bread-and-butter ones.[13] Or, equally conceivable, voters may consider one issue to be so important that they evaluate the party on only that one policy dimension.

The distinction between low and high congruency of stored political information is somewhat related to the usual division that is made between "weak" and "strong" party identifiers. The concept of perceptual congruency is preferred, however, because it more precisely specifies which dimension of party identification is being considered. The "weak-strong" division connotes an emotive attachment to the party which is analytically distinct from any perceived congruency between the voter's and the party's schedule of preferred policy outcomes. Moreover, it is important to emphasize that the congruency of stored political information has nothing to do with the ability of the voter to perceive *accurately* the various parties' policy positions. In its most basic form the concept refers to the voter's belief (for whatever reason and however inaccurately) that his party best represents his system of preferred policy alternatives (regardless of how vague these preferred alternatives may be in the cognitive structure of the voter).

The second intervening variable, the direction of the partisan information flow, measures the voter's perception of the political information context. There are, however, two dimensions to this perception. First, there is the voter's perception of the total *amount* of political information that is available to him in the formal (and/or informal) communication channels. Ranked by sheer volume of available information, elections could be dichotomized into low and high stimulus ones.[14] The second dimension refers to the voter's perception of the degree to which the amount of political information in the community reinforces his party identification. This dimension is in effect a measure of the perceived relative *congruency* of political informational cues.[15]

[13] Historically, a classic example of this phenomenon was the failure of the Southern Populists to build an interracial alliance in the South during the 1890's.

[14] The distinction between low and high stimulus elections that is used here differs significantly from Campbell's original usage of the terms. For Campbell the essential difference between the two types is the degree of importance that the voters attach to the choice among the alternatives. He in effect uses the term "stimulus" as a way to *summarize* the voters' perception of the quantity and qualitative nature of the electoral environment (of which the volume of information is only a part) which affects the voters' electoral calculus (including the decision even to vote). Angus Campbell, "Surge and Decline: A Study of Electoral Change," *Public Opinion Quarterly*, 24 (Fall, 1960), pp. 397–418.

[15] It is being assumed, of course, that congruent information cues reinforce the preexisting partisan identification. Given selective attention to stimuli, however, incon-

These two dimensions of the voter's perception of the information context can be combined in order to classify the variable, partisan information flow, into three possible directional categories. Briefly, the partisan information flow is *negative* if there is a high amount of *incongruent* political information perceived by the voter. Regardless of the amount, however, the partisan information flow is *positive* if the information is congruent with the voter's party identification. Finally, the partisan information flow is *uncertain* if the amount of information is both low and incongruent.

The basic model can now be reformulated to reflect (a) the variation in congruent stored political information and (b) the possible directions of the partisan information flow. The problem is now stated in the following manner: to what extent (and in what direction) will the party identification-party vote relationship vary as the congruency of stored political information and the direction of the partisan information flow varies?

If both intervening variables are conceptualized as affecting the probability that party identification will produce a party vote, the effect of their multivariance can be specified. While the expected effects will be stated in probabilistic terms, it should be noted that the probabilities listed in Table 1 are only *theoretically* assigned and not mathematically derived. Based on a model which postulates a perfect positive correlation between party identification and party vote, the assigned probabilities indicate the expected effect of the two intervening variables on the relationship.

Ideally, the probability of the relationship occurring is 1.0. If the two intervening conditions are varied, however, the probability that the relationship will continue to hold will gradually decrease (in three of the six situations) to the point at which the probability of a party vote is no

TABLE 1

Expected Relationship Between Party Identification and Party Vote

Partisan Information Flow	Congruency of Stored Political Information	
	High	Low
Positive	1.00	1.00
Uncertain	1.00	.75
Negative	.75	.50

gruent information may not necessarily reduce the partisan identification. For example, research on the effects of the Kennedy-Nixon debates indicate that partisans selectively interpreted the exchanges to fit their partisan expectations. Elihu Katz and Jacob J. Feldman, "The Kennedy-Nixon Debates: A Survey of Surveys," *Studies in Public Communication*, 4 (Autumn, 1962), pp. 127–163.

greater than it would be if random decision-making were assumed (and if there were only two voting choices).[16]

Five major propositions can be derived from Table 1. Each proposition reflects the variation in the two intervening variables.

(1) The perfect relationship between party identification and party vote will hold regardless of whether the voters' congruency of stored political information is high or low so long as the direction of the partisan information flow is positive;

(2) the perfect relationship will be maintained under conditions of an uncertain partisan information flow so long as the congruency of stored political information remains high;

(3) the relationship between party identification and party vote will be weakened if a low congruency of stored political information is combined with the condition of an uncertain partisan information flow;

(4) the relationship will be equally weakened if the congruency of stored political information is high but the voter perceives a negative partisan information flow; and

(5) the voter will make a random voting choice under the condition of a negative partisan information flow when his congruency of stored political information is low.

While the model originally postulated a perfect positive correlation between party identification and party vote, we know that there are few perfect correlations in the empirical world. Hence, we should not be surprised if the existing research cannot provide this major proposition with substantiating evidence. What we should expect, however, is that the same rank-order of probabilities exist (as indicated in Table 1) if the model is a useful conceptualization of the real political world.

EVIDENCE SUPPORTING THE MODEL

Existing research directly applicable to testing these propositions (as specifically defined by the model) is limited. Some of the available research can, however, be reinterpreted to provide at least some inferential evidence that the propositions are indeed valid.

Survey analyses have revealed three relevant findings about the American voter. First, the average voter has a low amount of accurate information about the political system. Second, few voters are able to formulate accurately the policy differences between the two major parties. Third, the voter's position on policy alternatives is a very poor predictor of the partisan direction of his vote.[17] Thus, under certain conditions at least, the

[16] There are normally four choices in a two-party system which confront the voter. The voter may (a) vote for his party, (b) vote for the other party, (c) vote for a "third" party, or (d) stay home and not vote at all. To assume a random decision on the part of the voter is to give each alternative a .25 chance of occurring. To simplify the model, however, it is assumed that there are only two alternatives (a vote for one of the two major parties). Assuming random decision-making, therefore, each party has a .50 chance of obtaining the individual's vote.

[17] Campbell, et al., American Voter, pp. 97–144.

degree of the voter's congruency of stored political information would not appear to be a decisive variable. For if the voter is ignorant of the *different* partisan positions, the variation in congruency between his preferred policy outcomes and his party's programs would appear to be irrelevant to his final voting decision.

Research has also indicated, however, that there appears to be a relationship between local party activity and an increased party vote. Increased party activity would presumably affect the direction of the partisan information flow. Hence, if the congruency of stored political information is held constant, we should expect an increased party vote with an increase in the positive direction of the partisan information flow.[18]

If the direction of the partisan information flow is uncertain, however, we would expect that the degree of the voter's congruency of stored political information would affect the probability of the party identification producing a party vote. This type of situation is most apparent in "nonpartisan" elections. The congruency and amount of partisan information is low (hence uncertain) while the saliency of party labels is reduced for some voters since the normal reference points are less applicable. Thus, we should expect a stronger partisan vote among individuals with a higher congruency of stored political information than among those voters with a lower congruency.

While it is based on primarily aggregate data, the research, nevertheless, does provide at least inferential support for this proposition.[19] Furthermore, the "breakage effect" could be interpreted as suggesting that voters of lower congruency are more vulnerable to partisan deviation under conditions where the partisan information flow does not positively (as defined) reinforce their party identification.[20]

Research on the effects of dominant one-party areas on voting behavior provides some important inferential evidence that the party identification-party vote relationship is seriously weakened if the direction of the partisan information flow is negative (high amount but low congruency). For in areas where a majority party overwhelmingly dominates the political context, the minority party loses votes over time even among its highly com-

---

[18] Daniel Katz and Samuel J. Eldersveld, "The Impact of Local Party Activity Upon the Electorate," *Public Opinion Quarterly*, 25 (Spring, 1961), pp. 1–24. See also, Raymond E. Wolfinger, "The Influence of Precinct Work on Voting Behavior," *Public Opinion Quarterly*, 27 (Fall, 1963), pp. 387–398.

[19] Oliver P. Williams and Charles R. Adrian, "The Insulation of Local Politics Under the Nonpartisan Ballot," *American Political Science Review*, 53 (Dec., 1959), pp. 1052–1063.

[20] Bernard R. Berelson, *et al.*, *Voting* (Chicago: University of Chicago Press, 1954), Chap. 6. The "breakage effect" occurs when the voter's proximal environment is divided in political preference. With his immediate environment divided, a voter will tend to "break" toward the majority preference in the larger (or distal) environment. Althought the variables are quite different from the ones being discussed here, it is interesting to note that Orbell found that low politically involved respondents are the most likely ones to conform to perceived partisan cues of their residential area. John M. Orbell, "An Information-Flow Theory of Community Influence," *Journal of Politics*, 32 (May, 1970), pp. 322–338.

mitted members. If a voter already perceives little congruency between his structure of preferred policy outcomes and his party's programs, we would expect an even higher rate of deviation.[21]

Finally, research on straight and split ticket voting would suggest that variations in the two intervening variables do in fact affect the probability that party identification will produce a party vote. Voters with a low congruency of stored political information tend to deviate from the party vote on non-national candidates in greater proportions than do voters with higher levels of congruency. Moreover, this tendency to deviate should be exaggerated if there is a negative partisan information flow with respect to the local candidates.[22]

A NOTE ON UNIDIRECTIONALITY

It should be noted that this model of the relationship between party identification and the party vote has assumed a unidirectional causal flow.[23] That is, in attempting to account for deviations from partisan voting, it has been assumed that (a) party identification causes party voting and (b) the two intervening variables affect the probability of this unidirectional causation.

Yet the research indicates that there may be a multidirectional causation involved with these variables. For example, continued partisan voting may reinforce partisan identification. In addition to the social and political integration argument, one reason why younger voters tend to be less stable than older voters in their partisan identification may be because of the short time period in which they have been participating in the electoral system. Likewise with the empirically established relationship between political participation in general and partisanship, there is a tendency to assume that partisanship leads to participation.[24] Yet equally reasonable is the suggestion that increased participation (e.g., work in a partisan campaign) leads to a stronger partisan identification.

In addition to this perhaps obvious bidirectional relationship between partisan identification and voting, the intervening variables can also be viewed in multicausal terms. We would expect, for example, that a continued exposure to a positive partisan information flow will lead to an increased voter perception that his party best represents his schedule of preferred policy alternatives. This increased perception of congruency

[21] Warren E. Miller, "One Party Politics and the Voter," *American Political Science Review*, 50 (Sept., 1956), pp. 707–725; Philip H. Ennis, "The Contextual Dimension of Voting," in William N. McPhee and William A. Glaser, eds., *Public Opinion and Congressional Elections* (New York: Free Press, 1962), pp. 180–211.

[22] Campbell and Miller, "Motivational Basis of Straight and Split Ticket Voting."

[23] It has also assumed a linear relationship among the variables (particularly in terms of the expected effect of the two intervening variables). Yet there may well be a "critical mass" of stored congruent political information (and/or partisan information flow) which accelerates the positive (or negative) impact of partisan identification on partisan voting.

[24] Lester W. Milbrath, *Political Participation* (Chicago: Rand McNally, 1965), Chap. 3.

will in turn presumably lead to a strengthening of his partisan identification.

Given this multidirectional causation among the variables, it is, nonetheless, quite appropriate to assume for purposes of the model a one-way causal flow. First, such an assumption simplifies considerably the presentation. Second, and more importantly, the assumption permits us to isolate for a more detailed examination the possible variables that may affect the probability of a voter electorally deviating from his partisan identification. Ideally, of course, research could be designed to test specifically this model of voting deviation for much of the existing research has not been designed to measure precisely the variables as they have been defined here. With the appropriate data, it would be possible to specify more precisely not only the variance in the party identification and party vote relationship that is explained by the variance in the two intervening variables, but also the proportional direction of the causation.

VOTING BEHAVIOR IN OPEN HOUSING REFERENDA[1]

HOWARD D. HAMILTON
Kent State University

OPEN HOUSING REFERENDA OCCURRED IN TWELVE CITIES AND TWO STATES during the 1960's. These referenda may be viewed as laboratories for checking the validity of major propositions of social research relative to attitudes on racial residential integration, for filling a lacuna of voting behavior literature, and for examining the implications of direct democracy in an extraordinarily vital sector of public policy.[2] The housing elections are also laboratories of reality rather than simulated situations in which so much social research necessarily occurs.[3] The purpose of this article is to examine and compare findings from four such laboratories: the Berkeley, California, Detroit and Toledo referenda, all of which were investigated by survey research procedures. Commercial poll data have been analyzed for the Berkeley and California referenda,[4] and Detroit data are from a post-referendum sample of 32 precincts.[5] The Toledo study was the only instance of a planned effort to capture data, with a city-wide sample of 455 (usable) interviews conducted during the week preceding the election.[6] Figure 1 presents the results of these four referenda in the

[1] The writer is indebted to Mrs. Duane Stranahan and the Bowling Green University Foundation for generous financial assistance.

[2] Cf. Lynn W. Eley, "Fair Housing Laws—Unfair Housing Practices," *Trans-Action*, 6 (June, 1969), pp. 56–61; Howard D. Hamilton, "Direct Legislation: Some Implications of Open Housing Referenda," *American Political Science Review*, 64 (March, 1970), pp. 124–137; and items in fn. 4, below.

[3] Discrepancies between the findings of social research on this topic and integration plebiscites can be documented. A 1967 survey for the Civil Disorders Commission reports that 40 per cent of whites in 15 unspecified cities endorsed open housing legislation, but simultaneously only about 20 per cent voted for it in Toledo, about 27 per cent in California, and evidently considerably less than 40 per cent in all the referenda prior to the federal open housing act of 1968. Compare the data in Figure 1 with those presented by Angus Campbell and Howard Schuman, "Racial Attitudes in 15 Cities," Supplemental Studies for the National Advisory Commission on Civil Disorders (1968), p. 83. The discrepancy probably cannot be assigned to the differences between voters and nonvoters, because the California referendum coincided with the presidential election and only two per cent passed up the issue ballot.

[4] T. W. Casstevens, *The Defeat of Berkeley's Fair Housing Ordinance* (1965) and *California's Rumford Act and Proposition 14* (1967), pamphlets published by the Institute of Governmental Studies, University of California; Raymond Wolfinger and Fred Greenstein, "The Repeal of Fair Housing in California," *American Political Science Review*, 62 (Dec., 1968), pp. 753–769; Harlan Hahn, "Northern Referenda on Fair Housing: The Response of White Voters," *Western Political Quarterly*, 21 (Sept., 1968), pp. 483–495.

[5] Hahn, "Northern Referenda on Fair Housing."

[6] Clusters of three housing units were drawn systematically. A randomizing device was used to locate the cluster within each block and another to select the interviewee. Interviews were completed in all but one cluster and two in most, with a completion rate of 76 per cent.

FIGURE 1

Vote on Open Housing Referenda

Per Cent For

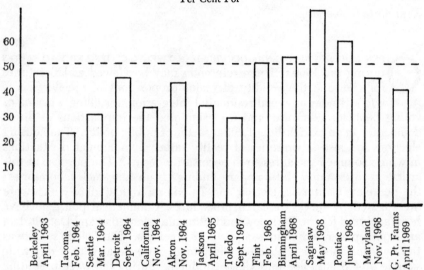

context of all open housing referenda which took place during the 1960's.

Voting Correlates: Age and Sex. Both conventional wisdom and political socialization literature point to a strong association of age with voting
on open housing, except for Negroes. Greenstein and Hess and Torney
have found that fundamental political orientations are acquired at an
early age, and early learning is very durable.[7] The revolution over the past
30 years in the content of the manifest socialization of children vis-à-vis
race probably has not always been supported by latent socialization forces,
but the teaching should make youth more "enlightened" than their parents
and much more than their grandparents. This should be one element of
the "generation gap." The spectacular rise in education level also should
contribute to a pronounced negative correlation of age and support of
open housing.

Table 1 shows the association of age and ethnicity which was so spectacular in Berkeley as to elicit a sanguine prophecy: "With birth rates and
death rates on the side of fair housing legislation, its long run prospects are
quite good."[8] However subsequent referenda in more typical cities furnish
less support for that prophecy. Hahn found "no discernible or consistent
pattern" between age and voting in Detroit,[9] but in Toledo and California
there was a moderate relationship, where integrated housing received

[7] Fred Greenstein, *Children and Politics* (New Haven: Yale University Press, 1965),
chap. 8; Robert D. Hess and Judith V. Torney, *Political Attitudes of Children* (Chicago: Aldine, 1968), chap. 2.

[8] Casstevens, *Defeat of Berkeley's Fair Housing Ordinance*, p. 108.

[9] Hahn, "Northern Referenda," p. 489. Hahn also interpreted his data on Proposition 14 as showing no age influence, but that was taking the pro responses as the
measure. The anti responses, Table 1 above, are contra.

TABLE 1

Caucasian Age, Religious Preference, Home Ownership, Occupation,
Education, Party Preference, and Position
Per Cent for Open Housing

	Berkeley	Calif.	Detroit	Toledo
Age				
21–29	69	25	----	28
30–39	57	24	----	27
40–49	38	26	----	27
50–59	--	17	----	--
50–64	14	--	----	20
60 up	--	15	----	--
65 up	9	--	----	16
N	(315)	(560)	----	(374)[a]
			[a].10>P>.05	
Religious Preference				
Protestant	23	19	----	24
Catholic	28	27	----	27
Jewish	90	53	----	36
No preference	73	36	----	13
N	(315)	(560)	----	(374)[b]
			[b] P>.50	
Home Ownership				
Owners	25	----	32	25
Renters	54	----	23	20
N	(315)	----	(164)	(374)[c]
			[c].05>P>.02	
Occupation				
Unskilled and unemployed	--	----	----	28
Semi-skilled workers	--	----	----	30
Skilled and foremen	--	----	----	18
Manual and clerical	33	----	----	--
Clerical and sales	--	----	----	16
Proprietors and executives	--	----	----	21
Sales, prop. and exec.	20	----	----	--
Professional	55	----	----	45
Retired	8	----	----	14
N	(315)	----	----	(374)[d]
			[d].05>P>.02	
Education				
0–8 grades	--	18	37	13
Some high school	12	--	33	21
High school grad.	--	20	23	25
Some college	26	29	28	26
College graduate	37	39	50	38
Graduate study	69	53	--	58
N	(315)	(1,000)	(179)	(374)[e]
			[e]P<.01	

TABLE 1 (Continued)

	Berkeley	Calif.	Detroit	Toledo
Party Preference				
Democrats	----	41	36	24
Republicans	----	22	18	26
Independents	----	--	--	24
N	--	(1,200)	(160)	(374)[f]
				[f]P>.80

Sources: For Age, Religious Preference, Home Ownership, and Occupation: Casstevens for Berkeley and California, Hahn for Detroit. For Education: Casstevens, Wolfinger and Greenstein (white gentiles only), and Hahn. For Party Preference: Wolfinger and Greenstein, Hahn.

about twice as much support from young adults as from their grandparents.

There evidently are no significant sex differences in attitudes on this issue. Although the Berkeley survey found higher male support for integration, no difference showed elsewhere. Graduate students may have been responsible for the Berkeley deviance.

Ethnicity and Religion. The salience of ethnicity and religion to this issue was exemplified by a respondent who used them as touchstones for identifying city council candidates. "Siegal is Jewish, he would be for it; Markowski is Polish, he would be against it; Savage is Slavic, he would be for it." What ethnic attributes other than race are consequential? Apparently few outside California where Orientals and Mexican-Americans displayed minority consciousness and solidarity by opposition to Proposition 14. Sixty-one per cent of Orientals and 53 per cent of Mexican-Americans expressed opposition to Proposition 14[10]; whereas only about 27 per cent of Caucasians voted against it.[11] In Toledo the only significant deviant group was the Polish, of whom only 13 per cent endorsed open housing, about half the rate of respondents of British or German stock.

Table 1 shows that support for open housing varied rather markedly among the principal religious categories in California but not in Toledo. There is a plausible explanation for the association of religious preference and voting on Proposition 14; that campaign was waged more along party and class lines than the Toledo referendum. Campaigns can have consequences. "Protestant," one suspects, is a poor category vis-à-vis this issue; perhaps fundamentalist and nonfundamentalist would be more significant.

The overwhelming defeat of the Toledo ordinance after church leaders

[10] The Mexican-American figure is of a Los Angeles County sample. Wolfinger and Greenstein, "Repeal of Fair Housing," p. 759. Corroborating data are in Casstevens, *Defeat of Berkeley's Fair Housing Ordinance*, p. 73.

[11] An estimate calculated by the writer from Wolfinger and Greenstein's data on Orientals and Mexican-Americans and the ethnic composition of California in 1960. The Field Poll reported 22 per cent of Caucasians opposed and 19 per cent Don't Know. Casstevens, *Defeat of Berkeley's Fair Housing Ordinance*, p. 73.

TABLE 2

Church Attendance and Position, Toledo FHO Referendum

	For	Against	DK	Per Cent For
Regularly	48	101	14	29
Frequently	21	48	7	28
Rarely	17	63	6	20
Not at all	4	33	6	9
Not ascertained	1	5	0	17

$$.05 > P > .02$$

had trumpeted for it conveys an impression that religious affiliation is inconsequential, but that is erroneous. The interview included a simple question which proved significant. "How frequently do you attend church?" Religion in terms of this objective indicator was one of the strongest correlates of voting in Toledo (see Table 2).

The Toledo data are at variance with research that has found less racial tolerance among church affiliated persons than the nonaffiliated.[12] Two explanations come to mind. Communication and exhortation were factors. The pro "Fair Housing" campaign reached the churchgoers more than the public and the target was not entirely unreceptive. Also, to compare the racial tolerance of affiliated and nonaffiliated may be using a poor litmus. Perhaps frequency of church attendance is a more valid criterion of affiliation than "have you a religious preference?"

Economic and Status Variables. Home ownership should be a potent variable in open housing plebiscites. The opposition campaign propaganda astutely capitalizes on two of the most prized values of the American creed, freedom of choice and the sanctity of property. The counter attack strategy devised by the realty associations is the "homeowners' bill of rights." The strategy is one of undercutting your opponent by changing the issue, by portraying open housing laws as arbitrary, "unconstitutional" assaults on freedom of choice and property. Hahn finds that the strategy has been successful. "Apparently a large proportion of the whites who voted on such questions as the Home Owners' Ordinance and Proposition 14 reacted primarily to the relatively superficial issues of free choice in the purchase or sale of property."[13]

However, Table 1 shows that the association of home ownership and voting was pronounced in only one of these referenda. In Berkeley, renters gave twice as much support for open housing as owners, but in Detroit and Toledo owners were distinctly more favorable than renters! The analyses

[12] See studies cited by Robin M. Williams, *Strangers Next Door* (Englewood Cliffs, N.J.: Prentice-Hall, 1964), pp. 57–60. But the Toledo data are closer to Williams' findings of a curvilinear relationship between religious activity and prejudice with low prejudice among the frequent attenders.

[13] Hahn, "Northern Referenda," p. 495.

of Proposition 14 are contradictory. One states that "homeowners were about 8 per cent more hostile" to integration, which is supported by another analysis, but the third user of the same cards reports that renters were 10 per cent more hostile.[14] Which, if either, is correct is obscured by the large volume of "Don't Knows."

There are explanations of this contrast in voting patterns. If Berkeley renters are preponderently university faculty and graduate students, education is the causal variable and the negative association of ownership and support is idiosyncratic. The campaigns had significant differences. Realty interests spearheaded the opposition campaigns in Berkeley and California, and political parties took conspicuously opposing positions on Proposition 14; whereas the Toledo referendum was a nonpartisan issue at a nonpartisan city primary, and realty associations were neutral (at least overtly). As noted previously, campaigns can affect voting. *Ceteris paribus,* homeowners should be expected to give greater support of open housing if education and social status are germane variables. Hahn offers twin explanations in a status anxiety hypothesis:

> For an individual who has not yet achieved the station of home ownership and who may live in closer proximity to Negroes, the fear of Negro dominance in the neighborhood may be more severe than for home owners who are ensconced in the relative security of their domains. The maintenance of existing patterns of housing discrimination, therefore, may be more critical for a renter who has not yet satisfied the dream of owning his home than for a person who has attained his ambitions of property ownership.[15]

This status anxiety hypothesis is a familiar one in the vernacular. As one Toledo respondent said, "It's easy for the rich folks in Ottawa Hills to be for that law." Some Toledo data are apropos but not definitive. White residents of integrated neighborhoods should exhibit a greater fear of Negro dominance of the neighborhood than other whites, but white respondents with Negro neighbors expressed slightly higher support for the FHO than those without Negro neighbors. However status anxiety might be most intense in segregated lower income neighborhoods. Also some whites in an integrated neighborhood might favor open housing legislation in order to prevent their neighborhood from becoming entirely Negro.

Unfortunately the California data are not very satisfactory for reading the impact of social status variables. Wolfinger and Greenstein found a slight correlation between Proposition 14 voting and the percentage of the labor force in manufacturing of California cities.[16] Hahn, however, construes the California poll data and his own Detroit data as "not corroborating" the familiar proposition that racial intolerance is greatest in the white urban working class.[17]

---

[14] Wolfinger and Greenstein, "Repeal of Fair Housing," p. 764; Casstevens, *Defeat of Berkeley's Fair Housing Ordinance,* p. 76; Hahn, "Northern Referenda," p. 489.

[15] *Ibid.,* p. 490.

[16] *Ibid.,* p. 758.

[17] *Ibid.,* pp. 490–491.

TABLE 3

Caucasian Income and Position on Open Housing

| Detroit | | Toledo[a] | |
Income	Per Cent For	Income	Per Cent For
Lower and lower middle	32	0–2999	14
Middle	21	3000–4999	22
Upper middle	24	5000–6999	20
Upper	52	7000–9999	31
N	(163)	10000–14999	28
		15000 up	26
		N	(374)
	Recapitulation		
Lower & middle	27	0–6999	19
Upper m. & upper	34	7000 up	29

Source: Hahn for Detroit.   [a]P$<$.05

The only vocational data are from Berkeley and Toledo. If the sequence of occupations in Table 1 is roughly their prestige ranks, voting correlates imperfectly with occupational rank. In neither city were blue collar workers in toto far from the Caucasian mean, and they exhibited less intolerance than white collars, exclusive of professionals, who are *sui generis*. In fact the most intolerant segment in Toledo was white collar workers with incomes below $7000, whose support rate was 3 per cent.[18] Evidently "working class" is an unsatisfactory category vis-à-vis open housing, and perhaps for civil rights. In Toledo the support rate of unskilled and semi-skilled was slightly above the city mean; whereas the least support was among white collar and skilled workers. Another conspicuous within-class contrast is between professionals and businessmen. It may be observed that the Toledo distribution comports well with Hahn's status anxiety theory.

Detroit and Toledo data indicate that the relationship between income and integrated housing is complex and confused (see Table 3). There is some positive association, demonstrated by dichotomizing the data, but the relationship was curvilinear in Detroit and Toledo. The data are clear that the greatest antagonism to integrated housing is in the middle income interval (except possibly the authentic poor), the bracket of skilled workers and numerous "business" people.

There are data for the Detroit and Toledo referenda relating voting and social class, employing a three dimensional SES index.[19] There certainly are no contradictions and perhaps the congruency would be complete if

[18] This is not a sampling fluke; the cell N is 31.

[19] The Toledo SES index was constructed by trichotomizing the constituent variables: education: below 12 years, high school graduates, over 12 years; income: below $5,000, $5–10,000, over $10,000; occupation: blue collar, clerical and sales, professionals and business executives.

TABLE 4

White Socioeconomic Status and Position
Per Cent for Open Housing

Detroit		Toledo[a]	
Status Level	Per Cent	Status Level	Per Cent
Lower and		1	16
lower		2	20
middle	27	3	25
Middle	23	4	12
Upper		5	25
middle	29	6	47
Upper	50	7	32
N	(161)		(374)

Source: Hahn for Detroit.   [a]$P<.001$

the intervals were identical. The two dips in the Toledo trend line of Table 4 are not mysterious. The fourth status level is populated by skilled blue collar and modest income white collar workers. The sixth level has the concentration of professionals; whereas the seventh has a larger proportion of business proprietors and executives.[20]

In Toledo the subjective SES voting pattern matched the objective SES pattern of Table 4.[21] The support rates of persons who classified themselves as belonging to the working, middle, and upper classes were 21 per cent, 28 per cent, and 40 per cent.

Hahn found the relationship of education and voting in Detroit to be curvilinear with high school graduates as the category most opposed,[22] a phenomenal contradiction of what has long been presumed to be one of the most solid propositions about American political culture, that racial tolerance correlates positively and decisively with educational attainment.[23] The other referenda, however, are unanimously and indubitably contra (see Table 1). In Berkeley, California, and Toledo the relationship of educational attainment and open housing voting was clearly linear and pronounced, and there is striking uniformity in the data of all four jurisdictions, except for the voting in Detroit of persons without high school diploma. Evidently in Detroit persons with less formal education (82 of the sample of 179) gave an extraordinary rate of support for open housing;

[20] Numerous professionals, notably teachers, did not make the seventh level, because their incomes were below $10,000.

[21] "What social class would you say you belong to?" Although few nominate themselves into the "lower" or "upper" classes, the "all American middle class" appears inaccurate. Half of the Toledo sample classified themselves as "working class."

[22] Hahn, "Northern Referenda," p. 490.

[23] Cf. Paul B. Sheatsley, "White Attitudes Toward the Negro," *Daedalus*, 95 (Winter, 1966), pp. 217–238; Hazel Gaudet Erskine, "The Polls: Negro Housing," *Public Opinion Quarterly*, 21 (Autumn, 1967), pp. 482–498.

perhaps Detroit is one place where the CIO influences attitudes and voting even on nonlabor issues.

The foregoing data and Figure 2 indicate that education is the paramout socioeconomic correlate of attitudes on residential integration, matched only by party identification in some instances. In this regard it should be observed that the education data of Table 1 understate the potency of education in the California and Detroit referenda, because of the counter influence of party identification.[24] The Toledo education column of Table 1 may be the best of the four mirrors, because of less distortion by other variables (party, union, or Mexican-Americans). The Toledo data display an interesting pattern of four plateaus. "Some high school" makes considerable difference, but "some college" has slight effect, whereas a full college exposure has the greatest effect.

Whether higher education really has a substantial effect on attitudes recently has been questioned by Langton and Jennings, who suggest that the attitudinal differences between high school and college graduates may be largely a function of selection.[25] The data of all four samples here indicate that the college experience does substantially modify attitudes on this issue, because support advances consistently with the number of years of college. If selection were the principal factor, the sharpest change should be between high school graduates and respondents with only some college.

For anyone who does not reject the analysis and judgments of the "Riot Commission," these data are bases for mixed feelings, of satisfaction and consternation. Table 1 education data present a success story in the perspective of the 1950's, when they could have been viewed as assuring a satisfactory resolution of the American dilemma in two or three generations, but the abrupt end of the gradualism era places the data in a radically different perspective. Now that degree of achievement is not success; it is failure. The significance of the data becomes not the amount of success but the amount of nonsuccess; even most college graduates, the people with the least basis for status anxiety, reject open housing legislation.

Political Variables. The manifest logic of the preceding data is that Republicans should be less frequently opposed to residential integration than Democrats, in view of the disparities in the distribution of all the status values. On the other hand, the Democratic Party has staked out a reputation as sponsor of civil rights legislation in state capitols as well as

[24] When Wolfinger and Greenstein segregated donkeys and elephants, the support for open housing within Republican ranks ranged from 10 per cent by persons with less than high school education to 33 per cent by those with more than two years of college, and from 29 per cent to 64 per cent within the Democratic ranks. "Repeal of Fair Housing," p. 760. They employ the data to demonstrate the potency of party, but that sword cuts both ways. Here would appear to be the root of Hahn's judgment, that the propositions about education and SES are dubious. Controlling for party might show distinctly different results than the curvilinear relationships which he reported.

[25] Kenneth P. Langton and M. Kent Jennings, "Political Socialization and the High School Civics Curriculum in the United States," *American Political Science Review*, 62 (Sept., 1968), p. 866.

FIGURE 2

Association of Four Variables with
Position on FHO of Toledo White Adults

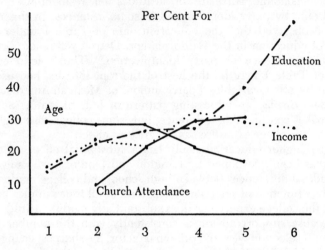

Intervals as per Tables 1, 2, 3

Washington, while Eisenhower and Goldwater fixed the position of the party of Lincoln as disapproval of integration by "legal fiat."[26] Furthermore the opposition usually is led by realty interests and waves symbols that have a Republican copyright. Consequently it would be rash to proclaim any law of the relationship of open housing voting and party affiliation.

A pronounced association of party and voting was found in Berkeley, Detroit, and California. Wolfinger and Greenstein state that party identification was "at least as strong an independent variable as education,"[27] which conspicuously was not true in Toledo (see Table 1). The contrast is plausible enough; there were critical differences in the circumstances and campaigns. The California battle was along party lines as the Democrats plumped against Proposition 14, coincident with the presidential election where party positions on civil rights were maximally salient and separate. Toledo was the antipodal, nonpartisan model.[28]

[26] The image of the Democratic Party as pro civil rights was manifested in Toledo. When asked the positions of several organizations, the Republican Party was perceived as pro FHO by 30 per cent of the sample, the Democratic by 40 per cent.

[27] Wolfinger and Greenstein, "Repeal of Fair Housing," p. 760. Their data actually show that party was quite significant for persons at each end of the educational attainment scale, but less so for those with between 8 and 14 years of education—where most reside. Also one cannot be certain that the 41 per cent/22 per cent ratio held up in the actual balloting, because unless the three minority groups failed to turn out for the 1964 presidential election, Caucasian voting against Proposition 14 was considerably less than 32 per cent.

[28] The unaminously enacted ordinance was sponsored by the mayor, who championed it in the referendum while one of his opponents campaigned on an anti-FHO platform and the other found flaws in the ordinance, as both party committees of-

That the Toledo FHO apparently got a slightly higher rate of support from Republicans than Democrats fits the nonpartisan model, but the difference was not statistically significant. Some other partisan measurements show larger differences. Applying the familiar seven categories of party identification, the most FHO support was by independent Republicans (40 per cent) and the least by strong Republicans (19 per cent). Not surprisingly, in Toledo and California, position correlated less with party than with 1964 presidential voting.[29]

Attitudinal Syndromes. An open housing plebiscite affords an opportunity to check out three of our most celebrated attitudinal constructs: authoritarianism, alienation, and political efficacy.[30] From the preceding data and the fact that political efficacy is so much a function of status and education,[31] one would anticipate the strong association of political efficacy and white (only) voting exhibited in the Toledo data. The same relationship has been noted in fluoridation referenda.[32]

The authoritarianism-ethnocentrism thesis of the *Authoritarian Personality* has been the topic of extensive controversy.[33] However, measured by an uncomplicated index, comprised of one item from the Rosenberg misanthropy scale[34] and three explicitly authoritarian expressions, the Toledo data display a strong and consistent relationship of authoritarianism with ethnocentric behavior in clearest form (Table 5).

Alienation has been detected as an undercurrent in some bond referenda[35] and has been advanced as a principal reason for the frequent rejection of fluoridation by local electorates.[36] The alienation referendum

---

ficially blessed the ordinance and lifted not a finger in its behalf. The mayor was not reelected.

[29] Wolfinger and Greenstein, "Repeal of Fair Housing," p. 760. The Toledo FHO was favored by 16 per cent of Goldwater voters and 27 per cent of Johnson voters.

[30] Indices were constructed from responses to these questions:
Authoritarian index: "Obedience and respect for authority are the most important things to teach children." "A few strong leaders could make this country better than all the laws and talk." "People can be trusted." "People are getting too soft and weak as a result of so much coddling."
Political Efficacy index: "I don't think public officials in this city care what people like me think." "The way people vote does not have much effect on the way things are run in this city."
Alienation index: the Political Efficacy index items plus "To succeed in politics around here, a man has to be dishonest."

[31] Angus Campbell, et al., *The American Voter* (New York: Wiley, 1960), pp. 479–81.

[32] William A. Gamson, "The Fluoridation Dialogue," *Public Opinion Quarterly*, 25 (Winter, 1961), pp. 534–36.

[33] T. W. Adorno et al., *The Authoritarian Personality* (New York: Harper, 1950); Richard Christie and Marie Jahoda, eds., *Studies in the Scope and Method of the Authoritarian Personality* (Glencoe: Free Press, 1954).

[34] Morris Rosenberg, "Misanthropy and Political Ideology," *American Sociological Review*, 21 (Dec., 1956), pp. 690–95.

[35] John Horton and Wayne Thompson, "Powerlessness and Political Negativism," *American Journal of Sociology*, 67 (March, 1962), pp. 485–493.

[36] Gamson, "Fluoridation Dialogue."

TABLE 5

Caucasian Attitudes and Position in Toledo FHO Referendum
Per cent in each level for Open Housing

Scale Level	Authoritarian Scale	Political Alienation Scale	Political Efficacy Scale
1 (low)	37	35	15
2	31	24	14
3	25	9	31
4	18	0	54
5 (high)	13	—	—
(N=374)			
	P<.02	P<.001	P<.001

model rests, of course, on the all too plausible premise that in many communities there is a reservoir of latent alienation. Most alienates are apathetic and hence vote infrequently in local—meaningless—elections, but occasionally they are catalyzed by the issue of a referendum and turn out to give vent to their frustrations and resentment of the establishment by torpedoing its pet policy plans: a bond issue, metropolitan government, fluoridation, or possibly open housing.[37]

Is alienation associated with white attitudes on housing and, if so, does it affect voting? The Detroit Area Study, 1958, disclosed such a relationship of moderate scale except among blue collar workers with only grammar school education.[38] The scenario of the Toledo FHO, and probably most others, fitted the alienation referendum model in several respects. The ordinance was conspicuously the handiwork of the Toledo establishment and the contest throughout was between members and foes of the establishment. The opposition propaganda exploited alienation sentiment. Consistent with the foregoing, application of a *political* alienation index to the Toledo data shows a strong relationship of alienation and voting (Table 5). The FHO was favored by 35 per cent of the white respondents with no trace of alienation, by only 9 per cent of the numerous persons manifesting substantial alienation, and by none of the few extremely alienated.

It would be folly, however, to credit alienation with much responsibility for the defeat of integrated housing in Toledo or anywhere for several reasons: (1) Open housing differs from the alienated referendum model in a critical respect: a large chunk of alienates—Negroes—engage in positive voting. (2) Even though the opposition plays alienation music and even if white alienates turn out and vote negatively, the campaign rhetoric may not be the actual basis of the voting. (3) The alienated referendum model equates high turnout with voluminous negative voting, and

[37] Clarence Stone, "Local Referendums; An Alternative to the Alienated Voter Model," *Public Opinion Quarterly,* 29 (Summer, 1965), pp. 213–222.

[38] Marvin E. Olson, "Alienation and Political Opinion," *Public Opinion Quarterly,* 29 (Summer, 1965), p. 258.

TABLE 6

Correlation of Variables with Position on Open Housing
of Caucasians in Toledo Sample

	Simple	Partial
Education	.19	.14
Income	.10	.03
SES Index	.14	.01
Age	—.10	.07
Party Preference	.01	—
Home Ownership	.05	.04
Church Attendance	.15	.07
Political Efficacy	.24	.05
Pol. Alienation	—.28	—.10
Authoritarianism	—.19	—.11

low turnout with alienate absentia and referendum success, but the turn-out was low in the Toledo referendum. (4) And, most importantly, as the foregoing data document, alienates have no corner on prejudice.

The measurements of the operation of these syndromes in the Toledo referendum convey two unmistakable messages. Authoritarianism and po-litical alienation are markedly associated negatively and political efficacy positively, quite consistent with the logic of each syndrome. Those smooth correlations, however, have an attenuated range. Most opposition to inte-grated housing is not the product of alienation, authoritiarianism, or feel-ings of political impotence. Integrated housing is rejected by most of those white adults who are subjectively efficacious, low on authoritarianism, and without a trace of alienation. Prejudice is an independent variable.

To compare the strengths of the associations of the preceding variables with position on open housing, and to ascertain how much they may be epiphenomenal, simple and partial coefficients of correlation were com-puted for the Toledo sample (Table 6).[39] Education and the attitudinal scales were the strongest correlates of voting in Toledo but the values of the coefficients of partial correlation indicate that none of these variables exerted a profound influence. The association of voting with income, social status, church attendance, and political efficacy was mostly epiphenomenal. Education was the only strong positive influence and the significant nega-tive influences were authoritarianism and political alienation.

CONCLUSION

There is no occasion for any extensive revision or agonizing reappraisal of the lore on race relations attitudes, because the referenda analyses dis-close little contradiction of previous research. On the contrary, they pro-vide strong reinforcement of several major propositions: that authoritari-

[39] Pearsonian correlation was used, although inappropriate for some of these vari-ables which are merely ordinal, in order to do partial correlation.

anism and alienation have an affinity with prejudice; that tolerance has distinctly a negative association with age and a positive one with income, education, and status; that there are occupational differences and that professionals are *sui generis*, the one group where one may find even majority support for integrated housing; that formal education is the pre-eminent contributor to the erosion of white racism in America, and that higher education is the most potent solvent. Here is a vivid confirmation of Lane's proposition that "the professional class serves as the staunchest defender of democracy's two greatest ideals, liberty and equality."[40]

The referenda data do indicate that some of the established propositions are inaccurate without some qualification or refinement. For example, the Berkeley and California data show that the usual black-white dichotomy is inapposite in California where the substantial Oriental and Mexican-American groups opposed Proposition 14, and the data contradict the notion that the latter minority is more intolerant than "caucasians."

Of the status variables, only education has a neat linear relationship with attitudes on integrated housing, and even that may not be fully visible in a referendum which involves counter variables strong enough to offset it in the voting of persons on the lower side of the education distribution—the Detroit case. The association of income and SES to voting on the issue is only gross and definitely is not linear, which is explained by the Toledo occupational analysis. The sharp occupational differences correlate very imperfectly with occupational rank.

All the referenda suport Hahn's observation in Detroit that the working class authoritarianism syndrome needs some reexamination. The highest incidence of antagonism to open housing is among white collar-low income workers not "the working class," whose support of the laws in the referenda somewhat exceeded that of their bosses and social superiors, the business proprietors and executives.[41] "Working class" and "middle class" are unsatisfactory categories for a taxonomy of attitudes on open housing. Consistent with the status anxiety hypothesis and the achievement norm, skilled workers are one of the most antagonistic sectors, whereas other blue-collars match or slightly exceed the white mean; and the poles on the issue are within the middles class, by its usual definition as all white collar occupations.

The referenda analyses provide at least one major augmentation and correction to the corpus of knowledge on this subject by disclosing that the significant independent variables are not exclusively status ones. Party affiliation was an important independent variable in three of the four cases. Indeed, the influence of party operating counter to the status variables may offset them to almost the vanishing point. Whether or not party changes attitudes, it certainly can influence the voting. But party is a contingent variable, which may not operate if not triggered by the context of a plebiscite, as in the Toledo case, where support for open housing was

[40] Robert Lane, *Political Ideology* (Glencoe: Free Press, 1962), p. 81.
[41] The Berkeley and Toledo data are explicit and unambiguous, and this is my deduction from Hahn's SES data for Detroit and California.

greatest among independent Republicans and least among strong Republicans.

Information about three other variables is provided by the referenda data. The strong association of support for integration and political efficacy is not startling, but the church attendance relationship is at variance with some previous findings. A distinct surprise is that property ownership is as likely to be positively related to support as negatively; in fact it was positive except within California. Here is additional evidence that the nature of campaigns makes a difference. The referenda data affirm the relevance if not the primacy of politics.

These analyses also demonstrate that the associations of all the variables, including education, party, and the attitudinal syndromes, influence attitudes and voting on residential integration only within a restricted range. Thus the bulk of whites at the upper reaches of the education, income or status scales do not support open housing. All these variables fall far short of explaining the voting. We have meticulously ferreted out the influence of about all the possible variables except the crucial one—prejudice.

The city and state referenda document that the Civil Rights Act of 1968 is a monumental instance of minority rule, promulgating a policy which our data indicate was favored by less than 30 per cent of the white voters in the several "northern" referenda. Analysis shows that the policy does not even enjoy the support of the elite sectors, of college graduates, businessmen, and the upper social strata. The data also demonstrate that education, although a strong influence, has had limited success to date, with a majority of white college graduates rejecting integrated housing. Although more open housing laws may be enacted, and may even be sustained in future referenda, will they be more than symbolic?

THE POLITICAL IMPACT OF SHIFTING ATTITUDES[1]

HARLAN HAHN

University of California, Riverside

P ERHAPS FEW ASPECTS OF PUBLIC OPINION HAVE RECEIVED GREATER AT-
tention from social scientists than the study of attitude changes. In
numerous investigations, shifting personal preferences. have been
related both to personality variables and to measures of social interaction.[2]
As a result, important conceptual and empirical progress has been made
in examining the process by which individuals alter their positions on
many issues.[3]

Despite the energy that has been devoted to the study of shifting opinions, however, relatively little social psychological research has focused
upon the behavioral implications of attitude changes.[4] In an essay that
chided social scientists for "quietly and placidly ignoring a very vital problem," Festinger reported that he discovered only three studies concerning
the behavioral effects of shifting attitudes and that the relationships between opinion change and self-reported personal actions, in each case,
appeared to be slightly inverse.[5] In addition to the criticism that it has
received for neglecting the impact of opinion shifts upon behavior, research on attitude change occasionally has been further criticized because
such studies usually have been conducted in experimental or laboratory
settings rather than in sample surveys of a general population. Consequently, a growing interest has emerged in the use of panel survey data
to investigate shifting preferences.

Surveys on opinion change have seemed to be of particular importance
in the study of political attitudes or voter preferences. In the early voting
studies, considerable attention was devoted to the investigation of attitude
changes during electoral campaigns.[6] Yet, the potential value of this ap-

[1] This research was supported by General Research Support Grants from the University of Michigan School of Public Health and by United States Public Health Service grant No. NIH DH 00151.

[2] For a survey of the findings from much of this research, see William J. McGuire,
"The Nature of Attitudes and Attitude Change," in Gardner Lindzey and Elliot Aron-
son, eds., *The Handbook of Social Psychology* (Reading, Massachusetts: Addison-
Wesley Co., 1969), II, pp. 136–314.

[3] For a recent critical review of the many theoretical approaches to the study of attitude change that have been developed thus far, see Charles A. Kiesler, Barry E. Col-
lins, and Norman Miller, *Attitude Change: A Critical Analysis of Theoretical Approaches* (New York: John Wiley, 1969).

[4] Arthur R. Cohen, *Attitude Change and Social Influence* (New York: Basic Books,
1964), pp. 137–138.

[5] Leon Festinger, "Behavioral Support for Opinion Change," *Public Opinion Quarterly*, 28 (Fall, 1964), pp. 404–417.

[6] See, for example, Paul F. Lazarsfeld, Bernard Berelson, and Hazel Gaudet, *The
People's Choice* (New York: Columbia University Press, 1948); Bernard R. Berelson,
Paul F. Lazarsfeld, and William N. McPhee, *Voting* (Chicago: University of Chicago

proach has been sharply limited by several factors. Perhaps most importantly, relatively few subsequent efforts have been made to explore shifting opinions in political controversies, especially at the local level. As one researcher concluded, "political analysts have yet to begin to mine the riches of knowledge available in panel studies."[7] In addition, perhaps a need has emerged for increased survey research on attitude changes between elections as well as during campaigns. Although many political issues have been subjected to periodic review by the voters, panel surveys seldom have examined shifting political preferences in more than one election.

Moreover, in the study of political attitudes as well as in many other areas of investigation, there is a general lack of evidence concerning the consequences of changing preferences. Relatively little research on the development or resolution of political controversies focuses upon the behavior of groups of voters who have experienced different kinds of opinion changes. Presumably, however, citizens who have changed their minds in various ways about an issue may exhibit contrasting forms of political involvement and participation. Those differences, in turn, could have an important impact upon the outcome of political conflict. A major research priority, therefore, might be assigned not only to the study of factors that may promote or retard attitude changes but also to investigations concerning the role in political controversies of groups of voters who have undergone various types of opinion shifts.

At least four major types of changing attitudes might be identified without reference to individual positions on a political issue.[8] Initially, there are persons whose attitudes about an issue remain stable or uniform in different elections. Individuals who assume continuous positions of support or opposition are termed *Consistents* in this study. Secondly, some voters,

---

Press, 1954). The Survey Research Center at the University of Michigan also has frequently cited a forthcoming volume which has been in preparation for several years based upon its panel surveys extending over a number of presidential elections, but only scattered reports of those data have appeared thus far.

[7] Robert E. Agger, "Panel Studies of Comparative Community Political Decision-Making: Dynamics of Urban Renewal," in M. Kent Jennings and L. Harmon Zeigler, eds., *The Electoral Process* (Englewood Cliffs, N.J.: Prentice-Hall, 1966), p. 288.

[8] The categories are both somewhat comparable with, and slightly different from, earlier attempts to classify changes in political preferences. In the pioneering research on Erie County, Ohio, respondents were coded as Party Changers; Crystallizers, individuals who expressed no preference early in the campaign but who subsequently stated a choice; and Waverers, or persons whose attitudes fluctuated during the course of the campaign. See Lazarsfeld, *et al.*, *The People's Choice*, pp. 65–66. In another major study, both turnout and political preferences were used to categorize voters as Standpatters, people whose voting decisions remained consistent between different elections; Switchers, who changed their partisan preferences; and New Voters, who either were ineligible to vote or who failed to vote in the preceding election. See V. O. Key, Jr., *The Responsible Electorate* (Cambridge: Harvard University Press, 1966), esp. p. 16. Neither classification, however, devoted major attention to a group comparable to the Indecisives, or voters who continued to express uncertainty about their positions in more than one survey.

who are called *Converts*, may switch their positions on the issue either from support to opposition or vice-versa. Another group of citizens might display uncertainty about the issue or fail to express an opinion in only one of the elections. They may change either from uncertainty in the first survey to a firm position in the second election or from an explicit position in the first election to uncertainty in the second survey. Those persons are referred to as *Ambivalents*. Finally, a segment of the population, which is identified as *Indecisives*, might remain undecided about the issue in both elections.

The impact of shifting preferences upon the outcome of a controversy eventually might be determined both by the relative size of the four groups and by their political activity prior to an election and at the polls.[9] During a political campaign, voters who have experienced various kinds of attitude changes may exert an influence upon the opinions of other persons. Some citizens, for example, may become sufficiently aroused by an issue to display a strong interest in the conflict, while others might remain relatively indifferent to the matter. Similarly, one group could actively engage in discussions of the issue, but another group might fail to do so. In addition, people may differ in the extent to which they attempt to read or gain additional information about the issue.

Perhaps even more significant, at least for issues that are submitted to a public vote, is the impact of attitude changes upon participation in an election. In order to maximize the influence of his convictions, whether they have changed or remained stable, a voter must master several crucial political acts on election day. Perhaps the chief prerequisite is that he appear at the polls. Regardless of the intensity of his opinions or the amount of energy that he has invested in persuading others of their merits, his efforts to promote the position that he favors might be diminished if he is absent from his critical stage of decision-making. Secondly, he must vote on the particular issue in question. The outcome of issues may be affected by what has been termed ballot "roll-off,"[10] or the tendency of voters to record their opinions only in the most prominent contests and to ignore questions with less visibility on the ballot. Finally, the citizen must vote in

---

[9] Although attitude changes and variations in voter turnout often have been regarded as opposing forces that may have separate and independent effects on election results, it seems clear that both factors may have an important impact upon the outcome of political controversies. As Agger comments, "The theoretical question . . . namely, whether decisional changes are a function of differential participation by citizens with relatively constant policy perspectives or a function of more or less constant participation levels by citizens with relatively changing policy perspectives—has only begun to be explored. . . . That both processes operated simultaneously . . . is clear. What is not clear, and what will not become clearer until many more such panel studies are conducted in larger samples of communities with larger numbers of respondents in each wave . . . , is whether or not there are particular patterns of such processes and in what combinations or under what conditions these processes occur." Agger, "Panel Studies," p. 288.

[10] The phrase was coined by Walter Dean Burnham, "The Changing Shape of the American Political Universe," *American Political Science Review*, 59 (March, 1965), pp. 9–10.

accordance with his own preferences on the issue. This condition may not be as trivial as it might appear. In many situations such as nonpartisan elections and referenda, the voter is deprived of the guidance of partisan labels or other political cues. As a result, the task of identifying the ballot choice that is most consistent with his own interests and preferences on an issue may not be an altogether easy one.

This investigation seeks to examine the association between political involvement or participaiton and the stability and certainty of public attitudes. Initially, the conduct of persons who retain consistent opinions and those who fail to reach a decision about an issue seems to be relatively predictable. While Consistents might be expected to display the highest levels of political activity and effectiveness both before and during an election, Indecisives may be the least effective participants in political controversies or voting. Since both groups maintain constant explicit or undecided preferences on an issue, however, perhaps the principal effects of changing attitudes are evident among Converts and Ambivalents. Perhaps the primary distinction between the latter two groups is reflected by the surety of their positions. While Converts tend to be certain of their opinions, Ambivalents are indecisive on at least one occasion. Major attention in this study, therefore, is devoted to the political activity of so-called Converts and Ambivalents.

An examination of the behavior of Converts and Ambivalents provides an opportunity to assess the role of changing opinions in shaping the outcome of a political controversy. Although the activities of both groups prior to an election may tend to influence the final results, perhaps their principal impact is exerted at the polls. This effect can be measured by the actions of Converts and Ambivalents, as well as other groups, in voting both in the election and on the issue and by assessing the correspondence between their actual ballot choices and their voting intentions. Presumably, if persons who switch their preferences on an issue have a greater impact at the polls than those who were undecided in at least one survey, the effects of conversion might be regarded as more critical in determining the results of an election than efforts to induce wavering voters to take a position on the issue. On the other hand, if Converts are less effective participants in elections than Ambivalents, the political consequences of definite attitude changes might appear to be somewhat limited.

The purpose of this research is to explore the impact of changing opinions upon forms of political involvement and participation that could shape the outcome of an issue. This study also focuses upon opinion changes in a community controversy, an area of research that has been "substantially untapped by analysts of local government."[11] Specifically, this investigation is based upon public attitudes concerning the fluoridation issue, which has raised some troubling questions about the stability of political preferences, voter turnout, and the results of urban conflict.[12]

[11] Agger, "Panel Studies," p. 265.
[12] James S. Coleman, *Community Conflict* (Glencoe, Ill.: The Free Press, 1957), p. 19; Maurice Pinard, "Structural Attachments and Political Support in Urban Politics:

Data for this study were collected in a panel survey, based initially upon an area probability sample, of adult residents of the city of Detroit. In two successive waves, interviews were conducted with 596 persons shortly after the mayoralty election of 1965 and with 406 of the same respondents after the mid-term elections of 1966.[13]

The surveys offered an unusual opportunity to explore changing public attitudes and behavior in a political controversy. In both the 1965 and the 1966 elections, the city of Detroit held nearly identical referenda on the fluoridation issue. In both surveys, the percentage of respondents who reported that they had voted for or against fluoridation closely approximated the actual referendum vote in the city. Although the results of the referenda yielded essentially similar but narrow victories for the proponents of fluoridation in both elections, an examination of the panel survey results revealed evidence of changes as well as stability in local opinions about this issue.[14]

Table 1 indicates the trends in public attitudes on fluoridation that emerged in Detroit from 1965 to 1966.[15] Although the total percentages

---

The Case of Fluoridation Referendums," *American Journal of Sociology*, 68 (March, 1963), pp. 195–212. For a review of the literature on the fluoridation controversy, see S. Stephen Kegeles, "Contributions of the Social Sciences to Fluoridation," *The Journal of the American Dental Association*, 65 (Nov., 1962), pp. 667–672; Harlan Hahn, "Fluoridation and Patterns in Community Politics," *Journal of Public Health Dentistry*, 25 (Fall, 1965), pp. 152–157.

[13] Sampling and interviewing for the first wave were performed by National Analysts, Inc., of Philadelphia; interviewing and field work for the second wave were conducted by the National Opinion Research Center of the University of Chicago. Although the difference in the sample size reflected some attrition between the first and second waves of the survey, the reinterview rate of 68 per cent in the Detroit survey was substantially higher than the rates obtained in comparable waves of panel studies conducted in two smaller Oregon communities, which were 42 per cent and 50 per cent, respectively. See Agger, "Panel Studies," pp. 267–268. It was also necessary to eliminate from the Detroit survey all persons who had moved outside the city limits between 1965 and 1966. When those persons were removed from the net sample size, the completion rate was computed at 79 per cent. Letter from Eve Weinberg, Field Director, National Opinion Research Center, to the author, January 5, 1967. In addition, a report on the national panel surveys conducted by the Survey Research Center indicated that, of the 1,763 persons who were interviewed twice during the 1956 presidential campaign, only slightly more than 1,100 were questioned again in the fall of 1960, representing a reinterview rate of only approximately 63 per cent. Philip E. Converse, Angus Campbell, Warren E. Miller, and Donald E. Stokes, "Stability and Change in 1960: A Reinstating Election," *American Political Science Review*, 55 (June, 1961), p. 270.

[14] The question used in assessing fluoridation attitudes was: "Would you say that you strongly support, support, oppose, strongly oppose, or are undecided about fluoridation?" Interestingly enough, 65 per cent of the respondents who remained consistent in their positions on the fluoridation issue also indicated that they had not changed the intensity of their feelings about the matter; that is, relatively few of the respondents shifted from strong to mild support or opposition concerning the proposal, or vice-versa.

[15] The responses of the 190 persons who were not located in the second wave of

TABLE 1

Shifting Attitudes on Fluoridation in Detroit, 1965–1966 (in Percentages)

Fluoridation Attitudes—1965	(N)	Fluoridation Attitudes—1966			Total 1965
		Support	Oppose	Undecided	
Support	(195)	65	26	9	49
Oppose	(104)	9	78	13	26
Undecided	(101)	32	34	33	25
Total 1966	(400)	42	42	16	

suggest that the opponents of fluoridation gained somewhat and the number of undecided respondents was simultaneously reduced between the two years, the city electorate appeared to be rather evenly divided by the issue in both elections. In addition, most of the respondents who supported or opposed fluoridation in 1965 maintained consistent positions in 1966; but those persons who were initially undecided seemed to be split into three roughly equal groups of supporters, opponents, and indecisives in the following year.

The results of the Detroit surveys seemed to be comparable with findings reported by panel surveys that have been conducted elsewhere.[16] The largest group of people, or 52 per cent of the 400 residents interviewed in

the survey due to death, sickness, moving, or other circumstances did not appear to differ appreciably from the attitudes of respondents who were successfully reinterviewed in 1966. In fact, a comparison of those who were not reinterviewed with the respondents who were included in the second wave revealed that the distributions of opinions on the fluoridation issue in 1965 among the two groups were identical: 49 per cent supported fluoridation, 26 per cent opposed it, and 25 per cent were undecided about the issue. Consequently, even though potential changes in attitudes could not be examined empirically, weighting procedures have not been employed in this study. In addition, the responses of persons who were not located and those who were reinterviewed in the second wave to several other questions concerning discussion of the issue, reading about it, voter turnout, and ballot "roll-off" also seemed to be comparable. As footnote 25 suggests, however, since the total proportion of persons who voted in accordance with their preferences on the fluoridation issue was somewhat higher in the 1965 election than in the 1966 referendum, persons who were interviewed only in 1965 were somewhat more likely to vote "correctly" in the referendum than those who were reinterviewed in 1966.

[16] See, for example, Agger, "Panel Studies," p. 270. Another panel survey of 95 respondents in a water control controversy in eastern Kansas discovered that 10 per cent were converted, 20 per cent were ambivalent, 20 per cent were indecisive, and 50 per cent were consistent. E. Jackson Bauer, "Opinion Change in a Public Controversy," *Public Opinion Quarterly*, 26 (Summer, 1962), pp. 213–215. A report on national panel surveys in 1956 and 1958, which combined measures of attitude change and voter turnout, indicated that 44 per cent of the voters expressed consistent partisan choices in both elections, 13 per cent were converted, 22 per cent failed to vote in one election, and 21 per cent did not vote in either election. Angus Campbell, "Surge and Decline: A Study of Electoral Change," in Angus Campbell, Philip E. Converse, Warren E. Miller, and Donald E. Stokes, eds., *Elections and the Political Order* (New York: John Wiley, 1966), pp. 52–55.

TABLE 2

Shifting Attitudes on Fluoridation and Discussion, Reading, or
Interest in the Issue (in Percentages)

	Shifting Attitudes on Fluoridation			
	Consistents	Converts	Ambivalents	Indecisives
Discussion of Fluoridation				
High or increasing	48	53	38	17
Low or decreasing	52	47	62	83
(N)	(206)	(59)	(97)	(33)
Reading about Fluoridation				
A great deal or some	61	44	46	21
Little or none	39	56	54	79
(N)	(204)	(59)	(98)	(34)
Interest in Fluoridation				
A great deal	48	25	27	13
Somewhat	31	24	28	16
Little or none	21	51	45	71
(N)	(193)	(59)	(108)	(31)

both years,[17] were Consistents. Ambivalents constituted approximately
one-fourth of the respondents. In addition, 15 per cent were classified as
Converts. Only eight per cent were Indecisives. Employing size as a criterion, therefore, the greatest potential effect upon the outcome of the
controversy may have been exerted by Consistents, followed by Ambivalents, Converts, and Indecisives, respectively.

Since this research seeks to explore the impact of shifting attitudes upon
general patterns of political involvement and participation rather than to
describe specific referenda, attention will be devoted in the remainder of
this study to respondents who underwent different types of attitude
changes, irrespective of their positions on the fluoridation issue. Major interest, therefore, will be focused upon four groups of persons: Ambivalents, Indecisives, Consistents, and Converts.

SHIFTING ATTITUDES AND POLITICAL INVOLVEMENT

While many types of behavior such as active participation in campaign
work usually are confined to relatively small segments of the electorate,
other forms of conduct are available to most citizens in a political controversy. Table 2 presents the associations between shifting attitudes on
fluoridation and several common forms of political activity such as discussion, reading, and interest concerning the issue.

The findings tended to confirm the results of earlier studies which have
indicated that people who switch their positions on an issue frequently discuss the matter with others.[18] Converts were most likely to participate in

[17] Six respondents who failed to answer the questions about fluoridation in either
1965 or 1966 have been omitted from this analysis.
[18] See, for example, Bauer, "Opinion Change," pp. 223–225; Berelson, et al., *Voting*,
pp. 119–120.

a relatively large or growing number of conversations about fluoridation, but the proportion of Converts who joined in such talks was only slightly greater than the percentage of Consistents who discussed the proposal. By contrast, discussions about fluoridation were somewhat infrequent among Ambivalents and relatively rare among Indecisives. Since personal communications generally are regarded as especially influential in molding political attitudes,[19] the activity displayed by Converts in informal discussions may have provided them with an important means not only of forming their own opinions but also of shaping the preferences of others and the eventual outcome of the controversy.

On the other hand, most Converts did not seem to engage in extensive reading about fluoridation. Although clear differences were apparent in the reading habits of Consistent and Indecisive respondents, no such distinctions were found between Converts and Ambivalents. Persons who had changed their opinions did not differ appreciably in the amount of reading that they devoted to the issue from those who expressed temporary uncertainty about fluoridation.

In addition, Converts generally did not exhibit a strong interest in fluoridation.[20] Again, perceptible differences were evident in the interest displayed by Consistent and Indecisive respondents. Although Consistents expressed the greatest interest in fluoridation, Indecisives seemed to be relatively indifferent to the issue. But similar discrepancies were not reflected in the responses of Converts and Ambivalents. In fact, Converts appeared to be slightly less interested in the issue than Ambivalents, while Converts ranked well below Consistents in the amount of interest in fluoridation that they disclosed.

Despite their active participation in personal conversations about fluoridation, the influence of Converts may have been limited both by their failure to become involved in other means of gaining information and by their relative disinterest in the issue. While slightly more than half of the Converts said that they engaged in frequent or increasing discussions of fluoridation, an equivalent proportion stated that they had "little or no" interest in the issue.[21] In addition, when the respondents were asked to

[19] See, for example, Elihu Katz and Paul F. Lazarsfeld, *Personal Influence* (Glencoe, Ill.: The Free Press, 1955).

[20] In the classic study of voter attitudes in Erie County, Ohio, it was found that persons who switched their partisan preferences during the 1940 presidential campaign exhibited less interest in the election than people who maintained a constant position or those who wavered between the two parties. See Lazarsfeld, et al., *The People's Choice*, pp. 67–69.

[21] As might have been anticipated, among persons who engaged in such conversations, Converts also were more likely than any other group to report that most of the people with whom they discussed fluoridation expressed opinions that differed from their attitudes about the issue. Whereas 68 per cent of the Converts reported that they had been "cross-pressured" in this way, only 42 per cent of the Ambivalents, 36 per of the Indecisives, and 26 per cent of the Consistents stated that most of their discussants disagreed with them about fluoridation. Sixty-five per cent of the Consistents said that most of the persons who spoke with them also agreed with their position on fluoridation, but 43 per cent of the Indecisives could not identify the opinions of persons

name the sources of information that were most important to them "in trying to decide" about the fluoridation issue, personal conversations did not appear to be highly salient to most Converts.[22] Only one-twelfth of the Converts ranked discussions with friends and neighbors as their most important source of information about fluoridation, and just one-fourth cited those talks as the second most important source of information. Converts, therefore, may have lacked the information and the interest necessary to maximize their opportunities to affect the opinions of other persons and the eventual outcome of the issue through extensive informal discussions.

SHIFTING ATTITUDES AND ELECTORAL PARTICIPATION

Perhaps the most direct effects of changing attitudes upon the outcome of a political controversy, however, are exerted by the behavior of voters at the polls. Data concerning the electoral participation of respondents who experienced different types of attitude changes on fluoridation are presented in Table 3.

TABLE 3

Shifting Attitudes on Fluoridation and Electoral Participation (in Percentages)

| | Shifting Attitudes on Fluoridation | | | | |
	Con-sistents	Con-verts	Am-bivalents	Indeci-sives	Total Percent
Turnout					
Voted in both elections	64	59	57	38	59
Voted in 1966 election only	10	8	16	26	13
Voted in 1965 election only	12	14	6	12	11
Did not vote in either election	14	19	21	24	17
(N)	(208)	(59)	(99)	(34)	(400)
Roll-Off					
Voted on fluoridation	94	87	68	32	82
Did not vote on fluoridation	6	13	32	68	18
(N)	(151)	(39)	(66)	(22)	(278)
Direction of Fluoridation Vote					
Correct	82	69	58	43	74
Error	18	31	42	57	26
(N)	(146)	(35)	(45)	(7)	(233)

with whom they discussed the issue. On the other hand, Converts were somewhat less likely than Consistents to report that they had been exposed to information that contradicted their own views about fluoridation. When the respondents were asked in 1966 if they had "heard or read anything about fluoridation during the past year that you did not agree with," 46 per cent of the Consistents, 42 per cent of the Converts, 27 per cent of the Ambivalents, and only 13 per cent of the Indecisives answered affirmatively.

[22] In citing their most important source of information about the fluoridation controversy, only the Indecisives appeared to disagree with the predominant choice of other respondents. Whereas a slight majority of all of the remaining groups selected newspapers as their principal source of information about fluoridation, only 38 per cent of the Indecisives responded similarly.

In general, even though other issues and contests may have aroused more excitement among voters in both elections, shifting attitudes on the fluoridation question apparently were related to patterns of electoral participation. Again, Consistent and Indecisive respondents seemed to exhibit sharply contrasting forms of voter turnout, while Converts and Ambivalents assumed an intermediate position on this measure. Yet, among those persons in the latter two groups who voted in only one election, Converts were slightly more apt to participate in the first vote, while Ambivalents were somewhat more likely to appear for the second election. In 1966, the proportion of Converts who arrived at the polls to support their newly formed convictions apparently was exceeded by the percentage of Ambivalents who voted after they may have resolved their doubts about the issue. Although Converts maintained a somewhat higher record of continuous voting than Ambivalents, the eventual impact of the processes of conversion upon the outcome of the controversy may have been partially diluted by the failure of many Converts to cast their ballots in the second election.

On the other hand, the effects of definite changes in voter attitudes were clearly evident in the proportion of voters who failed to record their choices on fluoridation. Among those persons who participated in the 1966 election, Converts were more likely to mark preferences on the fluoridation proposal than Ambivalents. In fact, the measurement of ballot "roll-off" was the only variable that produced a statistically significant difference between the political conduct of Ambivalents and Converts ($p > .05$, two-tailed test).[23] In addition to the striking distinctions between Consistents and Indecisives, Converts and Ambivalents exhibited different rates of ballot "roll-off" that may have enhanced the impact of definite attitude changes upon the results of the election.[24]

The Detroit elections also provided an unusual opportunity to examine the accuracy with which voters express their preferences. In both referenda, the ballot wording of the fluoridation propositions was inverted, so that persons who desired to support fluoridation had to vote "No" on the issue and those who wished to oppose fluoridation were required to vote "Yes." In the surveys, voters were questioned carefully about whether they had voted "Yes" or "No" on the fluoridation question; and, at another point in the interviews, they were asked if they had intended to vote for or against fluoridation. As the total percentages for the 1966 referendum indicate, nearly three-fourths of the voters were not confused by the negative wording of the ballot proposal, and they voted in a manner that was con-

[23] Of course, nearly all of the differences between Consistents and Indecisives, and several of the differences between Consistents and Ambivalents, also were statistically significant at the .05 level.

[24] This pattern partially confirmed the findings of a national survey concerning the 1956 and 1958 elections which indicated that persons who switched parties or who failed to participate in one of the elections were less apt to vote a straight ticket or to mark a complete ballot than relatively consistent voters. Campbell, "Surge and Decline," pp. 57–59.

sistent with their own views about fluoridation.[25] As Table 3 indicates, not only were there major differences in the proporations of Consistents and Indecisives who voted "correctly" on the issue, but Converts also were somewhat less likely to commit "errors" in marking their ballots than Ambivalents. The Converts, therefore, also may have enjoyed a slight advantage in contributing to the final tally of the vote as a result of the accuracy with which they recorded their opinions in the polling booth.

In general, the effects of shifting attitudes upon election results seemed to be associated both with the stability of voter preferences and with their willingness to endorse a definite position on the issue. Consistents (who exhibited stable convictions) and Converts (who at least expressed a specific preference in both surveys, even though their preferences were reversed) apparently were what might be termed more effective voters than Ambivalents (who adopted a firm position only once) and Indecisives (who failed to take a stand in either survey). As the tendency to state a constant and categorical opinion on the fluoridation issue increased, several factors that might have weakened the impact of electoral choices such as persistent non-voting, ballot "roll-off," and "error" seemed to decline. On each of those measures, Consistents appeared to display the greatest effectiveness in shaping the outcome of the vote, followed by Converts, Ambivalents, and Indecisives, respectively.

SUMMARY AND DISCUSSION

The political impact of shifting atttiudes, therefore, seemed to reflect some important implications for the outcome of an issue. The emergence of stable or changing opinions apparently was not only associated with factors that might indirectly affect the results such as the involvement of persons in a controversy, but it also was related to political activity that could have a direct impact upon the outcome such as voting behavior and electoral participation.

Perhaps the clearest differences were reflected by the actions of Consistent and Indecisive respondents. Consistents were greatly interested in fluoridation, they discussed the issue frequently, and they made relatively intensive efforts to read additional information about it. Consistents also scored the highest rate of continual participation in the elections, an overwhelming proportion of them voted on the fluoridation proposal as well as on other contests, and they committed few "errors" in casting their ballots. Consistents, therefore, appeared to possess many characteristics of the active, alert, and interested voter.

[25] In 1965, when the ballot wording of the fluoridation proposition also was inverted, a slightly larger proportion of all respondents voted in accordance with their own preferences in the fluoridation referendum. In that year, the total percentage of voters who cast their ballots "correctly" on fluoridation was 87 per cent. For a discussion of the impact of voting "error" upon the outcome of another controversy, see Raymond E. Wolfinger and Fred I. Greenstein, "The Repeal of Fair Housing in California: An Analysis of Referendum Voting," *American Political Science Review*, 62 (Sept., 1968), pp. 755–757.

By contrast, Indecisives appeared to display attributes of the indifferent and uninvolved citizen who tends to withdraw from political controversies. Indecisives seemed to be highly disinterested in the fluoridation issue, they were not inclined to discuss it with others, they did not read much further information about it, and they were not prone to participate in elections. Moreover, if they did vote, they tended to skip the fluoridation proposal; and, even if they voted on fluoridation, they were liable to vote "incorrectly."

Ambivalent respondents appeared to reflect the classic stance of the wavering citizen, uncertain not only about his position on the issue but also about his willingness to enter the controversy. Before an election, Ambivalents seemed to occupy an intermediate position on several measures of political involvement. At the polls, however, they revealed relatively low rates of constant turnout, voting on the referendum proposal, and accuracy in their electoral choices.

Similarly, the political involvement of Converts prior to a vote seemed to convey the image of relatively malleable citizens who lacked a strong interest in the fluoridation issue but who may have been particularly susceptible to persuasion by others during the relatively large number of informal discussions in which they engaged. Converts, therefore, may have been unable to maximize the opportunities afforded by those conversations to influence the opinions of other voters. Yet, on election day, Converts were somewhat more likely than Ambivalents to participate continually in the voting, to mark their ballots on the referendum issue, and to vote "correctly." As a result, persons who changed definite opinions on the issue probably were somewhat more influential in shaping the final distribution of the vote than those who fluctuated between uncertainty and a firm position on the issue.

This research has attempted to explore the political consequences of changing attitudes. Although there is a need for additional investigations of the characteristics of persons who experience various sorts of opinion changes, as well as for studies of variables that might facilitate or impede those changes, increasing emphasis also might profitably be devoted to the political ramifications of shifting attitudes. The findings of this study suggest that different kinds of attitude changes can have an impact upon the outcome of political conflict. A relatively high priority in future work, therefore, might be assigned to a precise measurement of the effects that those changes can have upon the results of elections and other controversies. In undertaking those studies, however, attention might be focused not only upon the effects of attitude changes during a political campaign but also upon their impact at the polls.

Perhaps the major effects of changing opinions upon the outcome of the controversy in this study were evident in patterns of electoral behavior and participation. While no accurate estimate can be made of the impact of such trends upon the final tally, the tendency of Converts to reveal lower rates of persistent non-voting, "roll-off," and "error" than Ambivalents represented the only case in which the actual electoral influence of a group may have exceeded its potential impact as measured by its size in the electorate. Consistents represented the largest group of voters, and they probably had the most potent impact upon the results of the election. Similarly, Indecisives formed the smallest group of respondents, and they may have had the least effect upon the outcome. Even though the proportion of Ambivalents in the city population was greater than the percentage of Converts, however, the Converts seemed to gain a slight advantage in making their votes count at the ballot box. The net effect of conversions upon the outcome of an issue, therefore, probably can not be dismissed or ignored in a close election.

CONSTITUENCY INFLUENCE IN CONGRESS[*]

WARREN E. MILLER and DONALD E. STOKES[**]
University of Michigan

S UBSTANTIAL CONSTITUENCY INFLUENCE OVER THE LOWER HOUSE OF CONGRESS is commonly thought to be both a normative principle and a factual truth of American government. From their draft constitution we may assume the Founding Fathers expected it, and many political scientists feel, regretfully, that the framers' wish has come all too true.[1] Nevertheless, much of the evidence of constituency control rests on inference. The fact that our House of Representatives, especially by comparison with the House of Commons, has irregular party voting does not of itself indicate that congressmen deviate from party in response to local pressure. And even more, the fact that many congressmen *feel* pressure from home does not of itself establish that the local constituency is performing any of the acts that a reasonable definition of control would imply.

I. CONSTITUENCY CONTROL IN THE NORMATIVE THEORY OF REPRESENTATION

Control by the local constituency is at one pole of *both* the great normative controversies about representation that have arisen in modern times. It is generally recognized that constituency control is opposite to the conception of representation associated with Edmund Burke. Burke wanted the representative to serve the constituency's *interest* but not its *will*, and the extent to which the representative should be compelled by electoral sanctions to follow the "mandate" of his constituents has been at the heart of the ensuing controversy as it has continued for a century and a half.[2] Constituency control also is opposite to the conception of govern-

[*]Reprinted by permission of the author and publisher, from Warren E. Miller and Donald E. Stokes, "Constituency Influence in Congress," *American Political Science Review*, 57 (March, 1963), pp. 45–56.

[**]The research reported here was made possible through grants of the Rockefeller Foundation and the Social Science Research Council, whose support is gratefully acknowledged. The authors are indebted also to Ralph Bisco and Gudmund R. Iversen for invaluable assistance.

[1]To be sure, the work of the Federal Convention has been supplemented in two critical respects. The first of these is the practice, virtually universal since the mid-nineteenth century, of choosing Representatives from single-member districts of limited geographic area. The second is the practice, which has also become virtually universal in our own century, of selecting party nominees for the House by direct primary election.

[2]In the language of Eulau, Wahlke, *et al.*, we speak here of the "style," not the "focus," of representation. See their "The Role of the Representative: Some Empirical Observations on the Theory of Edmund Burke," *American Political Science Review*, 53 (Sept., 1959), pp. 742–756. An excellent review of the mandate-independence controversy is given by Hanna Fenichel Pitkin, "The Theory of Representation," Ph.D. dissertation, University of California, Berkeley, 1961. For other contemporary discussions of representation, see Alfred de Grazia, *Public and Republic* (New York: Knopf, 1951), and John A. Fairlie, "The Nature of Political

ment by responsible national parties. This is widely seen, yet the point is rarely connected with normative discussions of representation. Indeed, it is remarkable how little attention has been given to the model of representation implicit in the doctrine of a "responsible two-party system." When the subject of representation is broached among political scientists the classical argument between Burke and his opponents is likely to come at once to mind. So great is Burke's influence that the antithesis he proposed still provides the categories of thought used in contemporary treatments of representation despite the fact that many students of politics today would advocate a relationship between representative and constituency that fits *neither* position of the mandate-independence controversy.

The conception of representation implicit in the doctrine of responsible parties shares the idea of popular control with the instructed-delegate model. Both are versions of popular sovereignty. But "the people" of the responsible two-party system are conceived in terms of a national rather than a local constituency. Candidates for legislative office appeal to the electorate in terms of a *national* party program and leadership, to which, if elected, they will be committed. Expressions of policy preference by the local district are reduced to endorsements of one or another of these programs, and the local district retains only the arithmetical significance that whichever party can rally to its program the greater number of supporters in the district will control its legislative seat.

No one tradition of representation has entirely dominated American practice. Elements of the Burkean, instructed-delegate, and responsible party models can all be found in our political life. Yet if the American system has elements of all three, a good deal depends on how they are combined. Especially critical is the question whether different models of representation apply to different public issues. Is the saliency of legislative action to the public so different in quality and degree on different issues that the legislator is subject to very different constraints from his constituency? Does the legislator have a single generalized mode of response to his constituency that is rooted in a normative belief about the representative's role or does the same legislator respond to his constituency differently on different issues? More evidence is needed on matters so fundamental to our system.

II. AN EMPIRICAL STUDY OF REPRESENTATION

To extend what we know of representation in the American Congress the Survey Research Center of the University of Michigan interviewed the incumbent congressman, his non-incumbent opponent (if any), and a sample of constituents in each of 116 congressional districts, which were themselves a probability sample of all districts.[3] These interviews, con-

---

Representation," *American Political Science Review*, 34 (April–June, 1940), pp. 236–248, 456–466.

[3] The sampling aspects of this research were complicated by the fact that the study of representation was a rider midway on a four-year panel study of the electorate whose primary sampling units were not congressional districts (although

ducted immediately after the congressional election of 1958, explored a wide range of attitudes and perceptions held by the individuals who play the reciprocal roles of the representative relation in national government. The distinguishing feature of this research is, of course, that it sought direct

there is no technical reason why they could not have been if the needs of the representation analysis had been foreseen when the design of the sample was fixed two years before). As a result, the districts in our sample had unequal probabilities of selection and unequal weights in the analysis, making the sample somewhat less efficient than an equal-probability sample of equivalent size.

It will be apparent in the discussion that follows that we have estimated characteristics of whole constituencies from our samples of constituents living in particular districts. In view of the fact that a sample of less than 2,000 constituents has been divided among 116 districts, the reader may wonder about the reliability of these estimates. After considerable investigation we have concluded that their sampling error is not so severe a problem for the analysis as we had thought it would be. Several comments may indicate why it is not.

To begin with, the weighting of our sample of districts has increased the reliability of the constituency estimates. The correct theoretical weight to be assigned each district in the analysis is the inverse of the probability of the district's selection, and it can be shown that this weight is approximately proportional to the number of interviews taken in the district. The result of this is that the greatest weight is assigned the districts with the largest number of interviews and, hence, the most reliable constituency estimates. Indeed, these weights increase by half again the (weighted) mean number of interviews taken per district. To put the matter another way: the introduction of differential weights trades some of our sample of congressional districts for more reliable constituency estimates.

How much of a problem the unreliability of these estimates is depends very much on the analytic uses to which the estimates are put. If our goal were case analyses of particular districts, the constituency samples would have to be much larger. Indeed, for most case analyses we would want several hundred interviews per district (at a cost, over 116 districts, of several small nuclear reactors). However, most of the findings reported here are based not on single districts but on many or all of the districts in our sample. For analyses of this sort the number of interviews per district can be much smaller.

Our investigation of the effect of the sampling variance of the constituency estimates is quite reassuring. When statistics computed from our constituency samples are compared with corresponding parameter values for the constituencies, the agreement of the two sets of figures is quite close. For example, when the proportions voting Democratic in the 116 constituencies in 1958, as computed from our sample data, are compared with the actual proportions voting Democratic, as recorded in official election statistics, a product moment correlation of 0.93 is obtained, and this figure is the more impressive since this test throws away non-voters, almost one-half of our total sample. We interpret the Pearsonian correlation as an appropriate measure of agreement in this case, since the associated regression equations are almost exactly the identity function. The alternative intraclass correlation coefficient has almost as high a value.

Although we believe that this analysis provides a textbook illustration of how misleading intuitive ideas (including our own) about the effects of sampling error can be, these figures ought not to be too beguiling. It is clear that how close such a correlation is to 1.0 for any given variable will depend on the ratio of the between-district variance to the total variance. When this ratio is as high as it is for Republican and Democratic voting, the effect of the unreliability of our constituency estimates is fairly trivial. Although the content of the study is quite different, this sampling problem has much in common with the problem of attenuation of correlation as it has been treated in psychological testing. See, for example, J. P. Guilford, *Fundamental Statistics in Psychology and Education* (New York: McGraw-Hill, 1956), pp. 475–478.

information from both constituent and legislator (actual and aspiring). To this fund of comparative interview data has been added information about the roll-call votes of our sample of congressmen and the political and social characteristics of the districts they represent.

Many students of politics, with excellent reason, have been sensitive to possible ties between representative and constituent that have little to do with issues of public policy. For example, ethnic identifications may cement a legislator in the affections of his district, whatever (within limits) his stands on issues. And many congressmen keep their tenure of office secure by skillful provision of district benefits ranging from free literature to major federal projects. In the full study of which this analysis is part we have explored several bases of constituency support that have little to do with policy issues. Nevertheless, the question how the representative should make up his mind on legislative issues is what the classical arguments over representation are all about, and we have given a central place to a comparison of the policy preferences of constituents and Representatives and to a causal analysis of the relation between the two.

In view of the electorate's scanty information about government it was not at all clear in advance that such a comparison could be made. Some of the more buoyant advocates of popular sovereignty have regarded the citizen as a kind of kibitzer who looks over the shoulder of his representative at the legislative game. Kibitzer and player may disagree as to which card should be played, but they were at least thought to share a common understanding of what the alternatives are.

No one familiar with the findings of research on mass electorates could accept this view of the citizen. Far from looking over the shoulder of their congressmen at the legislative game, most Americans are almost totally uninformed about legislative issues in Washington. At best the average citizen may be said to have some general ideas about how the country should be run, which he is able to use in responding to particular questions about what the government ought to do. For example, survey studies have shown that most people have a general (though differing) conception of how far government should go to achieve social and economic welfare objectives and that these convictions fix their response to various particular questions about actions government might take.[4]

What makes it possible to compare the policy preferences of constituents and Representatives despite the public's low awareness of legislative affairs is the fact that congressmen themselves respond to many issues in terms of fairly broad evaluative dimensions. Undoubtedly policy alternatives are judged in the executive agencies and the specialized committees of the Congress by criteria that are relatively complex and specific to the policies at issue. But a good deal of evidence goes to show that when proposals come before the House as a whole they are judged on the basis of more general evaluative dimensions.[5] For example, most congressmen,

---

[4]See Angus Campbell, Philip E. Converse, Warren E. Miller, and Donald E. Stokes, *The American Voter* (New York: John Wiley and Sons, 1960), pp. 194–209.

[5]This conclusion, fully supported by our own work for later Congresses, is one of the main findings to be drawn from the work of Duncan MacRae on roll-call voting

too, seem to have a general conception of how far government should go in the area of domestic social and economic welfare, and these general positions apparently orient their roll-call votes on a number of particular social welfare issues.

It follows that such a broad evaluative dimension can be used to compare the policy preferences of constituents and Representatives despite the low state of the public's information about politics. In this study three such dimensions have been drawn from our voter interviews and from congressional interviews and roll-call records. As suggested above, one of these has to do with approval of government action in the social welfare field, the primary domestic issue of the New Deal–Fair Deal (and New Frontier) eras. A second dimension has to do with support for American involvement in foreign affairs, a latter-day version of the isolationist-international continuum. A third dimension has to do with approval of federal action to protect the civil rights of Negroes.[6]

Because our research focused on these three dimensions, our analysis of constituency influence is limited to these areas of policy. No point has been more energetically or usefully made by those who have sought to clarify the concepts of power and influence than the necessity of specifying the acts *with respect to which* one actor has power or influence or control over another.[7] Therefore, the scope or range of influence for our analysis is

---

in the House of Representatives. See his *Dimensions of Congressional Voting: A Statistical Study of the House of Representatives in the Eighty-First Congress* (Berkeley and Los Angeles: University of California Press, 1958). For additional evidence of the existence of scale dimensions in legislative behavior, see N. L. Gage and Ben Shimberg, "Measuring Senatorial Progressivism," *Journal of Abnormal and Social Psychology*, 44 (Jan., 1949), pp. 112–117; George M. Belknap, "A Study of Senatorial Voting by Scale Analysis," Ph.D. dissertation, University of Chicago, 1951, and "A Method for Analyzing Legislative Behavior," *Midwest Journal of Political Science*, 2 (1958), pp. 377–402; two other articles by MacRae, "The Role of the State Legislator in Massachusetts," *American Sociological Review*, 19 (April, 1954), pp. 185–194, and "Roll Call Votes and Leadership," *Public Opinion Quarterly*, 20 (1956), pp. 543–558; Charles D. Farris, "A Method of Determining Ideological Groups in Congress," *Journal of Politics*, 20 (1958), pp. 308–338; and Leroy N. Rieselbach, "Quantitative Techniques for Studying Voting Behavior in the U.N. General Assembly," *International Organization*, 14 (1960), pp. 291–306.

[6] The content of the three issue domains may be suggested by some of the roll-call and interview items used. In the area of social welfare these included the issues of public housing, public power, aid to education, and government's role in maintaining full employment. In the area of foreign involvement the items included the issues of foreign economic aid, military aid, sending troops abroad, and aid to neutrals. In the area of civil rights the items included the issues of school desegregation, fair employment, and the protection of Negro voting rights.

[7] Because this point has been so widely discussed it has inevitably attracted a variety of terms. Dahl denotes the acts of *a* whose performance *A* is able to influence as the *scope* of *A*'s power. See Robert A. Dahl, "The Concept of Power," *Behavioral Science*, 2 (July, 1957), pp. 201–215. This usage is similar to that of Harold D. Lasswell and Abraham Kaplan, *Power and Society* (New Haven: Yale University Press, 1950), pp. 71–73. Dorwin Cartwright, however, denotes the behavioral or psychological changes in *P* which *O* is able to induce as the *range* of *O*'s power: "A Field Theoretical Conception of Power," *Studies in Social Power* (Ann Arbor: Research Center for Group Dynamics, Institute for Social Research, The University of Michigan, 1959), pp. 183–220.

the collection of legislative issues falling within our three policy domains. We are not able to say how much control the local constituency may or may not have over *all* actions of its Representative, and there may well be pork-barrel issues or other matters of peculiar relevance to the district on which the relation of congressman to constituency is quite distinctive. However, few observers of contemporary politics would regard the issues of government provision of social and economic welfare, of American involvement in world affairs, and of federal action in behalf of the Negro as constituting a trivial range of action. Indeed, these domains together include most of the great issues that have come before Congress in recent years.

In each policy domain we have used the procedures of cumulative scaling, as developed by Louis Guttman and others, to order our samples of congressmen, of opposing candidates, and of voters. In each domain congressmen were ranked once according to their roll-call votes in the House and again according to the attitudes they revealed in our confidential interviews. These two orderings are by no means identical, nor are the discrepancies due simply to uncertainties of measurement.[8] Opposing candidates also were ranked in each policy domain according to the attitudes they revealed in our interviews. The nationwide sample of constituents was ordered in each domain, and by averaging the attitude scores of all constituents living in the same districts, whole constituencies were ranked on each dimension so that the views of congressmen could be compared with those of their constituencies.[9] Finally, by considering only the constituents in each district who share some characteristic (voting for the incumbent, say) we were able to order these fractions of districts so that the opinions of congressmen could be compared with those, for example, of the dominant electoral elements of their districts.

In each policy domain, crossing the rankings of congressmen and their

[8] That the Representative's roll-call votes can diverge from his true opinion is borne out by a number of findings of the study (some of which are reported here) as to the conditions under which agreement between the congressman's roll-call position and his private attitude will be high or low. However, a direct confirmation that these two sets of measurements are not simply getting at the same thing is given by differences in attitude–roll-call agreement according to the congressman's sense of how well his roll-call votes have expressed his real views. In the domain of foreign involvement, for example, the correlation of our attitudinal and roll-call measurements was .75 among Representatives who said that their roll-call votes had expressed their real views fairly well. But this correlation was only .04 among those who said that their roll-call votes had expressed their views poorly. In the other policy domains, too, attitude–roll-call agreement is higher among congressmen who are well satisfied with their roll-call votes than it is among congressmen who are not.

[9] During the analysis we have formed constituency scores out of the scores of constituents living in the same district by several devices other than calculating average constituent scores. In particular, in view of the ordinal character of our scales we have frequently used the *median* constituent score as a central value for the constituency as a whole. However, the ordering of constituencies differs very little according to which of several reasonable alternatives for obtaining constituency scores is chosen. As a result, we have preferred mean scores for the greater number of ranks they give.

constituencies gives an empirical measure of the extent of policy agreement between legislator and district.[10] In the period of our research this procedure reveals very different degrees of policy congruence across the three issue domains. On questions of social and economic welfare there is considerable agreement between Representative and district, expressed by a

[10]The meaning of this procedure can be suggested by two percentage tables standing for hypothetical extreme cases, the first that of full agreement, the second that of no agreement whatever. For convenience, these illustrative tables categorize both congressmen and their districts in terms of only three degrees of favor and assume for both a nearly uniform distribution across the three categories. The terms "pro," "neutral," and "con" indicate a relative rather than an absolute opinion. In Case I, full agreement, all districts relatively favorable to social welfare action have congressmen who are so too, etc.; whereas in Case II, or that of no agreement, the ordering of constituencies is independent in a statistical sense of the ranking of congressmen: knowing the policy orientation of a district gives no clue at all to the orientation of its congressman. Of course, it is possible for the orders of legislators and districts to be *inversely* related, and this possibility is of some importance, as indicated below, when the policy position of non-incumbent candidates as well as incumbents is taken into account. To summarize the degree of congruence between legislators and voters, a measure of correlation is introduced. Although we have used a variety of measures of association in our analysis, the values reported in this article all refer to product moment correlation coefficients. For our hypothetical Case I a measure of correlation would have the value 1.0; for Case II, the value 0.0. When it is applied to actual data this convenient indicator is likely to have a value somewhere in between. The question is where.

Case I: Full Policy Agreement

Congressmen	Constituencies		
	Pro	Neutral	Con
Pro	33	0	0	33
Neutral	0	34	0	34
Con	0	0	33	33
	33	34	33	100%

Correlation = 1.0

Case II: No Policy Agreement

Congressmen	Constituencies		
	Pro	Neutral	Con
Pro	11	11	11	33
Neutral	11	12	11	34
Con	11	11	11	33
	33	34	33	100%

Correlation = 0.0

correlation of approximately 0.3. This coefficient is, of course, very much less than the limiting value of 1.0, indicating that a number of congressmen are, relatively speaking, more or less "liberal" than their districts. However, on the question of foreign involvement there is no discernible agreement between legislator and district whatever. Indeed, as if to emphasize the point, the coefficient expressing this relation is slightly negative (− 0.09), although not significantly so in a statistical sense. It is in the domain of civil rights that the rankings of congressmen and constituencies most nearly agree. When we took our measurements in the late 1950s the correlation of congressional roll-call behavior with constituency opinion on questions affecting the Negro was nearly 0.6.

The description of policy agreement that these three simple correlations give can be a starting-point for a wide range of analyses. For example, the significance of party competition in the district for policy representation can be explored by comparing the agreement between district and congressman with the agreement between the district and the congressman's non-incumbent opponent. Alternatively, the significance of choosing Representatives from single-member districts by popular majority can be explored by comparing the agreement between the congressman and his own supporters with the agreement between the congressman and the supporters of his opponent. Taking *both* party competition and majority rule into account magnifies rather spectacularly some of the coefficients reported here. This is most true in the domain of social welfare, where attitudes both of candidates and of voters are most polarized along party lines. Whereas the correlation between the constituency majority and congressional roll-call votes is nearly +0.4 on social welfare policy, the correlation of the district majority with the non-incumbent candidate is − 0.4. This difference, amounting to almost 0.8, between these two coefficient is an indicator of what the dominant electoral element of the consistuency gets on the average by choosing the congressman it has and excluding his opponent from office.[11]

These three coefficients are also the starting point for a causal analysis of the relation of constituency to representative, the main problem of this paper. At least on social welfare and Negro rights a measurable degree of congruence is found between district and legislator. Is this agreement due to constituency influence in Congress, or is it to be attributed to other causes? If this question is to have a satisfactory answer the conditions that are necessary and sufficient to assure constituency control must be stated and compared with the available empirical evidence.

[11] A word of caution is in order, lest we compare things that are not strictly comparable. For obvious reasons, most non-incumbent candidates have no roll-call record, and we have had to measure their policy agreement with the district entirely in terms of the attitudes they have revealed in interviews. However, the difference of coefficients given here is almost as great when the policy agreement between the incumbent congressman and his district is also measured in terms of the attitudes conveyed in confidential interviews.

III. THE CONDITIONS OF CONSTITUENCY INFLUENCE

Broadly speaking, the constituency can control the policy actions of the Representative in two alternative ways. The first of these is for the district to choose a Representative who so shares its views that in following his own convictions he does his constituents' will. In this case district opinion and the congressman's actions are connected through the Representative's own policy attitudes. The second means of constituency control is for the congressman to follow his (at least tolerably accurate) perceptions of district attitude in order to win re-election. In this case constituency opinion and the congressman's actions are connected through his perception of what the district wants.[12]

These two paths of constituency control are presented schematically in Figure 1. As the figure suggests, each path has two steps, one connecting

FIGURE 1

Connections Between a Constituency's Attitude and Its Representative's Roll-Call Behavior

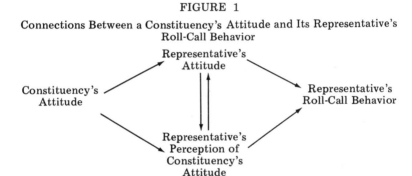

the constituency's attitude with an "intervening" attitude or perception, the other connecting this attitude or perception with the Representative's roll-call behavior. Out of respect for the processes by which the human actor achieves cognitive congruence we have also drawn arrows between the two intervening factors, since the congressman probably tends to see his district as having the same opinion as his own and also tends, over time, to bring his own opinion into line with the district's. The inclusion of these arrows calls attention to two other possible influence paths, each consisting of *three* steps, although these additional paths will turn out to be of relatively slight importance empirically.

[12] A third type of connection, excluded here, might obtain between district and congressman if the Representative accedes to what he thinks the district wants because he believes that to be what a representative *ought* to do, whether or not it is necessary for re-election. We leave this type of connection out of our account here because we conceive an influence relation as one in which control is not voluntarily accepted or rejected by someone subject to it. Of course, this possible connection between district and Representative is not any the less interesting because it falls outside our definition of influence or control, and we have a given a good deal of attention to it in the broader study of which this analysis is part.

Neither of the main influence paths of Figure 1 will connect the final roll-call vote to the constituency's views if either of its steps is blocked. From this, two necessary conditions of constituency influence can be stated: *first*, the Representative's votes in the House must agree substantially with his own policy views or his perceptions of the district's views, and not be determined entirely by other influences to which the congressman is exposed; and, *second*, the attitudes or perceptions governing the Representative's acts must correspond, at least imperfectly, to the district's actual opinions. It would be difficult to describe the relation of constituency to Representative as one of control unless these conditions are met.[13]

Yet these two requirements are not sufficient to assure control. A *third* condition must also be satisfied: the constituency must in some measure take the policy views of candidates into account in choosing a Representative. If it does not, agreement between district and congressman may arise for reasons that cannot rationally be brought within the idea of control. For example, such agreement may simply reflect the fact that a Representative drawn from a given area is likely, by pure statistical probability, to share its dominant values, without his acceptance or rejection of these ever having better a matter of consequence to his electors.

IV. EVIDENCE OF CONTROL: CONGRESSIONAL
ATTITUDES AND PERCEPTIONS

How well are these conditions met in the relation of American congressmen to their constituents? There is little question that the first is substantially satisfied; the evidence of our research indicates that members of the House do in fact vote both their own policy views and their perceptions of their constituents' views, at least on issues of social welfare, foreign involvement, and civil rights. If these two intervening factors are used to predict roll-call votes, the prediction is quite successful. Their multiple correlation with roll-call position is 0.7 for social welfare, 0.6 for foreign involvement, and 0.9 for civil rights; the last figure is especially persuasive. What is more, both the congressman's own convictions and his perceptions of district opinion make a distinct contribution to his roll-call behavior. In each of the three domains the prediction of roll-call votes is surer if it is made from both factors rather than from either alone.

Lest the strong influence that the congressman's views and his perception of district views have on roll-call behavior appear somehow foreordained— and, consequently, this finding seems a trivial one—it is worth taking a sidewise glance at the potency of possible other forces on the Representative's vote. In the area of foreign policy, for example, a number of congressmen are disposed to follow the administration's advice, whatever they or

---

[13] It scarcely needs to be said that demonstrating *some* constituency influence would not imply that the Representative's behavior is *wholly* determined by constituency pressures. The legislator acts in a complex institutional setting in which he is subject to a wide variety of influences. The constituency can exercise a genuine measure of control without driving all other influences from the Representative's life space.

their districts think. For those who are, the multiple correlation of roll-call behavior with the Representative's own foreign policy views and his perception of district views is a mere 0.2. Other findings could be cited to support the point that the influence of the congressman's own preferences and those he attributes to the district is extremely variable. Yet in the House as a whole over the three policy domains the influence of these forces is quite strong.

The connections of congressional attitudes and perceptions with actual constituency opinion are weaker. If policy agreement between district and Representative is moderate and variable across the policy domains, as it is, this is to be explained much more in terms of the second condition of constituency control than the first. The Representative's attitudes and perceptions most nearly match true opinion in his district on the issues of Negro rights. Reflecting the charged and polarized nature of this area, the correlation of actual district opinion with perceived opinion is greater than 0.6, and the correlation of district attitude with the Representative's own attitude is nearly 0.4, as shown by Table 1. But the comparable corre-

TABLE 1

Correlations of Constituency Attitudes

Policy Domain	Correlation of Constituency Attitude with	
	Representative's Perception of Constituency Attitude	Representatives Own Attitude
Social welfare	.17	.21
Foreign involvement	.19	.06
Civil rights	.63	.39

lations for foreign involvement are much smaller—indeed almost negligible. And the coefficients for social welfare are also smaller, although a detailed presentation of findings in this area would show that the Representative's perceptions and attitudes are more strongly associated with the attitude of his electoral *majority* than they are with the attitudes of the constituency as a whole.

Knowing this much about the various paths that may lead, directly or indirectly, from constituency attitude to roll-call vote, we can assess their relative importance. Since the alternative influence chains have links of unequal strength, the full chains will not in general be equally strong, and these differences are of great importance in the relation of Representative to constituency. For the domain of civil rights Figure 2 assembles all the intercorrelations of the variables of our system. As the figure shows,

FIGURE 2

Intercorrelations of Variables Pertaining to Civil Rights

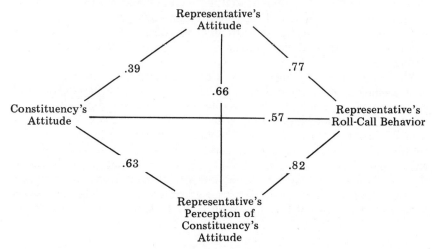

the root correlation of constituency attitude with roll-call behavior in this domain is 0.57. How much of this policy congruence can be accounted for by the influence path involving the Representative's attitude? And how much by the path involving his perception of constituency opinion? When the intercorrelations of the system are interpreted in the light of what we assume its causal structure to be, it is influence passing through the congressman's perception of the district's views that is found to be preeminently important.[14] Under the least favorable assumption as to its

---

[14] We have done this by a variance-component technique similar to several others proposed for dealing with problems of this type. See especially Herbert A. Simon, "Spurious Correlation: A Causal Interpretation," *Journal of the American Statistical Association*, 49 (1954), pp., 407–479; Hubert M. Blalock, Jr., "The Relative Importance of Variables," *American Sociological Review*, 26 (1961), pp. 866–874; and the almost forgotten work of Sewall Wright, "Correlation and Causation," *Journal of Agricultural Research*, 20 (1920), pp. 557–585. Under this technique a "path coefficient" (to use Wright's terminology, although not his theory) is assigned to each of the causal arrows by solving a set of equations involving the correlations of the variables of the model. The weight assigned to a full path is then the product of its several path coefficients, and this product may be interpreted as the proportion of the variance of the dependent variable (roll-call behavior, here) that is explained by a given path.

A special problem arises because influence may flow in either direction between the Congressman's attitude and his perception of district attitude (as noted above, the Representative may tend both to perceive his constituency's view selectively, as consistent with his own, and to change his own view to be consistent with the perceived constituency view). Hence, we have not a single causal model but a whole family of models, varying according to the relative importance of influence from attitude to perception and from perception to attitude. Our solution to this problem has been to calculate influence coefficients for the two extreme models in order to see how much our results could vary according to which model is chosen from our family of models. Since the systems of equations in this analysis are linear

importance, this path is found to account for more than twice as much of the variance of roll-call behavior as the paths involving the Representative's own attitude.[15] However, when this same procedure is applied to our

it can be shown that the coefficients we seek have their maximum and minimum values under one or the other of the limiting models. Therefore, computing any given coefficient for each of these limiting cases defines an interval in which the true value of the coefficient must lie. In fact these intervals turn out to be fairly small; our findings as to the relative importance of alternative influence paths would change little according to which model is selected.

The two limiting models with their associated systems of equations and the formulas for computing the relative importance of the three possible influence paths under each model are given below.

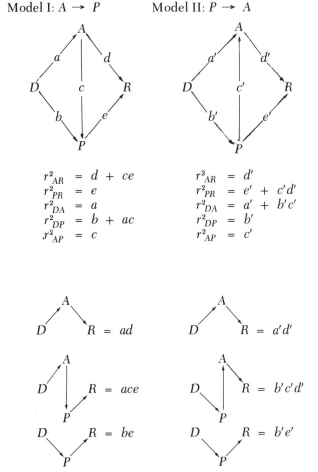

Model I: $A \rightarrow P$ Model II: $P \rightarrow A$

$$r^2_{AR} = d + ce \qquad r^2_{AR} = d'$$
$$r^2_{PR} = e \qquad r^2_{PR} = e' + c'd'$$
$$r^2_{DA} = a \qquad r^2_{DA} = a' + b'c'$$
$$r^2_{DP} = b + ac \qquad r^2_{DP} = b'$$
$$r^2_{AP} = c \qquad r^2_{AP} = c'$$

$D \nearrow A \searrow R = ad \qquad D \nearrow A \searrow R = a'd'$

$D \nearrow A \searrow R = ace \qquad D \nearrow A \searrow R = b'c'd'$

$D \searrow R = be \qquad D \searrow R = b'e'$

[15] By "least favorable" we mean the assumption that influence goes only from the congressman's attitude to his perception of district attitude (Model I) and not the other way round. Under this assumption, the proportions of the variance of roll-call behavior accounted for by the three alternative paths, expressed as proportions

social welfare data, the results suggest that the direct connection of constituency and roll-call through the congressman's own attitude is the most
important of the alternative paths.[16] The reversal of the relative importance of the two paths as we move from civil rights to social welfare is one
of the most striking findings of this analysis.

V. EVIDENCE OF CONTROL: ELECTORAL BEHAVIOR

Of the three conditions of constituency influence, the requirement that
the electorate take account of the policy positions of the candidates is the
hardest to match with empirical evidence. Indeed, given the limited information the average voter carries to the polls, the public might be
thought incompetent to perform any task of appraisal. Of constituents
living in congressional districts where there was a contest between a Republican and a Democrat in 1958, less than one in five said they had read
or heard something about both candidates, and well over half conceded
they had read or heard nothing about either. And these proportions are
not much better when they are based only on the part of the sample, not
much more than half, that reported voting for Congress in 1958. The
extent of awareness of the candidates among voters is indicated in Table 2.
As the table shows, even of the portion of the public that was sufficiently
interested to vote, almost half had read or heard nothing about either
candidate.

Just how low a hurdle our respondents had to clear in saying they had
read or heard something about a candidate is indicated by detailed qualitative analysis of the information constitutents *were* able to associate with

---

of the part of the variance of roll-call votes that is explained by district attitude, are
these:

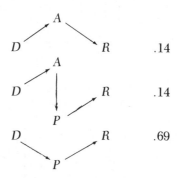

Inverting the assumed direction of influence between the congressman's own attitude and district attitude (Model II) eliminates altogether the effect that the Representative's attitude can have had on his votes, independently of his perception
of district attitude.

[16]Under both Models I and II the proportion of the variance of roll-call voting
explained by the influence path involving the Representative's own attitude is
twice as great as the proportion explained by influence passing through his perception of district attitude.

TABLE 2

Awareness of Congressional Candidates Among Voters, 1958

		Read or Heard Something About Incumbent[a]		
		Yes	No	
Read or Heard Something About Non-Incumbent	Yes	24	5	29
	No	25	46	71
		49	51	100%

[a]In order to include all districts where the House seat was contested in 1958 this table retains ten constituencies in which the incumbent congressman did not seek re-election. Candidates of the retiring incumbent's party in these districts are treated here as if they were incumbents. Were these figures to be calculated only for constituencies in which an incumbent sought re-election, no entry in this four-fold table would differ from that given by more than 2 per cent.

congressional candidates. Except in rare cases, what the voters "knew" was confined to diffuse evaluative judgments about the candidate: "he's a good man," "he understands the problems," and so forth. Of detailed information about policy stands not more than a chemical trace was found. Among the comments about the candidates given in response to an extended series of free-answer questions, less than 2 per cent had to do with stands in our three policy domains; indeed, only about three comments in every hundred had to do with legislative issues of *any* description.[17]

This evidence that the behavior of the electorate is largely unaffected by knowledge of the policy positions of the candidates is complemented by evidence about the forces that *do* shape the voters' choices among congressional candidates. The primary basis of voting in American congressional elections is identification with party. In 1958 only one vote in twenty was cast by persons without any sort of party loyalty. And among those who did have a party identification, only one in ten voted against their party. As a result, something like 84 per cent of the vote that year was cast by party identifiers voting their usual party line. What is more, traditional party voting is seldom connected with current legislative issues. As the party loyalists in a nationwide sample of voters told us what they liked and disliked about the parties in 1958, only a small fraction

[17]What is more, the electorate's awareness of Congress as a whole appears quite limited. A majority of the public was unable to say in 1958 which of the two parties had controlled the Congress during the preceding two years. Some people were confused by the coexistence of a Republican President and a Democratic Congress. But for most people this was simply an elementary fact about congressional affairs to which they were not privy.

of the comments (about 15 per cent) dealt with current issues of public policy.[18]

Yet the idea of reward or punishment at the polls for legislative stands is familiar to members of Congress, who feel that they and their records are quite visible to their constituents. Of our sample of congressmen who were opposed for re-election in 1958, more than four-fifths said the outcome in their districts had been strongly influenced by the electorate's response to their records and personal standing. Indeed, this belief is clear enough to present a notable contradiction: congressmen feel that their individual legislative actions may have considerable impact on the electorate, yet some simple facts about the Representative's salience to his constituents imply that this could hardly be true.

In some measure this contradiction is to be explained by the tendency of congressmen to overestimate their visibility to the local public, a tendency that reflects the difficulties of the Representative in forming a correct judgment of constituent opinion. The communication most congressmen have with their districts inevitably puts them in touch with organized groups and with individuals who are relatively well informed about politics. The Representative knows his constituents mostly from dealing with people who *do* write letters, who *will* attend meetings, who *have* an interest in his legislative stands. As a result, his sample of contacts with a constituency of several hundred thousand people is heavily biased: even the contacts he apparently makes at random are likely to be with people who grossly over-represent the degree of political information and interest in the constituency as a whole.

But the contradiction is also to be explained by several aspects of the Representative's electoral situation that are of great importance to the question of constituency influence. The first of these is implicit in what has already been said. Because of the pervasive effects of party loyalties, no candidate for Congress starts from scratch in putting together an electoral majority. The congressman is a dealer in increments and margins. He starts with a stratum of hardened party voters, and if the stratum is broad enough he can have a measurable influence on his chance of survival simply by attracting a small additional element of the electorate —or by not losing a larger one. Therefore, his record may have a very real bearing on his electoral success or failure without most of his constituents ever knowing what that record is.

Second, the relation of congressman to voter is not a simple bilateral one but is complicated by the presence of all manner of intermediaries: the local party, economic interests, the news media, racial and nationality organizations, and so forth. Such is the lore of American politics, as it is known to any political scientist. Very often the Representative reaches the mass public through these mediating agencies, and the information

[18] For a more extended analysis of forces on the congressional vote, see Donald E. Stokes and Warren E. Miller, "Party Government and the Saliency of Congress," *Public Opinion Quarterly*, 26 (Winter, 1962), pp. 531–546.

about himself and his record may be considerably transformed as it diffuses out to the electorate in two or more stages. As a result, the public—or parts of it—may get simple positive or negative cues about the congressman which were provoked by his legislative actions but which no longer have a recognizable issue content.

Third, for most congressmen most of the time the electorate's sanctions are potential rather than actual. Particularly the Representative from a safe district may feel his proper legislative strategy is to avoid giving opponents in his own party or outside of it material they can use against him. As the congressman pursues this strategy he may write a legislative record that never becomes very well known to his constituents; if it doesn't win votes, neither will it lose any. This is clearly the situation of most southern congressmen in dealing with the issue of Negro rights. By voting correctly on the issue they are unlikely to increase their visibility to constituents. Nevertheless, the fact of constituency influence, backed by potential sanctions at the polls, is real enough.

That these potential sanctions are all too real is best illustrated in the election of 1958 by the reprisal against Representative Brooks Hays in Arkansas' Fifth District.[19] Although the perception of Congressman Hays as too moderate on civil rights resulted more from his service as intermediary between the White House and Governor Faubus in the Little Rock school crisis than from his record in the House, the victory of Dale Alford as a write-in candidate was a striking reminder of what can happen to a congressman who gives his foes a powerful issue to use against him. The extraordinary involvement of the public in this race can be seen by comparing how well the candidates were known in this constituency with the awareness of the candidates shown by Table 2 above for the country

TABLE 3

Awareness of Congressional Candidates Among Voters in Arkansas
Fifth District, 1958

		Read or Heard Something About Hays		
		Yes	No	
Read or Heard Something About Alford	Yes	100	0	100
	No	0	0	0
		100	0	100%

[19] For an account of this episode see Corinne Silverman, "The Little Rock Story," Inter-University Case Program series, reprinted in Edwin A. Bock and Alan K. Campbell, eds., *Case Studies in American Government* (Englewood Cliffs: Prentice-Hall, 1962), pp. 1–46.

as a whole. As Table 3 indicates, not a single voter in our sample of Arkansas' Fifth District was unaware of either candidate.[20] What is more, these interviews show that Hays was regarded both by his supporters and his opponents as more moderate than Alford on civil rights and that this perception brought his defeat. In some measure, what happened in Little Rock in 1958 can happen anywhere, and our congressmen ought not to be entirely disbelieved in what they say about their impact at the polls. Indeed, they may be under genuine pressure from the voters even while they are the forgotten men of national elections.[21]

VI. CONCLUSION

Therefore, although the conditions of constituency influence are not equally satisfied, they are met well enough to give the local constituency a measure of control over the actions of its Representatives. Best satisfied is the requirement about motivational influences on the congressman: our evidence shows that the Representative's roll-call behavior is strongly influenced by his own policy preferences and by his perception of preferences held by the constituency. However, the conditions of influence that presuppose effective communication between congressman and district are much less well met. The Representative has very imperfect information about the issue preferences of his constituency, and the constituency's awareness of the policy stands of the Representative ordinarily is slight.

The findings of this analysis heavily underscore the fact that no single tradition of representation fully accords with the realities of American legislative politics. The American system *is* a mixture, to which the Burkean, instructed-delegate, and responsible-party models all can be said to have contributed elements. Moreover, variations in the representative relation are most likely to occur as we move from one policy domain to another. No single generalized configuration of attitudes and perceptions links Representative with constituency but rather several distinct

[20]The sample of this constituency was limited to twenty-three persons of whom thirteen voted. However, despite the small number of cases the probability that the difference in awareness between this constituency and the country generally is the result only of sampling variations is much less than one in a thousand.

[21]In view of the potential nature of the constituency's sanctions, it is relevant to characterize its influence over the Representative in terms of several distinctions drawn by recent theorists of power, especially the difference between actual and potential power, between influence and coercive power, and between influence and purposive control. Observing these distinctions, we might say that the constituency's influence is *actual* and not merely *potential* since it is the sanction behavior rather than the conforming behavior that is infrequent (Dahl). That is, the congressman is influenced by his calculus of potential sanctions, following the "rule of anticipated reactions" (Friedrich), however oblivious of his behavior the constituency ordinarily may be. We might also say that the constituency has *power* since its influence depends partly on sanctions (Lasswell and Kaplan), although it rarely exercises *control* since its influence is rarely conscious or intended (Cartwright). In the discussion above we have of course used the terms "influence" and "control" interchangeably.

patterns, and which of them is involved depends very much on the issue involved.

The issue domain in which the relation of congressman to constituency most nearly conforms to the instructed-delegate model is that of civil rights. This conclusion is supported by the importance of the influence-path passing through the Representative's perception of district opinion, although even in this domain the sense in which the constituency may be said to take the position of the candidate into account in reaching its electoral judgment should be carefully qualified.

The representative relation conforms most closely to the responsible-party model in the domain of social welfare. In this issue area, the arena of partisan conflict for a generation, the party symbol helps both constituency and Representative in the difficult process of communication between them. On the one hand, because Republican and Democratic voters tend to differ in what they would have government do, the Representative has some guide to district opinion simply by looking at the partisan division of the vote. On the other hand, because the two parties tend to recruit candidates who differ on the social welfare role of government, the constituency can infer the candidates' position with more than random accuracy from their party affiliation, even though what the constituency has learned directly about these stands is almost nothing. How faithful the representation of social welfare views is to the responsible-party model should not be exaggerated. Even in this policy domain, American practice departs widely from an ideal conception of party government.[22] But in this domain, more than any other, political conflict has become a conflict of national parties in which constituency and Representative are known to each other primarily by their party association.

It would be too pat to say that the domain of foreign involvement conforms to the third model of representation, the conception promoted by Edmund Burke. Clearly it does in the sense that the congressman looks elsewhere than to his district in making up his mind on foreign issues. However, the reliance he puts on the President and the Administration suggests that the calculation of where the public interest lies is often passed to the Executive on matters of foreign policy. Ironically, legislative initiative in foreign affairs has fallen victim to the very difficulties of gathering and appraising information that led Burke to argue that Parliament rather than the public ought to hold the power of decision. The background information and predictive skills that Burke thought the people lacked are held primarily by the modern Executive. As a result, the present role of the legislature in foreign affairs bears some resemblance to the role that Burke had in mind for the elitist, highly restricted *electorate* of his own day.

---

[22] The factors in American electoral behavior that encourage such a departure are discussed in Stokes and Miller, "Party Government and the Saliency of Congress."

CONGRESSIONAL RESPONSIBILITY AND THE ORGANIZATION OF CONSTITUENCY ATTITUDES[1]

DAVID R. SEGAL

The University of Michigan

THOMAS S. SMITH

The University of Michigan

A BASIC ASSUMPTION OF THE DEMOCRATIC MODEL OF LEGISLATIVE REPRE-
sentation is that the behavior of a legislator is both guided and constrained by the attitudes of his constituents regarding the issues
that confront him. He is presumed to have been elected in the first instance because his position on public issues reflected the views of his constituents. If his position on issues ceases to be in accord with those he represents, it is assumed that attempts at re-election will fail.

Such a model assumes further that there is some mechanism by which
the legislator may know the issue preferences of his constituency. He gets
some indications from visits home, from polls that he may conduct, from
the mail he receives from constituents, and from the home town press.
However, he is called upon to make decisions on a wide range of specific
issues on which he has received no direct feedback from constituents. He
must base his decisions regarding these issues on inferences from what
he does know about the positions of those he represents.

The attitudes of people are presumed to be organized on the basis of
principles that are subjectively meaningful.[2] It is this organization that
makes inference possible. If a legislator knows how his constituents feel
on some set of issues, and if there is an underlying logic to the organization of their attitudes, then he should be able to estimate their positions
on related issues.

The principles underlying the organization of constituency attitudes,
however, have not been well defined. Early research on political attitudes dealt with a single dimension of liberalism vs. conservatism.[3] Downs

[1] This study was supported in part by faculty research grants to each of the authors
from the Horace H. Rackham School of Graduate Studies, University of Michigan. We
are indebted to Ronald Inglehart, who commented extensively and incisively on a much
longer draft of this paper. Duncan MacRae also read the longer draft, and urged us to
throw most of it away in order to stress that which was interesting. We have followed
his advice but have not let him read the revised paper. John Fox and Jean Schneider
provided research assistance. Our data were provided by the Inter-University Consortium for Political Research.

[2] See for example William N. McPhee *et al.*, "Attitude Consistency," in William N.
McPhee and William A. Glaser, eds., *Public Opinion and Congressional Elections* (New
York: Free Press, 1962), pp. 78–120.

[3] This traditional "left-right" continuum still recurs in the literature. See Jean A. La-
Ponce, "Note on the Use of the Left-Right Dimension," *Comparative Political Studies*,
2 (Jan., 1970), pp. 481–502.

defines this dimension in terms of scope of governmental power, i.e., how much governmental control an individual feels is proper.[4] Other researchers, however, have argued that this single dimension is insufficient to describe political orientations in the modern world.[5]

Recent research has attempted to define attitude structures within substantive areas of issue content. We shall argue below that the notion of liberalism-conservatism as defined by Downs may well be as powerful a predictor of legislative behavior as the more issue-specific dimensions dealt with in the current literature.

THE ORGANIZATION OF ELECTORAL ATTITUDES

There exists a contradiction between current theory regarding the rather precise linkages that are presumed to exist between constituency attitudes and congressional behavior in specific issue areas, on the one hand, and research on attitude organization among the mass electorate on the other. In particular, research suggests that popular attitudes are not highly enough structured to place the kinds of specific constraints on legislative behavior that are postulated to exist.

In their analysis of American political attitudes, Campbell and his colleagues report that 1956 data on issues relating to domestic welfare, as well as data on foreign policy issues, scale according to Guttman's criteria, with no relationship between scales.[6] Axelrod, however, returning to the Survey Research Center's 1956 election study, and substituting cluster analysis for more conventional scaling techniques, found no strong structuring of political attitudes.[7] Indeed, the domestic welfare issues could only be regarded as scalable if a criterion value of $\phi/_{\phi\,max}$ of .14 were acceptable. This value tends to be greater than a correlation coefficient for the same data, and a value of .75 generally regarded as necessary for Guttman scaling. Axelrod's analysis did produce a cluster of items including domestic welfare and non-welfare issues, and foreign policy issues, that were more highly interrelated than the items in Campbell's scales. He defined this cluster as "populism."[8]

[4] Anthony Downs, *An Economic Theory of Democracy* (New York: Harper and Row, 1957).

[5] See for example Seymour Martin Lipset, *Revolution and Counter-Revolution* (New York: Basic Books, 1968); Donald E. Stokes, "Spatial Models of Party Competition," in Angus Campbell *et al.*, *Elections and the Political Order* (New York: Wiley, 1966), pp. 161–179; Edward A. Shils, "Authoritarianism: 'Right' and 'Left,'" in Richard Christie and Marie Jahoda, eds., *Studies in the Scope and Method of the Authoritarian Personality* (Glencoe: Free Press, 1954).

[6] Angus Campbell *et al.*, *The American Voter* (New York: Wiley, 1960). For a discussion of Guttman scaling techniques, see L. Guttman, "The Basis for Scalogram Analysis," in S. A. Stouffer *et al.*, *Measurement and Prediction* (Princeton: Princeton University Press, 1950).

[7] Robert Axelrod, "The Structure of Public Opinion on Policy Issues," *Public Opinion Quarterly*, 31 (Spring, 1967), pp. 55–60. For a discussion of cluster analysis, see R. E. Bonner, "On Some Clustering Techniques," *I.B.M. Journal of Research and Development*, 8 (Jan., 1964), pp. 22–32.

[8] Edward E. Cureton, "Note on $\phi/_{\phi\,max}$" *Psychometrika*, 24 (March, 1959), pp.

Converse's analysis of belief systems using Survey Research Center data similarly failed to discover the degree of mutual constraint among political attitudes that would be expected to appear in a unidimensional space.[9] While his report on data collected in a study of the 1958 congressional election show that the relationships between attitudes *within* domestic or foreign arenas were stronger than relationships between attitudes cross-cutting domestic and foreign issues, even the former associations were weak. The mean tau-gamma coefficient among attitudes, within both domestic and foreign realms was .23. Moreover, McClosky, *et al.* have previously demonstrated that among members of the mass public, even such a manifest political cue as party choice is not an important constraint on issue position.[10]

Luttbeg takes issue with Converse's findings.[11] In a factor analytic study of survey data collected in two Oregon communities, he finds no difference in the mutual constraint of attitudes between leaders and followers. The items he used, however, refer to local rather than national political issues, and hence pose no problems for us. The notion that people have more structured beliefs on local rather than national political issues is not incompatible with our formulation. Bobrow has previously demonstrated that attitudes on international affairs regarding even the relatively narrow issue of national security are not highly structured.[12]

ISSUE LINKAGES BETWEEN LEGISLATOR AND CONSTITUENCY

This apparent weakness of attitude structure notwithstanding, Miller and Stokes, analyzing the same data that Converse used, report the construction of three scales, using techniques developed by Guttman and

---

89–91. The items that fell into Axelrod's "populism" cluster were:

1. The government ought to cut taxes even if it means putting off important things that need to be done;

2. The government in Washington ought to see to it that everybody who wants to work can find a job;

3. This country would be better off if we just stayed home and did not concern ourselves with problems in other parts of the world;

4. The government ought to help people get doctors' and hospital care at low cost;

5. If cities and towns around the country need help to build more schools, the government in Washington ought to give them the money they need;

6. The government ought to fire any government worker who is accused of being a Communist even though they don't prove it.

[9] Philip E. Converse, "The Structure of Belief Systems in Mass Publics," in David Apter, ed., *Ideology and Discontent* (New York: Free Press, 1964), pp. 206–261. For a general discussion of the structure of belief systems, see Giovanni Sartori, "Politics, Ideology and Belief Systems," *American Political Science Review*, 63 (June, 1969), pp. 398–411.

[10] Herbert McClosky *et al.*, "Issue Conflict and Consensus Among Party Leaders and Followers," *American Political Science Review*, 54 (June, 1960), pp. 406–427.

[11] Norman R. Luttbeg, "The Structure of Beliefs Among Leaders and the Public," *Public Opinion Quarterly*, 32 (Fall, 1968), pp. 398–409.

[12] Davis B. Bobrow, "Organization of American National Security Opinions," *Public Opinion Quarterly*, 33 (Summer, 1969), pp. 223–239.

others, covering three issue domains: social welfare, American involvement in foreign affairs, and civil rights.[13]

Eight attitude items had been included in the 1958 survey. Each of them appeared in one of the scales. The three scales defined by Miller and Stokes' analysis were:[14]

A. Social Welfare Scale.
   1. The government should leave things like electric power and housing for private businessmen to handle.
   2. The government in Washington ought to see to it that everybody who wants to work can find a job.
   3. If cities and towns around the country need help to build more schools, the government in Washington ought to give them the money they need.

B. Internationalism Scale.
   1. This country would be better off if we just stayed home and did not concern ourselves with problems in other parts of the world.
   2. The United States should give economic help to the poorer countries of the world even if those countries can't pay for it.
   3. The United States should keep soldiers overseas where they can help countries that are against communism.

C. Civil Rights Scale.
   1. If Negroes are not getting fair treatment in jobs and housing, the government should see to it that they do.
   2. The government in Washington should stay out of the question of whether white and colored children go to the same school.

For the 116 congressional districts in which interviews were conducted by the Survey Research Center in 1958, mean constituency scores were computed, and correlated with the attitudes and roll-call behavior of congressmen with weights being assigned to each district approximately proportional to the number of interviews taken. The relationship between constituency opinion and roll-call votes in the area of civil rights was about .65, the highest correlation attained. The agreement between congressmen and their constituents on economic welfare was approximately .4, and on the question of foreign involvement, the correlation was less than .2.

RESCALING THE 1958 DATA

The seeming contradiction between the absence of highly structured

[13] Warren E. Miller and Donald E. Stokes, "Constituency Influence in Congress," in Angus Campbell et al., Elections and the Political Order (New York: Wiley, 1966), pp. 351–372.

[14] Guttman suggests ten items as the minimum that can be used to define a unidimensional space. While we have never seen a scale that meets this criterion, we are uneasy about using the rhetoric of scalogram analysis to describe two or three item sets. High coefficients of reproducibility can be obtained among small numbers of interrelated but non-unidimensional attributes, and it thus seems safer here to utilize the techniques of scaling to construct an index that is not assumed to be unidimensional.

political attitudes, on the one hand, and the constraints that seem to be placed on congressional behavior by constituency opinion which was scalable, on the other, led us to further explore the data utilized by Miller and Stokes. An attempt was made to replicate their three scales, using the multi-scaling program developed by the Institute for Social Research for use on the IBM 7090 computer at the University of Michigan. The eight attitude items, which had five point Likert response categories, were dichotomized by collapsing the strongly agree and agree categories, and the strongly disagree and disagree categories. Undecided responses were treated as missing data. This is consistent with the logic of Guttman scaling, which suggests that the selection of a cutting point will not affect the scalability of an item, although it may affect that item's position on the scale. The eight items were submitted as a single data set with no *a priori* assumption of unidimensionality. The minimum coefficient of reproducibility was set at .85, and adjacent items were tested for statistical independence using the chi-square distribution as a criterion. Adjacent items not related to each other at the .01 level or better were discarded.

Given these constraints, a single three item index, containing one item from each of the three scales derived by Miller and Stokes, was generated.[15] The items included were:

1. If Negroes are not getting fair treatment in jobs and housing, the government should see to it that they do.

2. If cities and towns around the country need help to build more schools, the government in Washington ought to give them the money they need.

3. The United States should give economic help to the poorer countries of the world even if those countries can't pay for it.

These items scaled with a coefficient of reproducibility of .979. While we do not suggest that they measure a unidimensional attitude space, they do seem to share as a common characteristic orientations toward federal governmental activity, regardless of policy area.

All three of these items measure attitudes that would seem to be in accord with Downs' definition of the left-right dimension, i.e., scope of governmental power. More specifically, two of the three items deal with government expenditure. We therefore used cumulated responses to these items as an index of liberalism. Our usage is compatible with that of Bowles and Richardson, who saw the liberalism-conservatism dimension as an underlying facet of attitude consistency.[16]

---

[15] We do not mean to suggest that our failure to replicate the scales utilized by Miller and Stokes indicates a misrepresentation of the data on their part. Indeed, it is quite probable that their scales were constructed utilizing methods more sophisticated than those developed by Guttman. We do take issue with their failure to present the criteria upon which these scales are based. Stokes states, in a paper prepared for the 1967 meetings of the American Political Science Association, that "the content of the attitude items and the methods by which they have been used to form these three attitude scales or dimensions" are reported in the original report. That they do not appear there is obviously an oversight, but we hope that these materials will be made available in their forthcoming volume, *Representation in the American Congress*.

[16] Roy T. Bowles and James T. Richardson, "Sources of Consistency of Political Opinion," *American Journal of Sociology*, 74 (May, 1969), pp. 676–684.

CONSTITUENCY LIBERALISM AND ECONOMIC ROLL-CALLS

To test this interpretation of our index, we analyzed the relationship between constituency attitudes and congressional votes on federal expenditures. Like Miller and Stokes, we computed mean index scores for constituencies. However, rather than weighting the 116 congressional districts in the total sample, we included in our analysis only data from the 36 districts in which 20 or more interviews were taken. Research by Segal and Wildstrom has shown that a cluster of 20 interviews produces a close estimate of population parameters.[17] Note that this is not a major discrepancy between our procedures and those of Miller and Stokes. Their constituency weights were roughly proportional to the number of interviews taken; so the districts we studied were those that played the greatest part in their analysis, while those in which only a few respondents were interviewed, which we omitted, presumably contributed little explanation or error variance to their study.

Our mean index scores were correlated with the percentage of 21 roll-calls in which each constituency's representative voted "yea" or "nay" in opposition to moves to limit federal spending in 1958.[18] Over the set of districts studied, the zero-order correlation between mean constituency opinion and congressional roll-call behavior was slightly greater than .18; roughly the same magnitude that Miller and Stokes found with regard to constituency-legislator agreement on foreign involvement.

Miller and Stokes suggest that constituency influence on legislators is based upon agreement between a legislator's votes and "his own policy views or his perceptions of the district views," and a correspondence between the "attitudes or perceptions governing the representative's acts," and the actual opinion of his constituency.

A corollary to this formulation of legislators representing the interests of their constituents is that if there is no correspondence between the legislator's acts and the opinions of his constituents, there will be dissatisfaction and the legislator will not be re-elected. To test this proposition, we computed the relationship between constituency attitudes and congressional roll-calls for those six districts in our set of 36 that elected someone other than the incumbent to Congress in 1958. The correlation for these six districts was −.63. The magnitude of this statistic must of course be interpreted in the light of the small case base. More importantly, with these cases excluded, the relationship between constituency attitude and roll-call behavior for the remaining 30 districts was .43. This is lower than the direct linkage found to exist between constituency attitudes and representatives' roll-call behavior in the area of civil rights by Miller and Stokes. It is greater than the relationship they found in the areas of domestic welfare and foreign involvement. Thus, once we take into account legislators who

[17] David R. Segal and Stephen H. Wildstrom, "Community Effects on Political Attitudes: Partisanship and Efficacy," *Sociological Quarterly*, 2 (Winter, 1970) pp. 67–86.

[18] Percentage scores for congressmen were taken from the *Congressional Quarterly Almanac* for 1958.

are punished by their constituencies for not voting in accordance with popular opinion, our index of liberalism becomes a better predictor of legislative roll-call behavior than are two of the three issue-related scales used by Miller and Stokes.

DISCUSSION

A legislator is frequently called upon to represent the positions of his constituents on issues about which he has received no direct advice from them. The tendency toward attitude consistency allows him to infer their probable position from direct knowledge of their positions on related issues.

Our review of the literature, and our failure to replicate the Miller and Stokes scales, suggest to us that the principles underlying the structure of political attitudes in the mass electorate are too diffuse and general for such inferences to be made within specific policy areas. Rather, the legislator must be guided by the position that his constituents have taken in the past with regard to the scope of governmental activity in general, and more particularly toward federal expenditures.

Our data suggest that legislative behavior is indeed constrained by these factors. There is also some evidence that if a legislator's behavior is not in accord with the attitudes of his constituents, he may soon terminate his career. Our small case base allows us to attach only heuristic importance to this finding.

We are not arguing that the liberalism dimension is sufficient to explain the constituency attitudes that are relevant for understanding legislative behavior. Our analysis leaves far too much variance unexplained for such a position to be viable. We anticipate that the identification of additional dimensions will result from research on general orientations toward the political world, rather than on the structure of beliefs with regard to specific political issues.